WITHDRAWAL

HANDBOOK OF ENGAGED SCHOLARSHIP

Transformations in Higher Education: The Scholarship of Engagement

HANDBOOK OF ENGAGED SCHOLARSHIP

CONTEMPORARY LANDSCAPES, FUTURE DIRECTIONS

VOLUME ONE

Institutional Change

EDITED BY

Hiram E. Fitzgerald, Cathy Burack, and Sarena D. Seifer

Michigan State University Press • *East Lansing*

Copyright © 2010 by Michigan State University

♾ The paper used in this publication meets the minimum requirements
of ANSI/NISO Z39.48-1992 (R 1997) (Permanence of Paper).

The Handbook of Engaged Scholarship is a joint project of Michigan State University's National Center for the Study of University
Engagement and the Higher Education Network for Community Engagement (HENCE).

Michigan State University Press
East Lansing, Michigan 48823-5245

Printed and bound in the United States of America.

16 15 14 13 12 11 10   1 2 3 4 5 6 7 8 9 10

LIBRARY OF CONGRESS CATALOGING-IN-PUBLICATION DATA

Handbook of engaged scholarship: contemporary landscapes, future directions / edited by Hiram E. Fitzgerald, Cathy Burack, and
Sarena Seifer.
v. cm.—(Transformations in Higher Education: The Scholarship of Engagement)
Includes bibliographical references and index.
ISBN 978-0-87013-974-1 (v. 1 : cloth : alk. paper)—ISBN 978-0-87013-975-8 (v. 2 : cloth : alk. paper) 1. Community and college—
United States—Handbooks, manuals, etc. 2. Service learning—United States—Handbooks, manuals, etc. 3. Education, Higher—Aims
and objectives—United States. I. Fitzgerald, Hiram E. II. Burack, Cathy. III. Seifer, Sarena D.
LC238.H36 2010
378.1'03—dc22
2010003500

Cover design by Adina Huda
Book design by Aptara

Michigan State University Press is a member of the Green Press Initiative and is committed to developing
and encouraging ecologically responsible publishing practices. For more information about the Green Press
Initiative and the use of recycled paper in book publishing, please visit www.greenpressinitiative.org.

———————————

Visit Michigan State University Press on the World Wide Web at: www.msupress.msu.edu

Transformations in Higher Education: The Engaged Scholar

Higher education is being challenged to connect with communities to develop solutions to major social and economic problems affecting contemporary society. Pressures to build strong university-community collaborations pose difficult problems for the academy because they demand interdisciplinary cooperation, rejection of provincial disciplinary turfism, changes in the faculty reward system, a re-focusing of unit and institution missions and the breaking down of firmly established and isolated silos. Partially in response to societal challenges to higher education, education-oriented social critics and reformists began to articulate a new vision for American higher education. Public support of higher education was being bound to public expectations that "their" colleges and universities would become more directly engaged in the transformation of society across the broad disciplinary domains that define higher education.

The Kellogg Commission's challenge for higher education to engage with communities was a significant catalyst for action. It built upon the work of individuals such as Boyer and Lynton and organizations such as the American Association for Higher Education's Forum on Faculty Roles and Rewards and Campus Compact and other activist events of the 1990s. These events funneled into a nexus around which both engaged scholarship and the scholarship of engagement could evolve and become distinctively defined scholarly approaches to campus-community partnerships. Engaged scholars study the processes, relationships, and impacts of outreach and engaged work on engaged faculty, the institution, disciplines, the academy as a whole, and the community partners with whom they work. Indeed, engaged scholars recognize that community based scholarship requires community involvement based on principles that reflect mutual respect, recognition that community knowledge is valid, and that sustainability must be an integral part of the partnership agenda.

Higher education has responded strongly to its critics. During the past decade, numerous conferences, journals (peer-reviewed and on-line open source), books, and visionary reports have been published. Countless evidence-based models for partnerships have been disseminated, and new individual and institutional membership associations have been formed. Clearly, a disciplinary aura around engaged scholarship and the scholarship of engagement is forming.

When leaders at Michigan State University's National Collaborative for the Study of University Engagement conceived of the idea for a Handbook of Engaged Scholarship, they approached the Higher Education Network for the Study of University Engagement to solicit its support for the project. The response was quick and positive. Across the two volumes, we have attempted to capture the rich diversity of institutions and partnerships that characterize the contemporary landscape and the aspirational future of engaged scholarship.

We are indebted to all of the authors and editors who have contributed their time and energy to create this seminal handbook. Each chapter was edited by one of the three volume editors, and chapters in each sub-section were also independently edited by the individuals who provide overviews for the section. When leaders from the National Collaborative for the Study of University Engagement proposed the *Transformations in Higher Education: Engaged Scholarship* book series to Gabriel Dotto, Director of the Michigan State University Press, he enthusiastically endorsed the project with little more than a page of descriptive information in support of the concept. We thank him for his enthusiastic support throughout the process of crafting the *Handbook of Engaged Scholarship* as the anchor volume in the series. We are equally indebted to Kristine M. Blakeslee, Project Editor at the MSU Press, whose difficult task was to guide over sixty authors through the production cycle. Lisa Devereaux worked diligently to assure that all chapters were in a common format for submission to the publisher, and Julie Crowgey tracked chapters through the final revision cycle. To each we owe special thanks. It is our hope that publication of the *Handbook* will be a catalyst for moving higher education closer to alignment with the call to action issued by the Kellogg Foundation task force, which challenged higher education to renew its covenant with society through engaged scholarship.

Hiram E. Fitzgerald
Cathy Burack
Sarena D. Seifer

Contents

Foreword

James C. Votruba

Over the past twenty years there has developed within American higher education a rich conversation concerning how colleges and universities can better utilize their vast knowledge resources to support public progress. Beyond the production of graduates, what is the value-added that we bring to such public goals as strengthening economic competitiveness, improving P–12 education, enhancing health care, and a host of other challenges that confront our nation and its communities? What form should this public engagement take? Who should be involved? How can this involvement contribute to our mission to educate students and produce cutting-edge research? The contributors to this handbook represent some of the most thoughtful and influential leaders in this national conversation. Together, their work represents the most comprehensive set of perspectives yet assembled on behalf of higher education's public engagement mission.

American higher education has a long and rich tradition of involvement in advancing public priorities. Over the past 150 years, our colleges and universities have brought science to agriculture, produced the workforce for economic expansion, provided the most direct pathway for intergenerational mobility, contributed to national defense, and produced cutting-edge research that has improved nearly every dimension of our lives. Our faculty members as well as our institutions themselves have often served as voices of reason and conscience related to highly charged matters of public concern. In short, American higher education has been both a catalyst and a launching pad for much of America's breathtaking economic and social progress.

Twenty years ago, I was part of an effort at Michigan State University to develop a deeper understanding of the scholarship of engagement and to determine what role such scholarship should play in the life of the university. Many of the contributors to this handbook were part of that effort, which helped launch similar efforts on campuses across the nation. Although often different in mission, size, focus, and funding, what these institutions shared in common was an interest in better defining the role of higher education in fostering citizenship and helping to address some of the difficult challenges confronting the public. In this sense, the focus was on higher education's public role, which is also the focus of this handbook.

We've come a long way in understanding the role of public engagement in the life of our colleges and universities. Still, we have a long way to go before the scholarship of engagement is fully embraced as a core campus mission.

Several years ago, I chaired a national task force on public engagement sponsored by the American Association of State Colleges and Universities. We surveyed more than four hundred universities to help us better understand the nature and extent of their public engagement involvement and how this work fits in the overall institutional mission. Two outcomes are particularly notable for our purposes here. First, we found that there was a vast array of public engagement activity being conducted by faculty across the full spectrum of the university, from arts and sciences to the professions. Second, we discovered that this work tends to be fragile and very person-dependent. That is, it tends to flourish when there is a president, provost, dean, or chair who champions the engagement mission and supports faculty involvement. However, when the leader departs, the engagement mission often flounders.

Contrast this fragility with the institutionalization of research and scholarship in the major research-intensive universities. In these institutions, presidents and provosts, deans and chairs may come and go, but the importance of the research mission is so deeply embedded in the fabric of the institution that it continues uninterrupted. The next great challenge for advocates of the public engagement mission is to achieve this same level of institutionalization: to so deeply embed the scholarship of engagement in the fabric of the campus at every level that it becomes a thoroughly integrated part of the institution's core academic mission.

What would such an institution look like? Public engagement would be grounded in a strong intellectual foundation that relates it to the other mission dimensions. The voice of the public would be institutionalized at every level. Key institutional leaders would be selected and evaluated based, at least in part, on their capacity to lead the public engagement function. Faculty and unit-level incentives and rewards would encourage and support the scholarship of engagement. Faculty selection, orientation, and development would highlight the importance of the public engagement mission. The curriculum would include public engagement as a way to both support community progress and enhance student learning. Institutional awards and recognitions would reflect the importance of excellence across the full breadth of the mission, including engagement. The planning and budgeting process would reflect the centrality of public engagement as a core institutional mission. And the university would take seriously its public intellectual role and have the courage to be a safe place for difficult public conversations.

The chapters that follow touch on many of these dimensions. They provide a rich overview of how the scholarship of engagement has emerged as an important higher education movement; how this work expresses itself in a variety of institutions and disciplines; the variety of forms that the scholarship of engagement can take; and how public engagement can result in enhanced student learning and a deeper public appreciation of the role that higher education can play in their lives and the lives of their communities.

I've followed the public engagement movement for well over twenty years, both as an observer and as a participant. As our nation and its communities struggle to cope with a broad range of complex and formidable challenges, it's time to take the public engagement movement to a new level of development and maturation. Let me suggest several areas that deserve special focus as we work to advance higher education's public engagement mission.

First, we need public policy that supports the scholarship of engagement. On most university campuses, the scholarship of engagement is a cost center, not a revenue center. I would argue that the reason research is so deeply embedded in the research-intensive universities is because there is a massive amount of federal funding that supports both the individual investigator and the institution itself. Until we have federal and state policy that supports the scholarship of engagement, this work is not likely to become institutionalized.

There are some encouraging signs that the federal agencies are broadening their funding focus to include what is being described in this handbook as engaged scholarship. For example, the National Institutes of Health (NIH) is placing greater emphasis on translational science as well as efforts directed at underserved and vulnerable populations. The National Science Foundation is requiring social significance as part of its review criteria. The point is that community-based research and scholarly activity are open to all research methodologies, including qualitative ones and mixed methods, and NIH and other agencies are funding such efforts. There are early signs that the new Obama administration values the role that engaged scholarship can play in advancing public progress. If this is the case, the higher education community must move quickly and strategically to make the case that engaged scholarship is an important element in advancing important public priorities.

There are also encouraging signs at the state policy level. For example, Kentucky recently became the first state to create a funding stream to support university public engagement work. Access to these funds requires both campus and community input and clearly defined and measurable public outcomes. In the first few years of the program, the focus has been on strengthening community economic competitiveness, improving P–12 education, enhancing the nonprofit sector, and improving health care access and delivery. We need more states to develop similar policies.

It is doubtful that public engagement will become a broadly accepted core campus mission until there is significant federal and state policy that supports it. Absent public policy support, the scholarship of engagement is less likely to attract sustained attention from large numbers of faculty members or from the institutions themselves. However, if significant support is forthcoming from both the federal and state levels, we can expect institutions to quickly adapt as they and their faculty members turn their attention to these new funding sources.

Second, we need to do a far better job of assessing our engagement work. We've made progress in this regard but, until we have reached agreement regarding what constitutes excellence in this domain, it will remain difficult to measure and reward. For example, should we focus on assessing activities or outcomes? What role does self-assessment play? How about peer assessment? Absent appropriate and generally accepted standards for evaluating the scholarship of engagement, faculty members are less likely to embrace it because of the risk that it will not be recognized and rewarded.

Third, we must do a better job of aligning our colleges and universities in a way that supports the institutionalization of this work. In their 1994 book *Built to Last*, Jim Collins and Jerry Porras studied the defining qualities of companies that achieved very high levels of success over a long period of time. What they found was that these high-performing companies had every organizational element aligned to support intended outcomes. If higher education is going to produce outstanding public engagement, every element of the institution must be aligned to support that outcome. To what extent are campus leadership, faculty incentives and rewards, planning and budgeting, annual evaluations, awards and recognitions, and public policy aligned to support the scholarship of engagement? Absent such alignment, involvement will more likely be based on *individual* faculty commitment rather than *institutional* commitment.

Fourth, it's time to focus on the development of professional standards related to the public engagement mission. Such standards exist for research and teaching. Public engagement needs generally accepted standards that can be used to guide the development, administration, and evaluation of public engagement initiatives. What should be the standards that a faculty member uses to define her or his involvement in a particular initiative? What standards should be applied when a campus is deciding whether to make an institution-wide commitment to a particular engagement focus? Well-defined and generally accepted standards for public engagement can provide guidance at both the individual and institutional level and can help avoid some of the major pitfalls that can develop as a result of pursuing this work.

Fifth, it's time for us to become far more intentional in the preparation of campus- and system-level leaders who are expected to lead on behalf of the public engagement mission. Department chairs, deans, vice presidents, and presidents generally assume their leadership positions with little or no involvement in the scholarship of engagement, yet we expect them to lead in this domain. Several months ago, I hosted a group of twenty-three university presidents for two days of discussion on their role in leading the engaged university. These leaders want their institutions to be deeply committed to public engagement. What they were looking for was insight on how to advance the scholarship of engagement as a core campus priority. As with any movement, leadership matters, and it will be indispensable as we move public engagement to the next level.

Sixth, the scholarship of engagement is more easily focused and carried out if it is conducted in response to a well-defined public agenda. A decade ago, Kentucky defined a public agenda for higher education that connected with a larger set of state goals. The agenda is focused on five questions. Are more Kentuckians ready for postsecondary education? Is Kentucky postsecondary education affordable for its citizens? Do more Kentuckians have certificates and degrees? Are college graduates prepared for life and work in Kentucky? Are Kentucky's people, communities, and economy benefiting? Each year, Kentucky's colleges and universities are asked to demonstrate their contributions to these overarching public priorities.

On a more local level, I recently co-chaired a regional planning process called Vision 2015. It involved hundreds of citizens from throughout the northern Kentucky region coming together to establish goals for regional progress and strategies for achieving them. Having these goals in hand, it became far easier to focus higher education's human and financial resources in a way that supported their achievement.

Universities can provide important leadership in helping to define and pursue state and regional priorities. We can conduct applied research to help better understand the nature of a problem. We can identify "best practice" from other locations and help test those practices in local settings. We can engage in outcomes assessment intended to measure the impact of problem interventions. We can help formulate public policy approaches that attempt to reduce or eliminate problems that influence public progress. And we can add the knowledge and experience of our faculty to help inform citizens who are attempting to frame goals for their state and communities.

Finally, the next level of public engagement will include a more cautious representation of higher education's capacity to impact matters of public concern. Too often, with our hearts in the right place, we overpromise related to problems that are far beyond our capacity or expertise to resolve. In doing so, we can create false hope among the public that often results in resentment because the college or university fails to deliver. In the most fundamental sense, we are learning institutions. We promote learning through the generation, transmission, and application of knowledge. In our public engagement work, our goal should be to promote learning so that the public can act from an informed position. In this sense, colleges and universities don't solve social problems, although we have an indispensable role to play in helping to understand a problem as well as frame a strategy for its resolution. It is when we promise to go beyond the promotion of learning that we embark on a slippery slope that can result in frustration and disappointment for both the campus and community.

The scholarship of engagement generates great benefit not only for the larger society but also for our colleges and universities themselves. By involving students in addressing complex "real-world" challenges, we can deepen their educational experience and better prepare them to assume the responsibilities of citizenship in a democratic society. By involving our faculty members, we can strengthen and enhance the link between their research and scholarship and the challenges that confront the larger society that we look to for support.

By having a robust public engagement mission, colleges and universities can help ensure that they will never lose touch with the public whom we serve. Back in the early 1980s, I was in a meeting with the recently retired chairman and CEO of the General Motors Corporation. He was asked what caused the American auto industry to fall so far, so fast during the 1970s. His response is never too far out of my mind. He said that it wasn't the unions. It wasn't plant obsolescence. It wasn't the time that it took to get design into production. Fundamentally, it was hubris. It was a belief that American auto manufacturers had always built the best vehicles and always would build the best vehicles—that the problem was a marketing problem, not a product problem. In fact, the industry had lost touch with their market, and their own arrogance created a filter that didn't allow them to see what was so clear to everyone else.

American higher education, like financial institutions and automobile manufacturers, is a mature industry. We are described as the best higher education in the world and we embrace this mantle with great pride and enthusiasm. The danger in all mature industries is that hubris can take hold and we can lose touch with the public whom we serve. The scholarship of engagement can help ensure that our colleges and universities will always remain deeply rooted in the larger world on which we depend.

The chapters that follow provide penetrating and often original insight into the scholarship of engagement. Although engagement with the larger society dates back to the beginning of the last century, it is only recently that the conversation has expanded to include all academic disciplines and professional fields. In the most fundamental sense, the scholarship of engagement challenges American higher education to move to a new level of civic involvement. It calls on us to be far more intentional in our approach to advancing public progress. And it requires us to think more deeply not just about public engagement but about every dimension of our academic mission and purpose. This handbook is a useful guide along this path.

PART 1

The Emerging Movement

Edited by Ann E. Austin

The Emerging Movement

Ann E. Austin

A handbook that examines engaged scholarship has the responsibility to look at the issue from many perspectives. A good starting point for understanding most phenomena is to consider definitions, context, and history, and this first part of this handbook takes up these very issues. Across the chapters, the authors consider what engaged scholarship means, taking care to acknowledge that the concept is enriched by recognizing various perspectives. They agree that core elements of the definition include connections between higher education institutions and their communities, attention to collaboration and reciprocal learning and benefits, and the relevance of engaged scholarship to teaching, research, and service. The chapters also offer insights into the history of the scholarship of engagement. Readers will gain an appreciation for the ways in which a commitment to linking universities with the community is woven throughout the history of American higher education. Certainly, specific factors in the current landscape have led to heightened interest in recent years in engagement as a key responsibility of higher education institutions. But the scholarship of engagement, as the authors in this part show, has deep historical roots.

In addition to providing definitions and setting the context for an examination of the scholarship of engagement, the authors in Part 1 open a discussion that continues throughout the *Handbook* concerning the future of engaged scholarship. Indeed, the past, present, and future connect in these chapters. Defining, conducting, theorizing, and conducting research about the scholarship of engagement is a dynamic activity. Although the handbook answers many questions, it also frames issues that deserve ongoing attention. These include, as the authors in Part 1 mention, questions about the characteristics of those who do this kind of scholarship and how institutional leaders can encourage and support them, strategies for preparing future faculty with commitment and skills to conduct this form of research, issues of assessing and rewarding this kind of work, the role of power in the relationships between higher education institutions and the community, and the importance of linking engaged scholarship to policy implications. Each chapter in this part provides the reader with background, context, and stimulating questions that provide a basis for further reading in the volume.

This Part opens with a chapter by Chris Glass and Hiram Fitzgerald in which their opening argument sets the tone for the handbook. Campuses and scholars, they explain, understand engagement in a "rich diversity of ways," various approaches that together offer excellent exemplars of ways in which higher education institutions and communities can interact and engage. Furthermore, they assert, "the dynamic tensions this diversity creates within the academy has not only been central to the intellectual vitality of the conversation—it embodies the very democratic values it seeks to advance." The chapter then proceeds to paint the landscape in which attention to the scholarship of engagement has developed and to highlight key aspects of the recent history of American higher education—Ernest Boyer's call in the 1990s for a broadening of conceptions about scholarship, wide and growing concern about the array of societal challenges, and a variety of calls for a renewed covenant between higher education and society. Glass and Fitzgerald then examine the meaning of engagement as it is used in the terms "engaged campuses" and "engaged scholarship." They argue that three qualities are essential: engagement is "scholarly," "cuts across the missions of teaching, research, and service," and "is reciprocal and mutually beneficial." They conclude their chapter by looking forward and framing four key areas for critically important continuing dialogue: (1) the meaning of being an engaged scholar, (2) how to reward engagement, (3) issues pertaining to the relationships between community and campus, and (4) how to benchmark, assess, and accredit engagement. Well-written, focused, and insightful, this chapter offers an excellent overview and conceptual framing of the issues taken up in the part and the handbook as a whole.

David Cox's essay then helps readers go deeper into the history of the scholarship of engagement in American higher education. Cox draws on Adrianna Kezar's 2001 work *Understanding and Facilitating Organizational Change in the 21st Century: Recent Research and Conceptualizations,* which concerned models of change. Cox uses each of her models as a lens through which to discuss how various factors have encouraged the scholarship of engagement and how higher education institutions have grappled, over time, with this form of scholarship. The evolutionary model of change highlights the external pressures on higher education institutions to engage with their communities to address physical, economic, and social issues and to seek external funding support. The teleological perspective emphasizes the way in which articulation of institutional purposes can foster change. For example, in regard to the scholarship of engagement, institutional leaders have called for engagement to be at the heart of the institutional missions of their institutions. The political model focuses on the ways in which change emerges in relationship to political tensions inherent in institutions. From the perspective of this model, calls for engagement are situated squarely within debates about the purpose and values of the academy—to be relevant to society or to stand apart from society as a critical observer. The scholarship of engagement movement has been advanced as associations, journals, and accrediting bodies have weighed in on this debate. The two other models for change—the social cognition and the culture models—both focus on how change occurs as different interpretations and understandings of the role of the organization develop. Public views that the university has a key role to play in promoting democracy and the increasing diversity of the faculty, many of whom have views consistent with the scholarship of engagement, have served as additional factors (highlighted by the social cognition and culture models) supporting this form of academic work. Cox concludes by asserting that, although various conditions and contexts may change, the array of factors in place and the recent interest suggest "an ever more promising future for the scholarship of engagement."

The third essay continues the process of setting context and history, as Kelly Ward and Tami Moore review the origins of community engagement in higher education and explore the various ways it is used "for describing how campuses and communities engage with one another." They remind the reader that early American higher education institutions in the seventeenth and eighteenth centuries embraced the idea that higher education should contribute to the common good; they highlight the notions of utility, usefulness, practicality, and service that characterized the emerging university in the nineteenth century; and they call up the image of the land-grant institution, with its emphasis on linking research and application. While recognizing the importance of the land-grant tradition, they also note that a range of institutional types, including liberal arts colleges, community colleges, and comprehensive and regional institutions, have contributed to the ongoing history of the role of engagement in American higher education. Ward and Moore continue their chapter by considering the relevance of the notion of engagement to different constituencies. In regard to students, engagement refers to the various activities students may do in the community, as well as to the outcome of an education in which students learn to be both local and global citizens, involved in democratic processes, and committed to volunteerism and community service. In regard to faculty work, they emphasize that, as faculty members integrate community-based work into their various forms of scholarship, engagement can relate to teaching, research, and service. Although they reference the important leadership provided by Ernest Boyer in naming and honoring multiple forms of scholarship, they also acknowledge that discussions of the meaning of engagement in faculty work continue and that engagement involves asking faculty members "to work differently." A third way to think about engagement concerns the institutional level. Here, the focus is on "engaged campuses" that link campus resources with needs in the community in diverse ways. Various associations and groups, including Campus Compact, the American Association of Colleges and Universities, the National Association of State University and Land-Grant Colleges (NASULGC), and an array of disciplinary societies, have encouraged higher education institutions to deepen their commitment to their communities. In the final section of their essay, Ward and Moore, like other authors in this part, look forward and encourage efforts to clarify, refine, and advance the notion of engagement in higher education. Specifically, they call for more use of critical theory in examining the implicit power relations associated with community-university relationships, exploration of a range of theories that may illuminate the relationships between higher education institutions and their communities, greater interest in interdisciplinary collaboration, and heightened attention to the perspectives of the community as approaches to engagement are developed.

Tony Chambers and Bryan Gopaul look closely at what engaged scholarship means from a social justice-centered approach. In fact, they argue that the main purpose of engaged scholarship is "to recognize, analyze, and seek resolution of socially unjust conditions for individuals and communities." In order to make a case for the centrality of social justice to the purposes of engaged scholarship, they systematically examine the concepts of "public good" and "social justice," and then argue that engaged scholarship involves the scholarship "of" engagement, the scholarship "on or about" engagement, and the scholarship "for" engagement. They conclude that engaged scholarship emphasizes collaboration, mutual learning, and reciprocity between communities and scholars, whose work together leads to societal transformation locally, nationally, and internationally. The chapter concludes with a useful enumeration of important issues that should be addressed in the continuing dialogue and practice of a social justice–centered engaged scholarship. These issues include, among others, the role of leaders in institutions, communities, and professional associations in regard to framing and nurturing the scholarship of engagement, the process of more fully institutionalizing this form of scholarship, the preparation of future scholars prepared to conduct engaged scholarship, and the importance of considering ethical issues related to the scholarship of engagement.

In the final chapter of Part 1, John Braxton and William Luckey take an empirical approach to examining patterns in faculty work in regard to the scholarship of engagement. Specifically, they look at faculty behaviors in regard to five types of studies illustrative of the scholarship of engagement (studies conducted for local organizations, those for a local nonacademic professional association, those for a local government agency, those that help solve a community problem, and those that solve a county or state problem). Referring to these forms of work, they ask: With what frequency do faculty members conduct the five different kinds of studies associated with the scholarship of engagement? Does the frequency of these different kinds of work vary by different institutional type or by academic discipline? Is there a relationship between various faculty characteristics and the frequency of the kinds of studies in which they engage? Do those who do the scholarship of engagement also pursue the other forms of scholarship laid out by Boyer—the scholarship of application, discovery, and integration? Working with a large sample of faculty members from different institutional types, Braxton and Luckey report that academic discipline is more closely related to doing the scholarship of engagement than the type of institution where one is situated. They also report that academic discipline and publication productivity (much more than gender, professional age, and tenure status) relate to the profile of faculty members likely to do the scholarship of engagement. In particular, sociologists and faculty who have done scholarship focused on application and integration are more likely than others to pursue the scholarship of engagement. The authors believe that more research should be conducted to clarify what the scholarship of engagement is, how it differs from the scholarship of application, and who does it. Their research raises the question, I believe, of how institutional leaders can best focus their efforts to encourage the scholarship of engagement. Different approaches to encouraging and supporting this kind of scholarship may be more or less effective depending on the discipline of the faculty member. Future research might explore this and other questions more fully.

Taken together, the first five chapters of the *Handbook* provide definitions, history, context, and questions relevant to a thorough consideration of the scholarship of engagement. Readers will gain a solid basis for further reading in the *Handbook* and a deep appreciation of the importance and relevance of the topic of engaged scholarship to institutional and community leaders and higher education faculty members today.

Engaged Scholarship: Historical Roots, Contemporary Challenges

Chris R. Glass and Hiram E. Fitzgerald

During the past twenty-five years, repeated efforts have been made to stimulate American higher education to more actively engage with society. Foundations and national organizations have provided leadership by creating commissions, issuing reports, and sponsoring visioning conferences. As part of its collective civic mission, America's higher education system has been challenged to partner with communities, organizations, schools, businesses and industries, government agencies, and funding agencies to address a wide range of societal problems and more actively engage with the open democratic society that supports the system.

This more active relationship has generated a fresh vision about the democratic purposes of higher education and the ways universities contribute to the public good (Boyte, 2004; Boyte & Kari, 1996). From the founding of Campus Compact in 1985, to reformist calls for higher education to renew its covenant with society in the 1990s, there have been significant advances in scholarship-based outreach and engagement across the teaching, research, and service missions of higher education. These advances have stirred active and deep debate about the meaning of engagement, the role of higher education in society, higher education's faculty reward system, the meaning of private-public partnerships, and the allocation of resources needed to redirect America's college students back to core democratic values. These discussions have become so wide-ranging that a perceived need arose to codify the foundations of engaged scholarship, to assess its vision, types of work, personnel, and barriers, and to address issues related to measurement, evaluation, standards of practice, and methodologies. The time seemed right for a handbook on engaged scholarship.

This handbook provides a sampling of the rich diversity of the ways in which campuses and scholars understand engagement. The dynamic tension this diversity creates within the academy has not only been central to the intellectual vitality of the conversation—it embodies the very democratic values it seeks to advance. There are differences in mission and resources among America's research universities and its historically minority-serving institutions, comprehensive universities, liberal arts colleges, and community colleges. Therefore, the emphases, structures, and practices in community-campus collaborations vary significantly among different institutions (Church, 2001). Nevertheless, each type of institution provides exemplars of community-campus engagement appropriate to its mission. In addition to diverse institutional practices, a wide range of scholars now identify themselves as engaged scholars. Scholars from the social sciences, humanities, natural sciences, and professional disciplines now integrate engagement as part of their research, teaching, and service roles and responsibilities at their institutions.

The handbook encourages leaders and scholars to thoughtfully enter into deliberative conversations about how community engagement is practiced in their context, in the hope that it will help to frame transformational change in higher education as it fully embraces the challenges of the twenty-first century. We open the discussion about engaged scholarship, in this chapter, by focusing on its history, the meaning and diversity of its practices, and the challenges it faces in contemporary higher education.

Historical Context

The distinguished philosopher Alfred North Whitehead (1947) noted that "unapplied knowledge is shorn of its meaning. Careful shielding of a university from the activities of the world around is the best way to chill interest and to defeat progress" (p. 267). The extraordinary government investment in science and technology that followed World War II prompted the creation of the National Science Foundation (1950) and the National Institute of Mental Health (1946) and vastly expanded the size and diversity of the National Institutes of Health. These events helped to transform America's universities from teaching institutions to "research intensive" institutions and elevated research productivity to primacy among the criteria used to reward faculty performance. The scholarship of application was devalued as disciplinary or basic research became the standard of practice for faculty promotion and rewards. Whitehead's warning about isolating knowledge generation from knowledge application was forgotten.

A movement to reinvigorate the civic purposes of higher education began in the mid-1980s when the presidents of Brown, Stanford, and Georgetown Universities and the president of the Education Commission of the United States founded Campus Compact. Campus Compact (2007) was created to help students "make a difference" through public and community service.

In the 1990s, education-oriented social critics and reformists began to articulate a new vision for American higher education. Public support of higher education was being bound to the expectation that the "public's universities" would become more directly engaged in the transformation of society across the broad disciplinary domains that define higher education. American higher education asked itself, "How well are we performing our obligations to the society that sustains us?" (Bok, 1990, p. 105).

Attention to the historical land-grant tradition surfaced amidst national concern that higher education had drifted too far from its teaching mission (Boyer, 1990) and, especially for land-grant institutions, too far from its historical commitment to help meet the broad and diverse needs of society (Bonnen, 1998; Lerner & Simon, 1998; Votruba, 1992). There was a desire to more closely link the university to the daily lives of citizens that earned the original land-grant institutions the designation "democracy's colleges" (Campbell, 1995). This mission would necessitate a broader definition of scholarship-based teaching, research, and service (Braxton, Luckey, & Helland, 2002) and a commitment to link universities solidly with community efforts to resolve a wide range of societal problems (McCall, Groark, Strauss, & Johnson, 1998).

Boyer (1990) and other critics challenged higher education to broaden its definition of scholarship to include the scholarship of discovery, integration, application, and teaching (see also Johnson & Wamser, 1997). The intent was to elevate the scholarship of teaching and the scholarship of application to the same level as the scholarship of discovery with respect to faculty roles and responsibilities.

Boyer also drew attention to a wide array of societal problems that threatened the stability and viability of American society. His comment was one of many warnings about the intolerable social, psychological, and environmental circumstances that surrounded the lives of millions of Americans. He challenged higher education to help find solutions to such pervasive social problems as infant mortality, child poverty, homelessness, substandard housing, failing schools, youth crime and violence, and teen pregnancy. Children and youth in particular were at high risk and had fewer life choices associated with escaping from these social problems (Garbarino, 1994; Lerner, 1995). In 1994, prevalence rates for children at risk included 768 children and adolescents killed by firearms; 2,243 children and youth suicides; 112,230 children younger than 18 arrested for violent crimes; 1 million babies born into poverty; and nearly 2,700,000 children reported as being abused or neglected (CDF Reports, 1994).

Boyer argued that it was time for higher education to renew its covenant with society and to directly address its problems by partnering with various communities to create transformational changes and preserve democracy. Arguing for a new community-campus relationship, Boyer urged higher education to more actively engage society:

> [W]hat I find most disturbing . . . is a growing feeling in this country that higher education is, in fact, part of the problem rather than the solution. Going still further, that it's become a private benefit, not a public good. Increasingly, the campus is being viewed as a place where students get credentialed and faculty get tenured while the overall work of the academy does not seem particularly relevant to the nation's most pressing civic, social, economic, and moral problems. (Boyer, 1996)

Although Boyer targeted land-grant institutions because of their historic commitment to applied research and the dissemination of knowledge (Bonnen, 1998), his message was intended for the whole American system of higher education.

Demonstrating the broadening nature of support for a more engaged relationship with society, a coalition of university presidents declared their commitment to leading the renewal of the civic mission of higher education in the *Fourth of July Declaration on the Civic*

11

Responsibility of Higher Education (Boyte & Hollander, 1999). Symbolically released on July 4, 1999, the declaration urged American higher education institutions to become "vital agents and architects of a flourishing democracy" (Boyte & Hollander, 1999).

Creating the Covenant

Within the context of the Zeitgeist just described, the National Association of State Universities and Land-Grant Colleges received a grant from the W. K. Kellogg Foundation to examine the extent to which public universities were prepared to meet societal needs for the twenty-first century. The Kellogg Commission, made up primarily of former and current university presidents, was designed to create an awareness among public universities of the kinds of reforms higher education required to meet the challenges of the new century. Drawing heavily on the ideas articulated by Boyer, the Kellogg Commission called on America's public universities to "renew their covenant" with society. This renewed covenant would refocus the scholarship agenda to place students at the forefront and elevate the status of teaching and public service within the context of institutional mission and faculty rewards.

This was a powerful challenge. A covenant is "a solemn and binding undertaking to do something or get something done" (Wyld, 1938), which, if embraced by higher education, would require substantive change within the academy. Such a covenant would place special demands on research universities. Indeed, the Kellogg Commission argued for "a redesign of basic university functions so the institution becomes even more productively involved with communities, however community is defined" (Kellogg Commission, 2000, p. 22). The report concluded that:

> our tried-and-true formula of *teaching, research,* and *service* no longer serves adequately as a statement of our mission and objectives. The growing democratization of higher education, the greater capacity of today's students to shape and guide their own learning, and the burgeoning demands of the modern world require us to think, instead, of *learning, discovery,* and *engagement.* (Kellogg Commission, 2001, p. 27)

Such a redesign of basic university functions goes beyond an elevation of the status of applied research and an investment in student service learning. As Boyte and Kari (1996) point out, "to create serious change at a research university requires change in the culture and understanding of research." It would also require changes in cultural values related to teaching and service (Braxton, Luckey, & Helland, 2002). For example, to fully implement a covenant with society to promote societal change, higher education would need to "embed change priorities in core reporting, budgetary, and accountability structures of the university" (London, 2002). Undoubtedly, liberal arts colleges, professional and technical colleges, and community colleges would be similarly challenged to restructure and reallocate limited resources to meet the covenant challenge.

From Outreach to Engagement

In urging higher education to more actively engage society, the Kellogg Commission distinguished "engagement" from the more familiar terms "public service," "outreach," and "extension." The new approach challenged faculty to move beyond "outreach," as it was conceptualized in the land-grant colleges with their agricultural roots. It also asked that the scholar go beyond "service," with its overtones of *noblesse oblige.* Whereas existing conceptions of "outreach" and "service" involved one-way transfers of university expertise, engagement necessitated a systemic, two-way relationship between higher education and society. Genuine collaboration emphasizes that "learning and the teaching be multidirectional and the expertise shared" (Rice, 2005, p. 28). The Commission made the distinction quite explicit:

> Engagement goes well beyond extension, conventional outreach, and even most conceptions of public service. Inherited concepts emphasize a one-way process in which the university transfers its expertise to key constituents. Embedded in the engagement ideal is a commitment to sharing and reciprocity. By engagement the Commission envisioned partnerships, two-way streets defined by mutual respect among the partners for what each brings to the table. (Kellogg Commission, 2001, p. 13)

The commission proposed seven guiding characteristics to give greater specificity to its definition (p. 16), and we have slightly rephrased them as follows:

- *Responsiveness:* Are we responsive to the communities that we serve?
- *Respect for partners:* Are we developing joint academic-community definitions of problems, solutions, and definitions of success?
- *Academic neutrality:* Are we playing the role of neutral facilitator and source of information in public policy?
- *Access:* Do we help potential partners navigate our complex structure?
- *Integration:* Are we integrating institutional scholarship with the service and teaching missions of the university?
- *Coordination:* Are we achieving alignment of the engagement agenda throughout the university?
- *Resource partnerships:* Are we identifying our partners in government, business, communities, and the nonprofit world?

The Kellogg Commission's seven characteristics, which we have rephrased as action steps for community partnering, set the boundaries for a national discussion about what it means to be an engaged institution. However, whereas the characteristics offered greater specificity, the reports did not translate easily into implementation strategies or address many of the core barriers to institutional change. For example, although clearly within the spirit of Boyer's redefinition of scholarship, the Kellogg definition of engagement did not easily translate into clear objectives relative to faculty roles and responsibilities, student learning environments, or institutional benchmarks for measuring institutional commitments as engaged universities. How would higher education know whether it had actually succeeded in "getting something done"? How would it know when the covenant had been fulfilled?

The Meaning of Engagement, the Engaged Campus, and Engaged Scholarship

The Kellogg Commission's call for a covenant with society necessitated the development of the meaning of engagement, the engaged campus, and engaged scholarship. Moving from outreach as a one-way transfer of knowledge to engagement as a two-way process of mutual knowledge creation and benefit has required extensive dialogue and development. What does it mean that scholars work on engaged campuses and that they are immersed in engaged scholarship? The importance of having a clear understanding of both terms is that scholars will know whether their campuses are indeed engaging a more two-way, systemic relationship with society. A critical step in developing of the meaning of engagement has been a shift in "the discourse about scholarly engagement from a linear notion of the university that extends itself to communities, to a systemic notion of discourse and praxis that is shared by the university, community, and service institutions" (Fear, Rosaen, Bawden, & Foster-Fishman, 2002, p. 10).

Both the engaged campus and engaged scholarship have three qualities that are central to an understanding of engagement's development, its language, and its practices (Fitzgerald, Smith, Book, Rodin, & the CIC Committee on Engagement, 2005). These three qualities manifest themselves organizationally through the *engaged campus* and academically through *engaged scholarship*.

1. Engagement is scholarly.

A scholarship-based model of engagement involves both the act of engaging (bringing universities and communities together) and the product of engagement (the spread of discipline-generated, evidence-based practices in communities). This emphasis on scholarship is what clearly distinguishes engaged scholarship from service. Service does not involve the creation of scholarly products. Because engagement places a significant emphasis on scholarship, institutions that track and measure engaged scholarship are able to demonstrate how they are contributing to the public good. Engagement fulfills higher education's civic mission—not just by educating students to be better citizens, but through engaging scholars with the public in creating knowledge that is of value to both scholars and society.

2. Engagement cuts across the missions of teaching, research, and service.

Engagement cannot be separated from the core missions of teaching, research, and service. It is an orientation toward those core missions. It is a mode of teaching, a method of research, and a form of service.

3. Engagement is reciprocal and mutually beneficial.

Engagement is not a one-way transmission or translation of scholarship. Nor is it a simple two-way exchange of information. It involves a two-way, systemic relationship. There is mutual planning, implementation, and assessment among engagement partners. Such a mutual and reciprocal relationship is aimed simultaneously at institutional and social transformation. By engaging a diverse set of stakeholders in dialogue, this participatory process is part of the process of inquiry itself (Habermas, 1987). It puts social interactions and human relationships, rather than technorationality, at the center of social transformation. It involves creating knowledge not just *about* the public, in policy reports, but *with* the public, empowering the critique of popular ideas as well as existing social and political arrangements with the same freedom of inquiry that exists in the academy.

The Engaged Campus

A committee comprising representatives from the Committee on Institutional Cooperation (CIC), a consortium of twelve research universities including the eleven members of the Big Ten Conference and the University of Chicago, developed a definition of engagement adopted by the CIC Members Committee (Provosts). The Committee drew on several member institutions' definitions of outreach and engagement to develop the following integrated definition:

> Engagement is the partnership of university knowledge and resources with those of the public and private sectors to enrich scholarship, research, and creative activity; enhance curriculum, teaching, and learning; prepare educated, engaged citizens; strengthen democratic values and civic responsibility; address critical societal issues; and contribute to the public good. (Fitzgerald et al., 2005, p. 2)

This definition provides a model from which each institution can develop a definition appropriate to its mission and context.

Engaged Scholarship

The Committee on Engagement also endorsed *engaged scholarship* as a critical defining characteristic of an *engaged campus*. They noted Holland's definition of engaged scholarship, namely:

> a specific conception of faculty work that connects the intellectual assets of the institution (i.e., faculty expertise) to public issues such as community, social, cultural, human, and economic development. Through engaged forms of teaching and research, faculty apply their academic expertise to public purposes, as a way of contributing to the fulfillment of the core mission of the institution. (Holland, 2005)

Both definitions embrace the concept of university-community partnership for mutual benefit; endorse scholarship as a critical defining characteristic of the university; allow for greater diversity of scholarship products; and view engaged student learning as critical to the mission of higher education.

Evoking the legacy of Ernest Boyer, Ellison and Eatman (2008) argue for the need to ground engaged scholarship in the notion of multiple scholarships. Their inclusive framework allows a scholarly continuum that recognizes many professional pathways. This framing allows faculty members to identify themselves within a range of options for what counts as scholarship on their campus. It allows each campus to decide how it might create knowledge "about, for, and with" (p. iv) the public appropriate to its mission and social context while maintaining principles of scholarly excellence (Ellison & Eatman, 2008). Figure 1 offers one example of how a campus might understand this continuum. Table 1 summarizes benchmarks for operationalizing engagement activities and tracking their outcomes. Different campuses may arrange the variety of forms of scholarship at different locations than the one presented in the figure, and they may select various indicators to measure their success. Likewise, they may choose to include or exclude some of the forms of scholarship listed. Yet, by naming a range of options for what counts as scholarship, they articulate the ways their campus's research, teaching, and service missions overlap with the community.

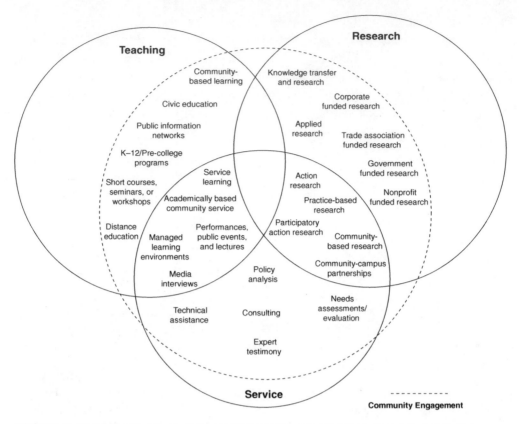

FIGURE 2.1 Examples of a Continuum of Engaged Scholarship across Teaching, Research, and Service

Current Challenges in Renewing the Covenant

The Kellogg Commission's call for a covenant with society necessitated enormous change in higher education. Since the Commission, scores of books have been written, journals published, and conferences organized. Networks of campuses and scholars now exist, each of which focuses on engaged scholarship and its impact on higher education's democratic mission. Although it may be presumptuous to expect consensus or consistency to be reached in such a loosely coupled movement of organizations and individuals, new languages have emerged that bridge the diversity in context and practice.

Significant progress has been made in advancing each of the Commission's recommendations, yet we are far from achieving full integration of engaged scholarship in the academy. According to its own self-evaluation, the emphasis on two-way engagement with society has stimulated conversations and led many campuses to include engagement as a central part of their mission, planning, and programs (Byrne, 2006). However, the same self-evaluation noted that although many campuses had adopted the language of engagement, some campuses still used "engagement" interchangeably with "outreach" (Byrne, 2006). The two-way relationship, involving mutual sharing and reciprocity, has not necessarily described the new plans and programs implemented at these institutions.

Table 1. Draft Recommendations for Engagement Benchmarks and Outcome Indicator Categories

1. Evidence of Institutional Commitment to Engagement
   1.1. The institution's commitment is reflected throughout its administrative structure.
   1.2. The institution's commitment is reflected in its reward structure for faculty and staff.
   1.3. The institution's commitment is reflected in its policies and procedures designed to facilitate outreach and engagement activities.
   1.4. The institution's commitment is reflected in its policies and procedures that are responsive to students.

2. Evidence of Institutional Resource Commitments to Engagement
   2.1. The institution shows evidence of leadership for engagement and outreach activities.
   2.2. The institution shows evidence of financial support for engagement through its budgetary process.
   2.3. The institution shows evidence that faculty and staff time is devoted to outreach and engagement activities.
   2.4. The institution includes engagement activities as part of its programs for faculty, student, and staff development.

3. Evidence That Students Are Involved in Engagement and Outreach Activities
   3.1. The institution shows evidence that engagement is both an implicit and an explicit component of the curriculum and co-curricular activities.
   3.2. The institution shows evidence that it attends to diverse communities, peoples, and geographic areas.
   3.3. The institution shows evidence that students are engaged in projects and programs that are centered in communities.
   3.4. The institution provides educational opportunities that clarify the engaged nature of research and scholarship.

4. Evidence That Faculty and Staff Are Engaged with External Constituents
   4.1. The institution shows evidence that faculty and staff are involved in scholarly activities related to the institution's engagement mission.
   4.2. The institution shows evidence that faculty and staff are engaged in community well-being and economic development initiatives in partnership with external constituents.
   4.3. The institution shows evidence that there is translation and transfer of new knowledge to external audiences.
   4.4. The institution has policies regarding intellectual property rights that foster the availability of knowledge and research as a public good.

5. Evidence That Institutions Are Engaged with Their Communities
   5.1. The institution shows evidence that it has established university-community partnerships with diverse entities.
   5.2. The institution shows evidence that it participates in environmental scanning in order to determine critical social needs.
   5.3. The institution shows evidence that communities have access to and use university resources and programs.
   5.4. The institution shows evidence that its partnerships strive to improve community well-being.

6. Evidence of Assessing the Impact and Outcomes of Engagement
   6.1. The institution shows evidence that it has assessment tools and assessment plans developed in collaboration with external partners.
   6.2. The institution shows evidence that its experiential learning programs are evaluated in partnership with constituents served.

7. Evidence of Resource/Revenue Opportunities Generated through Engagement
   7.1. The institution shows evidence that it generates additional tuition and fee revenues from educational experiences that serve external audiences.
   7.2. The institution shows evidence that it generates economic impact from its engagement activities.

Innovations in higher education are slow to be implemented. Lasting institutional change does not occur without robust debate, disagreement, and the emergence of diverse pathways and practices. To continually develop a more reciprocal engagement with society will require active dialogue in four areas: (1) what it means to be an engaged scholar, (2) rewarding faculty engagement, (3) linking community and campus, and (4) benchmarking institutional engagement.

1. A Broader Definition of the Community of Scholars

What does it mean to be a scholar? A scholar is "a person regarded as acquiring experience or information . . . a learned individual, one trained in accuracy and critical method, and who possesses a mastery of some subject, especially some branch of humane learning" (Wyld, 1938). The engaged scholar embraces values and beliefs regarding the social role and social responsibility of the community of scholars. And although the contextual setting for societal problems may change over generations, the value of social responsibility endures.

Society requires that its community of scholars develop innovations to resolve a variety of problems, across multiple contexts. These problems relate to: competitiveness in a global economy; the quality of early childhood, pre-K, and K–12 education; health care access and delivery; family and community stability and security; security of food and water supplies; effective land use and sustainable, built environments; community and interpersonal violence and antisocial behavior; and tolerance for diversity in all of its forms, among others. Depressingly, children, adolescents, and families continue to live in high-risk circumstances (Fitzgerald, Zucker, & Freeark, 2006) at rates that many view as the single most threatening challenge to the preservation of American democratic life. For example, poverty surrounds the lives of millions of American children and families and contributes directly and indirectly to high rates of (1) infant morbidity and mortality, particularly among African American families, (2) teenage pregnancy, and (3) substance abuse and antisocial behavior (Fitzgerald, McKelvey, Schiffman, & Montanez, 2006; Fitzgerald & Zucker, 2006; Hussong, Zucker, Wong, Fitzgerald, & Puttler, 2005), and (4) social injustices in many ethno-racial populations. The combination of adolescent parenthood and substance abuse is especially endangering to the mental and physical health of infants and young children (Fitzgerald & Eiden, 2007).

However, the community of scholars cannot contribute fully to the resolution of such problems while surrounded by the artificial walls that separate campus and community (Fitzgerald et al., 2005). The problems are *in* the community, and scholars must work *with* the community to effect sustainable solutions. Community change requires a much broader conceptualization of the community of scholars, one that recognizes nonacademic, experiential knowledge as being as important for resolution of community problems as is knowledge from campus. Resolution of societal problems will not come either from the community of scholars or from politicians, school superintendents, fire marshals, or corporate CEOs alone. The complexities and interdependencies of social, economic, political, educational, and health systems require the integration of the knowledge resources of both campus and community to create solution-focused programs that benefit all.

2. A Broader Definition of Scholarship

In addition to a broader definition of what it means to be in the community of scholars, community-campus partnerships require a broader definition of scholarship within that community. Today, faculty in research-oriented colleges and universities typically are evaluated on three aspects of their work—research (scholarship of discovery), teaching, and service, precisely in that hierarchical order. Assessment of faculty starts with an evaluation of their published works, on the "products" they produce. But the products are in-house, peer-reviewed, and peer-judged. Has an article been published in a Tier 1 peer-reviewed journal? Was it cited heavily by other members of the discipline? Was the performance judged to be of value by critics? The criteria guiding such assessments are product-oriented, disciplinary-specific, increasingly narrow, and often shielded from public dissemination.

The limitations of the discipline-based peer review are more evident in evaluating engaged scholarship. Community-campus partnerships require a broader set of criteria to assess scholarly work (Braxton, Luckey, & Helland, 2002). Because engagement involves producing knowledge with communities, organizations, or agencies, external peers need to provide assessment of the quality and efficacy of the scholarship produced. Colleges and universities must wrestle with how and in what way these stakeholders assess the quality and efficacy of the scholarship produced. Glassick, Huber, and Maeroff (1997) identified six standards common to any domain of scholarship (i.e., clear goals, adequate preparation, appropriate methods, significant results, effective presentation, and reflective critique) that are potentially useful in evaluating faculty performance and that also translate well when applied to community-campus partnerships. For example, has the partnership developed clear goals? Has it prepared adequately? Is it using appropriate methods? What results have been obtained? How have they been disseminated? What has been learned as a result of the attempt at system change?

Work is still needed to give engaged scholarship full standing in promotion and rewards. Some universities have created new incentives for faculty involvement in reward structures; however, tenure and promotion policies at many institutions still discourage faculty from doing engaged scholarship (Church, Zimmerman, Bargerstock, & Kenney, 2003).

For faculty who report engaged scholarship as part of their promotion and tenure forms, Community-Campus Partnerships for Health (CCPH) has created a guide that describes and documents quality community-engaged scholarship for faculty in the promotion and tenure process (Jordan, 2007). CCPH is a nonprofit organization that promotes health through service-learning, community-based participatory research, and university-community partnerships (CCPH, 2008). The guide provides examples of portfolios that evidence high-quality, rigorously engaged scholarship and have been used by other faculty in the promotion and tenure process. Institutions may also choose to review a faculty's engaged scholarship via the National Clearinghouse on Engaged Scholarship, which provides written feedback and an assessment of quality.

Imagining America, a national consortium of colleges and universities committed to public scholarship, has led a national effort to advocate changes to reward policies that include a continuum of scholarly products, professional pathways, and ways to value public engagement (Ellison & Eatman, 2008). Its publicly available report, *Scholarship in Public: Knowledge Creation and Tenure Policy in the Engaged University*, is currently being used to

19

discuss changes to faculty reward and promotion structures. Its unique approach allows universities and faculty to determine where on the spectrum they want to include engaged scholarship in decisions on promotion and tenure.

3. Connecting Community and Campus

Many campuses have included engagement as part of their university's strategic or academic planning process. Several universities have created high-level offices to administer their engagement activities. Institutions are considering how their "intellectual assets should or should not be focused on the exploration of questions with public dimensions" (Holland, 2005). This move toward more collaborative scholarship led Barbara Holland to suggest that a new generation of scholars may grow up hearing "partner or perish" rather than "publish or perish" (Holland, 2005). Still, the challenge remains for campuses to strengthen these organizational structures and create a more effective means of tracking and assessing their commitments beyond individual faculty projects, course assessments, or departmental reviews (Driscoll, 2008a).

Silka (1999) has framed a number of paradoxes about community-campus partnerships, each of which could critically impact the extent to which university faculty would be willing to invest energy and resources into building community collaborations (see table 2). To call for increased community-campus partnerships is easy; to put them into effect presents a set of systemic issues both within the campus and within the community in order to make such partnerships effective and sustainable.

Table 2. Silka's Ten Paradoxes of Partnerships That Capture the Polarities That Frame Institutional Dialogue about the Value of Engaged Scholarship

1. University partnerships are new, untried experiments/Partnerships are old, commonplace institutional practices

2. Partnerships are robust/Partnerships are fragile

3. Successful partnerships are easy to achieve/Partnerships are rarely successful

4. Partnerships should be choreographed, planned relationships/Partnerships should be allowed to be evolving, emergent relationships

5. The university's commitment to the community is short term/The university's involvement is long term

6. Partnerships are collaborations between organizations/Partnerships are relationships between individuals

7. Partnerships are vehicles for local application and improvement/Partnerships are opportunities for faculty innovation and advancement

8. Successful partnerships will depend on the involvement of new faculty/Partnerships will be successful only if they draw on mature faculty

9. Partnerships need faculty as experts/Partnerships need faculty as generalists

10. Partnerships are valuable for researchers/Partnerships are primarily of use for faculty in their role as teachers

SOURCE: Adapted from Silka, L. (1999). Paradoxes of partnerships: Reflections on university-community collaborations. *Research in Politics and Society, 7,* 335–359.

Portland State University hosted a Partnership Forum in 2008. The forum developed a definition of community-campus partnerships:

> Partnerships develop out of relationships and result in mutual transformation and cooperation between parties. They are motivated by a desire to combine forces that address their own best interests/mission and ideally result in outcomes greater than any one organization could achieve alone. They create a sense of shared purpose that serves the common good. (Driscoll, 2008b)

The forum also identified six different types of partnerships that these offices are coordinating with their surrounding community: (1) higher education institution/community partnerships, (2) college, department, program/community partnerships, (3) individual faculty/community partnerships for service-learning, (4) individual faculty/community partnerships for community-based research, (5) student(s)/community partnerships, and (6) student organization/community partnerships (Driscoll, 2008b).

4. Measuring, Assessing, and Accrediting Engagement

A significant amount of progress has been made in regard to institutional tracking and assessment of university-community engagement. In 2002, Campus Compact received a three-year grant from the Carnegie Corporation to develop indicators of engagement to help campuses with organizing more effective practices. Recognizing that institutions approach engagement based on their particular context and mission, the indicators were designed to identify effective practices of community engagement. The indicators focus on institutional culture, curriculum and pedagogy, faculty roles and rewards, mechanisms and resources, and community-campus exchange.

Not only have national organizations developed means of tracking and assessment; individual institutions have also developed new tools that track and assess faculty engagement. Michigan State University, for example, has created the Outreach and Engagement Measurement Instrument (OEMI), which is now used to track and measure community engagement at several large research universities. Data from the OEMI provides evidence to stakeholders, such as administrators, alumni, and legislators, on how each university is contributing to the development of its region and state, the nation, and beyond.

In 2005, the Higher Learning Commission of the North Central Association of Colleges and Schools included "Engagement and Service" as one of the five criteria linked to accreditation, requiring institutions to demonstrate responsiveness to the constituencies and communities they serve, including connecting students with external communities through their educational programs.

In addition, engagement received national visibility when the Carnegie Foundation for the Advancement of Teaching developed a "Community Engagement" elective classification for institutions that demonstrate an exchange of knowledge and resources between higher education institutions and their larger communities in a context of partnership and reciprocity. The classification's framework is intended to "respect the diversity of institutional contexts and approaches to engagement, to encourage reflective inquiry and [a] self-assessment process that is practical and provides useful data, and to affirm good work while urging even better" (Driscoll, 2008a).

In 2006, seventy-six U.S. colleges and universities were listed as "institutions of community engagement": forty-four public, thirty-two private, thirty-six doctorate-granting, and twenty-one master's-granting colleges and universities, as well as baccalaureate colleges, five community colleges, and one specialized arts college (Driscoll, 2008a). Each institution was asked to provide documentation in two sections: foundational indicators and categories of engagement. In 2008, 120 colleges and universities were approved as engaged institutions. The diversity of institutions and the diversity of engagement reflects in the Carnegie classifications ranges from research-intensive and comprehensive universities to faith-based, minority-serving, and liberal arts colleges.

Engagement into the Twenty-First Century

We opened this chapter's discussion about engaged scholarship by focusing on its history, the meaning and diversity of its practices, and the challenges it faces in contemporary higher education. We framed how specific practices or questions fit within the larger historical context. Yet, this is only one starting point for the conversation. Engaged scholarship involves a rich diversity of campus and scholarly perspectives. Understanding the varieties of practice and critical questions allows each person to thoughtfully consider how engagement might be integrated into his or her discipline, department, or campus.

Administrators and department chairs may enter the conversation by exploring examples of how different institution types incorporate engagement into their structures and cultures. They may consider the national organizational models that are being developed to coordinate efforts across campuses and between communities and campuses.

Department chairs and faculty may have critical questions about engaged scholarship. For example: How do departments measure or reward engaged scholarship in the promotion and tenure process? How does engaged scholarship develop over faculty career stages? How do departments prepare current and future faculty to be scholars who practice engaged research and teaching? How do students learn in the engaged academy?

Finally, faculty who already practice engaged scholarship may consider reading more about scholarship-focused research to increase its academic and community impact. Other faculty may examine student trends that will impact engaged teaching and learning practices in the future.

The diversity and practices of engaged scholarship have grown significantly over the past twenty-five years. As the conversation continues, it will reinvigorate the democratic purposes of higher education. It is in this democratic spirit that we invite you to enter the conversation. Read thoughtfully and critically. Ultimately, however, consider how you might take action and continue the conversation in your context, whether it be a community organization, college or university department, or disciplinary organization.

References

Bok, D. (1990). *Universities and the future of America.* Durham, NC: Duke University Press.

Bonnen, J. T. (1998). The land-grant idea and the evolving outreach university. In R. M. Lerner & L. A. K. Simon (Eds.), *University-community collaborations for the twenty-first century* (pp. 25–70). New York: Garland.

Boyer, E. L. (1990). *Scholarship reconsidered: Priorities of the professoriate.* Princeton, NJ: The Carnegie Foundation for the Advancement of Teaching.

Boyer, E. L. (1996). The scholarship of engagement. *Journal of Public Service and Outreach, 1,* 11–20.

Boyte, H. (2004). *Everyday politics: Reconnecting citizens and public life.* Philadelphia: University of Pennsylvania Press.

Boyte, H., & Hollander, E. (1999). *Wingspread declaration on renewing the civic mission of the American research university.* The Wingspread Conference, Racine, WI, p. 16.

Boyte, H., & Kari, N. (1996). *Building America: The democratic promise of public work.* Philadelphia: Temple University Press.

Braxton, J. M., Luckey, W., & Helland, P. (2002). *Institutionalizing a broader view of scholarship through Boyer's four domains.* San Francisco: Jossey-Bass.

Byrne, J. V. (2006). *Public higher education reform five years after The Kellogg Commission on the Future of State and Land-Grant Universities.* Battle Creek, MI: W.K. Kellogg Foundation.

Campbell, J. R. (1995). *Reclaiming a lost heritage: Land-grant and other higher education initiatives for the twenty-first century.* Ames: Iowa State Press.

CDF Reports. (1994, March). *15*(4), 11.

Church, R. L. (2001, November). *Counting public service: Can we make meaningful comparisons within and among institutions.* Paper presented at the symposium "Broadening the Carnegie Classification's Attention to Mission: Incorporating Public Service," at the annual meeting of the Association for the Study of Higher Education.

Church, R. L., Zimmerman, D. L., Bargerstock, B. A., & Kenney, P. A. (2003). Measuring scholarly outreach at Michigan State University: Definition, challenges, tools. *Journal of Higher Education Outreach and Engagement, 6,* 141–152.

Community-Campus Partnerships for Health (CCPH). (2008). Retrieved August 18, 2008, from http://depts.washington.edu/ccph/index.html.

Driscoll, A. (2008a, January/February). Carnegie's Community-Engagement Classification: Intentions and insights. *Change, 40,* 4.

Driscoll, A. (2008b, March 6–8). *A guide to reciprocal community-campus partnerships.* Paper presented at the Partnership Forum, Portland State University.

Ellison, J., & Eatman, T. (2008). *Scholarship in public: Knowledge creation and tenure policy in the engaged university: A resource on promotion and tenure in the arts, humanities, and design.* Syracuse, NY: Syracuse University.

Fear, F. A., Rosaen, C., Bawden, R. J., & Foster-Fishman, P. G. (2006). *Coming to Critical Engagement.* Lanham, MD: University Press of America.

Fitzgerald, H. E., & Eiden, R. D. (2007). Paternal alcoholism, family functioning, and infant mental health. *Zero to Three, 27,* 20–26.

Fitzgerald, H. E., McKelvey, L. M., Schiffman, R. F., & Montanez, M. (2006). Effects of exposure to neighborhood violence and paternal antisocial behavior on low-income families and their children. *Parenting: Research and Practice, 6,* 243–258.

Fitzgerald, H. E., Smith, P., Book, P., Rodin, K., & the CIC Committee on Engagement. (2005, February). *Draft CIC Report: Resource guide and recommendations for defining and benchmarking engagement.* Champaign, IL: CIC.

Fitzgerald, H. E., & Zucker, R. A. (2006). Growing up in an alcoholic family: Pathways of risk aggregation for alcohol use disorders. In K. Freeark & W. Davidson III (Eds.), *The crisis in youth mental health: Critical issues and effective program: Vol. 3. Families, children and communities* (pp. 249–271). Westport, CT: Praeger.

Fitzgerald, H. E., Zucker, R. A., & Freeark, K. (2006). *The crisis in youth mental health: Critical issues and effective programs.* Westport, CT: Praeger.

Garbarino, J. (1994). What children and youth can tell us about violence and trauma. *The Child, Youth, and Family Services Quarterly, 39,* 2–4.

Glassick, C. E., Huber, M. T., & Maeroff, G. I. (1997). *Scholarship assessed: Evaluation of the professoriate.* San Francisco: Jossey-Bass.

Habermas, J. (1987). *The theory of communicative action: Vol. 2. Lifeword and system: A critique of functionalist reason.* Boston: Beacon Press.

History of Campus Compact. (2007). Retrieved September 30, 2008, from http://www.compact.org/about/history.

Holland, B. (2005, July). *Scholarship and mission in the 21st century university: The role of engagement.* Paper presented at the Australian Universities Quality Forum, Sydney.

Hussong, A. M., Zucker, R. A., Wong, M. W., Fitzgerald, H. E., & Puttler, L. I. (2005). Social competence in children of alcoholic parents over time. *Developmental Psychology, 41,* 747–759.

Johnson, R. N., & Wamser, C. C. (1997). Respecting diverse scholarly work: The key to advancing the multiple missions of the urban university. *Metropolitan Universities, 7,* 43–59.

Jordan, C. (Ed.). (2007). *Community-engaged scholarship review, promotion & tenure package.* Peer review workgroup, community-engaged scholarship for health collaborative. Seattle, WA: Community-Campus Partnerships for Health.

Kellogg Commission. (2000). *Renewing the covenant: Learning, discovery, and engagement in a new age and different world.* Washington, DC: National Association of State Universities and Land-Grant Colleges.

Kellogg Commission. (2001). *Returning to our roots: Executive summaries of the reports of the Kellogg Commission on the Future of State and Land-Grant Universities.* Washington, DC: National Association of State Universities and Land-Grant Colleges.

Lerner, R. M. (1995). *America's youth in crisis: Challenges and options for programs and policies.* Thousand Oaks, CA: Sage.

Lerner, R. L. & Simon, L. A. (Eds,). (1998). *University-community collaborations for the twenty-first century.* New York: Garland.

London, S. (2002). *Practical strategies for institutional civic engagement and institutional leadership that reflect and shape the covenant between higher education and society.* Monticello, MN: Kellogg Forum on Higher Education for the Public Good.

McCall, R. B., Groark, C. J., Strauss, M. S., & Johnson, C. N. (1998). Challenges of university-community outreach to traditional research universities. Lerner, R. L., & Simon, L. A. (Eds.), *University-community collaborations for the twenty-first century* (pp. 203–230). New York: Garland.

Rice, R. E. (2005). "Scholarship reconsidered": History and context. In K. A. O'Meara & R. E. Rice (Eds.), *Faculty priorities reconsidered* (pp. 17–31). San Francisco: Jossey-Bass.

Silka, L. (1999). Paradoxes of partnerships: reflections on university-community collaborations. *Politics and Society, 7,* 335–359.

Votruba, J. C. (1992). Promoting the extension of knowledge in service to society. *Metropolitan Universities, 3*(3), 72–80.

Whitehead, A. N. (1947). *Essays in science and philosophy.* New York: Philosophical Library.

Wyld, H. C. (Ed.). (1938). *The universal dictionary of the English language.* Chicago: Standard American Corporation.

History of the Scholarship of Engagement Movement

David Cox

Loosely defined, history is a narrative, a record through time often accompanied by an explanation of that time. That narrative may come in many forms. Presented as biography or autobiography, history is viewed through the lens of a person. Approached as an event, history may be seen as the unfolding of a conflict or an idea or ideology. Explored as a particular period of time, history may be presented as an era of economic plenty or upheaval. Focused on an institution, history may be the story of a nation or an organization.

Biography, events, period of time, and institutions all offer frameworks for exploring the history of the scholarship of engagement movement. Boyer (1990), Dewey (1938), and Lynton (1983) are just a few of the authors whose biography would inform that history. Events such as the creation and development of the land-grant movement offer a means of viewing that history (Committee on the Future of the Colleges of Agriculture in the Land Grant University System, 1995). The time from the introduction of higher education in the United States in the colonies to the present day is a time period in which to view that history (Bender, 1988). Similarly, institutions from the turn-of-the century Hull House, to individual higher education campuses, to the rise of associations such as Campus Compact provide institutional frameworks through which to explore the history of the scholarship of engagement (Gearan, 2005).

At its core, though, this book has two foci. One is about change. Volume 1, *Institutional Change*, is explicit on that point. It explores change within higher educational institutions in response to changes in their relationships with communities. The other is about the relationships. Volume 2, *Community-Campus Partnerships*, focuses on the nature of the engagement between campuses and their external communities. As a consequence of these foci, the historical frame for this chapter will be about change: change in institutions of higher learning related to the scholarship of engagement. What processes of change are in place within higher education institutions? How do those processes involve the scholarship of engagement? And what might that involvement tell us about the future of the scholarship of engagement?

Defining the Scholarship of Engagement

A first step is defining what we mean by the scholarship of engagement. Scholarship is a process. It is purposeful, executed using appropriate rigor and methodological standards, and adds to the body of knowledge (Diamond & Adam, 1993; Glassick, Huber, & Maeroff, 1997). Engagement connotes connection and perseverance. As noted by Bender (1988), higher education institutions have been connected with and committed to the communities and societies in which they exist for centuries. Scholarship may be connected to external communities through the transmission of resulting knowledge to those communities. It may occur when external communities are used as laboratories for the conduct of that scholarship.

The scholarship of engagement, though, is distinguished by the reciprocal nature of that connection and commitment in the production of knowledge. External partners are actively involved as reciprocal partners in the execution of the work. That participation may occur in defining the issue to be addressed. It may involve design and execution of the project and inquiry producing knowledge. Or, it may take place in the analysis of results and dissemination of the resulting learning. That participation may take place at some or at all the stages of the work. The critical point is that scholarship takes place and that it involves meaningful collaboration between higher education and community partners (Cox, 2006; Van de Ven, 2007).

Understanding Institutional Change

A second step is defining the models or lenses for viewing the processes of change. Change as a concept for understanding institutions has not been easy to define. It may be seen as change within an organization, change in an organization's relations with others, change in behaviors of an organization, or even change in perceptions about an organization (Burnes, 1996; Senge, 1990; Van de Ven & Poole, 1995). It may result from intentional acts or it might result by accident (Carr, Hard, & Trahant, 1996; Weick, 1979). How one conceptualizes change matters to a history of change. The model or lens of change that one uses directs where to look for change. Where one looks for change shapes the understanding of how and whether change occurred and the meaning of that change.

Recently, Kezar (2001) offered a synthesis of work on analyzing institutional change by Burnes (1996), Rajagopalan and Spreitzer (1996), Van de Ven and Poole (1995), and others. The synthesis is based on a four-question framework (Kezar, 2001): Why did change occur, what processes were involved in the change, what were the outcomes of the change, and what is the key metaphor for understanding that change? Kezar's answers led her to identify six models of change: evolutionary, teleological, life cycle, political, social cognition, and cultural.

Although connections between higher education institutions and communities in the form of engaged scholarship have been at issue since the appearance of universities in the later middle ages (Bender, 1988), recent attention has been a response to a set of critiques of the role of higher education institutions in society during the past generation (Bok, 1982; Boyer, 1990). The focus of this history, therefore, is on change during the past several decades. As a result, Kezar's life cycle model, which involves a much longer period of time, is not included in our analysis.

Four differences appear among the remaining five models. Three among the five models differ in the forces they identify as keys to understanding recent change and the effect of those changes related to the scholarship of engagement. Those differing forces point to different forms of response and resulting differing futures within the models. The other two models offer different sources as key to driving that change. But they reach the same conclusion as to the direction of the resulting change on higher education institutions' approach to the scholarship of engagement and its future.

In one model, the external environment is the source of change. The result is an evolutionary model, organizational change in response to external environmental stimuli. Change in this model tends to be slow, adaptive, and nonintentional. New structures and processes may result from the change. The metaphor is the institution as an organism. Adaptation for survival directs the change.

In a second model, purpose set within the institution drives change. Change therefore is teleological or intentional. Organizations are seen as having purpose. Change occurs because of leaders who see a need to direct the organization to better serve or in some cases change that purpose. Change is an internal decision. Planning, assessment, incentives and rewards, stakeholder analysis, goals, and strategies are all key elements in accomplishing change. The outcome may be new structures or processes. The metaphor is the leader as change master.

In a third model, competing values, ideals, or norms within an organization are the force for change. Resolution of those differences occurs through processes of negotiation and power. The result is a political model. An outcome of those negotiations or power processes may be a new ideology directing the institution. A metaphor for this model has been social movements.

With the two remaining models, social cognition and culture, the sources for change differ. But for each, the response to those forces is the same. It is a fundamental reframing of how the organization comes to be understood or defined. Change toward the scholarship of engagement is the product of that new understanding.

Social cognition finds the force for that change in the process of learning. People involved with the organization gain information leading to a reinterpretation of the organization. Or, resolution of conflicts within an organization may involve new interpretations of the role of that organization. Whether through internal learning or conflict resolution, the consequence of these forces is a new understanding of the fundamental role of the organization in society. Given the role of learning, the brain is the metaphor for the social cognition model.

In the cultural model, change in the broader social setting produces the change in perceptions of the organization. Cultural changes outside of and permeating the organization

27

lead to a reinterpretation of the organization. As with social cognition, the result is a new understanding of the fundamental role of the organization with resulting changes in behavior. Social movement is the metaphor for the cultural model. In both models, change tends to be slow, and the outcome is a new frame of mind and behaviors.

Histories of Higher Institutional Change and the Scholarship of Engagement

Evolutionary History of the Scholarship of Engagement

External forces are the source of change within the evolutionary models of change for institutions. Several external factors have been associated with the development of the scholarship of engagement in higher education institutions during the past several decades.

One external force is found in the physical, economic, and social environments of their settings, especially for many urban-based higher education institutions. Whatever the circumstances of the communities when they were originally located, increases in poverty, crime, and physical deterioration, often on their doorstep, began to threaten their existence (Webber, 2005). Those conditions become a threat to the ability of those institutions to attract students, faculty members, and staff and to maintain their level of performance (Cisneros, 1996; Harkavy, 1997; Jackson & Meyers, 2000).

Their challenge was as anchored institutions; they could not pick up and leave. That left two choices. They could try to build walls to insulate themselves from the changes occurring in their environment. Or, using their resources, they could try to address the surrounding deterioration (Maurrasse, 2007).

Armed with advantages in access to public and private funds, many have sought to address that deterioration. Some simply developed their own plans for doing so. Often that included removing the poor and clearing the physical deterioration. Those efforts did not include engagement and reciprocity with the affected communities (Perry & Wiewel, 2005).

For others, though, the threats became an important stimulus to engage with communities. The resulting engagement took many forms (Dubb & Howard, 2007). In Philadelphia, it involved engagement between residents of West Philadelphia and the University of Pennsylvania, located in the area, to make neighborhood schools better as a means of neighborhood improvement (Harkavy, 1997). Engagement became critical to the success of neighborhood revitalization next to the Ohio State University campus (Jackson & Meyers, 2000). In these and many other examples, surrounding deterioration was a stimulus for higher education institutions to act, and engagement with community was necessary for success.

Another form of external pressure was found in increasing expectations by public officials and city and state leaders for higher education institutions to be responsible and become more involved in addressing social and economic conditions, no matter the locale. That is particularly the case for urban and for public higher education institutions. As an example, when a representative of an economically distressed city in Illinois became chairperson of the state legislature's Joint Committee on Higher Education Finance, she challenged the state's public higher education leadership to demonstrate its commitment and responsibility to the state by addressing that distress. In response, students and faculty members at the University of Illinois became engaged with community residents and municipal officials in an extensive engaged partnership to improve living conditions in East St. Louis, Illinois (Reardon, 2000).

A third form of environmental pressure came from higher education's continuing need for resources. Rising personnel, facilities, and equipment costs lead to an ongoing quest for additional and new sources of revenue. Partnerships provide access to new sources of revenue. Partnerships can increase an institution's competitive position to acquire new revenues. Indeed, through time, partnerships and engagement with communities have become requirements for eligibility for governmental and foundation funding ranging from the U.S. Department of Housing and Urban Development and National Institute of Health, to national foundations such as the Robert Wood Johnson Foundation and the W. K. Kellogg Foundation, to numerous local and community foundations. As a consequence, engaged scholarship has become an important element in higher education institutions' strategies for obtaining additional and new revenues.

Consistent with the evolutionary model, all of these pressures have led to new structures within higher education institutions (Holland, 1997). The most salient change has been the creation of offices or centers with responsibility for advancing engagement. An example can be found in the evolution of the U.S. Department of Housing and Urban Development's (HUD) Community Outreach Partnership Center (COPC) program. Launched in 1994, the program became one of the federal government's major initiatives to encourage and support higher education engagement with economically distressed neighborhoods, eventually funding several hundred partnerships before its ending in 2006. As the program progressed, HUD increased attention to institutionalization of those partnerships to sustain its investments. Institutionalization eventually became one of the required components of a successful application. One component of that institutionalization was strengthening infrastructure in support of those partnerships. A common response was creation of a center focusing on community outreach (Vidal, Nye, Walker, Manjarrez, & Romanik, 2002). Consistent with the COPC program's stimulus for structural change, there has been a rapid growth in the number of higher education institutions establishing a center or office responsible for guiding and enhancing engagement. Indicative of that pattern and expectation, structural forms listed as "Foundational Indicators" are a component of evidence of infrastructure for engaged scholarship in the recently created Carnegie Foundation for the Advancement of Teaching Community Engagement classification (Driscoll, 2007). Consistent with the evolutionary model, the scholarship of engagement was an adaptation to continue the survival of the organization.

Teleological History of the Scholarship of Engagement

In this model, institutional purpose drives change, internal leadership is the force accomplishing that change. One example of this view of the history of the scholarship of engagement may be found in the creation and development of National Campus Compact. Formed in 1985, its impetus was a group of university presidents who believed that developing their students' social awareness and involvement in community and society was a responsibility of higher education institutions (Presidents' Declaration, n.d.). Working from that purpose and with an initial focus on a component of engagement, service learning, Campus Compact has recruited more than one thousand presidents and institutions in support of engagement. In another example, in a 1999 report to the Kellogg Commission (Kellogg Commission on the Future of State and Land Grant Universities, 1999), presidents and chancellors of twenty-five public universities repeated the call for engagement to become central to the mission of higher education. Reflecting that senior executive-level institutional commitment to engagement, the Carnegie Foundation for the Advancement of Teaching Community Engagement classification has identified more than two hundred higher education institutions that now include engagement as an explicit component of their mission statements (Driscoll, 2007).

Purposeful leadership supporting the scholarship of engagement has also developed among higher education institution associations. Some of that leadership has come from existing higher education groups and associations adopting and advancing engagement. Traditional associations such as the Council of Independent Colleges (CIC), the American Association of Community Colleges (AACC), the American Association of State Colleges and Universities (AASCU), and the Association of Public and Land-grant Universities (APLU) have all endorsed engaged scholarship and sponsored it in their commissions and conferences. Professional associations built around disciplines have advocated engagement in advancing their field of knowledge. Postsecondary accrediting associations from regional institutional accrediting bodies to discipline councils have included engagement as an accreditation criterion. Representing a very clear form of intentionality, higher education planning associations such as the Society for College and University Planning (SCUP) have integrated the scholarship of engagement into their programming, professional development, and publications (Peterson, 2004).

As important, the desire to advance the scholarship of engagement has stimulated the creation of a number of new associations, networks and journals. Campus Compact has been cited as one of those new associations. Not only is Campus Compact a national organization, it has encouraged the creation of state level Campus Compact associations. Other newly created national associations include the Community-Campus Partnership for Health (CCPH) focused on academic health connections to communities and the HBCU Faculty Development for Civic Engagement and Social Responsibility representing historically Black colleges and universities. Groups advancing components of engagement such as the Corporation for National and Community Service and the National Service-Learning Clearinghouse, with its focus on volunteerism and service learning, are a part of that network. Indeed, representing a culmination of the growth of organized efforts to advance the scholarship of engagement, the Johnson Foundation, a long-time supporter of engagement, supported a conference of leaders representing thirty-three higher education associations and institutions in 2006. The outcome of the conference was creation of the Higher Education Network for Community Engagement (HENCE) with the explicit purpose to "intentionally connect academic work to public purposes through extensive partnerships that involve faculty members, staff, and students in active collaboration with communities" (HENCE, 2006).

Academic journals are also important to the advancement of a discipline or approach in higher education. Accordingly, the scholarship of engagement has given rise to new journals and has been the focus of established publications. New journals that directly address issues in engaged scholarship are the *Journal of Higher Education Outreach and Engagement* and the *Michigan Journal of Community Service-Learning.* Other journals such as the *Metropolitan Universities Journal* regularly publish articles and special volumes on the scholarship of engagement (Caret, 2007).

Intentional structures in support of the scholarship of engagement can also be found within individual institutions. The scholarship of engagement has been one of three foci of The University of Massachusetts Boston's New England Resource Center for Higher Education (NERCHE). The Barbara and Edward Netter Center for Community Partnerships (BENCCP) at the University of Pennsylvania, aimed at supporting engagement with West Philadelphia, is an example of another early creation. These and many other centers are coordinating projects, publishing and disseminating learning and results, and offering conferences and professional development in support of engaged scholarship.

Finally, at the heart of any intention of an institution is how it rewards the behaviors it expects. For higher education institutions, that is found in how they go about merit awards, tenure, and promotion. What are the criteria, and what are the processes to properly assess engaged scholarship performance? A number of steps have been taken to address those questions. Glassick, Huber, and Maeroff (1997) provided an initial set of criteria that has influenced the answers. It included clear goals, adequate preparation, appropriate methods, significant results, effective communication, and reflective critique in the work. Building on that start, Driscoll and Lynton (1999) offered processes for documenting and assessing performance on those criteria. Through time, a number of publications, conferences, workshops, and institutions have come forward to offer engaged scholarship merit, tenure, and promotion guidelines and are a regular part of the portfolios of the many supportive higher education institutions. Reflecting that work, the National Review Board for the Scholarship of Engagement was created to serve as a national clearinghouse, advance guidelines, and assist in reviews. Consistent with the intentional model, change supporting the scholarship of engagement is coming about through purposeful leadership in higher education institutions and associated organizations.

Political History of the Scholarship of Engagement

The political model of change rests on the idea that there are internal political tensions within an institution. Change is a result of the interaction of those tensions. Engagement as a component of scholarship is a tension within higher education institutions.

One means of viewing this tension is in the competing views toward engagement of Ernest Boyer (1990) and Allan Bloom (1987). Scholarship, according to Boyer, encompasses discovery, integration, application, and teaching. Although the scholarship of engagement has come to include community in any of these components, Boyer particularly emphasized that connection in application. It is at that point that the higher education scholar was required to step outside of the ivory tower. Applied engagement is important to scholarship and higher education in several ways. One, it contributes to questions and new

31

understanding. Two, it leads higher education institutions toward the production of knowl-edge more relevant to the issues facing society. Three, it therefore improves the quality of and the value of higher education to the communities and society it serves (Boyer, 1990).

Bloom, on the other hand, took a very different view. Instead of opening higher education institutions to new insights and knowledge, the scholarship of engagement poses two threats. First, integration and reciprocity with the external world blurs the distinct role that higher education institutions play in society. Rather than remaining places of careful, disengaged, objective exploration and reasoning, engagement leads them to become carriers and exponents of the values and issues of the day. In so doing, they lose their special capacity for independent intellectual development and transmission of knowledge, a critical role for society. Second and correspondingly, by bringing in the issues of the day, engagement lowers the standards and quality of what higher education institutions produce and stand for, pure thought and reason-ing. Engagement thereby leads to a vulgarization of scholarship (Bloom, 1987).

Neither of these views is new to the history of higher education. Bender (1988) finds higher education institutions following separate and parallel paths toward engagement with community in the conduct of scholarship since the rise of the modern university in the middle century. The conflict continues today (Fish, 2003a, 2003b). Consistent with the polit-ical model, the two views represent competing values, ideals, and norms among higher education institutions, within higher education institutions, and within disciplines and units within higher education institutions.

Resolution continues to be a process of negotiation and power. That resolution has taken various shapes. In some cases, it has occurred at the institutional level. Some higher educa-tion institutions have chosen the Boyer view and have embraced engagement. That is the case for many who have opted to participate in the Carnegie Foundation for the Advance-ment of Teaching Community Engagement classification. Reflecting ongoing negotiation, some practice engagement but have not fully accepted it as central to or reflective of their institutions. Others, on the other hand, adhere to the Bloom approach. Another form of resolution is occurring at unit or departmental levels within given institutions. Some units or departments choose to pursue engaged scholarship, whereas others do not.

The metaphor for the political model is the social movement. Porta and Diani (2006) have described a set of characteristics of a social movement. Its actors are engaged in social action with a clear, distinct collective identity built around a core of shared values and beliefs; are involved in conflictual relations with clearly identified opponents; and are linked by dense informal networks. That description can be applied to the proponents for the scholarship of engagement with this model and the resulting resistance and response. Given the long history of that debate, tension over the role of the scholarship of engagement can be expected to be intense and ongoing.

Social Cognition and Cultural Models History of the Scholarship of Engagement
In the social cognition model, learning or conflict resolution within the organization are sources of change. In the cultural models, cultural changes outside of and permeating the organization are the source of change. The point in both models is that change occurs because of different interpretations of the role of the organization. By this view, support for

the scholarship of engagement results from a fundamental reinterpretation of the role of higher education institutions in our society. Both the social cognition and cultural models provide understandings of how these reinterpretations have occurred.

Regarding social cognition, Kennedy (1997) and Benson and Harkavy (2000) have described how American higher education has moved through several stages. At its earliest point, higher education was morally based training for a small elite to lead a mainly agrarian society. Subsequent stages involved creation of the research university leading to the "big science, Cold War, entrepreneurial university" by the middle of the twentieth century. Although not all American higher education institutions are research universities, the values of those institutions substantially shaped expectations for the behavior across higher education institutions. Driven by post–World War II dollars for big science, a key value for these institutions was the creation and transmission of universal knowledge: that is, knowledge and theory building for its own sake, regardless of its applications and unsullied by influences of "real and immediate world" issues or questions (Stokes, 1997). Along the way, higher education researchers and teachers came to be seen as the experts. Communities external to those institutions were viewed as laboratories, not partners in shaping the questions to be asked or in the creation or dissemination of knowledge (Harkavy, 1997).

By the 1960s, a set of circumstances began to intrude on this understanding of the role of higher education institutions. Contradictions between the wealth, status, and power of higher education institutions and the real conditions of society were becoming more obvious. Those contradictions were especially apparent in urban settings, where privileged colleges and universities often sat side by side with increasingly economically distressed and socially isolated communities. At the same time, declining levels of participation in and understanding of governing processes were seen as basic threats to our democratic society.

From those contradictions and threats rose a gradual awareness leading to a reexamination of the very roles and responsibilities of higher education institutions to society (Bok, 1982; Lynton & Elman, 1987). Were they mainly institutions for generating theory-driven knowledge and preparing a more advanced work force? Or, did they have more a more fundamental and direct responsibility in addressing the issues of society and in support of a more democratic and just society? Was their focus only on universal generalizable knowledge? Or, did they have a responsibility to produce and disseminate knowledge addressing immediate real-world issues, problems, and solutions?

From this framework, many of the calls for change and actions to bring about change can be seen as higher education institutions learning from these experiences and contradictions. A result was efforts to reframe the understanding of their role in society. Titles of the work of some of the leaders calling for change, Bok's *Beyond the Ivory Tower: Social Responsibilities of the Modern University*, Boyer's *Scholarship Reconsidered: Priorities of the Professoriate*, or Lynton's "A Crisis of Purpose: Reexamining the Role of the University," spoke to the need to redefine the very meaning and purpose of higher education institutions as connection to community. They were direct calls for real-world relevance and application.

But, how was this to be accomplished? The key was to reconnect with the communities experiencing these issues. Only through connection could higher education institutions

33

develop that relevance and impact (Gibson, 2006). That connection involved the tenets of the scholarship of engagement, collaboration, and reciprocity with external partners and multidisciplinary scholarship. Engaged scholarship became the cornerstone in redefining higher education institutions.

Consistent with those new understandings, a number of initiatives have arisen seeking to advance engaged scholarship as a part of reframing the role of higher education institutions. One approach has been to emphasize the role of higher education institutions in supporting democracy. As one example, the American Democracy Project, sponsored by the AASCU, is explicit in that purpose, focused on expanding the number of undergraduate students actively engaged in "civic projects" as an integral part of their education. Its purpose is to assert the role of higher education institutions in fostering democracy and democratic practices. Another is to seek that advance through disciplines. An example is the Imagining America Project, sponsored by the American Studies Association (ASA), advancing the role of the humanities and creative arts as a part of higher education in support of democratic practices.

Whereas within the social cognition model, learning can be observed as leading to reinterpretation of the role of higher education institutions and support for the scholarship of engagement, external changes can be seen as factors driving change within the cultural model, leading to the same result. A set of important factors have driven that change. One factor, concomitant with the recognition of contradictions between higher education institutions' performance and the conditions of society, was a broad cultural change in expectations and beliefs about the appropriate role of higher education institutions in society. The work by Bok (1982), Boyer (1990), Lynton (1995), and others can be seen as an expression of that change. A second factor, correspondingly and importantly, was that after World War II, there was a rapid expansion in the numbers of persons attending higher education institutions. That expansion led to greater diversity and a wider range of life experiences in those attending those institutions. Though the professoriate today is not reflective of the socioeconomic makeup of the broader population, it is far more diverse that a half century before (Lindholm, Szelenyi, Hurtado, & Korn, 2006). As a consequence, many of the faculty members entering institutions of higher education in the latter part of the twenty-first century brought with them direct experience and interest in the conditions of society. The result was a cultural change within the professoriate in higher education, an interest in social issues, and a commitment to engagement in the scholarship to address those issues. Cultural changes outside and inside higher education institutions therefore led to support for the scholarship of engagement.

As with the political model, the metaphor Kezar suggests for the cultural model is social movement. The metaphor is particularly relevant in that culture is in part defined by a core set of shared values and beliefs. Whether stimulated by changing values and beliefs in the broader society or reflecting changing values and beliefs of faculty members, students, and staff within higher education institutions, cultural changes have led to a new definition of the role of those institutions. The scholarship of engagement is central to fulfilling that role. Thus, whether it is the result of learning on the part of higher education institutions or in response to cultural changes, the central point from both of the social cognition and cultural models is that change is a redefinition of those institutions. The scholarship of engagement flows from that redefinition.

Projecting the Future for the Scholarship of Engagement

This chapter began with the assertion that history can be viewed through various frames. The frame chosen for this history of the scholarship of engagement was recent changes in higher education institutions related to the scholarship of engagement. Four separate models were used for viewing that change: evolutionary, teleological, political, and social cognition/cultural. The separate models helped identify different factors affecting the scholarship of engagement, offered differing explanations for the recent interest in the scholarship of engagement, and suggest different trajectories for its future.

According to the evolutionary model, the movement to engaged scholarship is the result of external threats to the viability of higher education institutions and the lure of external funding opportunities. In response, higher education institutions structured themselves to address those threats and capture those opportunities. According to the teleological model, leaders internal to higher education institutions came to see engagement as one of a set of responsibilities of their institutions. Engagement was made more explicit to their institutional missions. Existing higher education associations adopted engagement, and new ones were created to support that engagement. Roles and rewards are being redefined to support engagement. By the political model, forces for and against engagement are an ongoing part of the history of higher education. Some see it as necessary to ensuring the relevance of higher education; others see it as a threat to a unique role for higher education. Accommodations for one side or the other have been made at various levels ranging from institutional to departmental. Finally, according to the social cognition and cultural models, the scholarship of engagement is associated with a more fundamental change. Support for a civic and democratic society is a fundamental role for higher education. That support can only occur through engagement with the communities that higher education institutions serve. The scholarship of engagement then is more than just a strategy. Instead, it is a critical part of the very definition of a higher education institution.

Taken separately, the different factors identified in the models can point to different futures for the scholarship of engagement. By the evolutionary model, external threats and incentives drove higher education institutions toward engaged scholarship. Were those threats or incentives to go away, support for engaged scholarship could go away. According to the teleological model, engaged scholarship results from a commitment to engagement by institutional leaders and associated organizations. Were that commitment to wane, support for engaged scholarship could wane. Given the long history of conflict over engagement within the higher education community, the political model does not suggest a consensus for or against engaged scholarship in any near future. The struggle will go on. Similar to the evolutionary model, external factors affecting learning in the case of the social cognition model, or broader culture in the case of the cultural model, have led to attempts to redefine higher education by its engagement. If that learning or that culture were to change, support for engaged scholarship would change.

The purpose of a model, though, is to provide a simplification of a more complex world. In contrast to applying each of the models separately, each can also be seen as offering its particular perspective to the whole of change in higher education institutions related to the scholarship of engagement. Applied collectively, they may offer a clearer trajectory for engagement.

Although the physical economic, social threats identified in the evolutionary model might be reduced in a given setting, the reality is that they are not likely to be reduced across the population of higher education institutions in any near future. The environmental pressures and incentives toward engagement continue. From the perspective of the social cognition and cultural models, the persistence of those threats and incentives will continue organizational learning and cultural support for engagement as a defining component of higher education. Simultaneously, those environmental pressures and redefinitions of higher education reinforce higher education institutional leaders' intentional efforts to integrate engagement into their organizations. Internal tensions over engagement with community recognized in the political models will continue. However, the constellation of evolutionary, teleological, social cognition, and cultural change processes point to advancement for engagement. As it has come forth from the past, its recent history suggests an ever more promising future for the scholarship of engagement.

References

Bender, T. (Ed.). (1988). Introduction. In *The university and the city: From medieval origins to the present* (pp. 3–12). New York: Oxford University Press.

Benson, L., & Harkavy, I. (2000). Higher education's third revolution: The emergence of the democratic cosmopolitan civic university. *Cityscape: A Journal of Policy Development and Research, 5*(1), 47–57.

Bloom, A. (1987). *The closing of the American mind: How higher education has failed democracy and impoverished the souls of today's students.* New York: Simon and Schuster.

Bok, D. (1982). *Beyond the ivory tower: Social responsibilities of the modern university.* Cambridge, MA: Harvard University Press.

Boyer, E. L. (1990). *Scholarship reconsidered: Priorities of the professoriate.* Princeton, NJ: Carnegie Foundation for the Advancement of Teaching.

Burnes, B. (1996). *Managing change: A strategic approach to organizational dynamics.* London: Pitman.

Caret, R. (2007). Metropolitan universities and community engagement [Special issue]. *Metropolitan Universities Journal, 19*(1), 3–13.

Carr, D., Hard, K., & Trahant, W. (1996). *Managing the change process: A field book for change agents, consultants, team leaders, and reengineering managers.* New York: McGraw-Hill.

Cisneros, H. G. (1996, December). The university and the urban challenge [Special issue]. *Cityscape: A Journal of Policy Development and Research,* 1–14.

Committee on the Future of the Colleges of Agriculture in the Land Grant University System. (1995). *Colleges of agriculture at the land grant universities: A profile.* Washington, DC: Board on Agriculture, National Research Council, National Academies Press.

Cox, D. (2006). The how and the why of the scholarship of engagement. In S. Percy, N. Zimpher, & M. J. Brukardt (Eds.), *Creating a new kind of university: Institutionalizing community-university engagement* (pp. 159–177). San Francisco: Jossey-Bass.

Dewey, J. (1938). *Experience and education.* New York: Macmillan.

Diamond, R., & Adam, A. (1993). *Recognizing faculty work: Reward systems for the year 2000.* San Francisco: Jossey-Bass.

Driscoll, A. (2007). *Carnegie's community engagement classification: Intentions and insights.* Stanford, CA: Carnegie Foundation for the Advancement of Teaching.

Driscoll, A., & Lynton, E. A. (1999). *Making outreach visible: A guide to documenting professional service and outreach.* Washington, DC: American Association for Higher Education.

Dubb, S., & Howard, T. (2007). *Linking colleges to communities: Engaging the university for community development.* College Park, MD: The Democracy Collaborative.

Fish, S. (2003a, May 16). Aim low. *Chronicle of Higher Education.*

Fish, S. (2003b, January 23). Save the world on your own time. *Chronicle of Higher Education.*

Gearan, M. D. (2005). Engaging communities: The campus compact model. *National Civic Review, 94*(Summer), 32–40.

Gibson, C. (Ed.). (2006). *New times demands new scholarship: A leadership agenda.* Conference on Research Universities and Civic Engagement. Boston: Campus Compact.

Glassick, C. E. E., Huber, M. T., & Maeroff, G. I. (1997). *Scholarship assessed. Evaluation of the professoriate.* Carnegie Foundation for the Advancement of Teaching. San Francisco: Jossey-Bass.

Harkavy, I. (1997). The demands of the times and the American research university. *Journal of Planning Literature, 11*(3), 333–336.

Higher Education Network for Community Engagement (HENCE). (2006). *About HENCE.* Available at http://www.henceonline.org/about.php.

Holland, B. (1997). Levels of commitment to community engagement. *Michigan Journal of Community Service Learning, 4*(Fall), 30–41.

Jackson, G., & Meyers, R. B. (2000). Challenges of institutional outreach: A COPC example. *Cityscape: A Journal of Policy Development and Research, 5*(1), 125–140.

Kellogg Commission on the Future of State and Land Grant Universities. (1999). *Returning to our roots: The engaged institution.* Washington, DC: National Association of State Universities and Land-Grant Colleges.

Kennedy, D. (1997). *Academic duty.* Cambridge, MA: Harvard University Press.

Kezar, A. (2001). *Understanding and facilitating organizational change in the 21st century: Recent research and conceptualizations.* San Francisco: Jossey-Bass.

Lindholm, J., Szelenyi, K., Hurtado, S., & Korn, W. (2006). *American college teacher: National norms for 2004–2006: The HERI faculty study.* Los Angeles: Higher Education Research Institute.

Lynton, E. (1983). A crisis of purpose: Reexamining the role of the university. *Change, 15,* 18–23.

Lynton, E. (1995). *Making the case for professional service.* Washington, DC: American Association for Higher Education.

Lynton, E., & Elman, S. (1987). *New priorities for the university: Meeting society's needs for applied knowledge and competent individuals.* San Francisco: Jossey-Bass.

Maurrasse, D. (2007, September). *City anchors: Leveraging anchor institutions for urban success.* Chicago: CEOs for Cities.

Perry, D., & Wiewel, W. (Eds.). (2005). *The university as urban developer: Case studies and analysis.* London: M. E. Sharpe.

Peterson, T. (2004). Community-based research and higher education: Principles and practices. *Planning for Higher Education, 32*(3), 51–53.

Porta, D. D., & Diani, M. (2006). *Social movements: An introduction* (2nd ed.). Malden, MA: Blackwell.

Presidents' Declaration on the Civic Responsibility of Higher Education. (n.d.). *Campus Compact.* Available at www.compact.org/presidential.

Rajagopalan, N., & Spreitzer, G. M. (1996). Toward a theory of strategic change: A multi-lens perspective and integrated framework. *Academy of Management Review, 22*(1), 48–79, 125–140.

Reardon, K. (2000). An experiential approach to creating an effective community-university partnership: The East St. Louis action research project. *Cityscape: A Journal of Policy Development and Research, 5*(1), 59–74.

Senge, P. (1990). *The fifth discipline: The art and practice of the learning organization.* New York: Doubleday.

Stokes, D. (1997). *Pasteur's quadrant.* Washington, DC: Brookings Institution.

Van de Ven, A. H. (2007). *Engaged scholarship: A guide for organizational and social research.* London: Oxford University Press.

Van de Ven, A. H., & Poole, M. S. (1995). Explaining development and change in organizations. *Academy of Management Review, 20*(3), 510–540.

Vidal, A., Nye, N., Walker, C., Manjarrez, C., & Romanik, C. (2002). *Lessons from the Community Outreach Partnership Center Program.* Report to the Office of Policy Development and Research. Washington, DC: U.S. Department of Housing and Urban Development.

Webber, H. S. (2005). The University of Chicago and its neighbors. In D. Perry & W. Wiewel (Eds.). *The university as urban developer: Case studies and analysis* (pp. 65–79). London: M. E. Sharpe.

Weick, K. E. (1979). *The social psychology of organizing* (2nd ed.). New York: McGraw-Hill.

Defining the "Engagement" in the Scholarship of Engagement

Kelly Ward and Tami L. Moore

The word "engagement" has many meanings and definitions within higher education. Engagement is typically used to refer to different aspects of campus and community partnership: that is, to engage with the community. It is also a term that has been used to refer to student involvement and campus and community environments, as in student engagement with academic and civic activities. It is also a way to describe faculty work, as in faculty participation in engaged scholarship. When we talk about engagement in this chapter, we mean specifically interactions between faculty, students, administrators, or other professional staff members on a given campus and the geographically delineated communities primarily located external to the university.

The goal of this chapter is to examine the origins of community engagement in higher education, and to begin to untangle and then define the multiple perspectives and uses of the term for describing how campuses and communities engage with one another. The intent is not so much to provide a precise definition for common usage but rather to provide foundational information about how the term "engagement" is used in discourse about the community engagement activities of students, faculty, and institutions.

Origins of Engagement

Community-university engagement has been widely endorsed for the powerful possibilities that may result from harnessing the university's rich resources to address society's problems (Boyer, 1996). Advocates consistently highlight a key element of engagement: the notion that college and university resources generated from teaching, research, and service should be put to use to respond to problems found outside the university (Boyer; 1996; Boyte, 2004;

39

Ehrlich, 2000). Community engagement is a focal point of contemporary higher education, with many campuses intentionally pursuing their outreach and engagement missions. To situate the term "engagement" and how it is used in higher education today, we examine the origins of the term.

Linking the outcomes of the knowledge produced by higher education to application for the common good is a foundational principle of the American college or university, dating to the institution's origins in the seventeenth century (Veysey, 1965). As a basis to discuss engagement, we start with Veysey's concept of "utility," a reform model for the nineteenth-century university in the United States. Veysey (1965) uses "utility" as a label for the common goals shared by proponents of practicality, usefulness, and/or service as the fundamental purpose of the university system in the United States. Behind the idea of utility as a goal is the assumption that "real life"—equated with the workings of a democratic society—happened beyond campuses, not on them. This same idea appears in current discussions about "renewing the civic mission of higher education" (Checkoway, 2001; see also Barber, 1992; Boyte, 2004; Ehrlich, 2000). Veysey defines utility as synonymous with definitions of democracy as a form of self-government and as in the notion of equal access to facilities, resources, and knowledge. Academic utilitarians supported the "wide diffusion of knowledge throughout society" (Veysey, 1965, p. 65), with technical skills, scientific knowledge, civic duty, and aesthetic values flowing down and out of the university and into society. It is with this in mind that the American university was established.

McDowell (2001) and others (Kerr, 1963; Ward, 2003) have described the passage of the Morrill Act as an almost teleological shift in the history of higher education in the United States. With this legislation came an unprecedented opening of higher education to a wider portion of the nation's population than ever before. Equally significant, the applied sciences became appropriate material for university study. This had a democratizing effect on the curriculum that was just as transformative as the opening up of college enrollment beyond the socially and economically privileged classes (Veysey, 1965). It also had the effect of directly linking the expertise of the university with the needs of communities in terms of access and knowledge development.

After the Civil War, as the new land-grant universities began to appear, the influence of the German model of higher education also became evident in the emergence of a new, particular type of institution: the research university. This model focused on links between national development and university research; graduate education in pursuit of the doctoral degree; and the establishment of clearly identified disciplines of knowledge to be pursued by experts in relatively narrowly defined fields (Ward, 2003). The land-grant university ideal created the pathway for this knowledge to be extended into providing expertise to address government and societal needs.

Although the Morrill Act created the foundations for engagement in the research university and is often referred to as key legislation to establish the link between campus and community, there is historical evidence and contemporary manifestations of engagement-type activities in other sectors of higher education as well. Liberal arts colleges are typically residential in nature and have long-established links with their communities (Potts, 1977). In the liberal arts colleges, students have been (and are) encouraged into volunteerism and other service activities connecting them to the community as a way of reinforcing the goals of the institutions to educate citizens and to help maintain community vitality. The community college sector is by definition closely linked to meeting community needs (Crosson, 1983). Community colleges are intentional in their mission to meet community needs through workforce development and expanded access to higher education. Comprehensive and regional institutions also have a long-standing connection to their communities. Historically, these institutions were founded to meet the need for teachers in a particular region (Cohen, 1998). This mission has evolved and now includes a broad base of disciplinary offerings, but commitment to the regional needs of a particular regional community has remained steadfast (Moore, 2008; Ramaley, 2000).

Walshok (1995) and others (Ramaley, 2000; Holland, 2005) continue to encourage institutions of all types to engage as appropriate to their mission statements. A commitment to community engagement is an evolving part of the mission of increasing numbers of institutions supported by the expanding impact of works such as Boyer's (1996) call for a scholarship of engagement, Lynton and Elman's (1987) early discussions of the structures necessary to make engagement possible in and by the academy, and Driscoll and Lynton's (1999) *Making Outreach Visible*, providing faculty with of examples for documenting their engaged scholarship within the frame of the research imperative. Although community engagement can be expressed differently depending on the location and mission of the institution, the concepts of utility, democratization, access, and applied knowledge all have the common link of making outcomes of higher education (e.g., knowledge, students) appropriate to connect with societal needs. These concepts are the precursor to the idea of engagement used in higher education today.

Current State of Affairs in the Definition of Engagement

> Civic engagement has soared to rhetorical heights. The statements are impressive. But there are also some extraordinary things happening across the county. Now is the time to bring together rhetoric, leadership, and hard work. (Rice, cited in Sandmann & Weerts, 2006)

With these words, Eugene Rice called participants at the 2006 Wingspread Conference to bring together the many organizations working on engagement into closer collaboration. We draw on Rice's words here to guide the articulation of a clearer definition of engagement; his call also provides impetus to clarify the definition and use of the concept of engagement. Rice describes the "rhetoric" of engagement as commonplace in higher education, but what this engagement means and whom it benefits is not always clear. We now turn to discussion of how the term "engagement" is used to refer to different constituencies within higher education—students, faculty, and institutions as a whole.

Engaged Students

The mission of educating students to be active citizens remains prominent in higher education today. The early history of U.S. institutions of higher education includes many stories of colleges and universities founded for the (sometimes express) purpose of educating the citizens of a new nation. As the institutions matured and others emerged, the rhetoric surrounding higher education continued to position a university degree as something like "citizenship training for democracy" (Stanton, Giles, & Cruz, 1999, p. 17). This theme continues to figure prominently in discussions of student involvement with community-based projects and scholarship. The term "engagement" with regard to students encompasses the activities students participate in to foster community engagement, and the term is also used to describe a state of being or outcome for students—that is, engaged students.

Furco's (1996) overview of student activities and pedagogical approaches that connect universities and the larger community reflects the variety of paths taken by instructors and program administrators to provide opportunities for students to engage with the community. He identifies five types of experiential education activities that can be a means for students to participate in the community: volunteerism, community service, internships, field work, and community service learning. In outlining the distinctions between these approaches, Furco plots the five categories on two continuums to reflect the beneficiary and the focus of the activity. Volunteerism, for example, is an activity focused on service where the primary beneficiary is the recipient of the assistance. Students completing internships benefit most from the experience, which focuses primarily on their learning. Community service learning, the middle point on both continuums, is characterized by its "intention to equally benefit the provider and the recipient of the service as well as to ensure equal focus on both the service being provided and the learning that is occurring" (Furco, 1996, p. 5). At the time of its publication, this classification rubric brought much-needed definition to the new field of service-learning, helping to differentiate volunteerism and other community service from student learning and formal curricula. Furco's distinctions continue to be useful to identify the ways students engage in community-oriented activities and learning. His rubric is also useful as a way to think about community engagement and beneficiaries of this engagement. For example, community service learning activities specifically have the intent of benefiting the community and thus support community engagement, whereas other forms of experiential education, although taking part in the community, can be more focused on benefiting student learning, than on the outcomes for the community.

Early student involvement in service-learning and community-engagement projects remained clustered in the social sciences and professional programs such as nursing and social work, where there was a natural and long-standing connection between the curriculum and the community (Stanton, Giles, & Cruz, 1999). Students in fields such as business, engineering, and the sciences have only recently become involved in service learning. Recent literature reveals a growing body of scholarship reflecting the integration of civic engagement experiences in a broad range of fields (see, for example, Coffey & Wang, 2006; Esson, Stevens-Truss, & Thomas, 2005; Laroder, Tippins, Handa, & Morano, 2007; Madsen & Turnbull, 2006; Newman, Bruyere, & Beh, 2007). Service learning as a form of community engagement has put countless numbers of students in connection to their local communities.

In the past ten years, the literature has been marked by greater agreement about the substance required to label a project "community service learning," as documented in the *Michigan Journal of Community Service Learning* and other publications. Even so, the historical focus on educating the citizenry has not disappeared. The most prominent location of this message is the focus of the Association of American Colleges and Universities (AAC&U) on civic engagement and its long-term impact on students' development as local and global citizens. Similarly, the American Association of State Colleges and Universities (AASCU) American Democracy Project, in partnership with the *New York Times*, supports member institutions in their efforts to educate a new generation of students who are informed and engaged in the democratic process.

This focus on citizenship education as a by-product of interaction with the community has returned civic engagement to something more like civics. For example, many equate civic engagement with civic participation, along the lines of Jacoby's (2006) discussion of voter behavior as strengthened by civic engagement. This is also the fundamental argument of Colby, Ehrlich, Beaumont, and Stephens (2003), whose *Educating Citizens* articulates the stakes in civic engagement as the education of future citizens and future voters. Reich (2005) even asks if "community service work [has] become a substitute for political activity . . . among young people" (p. 23). By conflating engagement with civics or citizenship in describing or discussing engaged students, the literature includes several things under the heading of "engagement" that others may well see as simply the kinds of things students should be gaining from a liberal education, rather than new activities reflective of their alma mater's commitment to community engagement.

The National Survey of Student Engagement (NSSE) has the expressed purpose of gathering information about "student participation in programs and activities that institutions provide for their learning and personal development" (NSSE. n.d.). The NSSE is not specifically tied to community engagement, but through the NSSE, the concepts of engagement and engaged students have gained a presence on college campuses and merit consideration here. *Student Success in College* (Kuh, 2005) talks about programs and policies that are tied to academic achievement and students' meaningful engagement in different types of activities, and many of these are tied to the community. Our point in mentioning this here is to point out that "engaged students" is phraseology that is often used in higher education, in part due to the good work of the NSSE, as well as those advocating for greater community engagement by students.

Engaged Faculty

In the past twenty years, research related to faculty involvement in community-oriented work has grown considerably. This literature documents the growing number of faculty across institution types who bridge research, teaching, and service through the integration of community-based work with their scholarly agendas. Given the broad base of activities that constitute faculty work in general and the array of activities that encompass community engagement, many campuses struggle with what it means for faculty to engage in the community as part of their scholarly agenda. Campuses also struggle with how to define engagement so it can be recognized as part of the faculty evaluation process. There is ample opportunity and need for greater clarity about the nuances and definitions of community engagement and faculty work.

Faculty typically document their work using traditional language that references easily understood roles: teaching, research, and service (Moore & Ward, 2008; Ward, 2003).

Although the service category was originally most closely linked with community engagement (i.e., community service), the term "engagement" has come to represent a broader construction of faculty work; thus, the call for greater definition. The term "engagement" can represent activities which integrate and subsequently transcend the teaching, research, service categorization. Because of this, the term is often misunderstood. Faculty can be involved in different activities that fall under the rubric of engagement (Cushman, 1999; Moore & Ward, 2008; Ward, 2005).

As part of the teaching role, faculty can adopt service learning as a pedagogical approach. For instance, an engineering faculty member involved freshman students in the design and construction of school playgrounds. A graphic design professor solicited design clients for her students' advanced coursework from community-based nonprofit organizations. A Spanish instructor asked student to volunteer in Spanish-speaking environments and use their experiences as a vehicle to develop their language skills, as well as an opportunity to reflect on issues related to Latino/a culture and politics around immigration issues. Student involvement in the community is directly linked to the teaching objectives of a course. Service learning is one expression of how faculty can include community engagement in their teaching.

As part of the research role of faculty, community-engaged topics generate opportunities for conducting research projects that, as Cruz (2007) suggests, draw on the wide store of community-based knowledge that is required to solve the problems facing today's world. A tenured professor of literacy has worked with a local agency to study adult literacy among non-native speakers of English through her involvement in the literacy tutoring program. A professor of education and ethnic studies formed a partnership with the community historical society to preserve the stories of ethnic groups in a large urban environment, and with communities of color to understand better the experience of parents in the metropolitan school system. A chemist approached the local timber industry, suggesting analyses and other resources from physical chemistry research for streamlining production; these relationships have led to expanded access to study the processes, as well as placement of advanced graduate students who are also involved in extending the knowledge base through research.

As part of the service role, engagement can mean different things. Consulting, or the practice of extending discipline-specific knowledge to corporate or community clients, falls under service on some vitae and could also be considered engagement (Ward, 2003). In some fields, presentations to local and state government provide opportunities to extend faculty expertise into the realm of public policy and community decision making. Education scholars occasionally advise local school districts on curriculum design/delivery, professional development, leadership, and other issues related to educating students and school administration that fall under the rubric of engagement. It is often through engagement activities falling under the service category of faculty work that faculty are able to readily extend their disciplinary expertise into broader community application.

One of the ongoing issues with the integration of engagement is the continuing need to articulate what it means for faculty to do service, how that service intersects with the traditional tripartite faculty roles, and how the service role is tied to meeting the outreach and engagement missions of campuses. Ward (2003) differentiates between internal and external service and links external service to opportunities for engagement with communities. The original impetus for this broadening understanding of faculty roles to include a scholarship of engagement comes from Boyer's (1990) expanded definition of scholarship. His writing moved the understanding of faculty work beyond the research imperative by calling for four different types of scholarship: discovery, integration, application, and teaching. These categories transcend traditional faculty roles by demonstrating that the four functions of scholarship he proposes are equally associated with research, teaching, or service. In 1996, Boyer proposed a fifth function of scholarship: engagement. He called specifically for the harnessing of institutional resources to address issues and opportunities facing communities. Continued attention to what it means for faculty to be of service and what it means to engage is necessary to highlight the ways in which faculty can be scholarly and engaged with the community. By keeping a focus on this discussion, it is possible to actively resist efforts to distinguish engagement as something different from "traditional" scholarship.

Ongoing definition of engagement and how it fits into faculty work is also necessary as campuses continue to grapple with how to reward faculty for work that supports outreach missions. Faculty are key actors in realizing engagement initiatives. Promotion and tenure guidelines at all types of institutions clarify for faculty how to spend their time and how to approach their work. Ward's (2003, 2005) work, and the examples of faculty engaging with communities that we offer here, makes clear that calls for engagement are not asking faculty to take on more work, but rather to work differently.

Engaged Institutions

The "engaged campus" is one that attempts to clearly tie the resources of campus to meeting community needs. Although the majority of campuses have clearly delineated service missions, this is typically not expressed as a stand-alone mission; instead, the commitment to service is expressed as functions of the teaching and research roles. That is, campuses become engaged in the community (i.e., give service) through their teaching and research missions. Throughout the past ten years there has been significant focus on the community engagement missions of college campuses. In part, this focus has been prompted by the work of the Carnegie Foundation for the Advancement of Teaching and also by the work of other associations dedicated to providing leadership and support for campuses to remain true to their long-standing missions to serve their communities.

The origins of community-university engagement are commonly connected to the university extension service model (McDowell, 2001, 2003). The Wisconsin Idea institutionalized a view of knowledge generated by university professors as imminently relevant and ideally accessible to the community served by the university. However, by tracing engagement exclusively through university extension, we risk excluding the contributions of the liberal arts college legacy cited earlier in discussing engaged students, and also the role of social scientists in political reform movements of the late nineteenth century (see, for example, Recchiuti, 2006). One hundred years later, beginning in the late 1980s, partner organizations in the nonprofit sector also contributed, calling for a refocusing of the mission of higher education on the tradition of engagement with the community.

Associations have been a catalyst to helping higher education rethink community engagement and re-enliven their service missions. Campus Compact, a consortium of presidents dedicated to civic engagement, community service, and service learning in higher education, has played a leadership role in providing resources for campuses to create an infrastructure to support their community efforts (www.compact.org). The Association of Public and Land-Grant Universities (APLU, formerly the National Association of State Universities and Land-Grant Colleges, or NASULGC) has played a leadership role in conversations about service missions in public and land-grant universities. Their work has not been limited to their direct constituency (public and land-grant universities); they serve other types of institutions as well, in part because of their publications. For example, *Returning to Our Roots*, published in 1999 (Kellogg Commission, 1999), specifically held up the land-grant ideal to be emulated in re-establishing connections between higher education and the communities it serves. Similar publications appeared in subsequent years, such as *Stepping Forward as Stewards of Place* (AASCU, 2002), and the series of publications from the American Association of Colleges and Universities (AACU) focusing primarily on the building of institutional supports for civic engagement by students (see, for example, Langseth & Plater, 2004). Pickeral and Peters's (1996) monograph, published by the Campus Compact National Center for Community Colleges, addressed the development of service learning programs in community colleges. The American Association for Higher Education (AAHE) Forum on Faculty Roles and Rewards played a key role in bringing attention to the connection between faculty work and institutional missions emphasizing engagement. Although the AAHE Forum is no longer in existence, the publications and leadership that emanated from this organization have had a lasting impact on defining engagement for faculty. These associations and resulting publications have played a key role in providing leadership for their constituent campuses to think about engagement as part of their mission. Disciplinary associations (e.g., Modern Language Association, American Chemical Society) have also taken up the topic of engaging with communities as an important discussion with their membership. The intent of these conversations has been to think about how the expertise that emanates from a particular discipline can be used to address community needs. These organizations continue to play key leadership roles in creating materials, providing verbiage, and prompting institutions to reexamine and enact the service mission that can, in part, be translated or interpreted as engagement.

As a result of these broad national calls for utility, and for applying knowledge and other resources to community issues, universities engage with the communities they serve in many ways. For example, Trinity College in Hartford, Connecticut, committed itself to community revitalization in the economically disadvantaged neighborhoods surrounding its campus. The University of Wisconsin-Milwaukee undertook an initiative to engage the city in developing what they have referred to as The Milwaukee Idea, outlining new roles and relationships linking the university and its community. The University of Central Oklahoma partnered with Oklahoma City in an effort to establish the city as an U.S. Olympic training site in conjunction with a much broader civic revitalization program already underway. These are just a few examples of particular campuses engaging with their communities. These initiatives are carried out in a multitude of ways—through faculty research, faculty service, and student involvement in different types of classroom activities (e.g., research projects, service learning).

Engagement is expressed at the campus level in the mission and is carried out by faculty and students. This broad involvement of actors in engagement necessitates a broad understanding of the term "engagement," requiring specific attention to engagement by students, by faculty, and by the administrators and other constituents who shape institutional mission and practice. The Kellogg Presidents' Commission, convened in 1996 by the NASULGC institutions, began its work by expressing concern that its member institutions were becoming increasingly irrelevant to the society in which they existed. The commission responded to this perceived crisis with a call for returning to the roots of the land-grant college, and purposefully reconnecting with the community (Kellogg Commission, 1999). Leaders involved in this work see it as the origin of the discussion of engagement, and the notion of "the engaged university" as connoting a two-way interaction between community and university. McDowell (2003) traces a bit of this history and points out that even immediately prior to the publication of *Returning to Our Roots,* national conferences (e.g., AAHE's Conference on Faculty Roles and Rewards), publications (e.g., *Daedalus'* 1997 issue focused on the American academic profession), and individual authors (e.g., Bok's ongoing critique of American higher education) have focused on this commitment to public service and interaction with the community as a unique, if under-studied, characteristic of the higher education system in the United States. We now turn to an examination of ongoing discussions and possibilities for new avenues in the scholarly literature on engagement at all three levels.

The Future of Engagement

The most widely referenced current definition of engagement is that offered by the Carnegie Foundation (2008): "Community engagement describes the collaboration between institutions of higher education and their larger communities (local, regional/state, national, global) for the mutually beneficial exchange of knowledge and resources in a context of partnership and reciprocity." The evolutionary nature of engagement's definition, and indeed the need for a chapter defining engagement in this handbook, calls for continued attention to the evolving understandings of Boyer's (1996) concept of the scholarship of engagement. As we have outlined, engagement has come to be consistently associated with campus and community partnerships and other relatively local initiatives to meet community needs. To continue pushing our thinking forward on what it means to be of service or, as Veysey (1965) would say, to be useful, and to engage, more is required of scholars and practitioners in this field. In the next two decades, this attention must continue, with specific attention to four issues/areas: critique, theory, cross/interdisciplinary scholarship, and community perspectives.

Critical Focus on Engagement
The body of literature associated with the field of engagement can be characterized in phases. Early writing included polemics and exhortations to engagement and public service (Boyer, 1996), accompanied by descriptive pieces documenting the efforts of already-prominent

institutions, their administrators, and faculty (Driscoll & Lynton, 1999; Ryan, 1998; Votruba, 1996) to engage and also to shape institutional culture to encourage and support this engagement (Lynton & Elman, 1987). The community voice is heard somewhat more often in the community service learning literature and in scholarly discussions of community-university interactions in general. More recently, authors have been focusing critical attention on engagement as a way to think about power in campus and community relationships.

By "critical focus," we mean bringing specific focus to the power relations inherent in community-university relationships, and using scholarship as a tool for bringing about change in these relationships. Fear, Rosaen, Bawden, and Foster-Fishman's (2006) definition of critical engagement provides a guide in these efforts. They propose a critical engagement approach, characterized by "opportunities to share . . . knowledge and learn with [all] those who struggle for social justice; and to collaborate . . . respectfully and responsibly for the purpose of improving life" (p. xiii). Fear et al. differentiate critical engagement from instrumental engagement, which focuses on completing tasks and projects. Critical engagement is, above all else, a transformative experience for all involved: "The primary value is the effect it has on participants, helping them think intentionally and deeply about themselves, their work, and how they approach their practice" (p. 257). Although their work focuses on community-engaged scholars, Fear et al. understand their discussion of critical engagement to apply to all participants in the engagement initiatives, representing the university as well as the larger community (F. Fear, personal communication, March 15, 2006). It is in this sense that we employ their definition of critical engagement as a transformative learning and community-building endeavor including diverse members of the larger community, and call for greater attention to these goals in both the scholarship and the practice of community university engagement.

Theory

To date, the interaction between community and university has largely been treated as either an organizational topic or an interpersonal one. For instance, Sandmann and Weerts (2008) draw on theories of boundary spanning, from the organizational development literature, to discuss engagement at four research universities located in both urban and rural settings. Bracken (2007) draws on theoretical constructs from collaboration to discuss the role of language, context, and communication in a partnership involving community groups, a community college campus, and federal funders. Van de Ven's (2007) background in business management and organizational theory influences his discussion of engagement as an institutional activity. These perspectives are indeed useful for thinking about engagement. However, by focusing too closely on the interaction from a university-centered perspective, research in this area has overlooked the potential of social and cultural theories to inform our scholarly understanding of all the components of university-community interaction.

A broad assumption undergirds this recommendation for future work in theorizing engagement: Engagement is constituted by activities involving people who live and work in specific geographic locations interacting with each other. The corollary assumption is that real engagement exists, and should be studied, beyond the rhetoric of returning to institutional roots, educating citizens, or renewing civic missions. By calling earlier for a more critical focus we join Fear et al. (2006) in drawing explicitly from critical theory as a tool to examine and address power relationships. For example, Moore and Avila (2007) have explored the potential for emancipatory engagement, drawing on the community organizing models of Saul Alinsky and the Industrial Areas Foundation. Moore (2008) examined the role of place, as it relates to building mutually beneficial partnerships, drawing from critical geography and Bourdieu's (1986, 1989, 1991) concepts of field and habitus.

By explicitly naming the community as the site of engagement, we can connect the scholarship of engagement to cultural geography. One might also view the university as traditionally acting upon the community rather than fully acting with it; to explore these ideas, or make sense of data that reflects such a situation, the researcher might access culture theories, postcolonial studies, or recent thinking in comparative ethnic studies. For example, Prashad's (2006) concept of polyculturalism suggests the possibility that the culture of the university and the culture of the community may come together in community-university partnerships to create a unique polyculture. This is a different way of understanding what happens within collaborative relationships which focuses more on the people than on the organizations. Cultural theory informs much of the writing about civic engagement and service learning in African contexts (Erasmus, 2007; Oldfield, 2008; Serpell, 2007) and suggests that the insights available from focusing on the interaction of people instead of institutions can enrich scholarship in the U.S. context as well.

Cross/Interdisciplinary Scholarship

The research questions faculty ask and the community problems they seek to address through engagement often do not present themselves in disciplinary packages. Scholars working with and in communities sometimes describe combining their academic background with previous professional experience in a related field, or partnering with faculty colleagues in other disciplines to bring multiple lenses to a project (Moore & Ward, 2007a, 2007b, 2008). Lattuca (2002) has explored how faculty learn interdisciplinarity, high-lighting an important "prior step" required for faculty to "take advantage of policies or pro-grams that encourage interdisciplinarity" (p. 711). Lattuca's discussion highlights a strong connection between the scholarship of engagement and increasing emphasis being placed on working interdisciplinarily in the academy. For example, at an institution where faculty are being encouraged to collaborate with colleagues outside their disciplines, a graphic designer took her expertise to a team of philosophy and law faculty and provided project management skills in a federally funded project to develop an online tribal law database.

Engagement helps the academic break out of disciplinary confines, and these impetuses to do so are being further supported by funding opportunities. The National Science Foundation, National Institutes of Health, and other federal agencies are encouraging and in some instances requiring interdisciplinarity in their funding guidelines. Proposals/funded projects are also expected to address the application of knowledge generated through the funded research to communities and other stakeholders external to the university.

We see this connection between interdisciplinarity and engagement as part of a larger ebb and flow of priorities in the academy. In the 1970s and 1980s, much attention was given to diversity. As the rhetoric and scholarship of engagement and focus on service learning developed, some institutions pointed to service learning projects in neighboring communities of color as opportunities for students on predominantly white campuses to engage with diverse populations and thereby further the institution's commitment to diversity (G. Hull, personal communication, September 4, 2006). Today, the multifaceted nature of community-engaged research reinforces the connection between engagement and interdisciplinary approaches to scholarship. Given this, scholars and practitioners in the field of engagement can benefit from expanded understandings of the why and how of interdisciplinary collaborations.

Community Perspectives

The literature on university engagement is ripe with rhetoric exhorting colleges and universities, as well as their faculty and students, to engage with the community (see, for example, Boyer, 1996; Checkoway, 2001; Kezar, Chambers, Burkhardt, & Associates, 2005). Too often missing from the dialogue—across all types of interaction between universities and communities—is the community voice. As a result, higher education dominates the conversation about engagement, posing a significant problem given the definition of community-university engagement as "direct, two-way interaction . . . through the development, exchange, and application of knowledge, information and expertise for mutual benefit" (American Association of State Colleges and Universities, 2002, p. 7).

The absence of the community voice in the scholarship related to engagement is not surprising, nor is it necessarily problematic in and of itself. The academy values writing and peer-reviewed publications; the community does not value the same things as tangible outcomes of engagement. The problem, per se, is the relative absence of community perspectives in the discussion of community-university engagement. The current situation is something like managers discussing and solving issues, where the solutions will be lived out by others. The souls of the institutions—those people and values that make the university and the community unique—are not communicating in a way that brings all the necessary perspectives to the conversation (Cruz, 2007; Moore, 2008). Without community involvement from the earliest stages of a project, the "mutually beneficial" nature of engagement is compromised. Although there are some notable examples of community voices in the scholarship of engagement, and the venues for such are growing, more is necessary. The *Journal of Community Engagement and Scholarship*, for example, is specifically prioritizing the solicitation of articles that equitably reflect the involvement of both community and university representatives in the projects themselves, and in writing about these projects.

Despite the need to move beyond rhetoric and definition, the multiple manifestations of engagement on college campuses means that these issues cannot be left unattended as the scholarship, theory and practice of community university engagement advances. Rice (2006; cited in Sandmann & Weerts, 2006) reminds us that it is important to be focused on definitions and appropriate nomenclature to further understandings of campus and community engagement, and we extend this point to emphasize the emerging need to consider new theory and different perspectives. Rhetoric, definition, and theorizing are all necessary to advance research and practice to uphold the spirit of engagement. Faculty, students, and institutions, however, need to move beyond the rhetoric and into the action of engaging more fully with communities and carrying out engagement initiatives.

References

American Association of State Colleges and Universities (AASCU). (2002). *Stepping forward as stewards of place*. Washington, DC: Author.

Barber, B. R. (1992). *An aristocracy of everyone: The politics of education and the future of America*. New York: Ballantine Books.

Bourdieu, P. (1986). The forms of capital. In J. G. Richardson (Ed.), *Handbook of theory and research for the sociology of education* (pp. 241–258). New York: Greenwood Press.

Bourdieu, P. (1989). Social space and symbolic power. *Sociological Theory, 7*(1), 14–25.

Bourdieu, P. (1991). On symbolic power. In J. B. Thompson (Ed.), *Language and symbolic power,* G. Raymond & M. Adamson, trans. (pp., 163–170). Cambridge, MA: Harvard University Press. (Original work published 1979).

Boyer, E. L. (1990). *Scholarship reconsidered: Priorities of the professorate*. Princeton, NJ: The Carnegie Foundation for the Advancement of Teaching.

Boyer, E. L. (1996). The scholarship of engagement. *Journal of Public Service and Outreach, 1*(1), 11–20.

Boyte, H. (2004). *Everyday politics: Reconnecting citizens and public life*. Philadelphia: University of Pennsylvania Press.

Bracken, J. (2007). The importance of language, context, and communication as components of successful partnership. *New Directions for Community Colleges, 139,* 41–47.

Carnegie Foundation. (2008). *Community Engagement elective classification*. Retrieved March 24, 2010, from http://www.carnegiefoundation.org/descriptions/community-engagement.php.

Checkoway, B. (2001). Renewing the civic mission of the American research university. *Journal of Higher Education, 72*(2), 125–147.

Coffey, B. S., & Wang, J. (2006). Service learning in a master of business administration (MBA) integrative project course: An experience in China. *Journal of Education for Business, 82,* 119–124.

Cohen, A. (1998). *The shaping of American higher education: Emergence and growth of the contemporary system*. San Francisco: Jossey-Bass.

Colby, A., Ehrlich, T., Beaumont, E., & Stephens, J. (2003). *Educating citizens: Preparing America's undergraduates for lives of moral and civic responsibility*. San Francisco: Jossey-Bass.

Crosson, P. (1983). *Public service in higher education: Practices and priorities*. ASHE-ERIC Higher Education Research Report. Washington, DC: George Washington University. (ERIC Document Reproduction Service No. ED284515)

Cruz, N. (2007, March). *Reflection and response to Katrina: Engaged educators on fire with urgency, clarity and hope*. Keynote address presented at the Gulf South Summit on Civic Engagement, New Orleans.

Cushman, E. (1999). The public intellectual, service learning, and activist research. *College English, 61*(3), 328–336.

Driscoll, A., & Lynton, E. A. (1999). *Making outreach visible: A guide to documenting professional service and outreach*. Washington, DC: American Association for Higher Education.

Ehrlich, T. (2000). *Civic responsibility and higher education*. Phoenix, AZ: Oryx Press for the American Council on Education.

51

Erasmus, M. (2007). Service learning: Preparing a new generation of scientists for a Mode 2 society. *Journal for New Generation Sciences, 5*(2), 26–40.

Esson, J. M., Stevens-Truss, R., & Thomas, A. (2005). Service-learning in introductory chemistry: Supplementing chemistry curriculum in elementary schools. *Journal of Chemical Education, 82*(8), 1168–1173.

Fear, F. A., Rosaen, C. L., Bawden, R. J, & Foster-Fishman, P. G. (2006). *Coming to critical engagement: An autoethnographic exploration.* Lanham, MD: University Press of America.

Furco, A. (1996). Service-learning: A balanced approach to experiential education. In Corporation for National Service (Ed.), *Expanding boundaries: Serving and learning* (pp. 2–6). Columbia, MD: Cooperative Education Association.

Holland, B. A. (2005). Institutional differences in pursuing the public good. In A. J. Kezar, T. C. Chambers, J. C. Burkhardt, and associates (Eds.), *Higher education for the public good: Emerging voices from a national movement* (pp. 235–259). San Francisco: Jossey-Bass.

Jacoby, B. (2006). Bottom line—making politics matter to students. *About Campus, 11*(4), 30–32.

Kellogg Commission on the Future of State and Land-Grant Universities. (1999). *Returning to our roots: The engaged institution.* Washington, DC: National Association of State Universities and Land-Grant Colleges.

Kerr, C. (1963). *Uses of the university.* Cambridge, MA: Harvard University Press.

Kezar, A. J., Chambers, T. C., Burkhardt, J. C., & Associates (Eds.) (2005). *Higher education for the public good.* San Francisco: Jossey-Bass.

Kuh, G. D. (2005). *Student success in college: Creating conditions that matter.* San Francisco: Jossey-Bass.

Langseth, M., & Plater, W. M. (2004). *Public work and the academy: An academic administrator's guide to civic engagement and service learning.* San Francisco: Jossey-Bass.

Laroder, A., Tippins, D., Handa, V., & Morano, L. (2007). Rock showdown: Learning science through service with the community. *Science Scope, 30*(7), 32–37.

Lattuca, L. R. (2002). Learning interdisciplinarity. *Journal of Higher Education, 73*(6), 711–739.

Lynton, E. A., & Elman, S. E. (1987). *New priorities for the university: Meeting society's needs for applied knowledge and competent individuals.* San Francisco: Jossey-Bass.

Madsen, S. R., & Turnbull, O. (2006). Academic service learning experiences of compensation and benefit course students. *Journal of Management Education, 30*(5), 724–742.

McDowell, G. R. (2001). *Land-grant universities and extension into the 21st century: Renegotiating or abandoning a social contract.* Ames: Iowa State University Press.

McDowell, G. (2003). Engaged universities: Lessons from the land-grant universities and extension. *Annals of the American Association of Political and Social Sciences, 585*, 31–50.

Moore, T. L. (2008). *Placing engagement: Critical readings of interaction between regional communities and comprehensive universities.* Unpublished doctoral dissertation, Washington State University, Pullman.

Moore, T. L., & Avila, M. (2007, April). *Community-university partnerships: Theoretical and community organizing models for transformation.* Paper presented at the meeting of the American Educational Research Association, Chicago, IL.

Moore, T. L., & Ward, K. A. (2007a, November). *Beyond exemplars and best practices: Reframing the discussion of community-engaged faculty.* Paper presented at the meeting of the Association for the Study of Higher Education, Louisville, KY.

Moore, T. L. & Ward, K. A. (2007b, April). *Faculty at work as teachers, scholars and citizens: Managing integration and complexity.* Paper presented at the meeting of the American Educational Research Association, Chicago, IL.

Moore, T. L., & Ward, K. A. (2008). Documenting engagement: Faculty perspectives on self-representation for promotion and tenure. *Journal of Higher Education Outreach and Engagement, 12*(4), 5–27.

National Survey of Student Engagement (NSSE). (n.d.). Available at http://nsse.iub.edu/.

Newman, P., Bruyere, B. L., & Beh, A. (2007). Service-learning and natural resource leadership. *Journal of Experiential Education, 30*(1), 54–69.

Oldfield, S. (2008). Who's serving whom? Partners, process, and products in service-learning projects in South African urban geography. *Journal of Geography in Higher Education, 32*(2), 269–285.

Pickeral, T., & Peters, K. (1996). *From the margin to the mainstream: The faculty role in advancing service-learning in community colleges.* Mesa, AZ: Campus Compact National Center for Community Colleges.

Potts, D. B. (1977). College enthusiasm! as public response: 1800–1860. *Harvard Educational Review, 47*(1), 149–161.

Prashad, V. (2006). Ethnic Studies inside out. *Journal of Asian American Studies, 9*(2), 157–176.

Ramaley, J. A. (2000). The perspective of a comprehensive university. In T. Ehrlich (Ed.), *Civic responsibility and higher education* (pp. 227–248). Phoenix, AZ: Oryx Press for the American Council on Education.

Recchiuti, J. L. (2006). *Civic engagement: Social science and Progressive-era reform in New York City.* Philadelphia: University of Pennsylvania Press.

Reich, R. (2005). Service learning and multiple models of engaged citizenship. *Journal of Education, 186*(1), 23–27.

Ryan, J. H. (1998). Creating an outreach culture. *Journal of Public Service and Outreach, 3*(2), 29–36.

Sandmann, L. R., & Weerts, D. J. (2006). Engagement in higher education: Building a federation for action. *Report of the proceedings for a Wingspread Conference establishing the Higher Education Network for Community Engagement (HENCE)*, Racine, WI.

Sandmann, L. R., & Weerts, D. J. (2008). Reshaping institutional boundaries to accommodate an engagement agenda. *Innovative Higher Education, 33*(3), 181–196.

Serpell, R. (2007). Bridging between orthodox western higher educational practices and an African sociocultural context. *Comparative Education, 43*(1), 23–51.

Stanton, T. K., Giles, D. E., & Cruz, N. I. (1999). *Service-learning: A movement's pioneers reflect on its origins, practice, and future.* San Francisco: Jossey-Bass.

Van de Ven, A. H. (2007). *Engaged scholarship.* New York: Oxford University Press.

Veysey, L. R. (1965). *The emergence of the American university.* Chicago: University of Chicago Press.

Votruba, J. C. (1996). Strengthening the university's alignment with society: Challenges and strategies. *Journal of Public Service and Outreach, 1*(1), 29–36.

Ward, K. A. (2003). Faculty service roles and the scholarship of engagement. *ASHE-ERIC Higher Education Report* (Vol. 29, No. 5). San Francisco: Jossey-Bass.

Ward, K. A. (2005). Rethinking faculty roles and rewards for the public good. In A. J. Kezar, T. C. Chambers, J. C. Burkhardt, and associates (Eds.), *Higher education for the public good* (pp. 217–234). San Francisco: Jossey-Bass.

Toward a Social Justice-Centered Engaged Scholarship: A Public and a Private Good

Tony Chambers and Bryan Gopaul

Throughout the history of higher education in the United States, there has been an ongoing debate about the role of higher education's contribution to a "just" society. In spite of the high participation rate in U.S. higher education, college goers still represent a relatively small number/percentage of the U.S. population. Further, if we consider the number of higher education graduates and those within certain population demographic groups (i.e., low income, students of color, first generation, etc.), the relative proportion of those acquiring the full benefit of a college education dwindles even further. Questions central to the debate include: How does one come to understand what is socially just, or what is a public or private good? How does the relative exclusive nature of higher education, specifically elite colleges and universities, go with their claim of being a public good and promoters of a "just" society? Is access, without completion, considered socially just? Are all public goods socially just? Can a private good be socially just? Is it even higher education's responsibility to promote a public good or social justice?

The guiding belief of this chapter is that the endgame for an engaged scholarship is the "just" recognition, analysis, and resolution of socially unjust conditions. Our fundamental position in this chapter is that scholarship that is void of a conscious social justice intent may be scholarship, but it is not engaged scholarship. Stated another way, we believe that all engaged scholarship is directed at the recognition, analysis, and resolution of socially unjust conditions. Within this chapter, as we struggle to respond to some of the central questions in the "higher education for social justice" debate within a framework of engaged scholarship, there are first several important concepts and practices that need to be examined. This chapter follows with an overview and interrogation of the issues and concepts central to the social justice dynamics of engaged scholarship in higher education; gives a brief critique of

55

efforts in higher education to promote and practice a social justice-centered engaged scholarship; and concludes with our sense of emerging patterns and concerns that need to be addressed in order to advance engaged scholarship from a social justice perspective.

Public and Private Good

The terms "public" and "good" represent important constructs that institutional leaders and supporters, as well as critics and opponents, use to frame the discourse about the role of higher education in a democratic society. Knowing the possible interpretations of these powerful constructs should assist institutional leaders, supporters, and public decision makers in setting an informed course of action for institutions of higher education. Additionally, social commentators, communities and others who are keen on framing higher education's efforts as contributions to social justice will have defined matrices to better gauge an institution's rhetoric against its impact. As well, knowing the possible interpretations of constructs central to the social purposes of higher education will provide scholars and their community partners will a clearer sense of the goals and expectations of their engagement with one another.

> Generally, the "public good" referred to the betterment of individuals and society. The public good was served when better-educated citizens advanced both their own lives and the standards of living within the communities. By advancing civilization and helping to drive economic development, higher education served the public good. . . . (Longanecker, 2005, p 57)
>
> The Public Good is an aspiration, a vision and destination of a "better state" that we can know in common that we cannot know alone. (Chambers & Gopaul, 2008)

The preceding quotes position the notion of "public good" as a collective or social process that impacts more than just those directly engaged in the specific public good activity. This notion is captured by the Latin phrase "non nobis solum," which is loosely translated as "not for ourselves alone" (Shapiro, 2005). Public good is also seen as a set of behaviors, outcomes, and aspirations. For an institution, service, or product to be a public good, it does not necessarily have to be provided by the "public," meaning provided by the *government.* Conceivably, public goods can be supplied by the private sector and private goods—by the public sector. According to Samuelson (1954), pure public goods are characterized by:

> *Nonrivalry.* The cost of extending the service or providing the good to another person is (close to) zero. Public goods are accessible to growing numbers of people without any additional marginal cost. This broad distribution of benefits from a public good makes them unsuitable for private entrepreneurship. It is impossible to recapture, or fully describe, the range of returns produced or influenced by them.
>
> *Nonexcludability.* It is impossible to exclude anyone from enjoying the benefits of a public good, or from contributing to its costs.
>
> *Externalities.* Public goods impose costs (negative externalities) or benefits (positive externalities) on others—individuals or organizations—outside the marketplace, and their effects are only partially reflected in prices and the market transactions.

Isolating higher education's public and private good roles are difficult to do because claims can be and are made that most of its activities serve public purposes in some way. Again, the argument can be made that along with higher education's resulting public good outcomes, there are considerable private outcomes as well. The *teaching charge*—and particularly the commitment to provide access to historically underrepresented populations—serves a general public purpose, in the sense that it creates opportunities for a diverse citizenry to realize their full social, economic, intellectual, cultural, and personal potential, which can also provide that same diverse citizenry with private gains and potentially contribute to private markets through increased financial and social access and expenditures. *Research* also is generally considered to be conducted in the public sphere and for the public good, although it is increasingly supported by private funds and yields outcomes that advance particular private markets. The traditional teaching, research, and service missions and activities within higher education are and should be measured according to the degree to which they contribute to improving human and social conditions. Whether these missions or activities are framed as purely public or private is secondary to the impact the activities have on the lives of those in the society who support higher education. As Shapiro (2005) rightfully forewarns, what's at stake is "the continued social relevance of institutions of higher education" (p. 11).

Matthews (2005) situated "good" in a democratic context and specifically expressed a "good" as "what citizens determine is most valuable in their common life—more precisely, what actions people deem most consistent with the things they hold dear" (p. 72). In this regard, conceptualizing a "good" is for individuals to reflect on that which is important. The notion of "public" involves a broader conceptualization than the idea of community or neighborhood. Here, "public" refers to a citizenry that is actively engaged in the work that self-government necessitate as well as to a set of interactions or practices rather than a static population (Matthews, 2005). The term "private" is usually associated with individual pursuits and achievements as well as themes of exclusivity and selectivity. In particular, some leaders suggest, "higher education is seen as a private good with the benefits accruing to the student in the form of higher future wages and quality of life" (Mattoon, 2006).

To situate these elements into a relationship with higher education, Bowen (1977) conducted analyses of individual and public benefits of higher education and subsequently developed a useful conceptual framework. In particular, Bowen's framework was later translated into a matrix with four intersecting dimensions that reflect broad individual and social benefits of higher education—public, private, economic, and social (Institute for Higher Education Policy, as cited in Chambers, 2005).

	Public	**Private**
Economic	Increased tax revenues	Higher salaries
	Greater productivity	Higher savings
	Increased consumption	Improved working conditions
	Increased workforce flexibility	Personal/professional mobility
Social	Reduced crime rate	Improved health
	Increased community service	Improved quality of life
	Increased quality of civic life	Better consumer decision making
	Social cohesion	More hobbies, leisure activities
	Appreciation of diversity	

FIGURE 5.1 The Array of Higher Education Benefits

SOURCE: The Institute for Higher Education Policy (1998)

In utilizing this conceptual framework, we are not suggesting that higher education is the panacea for these social, economic, public, and private benefits. To do so would be to risk trivializing the significance of other social institutions in society that can also contribute to these and other outcomes (Chambers, 2005). In addition, we recognize that the complexities of the human condition and social institutions cannot be neatly categorized in a two-by-two matrix. Clearly, it can be argued that all economic and social outcomes are the result of interactions between individual and social forces. Likewise, it can be argued that all individual and social outcomes are the result of interactions among economic and social forces.

Although scholars recognize that higher education contributes to all of these dimensions, recent discussions concern the increased orientation of higher education to market and economic goals (Kezar, 2005; Bok, 2003). The economic advancement of developing societies has been a top political agenda item, and governments define public good as private advancement and economic attainment rather than the historical commitments of social development, social justice, and democratic engagement (Kezar, 2005). Hence, the emphasis on *public good* does not negate the economic benefits of and imperatives to higher education, but rather acts as a lens through which the relationship between higher education and society can be viewed and understood.

From a public policy perspective, Longanecker (2005) reframed the traditional discussion that connects higher education's public role with broader public policy. His sense is that instead of thinking about "supporting public higher education as a public good," we should focus on "finding a balance for public higher education between its public and private purposes" (p. 59). Accordingly, Longanecker outlined three distinct public policy paths through which this shift from "serving the public good" to "balancing public and private purposes" has evolved:

Conjoining public activities with private interests: Public higher education contracts with private interests to provide "peripheral" institutional services that cut cost and increase benefits. Problems surface when institutions began contracting with private sources to provide "essential" educational services (i.e., curriculum, student services, educational facilities management, etc.). Questions emerge regarding the degree to which institutions maintain control over the shape of their core business.

Courting private gain to achieve the public good: Aggressively seeking support from private sources for constructing customized curriculum (that focus on specific proprietary ends for the private sources [i.e., businesses]) and engaging in customized applied research (again, often with specific proprietary ends in mind for businesses). These activities may have public value; however, the concern remains whether higher education institutions that engage, or overengage, in these types of activities release control of the destiny of their institutions, thereby jeopardizing the public good role to which they are committed.

Privatization of the public enterprise: Transitioning from a publicly governed and focused institution to an institution with primarily (if not exclusively) private financial intentions. This path is reflected in the continuum from establishing "charter" institutions with implied public good intentions, to establishing "for-profit" ventures that are a part of public institutions, some of which emerge from various types of profit-oriented research (private and publicly funded) that was mentioned in the previous path. (pp. 60–65).

Kezar (2005) posits a set of critical questions that are central to the dialogue regarding higher education's public and private interests and relationships:

1. At what level should higher education institutions adapt to market forces and to what level should they retain their historic functions and longer-term public interests?
2. What are some of the historic social functions that need to be considered in this dialogue? How can new social functions such as educating for a diverse society and creating reciprocal partnerships with community be incorporated?
3. To what degree should higher education become private and what is the impact of this shift? Is public higher education part of the state or is it independent? What type of autonomy or regulation should be exerted?
4. How can we think about private and public in complex ways that still maintain the social role of higher education?
5. To what degree is the dilemma of values and priorities internal, institutional rather than external, corporate?
6. How can the public be engaged in a reciprocal relationship around the social charter?

Finally, we would question whether *private goods, resulting from higher education initiatives, can be socially just, or even more fundamentally, whether all public goods, resulting from higher education initiatives, are socially just,* particularly during times of severe economic and social stress, and increasing commercialization within higher education.

Social Justice

The notion of social justice has received considerable scholarly and public attention. Although social justice has been theorized differently in philosophy, political science, and other disciplines, our initial intention here is to map out some of the major theoretical movements that have informed social justice in its current articulation. Social justice is interpreted and practiced in different ways depending on the principles or criteria used to define what is "just." The artificial distinction that is often presented is whether justice refers to "a just distribution of resources" or a "just outcome." The entry point for our notion of social justice begins with Rawls's understanding of justice in *A Theory of Justice* (1971). Traditionally, a Rawlsian approach to justice has been labeled a distributive theory of justice. Specifically, Rawls (1971) imagined how people would respond if their starting positions in life were equal and they had no knowledge of what positions they would occupy later (Gale, 2000). In considering this notion, Rawls (1971) argued that social justice has two principles: (1) liberty or individual freedom and (2) equal distribution of material and social goods. Hence, this emphasis on distribution anoints the Rawlsian notion of social justice as distributive justice.

An alternative interpretation of social justice that was initially posited by Nozick (1976) considered a reworking of liberty and freedom in social interactions. Nozick (1976) charged Rawls with an overemphasis on the social good possessed by individuals with little to no attention to the processes by which individuals acquire these goods (Gale, 2000). In this interpretation, "social justice is primarily concerned with fairness in the competition for goods and is not a matter of equalizing possessions" (Gale, 2000, p. 256). Unfairness, or injustice, according to Nozick (1976), would be "measures that both limit individuals' freedoms to exercise their talents and efforts as well as those which limit the rewards individuals receive from them" (Gale, 2000, p. 257). Many scholars (Apple, 1998; Rizvi & Lingard, 1996; Taylor, Rizvi, Lingard, & Henry, 1997) have criticized this approach as market-oriented in its privileging of property rights over person rights as well as a narrowing of the notion of liberty.

Another branch of social justice that grew out of these traditions was entitled the *recognitive* approach. Broadly, this approach is interested in reconsidering the origins of social justice as a "radical response to redress its restrictive conceptions" (Gale, 2000, p. 259). This work suggests that differences and areas of commonality among cultural groups are significant entry points. Building on the ideas of Young (1990) and Fraser (1995), the *recognitive* justice perspective is based upon (a) rethinking what is meant by social justice and; (b) acknowledging the place of social groups within this notion (Gale, 2000). Advocates of this *recognitive* approach emphasize issues which draw attention to actions and not simply to the outcomes of those actions (Gale, 2000).

A final approach we recognize here is the capabilities approach developed by Sen (1999) and then further elaborated upon by Martha Nussbaum (1999). The fundamental question in this approach is: "Is this person capable of this, or not?" The impetus for this approach originates from two main ideas: First, there are particular functions that are central in human life and whose presence or absence is understood to be an indicator of the presence or absence of human life; and second, there is something that has to do these functions in a truly human way, not simply an animal way (Nussbaum, 1999). A critical aspect of this approach is that human beings are free entities who shape their own lives, instead of being molded or herded like animals by the world and subsequent forces around them. Nussbaum (1999) outlined a range of ten capabilities that are essential for an individual to create a fulfilling life, which includes the spheres of the economic, personal, social, and environmental. The ten capabilities include life, bodily health, bodily integrity, senses, imagination and thought, emotions, practical reason, affiliation, other species, play, and control over one's environment (Nussbaum, 1999). Walker (2005) reviewed this list of capabilities and offered some insights into their applicability and integration into the purposes of higher education. Specifically, Walker (2005) wrote, "this approach suggests a view of higher education as more than education for economic development, and incorporates an implicit view of education both as and for democratic citizenship, and understanding and solidarity under conditions of cultural difference and diversity" (p. 170).

Engaged Scholarship

Although the definition of engaged scholarship or the scholarship of engagement has been shaped by considerable reflection and practice, we nonetheless had a few concerns about how it might be framed within our emergent sense of a social justice-centered engaged scholarship. The distinctions we think are worth making, for purposes of this chapter, are among what we call the scholarship *of* engagement, the scholarship *on or about* engagement, and the scholarship *for* engagement.

The scholarship *of* engagement involves partnerships between researchers and communities that are designed and implemented to address social or community needs. The interaction among partners for some socially defined outcome itself is a form of scholarship. The scholarship is undertaken by those engaged in the partnership. The scholarship *on* or *about* engagement is the study of the processes of collaboration, decision making, research, and action within this relationship between scholars and communities. The partnerships or engagement dynamics are the subjects of study. The scholarship is not necessarily undertaken by those involved in the partnerships. It may be undertaken by third parties not directly a part of the engaging partnerships. Finally, the scholarship *for* engagement has the sole purpose of preparing for and supporting engagement between higher education scholars and communities toward specific social (justice) outcomes and impacts. The unit of focus in the scholarship for engagement is the intended social outcome and impact. The partnerships and engagement dynamics are variables influencing the outcomes and impacts. The common framing of the scholarship of engagement implies the integration of the three forms of engaged scholarship. It's important to know the parameters and intent of one's involvement in engaged scholarship, and our distinctions provide a ground upon which discernments can be made by scholars and communities. For purposes of this chapter, what we mean by a social justice-centered engaged scholarship or scholarship of engagement is a combination of the scholarship *of* engagement and the scholarship *for* engagement, where the interactions among partners and the intended outcomes and impacts are the subjects of scholarly focus and action.

Engaged scholarship has been a relatively recent frame to consider the work of faculty members in academic institutions. The term has its roots in the work of Ernest L. Boyer, who suggested a broader definition of what activities and deliverables constitute scholarship. Boyer (1996) writes, "the academy must become a more vigorous partner in the search for answers to our most pressing social, civic, economic and moral problems, and must affirm its historic commitment to . . . the scholarship of engagement" (p. 11). The traditional conception of scholarship that was recognized and rewarded in universities was research that was original, was peer-reviewed, and constituted a contribution to the knowledge within a particular disciplinary field. Although these attributes are extremely important to the history of the university and the disciplinary and professional guilds that constitute academe, Boyer's suggestion required a reconceptualization not only of the work of faculty members, but also of the relationship of the university to society and, even more broadly, the purposes of the university. Hence, this emphasis on a new, broader notion of scholarship (that is, the scholarship of engagement) required focusing on the relationship between university and society.

The scholarship of engagement, meanwhile, encourages a break from the "top-down" or "expert-driven" model of partnership between universities, scholars, and communities. Various scholars (Lynton, 1995; Lynton & Driscoll, 1999) have further developed the scholarship of engagement by recognizing that the dynamic between faculty members and communities cannot be framed as outreach or even service. The scholarship of engagement seeks more than characterizations of service or outreach—it emphasizes collaboration. An important first step in distinguishing an engaged scholarship approach from the traditional research approach was to emphasize a bidirectional reciprocity between communities and scholars (Sandmann, 2007). Here, the co-constructed and multidirectional nature of learning and instruction is highlighted and the notion of expertise is shared (Rice, 2002).

Pinning down a precise definition of the scholarship of engagement requires a layering of notions that encapsulates the alternative epistemological underpinnings as well as the rearticulated mission of the university. Specifically, Boyer (1996) writes, "the scholarship of engagement means connecting the rich resources of the university to our most pressing social, civic and ethical problems" (p. 20), which provides an operationalization of the notion; but Boyer continues to say, "what's also needed is not just more programs, but a larger purpose, a larger sense of mission, a larger clarity of direction in the nation's life" (p. 20). Finally, Boyer (1996) adds, "the scholarship of engagement also means creating a special climate in which the academic and civic cultures communicate more continuously and more creatively with each other, helping to enlarge the universe of human discourse and enriching the quality of life for all of us" (p. 20). Most recently, Barker (2004) moved significantly closer to conceptual clarity by suggesting that the scholarship of engagement consists of "(a) research, teaching, integration and application scholarship that (b) incorporate reciprocal practices of civic engagement into the production of knowledge" (p. 124). For Boyer, engaged scholarship meant that faculty as scholars are taking on world problems through disciplinary means, fulfilling campus mission, and incorporating teaching, research, and service as vehicles to address the public good.

Social Justice-Centered Engaged Scholarship

The *social justice*-centered perspective of engaged scholarship involves working with community groups and individuals in need, but possesses significantly greater reflective and social-action components than traditional scholarship. Key points presented by Marullo and Edwards (2000), when talking about a social justice approach to service learning, can be directly applied to a social justice-centered engaged scholarship. Engaged scholarship should be about empowering those in communities as equal partners. Root causes of social injustice are examined and addressed, and the individuals who are targets of injustice are not blamed for their situation. Social justice-centered engaged scholarship should build community, increase social capital, and enhance diversity, and it is particularly crucial to engage all participants in problem solving and opportunity seeking. Individuals and communities that base their scholarship on a social justice approach adhere to the principle that "we must ensure that the educational institution is not merely using the community as a social laboratory with human guinea pigs" (p. 908). Social justice is interpreted and practiced in different ways depending on the principles or criteria used to define what is "just." The artificial distinction that is often presented is whether justice refers to "a just distribution of resources" or a "just outcome." Along the resource/outcome continuum are several popular ways of interpreting and practicing the notion of justice. Included among the interpretations are the "just" notions of *Liberty, Equity, Equality, Need,* and *Solidarity* (Chesler, 1993).

Liberty

The notion of liberty reflects the ability of people to freely make decisions about their own activities and options in a just society. The freedom to make decisions about one's own life is the central element in the ability to control one's fate and pursue satisfaction on one's own terms. Central to this interpretation of justice is the notion of individual free will.

Equity

Justice, within an equity framework, suggests that differences in individual talent, effort, or investment should be rewarded by differences in outcomes or rewards. Those who work hard, have valued talents, and use them well contribute more to the public good and should get greater rewards than those with less valued talents who work less hard.

Equality

Within an equality interpretation of justice, there should be a relatively equal distribution of societal resources that recognizes the inherent value of every individual regardless of his or her particular talent, effort, and contribution. This criterion helps to overcome the cultural and structural inequalities that give unfair advantages and liberties to some and disadvantages to others.

Need

A need perspective of justice recognizes that equality itself fails to respond to the reality that people are not equal with respect to their needs, and therefore certain inequalities may be legitimate if they are tied tightly to differential need.

Solidarity

Solidarity is less of a perspective than it is an approach to scholars and communities working together. Within the solidarity notion of justice, communicating with, caring about, and solving problems and seeking opportunities with others are essential to building respectful collaborations between scholars and communities around engaged scholarship efforts.

A social justice-centered engaged scholarship assists scholars and community partners in making decisions about what type of scholarship would best serve the needs of society; serve as models or lessons for others to replicate and further disseminate; prepare students with skills, knowledge, and commitments to engage in socially just activities; and, it may be hoped, establish sustainable relationships between scholars and communities to collectively address ongoing issues of injustice. Inherent in our notion of a social justice-centered engaged scholarship is that rigorous, collaborative, and intentional attention to justice through scholarship will lead to societal transformations at local, national, and international levels.

A social justice-centered engaged scholarship examines the broad systemic factors that contribute to the causes and continuation of social inequities and explores the means to undertake multilevel transformation that not only addresses the apparent causes of problems, but also challenges the assumptions and mindsets that sustain the problematic conditions. Transformation and change have been distinguished from one another by several scholars (Green, Eckel, & Hill, 1998). The position we take to transformation that results from a social justice-centered engaged scholarship is consistent with that of Green et al.:

> Transformation (1) alters the culture of the institution by changing select underlying assumptions and institutional behaviors, processes, and products; (2) is deep and pervasive, affecting the whole institution; (3) is intentional; and (4) occurs over time.
>
> Transformation requires major shifts in an institution's culture—the common set of beliefs and values that create a shared interpretation and understanding of events and actions. Institution-wide patterns of perceiving, thinking, and feeling; shared understandings; collective assumptions; and common interpretive frameworks are the ingredients of this "invisible glue" called institutional culture (Kuh & Whitt, 1988; Schein, 1992). Organizational culture is not monolithic. In organizations as complex as colleges and universities, it often is a composite of many different subcultures rather than a single culture. (p. 3)

Influenced by theories of libratory pedagogy and scholarship, a central goal of the social justice-centered engaged scholarship is that learners (scholars and communities) change and challenge the world rather than adapting themselves to it without critical thought. Political, economic, and personal empowerment is sought through dialogue between scholars, learners, and community members engaged in an effort to address broader social issues (Freire, 1970). Within a social justice-centered engaged scholarship approach, there are several dimensions that further distinguish it from other forms of scholarship. Among those dimensions are (1) *the primary "targets" of analyses*—the intended focus of the scholarship, as well as the primary partners working toward some form of transformation of unjust conditions; (2) *learning*—the process and outcomes of developing critical knowledge and understanding about social injustices; (3) *community*—a collection of individuals, organizations, and institutions that impact and are impacted by socially unjust conditions; (4) *change*—a signal of what will be different and how it will be different when communities and scholars address problems from a social justice-centered engaged scholarship approach; (5) *outcomes*—the expected (and unexpected) results of social justice-centered engaged scholarship efforts; and (6) *power*—the artifacts, relationships, and opportunities that provide individuals and institutions the privilege to decide and act on what is just and unjust for themselves and others.

For scholars and communities that adapt a social justice-centered engaged scholarship approach, the *primary "targets" of analyses* are the individual and/or a social group and systems and networks that contribute to and sustain the social conditions that are in need of transformation. Within the social justice-centered approach, *learning* is assumed to occur through a critical understanding of the history and contemporary conditions and circumstances that are experienced by populations that are, and have historically been, the target of injustices and inequality, as well as a critical understanding of ways in which institutions/organizations as a whole contribute to and benefit from the creation and continuation of social problems. *Community* comprises individuals and groups that have been "wronged" and are in need of support to "right" the wrong and develop capacity to sustain an improved social status. Community is also viewed as having "assets" and is engaged as a partner in the service-learning process. Broadly, community is viewed as a part of a larger, more complex system of institutions and networks that is both a contributor to and a recipient of social injustices. Desired *change* will occur when the group that is wronged is no longer the target of the wrongdoers and may receive some form of compensation for past inequities. Structures are also put in place to signal the end of the injustice and to provide an avenue for redress if the injustice occurs again. Further, desired change will occur when components of the system acknowledge their role in contributing to the social problem and participate actively in deploying resources, with others in the system, to address the core and manifestations of the problem. There needs to be an alteration of the mindset and social and institutional conditions that contributed to the problem in the first place. The intended *outcomes* of a social justice-centered approach to engaged scholarship is for the elimination or reduction in unjust treatment toward groups or individuals, and the development of processes for the various components of a social system to work together toward addressing complex social problems that they have contributed to creating and sustaining. Communities, scholars, and others become conscious of the complexity of social problems and begin thinking and acting in more complex and creative ways to address these problems through scholarship and action. Finally, within a social justice-centered engaged scholarship, *power* is seen to reside within the laws and codified structures that address inequalities and injustice. Power also resides within the partnerships between those targeted for injustice and those who consider themselves allies and within the network of institutions and organizations in a broad system. The power that exists within the network is much stronger than power within any component of the network alone. Power also exists within the formal and informal structures of the network, as well as within each component (institution/organization) of the network. These and other dimensions of a social justice-centered engaged scholarship approach define some of the significant dynamics of the scholar and community relationship, as well as the intentions, expectations, and potential impacts of engaged scholarship efforts. How will these dynamics and potential impacts be reflected in the future of engaged scholarship? What will need to happen in order for a social justice-centered engaged scholarship to be sustained among scholars and communities? Following is a brief set of evolving patterns and concerns that we believe will need to be addressed in order to further define and advance a social justice-centered engaged scholarship approach.

Evolving Patterns and Concerns

Leadership

Critical to any institutional or social endeavor is the presence of forward-thinking and -acting leadership. Leadership within higher education institutions that sets a tone for how engaged scholarship and other forms of social engagement are valued and aligns with the institution's mission is essential to establishing a culture of engagement on any campus. Of course, institutional leaders need to demonstrate the value for engagement as much as verbalize the value of engagement. Demonstration of the value of engagement can take the form of providing financial incentives for creative forms of engagement and recognizing engaged scholarship that impacts a surrounding community or serves as the foundation for addressing significant social challenges. Community leadership is as important as

65

institutional leadership, because engaged scholarship and other forms of social engagement require partnerships among institutional and community members. Community leaders need to be able to work with multiple community constituencies to define and prioritize the issues and opportunities that communities want to address in their partnerships with scholars. Leadership from the various professional disciplinary organizations where faculty scholars look for peer validation of their work is also essential. Disciplinary guilds, more than higher education institutions in many cases, are the places where scholars establish a sense of professional worth and develop their sense of the scholarly worth of their engaged scholarship with communities. Peer-reviewed journals are products of professional guilds that frequently shape fields of scholarship by what is selected for publication in the journals. Leadership in the professional organizations that recognize, promote, and reward scholarship and professional service that addresses social justice-centered issues with communities could result in a shift in the professional value of engaged scholarship, and perhaps foster increased social justice-centered engaged scholarly efforts.

Institutionalization

Related to institutional leadership, social justice-centered engaged scholarship is frequently relegated to the periphery of institutionally recognized and rewarded scholarship. In order for this special form of scholarship and engagement to be considered central to an institution's purpose and mission, it has to be seen and experienced by all in the institution as a standard and essential component of the day-to-day functioning of the institution. This day-to-day institutional standard needs to be reflected in several areas: the institution's system of faculty rewards and recognition, including the tenure, promotion, and review process; provision of resources to carry out various forms of engagement with communities; student learning outcomes and assessments; acknowledgments at institution-wide recognitions and ceremonies; involvement of community members on important institutional boards; contracting and purchasing decisions for goods and services; fund-raising campaigns; expectations of new hires; accessibility of campus events and facilities to members of the surrounding communities; and the public recognition through speeches, news releases, interviews, etc., of the central value of scholarly, pedagogical, and social engagement with community partners. These are all ways to institutionalize engaged scholarship.

Preparation of Future Scholars

Another critical issue that needs to be addressed in order to advance a social justice-centered engaged scholarship is academic preparation of students, particularly graduate students who are considering professions as educators and scholars in higher education. Research and pedagogical preparation for these future scholars needs to include conceptual and theoretical as well as practical and reflective knowledge and skills in the area of engaged scholarship and pedagogies. We strongly believe that distributing these types of knowledge and skills throughout the curriculum, instead of isolating them in specific fields of study, is the most appropriate way of preparing future educators and scholars (and other professionals) with skills, knowledge, and sensitivities to engage communities in addressing social (justice) issues.

Public Policy Development

Systemic change that targets social justice issues needs systems-level policy (institutional and governmental) to ensure a degree of sustainability and enforcement, where and when appropriate. The results of social justice-centered engaged scholarship can be very persuasive to both institutional and government bodies to create, revise, adopt, implement, and enforce regulations, practices, and laws that address important justice issues locally, nationally, and internationally. Scholars and members of communities need to develop a deeper understanding and appreciation for the values of their engaged scholarship policy implications. Additionally, along with developing the skills, knowledge, and sensitivities to address social justice issues through engaged scholarship activities, they should develop skills, knowledge, and experience in translating their engaged scholarship into policy-level creation and change. To achieve broad, sustainable transformation on complex social issues, it may not be enough to confine the social change efforts and expectations to specific episodes or communities for undetermined periods of time.

Influencing Market Forces

Higher education institutions, scholars, and communities need to influence market processes to be more responsive to the concerns and needs of communities that have been stressed economically and socially by unjust policies and practices. Many of these communities have been either exploited or ignored by market processes. Not only should engaged scholarship critically examine the effects of markets on stressed communities, but those involved in engaged scholarship should leverage the knowledge gained from their scholarship to influence market behavior, market access, and the distribution of market benefits to those in most need.

Internationalization

Paul Collier (2007) points out that global poverty is actually falling in relative terms for about 80 percent of the world. The real crisis, he claims, is with a group of about fifty failing countries, which he dubs "The Bottom Billion," whose problems defy traditional approaches to eliminating poverty. What Collier, and others, point out is that life conditions for local neighborhoods and communities are tied inextricably to struggling neighborhoods and communities around the world. The degree to which scholars and communities engage in both a local and global inter-rogation of the conditions that are in need of change is of concern to us. Clearly, there are multiple examples of border-spanning justice issues that originated elsewhere, yet manifest themselves close to home. Engaged scholars would do well to expand their critique and analysis of local social justice issues to include correlate global social justice issues.

In addition to the concerns we've offered from fairly broad and general perspectives, at a very practical level, Minkler (2004) raised several key ethical challenges posed by actually participating in various forms of engaged scholarship. Among her challenges are the following.

Achieving a True "Community-Driven" Agenda

Is it possible or practical to set a collective agenda that focuses primarily or solely on what communities determine as important?

Insider-Outsider "Tensions"

How are tensions and perceptions managed when community members are frequently considered outsiders to the academic culture and academic scholars are frequently considered outsiders to community cultures?

The Limitations of Participation

As open and inviting as engaged scholarship is conceptually, everyone cannot participate in the same project at the same time. Likewise, there are occasions when communities and/or academic scholars choose not to participate at all, leaving the project without a "partnership."

Issues Involving Sharing, Ownership, and Use of Findings for Action

How do engaged scholars (community and institutional) transcend and transform political and parochial tendencies when working together toward social change?

Although considerable promise has been demonstrated by social justice-centered engaged scholarship, there are still many issues in need of attention in order to fully realize the potential impact of the process.

Conclusion

In this chapter, we set out to present a perspective on engaged scholarship that is situated as a process aimed toward social justice transformation. Our take on the concepts and theories that serve as a foundation for a social justice-centered engaged scholarship reflects our deep belief in the central purposes of engaged scholarship: that is, to recognize, analyze, and seek resolution of socially unjust conditions for individuals and communities. We also acknowledge the complexities of labeling engaged scholarship as a public good or private good. If asked whether engaged scholarship is a public or private good, our resounding response would be "Yes!" But at the end of the day, the life circumstances of people and communities would be significantly improved because of our collective engagement in this type of scholarship.

Social justice-centered engaged scholarship is approached in as complex and creative a fashion as the circumstances that inspired a need for the scholarship in the first place. In fact, there are varying interpretations of what constitutes social justice, and thus considerable variation in how scholars and communities frame and approach their efforts to address unjust conditions. Certainly, higher education institutions and professional guilds need to recognize and appropriately reward scholars who seek ways in which their scholarship can make a difference in moving toward a just society. Communities need to embrace the local-to-global complexities of their challenges, remain open to partnerships with academic scholars and institutions, and develop the capacities necessary to translate their considerable knowledge and experience into efforts for sustainable change. As Boyer (1996), so prophetically pronounced:

- at a deeper level, I have this growing conviction that what's also needed is not just more programs, but a larger purpose, a larger sense of mission, a larger clarity of direction in the nation's life. . . .

- I'm convinced that ultimately, the scholarship of engagement also means creating a special climate in which the academic and civic cultures communicate more continuously and more creatively with each other, helping to enlarge what anthropologist Clifford Geetz describes as the universe of human discourse and enrich the quality of life for all of us. (pp. 19–20)

References

Apple, M. (1998). Equality and the politics of commonsense. In W. Secada (Ed.), *Equity in education.* London: Falmer Press.

Barker, D. (2004).The scholarship of engagement: A taxonomy of five emerging practices. *Journal of Higher Education Outreach and Engagement, 9*(2), 123–137.

Bok, D. (2003). *Universities in the marketplace.* Princeton, NJ: Princeton University Press.

Bowen, H. (1977). *Investment in learning.* San Francisco: Jossey-Bass.

Boyer, E. L. (1996). The scholarship of engagement. *Journal of Public Service and Outreach, 1,* 11–20.

Chambers, T. C. (2005). The special role of higher education in society: As a public good for the public good. In A. J. Kezar, T. C. Chambers, & J. C. Burkhardt (Eds.), *Higher education for the public good: Emerging voices from a national movement* (pp. 3–22). San Francisco: Jossey-Bass.

Chambers, T., & Gopaul, B. (2008). Decoding the public good of higher education. *Journal of Higher Education Outreach and Engagement, 12*(4), 59–91.

Chesler, M. A. (1993). Alternative dispute resolution and social justice. In E. Lewis & E. Douvan (Eds.), *Injustice, conflict, and social Change.* Westport, CT: Greenwood.

Collier, P. (2007). *The bottom billion: Why the poorest countries are failing and what can be done about it.* New York: Oxford University Press.

Fraser, N. (1995). From redistribution to recognition: Dilemmas of justice in a "post-socialist" society. *New Left Review, 212,* 68–93.

Freire, P. (1970). *Pedagogy of the oppressed.* New York: Herder and Herder.

Gale, T. (2000). Rethinking social justice in schools: How will we know we recognize it when we see it? *International Journal of Inclusive Education, 4*(3), 253–269.

Green, M., Eckel, P., & Hill, B. (1998). On change: En route to transformation. An occasional paper series of the ACE project on leadership and institutional transformation. Washington, DC: American Council on Education.

Institute for Higher Education Policy. (1998). *Reaping the benefits: Defining the public and private value of going to college.* Washington, DC: Author.

Kezar, A. J. (2005). Challenges for higher education in serving the public good. In A. J. Kezar, T. C. Chambers, & J. C. Burkhardt (Eds.), *Higher education for the public good: Emerging voices from a national movement* (pp. 23–42). San Francisco: Jossey-Bass.

Kuh, G. D., & Whitt, E. J. (1988). *The invisible tapestry: Culture in American colleges and universities.* Washington, DC: ASHE-ERIC Higher Education Reports.

Longanecker, D. (2005). State governance and the public good. In A. J. Kezar, T. C. Chambers, & J. C. Burkhardt (Eds.), *Higher education for the public good: Emerging voices from a national movement* (pp. 57–70). San Francisco: Jossey-Bass.

Lynton, E. (1995). *Making a case for professional service.* Washington, DC: American Association for Higher Education.

Lynton, E., & Driscoll, A. (1999). *Making outreach visible: A guide to documenting professional service and outreach*. Washington, DC: American Association for Higher Education.

Marullo, S., & Edwards, B. (2000). From charity to justice: The potential for university-community collaboration for social change. *American Behavioral Scientist, 43*, 895–912.

Mathews, D. (2005). Listening to the public: A new agenda for higher education. In A. J. Kezar, T. C. Chambers, & J. C. Burkhardt (Eds.), *Higher education for the public good: Emerging voices from a national movement* (pp. 71–86). San Francisco: Jossey-Bass.

Mattoon, R. (2006, January). Higher education and economic growth. *Chicago Fed Letter, Federal Reserve Bank of Chicago*, No. 222. Available at http://www.chicagofed.org/publications/fedletter/cfljanuary2006_222b.pdf.

Minkler, M. (2004). Ethical challenges for the "Outside" researcher in community-based participatory research. *Health Education and Behavior, 31*(6), 684–697.

Nozick, R. (1976). *Anarchy, state and utopia*. Oxford, England: Blackwell.

Nussbaum, M. (1999). Women and equality: The capabilities approach. *International Labour Review, 138*(3), 227–245.

Rawls, J. (1971). *A theory of justice*. Oxford, England: Oxford University Press.

Rice, R. E. (2002). Beyond scholarship reconsidered: Toward an enlarged vision of the scholarly work of faculty members. *New Directions for Teaching and Learning, 90*, 7–17.

Rizvi, F., & Lingard, B. (1996). Disability, education and the discourses of justice. In C. Christensen and F. Rizvi (Eds.), *Disability and the dilemmas of education and justice* (pp. 9–26). London: Open University Press.

Samuelson, P. A. (1954). The pure theory of public expenditure. *Review of Economic Statistics, 36*(4), 387–389.

Sandmann, L. R. (2007). Conceptualization of the scholarship of engagement in higher education: A ten-year retrospective. In L. Servage & T. Fenwick (Eds.), *Learning in community* (pp. 547–552). Proceedings of the Joint International Conference of the Adult Education Research Conference (AERC) and the Canadian Association for the Study of Adult Education (CASAE). Halifax, Nova Scotia, Canada.

Schein, E. H. (1992). *Organizational culture and leadership* (2nd ed.). San Francisco: Jossey-Bass.

Sen, A. K. (1999). *Development as freedom*. Oxford, England: Oxford University Press.

Shapiro, H. T. (2005). *A larger sense of purpose: Higher education and society*. Princeton, NJ: Princeton University Press.

Taylor, S., Rizvi, F., Lingard, B., & Henry, M. (1997). *Educational policy and politics of change*. London: Routledge.

Walker, M. (2003). Framing social justice in education: What does the "capabilities" approach offer? *British Journal of Educational Studies, 51*(2), 168–187.

Young, I. M. (1990). *Justice and the politics of difference*. Princeton, NJ: Princeton University Press.

Ernest Boyer and the Scholarship of Engagement

John M. Braxton and William Luckey

In his influential work in 1990, Ernest Boyer introduced us to his four domains of scholarship—the scholarship of discovery, the scholarship of integration, the scholarship of application, and the scholarship of teaching. After a three-year battle with cancer just fifty-eight days before his death, Boyer delivered a compelling speech to a room full of educators at the Induction Ceremony of the American Academy of Arts and Sciences in Cambridge, Massachusetts. In his parting words of wisdom, Boyer stated his firm belief in our colleges and universities as our greatest hope for intellectual and civic progress for this nation. He believed that in order for this potential to be fulfilled, "the academy must become a more vigorous partner in the search for answers to our most pressing social, civic, economic, and moral problems, and must reaffirm its historic commitment to what I call the scholarship of engagement" (Boyer, 1996, p. 11).

Why just two months before his death did Boyer, who had previously advocated for the scholarship of application in his words and writings, instead campaign for the scholarship of engagement? What is the difference, if any, between the scholarship of engagement and the scholarship of application? In order to best respond to these questions, one must first return to Boyer's *Scholarship Reconsidered*, where he states "the application of knowledge moves toward engagement" (Boyer, 1990, p. 21) as the scholar asks how knowledge can be helpful to individuals as well as institutions. This *application* of knowledge moves toward engagement as the scholar asks, "How can knowledge be responsibly applied to consequential problems?" (Boyer, 1990, p. 21).

Boyer points out the gap between the values of the academy, research, and the needs of the larger world. In fact, he notes that service in the academy is routinely praised but often ignored in tenure decisions. Consequently, scholars tend to invest their time and talents in ways that are most beneficial to the individual researcher rather than improving the human condition. In Boyer's mind, the scholarship of application is a dynamic process where theory and practice interact and renew each other. He felt this scholarly service that both applies and contributes to human knowledge was "particularly needed in a world in which huge, almost intractable problems call for the skills and insights only the academy can provide" (Boyer, 1990, p. 23).

Boyer made sure to distinguish between doing good and doing scholarship. He appropriately drew a sharp distinction between citizenship activities related to various social and civic organizations such as Rotary, Kiwanis, town councils, and youth clubs and the professional service activities tied directly to one's special field of knowledge.

In his speech just months before his death, Boyer mentioned that "for more than 350 years, higher learning and the larger purposes of American society have been inextricably interlocked" (Boyer, 1996, p. 11). He cited the colonial colleges and the preparation of civic and religious leaders; the impact of the historic Land Grant Act, passed during our nation's darkest hour in the Civil War, which linked higher learning to our country's agricultural, technological, and industrial revolutions; and the development of radar and penicillin as examples to demonstrate how our scholars had provided practical service to the nation (Boyer, 1996).

Less than one hundred years ago, the mission of higher education was the scholarship of engagement as described by Boyer. Colleges and universities were relevant and had a seat at the table when the great issues of the day were being discussed, debated, and decided. As a forty-year-old Princeton professor, Woodrow Wilson insisted that colleges and universities must continue their spirit of service to maintain their place in the public annals of the nation. "We dare not keep aloof and closet ourselves while a nation comes to its maturity" (Boyer, 1996, p. 12). In fact, it is Boyer's contention that, with the emphasis on the work of individual scholars as researchers, as well as the increasing value given to teaching, the historic commitment to the scholarship of engagement has dramatically declined, to our nation's peril. Higher education, which has historically been viewed as a partner during turbulent times, is often seen today as part of the problem rather than the solution. Boyer mentions that increasingly "the campus is being viewed as a place where students get credentialed and faculty get tenured" (Boyer, 1996, p. 14)—while, as researchers chase grant dollars and their individual scholarly pursuits, the great issues of our time go largely ignored by the academy. In effect, Boyer states that education is currently perceived as a private benefit, rather than a public good. He laments that at one time higher education was viewed as an investment in the future of our nation, with this national intellect perceived as too valuable to lose (Boyer, 1996).

At the time of this writing, our nation is experiencing its most difficult financial challenge since the Great Depression. Major banking institutions are closing or have asked for a financial bailout. The big three in the American automobile industry are asking to be rescued. At the same time, we have become a society with news around the clock. If Boyer were alive today, he would be asking where the academy is in engaging with the great issues of our time. Every Sunday morning millions of Americans tune in to *Meet the Press*, *Face the Nation*, or *This Week with George Stephanopoulos*. Today's issues are being debated and discussed by politicians and other political pundits rather than university scholars. Boyer described this endless discussion as "impoverished public discourse" (Boyer, 1996, p. 15) and cautioned that scholars and practitioners must speak and listen carefully to each other for the health of our civic and academic culture.

Boyer's primary concern was that the work of the academy would be directed toward humane ends. He was convinced "higher education in this country has an urgent obligation to become more vigorously engaged in the issues of our day, just as the land-grant colleges helped farmers and technicians a century ago" (Boyer, 1996, p. 17). No longer, he claimed, can our great universities remain "islands of affluence, self-importance, and horticultural beauty in seas of squalor, violence, and despair" (p. 19).

One essential difference between the scholarship of application and the scholarship of engagement is the urgency and the magnitude of the problems needing to be addressed. Real engagement takes time and an emotional commitment that is not as evident with simply applying disciplinary knowledge to solve problems. Boyer states that "what's also needed is not just more programs, but a larger purpose, a larger sense of mission, a larger clarity of direction in the nation's life as we move toward century twenty-one" (Boyer, 1996, p. 20). He concluded his remarks by quoting Oscar Handlin: "A troubled universe can no longer afford the luxury of pursuits confined to an ivory tower . . . scholarship has to prove its worth not on its terms, but by service to the nation and the world" (p. 21). This, according to Boyer, is what the scholarship of engagement is all about.

In addition to the urgency and magnitude of the problems needing to be addressed, the beneficiary of the scholarship conducted further differentiates the scholarship of application from the scholarship of engagement. When faculty members serve on a departmental curriculum committee, a program review committee, or an institutional self-study committee for accreditation purposes, they are involved in the scholarship of application. However, when a faculty member ventures into the local community to apply disciplinary knowledge to solve a problem, then the scholarship of engagement is occurring. Real engagement takes time and an emotional commitment to assist a local organization or solve a county- or state-level problem.

Although few in the academy will ever impact the world, we are often reminded to think globally and act locally. Faculty members are often encouraged to participate in a departmental self-study, a college-wide curriculum committee, or a program review committee— all on-campus scholarly activities that could be considered as indicative of the scholarship of application. However, how frequently do academics venture outside the ivory tower to engage in the challenges of even their local communities to perform what Boyer referred to as the scholarship of engagement? Studies conducted for local organizations, local nonacademic professional associations, and local governmental associations, as well studies conducted to solve a community problem or to solve a county- or state-level problem, constitute forms of scholarship engaged in matters of concern to the lay community.

Although some research and scholarship focused on the scholarship of application exists (Braxton, Luckey, & Helland, 2002, 2006; O' Meara, 2006), little research has focused on faculty participation in the scholarship of engagement in the form of studies conducted for a local organization, for a local nonacademic professional association, for a local government organization, to solve a community problem, and to solve a county- or state-level problem. As previously indicated, these five types of studies are illustrative of the scholarship of engagement. This chapter addresses this void by concentrating on the five research questions delineated in the following section.

Research Questions

The following five research questions guided this study:

1. **How frequently have college and university faculty members conducted each of the five types of studies illustrative of the scholarship of engagement during the past three years?**

This question simply emerges from a paucity of research.

2. **Does the frequency of faculty members conducting each of the five types of studies illustrative of the scholarship of engagement vary across different types of colleges and universities?**

The mission of colleges and universities wields a strong influence on the level of scholarly role performance of college and university faculty members (Ruscio, 1987). Levels of publication productivity (Blackburn & Lawrence, 1995; Finkelstein, 1984; Fox, 1985; Fulton & Trow, 1974; Ruscio, 1987) and the work styles, attitudes, beliefs, values, and reference groups of academic professionals (Blackburn & Lawrence, 1995; Fulton & Trow, 1974; Ruscio, 1987) that vary across different types of colleges and universities offer evidence of the influence of institutional missions. Moreover, Braxton et al. (2002) found that faculty members in research and doctoral-granting universities register more publications indicative of the scholarship of application than do faculty members in teaching-oriented colleges and universities. Thus, we might expect that the frequency of the five types of studies illustrative of the scholarship of engagement will vary across different types of colleges and universities.

3. **Does the frequency of faculty members conducting each of the five types of studies illustrative of the scholarship of engagement vary across different academic disciplines?**

Academic disciplines vary in their level of consensus (high versus low) on such dimensions as theoretical orientation, appropriate research methods, and the importance of various research questions to the advancement of the discipline (Biglan, 1973; Kuhn, 1962; 1970; Lodahl & Gordon, 1972). Braxton and Hargens (1996) conclude from an extensive review of empirical research on discipline differences that faculty in high-consensus fields are more oriented to research than faculty in low-consensus fields. In addition, faculty in high-consensus fields experience higher rates of publication, lower journal rejection rates, and greater availability of external funding for research than do their low-consensus faculty counterparts. Braxton et al. (2002) failed to observe distinctions between high- and low-consensus academic disciplines on publications reflective of the scholarship of application. However, we might find differences in the frequency of faculty members conducting each of the five types of studies illustrative of the scholarship of engagement across the four academic disciplines of biology, chemistry, history, and sociology that are represented in this study.

4. **Is there a relationship between various faculty characteristics and the frequency of conducting each of the five types of studies illustrative of the scholarship of engagement?**

Research by Blackburn and Lawrence (1995) as well as reviews of literature (Creamer, 1998; Creswell, 1985; Fox, 1985) delineate one or more of the following individual faculty characteristics as related to publication productivity: gender, race, professional age, and tenure status. Although race and tenure status hold little or no relationship to faculty publication productivity related to the scholarship of application, Braxton et al. (2002) found that gender and professional age bear a relationship. More specially, male academics tend to publish more application-focused scholarship than women academics (Braxton et al., 2002). In addition, they found a negative relationship between professional age and publication directed toward application (Braxton, Luckey, & Helland, 2002). Consequently, we might identify relationships between one or more of these faculty characteristics and the frequency of conducting each of the five types of studies reflective of the scholarship of engagement.

5. **Do faculty members who conduct studies illustrative of the scholarship of engagement also publish scholarship related to the domains of application, discovery, and integration?**

Given that three-fourths (74.7 percent) of faculty members have not published any of their scholarship focused on teaching during the past three years (Braxton et al., 2002), we do not include the scholarship of teaching in this research question. Two issues give rise to this question. First, Rice (2006) asserts that the scholarships of application, discovery, integration, and teaching are interconnected and should not be viewed as distinct and independent from another. If faculty who are conducting studies illustrative of the scholarship of engagement are also publishing scholarship reflective of the domains of application, discovery, and integration, then support for Rice's assertion obtains. The second issue pertains to the mechanisms through which opportunities emerge for faculty members to conduct one or more of the five types of studies illustrative of the scholarship of engagement. More specifically, publications reflective of the three domains of scholarship may provide visibility for faculty members that results in opportunities to conduct such studies.

Methodology

Data Collection

Full-time faculty members holding tenure-track academic appointments, either tenured or pre-tenure, at five types of colleges and universities and four academic disciplines make up the population of inference for this inquiry. The five types of colleges represent the following categories of the 1994 Carnegie Classification of Institutions: research I universities, doctoral-granting universities—I, comprehensive universities and colleges—I, and baccalaureate liberal arts colleges—selectivity I and baccalaureate liberal arts colleges—selectivity II. Biology, chemistry, history, and sociology constitute the four academic disciplines represented in this study.

A sample of four thousand faculty members was randomly selected from this population. More specifically, two hundred individuals were selected from each of the four academic disciplines at each of the five types of colleges and universities. In spring 1999, the *Faculty Professional Performance Survey* was mailed to this sample of four thousand faculty members. In addition to behaviors reflective of the five types of studies illustrative of the scholarship of engagement, this survey also includes other professional behaviors indicative of the four domains of scholarship delineated by Boyer (1990). The work of Boyer (1990), Braxton and Toombs (1982), and Pellino, Blackburn, and Boberg (1984) provided the foundation for the development of these behaviors in the items for this survey. Two experts on faculty scholarship performance ascertained the face validity of the various behaviors included in this survey.

An initial mailing and two additional mailings to nonrespondents resulted in a sample of 1,424 faculty members for a response rate of 35.6 percent. This sample was further reduced to 1,362 faculty members by selecting only full-time tenure-track faculty members, tenured or untenured. We conducted t-tests and chi square analyses that compared initial survey respondents to those individuals who responded to subsequent mailings that included items on the five types of studies reflective of the scholarship of engagement, academic discipline, institutional type, gender, tenure status, racial/ethnic group membership, and professional age. This approach to determining sample bias is consistent with the formulations of Goode and Hatt (1952) and Leslie (1972). These tests indicate that the sample of 1,362 faculty members used in this study tend to be representative of the population of inference on the five types of studies representative of the scholarship of engagement, academic discipline, institutional type, gender, tenure status, and professional age. However, White Caucasian faculty members are overrepresented in this sample.

Research Design

This study's research design consists of the five dependent variables and nine independent variables. The five dependent variables measure the frequency with which faculty members conducted each of the five types of studies illustrative of the scholarship of engagement previously delineated. Each of these five types of studies fit the category of unpublished but publicly observable forms of scholarship. Given the high probability that the outcomes of these studies were put in the form of a report, it seems plausible that each of these five types of studies meet the three necessary criteria delineated by Shulman and Hutchings (1998) for a scholarly form to be labeled as scholarship. These indispensable characteristics are as follows: (1) it must be public, (2) it must be amenable to critical appraisal, and (3) it must be in a form that permits exchange and use by other members of the scholarly community. Items on the *Faculty Professional Performance Survey* asked respondents to indicate how many times within the past three years they have conducted each of these five types of studies. The following five-point scale was used to respond: 1 = none, 2 = 1 to 2 times, 3 = 3 to 5 times, 4 = 6 to 10 times, and 5 = 11 or more times.

The nine independent variables in this inquiry include institutional type, academic discipline, gender, race/ethnicity, tenure status, professional age, publications related to the scholarship of application, publications related to the scholarship of discovery, and publications related to the scholarship of integration. These variables were formed using items included in the *Faculty Professional Performance Survey.*

Institutional Type

The five categories of colleges and universities of the Carnegie Classification of Institutions (1994) represented in this study's sample present a basis for the construction of Institutional Type as an independent variable. These categories vary in terms of their institutional missions. At one extreme, liberal arts colleges—II are predominately oriented toward teaching. At the other extreme, research I universities and doctoral-granting universities—I are primarily oriented toward research. Comprehensive universities and colleges—I and liberal arts colleges—I occupy a middle ground, given that their missions tend to be oriented toward both teaching and research (Finnegan, 1993; McGee, 1971).

Academic Discipline

The four academic disciplines of this study—biology, chemistry, history, and sociology—serve as the categories that comprise the variable academic discipline. These four disciplines are among those that may be classified as high- and low-consensus (Biglan, 1973; Lodahl & Gordon, 1972). Biology and chemistry are high consensus disciplines, whereas history and sociology are low consensus disciplines.

Gender

Gender is measured in the following way: female respondents are coded as "1," whereas male respondents are coded as "2."

Race/Ethnicity

Race/ethnicity is measured using the following four racial/ethnic categories: White-Caucasian, African American, Asian, and Hispanic.

Tenure Status

The variable tenure status is measured with tenured faculty coded as a "1," and untenured, but tenure-track, faculty coded as a "0."

Professional Age

This variable was constructed using the survey item: year highest earned degree received. This year was subtracted from 1999 to compute the variable professional age. We grouped faculty into three categories: 0 to 10 years, 11 to 27 years, and 28 years and beyond. These groups represent the quartile distribution of faculty professional age in our sample.

Publications Related to the Scholarship of Application

The forms of publications we use in constructing this measure correspond to Boyer's (1990) earlier formulations regarding the domain of the scholarship of application. He stated that the scholarship of application entails the application of disciplinary knowledge and skill to address important societal problems (Boyer, 1990). He also contended that new theoretical understandings and knowledge can result from such application of disciplinary knowledge and skill (Boyer, 1990). The forms of publications we use reflect these formulations.

The construction of this variable involves two steps. The first step entailed the summing of individual responses to the following five forms of publication related to the scholarship of application, and then dividing this sum by five: an article that outlines a new research problem identified through the application of the knowledge and skill of one's academic discipline to a practical problem, an article that describes new knowledge obtained through the application of the knowledge and skill of one's academic discipline to a practical problem, an article that applies new disciplinary knowledge to a practical problem, an article that proposes an approach to the bridging of theory and practice, and an article reporting findings of research designed to solve a practical problem. Respondents registered how many times within the past three years they had published each of these forms using the following five-point scale: 1 = none, 2 = 1 to 2 times, 3 = 3 to 5 times, 4 = 6 to 10 times, and 5 = 11 or more times.

The second step involved grouping faculty respondents into two categories based on the resulting composite scores of the first step: those who did not have any publications during the past three years, and those who had one or more publications during the past three years (an average score of 1.01 or higher on the five-point scale just indicated).

Publications Related to the Scholarship of Discovery

The construction of this variable involves two steps. The first step entailed the summing of individual responses to the following five forms of publication related to the scholarship of discovery, and then dividing this sum by 5: a book chapter describing a new theory developed by the author, a refereed journal article reporting findings of research designed to gain new knowledge, a book reporting findings of research designed to gain new knowledge, a book describing a new theory developed by the author, and a refereed journal article describing a new theory developed by the author. Respondents registered how many times within the past three years they had published each of these forms using the following five-point scale: 1 = none, 2 = 1 to 2 times, 3 = 3 to 5 times, 4 = 6 to 10 times, and 5 = 11 or more times.

The second step involved grouping faculty respondents into two categories based on the resulting composite scores of the first step: those who did not have any publications during the past three years, and those who had one or more publications during the past three years (an average score of 1.01 or higher on the five-point scale just indicated).

Publications Related to the Scholarship of Integration

The construction of this variable involves two steps. The first step entailed the summing of individual responses to the twenty forms of publication related to the scholarship of integration and then dividing this sum by twenty. Examples of these forms of publications are a review of literature on a disciplinary topic, a review of literature on an interdisciplinary topic, a review essay of two or more books on similar topics, an article on the application of a theory borrowed from another academic discipline to problems in one's own discipline, a book addressing a disciplinary/interdisciplinary topic published by the popular press, a book published reporting research findings to the lay reader, and a published textbook. Respondents registered how many times within the past three years they had published each of the twenty forms of publications oriented toward the scholarship of integration using the following five-point scale: 1 = none, 2 = 1 to 2 times, 3 = 3 to 5 times, 4 = 6 to 10 times, and 5 = 11 or more times.

The second step involved grouping faculty respondents into two categories based on the resulting composite scores of the first step: those who did not have any publications during the past three years, and those who had one or more publications during the past three years (an average score of 1.01 or higher on the five-point scale just indicated).

Statistical Design

We used several types of statistical techniques to address the research questions that guided this study. We used a frequency distribution for each of the five types of studies illustrative of the scholarship of engagement to address the first research question. We addressed the second and third research questions by conducting five 4 × d5 analyses of variance, one for each of the five types of studies. The four levels of the first factor consist of the four academic disciplines included in this study, whereas the five types of colleges and universities represented in this study make up the five levels of the second factor. Because a preliminary test identified heterogeneous variance for each of the five analyses of variance, we chose the .01 level of statistical significance to reduce the probability of type I errors. Following statistically significant main effects, we used the Scheffe method of post-hoc mean comparisons to identify statistically significant group mean differences.

Two statistical techniques were used to address the fourth research question. We used t-tests to address the fourth research question as it pertains to gender and tenure status. For race/ethnicity and professional age, we used a one-factor analysis of variance. A preliminary test revealed heterogeneous variances for each of the two analyses of variance. To reduce the probability of committing type I errors, we chose the .01 level of statistical significance. Following statistically significant main effects, we used the Scheffe method of post-hoc mean comparisons to identify statistically significant group mean differences.

The fifth research question dictated the use of t-tests. A total of fifteen t-tests were conducted. More specifically, t-tests were executed to test for differences between faculty who have not published and those who have published scholarship oriented toward the scholarship of application. Five t-tests were conducted, one for each of the five types of studies descriptive of the scholarship of engagement. Tests for such differences were also made for scholarship oriented toward discovery and scholarship oriented toward integration.

We used the .01 level of statistical significance for all statistical tests conducted. Because our tests using analyses of variance required this level, we applied it to all tests to maintain consistency. We also used this more conservative level because of our relatively large sample size of 1,362 faculty members.

Findings

We organize the presentation of the findings by research question. Tables contain the results of statistical tests conducted for each research question designated below.

1. **How frequently have college and university faculty members conducted each of the five types of studies illustrative of the scholarship of engagement during the past three years?**

Table 1 displays the frequency distributions for each of the five types of studies conducted that reflect the scholarship of engagement that we used to address this question. The vast majority of faculty members did not conduct any of the five types of studies during the past three years. The percent of faculty who did not conduct studies related to the scholarship of engagement ranged from 78.5 percent who did not conduct a study to solve a community problem to 93.5 percent of faculty who did not conduct a study for a local nonacademic professional organization during the past three years.

Nevertheless, a minority of faculty respondents report that they have conducted each of the five types of studies one to two times during the past three years. Whereas only 4.8 percent of faculty conducted a study for a local nonacademic professional association one to two times, 16.8 percent of faculty conducted a study to help solve a community problem one to two times during the past three years.

2. **Does the frequency of faculty members conducting each of the five types of studies illustrative of the scholarship of engagement vary across different types of colleges and universities?**

Table 2 exhibits the results of the analyses of variance conducted to focus on this question.

The frequency of faculty members conducting four of the five types of studies that embody the scholarship of engagement show little or no variation across the five types of colleges and universities represented in this study. However, faculty members in comprehensive universities and colleges—I tend to exhibit a statistically significant higher frequency of studies conducted for a local organization (mean = 1.29) than did faculty members in research I universities (mean = 1.11). Faculty members in doctoral-granting universities—I, liberal arts colleges—I, and liberal arts colleges—II show similar frequencies for this type of study.

Table 1. Frequency of Conducting Studies Illustrative of the Scholarship of Engagement within the Past Three Years (n = 1,362)

Times Conducted	For a Local Organization	For a Local Nonacademic Professional Association	For a Local Government Organization	To Solve a Community Problem	To Solve a County/State-Level Problem
0	83.4%	93.5%	88.5%	78.5%	85.0%
1–2	13.0%	4.8%	9.0%	16.8%	11.5%
3–5	3.2%	1.5%	1.9%	4.1%	2.9%
6–10	0.3%	0.2%	0.4%	0.5%	0.2%
11+	0.1%	0.0%	0.1%	0.2%	0.3%

Table 2. Results of the Analyses of Variance of the Five Types of Studies Illustrative of the Scholarship of Engagement by Institutional Type

Type of Study	F-Ratio*	RU-I	DOC-I	CUC-I	BA-I	BA-II	Post-Hoc Mean Comparisons
For a Local Organization	4.56**	1.11	1.19	1.29	1.21	1.25	CUC-I greater than RU-I‡
For a Local Nonacademic Professional Association	0.86	1.07	1.08	1.09	1.06	1.11	No statistically significant mean group differences
For a Local Government Organization	1.03	1.14	1.12	1.18	1.12	1.16	No statistically significant mean group differences
To Solve a Community Problem	3.48‡	1.18	1.22	1.33	1.26	1.32	No statistically significant mean group differences
To Solve a County/ State-Level Problem	1.55	1.19	1.18	1.23	1.13	1.21	No statistically significant mean group differences

Note: The response scale used to conduct the analyses of variance and compute means is $1 = 0$, $2 = 1$–2, $3 = 3$–5, $4 = 6$–10, and $5 = 11+$.

*F-Ratio for institutional type is independent of the F-ratio for academic discipline

**$p < .001$

‡$p < .01$

3. Does the frequency of faculty members conducting each of the five types of studies illustrative of the scholarship of engagement vary across different academic disciplines?

Discipline differences in the frequency of faculty members conducting each of the five types of studies embodying the scholarship of engagement exist. For all five types of studies, academic sociologists tend to show a higher frequency during the past three years in a statistically significant way. In the case of studies conducted for a local organization, sociologists (mean = 1.46) more frequently conducted such studies than chemists (mean = 1.08), biologists (mean = 1.17), and historians (mean = 1.13). Academic sociologists (mean = 1.14) also more frequently conducted studies for a local nonacademic professional association than did their academic counterparts in chemistry (mean = 1.03). However, sociologists did not differ in a statistically reliable way from biologists (mean = 1.06) and historians (mean = 1.08). Moreover, sociologists (mean = 1.25) more frequently conducted studies for a local governmental organization than did chemists (mean = 1.09) and historians (mean = 1.08), whereas academic biologists (mean = 1.16) exhibited a similar frequency to that of sociologists. Likewise, studies conducted to solve a community problem were also more frequently done by sociologists (mean = 1.55) than their counterparts in the disciplines of biology (mean = 1.22), chemistry (mean = 1.14), and history (mean = 1.14). For studies conducted to solve a county- or state-level problem, biologists (mean = 1.26) and sociologists (mean = 1.31) did not differ in a statistically significant manner. However, both biologists and sociologists conducted such studies more frequently than chemists (mean = 1.09) and historians (mean = 1.10). Table 3 displays the results of the analyses of variance that yielded these patterns of difference.

81

Table 3. Results of the Analyses of Variance of the Five Types of Studies Illustrative of the Scholarship of Engagement by Academic Discipline

Type of Study	F-Ratio*	Biology	Chemistry	History	Sociology	Post-Hoc Mean Comparisons
For a Local Organization	36.8**	1.17	1.08	1.13	1.46	Sociology greater than biology, chemistry, and history
For a Local Nonacademic Professional Association	6.29**	1.06	1.03	1.08	1.14	Sociology greater than chemistry
For a Local Government Organization	9.81**	1.16	1.09	1.08	1.25	Sociology greater than chemistry and history
To Solve a Community Problem	41.99**	1.22	1.14	1.14	1.55	Sociology greater than biology, chemistry, and history
To Solve a County/State-Level Problem	15.34**	1.26	1.09	1.10	1.31	Sociology greater than chemistry and history

Note: The response scale used to conduct the analyses of variance and compute means is: $1 = 0$, $2 = 1–2$, $3 = 3–5$, $4 = 6–10$, and $5 = 11+$.

*F-Ratio for academic discipline is independent of the F-Ratio for institutional type

**$p < .001$

4. **Is there a relationship between various faculty characteristics and the frequency of conducting each of the five types of studies illustrative of the scholarship of engagement?**

Faculty characteristics such as gender (see table 4), professional age (see table 5), and tenure status (see table 6) make little or no difference in the frequency with which faculty members conducted each of the five types of studies descriptive of the scholarship of engagement.

On the other hand, African American academics (mean = 1.50) more frequently conducted studies to solve a county or state-level problem than did their White-Caucasian faculty counterparts (mean = 1.18). However, Asian (mean = 1.27) and Hispanic (mean = 1.42) academics carried out such studies at a rate similar to that of African American faculty members. Nonetheless, the racial/ethnic group membership of college and university faculty bears little or no relationship to the frequency of conducting the other four types of studies emblematic of the scholarship of engagement: studies conducted for a local organization, for a nonacademic professional association, for a local governmental organization, or to solve a community problem. Table 7 corroborates these assertions.

Table 4. Gender Differences in the Frequency of Conducting Studies Illustrative of the Scholarship of Engagement

Type of Study	Mean Women	Mean Men	t-Value
For a Local Organization	1.26	1.19	2.07
For a Local Nonacademic Professional Association	1.09	1.08	0.58
For a Local Government Organization	1.14	1.15	0.38
To Solve a Community Problem	1.29	1.26	0.76
To Solve a County/State-Level Problem	1.16	1.21	1.56

Note: The response scale used to conduct the t-test and compute means is: $1 = 0$, $2 = 1$–2, $3 = 3$–5, $4 = 6$–10, and $5 = 11+$.

Table 5. Results of the Analyses of Variance of the Five Types of Studies Illustrative of the Scholarship of Engagement by Professional Age

Type of Study	F-Ratio	0–10 Years	11–27 Years	28+ Years	Post-Hoc Mean Comparisons
For a Local Organization	2.97	1.23	1.23	1.15	None
For a Local Nonacademic Professional Association	1.11	1.09	1.08	1.06	None
For a Local Government Organization	0.02	1.14	1.14	1.14	None
To Solve a Community Problem	2.86	1.26	1.30	1.21	None
To Solve a County/State-Level Problem	0.36	1.18	1.20	1.18	None

Note: The response scale used to conduct the analyses of variance and compute means is: $1 = 0$, $2 = 1$–2, $3 = 3$–5, $4 = 6$–10, and $5 = 11+$.

5. **Do faculty members who conduct studies illustrative of the scholarship of engagement also publish scholarship related to the domains of application, discovery, and integration?**

Having one or more publications during the past three years tends to make a difference in the frequency of conducting studies that typify the scholarship of engagement. This assertion particularly pertains to publications related to the scholarship of integration, because

Table 6. Tenure Status Differences in the Frequency of Conducting Studies Illustrative of the Scholarship of Engagement

Type of Study	Mean Tenured	Mean Untenured	t-Value
For a Local Organization	1.21	1.19	0.82
For a Local Nonacademic Professional Association	1.08	1.09	0.46
For a Local Government Organization	1.15	1.12	0.96
To Solve a Community Problem	1.27	1.26	0.43
To Solve a County/State-Level Problem	1.20	1.17	0.88

Note: The response scale used to conduct the t-test and compute means is: $1 = 0$, $2 = 1–2$, $3 = 3–5$, $4 = 6–10$, and $5 = 11+$.

Table 7. Results of the Analyses of Variance of Five Types of Studies Illustrative of the Scholarship of Engagement by Race/Ethnicity

Type of Study	F-Ratio	African American	Asian	Hispanic	White-Caucasian	Post-Hoc Mean Comparisons
For a Local Organization	1.98	1.38	1.09`	1.10	1.21	None
For a Local Nonacademic Professional Association	3.57	1.25	1.09	1.18	1.07	None
For a Local Government Organization	3.63	1.28	1.00	1.42	1.15	None
To Solve a Community Problem	3.27	1.54	1.31	1.36	1.25	None
To Solve a County/State-Level Problem	5.58*	1.50	1.27	1.42	1.18	African Americans greater than White-Caucasian

Note: The response scale used to conduct the analyses of variance and compute means is: $1 = 0$, $2 = 1–2$, $3 = 3–5$, $4 = 6–10$, and $5 = 11+$.
*$p < .001$

faculty with one or more publications in this domain also carried out each of the five types of studies with greater frequency than faculty with no integration-oriented publications during the past three years. Table 8 displays the results of the t-tests conducted and the exemplifying means.

This note also relates to publications within the domain of the scholarship of application for four of the five types of studies reflective of the scholarship of engagement. Put differently,

Table 8. Differences in the Frequency of Conducting Studies Illustrative of the Scholarship of Engagement by Integration-Oriented Publications

Type of Study	Mean Number of Publications	Mean One or More Publications	t-Value
For a Local Organization	1.13	1.23	3.84*
For a Local Nonacademic Professional Association	1.04	1.10	3.17**
For a Local Government Association	1.09	1.16	2.69**
To Solve a Community Problem	1.17	1.30	4.24*
To Solve a County/State-Level Problem	1.10	1.22	4.54*

Note: The response scale used to compute means is: $1 = 0$, $2 = 1–2$, $3 = 3–5$, $4 = 6–10$, and $5 = 11+$.

*p.<.001

**p < .01

faculty members with one or more publications stressing application tended to more frequently carry out these four types of studies than did academics with no publications related to the scholarship of application during the past three years. However, studies conducted for a local nonacademic professional association stands as the one type of study where the number of publications related to the scholarship of application in the past three years made little or no difference in the frequency with which such studies were conducted. Publications with the scholarship of application resonate with Boyer's 1990 formulations regarding this domain of scholarship as the application of disciplinary knowledge and skill to solve a societal or institutional problem (Boyer, 1990). Table 9 supports these observations.

Table 9. Differences in the Frequency of Conducting Studies Illustrative of the Scholarship of Engagement by Application-Oriented Publications

Type of Study	Mean Number of Publications	Mean One or More Publications	t-Value
For a Local Organization	1.17	1.25	2.84*
For a Local Nonacademic Professional Association	1.07	1.10	2.07
For a Local Government Association	1.10	1.20	3.98**
To Solve a Community Problem	1.21	1.35	4.54**
To Solve a County/State-Level Problem	1.13	1.27	4.70**

Note: The response scale used to compute means is as follows: $1 = $ none, $2 = 1–2$, $3 = 3–5$, $4 = 6–10$, and $5 = 11+$.

*p < .01

**p < .001

85

Table 10. Differences in the Frequency of Conducting Studies Illustrative of the Scholarship of Engagement by Discovery-Oriented Publications

Type of Study	Mean Number of Publications	Mean One or More Publications	t-Value
For a Local Organization	1.22	1.21	0.35
For a Local Nonacademic Professional Association	1.08	1.08	0.39
For a Local Government Association	1.11	1.16	1.71
To Solve a Community Problem	1.29	1.26	0.84
To Solve a County/State-Level Problem	1.14	1.21	2.64*

Note: The response scale used to compute means is as follows: 1 = 0, 2 = 1–2, 3 = 3–5, 4 = 6–10, and 5 = 11+.

*p < .01

In contrast to publications within the scholarly domains of application and integration, recent discovery-oriented publications played little or no part in the frequency with which four of the five studies illustrative of the scholarship of engagement had been accomplished during the past three years. However, faculty members having one or more publications (mean = 1.21) within this domain of scholarship tended to carry out more frequent studies to solve a county or state problem than did their counters with no recent discovery-oriented publications. Support for this assertion comes from table 10.

Limitations

Several limitations of this study moderate the discussion of findings, conclusions, and recommendations for policy and practice that we offer. These limitations are as follows:

1. The five types of studies reflective of the scholarship of engagement are not exhaustive of the types of studies that typify this domain of scholarship. For example, Boyer called for faculty to tackle problems that are consequential to society.
2. The rate of response of 35.6 percent to the *Faculty Professional Performance Survey* is relatively low. A higher rate of response might have resulted in a different configuration of findings. However, this limitation is blunted to some extent because the obtained sample is judged to be representative of the population of inference of this inquiry on the vast majority of variables included in this study's research design. Nevertheless, some bias exists in the obtained sample, because White-Caucasian faculty are overrepresented in this sample and Asian faculty members are underrepresented.
3. The sample obtained for this piece of research is limited to five categories of the Carnegie Classification of Institutions. The use of the full Carnegie Classification system might produce some differences in the findings. For example, the inclusion of two-year colleges might have resulted in a different configuration of findings regarding how frequently

studies illustrative of the scholarship of engagement are conducted by faculty members.

4. The four disciplines represented in this study may be classified as pure academic disciplines according to Biglan's (1973) classification of academic disciplines. The extension of the current research to applied academic disciplines might result in different findings regarding studies reflective of the scholarship of engagement.

Discussion

In his 1990 volume *Scholarship Reconsidered: Priorities of the Professoriate*, Boyer asserted that colleges and universities should stress the domain of scholarship most directly related to their institutional mission. In the case of the scholarship of application, Boyer (1990) viewed this form of scholarship as befitting the institutional mission of doctoral-granting universities and comprehensive universities and colleges. This study's finding that comprehensive universities and colleges—I tend to exhibit a statistically significant higher frequency of studies conducted for a local organization (mean = 1.29) than do faculty members in research I universities (mean = 1.11) resonates with Boyer's prescription for domain emphasis. For the remaining four types of studies indicative of the scholarship of engagement, Boyer's prescription fails to receive affirmation. Moreover, the faculty members' institutional type appears to make little or no difference in the frequency with which studies for a local nonacademic professional association and for a local government agency are conducted. In addition, similar frequencies across institutional type also obtain for studies conducted to help solve a community problem and to help solve a county or a state problem.

Independent of the effects of institutional type, faculty members' academic discipline plays a part of some significance in the scholarship of engagement. In particular, academic sociologists play the most prominent part among the academic disciplines represented in this study. Such a pronounced role for sociologists in the scholarship of engagement finds grounding in the themes or ideology of the discipline of sociology. Calhoun (2007) notes that, from its beginnings, sociology demonstrated an engagement with projects of social reform. Moreover, progress constituted a central theme for sociology (Calhoun, 2007). Such themes echo Boyer's formulations regarding the scholarship of engagement.

As previously noted, faculty characteristics such as gender, professional age, and tenure status make little or no difference in the frequency with which faculty members conducted each of the five types of studies descriptive of the scholarship of engagement. With regard to gender, this pattern of findings fails to correspond to gender differences in general publication productivity found in previous research (Creamer, 1998; Creswell, 1985; Fox, 1985). It also conflicts with the findings of Braxton et al. (2002) that male academics publish more application-oriented scholarship than do women academics.

Creswell (1985) concluded from his review of research that tenure wields little or no influence on general publication productivity. The findings of this study resonate with Creswell's conclusion, given that tenured and untenured, tenure-track faculty show similar patterns in the frequency with which they conducted the five types of studies indicative of the scholarship of engagement.

This study's finding that professional age matters little in the frequency with which the five types of studies illustrative of the scholarship of engagement are conducted by faculty members fails to coincide with Finkelstein's (1984) conclusion from his review of research that a negative relationship exists between professional age and publication productivity. However, this study's finding supports the perspective of both Creswell (1985) and Fox (1985) that the relationship between professional age and productivity should not serve as a basis for policy formulation.

Research by Blackburn and Lawrence (1995) and Creamer's (1998) review of research both indicate that race/ethnicity bears little or no relationship to publication productivity. This study's configuration of findings lends support to their conclusion in the case of four of the five studies that embody the scholarship of engagement. However, the finding regarding studies conducted to solve a county- or state-level problem deviates from the conclusion of Creamer, as well as that of Blackburn and Lawrence, given our finding that African American academics more frequently conducted such studies than did their White-Caucasian faculty counterparts.

Faculty members who have not published, within the past three years, any scholarship related to the domains of application, discovery, and integration have, however, conducted one or more studies illustrative of the scholarship of engagement. Nevertheless, publications within the past three years within these domains tend to provide authors with more well-developed channels of opportunity for them to conduct studies that embody the scholarship of engagement. Visibility attained through one's published scholarship contributes to the formation of such channels of opportunity. Moreover, this study's configuration of findings suggests that publications reflective of the scholarships of application and integration afford greater visibility than do discovery-focused published scholarship. In addition to greater visibility, publications also provide an index of the academic skills and knowledge that potential sponsors of studies oriented toward the scholarship of engagement need to commission such studies (Light, Marsden, & Corl, 1972).

The findings of this study also indicate that the vast majority of faculty members have not conducted any of the five types of studies illustrative of the scholarship of engagement represented in this study during the past three years. Such infrequency raises a significant concern about the engagement of the academic profession in matters that are important to the lay community. Do prevailing academic reward structures discourage faculty from conducting such studies? Although prevailing reward structures provide one explanation for such infrequencies, another possible explanation is that many faculty members may not have opportunities to conduct such studies because of their lack of recent publication activity. As discussed earlier, current publication activity accords a faculty member visibility in the lay community. Publications also suggest to members of the lay community that a given academic possesses the academic knowledge and skills needed to conduct studies that serve the lay community.

Conclusions

This study's pattern of findings gives rise to three conclusions:

1. The tendency of college and university faculty members to execute studies illustrative of the scholarship of engagement depends more on their academic discipline than on the

type of college or university where they hold their professorial appointment. Although Boyer (1990) offered prescriptions for domain emphasis by different types of colleges and universities, it appears that, in the case of the scholarship of engagement, academic disciplines temper such domain emphases by colleges and universities. In particular, the discipline of sociology plays such an attenuating role.

2. Individual faculty characteristics such as gender, professional age, and tenure status provide little guidance in the construction of a profile of faculty members likely to participate in the scholarship of engagement. However, academic discipline and publication productivity supply elements of such a faculty profile. Specifically, college and university faculty members who are sociologists and have published scholarship oriented toward application and integration during the past three years are more likely participants in the scholarship of engagement than faculty members displaying other attributes.

3. Rice (2006) asserts that the scholarships of application, discovery, integration, and teaching are interconnected and should not be viewed as distinct and independent from another. Our configuration of findings lends support to Rice's contention in the case of the scholarship of engagement. To elaborate, the findings of this study tend to indicate that faculty members who published during the past three years within the domains of the scholarship of application and integration and to a limited extent within the scholarship of discovery also tended to more frequently conduct the type of studies that embody the scholarship of engagement than did faculty members who had not published during the past three years. Put differently, the execution of studies related to the scholarship of engagement does not occur in isolation from other forms of scholarship that result in published work.

Implications for Policy and Practice

Based on their empirical analysis of the extent to which the academic reward structure corresponds to the ideal characteristics for reward structures in different types of colleges and universities, Braxton et al. (2006) have recommended that the scholarship of application become the primary domain of scholarship stressed by comprehensive colleges and universities. The findings of this study indicate that this recommendation requires revision, given the thrust of the first conclusion of this inquiry. Although comprehensive colleges and universities might put a primary emphasis on the scholarship of application, sociologists in this type of college or university may be the most likely faculty members to participate in the scholarship of engagement as distinct from the scholarship of application. By extension, faculty members in other disciplines that evince a similar ideology of social reform and progress may also participate. In addition, faculty members in other types of disciplines may not have the opportunities to conduct studies illustrative of the scholarship of engagement (Adam & Roberts, 1993; Diamond & Adam, 1995; O'Meara, 2005). Thus, the central administration of comprehensive universities and colleges that desire a primary emphasis on the scholarship of application may hold unrealistic expectations of the extent of faculty participation in the scholarship of engagement if they do not take disciplinary differences into account.

Reflections upon Closing

The findings of the study described in this chapter indicate the extent to which college and university faculty members conduct studies embodying the scholarship of engagement. These findings also point to the role of institutional type, academic discipline, and the characteristics of faculty in faculty participation in the scholarship of engagement. Although the five types of studies employed in this study as indicative of the scholarship of engagement resonate with Boyer's perspective on the scholarship of engagement, much work remains. Future studies should focus on the extent to which college and university faculty members grapple with the types of problems delineated by Boyer in his later formulations that differentiated the scholarship of application from the scholarship of engagement. Such studies would give the academic community a fuller understanding of the fulfillment of Boyer's call for a scholarship of engagement.

References

Adam, B., & Roberts, A. (1993). Differences among the disciplines. *New Directions for Higher Education, 81,* 23–62.

Biglan, A. (1973). Relationships between subject matter characteristics and the structure and output of university departments. *Journal of Applied Psychology, 57*(3), 204–213.

Blackburn, R. T., & Lawrence, J. H. (1995). *Faculty at work: Motivation, expectation, satisfaction.* Baltimore: Johns Hopkins University Press.

Boyer, E. L. (1990). *Scholarship reconsidered: Priorities of the professoriate.* Princeton, NJ: Carnegie Foundation for the Advancement of Teaching.

Boyer, E. L. (1996). The scholarship of engagement. *Journal of Public Service and Outreach, I*(1), 11–20.

Braxton, J. M., & Hargens, L. (1996). Variation among academic disciplines: Analytical frameworks and research. In J. Smart (Ed.), *Higher education: Handbook of research and theory* (Vol. 11, pp. 1–46). New York: Agathon Press.

Braxton, J. M., Luckey, W., & Helland, P. (2002). *Institutionalizing a broader view of scholarship through Boyer's four domains.* San Francisco: Jossey-Bass.

Braxton, J. M., Luckey, W., & Helland, P. (2006). Ideal and actual value patterns toward domains of scholarship in three types of colleges and universities. *New Directions for Institutional Research, 129,* 67–76.

Braxton, J. M., & Toombs, W. (1982). Faculty uses of doctoral training: Consideration of a technique for the differentiation of scholarly effort from research activity. *Research in Higher Education, 16*(3), 265–282.

Calhoun, C. (2007). Sociology in America: an introduction. In C. Calhoun (Ed.), *Sociology in America: A history* (pp.1–38). Chicago: University of Chicago Press.

Creamer, E. G. (1998). *Assessing faculty publication productivity: Issues of equity.* Washington, DC: Graduate School of Education and Human Development, George Washington University.

Creswell, J. W. (1985). *Faculty research performance, lessons from the sciences and social sciences.* Washington, DC: Association for the Study of Higher Education.

Diamond, R., & Adam, B. (Eds.). (1995). *The disciplines speak: Rewarding the scholarly, professional, and creative work of faculty.* Washington, DC: American Association for Higher Education.

Finkelstein, M. J. (1984). *The American academic profession: A synthesis of social scientific inquiry since World War II*. Columbus: Ohio State University Press.

Finnegan, D. (1993). Segmentation in the academic labor market. *Journal of Higher Education, 64*(6), 621–656.

Fox, M. (1985). Publication, performance, and reward in science and scholarship. In J. C. Smart (Ed.), *Higher education: Handbook of theory and research* (Vol. 1, pp. 255–282). New York: Agathon Press.

Fulton, O., & Trow, M. (1974, Winter). Research activity in American higher education. *Sociology of Education, 47*, 29–73.

Goode, W. J., & Hatt, P. K. (1952). *Methods in social research* (1st ed.). New York: McGraw-Hill.

Kuhn, T. S. (1962). *The structure of scientific revolutions* (1st ed.). Chicago: University of Chicago Press.

Kuhn, T. S. (1970). *The structure of scientific revolutions* (2nd ed.). Chicago: University of Chicago Press.

Leslie, L. (1972). Are high response rates essential to valid surveys? *Social Science Research, 1*(3), 323–334.

Light, D., Jr., Marsden, L. R., & Corl, T. C. (1973). *The impact of the academic revolution on faculty careers*. Washington, DC: American Association for Higher Education.

Lodahl, J., & Gordon, G. (1972). The structure of scientific fields and the functioning of university graduate departments. *American Sociological Review, 37*(2), 57–72.

McGee, R. (1971). *Academic Janus: The private college and its faculty*. San Francisco: Jossey-Bass.

O'Meara, K. (2005). Encouraging multiple forms of scholarship in faculty reward systems: Does it make a difference? *Research in Higher Education, 46*(5), 479–510.

O'Meara, K. (2006). Encouraging multiple forms of scholarship in faculty reward systems: Have academic cultures really changed? *New Directions for Institutional Research, 129*, 77–95.

Pellino, G., Blackburn, R., & Boberg, A. (1984). The dimensions of academic scholarship: Faculty and administrator views. *Research in Higher Education, 20*(1), 103–115.

Rice, R. (2006). Enhancing the quality of teaching and learning: The U.S. experience. *New Directions for Higher Education, 133*, 13–22.

Ruscio, K. (1987). The distinctive scholarship of the selective liberal arts college. *Journal of Higher Education, 58*(2), 205–222.

Shulman, L., & Hutchings, P. (1998). *About the scholarship of teaching and learning*. Menlo Park, CA: The Carnegie Foundation for the Advancement of Teaching.

PART 2

Across the Higher Education Landscape

Edited by Hiram E. Fitzgerald

Across the Higher Education Landscape

Hiram E. Fitzgerald

Although changes in higher education often appear to be implemented slowly, in America this impression must be tempered by the development of the country as a whole. In 1636, Harvard College became America's first institution of higher education. Soon thereafter the College of William and Mary was founded (1693), followed during the 1700s by a number of sectarian and religiously affiliated (Puritan, Moravian, Presbyterian, Disciples of Christ, Church of England, Baptist, and Catholic) colonial colleges. However, during the 1800s the face of America's higher education system was to change rather dramatically. The Organic Act of 1837 officially established the University of Michigan as a public university, and a university that was anchored in the German Humboldtian tradition of discipline-based research. The University of Michigan, therefore, became a model for public research universities quite distinct from the colonial college model of liberal education.

Shortly thereafter, yet another model of higher education was to emerge, led by the founding of the Agricultural College of the State of Michigan (Michigan State University) on September 12, 1855, and followed ten days later by the founding of the Farmer's High School of Pennsylvania (Pennsylvania State University). These two institutions were forerunners of the Morrill Act of 1862, which established each as land-grant institutions, a distinctive and unique approach to higher education fashioned by an emerging nation. The public-good mission of land-grant institutions was further defined by the Hatch Act of 1887 (establishing Agricultural Experiment Stations) and the Smith-Lever Act of 1914 (establishing Cooperative Extension). The Morrill Act was expanded in 1890 to include seventy additional colleges and universities now collectively referred to as the Historic Black Colleges and Universities. In 1992, reauthorization of the Higher Education Act formally recognized Hispanic Serving Institutions, and in 1994 funding was provided to establish a system of Tribal Colleges and Universities.

Therefore, within a 132-year span (1862–1994), America established a vast system of publicly supported institutions of higher education with applied research and scholarship embedded within their core missions. In 1900, twelve institutions (three public: University of Michigan, University of California Berkeley, and University of Wisconsin) established the Association of American Universities (AAU) with the explicit intent to advance academic (disciplinary) research and scholarship (the Humboldt model). Following World War II, the U.S. government invested heavily to expand the research intensiveness of America's higher education system, in effect giving emphasis to the AAU focus on academic scholarship, with a number of land-grant institutions also receiving status as AAU institutions. The 363 years spanning higher education in the United States, therefore, created what is now approximately 4,350 colleges, universities, and community (junior) colleges with rich and diverse histories and missions.

The most recent innovation to higher education's diverse history and contemporary practices occurred in the 1990s, when social/educational critics and national commissions called for a renewed emphasis on higher education's covenant or social contract to generate knowledge for the public good. But this innovation added a new twist. Generation of knowledge for the public good was also to involve the public in the knowledge-generation process. This call to reconnect higher education to societal issues was especially directed toward public institutions. Critics challenged higher education to become more directly involved with efforts to resolve societal problems, such as high-risk infants, disabled children, troubled youth and adolescents, single parenthood, substance abuse, failing schools, poverty, family illiteracy, family and neighborhood violence, nutritional disorders, environmental contaminants, and economic decline. Partially in response to societal challenges to higher education, education-oriented social critics and reformists began to articulate a new vision for American higher education that would replace the current system's emphasis on disciplinary-focused research with greater emphasis on a student-oriented mission; a broader definition of scholarship-based teaching, research, and service; university-community partnerships based on reciprocity and mutual benefit; and commitment to link universities with community efforts to resolve a wide range of societal problems. Public support of higher education was being bound to public expectations that "their" colleges and universities would become more directly involved in social change and reemphasizing the public good implicit in the original land-grant philosophy.

Chapters in this part of the handbook are anchored in the history and diversity of America's system of higher education. Included are chapters providing perspectives on engaged scholarship applicable to land-grant (Simon), private (Hartley & Harkavy), AAU universities (Simon; Hartley & Harkavy), private liberal arts colleges (VanderStoep, Wise, & Blaich), community colleges (Franco), faith-based institutions (Eby), Historically Black Colleges and Universities (Rozman), Hispanic-Serving Institutions (Chahin & Ortega), and Tribal Colleges and Universities (Sarche, Novins, & Belcourt-Dittloff). Despite the diversity represented in these chapters, there are some common themes. All emphasize a scholarship-focused approach to engaged research, engaged teaching/learning, or engaged service. All note that engagement is anchored in concepts of public good; civic responsibility; the need to build trust and respect with community partners; use of participatory engagement methods; acknowledging and respecting community knowledge; stimulating critical reflection in faculty, students, and community members; and taking risks so that as much can be learned from unsuccessful efforts for transformational change as is learned from successful efforts.

These chapters reflect a system-wide response to individuals who have challenged American higher education to play a key role in transforming society for success in the twenty-first century. America's attempt to recreate itself as a knowledge-driven economy, emphasizing innovation, connectivity, inclusion, and quality of life for all of its citizens, cannot be accomplished unless its system of higher education leads the way. The landscape of American higher education has changed over its 373-year history. Perhaps the safest bet for the twenty-first century is that it will surely change again.

Engaged Scholarship in Land-Grant and Research Universities

Lou Anna Kimsey Simon

Engaging to Empower: Serving as an engine of prosperity for the common global good by leveraging the land-grant conviction that extraordinary potential lies in ordinary individuals and creating circumstances in which that potential can be achieved. Creating prosperity that goes well beyond finances and fortune is at the heart of Michigan State University's purpose, vision, and our twenty-first-century engaged scholarship.

Throughout our nation's history, the challenges and opportunities inherent in monumental economic and demographic shifts have fueled fundamental changes in the shared covenant between institutions of higher education and the public they serve. Today, our nation must transform from a manufacturing-based, national economy into a knowledge-based, global economy well positioned in the green revolution, generating national capacity to light our future (Friedman, 2008) in new and innovative ways. Further, we must both meet these challenges and create opportunities in the midst of national and global economic and social stresses (Duderstadt, 2000; Duderstadt & Womack, 2003; Wegner, 2008; Zemsky, Wegner, & Massy, 2005).

Changes driven, in part, by this economic chill call us to develop and use cutting-edge knowledge to power and empower an improved quality of life for all people through clean and sustainable energy, access to quality education, safe and plentiful food, affordable health care, an enduring sense of humanity, and undaunted hope. As democratizers of knowledge and education, research-intensive universities with land-grant heritage and values collaborate with their partners to play critical roles in empowering individuals and the communities in which they live and work. Similarly, we are engaged with and empowered by ideas, energy, and the support of our partners outside the university. Connecting these engagements is at the heart of the partner relationships and the work of engaged scholarship.

At Michigan State University (MSU), we have embraced an approach to engagement that arises directly from our land-grant traditions and values—an asset-based, action-driven approach that places a premium on collaboration with and within communities to identify problems and find solutions. The articulation of research questions and development of innovative solutions through evidence-based scholarship requires embracing a full range of community-based approaches and integrating them into the university's academic approach to engaged scholarship, and vice versa (MSU, 1993). This approach engages students as agents of change along with faculty and is inclusive of our community, government, and business partners. It takes on the difficult but essential work of embedding an ever-increasing capacity for discovery, analysis, and innovation in the community. The diverse disciplines and interdisciplinary activities that comprise highly regarded and relevant research-intensive land-grant universities, coupled with a commitment to education that is both practical and theoretical, not only make this approach feasible but also help create a potent lever for creating sustainable global prosperity.

In this chapter, I describe and consider MSU's approach to engaged scholarship, particularly the institutional imperatives that anchor this work in our land-grant philosophy. I then address how Michigan State is building on its founding values and, through collaborative work, has established itself as a globally engaged research-intensive university for the twenty-first century. I describe several grassroots examples of engaged scholarship to illustrate our action-driven approach. Finally, I identify a set of organic tensions that are reframing higher education and engaged scholarship.

Core Land-Grant Values—Quality, Inclusiveness, and Connectivity: Good Enough for the Proudest and Open to the Poorest

Abraham Lincoln's signature on the Morrill Act of 1862 created the legislative mandate to found land-grant institutions, whose covenant with society included advocating for the public good. At its essence, the land-grant idea is a set of beliefs about the university's social role (Anderson, 1976; Bonnen, 1992; Campbell, 1998; Cross, 1999).

Michigan State's visionaries imagined a learning institution unlike any other the world had ever seen. Like other land-grant institutions, Michigan State was founded on the innovative idea that practical knowledge could be united with traditional scientific and classical studies to create a rigorous curriculum that melded the liberal arts tradition of knowing and being with the practical capacity for thinking and doing. We were created to be elite without being elitist, to provide access to knowledge and education to those previously denied such access.

> The Land-Grant Idea is not just access to higher education for those with limited resources. It is not just good science. It is not just science applied to practical problems. It is not just extension education for people out in the state who have practical problems to solve. It was *all of this and more* [italics added]. (Bonnen, 1992)

In the middle of the nineteenth century, the land-grant idea was a bold experiment, and history has shown it was—and continues to be—overwhelmingly successful. Over more than

150 years, Michigan State has grown in size, scope, and stature. Today, MSU is recognized as among the best research-intensive, globally engaged universities in the world.

Great universities, like great companies, are rooted in fundamental values that define their contributions to society and endure regardless of who is at the helm (Kanter, 2008). We believe that keeping our core land-grant values relevant to society's changing needs is the source of meaningful distinction. As we deepen our engagement with society, our aspirations and our actions stem from three interwoven values: quality, inclusiveness, and connectivity.

Our commitment to quality means we shun complacency and continually strive to be among the best in all we do. Although we realize no university can be everything to everybody, we can be the university *for* everybody and the best in key areas. Great businesses, great communities, and great universities ask everyone to be better and to reject lack of aspiration as unacceptable.

We must remain competitive with the classically defined universities of distinction while adding value through our resolve to advance the common good through our work. In our work, MSU is world class; however, our distinction grows more through how our work is accomplished as we engage with our students, partners, and constituents, rather than through any particular programs. Because world-class universities are much more alike than different, our distinction comes from how and with whom we build capacity for high-quality discovery, analysis, and innovation in communities in Michigan and throughout our nation and the world. MSU's core value of exceptional quality expresses itself in the institutional hallmark to be good enough for the proudest, recognized as among the best, yet ever open to the poorest to the benefit of all.

Inclusiveness underpins and stems from our commitment to quality. Valuing inclusion means we embrace a mindset open to learning from one another, regardless of socioeconomic or social status. It means that MSU scholars benefit as they advance knowledge by exploring the vast range of questions that result from human differences throughout the world. Inclusion also benefits our engaged scholarship, as partners, faculty, students, and staff gain from the full spectrum of experiences, viewpoints, and intellectual approaches enriching our conversations and work together. Valuing inclusion means we embrace access to success for all and treat all members of our extended community with fairness and dignity. We recognize that cross-cultural interactions may sometimes create moments of surprise or discomfort, but when perspectives and expectations clash, we possess an individual and shared responsibility to guard against behaviors that demean or harm individuals, communities, and the trust inherent in relationships that support sustainable engagements characterized by respect for and civility toward one another. Fostering and sustaining relationships of trust develops partners who are intellectually curious about different perspectives, who are culturally competent, and who have the passion and skills to contribute to a global society. Embedded in our core value of inclusiveness is our commitment to cocreate opportunities for learners and partners from all backgrounds, multiply the benefits of cutting-edge knowledge, and grow the rewards of cocreated knowledge in the lives of individuals and in the communities in which they work and live.

Connectivity—with one another in academic enterprises and with those we serve locally, nationally, and globally—obliges us not only to prioritize the use of our assets but also to align them so they foster and reinforce collaborations that look to future advances and accomplishments. Connectivity is the nexus of a "can-do" attitude, of the sharing and cocreation of new assets, and of the alignment of those assets with others to create visions and solutions that are more than a sum of the individual parts. In the context of connectivity, collaboration is a new way of building sustainable relationships, earning public trust, and strengthening the alignment of resources, especially of people and programs, in the public interest. Connectivity cuts across boundaries—disciplinary, geographical, and political—to tackle the most difficult societal problems and to address the intellectual needs of talented and aspiring citizens, regardless of socioeconomic circumstances. Valuing connectivity requires anticipating tomorrow's issues while addressing today's. For MSU, connectivity means that we are committed to being a part of the local and global communities where we have a presence and to effecting both incremental and transformational changes that are sustainable in those communities.

Core Values and Strategic Positioning for Relevance: Boldness by Design

Unrelenting focus on our core values is absolutely essential to our approach to engaged scholarship. But core values alone are not sufficient. Coupling these values with a strategic vision is necessary for twenty-first-century relevance and distinction. When I assumed the presidency, I began this work by engaging with the MSU governing board; my leadership team; students, faculty, and staff; alumni, donors, and friends; community, government, and business leaders; presidents of peer institutions; and strategic partners. It was a team approach to strategically positioning MSU for relevance in the new century. I traveled widely around the state, across the nation, and abroad, listening to and reflecting on the expectations, perceptions, and advice of these partners, constituents, and colleagues on how to position MSU for the future. What I heard was the following:

- Focus.
- Simplify.
- Become more nimble.
- Play to your extraordinary strengths.
- Recast what is true about MSU to address twenty-first-century realities.
- Be the university that defines the land-grant mission's relevance for the twenty-first-century.

From these ideas, five imperatives were developed to guide Michigan State in fulfilling its strategic commitments and shared covenant with society:

- **Enhance the student experience** by continually improving the quality of academic programs and the value of an MSU degree for undergraduate and graduate students.
- **Enrich community, economic, and family life** through research, outreach, engagement, entrepreneurship, innovation, and diversity.

- **Expand international reach** through academic, research, and economic development initiatives and global, national, and local strategic alliances.
- **Increase research opportunities** by significantly expanding research funding and graduate and undergraduate students' involvement in research and scholarship.
- **Strengthen stewardship** by appreciating and nurturing the university's people, financial assets, and campus infrastructure for optimal effectiveness today and tomorrow.

These five imperatives, built on our historical strengths and core values, are now used to align existing initiatives, guide decisions on investing in new priorities, and focus our collective work along with that of our colleges and the centers of creativity and strength that cut across the university.

These imperatives, when supported by our core values, became the foundation of our visionary plan for strategic positioning, *Boldness by Design*. *Boldness by Design* (Michigan State University, 2005) is the framework for bringing our land-grant heritage to bear on society's needs, for acting on today's issues, and for anticipating and preparing for future challenges. *Boldness by Design* calls upon the entire campus community to be bold—in design, implementation, and values—and structures MSU's approach to engaged scholarship for the twenty-first century.

Persistence with Bold Purpose: Engaging to Empower

We entered the twenty-first century with society increasingly looking for research-intensive public universities to expand their roles in national, local, and international economic development; deliver more breakthrough discoveries; disseminate new knowledge more quickly; and partner with nonuniversity leaders to address the world's most urgent and complex problems.

As we grow in our understanding of engaged scholarship for the twenty-first century, we are influenced, but not driven, by current economic, political, and social circumstances. As we become engaged with society more effectively, there are four formational perspectives that deserve comment in the context of research-intensive land-grant universities:

1. The persistence of purpose to constantly refresh but not change our core values as the frontiers of society and knowledge change over time
2. The global overlay of bringing the best of the world to Michigan and the best of Michigan to the world
3. The expansion of the definition of community beyond place
4. The alignment of our bold "can-do" spirit with community- and university-based assets

Persistence of Purpose: Refreshing, but Not Changing, Our Core Values

Our decades-long success in becoming a more engaged institution rests upon our persistence in adhering to our historical foundation and purpose. At each stage of development, we have remained true to our core values of quality, inclusiveness, and connectivity, keeping them relevant but fundamentally unchanged. Through participation in the Knight Collaborative's Wharton–Institute for Research on Higher Education Executive Education programs in the

1990s, we began to better understand the Wharton School's construct of directional truth in an environment of perpetual white water and how this construct fits with our long-held perspective on persistence of purpose (Wegner & Knight Higher Education Collaborative, 2002). Directional truth provides a clear vision even when there are a variety of paths to pursue, emphasizing strategic intent instead of tightly specified plans and prescribed goals. It also focuses on the positive energy and can-do spirit created by the enormous internal and external tensions of being Bonnen's land-grant and more (1992) university in this century and on proactive sensitivity to small changes as tipping points for large transformational changes (Gladwell, 2002). Directional truth seizes opportunities inherent in the turbulence of a fast-changing world and recognizes the need to find alignments and make synergies a conscious part of the dialogue between partners. Overall, directional truth recognizes the uneven pace of change in a perpetually changing environment (Vaill, 1996) for the betterment of all.

MSU's long history in continuing education, lifelong education, Extension, public service, outreach, engagement, service learning, and engaged scholarship is rich in lessons learned and provides momentum for the future. We have influenced and been influenced by our long working relationship with the W. K. Kellogg Foundation and through our leadership in national conversations and initiatives to become an increasingly effective engaged institution. Our pioneering work, supported by the Kellogg Foundation, to define outreach as a form of scholarship across the institutional mission and within the work of faculty served as the foundation for the Committee on Institutional Cooperation's (CIC) definition of outreach and engagement (Fitzgerald, Smith, Book, Rodin, & the CIC Committee on Engagement, 2005). Similarly, our work helped shape the new definition for engaged institutions in the Carnegie Classification framework used to identify groups of roughly comparable institutions for research and analysis purposes (Giles, Sandmann, & Saltmarsh, 2010). Further, our work was pivotal in renaming the Association of Public and Land-Grant Universities' (APLU, formerly the National Association of State Universities and Land-Grant Colleges) Council on Extension, Continuing Education and Public Service to the Council on Engagement and Outreach. In the late 1990s, the relevance and impact of our leadership was validated by an invitation to participate on the Kellogg Commission on the Future of State and Land-Grant Universities. Their third report, *Returning to our Roots, The Engaged Institution* (Kellogg Commission, 1999), affirmed and strengthened our resolve that we can and must continue to do better in serving local, national, and global needs.

Our history suggests that outreach may well be the most complex and interconnected dimension of our mission and vision to be the leading land-grant university for the twenty-first century: research-intensive, globally engaged, and locally relevant. For example, rethinking Extension, organizationally and programmatically, particularly as funding patterns change, will be a major challenge across the entire institution to the ways in which we have been and are engaged with our state and regional partners. Historically, Extension has dominated our outreach agenda. It has been—and continues to be—a strong knowledge-delivery system in the state, especially because it broadened its reach into urban communities. But in the twenty-first century, Extension must evolve beyond the local and regional into international arenas. MSU is doing some of this, but much remains to be accomplished as Extension develops new and more effective roles to bring the best of the world to Michigan and the best of Michigan to the world. Extension's international dimensions must strengthen and grow as we engage the dominant societal issues of this century. It must add new partners and connect with existing partners in new ways, and its projects and programs must tie into a powerful system for profound change.

We will need to bring different voices into the conversations, voices that are sometimes at odds with our legacy of particular programs and relationships. Although the MSU approach to collaborations embedded in communities, stressing asset-based solutions, building community capacity, and creating sustainable collaborative networks will continue to be our hallmark in the years ahead, we must do more. We will not be able to fully optimize the assets of engaged scholarship if we simply keep doing the same things with the same partners.

MSU's founding values of quality, inclusiveness, and connectivity will continue to refresh our energies and passions and will drive our bold thinking to design changes that advance knowledge and transform lives—here in Michigan's counties and communities as well as around the world.

A detailed chronology of key events is beyond the scope of this chapter, but it is a significant context for engaged scholarship at MSU (Fear, 1994; Fitzgerald, Allen, & Roberts, 2010; Simon, 1999; Votruba, 2010). As our history illustrates, MSU's land-grant, value-centric approach to engagement with society has remained our persistent focus since our founding, even as the challenges and complexities of particular historical eras have changed (Thomas, 2008; Widder, 2005). As we have grown in stature, size, and scope, we have stayed in step with the society we serve. However, often our paths have differed from those of our traditional peers or the classical definitions by which institutional quality is measured. In this new century, our route will continue to evolve to reflect changing circumstances, but our destination will remain constant—creating sustainable prosperity for the common global good that goes well beyond finances and fortune.

The Global Overlay of Engaged Scholarship: Bringing the Best of the World to Michigan and the Best of Michigan to the World

Being globally engaged means more than recruiting faculty and students from other countries to come to MSU. It is more than our faculty working internationally and our students studying abroad. It is more than internationalizing the curriculum. It is more than creating a presence in China or Dubai or Africa. It is all of this and more. Being globally engaged has become a frame of reference for all that we do, a frame of reference that recognizes that fulfilling our aspirations and shared covenant with society requires dynamic and interconnected actions that extend across boundaries and borders.

A global overlay is a twenty-first-century necessity in our commitment to address the world's most intractable problems around issues common to all communities and countries—issues of the environment, food, education, health, energy, humanity, and hope. The impact of these problems is both immediate and long-range. And whereas the consequences are felt locally and personally, solutions must be global as well as local. Recognizing our interconnectedness—and acting in ways that improve quality of life broadly—is essential to creating a sustainable future.

In the same way that MSU was a pioneer land-grant institution in the nineteenth century, we are a pioneer of land-grant work around the world in the twenty-first century—a way of working I have called "world grant." We bring the same purpose—to open opportunities for development and prosperity and to increase the capacity of communities and countries to chart their own course toward self-sufficiency—to our work today as the early leaders of the land-grant movement brought to a young nation preparing for a new age. By building the capacity of others, we extend to the world the same covenant MSU had with the citizens of Michigan when it was established. Our historical obligation to democratize knowledge and help translate knowledge across the state in ways that drove innovation and prosperity now animates our engaged scholarship across geographical and political boundaries.

Standards for judging the significance of contributions for addressing problems surrounding health, food, energy, education, and the environment are becoming global and raise questions about the transnationalism of knowledge. Effective global engagement requires us to learn new ways to make local projects applicable in other places. In this global setting, both the project and process variables increase with the inherent complexities of different cultural community contexts; our faculty and partners must struggle with the applicability principles between developing and more developed countries.

Our global engagement is sharpening our questions both at home and abroad. How can we effectively move beyond project activities to become catalysts for broader change? From individual project activities to cocreating dreams with communities about all that can be accomplished? From project activity to the development of related public policy? How can we strengthen social networks that facilitate the specific project or projects at hand but also develop and sustain the next generation of work?

Creating bridges between policy development and capacity building is crucial for achieving the synergies of a multiplier effect, especially in developing countries, where public policy agendas are evolving. In these settings, it is often difficult and arduous to link a project's related activities together: the supply chains of materials, people, and human capital that are necessary to sustain successful projects. We have learned that the project activities and the process successes must be designed to inform and propel policy development.

Work here and abroad has been animated by many of the same threads identified by Kanter (2008) in her study of some of the world's biggest companies that are giving primacy to their plans to improve the world. They globalize and localize, deriving benefits from the intersections, producing business and societal value, and bringing together the soft areas of people, culture, and community responsibility with the hard areas of technology and product innovation. Kanter confirms what MSU has long experienced—that people are more inclined to be creative when the community's and institution's values stress innovation that helps the world. By focusing MSU's approach to engaged scholarship on the problems that impede prosperity, we enhance and protect the quality of life in Michigan and around the world.

Defining Community: Beyond Place or Locale

The expanded definition of community, that is, that it extends beyond place or locale, aligns with the global overlay of engaged scholarship. Originally, land-grant institutions were highly place-bound in their responsibilities and aspirations, society's expectations, and natural partnership areas. The powerful national economic engine envisioned in 1862 worked well in geographically contiguous areas of the nation's land-grant institutions; however, as the nation's number and kind of higher education institutions increased, they differentiated themselves in national competition for prestige, faculty, and students. Even as our recruitment of faculty and students expanded to reach competitively across the nation and world, the boundaries that defined our natural partnership areas remained relatively unchanged. Only recently has the understanding of "what is good for the world is also good for Michigan" begun to gain traction. Identity in a geographical place is deeply rooted and difficult to change.

The economic engine of the twenty-first century is fueled less by place than by connections and networks. Our founders, who saw the assets of place as the source of results, sought to establish the university throughout the state in every county via Extension agents and offices. They saw only two dots to connect to advance quality of life and drive economic prosperity: the institution and the problem site.

Today, engaged scholarship connects numerous dots, including students, faculty teams, interdisciplinary teams, community partners and community networks, businesses, and government agencies, without depending on the infrastructure of organization, institution, community, or discipline. In this approach, dependence on place as the interaction space shifts into the social milieu of consortia, networks, faculty-student teams, coalitions, collaborations, and partnerships. As partners participate in defining problems and developing solutions, ideas emerge across disciplinary, organizational, and community boundaries. Today's results stem from relationships intentionally designed to speed the dissemination of information, fuel future innovation, and build a platform of trust and confidence for potential future engagements. An example of such a campus-community partnership is illustrated by the Power of We Consortium (Fitzgerald, Allen, & Roberts, 2010).

The Mindset of the Research-Intensive, Globally Engaged University: A Bold Can-Do Spirit

In a highly competitive world in the throes of severe economic and social stresses, the willingness to try things that are boldly transformational requires a mindset grounded in a can-do spirit supported by cutting-edge knowledge. It is this mindset that builds and infuses hope into our work and the relationships we build with our partners. This bold can-do spirit has empowered MSU from its earliest years.

MSU's approach to engaged scholarship continues to align our assets with an action-driven mindset in which the best professional and disciplinary knowledge is mapped onto the needs of society and then taken around the globe to empower new communities. This alignment is a commitment to prioritize, redefine, and refine key questions for new contexts that in turn impels us to listen to all voices that should have a role in shaping the questions and agenda. It propels us forward in the difficult task of getting everyone thinking and doing boldly. That is our covenant with society.

The spirit that drives this shared covenant requires both a common vision and a common set of values. Part of this covenant is intangible. In the context of engaged scholarship, this means it is not merely a return-on-the-investment, businesslike transaction primarily concerned with funding. It is about the creation of a renewable resource of hope. Over time,

107

society has given us its trust and accepted our aspirations and capacity both to leapfrog ahead with information and to move knowledge forward via incremental discoveries. Engaged institutions and the communities they serve have a shared belief that it is possible to accomplish things that are difficult to envision but can nevertheless be done. It is a shared belief in society's capacity to develop to its fullest potential—not via a bartered or transactional exchange but in a collaborative we-can-get-this-done system.

This can-do attitude, aligned with our assets, requires us to form what I call "rebounding partnerships": partnerships that not only create an immediate impact on Michigan but also take a long view of Michigan and the world's future. These partnerships rebound from Michigan into the world and from the world back into Michigan. Rebounding partnerships call for creativity and engaged scholarship; confidence and conviction; innovation, boldness, and risk-taking; and the courage to try solutions that feel like they might not fit at the beginning, but that we—and the society we serve—will grow into.

The convergence of thinking and acting boldly with people requires that our communities' and our institution's assets be used to create possibilities as well as discover them. We've learned that addressing some of the most difficult societal problems affecting individuals and communities requires a multidimensional view—seeing not only what others see but also the new relationships and new dimensions of complex problems and potential solutions.

Twenty-First-Century Variations within the MSU Approach to Engaged Scholarship

The variations are many within MSU's approach to engaged scholarship (Michigan State University, 2009). Our approach is asset based, places a premium on collaboration within communities in both problem identification and strategic solutions and innovations, and works to create cutting-edge knowledge while embedding in the community an ever-increasing capacity for discovery, analysis, and innovation independent of the university's local presence. The following examples illustrate the diversity of work and the multiple approaches that characterize MSU's engaged scholarship.

Pioneering Prototype: Providing Access to Knowledge

One international example of MSU's engaged scholarship is in Tanzania. As is the reality in many developing countries, remote Tanzanian villages lack not only computers but also the electricity to power them. Books and other educational materials are scarce, and traditional ways of life are slowly disappearing. Many community elders believe that the future depends on educating their children to participate in public discourse so they can influence government decisions, ultimately protecting their land and way of life as well as broadening their life choices. In collaboration with Tanzanian colleagues, a community, university, and industry partnership designed a low-cost computer system that runs on solar energy to give children access to the Internet's vast educational and informational resources to empower them for twenty-first-century life. The design-and-install team for this prototyping engagement included the computer manufacturing partner, MSU faculty in engineering and communication arts and sciences, MSU students studying Swahili, and university faculty and students in Tanzania. The team worked with and trained community members, ultimately giving responsibility for the computer system to the village. Once young Tanzanian students learn to navigate the computer, the village's first goal is to prepare older students for the secondary school entrance examination. If the community has access to education, its members can become doctors, teachers, and entrepreneurs, all of which are needed throughout the region. This computer system, therefore, can help the community advance, perhaps even saving its village from destruction, just by preparing a higher proportion of students for secondary school. This program is the starting point to providing a better quality of life for future generations.

Closer to home, but also arising from that collaboration, is a new MSU undergraduate specialization entitled "Information and Communication Technologies for Development." Students in this new specialization will take two classes focused on the developing world and one class on technology for use in developing countries. Additionally, they will participate in a field experience that extends the work begun in Tanzania. This work will prepare them to understand and work in a global context, a skill set that is increasingly in demand.

Both at home and abroad, this is a pioneering prototype that is already democratizing knowledge in one village and has the potential to transform lives around the globe.

Impact That Improves Lives: Transformational Facilities for the World

The U.S. Department of Energy's selection of MSU to design, build, and run the Facility for Rare Isotope Beams (FRIB) brings together an international community of top scientists to advance understanding of rare isotopes, helping to unlock the origins of the universe and fueling potential breakthrough applications in medicine, national security, engineering, materials science, and the environment.

Rare isotopes are fleeting bits of matter created primarily in the extreme environment of stars. Despite their ephemeral nature, these short-lived isotopes are critical in the world of science and could affect lives around the globe. Rare isotope research has already led to the development of technologies that make the world safer, including a high-precision handheld device that detects a host of destructive elements, from lead paint on children's toys to an aluminum alloy used only in nuclear weapons production. Advances in accelerator technology used in nuclear and high-energy particle physics are also leading to innovations in proton therapy, which is showing promise in treating certain types of cancer.

Our vision for FRIB is to build on past successes. For years, MSU has operated a world-class rare isotope research facility, the National Superconducting Cyclotron Laboratory, that has served seven hundred researchers from a hundred institutions in more than thirty countries. FRIB is expected to expand the quality and quantity of research opportunities for approximately one thousand university and laboratory scientists, postdoctoral associates, and graduate students from around the globe. In doing so, FRIB is expected to provide economic benefits, too. This science venture will bring an estimated $1 billion in economic activity to Michigan over two decades, and the economic benefits from the application of new discoveries are incalculable.

The FRIB competition included grassroots community initiatives to build an appreciation for basic science research that recognized that the impact and discovery potential of such research may not be known for another ten to twenty years. Because MSU is both a research-intensive and a globally engaged institution, we used the FRIB competition as an opportunity for engaged scholarship, strengthening our outreach to K–12 students, educating the community about nuclear science and rare isotopes, building enthusiasm about sophisticated science, and positioning with our community partners to support esoteric science research. The competition for FRIB built community capacity to appreciate the long-term potential of basic research.

Multiple Solutions, Multiple Partners, Multiple Impacts

Transportation accounts for approximately two-thirds of oil consumption in the United States and approximately one-third of the nation's total energy use. The critical need to reduce our country's dependence on oil imports, combined with today's use of the same efficiency-limited combustion system that powered the first automobiles more than a century ago, present significant challenges and opportunities. There is no single solution to the world's fossil fuel shortage. In collaboration with partners in government and the transportation industry, MSU researchers in agriculture, plant sciences, and engineering are working on multiple approaches to finding environmentally responsible and economical ways to power transportation. One of these approaches involves developing powerful new biofuels in tandem with specially designed engines, a distinctly integrated approach that could drive the next automotive revolution, reduce the nation's dependence on oil imports, and dramatically contribute to reducing emissions and improving air quality, especially in large metropolitan areas. MSU's Energy and Automotive Research Laboratories, housed in a dynamic 29,000-square feet research complex on the MSU campus, have provided the necessary infrastructure to integrate these research projects. Such collaboration holds the potential to improve the environment and economic outlook for the region.

Rapidly Deployable Solutions: Parts of the Puzzle

Pollinators are to thank for one of every three bites of food consumed in the world. In recent years, however, honeybees—the powerhouses of agricultural pollination—have been disappearing at alarming rates, leaving beekeepers and scientists perplexed. With as much as 80 percent of Earth's crops at stake, MSU researchers working closely with beekeepers are seeking rapidly deployable solutions for protecting honeybees from colony collapse disorder (CCD), the complex bee disease characterized by the disappearance of all adult honeybees in a hive, while concurrently finding new ways to attract other pollinators to help ensure crop survival. Work with researchers and growers from countries including Tajikistan, Kyrgyzstan, and Uzbekistan has yielded new knowledge about the ways plants can be used to attract various species of native bees as well as natural enemies of insects that attack crops, allowing growers to control pests without chemicals that harm honeybees.

As growers, beekeepers, and scientists collaborate on research about pollinators, they contribute important knowledge to solving the larger puzzle of pollinating crops. Each additional puzzle piece also advances specific knowledge that will help beekeepers in Michigan, across the country, and internationally address CCD. MSU's pollinator studies also intersect with biofuel crops research. Sharing knowledge and working with other researchers as well as with crop producers and beekeepers, MSU entomologists and their partners are finding practical solutions that will sustain pollinators and the crops they support throughout Michigan and the world.

Connecting Cultures, Sharing Values

MATRIX, the Center for Humane Arts, Letters, and Social Sciences Online (Michigan State University, n.d.), uses Internet technologies to improve education and increase the democratic flow of information throughout the world. The group makes use of a variety of technology applications—from building online archives to developing interactive educational opportunities for increasing understanding of social justice issues—to connect cultures and share values across time and geography.

A similar initiative that ties into our work with the African National Congress to document their culture and the South African struggle against colonialism and white minority rule involved a collaborative team from MSU's Museum and the Nelson Mandela Museum in South Africa. Together, they created an interactive exhibit that is inspiring young people around the world with its message of *ubuntu*, a Zulu word that means "humanity to others."

Dear Mr. Mandela, Dear Mrs. Parks: Children's Letters, Global Lessons opened in South Africa in July 2008 and then at the MSU Museum before touring the United States. The exhibit features a collection of letters written by children from around the world to renowned human rights leaders Nelson Mandela and Rosa Parks. Designed to raise awareness of the social justice challenges that South Africans and Americans have faced, the multifaceted exhibit provides visitors with opportunities to read the children's letters alongside biographies of the human rights heroes and to listen to video messages from Mandela and others. Visitors can also write their own letters. By helping bring to life Mandela's and Parks's courage and social and cultural ideals, and by showing how they made a real difference in the world, MSU is strengthening a global community rooted in core values much like its own: quality, inclusiveness, and connectivity.

Organic Tensions and Their Role in Redefining Engaged Scholarship

As I observe research-intensive land-grant institutions change the scope of their engagement and address society's needs and expectations more effectively, I see a set of issues emerging as dominant themes characterizing the work and impact of the twenty-first-century engaged university:

- Variability, especially in large institutions, that has all the advantages of pushing engagement deep into colleges and across disciplines while accommodating the challenges of hundreds of potentially disparate approaches.
- Pursuit of institutional and community capacity-building models.
- Metrics that are relevant units of measurement and reflect direct and indirect impact beyond a project's life.
- Appropriate use of technology, particularly as issues of cost, time, distance, and transnational partners and projects increasingly dominate.
- Ways to honor and learn from less successful or even failed, but nevertheless bold, initiatives.

111

Embedded in these issues are organic tensions with the potential for constructive opportunities as well as significant problems. Framing them as questions to be addressed is a useful way to use them productively.

Variability

Varied approaches to knowledge creation, different principles and priorities driving any particular project, and different organizational and cooperative-competitive arrangements all interact dynamically. Even as people do the right things, institutions as large and complex as MSU have inherent variability that can appear as organizational incoherence. For MSU, *Points of Distinction* (Michigan State University & Zimmerman, 1996) created initial momentum to reduce variability through the creation of touchstones to help deans, unit chairs, directors, and individual faculty members define, plan, evaluate, and document quality outreach. However, there is a highly dynamic balance across the different organizational and professional contexts in which faculty and community partners find meaning and establish policy frameworks for the planning, evaluation, and reward of quality engagement. Balancing the tension between organizational coherence and the variations inherent in creative processes consumes considerable organizational energy. Although the appropriate promotion and tenure policies and organizational structures are in place at MSU to motivate and protect faculty who do the work, we continue to be challenged to avoid compromising the grassroots energy and joy that animates faculty taking on engagement in communities, while sustaining robust outreach planning, evaluation, and documentation frameworks. Nevertheless, it is clear that MSU has come a long way in making outreach and engaged scholarship a legitimate part of its institutional conversations.

We are considering new ways to make engaged scholarship's collective impact effective beyond a particular project, to create multiplier effects through policy and community infrastructures. We are headed in the right direction and speaking the same language within a commonly held definition of outreach as engaged scholarship. The work led by the MSU Office of University Outreach and Engagement is advancing the underpinning scholarship of cutting-edge knowledge necessary to build the policy- and best-practice basis of engaged scholarship, and to foster organizational coherence while recognizing variability across disciplines and programs. Meanwhile, we continue to struggle to better align the policies and incentives that drive faculty work.

How can the often vexing variability inherent in large institutions and in campus-community partnerships function to expand the capacity for creativity, innovation, and trust within the institution and with our partners?

Capacity Building

Engaged scholarship that builds robust capacity for discovery, analysis, and innovation is complicated by the long history of outreach as hands-on delivery of particular services or programs into communities, followed by the exit of faculty upon project completion. There is persistent tension in determining how to construct approaches to projects that are faculty-led yet simultaneously build a community's capacity to take on projects without a traditional faculty presence. I often think of this in a team metaphor. High-performing sports teams build appreciation for and create momentum from the contributions not just from the players who score, but also those who are assistant leaders and play makers, and those who add special team or bench strength. The whole team performs at levels higher than the skills of the individual players, increasing understanding of the sport as well as the game, recruiting players and integrating them into the team, and above all, developing the capacity to play a winning game in the absence of the coaching staff. The sports team metaphor is akin to the significant challenges and opportunities that arise in determining ways to develop a community's capacity to chart its own course and improve the quality of its citizens' lives.

Capacity building entails more than project-specific activities. Engaged scholarship must be designed to yield an impact beyond a particular community and the initial partnership's time frame, long after a specific project is complete. Capacity building helps capture the "scholarship lost" because we insufficiently document the macro impact of projects and the process of engagement. The engagement portfolio must be designed to reflect both an immediate return on the investment and returns over long periods of time—perhaps decades.

Capacity building entails working on solutions to local problems without being constrained by the local definition of the problem. It is knitting together networks across the country and around the world, recognizing that engaged scholarship is always about working together to define problems and priorities, without designating winners and losers and without being dependent on structures of authority, control, and power. Capacity building means embedding both the process and the activities into the community. Engaged empowering ensures that the focus is on path-breaking research, not just incremental community-maintenance discoveries. Building capacity bridges the gap between academic quality and community relevancy, creating a new sense of the discovery agenda. Closing the gap allows the academic definition of quality and the community definition of relevancy not only to fit together but also to create energy for further innovation. It is this fit between academic quality and community relevancy that underpins trust. By definition, capacity building is an iterative cycle fueled by trust based on continuous forward momentum as ideas are refined and developed. Engaged scholarship requires commitment to the full cycle of long-time horizon iterations that move through the shorter-time horizon increments and toward strategic and visionary innovative changes.

Without a doubt, institutional policies must recognize and foster interdependent and interdisciplinary work on campus and in the community. Initial momentum for building capacity within the community comes from individual projects. Sustaining the momentum in the community and in the university is increasingly complex, with multiple stakeholders, constituents, and partners as participants.

How can institutional and community capacity building be pursued as a central organizational responsibility and policy imperative as well as at grassroots project levels?

Metrics

The development of metrics for assessing the overall value of engagement continues to lag point-in-time project and institutional measurements. Breakthrough progress is needed in establishing metrics that are applicable across institutions as well as analyses

113

that are relevant at both institutional and project levels. Indicators of academic and community value that push outside the box of current circumstances or project activities and are "instruments of prospective strategy, not weapons of turf defense" (Zemsky, 2000) are largely absent in the documentation of engaged scholarship. Metrics are needed that not only demonstrate real impact over time but also continue the scholarship of learning about the nature, scope, and sustainability of the impact. Even the recent work by APLU and the American Association of State Colleges and Universities to create a Voluntary System of Accountability (AASCU & NASULGC, 2007) has not successfully addressed the issue of credit for adding significant value in a secondary or assistant role or as a broker of substantial engagement. There is much work to be done. Highlighting revenue sources or who paid for particular projects has limited utility in assessing and understanding the value the engagement created. Our current analyses are better at reflecting the university's work, but engaged scholarship requires us to think through how to reflect the work of and in the community and to develop indicators that show when engagement is no longer about the faculty or the funding source. Documentation must be developed to indicate the community-embedded ownership of ideas and processes as a measure of capacity.

The evidence of our success as a research-intensive, engaged university is the value we cocreate with our partners and the students we educate. Our success lies in the legacy of engaged empowerment that improves the quality of life for people in Michigan and throughout the world.

How can the work of the university and the work of the community be reflected in metrics that reveal both direct and derived impact over time?

Technology

Technology is becoming more ubiquitous in its capacity and reach into all socioeconomic strata apart from geographical; further, its extensive use raises ethical questions in all fields of endeavor. Traditionally, outreach has been hands-on in the delivery of knowledge. The deepening of our engagement with society now requires not only the delivery of cutting-edge knowledge to partners outside the institution but also the cocreation of knowledge with them. Technology facilitates both of these obligations, bringing people who have never met or worked together into direct conversation. Nonetheless, it is shifting the traditional strengths and satisfaction of hands-on and face-to-face engagements. The social milieu of the Internet is often at odds with our legacy practices because all ideas compete on an equal footing; contribution counts for more than credentials; hierarchies are natural and not prescribed; leaders serve rather than preside; tasks are chosen, not assigned; groups are self-defining and self-organizing; resources get attracted, not allocated; power comes from sharing information, not hoarding it; opinions compound and decisions are peer reviewed; users can veto most policy decisions; intrinsic rewards matter most; and hackers are heroes (Hamel, 2009).

Especially as partners and projects become more transnational, how can technology be used appropriately and effectively to build sustainable relationships and engaged scholarship's grassroots capacity?

Honoring and Learning from Less-Than-Successful Engagements

We need to discover ways not only to learn from but also to honor less successful or even failed projects. Engagement that is innovative presses against the usual ways of accomplishing change. A commitment to have a potentially profound impact on intractable problems generates a level of discomfort among partners, especially when risking failure. The drive and motivation to report successes often runs counter to our drive to be innovative and risk taking. Yet engagement with a community's most complex and difficult problems is central to our shared covenant with society. It demands a deep institutional culture of boldness, courage, perseverance, and risk taking. Historically, the farm and faculty partners understood that a demonstration project did not always yield the desired results. In fact, a demonstration project's power rested on the mutual understanding that some things would not work. With this understanding, partners grew in their trust of one another, enabling them to make judgments about the potential cost-benefit of the demonstration without being rigidly attached to always showing positive results.

How can we deal positively with our failures as well as our successes, finding ways to celebrate and build sustainable relationships through less successful but bold initiatives as well as those that are successful?

Conclusion

I have come to believe that these tensions and the questions they generate are tools for building the renewable resources of hope and the human capacity to chart the course of one's own life and community toward sustainable prosperity. These tensions propel faculty, partners, and communities beyond their individual passions, building the networks and relationships that, when fueled by emerging knowledge, refine ideas and innovations and move new ideas forward. As tools, they are based on the shared understanding that engaged scholarship is about:

- Knowledge that continually pushes the boundaries of understanding
- Knowledge that is at the frontier of relevancy, innovation, and creativity
- Knowledge that is organized and openly communicated to build capacity for innovation and creativity
- Knowledge that creates energy, synergy, and community independence to assess projects and processes, providing a reason and a capacity to gain new knowledge
- Knowledge that is accessible across the chasms of geographic boundaries and socioeconomic situations

In this context, the organic tensions around variability, capacity building, metrics, technology, and honoring innovation in less-than-successful initiatives are consequences of our initial successes on the journey of engagement with society that began, for MSU, in 1855. They are rooted in a fundamental commitment to broaden and to make effective the number and variety of voices that define relevant problems and to position our partners and the communities in which they live and work at the forefront of knowledge. Cocreating and using cutting-edge knowledge are fundamental to engaged empowering for sustainable economic prosperity for the common good of the citizens with whom we are intertwined, locally and globally.

Summary

This chapter has described and reflected on MSU's approach to engaged scholarship and commented on the institutional values and imperatives anchoring our work as we seek to transform the quality of life in Michigan and in communities around the globe. I have also used examples to illustrate a variety of themes in engaged scholarship. Finally, I have identified a set of organic tensions and a mindset that I believe are reframing higher education and engaged scholarship.

More than 150 years ago, reframing higher education and creating land-grant institutions required bold thinking, a passion for both thinking and doing in order to advance knowledge across traditional boundaries, and a commitment to transforming lives through access to new and applicable knowledge. Well before the Morrill Act was signed by Abraham Lincoln, Michigan State was engaged in pioneering work. In this century, I have called on MSU to be the exemplar as a world-grant institution in extending our land-grant work and values around the world, cocreating opportunities for prosperity and increasing communities' and countries' respective capacities to chart their own courses toward self-sufficiency through enabled empowerment based on shared ideas, talent, and innovation.

Engaged scholarship in twenty-first-century, research-intensive land-grant universities requires the same bold thinking, passion, and commitment demonstrated by nineteenth-century visionaries. How we fulfill the destiny derived from this legacy will depend on daring to be who we are and who we were created to be, and then "doing" even more boldly and better than we do now. We are recasting our land-grant values and traditions and our research-intensive mission to meet twenty-first-century challenges and opportunities, honoring the values of our past and drawing from them the energy to innovate our future—around the world, across the nation, and at home.

References

American Association of State Colleges and Universities, & National Association of State Universities and Land Grant Colleges. (2007). *Voluntary system of accountability program*. Retrieved April 21, 2009, from http://www.voluntarysystem.org/index.cfm.

Anderson, G. L. (Ed.). (1976). *Land-grant universities and their continuing challenge*. East Lansing: Michigan State University Press.

Bonnen, J. (1992, Spring). Reflections on the land-grant idea. *The Graduate Post: A Newsletter of the Graduate School, Michigan State University, 2*(2), 10–13.

Campbell, J. R. (1998). *Reclaiming a lost heritage: Land-grant and other higher education initiatives for the twenty-first century*. East Lansing: Michigan State University Press.

Cross, C. F. (1999). *Justin Smith Morrill, father of the land-grant colleges*. East Lansing: Michigan State University Press.

Duderstadt, J. J. (2000). *A university for the 21st century*. Ann Arbor: University of Michigan Press.

Duderstadt, J. J., & Womack, F. W. (2003). *The future of the public university in America: Beyond the crossroads*. Baltimore: Johns Hopkins University Press.

Fear, F. (1994). A selective history of outreach at Michigan State University. In F. Fear (Ed.), *Background papers: University outreach at Michigan State University: Extending knowledge to serve society* (pp. 27–43). Unpublished manuscript, Michigan State University, Office of the Provost.

Fitzgerald, H. E., Allen, A., & Roberts, P. (2010). Campus-community partnerships: Perspectives on engaged research. In H. E. Fitzgerald, C. Burack, & S. Seifer (Eds.), *Handbook of engaged scholarship: The contemporary landscape: Vol. 2. Community-campus partnerships*. East Lansing: Michigan State University Press.

Fitzgerald, H. E., Smith, P., Book P., Rodin, K., & the CIC Committee on Engagement. (2005). *CIC Reports: Resource guide and recommendations for defining benchmarking and engagement*. Champaign, IL: CIC.

Friedman, T. L. (2008). *Hot, flat, and crowded: Why we need a green revolution—and how it can renew America*. New York: Farrar, Straus and Giroux.

Giles, D. E., Jr., Sandmann, L. R., & Saltmarsh, J. (2010). Engagement and the Carnegie classification system. In H. E. Fitzgerald, C. Burack, & S. Seifer (Eds.). *Handbook of engaged scholarship: The contemporary landscape: Vol. 2. Community-campus partnerships*. East Lansing: Michigan State University Press.

Gladwell, M. (2002). *The tipping point: How little things can make a big difference*. Boston: Little, Brown & Company.

Hamel, G. (2009, March 24). The *Wall Street Journal* blog. Retrieved March 30, 2009, from http://blogs.wsj.com/management/2009/03/24.

Kanter, R. M. (2008). Transforming giants. *Harvard Business Review, 86*(1), 43–52.

Kellogg Commission on the Future of State and Land-Grant Universities. (1999). *Returning to our roots: The engaged institution*. Washington, DC: National Association of State Universities and Land-Grant Colleges, Office of Public Affairs. Retrieved March 30, 2009, from http://www.aplu.org/NetCommunity/Document.Doc?id=183

Michigan State University. (n.d.). *MATRIX: The center for humane arts, letters, and social sciences online*. Retrieved April 21, 2009, from http://www2.matrix.msu.edu/.

Michigan State University. (1993). *University outreach at Michigan State University: Extending knowledge to serve society*. Washington, DC: ERIC Clearinghouse mirofiches. Retrieved April 21, 2009, from http://www.eric.ed.gov/ERICDocs/data/ericdocs2sql/content_storage_01/0000019b/80/16/14/bb.pdf.

Michigan State University. (2005). *Boldness by design: Strategic positioning of Michigan State University*. Retrieved April 21, 2009, from http://boldnessbydesign.msu.edu/.

Michigan State University. (2009). *President's report, 2008: Powering and empowering prosperity*. Retrieved April 21, 2009, from http://report.president.msu.edu.

Michigan State University & Zimmerman, D. (1996). *Points of distinction: A guidebook for planning and evaluating quality outreach*. Washington, D.C.: ERIC Clearinghouse mirofiches. Retrieved April 21, 2009, from"http://www.eric.ed.gov/ERICDocs/data/ericdocs2sql/content_storage_01/0000019b/80/16/14/bb.pdf"

Simon, L. A. K. (1999). Constructive and complex tensions in the art of engagement. *Journal of Public Service and Outreach, 4*(2), 2–6.

Thomas, D. A. (2008). *Michigan State College, John Hannah and the creation of a world university, 1926–1969*. East Lansing: Michigan State University Press.

Vaill, P. B. (1996). *Learning as a way of being: Strategies for survival in a world of permanent white water.* San Francisco: Jossey-Bass.

Votruba, J. C. (2010). Foreword. In H. E. Fitzgerald, C. Burack, and S. Seifer (Eds.). *Handbook of engaged scholarship: The contemporary landscape: Vol. 1. Institutional change.* East Lansing: Michigan State University Press.

Wegner, G. R. (2008). *Engaging higher education in societal challenges of the 21st century.* San Jose, CA: The National Center for Public Policy and Higher Education. Retrieved April 21, 2009, from http://www.highereducation.org/reports/wegner/wegner.pdf.

Wegner, G. & Knight Higher Education Collaborative. (2002, August). *Michigan State University: Strategy without deep pockets* (microform): *Enhancing institutional capacity from within policy perspectives.* Washington, DC: ERIC Clearinghouse microfiches.

Widder, K. R. (2005). *Michigan Agricultural College, the evolution of a land-grant philosophy, 1855–1925.* East Lansing: Michigan State University Press.

Zemsky, R. (Ed.). (2000). The data made me do it. *Policy Perspectives, 9*(2), 1–11.

Zemsky, R., Wegner, G. R., & Massy, W. F. (2005). *Remaking the American university: Market-smart and mission-centered.* New Brunswick, NJ: Rutgers University Press.

Engaged Scholarship and the Urban University

Matthew Hartley and Ira Harkavy

As other chapters in this volume have underscored, the civic aims of American colleges and universities extend back to their origins. This is certainly true for urban universities. With the addition of a medical school in 1765, the University of Pennsylvania became America's first university. Penn was, of course, founded by Benjamin Franklin as the Academy of Philadelphia in 1740 in the largest and arguably the most important city in the American colonies. In 1749, Franklin published a pamphlet entitled "Proposals Relating to the Education of Youth in Pensilvania [sic]," and in it he articulated a vision of an institution predicated not on classical education for the elites but on serving all students of ability in the interest of fostering an "*Inclination* join'd with an *Ability* to serve mankind, one's country, Friends and Family" [emphasis in the original]. A similar civic-minded sentiment was echoed over a century later by the founders of many land-grant colleges. In the founding documents of Ohio State University, located in the capital Columbus, the trustees stated that they intended not only to prepare graduates to be successful "farmers or mechanics, but as men, fitted by education and attainments for the greater usefulness and higher duties of citizenship" (Boyte & Kari, 2000, p. 47).

It was the late nineteenth century that saw the dawn of the modern research university. The fortunes of many of these institutions were tied to their urban contexts. In 1876, Daniel Coit Gilman, first president of Johns Hopkins University, asserted in his inaugural address that the mission of urban universities was to "make for less misery among the poor, less ignorance in the schools, less bigotry in the temple, less suffering in the hospitals, less fraud in business, less folly in politics." In like manner in 1902, William Rainey Harper, the University of Chicago's first president, gave a speech at Nicholas Murray Butler's inauguration as president of Columbia University. Harper envisioned the emergence of the urban "Great

University" (his term) "which will adapt itself to urban influence, which will undertake to serve as an expression of urban civilization, and which is compelled to meet the demands of an urban environment . . . will ultimately form a new type of university" (Harper, 1905, p. 158).

Harper meant far more than being attentive to local surroundings or being a responsible institutional neighbor. He believed that only by using their intellectual resources to solve the pressing problems of the day would universities fulfill their promise. "Just as the great cities of the country represent the national life in its fullness and variety, so the urban universities are in the truest sense . . . national universities" (Harper, 1905, p. 160). This was no mere idealistic flight of fancy. Harper was convinced that such an emphasis would secure the support of wealthy Chicago elites, especially those committed to improving the city's public schools. Such enlightened self-interest was highly compatible with and powerfully reinforced by his theoretical conviction that collaborative, action-oriented, real-world problem solving was by far the best strategy to advance knowledge and learning and the interests of Chicago (both the city and the university) (Benson, Harkavy & Puckett, 2007).

That said, the civic vision embraced by the leaders of these urban universities was very much a contested one (Hartley & Hollander, 2005). There were competing notions about the purposes of the university. As historian Julie Reuben has documented, by the end of the nineteenth century the emphasis on moral instruction was replaced by a commitment to advancing knowledge and an adherence to emerging scientific standards (Reuben, 1996). Scholarship was increasingly defined (and its legitimacy derived) from its commitment to scientific objectivity and value-neutrality. Indeed, in 1889, G. Stanley Hall, the first president of Clark University in Worcester, Massachusetts, argued that faculty members should "live only for pure science and high scholarship." Such attitudes exemplified an important aspect of the German university model—learning for learning's sake and the establishment of a hierarchy of knowledge in which pure science was elevated above its application. The rise of the academic disciplines transformed the work of the professoriate at research universities. Greater specialization and expertise (as defined by the various disciplines) formed the basis for the increased legitimacy and authority of faculty members at these institutions.

The disciplines were, however, founded as a means to better understand specified aspects of society (e.g., economy and politics) in order to change society for the better. But an activist, engaged social science largely vanished after 1918. World War I was the catalyst for a retreat from an action-oriented, reformist social science. The brutality and horror of that conflict ended the buoyant optimism and faith in human progress and social improvement that had marked the Progressive Era. American academics were not immune to the general disillusion with progress. Scholarly inquiry directed toward creating a better world was increasingly deemed anachronistic and quixotic. The discipline, simply put, became an end in itself (Harkavy & Puckett, 1994, p. 306).

Over the past two decades, however, a host of colleges and universities have sought to recapture their civic purposes (Harkavy & Hartley, 2008). (See, for example, the list of 120 institutions that have received the community engagement classification from the Carnegie Foundation for the Advancement of teaching, available at http://www.carnegiefoundation. org/files/assets/2008-community_engagement.pdf.) Many have predicated their efforts on developing sustainable partnerships within their urban communities (Harkavy & Wiewel, 1995; Maurasse, 2001). The most promising of these efforts have focused on linking the civic and urban mission of the institution with core academic activities—especially the work of the professoriate. In some instances this has produced exciting new innovations in institutional policies, such as broadening the definition of scholarly work to include (or even encourage) engaged scholarship (Boyer, 1990; O'Meara & Rice, 2005). Other universities have sought to encourage and support this work *despite* a faculty culture that adheres to traditional norms of the academy and prizes certain specific expressions of scholarship (i.e., peer-reviewed journals) to the exclusion of all others.

In this chapter we examine the challenges facing engaged scholars at urban universities. Our central argument is that engagement efforts must be supported in ways that are mindful of the predominant norms of the institutions in which faculty members work. There are powerful normative forces that inhibit engagement at these institutions. However, there are also effective strategies institutions can use to encourage such work. Finally, we note a particularly promising development at a number of urban universities, the alignment of efforts by multiple faculty members from across disciplines to address pressing real-world problems.

The Role of Universities in Responding to Contemporary Urban Challenges

Universities are well positioned to play a role in responding to the challenges facing our nation's cities. More than half of all institutions of higher learning are located within or immediately outside urban areas (Hahn, with Coonerty & Peaslee, 2003). Research universities are powerful and resource rich institutions. In many cities, universities and hospitals ("eds and meds") are the largest private employers (Harkavy & Zuckerman, 1999). According to a recent estimate, urban colleges and universities employ three million people, and fully two-thirds are administrative, clerical, or support staff (Hahn et al., 2003). One study concluded, "[o]lder core cities have a significant concentration of jobs in education and health services. . . . These industries account for over 20 percent of the jobs in the case study cities, compared to 15 percent of jobs nationally" (Fox & Trouhaft, 2006, p. 41). As such, they serve as anchor institutions that provide significant economic stability to their local areas (Harkavy & Zuckerman, 1999). This status also gives them considerable leverage in encouraging and participating in systemic reform.

Although the institutions of higher learning described in this chapter have similarities (they offer both undergraduate and graduate programs, and they expect faculty members to spend a portion of their time conducting original research, in contrast to more teaching-centered institutions), there is variation among this group. First, some of these institutions are what Ernest Lynton termed metropolitan universities, comprehensive institutions that are "post-war creations or transformations of normal schools." Lynton argues that these institutions "are groping to define their mission in terms of what they are rather than what they are not, namely traditional research universities" (Lynton, 1991, p. 1). Such institutions offer a relatively greater emphasis on teaching and fewer graduate programs. Within public systems, these are not the flagships (based on traditional academic criteria), and a significant challenge of their leaders is carving out a distinctive niche. At the time Lynton was writing, institutional missions were often defined in geographic terms. (Admissions recruitment continues to be regional or statewide rather than national for many of these universities.) However, in the intervening decades many urban institutions have begun to alter and align their core academic work around a commitment to meaningful engagement. (The Coalition of Urban and Metropolitan Universities, which currently has eighty-nine members, offers many illustrative examples.) Traditional research universities make substantially greater demands on faculty with regard to research, and a significant proportion of their institutional budgets comes from external grants. These institutions tend to be dominated by traditional academic culture (as we discuss shortly). Nevertheless, some research universities have attempted to weave a commitment to the local community and to engagement into their core activities.

Impediments to Engaged Scholarship at the Urban University

Given the clear challenges facing neighborhoods right outside the walls of our urban universities, why is it that scholarship directed at addressing this state of affairs is not more prevalent? At many institutions, a number of factors conspire to prevent faculty from engagement work. First, universities are "loosely coupled" organizations (Weick, 1976). Each is divided into colleges, departments, centers, and schools, which are further divided into departments populated by largely autonomous faculty members. This atomization is the legacy of the German research university model, and though differentiation has certainly proven to be a useful strategy for developing new bodies of knowledge, it has splintered the faculty. It is also the case that power is diffuse in loosely coupled systems. Because the units have specialized knowledge (neither the board of trustees nor the president is about to tell the biochemistry department what to teach), any change must occur through discussion and persuasion rather than dictates from above.

A second factor impeding such change has to do with predominant academic norms, what we call Platonization (Benson, Harkavy, & Hartley, 2005). Plato advocated the search for theoretical knowledge as the primary end of the academy—knowledge for knowledge's sake. The dead hand of Plato stretches out across the academy even today. The system of peer review rewards (and publishes) scholarship that reflects familiar modes of inquiry and clearly advances disciplinary interests. Although there are scholarly venues for practice-oriented research as well as applied research, often these are not accorded equivalent status when promotion and tenure decisions are made. This is particularly true in academic disciplines outside of the professions. In her study examining faculty attitudes, O'Meara (2002) concludes that "many faculty hold values and beliefs about service scholarship that doubt and devalue its scholarly purpose, nature, and products" (p. 76). Although Boyer's ideas have sparked debate at many institutions, it has influenced expectations of scholarly production at comparatively few research universities (Braxton, Luckey, & Holland, 2002). Even if a report to the board of a community agency demonstrates disciplinary virtuosity, at the vast majority of research universities it does not count as scholarship: small wonder that faculty members, particularly those working toward promotion and tenure, are cautious about becoming involved. They are bound by "ancient Customs and Habitudes," the same enemy of educational progress that Franklin pointed to in 1789 (Best, 1962, p. 173). Even at institutions that promote engaged scholarship, faculty face competing commitments. As Daly and Dee (2006) note in their examination of turnover at urban public universities, faculty members experience "tensions between institutional priorities for applied scholarship and research traditions within academic disciplines. The result is often a conflict between the values of traditional discipline-based scholarship and institutional emphasis on social problems that by their very nature are interdisciplinary" (p. 784). Institutions experience role conflict as well: "Espoused commitments to access, applied research, and community outreach may be diminished by efforts to advance upward in the prestige hierarchy" (p. 784).

This brings us to a third factor mitigating against an engagement agenda—the reckless pursuit of research dollars. Late in 1944, President Roosevelt, highly impressed by the accomplishments of the Office of Scientific Research and Development, asked Vannevar Bush to draft a long-term plan for postwar science. Bush's report, *Science, the Endless Frontier,* which he delivered in 1945, profoundly influenced America's science policy. This investment produced new knowledge and resulted in the dramatic expansion of many universities. However, it also produced distortions of the academic mission of many institutions. Derek Bok (2003) explored the potential of commercialization to distort fundamental academic values to subsume a broader public purpose. According to Bok, "the commercialization of higher education" not only fundamentally contradicts traditional "academic standards and institutional integrity" but, in a "process [which] may be irreversible," threatens to sacrifice "essential values that are all but impossible to restore" (p. 208).

Community-based participatory research that is rooted in sustained and reciprocal partnerships often takes considerably more time to bear fruit than a research project in which the principal investigator (the faculty member) defines the questions and determines who ought to be consulted and what is relevant to report. This is a challenge for faculty who want to work collaboratively with community members but must demonstrate scholarly productivity by conventional measures (i.e., numbers of publications). It is particularly perilous for those marching to the insistent beat of the tenure clock. Although each discipline has the capacity to speak to real-world problems, real-world problems are highly complex, and interventions are unlikely to yield measurable (and therefore publishable) results in the short term. And when findings are published, they address concerns and audiences that tend to be outside of disciplinary boundaries. Thus, engaged scholarship is a risky proposition for assistant professors at institutions where the number of publications and the placement of those publications determines a professor's future. Absent publications—or publications in the "right" journals—faculty colleagues tend to view community-based work, even if it requires disciplinary expertise, as fitting squarely into the category of "service," a vastly subordinate consideration in the calculus of promotion and tenure at research universities.

Finally, it should be noted that some senior faculty members at urban universities question the very propriety of engagement. The attitude is aptly summed up in the comment made by a senior administrator at one institution we have visited: "This is a university, not a social service agency." We agree. What is problematic is that such attitudes reflect a profound misunderstanding of the nature of engaged scholarship, which has the capacity to produce knowledge that can resolve real-world problems *and* advance the discipline. Fortunately, significant numbers of faculty members are predisposed to supporting engagement work generally. For example, a recent survey of 32,840 faculty found that 60 percent believed it is important to "prepare students for responsible citizenship," and one in five (21.7 percent) reported that they had taught a service-learning course in the past two years (Lindholm, Astin, Sax, & Korn, 2002). Others, however, contend that higher education ought to focus solely on producing and conveying knowledge. What purpose that knowledge serves (if any) is, from this perspective, immaterial (Fish, 2003). This takes us to the heart of the matter. The idea of value neutrality is a potent inhibiting force to engagement work. Needless to say, such a stance rests uneasily with the notion of working alongside community partners toward a common cause or a more just community or society. As historians Benson and Harkavy (2002) put it:

> [Although] "value-free" advocates did not completely dominate American universities during the 1914–1989 period . . . they were numerous enough to strongly reinforce traditional academic opposition to real-world problem-solving activity, and they significantly helped bring about the rapid civic disengagement of American universities. (p. 13)

In sum, promoting change as inherently value laden as engagement requires a shift not only in organizational policies or structures, but also in the very norms that shape institutional life (Hartley, 2003).

Promoting Engaged Scholarship at Urban Universities

Successful efforts to promote engaged scholarship must ensure that these activities are aligned with institutional norms. Some institutions have accomplished this by broadening their definition of scholarship, for example building on the vision Ernest Boyer presented in *Scholarship Reconsidered* (Boyer, 1996; O'Meara & Rice, 2005). The University of Wisconsin, Milwaukee, for example, recognizes and rewards teaching as an important scholarly activity (Ciccone, 2006). In many instances this involves placing engagement activities within the existing faculty assessment framework of research, teaching, and service. Indiana University Purdue University at Indianapolis (IUPUI) underwent a significant institutional transformation under the leadership of William Plater, who served as Executive Vice Chancellor and Dean of the Faculties from 1987 to 2006 (Bringle, Hatcher, & Holland, 2007). The university's tenure and promotion guidelines were reshaped to encourage engagement in its urban surroundings: "As the state's only designated metropolitan university, IUPUI has specific opportunities and responsibilities to engage in research that draw on and supports the urban environment" (Bringle et al., 2007, p. 65). In addition to encouraging applied research, faculty members who use their scholarly expertise in the service of the community can document these activities and use them as a basis for a tenure and promotion decision. Between a fifth and a third of all faculty members promoted or granted tenure each year do so by demonstrating excellence in professional service (as well as competency in teaching and research) (Bringle et al., 2007).

At the vast majority of research universities, however, the scholarship of discovery remains the predominant model (Braxton et al., 2002). A comprehensive report generated by a faculty member for a community agency that demonstrates disciplinary acumen might be an acceptable document in a tenure and promotion dossier at some institutions. However, for many more-traditional research universities, peer-reviewed articles in top-tier journals remain the gold standard. At these institutions, institutional conceptions of what constitutes "scholarship" are quite narrow. Some faculty members are able to navigate these circumstances by applying certain methodological approaches that allow for collaboration with community members, such as participatory action research. Of course, such methods may be met with a measure of skepticism by departments populated by more-traditional scholars. Alternatively, faculty members may choose to engage in community-based research knowing that along with activities they engaged in that are useful to their community partners (e.g., providing expertise or producing reports), they will also need to produce peer-reviewed articles. It should be noted that even in circumstances where the definition of scholarship is constrained, an institutional identity that underscores the value of community-based or problem-solving research can create an environment that is conducive to engaged scholarship. When distinguished political philosopher Amy Gutmann assumed the presidency of the University of Pennsylvania, building on work of her predecessors Judith Rodin and Sheldon Hackney, Gutmann unveiled her vision for the university termed the Penn Compact. The Compact emphasizes the University's Franklinian roots through its tripartite goals of increased access, integrating knowledge (using experts from many disciplines to solve pressing real-world problems), and engaging locally and globally. The powerful symbolism of the Penn Compact, which has been backed up by a variety of initiatives, has produced an environment that encourages community-based teaching and research.

There are numerous other ways that urban universities (even traditional ones) can support and encourage engaged scholarship. First, some faculty members are unsure how to make connections with appropriate potential partners. Many universities have centers whose role is to promote civic or community engagement. These centers typically have developed a range of long-standing mutually beneficial relationships with community, civic, and governmental organizations (Maurasse, 2001). They therefore have the expertise to help faculty identify community partners whose interests are aligned with their scholarly agendas. This is particularly important in large urban areas where community organizations, especially public schools, face daunting challenges and have many demands on their time. The presence of an existing partnership can spell the difference between a faculty member being granted access or not.

Institutions can also provide tangible support. Many institutions now have internal grants programs. Tufts University's Jonathan M. Tisch College of Citizenship and Public Service provides seed money to faculty to promote engaged research in four distinct areas: "research about processes of civic participation; research about how young people develop civic values and skills; research that is civically engaged, produced in collaboration with community representatives; and research about public problems (public policy research)" (Hollister, Mead, & Wilson, 2006, p. 43). Penn has a long-standing program that provides grants for faculty to develop Academically Based Community Service (ABCS) courses (Penn's term for service-learning.) Faculty who receive these grants receive support on campus and in the community from the Netter Center for Community Partnerships staff. Often, these experiences lead to research opportunities in the urban context.

To offer one example, William Labov is a distinguished professor of sociolinguistics. A number of years ago Labov received a grant to develop an ABCS course working in several West Philadelphia schools. In the context of the course, Labov and his students conducted literacy research. Over time, they created a reading program designed to isolate each student's particular reading errors. They created a series of linguistically appropriate and culturally engaging reading materials whose themes were based on life in West Philadelphia and neighborhoods with which the children were familiar. This pilot research led to grants from the U.S. Department of Education and the National Science Foundation that enabled Labov to expand his research in Philadelphia and to several other cities. The Netter Center helped Labov recruit work-study students to be tutors and trained them in his methodology. The Individualized Reading Program (IRP) developed in Penn's Linguistics Laboratory by William Labov and his colleague Bettina Baker for use by America Reads tutors and teachers has been the main vehicle of instruction for the program. From 1997 to 2009, approximately 1,190 students have worked with Labov in the West Philadelphia community to raise reading levels of inner-city children. Not only has Labov's engaged scholarship made a difference in the lives of children in Philadelphia and beyond, it also positioned him to make important contributions to the field of sociolinguistics.

Looking Toward the Future

Creating programs to support individual faculty members is an important part of an effective engagement strategy. Looking forward we are convinced that one of the significant areas for growth in engaged scholarship involves drawing together scholars from a range of disciplines to address significant real-world problems. In 1910, John Dewey (1997) argued that knowledge and learning are most effective when human beings work collaboratively to solve specific, strategic, real-world problems. "Thinking," he wrote, "begins in . . . a *forked road* situation, a situation which is ambiguous, which presents a dilemma, which poses alternatives" (p. 9). A focus on universal problems (such as poverty, unequal health care, substandard housing, hunger, and inadequate, unequal education) as they are manifested locally is, in our judgment, the best way to apply Dewey's proposition in practice, and it is also the best way for research universities to transcend narrow disciplinary interests and fulfill their intellectual and civic promise.

The increased emphasis on interdisciplinary work to solve pressing real-world problems is leading to more broad-based research efforts. Tufts University is bringing together faculty from a number of disciplines to collaborate on projects (Hollister et al., 2006). Borrowing (and slightly amending) Singleton, Burack, and Hirsch's (1997) term, establishing and supporting such groups creates "enclaves" of engaged scholars who can lend mutual aid and support through shared research projects.

Consider the experience of Mary Summers, a senior fellow at Penn's Fels institute of Government at Penn. A few years ago, Summers developed an ABCS course with the support of the Netter Center. Summers and her students began with a simple and powerful question: Why do only 60 percent of Philadelphia residents eligible for food stamps participate in the program? The initial research led Summers to seek additional partners. Working with the Greater Philadelphia Coalition Against Hunger and the Philadelphia Higher Education Network for Neighborhood Development (PHENND), a network of thirty-six colleges and universities in the greater Philadelphia area that support community-based work, Summers became principal investigator for a research project funded by the USDA that ultimately involved faculty and students from fourteen area colleges and universities (Porter, Summers, Toton, & Aisenstein, 2008). The campaign successfully screened 7,463 potential clients and enrolled 2,123 people. Not only did the research produced by the group identify bureaucratic hurdles that prevented greater enrollment, but the researchers were able to use their findings to exert pressure to change policies in order to eliminate those barriers. (For example, County Assistance Offices expanded the use of phone interviews rather than requiring face-to-face interviews to become enrolled.) Helping someone eligible for food stamps enroll is a worthwhile service (and Summers and her collaborators certainly succeeded on that count), but collaborating with colleagues from institutions across the city, community members, and local agencies in order to conduct research and, in addition to producing publications, being able to use the resulting new knowledge to challenge and change public policy is exemplary scholarly engagement.

Such examples point to a tremendous potential opportunity. Many cities have more than one institution of higher learning. Imagine what collaborative research projects might be possible if faculty from various institutions with similar interests but disparate disciplinary backgrounds could be brought together to address pressing local problems. Such efforts have the capacity not only to legitimize engaged scholarship but to bring to fulfillment William Rainey Harper's vision of a "new type of university," one that exists not merely to advance narrow disciplinary interests or one hobbled by popular media-driven (and ultimately, highly dubious) yardsticks of merit, but as the true "expression of urban civilization, and which is compelled to meet the demands of an urban environment" (Harper, 1905, p. 158).

References

Benson, L., & Harkavy, I. (2002, October 6–7). *Truly engaged and truly democratic cosmopolitan civic universities, community schools, and development of the democratic good of society in the 21st century.* Paper presented at the Seminar on the Research University as Local Citizen, University of California, San Diego.

Benson, L., Harkavy, I., & Hartley, M. (2005). Integrating a commitment to the public good into the institutional fabric. In A. J. Kezar, T. Chambers, & J. Burkhardt (Eds.), *Higher education for the public good: Emerging voices from a national movement* (pp. 185–216). San Francisco: Jossey-Bass.

Benson, L., Harkavy, I., & Puckett, J. (2007) Dewey's Dream Universities and Democracies in an age of Education Reform. Philadelphia, PA: Temple University Press.

Bok, D. (2003). *Universities in the marketplace: The commercialization of higher education.* Princeton, NJ: Princeton University Press.

Boyer, E. (1990). *Scholarship reconsidered.* Princeton, NJ: The Carnegie Foundation for the Advancement of Teaching.

Boyer, E. (1996). The scholarship of engagement. *Journal of Public Service and Outreach, 1*(Spring).

Boyte, H. C., & Kari, N. N. (2000). Renewing the democratic spirit in American colleges and universities. In T. Ehrlich (Ed.), *Civic Responsibility and higher education* (pp. 36–59). Phoenix, AZ: Orynx Press.

Braxton, J., Luckey, W., & Holland, P. (2002). *Institutionalizing a broader view of scholarship through Boyer's four domains* (Vol. 29). San Francisco: Jossey-Bass.

Bringle, R. G., Hatcher, J. A., & Holland, B. (2007). Conceptualizing civic engagement: Orchestrating change at a metropolitan university. *Metropolitan Universities, 18*(3), 57–74.

Ciccone, A. (2006). The scholarship of teaching and learning in the engaged university. In S. L. Percy, N. L. Zimpher, & M. J. Bruckardt (Eds.), *Creating a new kind of university* (pp. 136–146). Bolton, MA: Anchor Publishing.

Cochran, T.C. (1972). *Business in American Life: A History.* New York: McGraw-Hill.

Daly, C. J., & Dee, J. R. (2006). Greener pastures: Faculty turnover intent in urban public universities. *Journal of Higher Education, 77*(5), 776–803.

Dewey, J. (1997). *How we think.* Boston: D.C. Heath.

Fish, S. (2003, March 16). Aim low. *The Chronicle of Higher Education.*

Fox, R. K., & Trouhaft, S. (2006). *Shared prosperity, stronger regions: An agenda for rebuilding America's older core cities.* Oakland, CA: PolicyLink.

Hahn, A., with Coonerty, C., & Peaslee, L. (2003). *Colleges and universities as economic anchors: Profiles of promising practices.* Waltham, MA: Brandeis University, Heller Graduate School of Social Policy and Management, Institute for Sustainable Development/ Center for Youth and Communities and POLICYLINK.

Harkavy, I., & Hartley, M. (2008). Pursuing Franklin's democratic vision for higher education. *Peer Review, 10*(23), 13–17.

Harkavy, I., & Puckett, J. (1994). Lessons from Hull House for the contemporary urban university. *Social Service Review, 68*(3), 299–321.

Harkavy, I., & Wiewel, W. (1995). Overview: University-community partnerships: Current state and future issues. *Metropolitan University, 6*(3), 7–14.

Harkavy, I., & Zuckerman, H. (1999). *Eds and meds: Cities' hidden assets.* Washington, DC: The Brookings Institution.

Harper, W. R. (1905). *The trend in higher education.* Chicago: University of Chicago Press.

Hartley, M. (2003). "There is no way without a because": Revitalization of purpose at three liberal arts colleges. *The Review of Higher Education, 27*(1), 75–102.

Hartley, M., & Hollander, E. (2005). The elusive ideal: Civic learning and higher education. In S. Fuhrman & M. Lazerson (Eds.), *Institutions of democracy: The public schools* (pp. 252–276). Oxford, England: Oxford University Press.

Hollister, R. M., Mead, M., & Wilson, N. (2006). Infusing active citizenship throughout a research university: The Tisch College of Citizenship and Public Service at Tufts University. *Metropolitan Universities, 17*(3), 38–55.

Lindholm, J. A., Astin, A. W., Sax, L. J., & Korn, W. S. (2002). *The American college teacher: National norms for 2001–2002.* Los Angeles: Higher Education Research Institute, UCLA Graduate School of Education & Information Studies.

Lynton, E. A. (1991). *The mission of metropolitan universities in the utilization of knowledge: A policy analysis* (No. 8). Boston: New England Resource Center for Higher Education, University of Massachusetts, Boston.

Maurasse, D. (2001). *Beyond the campus: How colleges and universities form partnerships with their communities.* New York: Routledge.

O'Meara, K. (2002). Uncovering the values in faculty evaluation of service as scholarship. *Review of Higher Education, 26*(1), 57–80.

O'Meara, K., & Rice, R. E. (Eds.). (2005). *Faculty priorities reconsidered.* San Francisco: Jossey-Bass.

Porter, J., Summers, M., Toton, S., & Aisenstein, H. (2008). Service-learning with a food stamp enrollment campaign: Community and student benefits. *Michigan Journal of Community Service Learning* (Spring), 66–75.

Reuben, J. (1996). *The making of the modern university: Intellectual transformation and the marginalization of morality.* Chicago: University of Chicago Press.

Singleton, S., Burack, C. A., & Hirsch, D. J. (1997). *Faculty service enclaves: A summary report.* Boston: University of Massachusetts, Boston.

Weick, K. E. (1976). Educational organizations as loosely coupled systems. *Administrative Science Quarterly, 21,* 1–19.

Student Engagement in Liberal Arts Colleges: Academic Rigor, Quality Teaching, Diversity, and Institutional Change

Scott VanderStoep, Kathleen S. Wise, and Charles Blaich

In this chapter, we explore the elements of a liberal arts education that have been shown to produce high student engagement. In the first section of the chapter we summarize the components that have been shown to maximize student engagement identified in the Wabash National Study of Liberal Arts Education (WNSLAE). The WNSLAE is emerging as the authoritative study of best practices that produce high levels of student achievement, motivation, and engagement. In the second part of the chapter we explore specific measures for which we believe liberal arts institutions should show higher percentages of students scoring high on the measure. For this section we use national data from the National Survey of Student Engagement (NSSE). In the third section of this chapter we explore a specific element on which we believe liberal arts institutions could have a unique advantage over research universities—institutional and curricular improvements. Being able to make flexible changes to educational delivery, we believe, puts liberal arts institutions in an advantageous position to increase student engagement; being able to identify areas of improvement, and to respond to these areas in a fashion that specifically addresses student engagement in a way that is consistent with an institution's mission, allows liberal arts colleges to respond to student-engagement needs more efficiently and effectively. For this section of the chapter, we use one liberal arts institution that has experienced success in responding well to student-engagement data that are not optimal. We describe the strategies that this institution has used to improve their student-engagement data, and the evidence that student engagement changed in response to these interventions.

Good Practices That Promote Student Engagement

What Is the Wabash National Study?

The Wabash National Study of Liberal Arts Education is a longitudinal project designed to investigate and assess the practices and institutional conditions that promote liberal arts education. This study is directed and sponsored by the Center of Inquiry in the Liberal Arts at Wabash College. The Wabash National Study began in 2006 and now includes more than 17,000 students from forty-nine colleges and universities across the country. This project is unique in its design to simultaneously measure, at the individual student level, both outcomes and experiences. This combination is critical because it enables institutions to gauge how students are changing on a variety of outcome measures and to identify the practices, conditions, and interactions that are supporting those changes. This, in turn, helps institutions locate practices, conditions, and interactions they could improve to strengthen student growth on outcomes.

The Wabash National Study has three other important qualities that are designed to facilitate its impact on campus assessment and student learning. First, all of the measures deployed in the study are psychometrically reliable and can be merged with institutional student-level data. Thus, individual scores on student outcome change or student experiences can be connected with grades, retention information, academic major, living unit, or any other information that institutions have about their students. Second, the fact that the project focuses on "liberal arts education" is manifest not in the type of institutions that participate in the study, but in the way that we analyze the data. Specifically, we take "liberal arts education" to be a form of education that, regardless of the institutional setting in which it occurs, aims to promote students' holistic development. A liberal arts education should at once benefit students' critical thinking, their interest in contributing to the arts and sciences, their moral reasoning, their capacity for leadership, their sense of well-being, their openness to different people and ideas, their interest in community involvement, and their curiosity about the world. In essence, it is an education of the mind and the heart. For the purposes of our analyses, this means that we look for high-impact teaching practices and institutional conditions that promote the development of multiple outcomes, from critical thinking to the interest in and openness to new ideas. Third, and finally, the Wabash National Study is not simply an enterprise that provides institutions with lots of data, although that is an essential part of our work. The Center of Inquiry staff, with the assistance of institutional researchers, assessment professionals, teaching center directors, educational researchers, and other faculty and staff from a variety of disciplines and departments, works with representatives from participating institutions to use study data to impact these institutions. This support comes in the form of site visits, on-campus presentations, workshops, institutional retreats, creating cross-institutional collaborations, and a host of other activities that are designed to bring the data into the institution so that people in the campus community can learn from and respond to it. Thus, providing data on student outcomes and experiences is only the first step in a process designed to strengthen institutions and improve student engagement.

In practical terms, then, these qualities mean that the Wabash National Study is intentionally designed to diagnose rather than rank. Our goal is to provide practitioners at institutions with information about conditions and practices that are benefiting their students and help them use that information to improve their institutions, instead of emphasizing how institutions rank relative to one another on any particular outcome.

How Is the Wabash National Study Implemented?

The Wabash National Study is administered to students three times during their college careers—when they first arrive on campus, at the end of their first year, and at the end of their fourth year. Students take about 1.5 hours to complete all of the tests and surveys. The first administration is designed to assess entering students' high school experiences, their demographic characteristics, their educational goals and values, and their scores on our outcome measures at the beginning of their college experience. Some of the questions in the first administration come from the Higher Education Research Institute's Cooperative Institutional Research Program (HERI CIRP) Freshman Survey and the Beginning College Survey of Student Engagement (BCSSE). The outcomes measures that students complete include the following:

- Collegiate Assessment of Academic Proficiency (CAAP) Critical Thinking Test
- Defining Issues Test, Version 2 (DIT-2)
- Ryff Scales of Psychological Well-Being
- Socially Responsible Leadership Scale—Revised Version II
- Need for Cognition Scale
- Miville-Guzman Universality-Diversity Scale—Short Form (M-GUDS-S)

We also administer a number of shorter scales to assess students' academic motivation, interest in contributing to the arts and sciences, openness to diversity and challenge, interest in community involvement, and interest in reading and writing.

The second and third administrations of the study, at the end of students' first and fourth years of college, respectively, include all of the surveys on educational goals and values from the first administration as well as all of the outcomes measures just listed. In addition, to gauge student experiences, we administer the National Survey of Student Engagement (NSSE) along with additional questions about what students are experiencing in and out of the classroom. (Full copies of all of these scales, with the exception of the CAAP Critical Thinking Test, as well as information about the reliability of each scale, are available at www.liberalarts.wabash.edu/.)

What Have We Found So Far?

Before we review our findings to date, it is important to note that we are now in the third year of this project, which means that we have not yet followed a cohort of students through four years of college. Therefore, the findings we describe here focus on the first year of college for students from the nineteen institutions in the first round of the Wabash National Study.

Overall, students evidenced small to modest growth in critical thinking and moral reasoning during their first year of college. Second, students changed little on our measures of leadership and well-being. Finally, students declined on our measures of their interest in and

133

openness to diversity, their interest in contributing to the arts and sciences, their interest in political and social involvement, and their academic motivation. As this project is still in its early stages, we do not yet know whether these declines are the result of the short-term impact of students' unrealistic expectations about college or if they are due to students' fatigue at the end of their first year, nor do we yet know whether these declines will be reversed in the second, third, and fourth years of college. However, given our approach, we are more interested in determining whether teaching practices and institutional conditions account for the individual variability in student growth, or decline, on the outcomes than we are in aggregate changes on the outcome measures. That is, are there student experiences that correlate with the extent to which students grow or decline on the outcomes?

To address this question, we factor analyzed approximately two hundred items from the Wabash National Study that asked students about their experiences at college. (The details of these analyses can be found at http://www.liberalarts.wabash.edu/study-research/.)

These questions covered a wide range of academic and cocurricular experiences, including items that asked students to report on the extent to which they thought that their faculty were interested in teaching, the amount of time they spent on homework, the frequency with which they interacted with student affairs staff, and extent to which they experienced positive and negative interactions with their peers. Ultimately, we identified six factors that focused on the following areas of student experience:

1. The quality of teaching and interactions with faculty
2. The level of academic challenge and expectations
3. The frequency of diversity experiences
4. The frequency of interactions with faculty and staff
5. The quality and frequency of interactions with peers
6. The frequency of cooperative learning

Of these factors, the first three have the strongest overall impact on our outcomes. Indeed, the first and the third are positively related to growth on over 90 percent of our various outcome measures. The second factor, focusing on academic challenge, is correlated with growth on over 80 percent of our outcome measures. Table 1 illustrates the correlations between these three factors and the outcome measures in the Wabash National Study.

A review of some of the specific questions that are included in each of these factors may provide a better picture of the kinds of effective experiences that emerged from our analyses.

1. Good Teaching and High-Quality Interactions with Faculty includes items such as:
   - Most faculty with whom I have had contact are genuinely interested in students.
   - Most faculty with whom I have had contact are interested in helping students grow in more than just academic areas.
   - I receive feedback from faculty on my level of performance in a timely manner.
   - Non-classroom interactions with faculty have had a positive influence on my personal growth, values, and attitudes.
   - Since coming to this institution, I have developed a close, personal relationship with at least one faculty member.

Table 10.1 Correlation between Good Practices and Outcomes

	Good Teaching	Academic Challenge	Diversity Experiences
CAAP Critical Thinking Test	+		
Defining Issues Test 2	+	+	+
Need for Cognition Scale	+	+	+
Ryff Scales of Psychological Well Being	+	+	+
Socially Responsible Leadership Scale	+	+	+
Miville-Guzman Universality-Diversity Scale	+	+	+
Life Goals and Orientation toward Learning Scales			
Contribution to the Arts			+
Contribution to the Sciences	+	+	+
Political and Social Involvement	+	+	+
Academic Motivation	+	+	+
Openness to Diversity and Challenge	+	+	+
Positive Attitude toward Literacy	+	+	+

+/– indicates significant positive or negative relationship.

- Faculty give clear explanations.
- Faculty effectively review and summarize the material.
- Class time is used effectively.

2. Academic Challenge and High Expectations includes items such as:
   - Worked harder than you thought you could to meet an instructor's standards or expectations.
   - The institution emphasizes spending significant amounts of time studying and on academic work.
   - Asked questions in class or contributed to class discussions.
   - Examinations or assignments required you to write essays.
   - Examinations or assignments required you to argue for or against a particular point of view and defend your argument.
   - Faculty challenged your ideas in class.
   - Courses have helped you understand the historical, political, and social connections of past events.
   - Worked on a paper or project that required integrating ideas or information from various sources.

3. Diversity Experiences includes items such as:
   - Attended a debate or lecture on a current political/social issue during this academic year.
   - Had serious discussions with student affairs staff (e.g., residence hall staff, career counselor, student union or campus activities staff) whose political, social, or religious opinions were different from your own.

135

- Institution emphasizes encouraging contact among students from different economic, social, and racial or ethnic backgrounds.
- Had meaningful and honest discussions about issues related to social justice with diverse students (e.g., students differing from you in race, national origin, values, religion, political views) while attending this college.

The experiences included in each of these factors simultaneously impact outcomes such as critical thinking, moral reasoning, leadership, well-being, interest in contributing to the arts and science, and a host of other measures. In essence, having faculty who are caring, challenging, and competent in the classroom, engaging in work that is both conceptually challenging and effortful, and having meaningful interactions with people and ideas that are different from your own promotes growth on a wide range of qualities. Thus, we see emerging in our analyses the kinds of teaching practices and institutional conditions that are at the heart of a liberal arts education.

To our surprise, the factors that focused on the frequency of student-faculty and student-staff interactions, on peer interactions, and on cooperative learning did not have a very strong impact on our outcome measures. There are a number of reasons why this may have occurred. For example, it is possible that our survey questions did not adequately assess the quality of the cooperative learning experiences in which students were engaged. Or, perhaps students with lower academic performance are more likely to have frequent interactions with faculty and staff than students who are doing well. It is also possible that the kinds of experiences in these last three factors matter more in the second, third, and fourth year of college. We will have more information about these factors after the last survey administration at the end of students' fourth year of college, and we will then be able to examine whether these factors have more of an impact on outcomes after the first year of college.

Another possible explanation for the limited effect of the factors of interactions with faculty/staff, interaction with peers, and cooperative learning may be that they are related in some way to the three factors of good teaching, academic challenge, and diversity experiences. For example, it may be that students see good teachers as those who also are more likely to use cooperative learning. We designed our analyses so that we could identify the unique effects of each factor. Using the example just given, we ask if cooperative learning has an impact after taking good teaching, academic challenge, diversity experiences, and the other two factors into account. It is, therefore, possible that after taking good teaching into account, cooperative learning does not account for any growth on the outcome measures. Similarly, once the quality of student-faculty interactions is taken into account, the frequency with which students interact with faculty may not account for additional growth on the outcomes.

What Are the Implications of These Good Practices for Improving Student Engagement?

The practices that we have identified will not surprise any faculty or staff member who is familiar with Chickering and Gamson's (1987) famous list of seven good practices. But there are important qualities about these findings that cut against the conventional wisdom that many teachers bring to their encounters with assessment data.

First, self-report data from students about their experiences are important. Even though students' impressions about the quality and substance of their interactions with faculty, staff, and their peers is surely subjective, in our analyses, it still matters. In this study, students' reports of what they experience predict their growth or decline on independent outcome measures. We are not arguing that students can accurately self-assess their growth on outcomes. Indeed, some of our findings indicate that they cannot (Bowman, 2008). However, students' reports on whether teaching is organized and clear or whether assignments are asking them to perform cognitively challenging tasks does tell us about something about whether or not they are learning.

When we talk to faculty at Wabash National Study institutions, we occasionally hear that students do not understand the more subtle and nuanced tactics that faculty may use in class, or that catering to a student's sense of organization or clarity may eliminate richer pedagogical approaches that will ultimately benefit the student. Although this may or may not be true, we have consistently been surprised in our many conversations with students by the degree to which they can describe complicated pedagogical approaches that their instructors use and why or why not these approaches are effective. Thus, data from the surveys and assessments in the Wabash National Study and information from our conversations with students seem to suggest that students may be in a better position to understand what they are experiencing than we are.

Second, there is exceptional variation within our institutions in the extent to which students experience good practices. As faculty, we often tacitly think of student experience at our institutions as having some core or signature qualities. Faculty will talk about "how we teach at Wabash" or "how we teach at Hope" and refer to some set of good practices or pedagogical strategies that are thought to be especially pervasive at their institution. Although we do not doubt that faculty at an institution may collectively value specific pedagogies or practices, Wabash National Study data are striking in the extraordinary degree to which students' experience of the good practices varies within institutions. Figure 1 illustrates

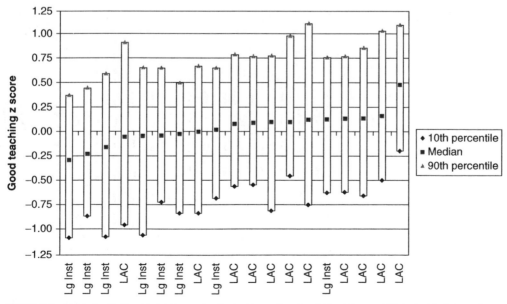

FIGURE 10.1. Within-Institution Variability in the Scale Measuring Good Teaching and High-Quality Interactions with Faculty for Nineteen Wabash National Study Institutions

this variability for one of the good practices—Good Teaching and High-Quality Interactions with Faculty—but tremendous variability exists within each institution for all of the high-impact practices identified in our study.

One way to think about this within-institution variability is that, rather than a singular "Wabash College" that all students experience, there are many different Wabash Colleges. Different groups of students attend these "different" colleges. Some students at Wabash report experiences that are as good as or better than those at any institution in the study. These are the students whom faculty imagine when they think of their best work in and out of the classroom. On the other hand, students in another group at Wabash experience a very different kind of institution than this first group of students. They report classroom experiences and interactions with faculty that are as poor as those at institutions with the lowest overall levels of the good practices. The range of experiences in our institutions may seem daunting, but it is, in fact, a reservoir of data from which we can draw information to improve student engagement. By examining the range of student experiences, we can attempt to answer the following questions: Who are the students in "good Wabash" and "bad Wabash"? What accounts for the powerful differences between these two groups? And what can we learn from the experiences of these students that can be profitably replicated or profitably reduced to improve the experience of all of our students?

Finally, there is considerable room for improvement even if we focus on what is typical rather than concentrating on the best and worst of what students are experiencing. For virtually every good practice that we measured, the majority of students, regardless of the type of institution they attended, reported experiencing these good practices only "sometimes" or "occasionally." This means that the modal response to questions about how often students have been asked to work on a paper or project that required integrating ideas or information from various sources, to take exams that required them to argue for or against a particular point of view and defend their arguments, and to have serious conversations with students who are different from them is "sometimes." This is not sufficient.

That students report generally moderate levels of the good practices provides another possible explanation for their lack of change on our outcome measures. On the whole, perhaps students are simply not encountering high-impact practices and experiences in college at the levels necessary for growth. In terms of increasing the level of good practices that students experience, every institution in our study has room for improvement, even those with the highest overall levels of good practices and student engagement. This suggests that many institutions can benefit from looking at the list of good practices identified in the Wabash National Study and finding ways to increase their students' exposure to them and, in turn, increase student engagement.

Engagement in Liberal Arts Compared to Research Universities

The Wabash National Study of Liberal Arts Education identifies the institutional best practices that promote students' cognitive and motivational growth. In this section, we identify ways in which liberal arts colleges are uniquely qualified to increase student engagement. That liberal arts college students experience advantages in student engagement is not a new finding (e.g., Astin, 1999; Kuh & Hu, 2001). In fact, some of the adaptive effects seem to persist beyond the college years (Pascarella, Cruce, Wolniak, & Blaich, 2005). Previous empirical work by the NSSE staff identified five clusters of student engagement—academic challenge, active and collaborative learning, student-faculty interaction, enriching educational experiences, and supportive campus environment. On all five of these measures, students at liberal arts colleges report experiencing greater levels than students at research universities.

As a framework to understand the potential impact of liberal arts colleges on student engagement, we use the indicators measured in the NSSE. Specifically, we have categorized the relevant NSSE measures into seven different domains of engagement. These domains are identified in the column headings of Table 2. (We recognize that these distinctions are somewhat arbitrary and that other scholars might construct different domains. Still, we postulate that student engagement is multidimensional. We simply propose it as a useful way to understand different types of engagement.) Down each column, then, are measures of the seven engagement domains, which we have taken from the NSSE. There are clearly other indicators of engagement, but given that many of the measures from the Wabash National Study also come from the NSSE, we have decided to use just the NSSE in constructing this framework. Clearly, other measures from other instruments besides the NSSE could be used, and we encourage this type of exploration to gain a deeper understanding of student engagement. For our purposes, we focus our discussion on the NSSE. In the table, we have coded the various indicators to correspond to the three best practices identified in the Wabash National Study, and described in the previous section. Those elements in italics correspond to academic rigor. Those elements that are underlined correspond to high-quality teaching. Those elements in bold correspond to diversity experiences. Next, we identify ways in which liberal arts colleges, because of the characteristics inherent in these institutions, could provide superior engagement experiences for their students. We then compare our hypotheses to national data from the NSSE.

It is important to remember, as pointed out earlier in the chapter, that although students at liberal arts colleges report greater amounts of experiences with the three best practices that produce high-quality student outcomes, a liberal arts setting is neither necessary nor sufficient to have these practices present on campus (and therefore to produce the subsequent student achievement). For example, there are liberal arts institutions that lack components of at least one of the best practices identified in the previous section of this chapter. Conversely, there are major research universities in which students report high levels of the best practices of rigor, quality teaching, and diversity experiences. However, the data from the WNSLAE indicate that the characteristics of liberal arts institutions—specifically with respect to size of institution, class size, and collaborative opportunities with faculty—make it more likely that students will experience these best practices in liberal arts settings.

To make our case that liberal arts colleges afford the opportunity for advantages in these three domains, we will, where appropriate, reference data from the *2008 Institutional Report* of the National Survey of Student Engagement (available online at http://nsse.iub.edu/2008_ Institutional_Report/). Although NSSE does not distinguish between research university and liberal arts college, per se, the report does disaggregate the data by Carnegie classification. Comparing Baccalaureate Arts/Sciences (Bac/A&S) institutions to Research University/Very

Table 10.2 Domains of Engagement

Academic Engagement in the Classroom	Academic Engagement outside the Classroom	Nonacademic Engagement	Mentoring	Service	Diversity Experiences	Peer Learning
Asking questions in class	*High-level writing*	Attending fine/performing arts events	Electronically communicated with professor	Tutoring	Discussed class ideas with other students outside of class	Worked with other students on projects during class
Class presentations	*Integrating multiple ideas*	Exercise	Electronically completed an assignment	Community-based learning	Serious conversations with students of different races or ethnicities	Worked with other students to prepare assignments
Diverse perspectives in class discussions	*Integrating different courses*	Spiritual life	Discussed academic progress with professor	Volunteer work	Serious conversations with students of different religious or political views	Participate in a learning community
Worked with others on class projects	Worked harder than you thought to meet professor's expectation	Quality of relationships with other students	Discussed career plans with professor		Examined your own views	
High-level coursework emphases (e.g., synthesis)	Number of assigned textbooks	Quality of relationships with faculty	Discussed course ideas with professor outside of class		**Imagine someone else's perspective**	
Senior experience	Number of assigned papers	Quality of relationships with college personnel	Worked with professor on activities besides coursework		**Learned something that changed the way you thought**	
Independent study	Number of assigned problem sets	Working for pay	Worked with professor on research		**Second language training**	
	Internship	Cocurricular involvement	High-quality academic advising		**Study abroad**	
	Preparing for class	Socializing				

Note. The elements in italics, bold, or underlined font indicate components of the undergraduate educational experiences on which liberal arts colleges could capitalize because of the features of the liberal arts setting. The components in italics correspond to academic rigor; the underlined components correspond to good teaching; the components in bold correspond to diversity experiences.

High Research Activity (RU/VH) institutions would provide indirect estimate of the differences between liberal arts colleges and larger universities. This is based on the assumptions a majority of Bac/A&S institutions are liberal arts colleges and that RU/VH institutions would normally not be liberal arts colleges.

Academic Rigor

The first element of successful student outcomes, as identified by the Wabash National Study, is academic rigor. Liberal arts colleges are particularly well suited for emphasizing high-level coursework such as analysis and synthesis. Liberal arts colleges would tend to have smaller class sizes. A possible manifestation, although not a necessary manifestation, of smaller class sizes would be assignments would be the advantage of assignments that require higher-level intellectual engagement. Table 2 identifies several elements, highlighted in italics, on which liberal arts institutions may show higher levels of rigor than research universities. The NSSE data indicate that, indeed, more liberal arts students than research university students report higher levels of rigor on these items (although the differences are not always large). Indeed, when comparing Bac/A&S institutions to Research University/ Very High Research Activity (RU/VH), slightly more students at Bac/A&S schools report high levels of engagement than at RU/VH institutions. Specifically, more students at Bac/A&S institutions reported that they "very often" engaged in *analyzing the basic elements of an idea* (43 percent vs. 35 percent), *synthesizing and organizing ideas, information, and experiences* (33 percent vs. 26 percent), and *making judgments of about the value of information* (31 percent vs. 24 percent).

One of the fundamental skills that can be developed in college is writing. Teaching writing and grading writing take time. It requires engagement on the part of both students and faculty. It would seem plausible that students in the liberal arts setting would provide more opportunities for writing. The NSSE data provide some support for this claim. Specifically, slightly more students at Bac/A&S than at RU/VH reported more often: writing between one to four 20+-page papers during an academic year (14 percent vs. 11 percent), writing at least 11 papers between 5 and 19 pages (12 percent vs. 8 percent), and writing at least 11 papers less than 5 pages (40 percent vs. 30 percent). Although these differences are not overwhelming, we see some evidence that the liberal arts setting provides a unique opportunity for engagement in the form of student writing.

Another measure of academic engagement is integrating multiple ideas. More students at Bac/A&S than at RU/VH institutions reported that they "very often" worked on *projects that involved integrating multiple ideas or sources* (36 percent vs. 26 percent). Similarly, but to a smaller degree, more students at Bac/A&S than at RU/VH institutions reported that they "very often" *put together ideas from different courses* (18 percent vs. 14 percent).

Good Teaching

The second element of successful student outcomes, as identified by the Wabash National Study, is good teaching and high-quality interaction with faculty. Table 10.2 has six indicators from the NSSE, set in underlined text, that presumably are related to good teaching and interaction with faculty. The national data indicate that students at Bac/A&S institutions show advantages over students at RU/VH institutions on all six of these measures, although it is also the case for several of these indicators that the difference between the two types of institutions is quite small.

The largest differences, in terms of percentage, between Bac/A&S and RU/VH institutions occurred for discussing progress with instructor and quality of advising. Specifically, 21 percent of students at Bac/A&S institutions reported that they "very often" *discussed academic progress* with their professor compared to 14 percent of students at RU/VH. Similarly, 35 percent of students Bac/A&S institutions reported that the quality of their academic advising was "excellent" compared to 29 percent of students at RU/VH.

On the other four dimensions, students at Bac/A&S institutions showed very slight advantages over students at RU/VH institutions. Specifically, compared to students at RU/VH institutions, more students at Bac/A&S institutions reported "very often" *discussing career plans* with faculty (11 percent vs. 8 percent), reported "very often" *discussing course ideas with a professor outside of class* and reported "very often" *working with a professor on activities outside of class* (8 percent vs. 5 percent); also, more students at Bac/A&S institutions reported that they either had conducted or intended to conduct research with a professor (45 percent vs. 43 percent). The differences in these four indicators are obviously quite small, so any one indicator by itself is not convincing evidence. However, taken together, coupled with the larger differences in *discussing academic progress* and receiving high-quality advising, the differences make a fairly strong case that students at liberal arts colleges have a unique opportunity to receive the positive engagement opportunities that correlate with increased cognitive and motivational outcomes.

Diversity Experiences

Examining the diversity experiences measured in the NSSE, several of the indicators relate to the good practice of promoting diversity experiences (set in bold in Table 2). More students at Bac/A&S than at RU/VH institutions reported that they very often *included diverse perspectives (e.g., race, religion) in class* (27 percent vs. 20 percent). More students at Bac/A&S than at RU/VH institutions reported that they very often *tried to better understand someone else's perspective* (25 percent vs. 20 percent). More students at Bac/A&S than at RU/VH institutions reported that they very often *learned something that changed the way they thought about an issue* (29 percent vs. 22 percent). More students at Bac/A&S than at RU/VH institutions reported that they either had completed or intended to complete second-language coursework (71 percent vs. 62 percent). There was only a small advantage for Bac/A&S students over RU/HV students in the percentage who had studied or intended to study abroad (60 percent vs. 56 percent).

The data from this analysis and other empirical investigations indicate that liberal arts institutions enjoy an advantage with respect to at least the opportunity to offer students higher levels of academic engagement than at research universities. However, one important point to bear in mind is that, despite the empirical edge demonstrated by liberal arts colleges, there is still much within-institution variation among all types and sizes of schools (as illustrated in Figure 10.1). For example, on level of academic challenge experienced by students at schools of sizes ranging from several hundred to more than 30,000, Kuh (2003) found that, at almost any given institutional size, at least some students at every institution could be found to have experienced high engagement. This particularly applies to schools the size of traditional liberal arts colleges.

Improving Student Engagement by Changing Institutional Practices

One of the features that we believe distinguishes liberal arts colleges from research universities is their ability to make changes to institutional structure and practice at a faster pace than research universities. In the final section of this paper, we present a case study to illustrate ways in which student engagement is improved through institutional changes. The engagement domain in this case study is improving academic rigor either inside or outside of the classroom. We have focused our discussion on three measures that this institution has examined over a six-year period—students preparing for class, time spent on academic work, and student effort relative to their own perceived capacity.

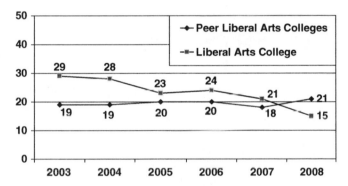

FIGURE 10.2. Percentage of Seniors Who Reported That They "Often" or "Very Often" Came to Class without Completing Assignments from NSSE-Participating Liberal Arts Colleges and the Case-Study Liberal Arts College

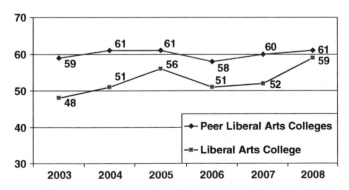

FIGURE 10.3. Percentage of Seniors Who Reported That They "Often" or "Very Often" Worked Harder Than They Thought They Could to Meet an Instructor's Expectations from NSSE-Participating Liberal Arts Colleges and the Case-Study Liberal Arts College

143

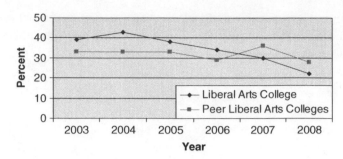

FIGURE 10.4. Percentage of Seniors Who Reported That They Spent Ten Hours per Week or Fewer Preparing for Class from NSSE-Participating Liberal Arts Colleges and the Case-Study Liberal Arts College

The Challenge Facing This Institution

This liberal arts institution received positive student reports on several dimensions it had assessed. This institution has performed well in students' perceptions of high-quality institutional contributions, spiritual development (a goal of this institution), academic advising, physical wellness, and overall satisfaction with their college selection. This liberal arts institution received poorer student reports on two dimensions: diversity experiences and academic rigor. In the final section of this chapter, we describe strategies this institution used to address the issue of increasing student academic engagement.

Strategies Employed by the Institution to Increase Student Engagement

Two Faculty Meetings

The institution first brought the data on student engagement to the faculty as a whole. It dedicated two faculty meetings to improving student engagement. The provost and faculty moderator called a special, extended, evening faculty meeting. Faculty heard a report of the NSSE data, and then broke into groups to discuss strategies for addressing this issue. Later that same academic year, a second faculty meeting was dedicated to the same issue. Prior to the meeting, departments were asked to generate strategies that could be used to increase student engagement. These suggestions were shared among faculty in the hopes that strategies designed in one department might prompt another department to fashion an idea that would fit the other department's needs. These two faculty meetings, taken together, did much to increase campus awareness of an important assessment issue and to encourage faculty to generate strategies for improving engagement in their departments.

Involvement from the Academic Affairs Board and Assessment Committee

The Academic Affairs Board, one of the three governing boards on the campus, sent a request to department chairs asking them to generate strategies to use in their major courses for increasing academic rigor and student engagement. The board also convened a student panel to discuss the issues of rigor and engagement. Students frankly shared some of their concerns about the issue. These concerns included (a) different standards for different majors, (b) students' lack of effort in general education courses, and (c) courses in which students are not held accountable for not doing the reading. Independently, the Assessment

Committee also convened a focus group of students to discuss the issues of rigor and engagement. The students interviewed by the Assessment Committee echoed similar concerns. The results of both of these student panels were shared with faculty at the second campus-wide faculty meeting discussed earlier.

Involvement from Departments

As stated previously, the Academic Affairs Board asked departments to identify ways in which their department could improve academic rigor. Departments were asked to provide the board with a written document describing the content of their department discussion. These documents varied widely in their coverage and focus. We reproduce here one example of a department's response to the board's inquiry, which highlights the vital role that a department can play in student engagement.

Our department met to discuss what role we can play in raising academic standards on campus. Based on anecdotal observations of classroom behavior in our department, we believe that some students are not doing the reading prior to coming to class. We discussed the possibility of introducing pop quizzes into course assessments to increase engagement outside of the class. When the switch was made from 3-hour to 4-hour classes, our department did not add 33% more course content. Rather, we introduced either a lab or practicum component to the class. This was another form of instruction that did not require the standard reading/testing that accompanies lecture courses. It is unclear how demanding these other forms of instruction are, and whether students are really engaged 33% more for 33% more credit. If this other kind of instruction does not require the same amount of what NSSE calls "preparing for class," our numbers may be low for that reason. (Of course, this is assuming that other colleges either have 4-credit classes with straight lecture/without alternative instruction or have 3-credit classes.)

We believe that administering the ETS Major Field Achievement test to our graduates will provide helpful information about this issue. Specifically, if our students are reporting lower levels of engagement than their peer groups at other schools (as documented in NSSE), but yet our students are still scoring at high percentile levels, our concern over the NSSE data may be attenuated or perhaps the data need to be reinterpreted.

Our department was clear that we didn't want to raise work levels simply for the sake or increasing work load. In other words, we don't want to assign busy work just to get our NSSE data to show higher engagement. Instead, we will be looking for indicators of meaningful student engagement both in and out of the classroom.

Our department felt that we would benefit from faculty "checking in" with each other at least once a semester on how our courses were going with respect to student engagement and academic rigor. We support the idea proposed at our faculty meetings of gradually increasing our demands in courses where we feel our academic engagement should be higher. Some professors volunteered that they could do better in making students work more in terms of high-level writing, synthesis of ideas, and presenting more complex material from primary sources.

We wondered if it would be useful to conduct detailed analyses of each course with respect to how much time students are engaged in various intellectual tasks. Does the amount of time students spend on our introductory course differ from our mid-level courses, and do they, in turn, differ in the demands of our advanced courses? We believe that they should, but we lack evidence to support the claim.

We speculated that faculty load has tempered our enthusiasm for adding extra work. Increasing student engagement also tends to increase the work load for faculty (e.g., large research papers). Have faculty demands on our time and the pressures to produce scholarship increased over the years, forcing faculty to make choices about how much academic engagement we require of our students?

The department affirmed the idea that we could increase student engagement by in assigning a larger number of primary research articles in our classes above Introductory. These primary sources are cognitively complex and require extensive independent work on the part of the students. This may be one relatively easy way to address this topic of engagement in our department.

Workshop for Department Chairs

The Director of Campus Assessment convened a workshop for department chairs to discuss student engagement as it was demonstrated in the data from the Wabash National Liberal Arts study. Upon collection of the fall data, the Wabash team delivered to the institution preliminary results from first-year students. The first goal of the workshop was to distribute more widely the findings of the Wabash study. The second goal was to challenge department chairs to identify ways in which they could use this information to inform and improve their curricula, pedagogy, and student academic engagement. The Assessment Director reviewed the Wabash materials. This was followed by two break-out sessions. In the first session, departments were split along divisional lines. In the second break-out session, department chairs "cross-pollinated" and shared ideas with department chairs from the other three divisions. After lunch, the large group reconvened, and they developed a list of general approaches that could be used campus-wide to address the issues shown in the Wabash study.

Summary

All of the efforts just described were completed in one academic year. Changes in student engagement on three measures are shown in Figures 10.2–10.4. Specifically, the percentage of seniors who reported that they "often" or "very often" came to class without completing their assignments dropped from 29 percent in 2003 to 15 percent in 2008; the percentage of seniors who reported that they "often" or "very often" worked harder than they thought they could to meet a professor's expectations rose from 48 percent in 2003 to 59 percent in 2008; the percentage of students who reported that they spent 10 hours per week or fewer studying for class decreased from 39 percent in 2003 to 22 percent in 2008.

The main point to glean from these data is not that certain interventions guarantee certain increases in engagement. Indeed, the relationship between the institution's efforts to improve student engagement and the actual increases in the percentage of students showing increased engagement is correlational not causal. Nor is the main point to glean from these data that this institution should be set apart for its accomplishments. Rather, the main point is to highlight ways in which a liberal arts institution can effect change that, it can be argued from the Wabash National Study and other research, is directly related to student engagement. We argue that liberal arts colleges, given their smaller size and uniform institutional mission, are in a better position than research universities to adapt to assessment data and thereby more quickly enact strategies to increase student engagement. Each institution highlighted in Part 2 of this volume has certain built-in advantages and disadvantages. We believe that liberal arts colleges have the advantages of smaller institutional size, smaller class sizes, more uniform institutional mission, and great nimbleness and ability to change instructional and curricular strategies. We believe, in turn, that those advantages can be parlayed into producing higher levels of student academic engagement.

Acknowledgment

The Center of Inquiry collaborates with a research team from the University of Iowa on the Wabash National Study. ACT, Inc. assists with the data collection and reporting for the study. Research teams from the University of Michigan and Miami University (Ohio) are also conducting annual interviews with a subset of students from six institutions in the 2006 round of the study. The Wabash National Study is funded through grants from the Lilly Endowment Inc., the Davis Educational Foundation, and the Teagle Foundation.

References

Astin, A. W. (1999). How the liberal arts college affects students. *Daedalus, 128,* 77–100.

Chickering, A. W., & Gamson, Z. (1987). Seven principles for good practice in undergraduate education. *AAHE Bulletin, 40*(7), 3–7.

Bowman, N. A. (2008, November). *Can first-year college students provide accurate self-reports about their learning and development?* Paper presented at the 33rd annual conference of the Association for the Study of Higher Education, Jacksonville, FL.

Kuh, G. D. (2003, November). *Built to engage: Liberal arts colleges and effective educational practice.* Paper presented at the ACLS Conference on Liberal Arts Colleges in American Higher Education, Williamstown, MA.

Kuh, G.D., & Hu, S. (2001). The effects of student-faculty interaction in the 1990s. *The Review of Higher Education, 24,* 309–332.

Pascarella, E. T., Cruce, T. M., Wolniak, G. C., & Blaich, C. F. (2005). *Liberal arts colleges and liberal arts education: New evidence on impacts.* ASHE Higher Education Report, No. 31.

Faculty Engagement in the Community Colleges: Constructing a New Ecology of Learning

Robert W. Franco

The following perspective on engagement in America's community colleges is shaped by more than thirty years as a practicing ecological anthropologist deeply concerned about the condition of new Samoan and Pacific Islander immigrants as they adapt to life in American cities. These "new neighbors" (MacPherson, Shore, & Franco, 1977) have unique and deep cultural and linguistic traditions shaped by sustaining and evolving cultures on distant islands, but they experience many of the same challenges that American minorities and immigrants have faced for centuries.

Most Asian immigrant groups originally came to the United States as immigrant labor in the late nineteenth century. At this same time, the United States was coming as a colonizer to Hawaii, American Samoa, and Guam. Native Hawaiians survived the initial American onslaught, are revitalized, and are attempting to establish their own sovereign nation. American Samoans are "U.S. nationals," who genuinely celebrated their centennial as an American territory in 2000. Samoans from the independent nation of Samoa and their kin from American Samoa now make up populations of more than 200,000 in many states in the western United States. Guam's residents are U.S. citizens, and Guam's indigenous Chamorros have survived western colonial dominance stretching back to 1522, when Magellan was the first European to discover the island. Of all the Asian American countries of origin, only the Philippines, including the Mindanao region that is primarily Muslim in religious and cultural background, was fully colonized after the Spanish-American War, whereas Japan, Korea, and Vietnam were settings for major warfare in the mid-to-late twentieth century. All these places have emerged in different places in a globalizing age.

For nearly twenty-five years, as a community college faculty member with extensive teaching and administrative responsibilities, I have been unable to sustain this research and have encouraged and mentored Hawaiian and Pacific Island scholars to pursue the equity and opportunity issues embedded in their history. Over this period, I have remained focused on the role of community colleges in meeting the challenge of equal opportunity in higher education for Americans of all ethnic, cultural, and class backgrounds.

My scholarly research has shaped my engagement in meeting this huge challenge. I have seen hundreds of Hawaiians, Samoans, and Pacific Islanders succeed in college, and I have celebrated their graduations with their families on the college's Great Lawn. I have also tracked their numbers in Hawaii's prisons and compared them with the number of two-year and four-year degree completers in the University of Hawaii system. I have also tracked health, housing, and employment indicators for these groups. There is much work ahead, both locally and nationally, even for these smaller ethnic groups.

After nearly thirty years as a practicing ecological anthropologist and community college faculty member, my greatest fear is that I have been an unwitting actor in a Darwinian dilemma. Has my career in the community college diverted my scholarly research and my ability to make a substantial difference in the social indicators I just described? Might I have done more to improve these numbers in a university research position?

The American Community College: Dreams Fulfilled or Diverted?

Within American higher education, only the community college is a community-based organization. Tracing their roots to the early 1900s, these colleges, initially called junior colleges, with reduced entrance requirements and tuition, support millions of worthy local students as they enter their "open doors" to pursue civic, career, and degree goals and dreams. Early proponents of the junior college referred to them as America's "democracy colleges," with a strong relationship to their communities, emphasizing equal opportunity and civic participation and valuing diversity (Gleazer, 1994; see also Franco, 2002; Zlotkowski et al., 2004).

Early in the twentieth century, Dean Alexis Lange of the University of California School of Education and other national leaders "urged the junior colleges to give high priority to programs that would prepare their students for effective participation in community life" (Gleazer, 1994, p. ix). According to Bogue (1950, pp. 336–337), Lange called for a junior college department of civic education with a curriculum that would "quicken" students' "communal sympathies," "deepen their sense of indissoluble oneness with their fellows," and encourage them "to participate vigorously, militantly, if need be, in advancing community welfare." Further, he suggested pedagogical innovations that would provide these students with suitable opportunities for "observation firsthand and for direct participation in the civic activities" of the community.

In a period of heightened attention to the urban migration of African Americans and international immigration of Southern and Eastern Europeans and East Asians, and an emerging social Darwinism, Lange and other elite university presidents also promulgated another, largely hidden mission for the community college. According to Brint and Karabel (1989, p. 208):

> fearing they would be "overrun" by hordes of unqualified students and yet recognizing the powerful political pressures for more open access to universities in a society emphasizing upward

mobility through education, the elite universities saw the junior college as an essential safety valve that would satisfy the demands for access while protecting their own institutions . . . they saw the two-year institution as existing less to offer new opportunities to obtain a bachelor's degree to excluded segments of the population than to divert them away from four-year colleges and universities.

In 1922, the American Association of Junior Colleges, in their first revision to their statement of purpose asserted: "The junior college may, and is likely to, develop a different type of curriculum, suited to the larger and ever changing civic, social and vocational needs of the entire community in which the college is located" (Gleazer, 1994, pp. viii–ix). The 1920s and 1930s saw the junior colleges deemphasizing their transfer role and stressing their role as a provider of terminal vocational education for marketable skills in local workforces (Brint & Karabel, 1989, pp. 205–206).

In 1936, Hollinshead reasserted that "the junior college should be a community college, meeting community needs; that it should serve to promote a greater social and civic intelligence in the community . . . that the work of the community college should be closely integrated with the work of the high school and the work of other community institutions" (p. 111). Hollinshead's assertion signals a critical realignment by junior colleges to high schools with less emphasis on strengthening linkages to baccalaureate transfer institutions.

Realignments toward vocational and terminal degrees and linkages with high schools gradually result in the reconceptualization of the "junior college" with a greater emphasis on getting local, diverse students to the "community college" with a balanced commitment to both transfer and vocational degrees. Two-year "technical colleges" focus largely on terminal associate degrees meeting local workforce needs.

In 1947, the Truman Commission called on "community colleges" to become "centers of learning for the entire community with or without the restrictions that surround formal course work in traditional institutions of higher education. It gears its programs and services to the needs and wishes of the people it serves" (President's Commission on Higher Education, 1947, pp. 69–70). Following from Langue's promotion of pedagogies that would provide students with opportunities for "firsthand observation" and "direct participation" in civic activities, the Truman Commission was also promoting less "formal course work" in community colleges as local "centers for learning." The Commission also boldly asserted the need for public education to be "made available, tuition-free, to all Americans able and willing to receive it, regardless of race, creed, color, sex, or economic and social status" (Gleazer, 1994, p. xi).

With millions of service personnel returning from the European and Pacific theaters of World War II, pressure to extend educational opportunities resulted in the passage of the GI Bill in 1944 and soaring enrollments in community colleges through 1948, and, according to Witt, Wattenberger, Gollattschek, and Suppiger (1994, p. 126), "By the fall of 1946, nearly 43 percent of all junior college students were veterans" (see Franco, 2002).

The 1950s and 1960s saw the return of Korean War veterans, a sustained baby boom, and rapid economic and technological growth leading to an explosion in demand for higher education. Individual state plans called for the creation of community college campuses within commuting distance of population centers, and the construction of these campuses became intertwined with urban and regional development and eventually contributed to suburban sprawl.

From 1950 to 1970, the number of American community colleges increased from 412 to 1,058, and throughout the 1960s, America built "nearly one community college per week." Located in every state in the union, community college enrollments soared to nearly 2.5 million students (Witt et al., 1994, p. 185).

In the 1960s, community colleges found themselves "in communities caught in the throes of change" and substantial ethnic, racial, and political unrest. Colleges and communities were "interfusing both spatially and functionally" with a wide range of other community-based organizations (Gleazer, 1994, p. xi). Throughout the 1970s, community colleges attempted to balance their university transfer and workforce development roles with their role as a "central hub of community educative and agencies and organizations" (Gleazer, 1994, p. xi).

In the 1980s, growth in the number of community colleges slowed, but their role in educating an unprecedented diversity of students accelerated. In many American cities, the community college campus was the setting for the first genuine and sustained interactions among racial and cultural groups. Also in the 1980s, "the community college vocationalizers . . . were finally having an impact" and "faced with a barrage of media images of Ph.D.s driving taxis and college graduates waiting in long lines in unemployment offices, community college students began to view the college transfer programs not as way stations on the road to success but as gateways to nowhere" (Brint & Karabel, 1989, p. 211). The community college's "sorting function" was reasserted as states concerned about budgets and a growing mass of "overeducated" workers came to view terminal vocational education as a mean to reduce university enrollments and provide students with practical skills "harnessed to larger state economic development strategies" (Brint & Karabel, 1989, p. 213).

In the 1990s, even with the end of the Cold War and the end of the War on Poverty, the number of community colleges climbed to 1,155. From 1972 to 1992, the percentage of American higher education students attending a community college increased from 28.7 percent to 37 percent. Over this same period, there was little or no improvement in the percentage of low-socioeconomic-status (SES) students attending four-year colleges, although there was a doubling, from 11 percent to 22 percent, in the percentage of low-SES students attending community colleges (Gladieux & Swail, 1998, pp. 102–105). In the period from 1970 to 2000, community colleges were still, to a large extent, merely masking and reproducing social structural inequalities, as Brint and Karabel argue.

Today, America's 1,195 community colleges (987 public, 177 independent, 31 Tribal) educate 11.5 million credit students, 41 percent of whom are full-time and 59 percent part-time (all current data from the American Association of Community Colleges).Women comprise 60 percent and men 40 percent of total national enrollment. The average age of community college students is 29, with a nearly equal percentage of students (43 percent) under the age of 21 and between the ages of 22 and 39 (42 percent), whereas 15 percent are over 40. Nearly half (46 percent) of all U.S. undergraduates are in community colleges. More than half of all Native American (55 percent) and Hispanic (55 percent) undergraduates and nearly half of all African American (46 percent) and Asian/Pacific Islander (46 percent) undergraduates are in community colleges.

The average annual cost for tuition and fees at public community colleges is $2,361. Nearly half (47 percent) of community college students receive financial aid: 23 percent receive federal grants, 11 percent federal loans, and 12 percent state aid, and more than 80 percent of all community college students are employed. Only 303 community colleges provide on-campus housing. The community colleges annually award more than 555,000 associate degrees and 295,000 certificates. Students at 41 percent of the public community colleges can earn an associate degree entirely online.

The community colleges are on the forefront of health care training: 59 percent of new nurses and the majority of other health care workers are educated at community colleges. Nearly 80 percent of firefighters, law enforcement officers, and emergency medical technicians are credentialed at community colleges. Nearly all (95 percent) of the businesses and other organizations that employ community college graduates support community college workforce development programs. The average expected lifetime earnings for a graduate with an associate degree are $1.6 million, about $0.4 million more than a high school graduate earns. Finally, 100,000 international students attend America's community colleges and these students comprise 39 percent of all international undergraduates in the United States.

The central engagement question for community college faculty and administrators, many of whom have doctoral degrees and substantial research experience, is how their colleges can help a broader, more diverse population of college students fulfill both their transfer and career dreams for the betterment of themselves and their communities. Community colleges can no longer merely mask and perpetuate social structural inequalities as "sorters" and "diverters" of lower SES students. The engagement imperative for faculty in the community colleges is simply this: How can we develop new "high impact" pedagogical approaches (AAC&U, 2008) that simultaneously prepare our increasingly diverse students for success in academic transfer, twenty-first-century careers, and as citizens in their communities, locally, nationally, and globally?

Engagement at Community Colleges

In 2002, Campus Compact, an organization that had been formed by a group of elite university presidents in the 1980s, contracted Dr. Donna Duffy of Middlesex Community College and myself to help guide a national team of researchers led by Dr. Edward Zlotkowski in the exploration of institutional civic engagement in America's two-year colleges. This research resulted in the Campus Compact publication *The Community's College: Indicators of Engagement at Two-Year Colleges* (Zlotkowski et al., 2004). This research would provide the framework for subsequent Campus Compact exploration of engagement in minority-serving institutions and in comprehensive universities (see Compact.org for references).

The research team, building on earlier research, identified thirteen indicators of engagement at community colleges, all of which impact the ability of community college faculty to engage with their students and their communities (Zlotkowski et al., 2004, pp. 5–6):

1. Mission and purpose explicitly articulate a commitment to the public purposes of higher education.

153

2. Administrative and academic leadership is in the forefront of institutional transformation that supports civic engagement.
3. Disciplines, departments, and interdisciplinary work have incorporated community-based education, allowing it to penetrate across disciplines and reach the institution's academic core.
4. Pedagogy and epistemology incorporate a community-based, public problem-solving approach to teaching and learning.
5. Faculty development opportunities are available for faculty to retool their teaching and redesign their curricula to incorporate community-based activities and reflect on those activities within the context of the course.
6. Faculty roles and rewards, including promotion and tenure guidelines and review, reflect a reconsideration of scholarship that embraces a scholarship of engagement.
7. Enabling mechanisms are present in the form of visible and easily accessible structures (e.g., centers, offices) on campus to assist faculty with community-based teaching and to broker community partnerships.
8. Internal resource allocation is adequate for establishing, enhancing, and deepening community-based work on campus—for faculty, students, and programs that involve community partners.
9. Community voice deepens the role of community partners in contributing to community-based education and shaping outcomes that benefit the community.
10. External resource allocation is made available for community partners to create richer learning environments for students and for community-building efforts in local communities.
11. Integrated and complimentary engagement activities weave together student service, service-learning, and other community engagement activities on campus.
12. Forums for fostering public dialogue are created that include multiple stakeholders in public problem-solving.
13. Student voice is cultivated in a way that recognizes students as key partners in their own education and civic development and supports their efforts to act on issues important to themselves and their peers.

The *Indicators of Engagement* research team recognized that the primary challenges to deeper community engagement facing community colleges faculty were:

1. Full-time, permanent faculty have a heavy teaching workload, on average five courses per term, as well as other responsibilities within their academic departments and campus-wide committees.
2. Part-time adjuncts make up nearly two-thirds of the faculty in two-year colleges, and they are usually hired to teach specific courses with syllabi, textbooks, and learning objectives identified by permanent faculty, and frequently at multiple campuses.
3. Community college students have diverse learning styles shaped by culture and experience, are frequently underprepared for college, and swirl in and out of college as familial responsibilities and job opportunities wax and wane.

4. Administrators focusing on workforce development and the achievement of specific workplace skills, and a host of other accountability measures, often underestimate the value of service and civic engagement.

For community college faculty, then, all thirteen indicators of engagement are necessary for their sustained and transformative civic and scholarly engagement. The *Indicators of Engagement* research team captured the need for this holistic support structure by developing an integrated chapter on "Faculty Culture" and identified six best practices and institutional examples to support faculty engagement in the two-year college (Zlotkowski et al., 2004, p. 53):

1. Centralize faculty development resources and build engagement into these development efforts.
2. Create a culture of service through hiring and buy-in from key academic administrators.
3. Provide on-campus training and incentives for participation.
4. Actively recruit adjunct faculty to participate in community-related activities.
5. Seek external funding to support engagement efforts.
6. Document results to justify resource allocations.

At Anne Arundel Community College (AACC) in Maryland, all new faculty must participate in a year-long Learning College implemented by the Institutional Professional Development office. Service-learning and other community-based pedagogies are presented by experienced faculty practitioners. AACC also offers service-learning faculty development opportunities within its three-day faculty orientation and in three-part faculty service-learning institutes.

At Brevard Community College in Florida, faculty engagement is strengthened through a broad-based "saturation" model initiated by the director for the Center for Service-Learning (CSL) and supported by the college's administration for nearly two decades. The CSL regularly offers a range of community-related opportunities, including workshops and courses, strengthens school partnerships, and supports faculty attendance at numerous annual conferences and publication opportunities. Brevard Community College and Miami-Dade Community College have instituted a "point system" that impacts a faculty member's contract status. Service-learning is a legitimate way for faculty to earn points toward future contract renewal.

Success in faculty community engagement at Kapiolani Community College in Hawaii is driven by a broad commitment to a "culture of service" as a way of life for faculty and students. The college's hiring practices result in the recruitment and retention of "a critical mass of faculty who see their own productivity, creativity, and commitment in relation to the greater community" (Zlotkowksi et al., 2004, p. 45). The Kapiolani culture of service results from the vision and the leadership of key administrators who also support a multipurpose Service-Learning Office to facilitate and formatively evaluate community partnerships, and cultivate a cadre of student leaders focused on "reducing the severity of issues" in the community.

Malcolm X Community College in Illinois and Yakima Valley Community College in Washington are also developing a broader culture of service for their faculty and tapping powerful minority cultures to forge a "sense of natural connectedness and social responsibility" (Zlotkowksi et al., 2004, p. 45).

At Portland Community College in Oregon, Brevard, and many other community colleges, there are strong intentional efforts to "mend the rift with adjuncts" (Zlotkowksi et al., 2004, p. 46). Recognizing that adjuncts may have other lives with community-based organizations in the nonprofit and private sectors, these colleges have viewed "adjunctness" as an asset that can help engage students with the wider community. Faculty mentoring models, such as the program at Chandler-Gilbert Community College in Arizona, also help junior and adjunct faculty develop into engaged full-time, permanent faculty.

At most successful community college campuses, faculty development for increased community engagements involves:

1. Sustained, on-campus training opportunities.
2. Sharing of publications, course models, and exemplary syllabi.
3. Opportunities for community immersion as learning experiences for faculty.
4. Opportunities to attend local conferences with engaged K–12 and university educators, and regional and national conferences with discipline-based community college colleagues.
5. Reduced course loads and mini-grants for revising courses and developing faculty collaboration, and summer institutes to immerse faculty in the complexities and richness of community engagement, in their nonduty periods.

Two major national organizations play a significant and sustained role in the development of community-engaged community college faculty. Since 1995, the American Association of Community Colleges' "Horizons Colleges" initiative has played a critical role in developing community-engaged faculty at hundreds of campuses nationally. AACC awards three-year subgrants to community colleges and has identified and trained dozens of faculty mentors who provide campus-based training and technical assistance for each new cohort of Horizons colleges.

The Community College National Center for Community Engagement (CCNCCE) produces publications, provides training, and assists community colleges in identifying external funding. Attendance at the CCNCCE annual conference is a major component of faculty development for dozens of community colleges annually. Since 2002, Campus Compact has also supported a Senior Faculty Fellow for the Community Colleges who has provided faculty engagement training at nearly two hundred colleges in thirty-four states and three U.S. territories.

At engaged community colleges, service-learning is explicitly grounded in an institution's commitment to teaching and learning. Further, service-learning as pedagogy is aligned with service-learning as an indicator of institutional civic commitment. As community-based, teaching institutions, community colleges can reward faculty for the integration of service-learning assignments into courses, and for serving the institutions' civic purposes.

The Miami-Dade Center for Community Involvement explicitly describes the many "maintenance of rank" options related to service-learning and provides workshops on integrating both service-learning and civic responsibility into the curriculum, as well as reflection and assessment workshops. By coupling engagement with career advancement,

Miami-Dade is implementing a long-term sustainable strategy for both faculty and community development.

At Kapiolani Community College, the chancellor has emphasized that "there is a palpable faculty peer pressure to do civically engaged work; excellence in this area sets the institutional tone, and this in turn results in a difference in faculty productivity, creativity, and commitment" (Zlotkowski et al., 2004, p. 50).

For most community-engaged faculty in two-year colleges, the primary motivations for engaging their students in community-based work are (a) improved learning of academic content (methods, theory, critical thinking); (b) personal development and especially career clarification and advancement; and (c) increased civic understanding, skills, and attitudes. To the extent that these learning outcomes are embedded in general education, degree, and college requirements, as well as institutional mission, vision, and values, faculty engagement can both deepen and expand. When these learning outcomes are less visible and less emphasized at the community college, faculty community engagement is likely to wither as just another passing higher education reform.

In December 2008, of 119 higher education institutions receiving the Carnegie Classification for Community Engagement, nine were community colleges:

For Curricular Engagement and Outreach and Partnerships

    Anne Arundel Community College, MD

    Bunker Hill Community College, MA

    Hocking College, OH

    Miami Dade College, FL

    Mount Wachusetts Community College, MA

    Northampton Community College, PA

    Northwest Florida State College, FL (formerly Okaloosa-Walton College)

    Raritan Valley Community College, NJ

For Outreach and Partnerships

    Owens Community College, OH

In 2006, five other community colleges received the Curricular Engagement and Outreach and Partnerships designation:

    Bristol Community College, MA

    Chandler-Gilbert CC, AZ

    Kapiolani CC, HI

    Middlesex CC, MA

    Richland College, TX

Scholarship of Engaged Teaching and Learning in the Two-Year College

In 2007, Campus Compact again contracted with Donna Duffy and myself, as well as Amy Hendricks and Marina Baratian from Brevard Community College and Tanya Renner from Kapiolani, to develop a follow-up publication entitled *Service-Learning Course Design for*

Community Colleges. Kay McClenney, Director of the Community College Survey of Student Engagement (CCSSE), contributed the Foreword to this publication and emphasized that "service-learning, properly conceived and executed, powerfully reflects those key elements of the student experience that we know are important to learning and success: collaboration with other students and community organizations; active involvement in planning, participating in, and rigorous reflection upon the service experience; and focused interaction with faculty, peers, and others" (Duffy et al., 2007, p. viii).

This publication represents a new direction in engaged scholarship for community college faculty and that is to explore the impact of community-based learning on "success" for diverse community college students. By "success" we mean (a) earning a "C" or better in courses, (b) completing a semester (retention), (c) reenrollment in continuous semesters (persistence), (d) degree completion and/or baccalaureate transfer, and (e) employment at mean national income or higher. All the papers in this course design volume provide convincing evidence that service-learning and other community-based pedagogies contribute positively to the success of community college students. These papers, taken as a whole, suggest that if two-year campuses are serious about student success, and about closing the gaps between lower, middle, and higher SES groups, then community engagement should be a primary pedagogical innovation advanced at their institutions.

Scholarship on Specific Issues in Community Colleges

Beyond the focus on service-learning and success for diverse students, which is the main topic of concern for community colleges, there are a number of specific civic issues that community college faculty are elucidating:

- From a psychology perspective, Donna Duffy, Middlesex Community College, has contributed important insights on the relationship between service-learning, engaged pedagogy, and the academic and personal "resilience" of community college students. She has also detailed a clear "route" to integrating service-learning into the Scholarship of Teaching and Learning (Duffy, 2007a, pp. 89–99).
- Tanya Renner, Kapiolani Community College, again from a psychology perspective, has developed a set of comprehensive methodologies to assess student learning, especially critical thinking gains, as well as authentic assessment strategies for community partners (Renner, 2007, pp. 79–88).
- Many community college faculty have developed service-learning best practices that have had significant impact on HIV/AIDS prevalence in their communities. These practices were developed within the AACC "Bridges to Healthy Communities" initiative.
- Community college faculty at Kapiolani and Miami-Dade have addressed "digital divide" issues in low-income, multiethnic communities they serve. Judith Kirkpatrick, Professor of English at Kapiolani, has developed a new publication for the HUD-Office of University Partnerships on the "Palolo Learning Center" established in 2008.
- Dennis Lehman, Science Professor at Harold Washington College in Illinois, has developed an asthma education learning community where students in both developmental and

college-level courses address the issue of urban asthma in Chicago. His engaged scholarship is recognized by the National Science Foundation project, Science for New Civic Engagements and Responsibilities (SENCER).

- Rudi Garcia, faculty and now dean at Central New Mexico Community College, is a nationally recognized expert on service-learning, career education, and community development.
- Neghin Modavi, Sociology Professor at Kapiolani, has developed instructional videos on the College's Palolo Educational Pipeline, and on its "Service-Learning and Long-Term Cares Pathway." With state legislature funding in 2006, the college established a long-term care center to address the needs of Hawaii's elderly.
- John Rand, science professor and NSF STEM Program Director at Kapiolani, has developed a SENCER model course on the "Science of Sleep" that explores the significant issue of sleep deprivation in young adults and its impact on student learning. Dr. Rand has also led innovations in undergraduate research by Native Hawaiian and other talented science, technology, engineering, and math students in the community colleges.

Finally, my own engaged research of more than thirty years focuses on America's new migrants from U.S. territories in Polynesia and Micronesia. These migrants enter Honolulu through our public housing facilities, schools, and colleges, or languish in homeless shelters, or worse, in prisons. Their experiences on the margins of American society are not very different from those of immigrants coming to America a century ago.

What is different is that today, community colleges have become central institutions in higher education, and they are expected to respond to these and numerous other issues confronting our communities and nation. At the same time, community colleges need to be accountable to student success in transfer, work, and civic life. Service-learning, and other community-engaged pedagogies, coupled with faculty research and scholarship on significant issues impacting our students, holds great promise for the future of the community college movement.

To address the new immigrant diversity, community colleges from La Guardia in New York, to Central Piedmont in North Carolina, to Richland in Texas, to Mesa in Arizona, to Costa Mesa in California, and to Edmonds in Washington are developing service-learning and other active and collaborative pedagogies to engage their students in and from these increasingly diverse cultural and linguistic communities. And many community colleges are developing two-year teacher preparation pathways, featuring service-learning across the first and second year of the undergraduate experience (Franco, 2000).

Future Engagement Challenges for America's Democracy Colleges

Closing the minority achievement gap will continue to be a pressing priority for community colleges into the second and third decades of this century. High level of underpreparedness in high school graduates and increased labor in-migration will continue to challenge community colleges as they try to meet higher levels of accountability to their boards and trustees, community stakeholders, legislatures, and accrediting bodies.

159

Full-time faculty and staff are already stretched, and they will need to work harder and smarter. Engaging talented students as service-learners, leaders, tutors, and mentors is clearly part of the solution to these challenges, which seem to exacerbate at an exponential rate. Community colleges will need to be at the forefront of the civic and workforce transformations that will accompany America's transitions to alternative energy and sustainable ecologies. They will also need to be primary drivers of the education and training that will shape the nation's civic and health care response to the multiple complex issues of aging in America. Finally, if past is indeed prologue, community colleges will also play a vital role in transitioning the citizen-soldiers (state National Guard men and women, as well as other military personnel) as they transition back to civilian life in a transforming economy.

The future of America's community colleges, and their ability to be transformative for individuals, communities and the nation, will depend to a great degree on the kinds of citizens they educate and create. Faculty engagement that connects students with real-world problem solving in relation to educational, environmental, health, housing, long-term care, and other community issues is the best preparation for lives of engaged citizenship. These future citizens will continue to value and support their community's college, and the community college movement will likely see a new resurgence across the American landscape.

Future Opportunities: Imagining and Constructing a New Ecology of Learning

As community-based organizations, community colleges have a unique role both within communities and within American higher education. Throughout the history of the American community college, there have been calls for innovative pedagogies that would provide students with opportunities for "firsthand observation" and "direct participation" in civic activities (Langue, early 1900s), position the community college as local "centers for learning" (Truman Commission, 1947), and interfuse community colleges "both spatially and functionally" as central hubs of "educative agencies and organizations" in local environments (Gleazer, 1994).

Since their inception, community colleges have always valued diversity and equal higher education opportunity for all. From the 1950s to the present, their role in educating an unprecedented diversity of students has accelerated, and in many American cities the community college campus was the setting for the first genuine and sustained interactions among racial and cultural groups (Brint & Karabel, 1989).

Throughout the first century of the American community college, these uniquely American institutions have attempted to balance liberal arts transfer and workforce development missions, and high school and university connections, while struggling to deliver on their historical commitment to prepare students for community engagement and the work of democracy.

Since the early 1990s, service-learning has been an innovative pedagogy that more than five hundred community colleges (AACC Service-Learning Clearinghouse, n.d.) have been implementing to deliver on this historical commitment. Still, for most two-year colleges, service-learning and student community engagement have remained on the margins of their mission.

Since the early 1990s, another trend, distance and technology-enhanced learning, has accelerated across the community college and higher education landscape, and as mentioned earlier, students at 41 percent of public community colleges can earn an associate degree entirely online. Developments in new technology and social media are fundamentally rattling the walls of the traditional classroom as the center for learning and altering the way student services are delivered to a technology-savvy generation.

One way to move community-based service-learning from the margins to the mainstream is to imagine and construct a new ecology of learning that seamlessly integrates current learning environments, that is, the classroom, centers and labs, campus, community (local, national, global), and cyberspace into one learning ecology in which faculty, students, staff, and administrators interact with each other and community stakeholders in three equally important purposes—liberal arts transfer, twenty-first-century career preparation, and community engagement.

Once this new ecology is constructed, it will need sustaining, through institutional commitment to civic engagement and faculty and staff development for student community engagement. The actors in this new ecology will need to behave differently with new tools and technologies available for shaping each other and the new learning spaces.

Once this new ecology is constructed, community is positioned in the middle, not on the margins, and community colleges, interfused in this ecology, can reassert their civic purposes and their central place in the genuine, sustained, and creative interactions among racial, cultural, socioeconomic, gender, and age groups.

Still, questions will linger: Is the American community college simply sorting and diverting the disadvantaged in these groups, masking perpetuated structures of inequality? The community college is increasingly challenged, and not nearly adequately funded, to close achievement gaps for disadvantaged groups in American higher education.

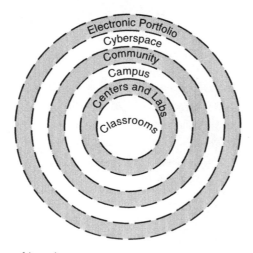

FIGURE 11.1 Kapi'olani Ecology of Learning

Closing this gap is America's central civic, democratic, and simultaneously global challenge. In this new ecology of learning, community college faculty, student services professionals, including service-learning coordinators, and technology specialists will need to engage in new and deeper ways with their high school and university colleagues. University researchers working with engaged community college faculty need to focus on baselining social indicators for disadvantaged groups (education, imprisonment, health, housing, employment statistics) and setting and achieving ambitious benchmarks for improvement by working more effectively with student services support staff and programs.

If this new ecology and all the individuals within it are going to thrive and grow to meet this challenge, community college, university, and higher education policy makers will also need to reassert their commitment to meeting this most important civic challenge. The ecology cannot be sustained and the challenge cannot be met without new financial, social, civic, and intellectual capital.

The sooner, the better; the career of this engaged ecological anthropologist and major community college advocate is almost over.

References

American Association of Community Colleges. (n.d.). *Homepage*. Retrieved December 15, 2008, from http://www.aacc.nche.edu.

American Association of Community Colleges. (n.d.). *Service-learning clearinghouse*. Retrieved December 15, 2008, from http://www.aacc.nche.edu.

Association of American Colleges and Universities (AAC&U). (2008). *High impact strategies*. Washington, DC: AAC&U Press.

Baratian, M. (2007). Stand-alone service-learning courses and models. In D. Duffy et al. (Eds.), *Service-learning course design for community colleges*. Providence, RI: Campus Compact.

Bogue, J. (1950). *The community college*. New York: McGraw-Hill.

Brint, S., & Karabel, J. (1989). *The diverted dream: Community colleges and the promise of educational opportunity in America, 1900–1985*. New York: Oxford University Press.

Duffy, D. (2007a). Campus Compact, service-learning, and community college engagement. In D. Duffy et al. (Eds.), *Service-learning course design for community colleges*. Providence, RI: Campus Compact.

Duffy, D. (2007b). Service-learning and the scholarship of teaching and learning. In D. Duffy et al. (Eds.), *Service-learning course design for community colleges*. Providence, RI: Campus Compact.

Duffy, D., Franco, R., Hendricks, A., Henry, R., Baratian, M., & Renner, T. (Eds.). (2007). *Service-learning course design for community colleges*. Providence, RI: Campus Compact.

Franco, R. W. (2000). *The community college conscience: Service-learning and training tomorrow's teachers* (ECS Issue Paper). Denver, CO: Education Commission of the States.

Franco, R. W. (2002). The civic role of community colleges: Preparing students for the work of democracy. *The Journal of Public Affairs, 6*(suppl. 1), 119–138.

Franco, R. W. (2007a). Using service-learning to build attainment pathways. In D. Duffy et al. (Eds.), *Service-learning course design for community colleges*. Providence, RI: Campus Compact.

Franco, R. W. (2007b). The next nexus: Classroom and community, community and world. In D. Duffy et al. (Eds.), *Service-learning course design for community colleges.* Providence, RI: Campus Compact.

Gladieux, L. E., & Swail, W. S. (1998). Postsecondary education: Student success, not just access. In S. Halpern (Ed.), *The forgotten half revisited: American youth and young families, 1988–2000.* Washington, DC: American Youth Policy Forum.

Gleazer, E. J. (1994). Foreword. In A. A. Witt et al. (Eds.), *America's community colleges: The first century.* Washington, DC: Community College Press.

Hendricks, A. (2007). Best practices for creating quality service-learning courses. In D. Duffy et al. (Eds.), *Service-learning course design for community colleges.* Providence, RI: Campus Compact.

Hollinshead, B. (1936). The community junior college program. *Junior College Journal 7*(3), 111–116.

Macpherson, C., Shore, B., & Franco, R. (1978). *New neighbors: Islanders in adaptation.* Santa Cruz, CA: Center for South Pacific Studies.

President's Commission on Higher Education. (1947). *Higher education for American democracy* (Vol. 1, pp. 69–70). Washington, DC: Superintendent of Documents.

Renner, T. (2007). Assessing service-learning outcomes. In D. Duffy et al. (Eds.), *Service-learning course design for community colleges.* Providence, RI: Campus Compact.

Witt, A., Wattenberger, J., Gollattschek, J., and Suppiger, J. (1994). *America's community colleges: The first century.* Washington, DC: Community College Press.

Zlotkowski, E., Duffy, D., Franco, R., Gelmon, S., Norvell, K., et al. (2004). *The community's college: Indicators of engagement at two-year institutions.* Providence, RI: Campus Compact.

Civic Engagement at Faith-Based Institutions

John W. Eby

Faith-based service-learning exists at the crossroads of several important contemporary conversations: conversations about the role of faith in the public square, the role of higher education in the development of communities, about the role of higher education in moral and civic development of students and about the integrity and spirituality of teaching and learning.
—Gail Gunst Heffner and Claudia DeVries Beversluis

One does not have to believe in a particular religion or be religious at all to recognize the important role religion plays in society. Many individuals use religious values to make important decisions. Society looks to religion for a moral base. Religious institutions exert significant influence on society. Nevertheless, higher education doesn't know how to deal with religion. Lee Schulman, retiring president of the Carnegie Foundation for the Advancement of Teaching, said in a recent interview, "Secular institutions have not yet come to terms with the central role of religion in society. They just pretend that religion is not there" (Selingo, 2008). Faith-based colleges and universities do not have this dilemma, though the overt presence of religion creates others.

Because of their particular character and mission, faith-based colleges and universities intentionally bring together things that the rest of the academy separates. They include spirituality and religion in their educational approach and community relationships in ways that open opportunities for holistic and integrated educational philosophies and effective community partnerships.

There are a number of ways this happens. Faith and religion inform understandings of service and civic engagement. Students serve because of the call of their faith and grow in maturity and commitment to their faith through their service. Because many community organizations share a faith perspective, faith-based colleges and universities develop deep, broadly rooted connections and relationships. They can be intentional about spirituality in teaching and learning as well as about the role spirituality plays in motivating students and community partners for engagement in service and social change. Faith and faith-based organizations form important parts of the social capital that makes communities strong and vital, and when absent weak and vulnerable.

The term "faith-based" is used here to refer to institutions that reflect a relationship to a particular faith and religious tradition or perspective. These institutions are sometimes called "religiously affiliated," "church-related," "religious," "denominational," or "Christian" colleges and universities. They vary greatly in the way they operationalize their faith perspective. Each brings a particular understanding of civic engagement, service, and learning and particular understandings of human nature, the world, the church, social issues, evil, and the meaning of faith. Together, they represent a rich diversity.

The activist social justice emphasis of the Jesuits contrasts in interesting ways with the contemplative tradition of Naropa University and its Buddhist tradition. The optimism of the Reformed tradition regarding the possibility of transforming social structures is balanced against the Anabaptist awareness of "two kingdoms" and its pessimism about how realistic it is to expect to incorporate Kingdom values into secular society. The emphasis on a social gospel of the Catholic tradition and of some Protestant traditions challenges the individualistic perspectives of others. The rich history of significant scholarship in the Catholic tradition contrasts with the suspicion of learning and education in some Evangelical traditions. Communal traditions balance more individualistic ones. Biblical traditions interact with philosophical ones. Some emphasize individual salvation and others social justice.

Most faith-based institutions would identify themselves as Christian and relate to Catholic or Protestant communities. There are several Buddhist and Jewish institutions in the United States. Some faith-based institutions identify with particular denominations or religious orders, whereas others are interdenominational or nondenominational. Some are owned and controlled by a denomination. Others show little specific influence from their denomination. There has been a general trend to move away from direct denominational influence. The thing that distinguishes these institutions from others is that their organizational culture and approach to education include an overt religious and spiritual dimension.

Jacobsen and Jacobsen (2008) give an overview of religiously affiliated colleges and universities based on statistics from the National Center for Education Statistics within the U.S. Department of Education. In 2004, according to their analysis, about one in eight undergraduate students attended religiously affiliated colleges and universities. Of the total undergraduate population, 27 percent attended public institutions, 40 per cent private nonreligious institutions, 9 percent Catholic institutions, 23 percent other Christian institutions, and 1 percent Jewish institutions. They compiled a breakdown of church-related colleges and universities that offer bachelor's degrees (Table 1). Although this table identifies larger institutions, most faith-based institutions are relatively small. More recent statistics from 2006 indicate that there are 925 institutions listed in the IPEDS list as religiously affiliated. The median size was 1,008 students. About three hundred institutions listed enrollments of fewer than five hundred students.

Table 1. Church-Related Colleges and Universities That Offer Bachelor's Degrees

Religious Identity	Number of Schools That Offer Bachelor's Degrees	Largest Schools
Roman Catholic	208 28.1% of church-related colleges and universities 8.9% of all colleges and universities	De Paul, IL St. John's, NY Saint Louis University Boston College, MA Loyola University, Chicago, IL Fordham University, NY Georgetown, University DC Saint Leo University, FL Marquette University Regis University, CO
Baptist	106 14.3 % of church-related colleges and universities 4.5% of all colleges and universities	Baylor University, TX Liberty University, VA Mercer University, GA Campbell University, NC Wayland Baptist University, TX
Methodist	95 12.8% of church-related colleges and universities 4.2% of all colleges and universities	Duke University, NC Emory University, GA American University, DC Southern Methodist University, TX
Presbyterian	58 7.8% of church-related colleges and universities 2.5% of all colleges and universities	University of Tulsa, OK Arcadia University, PA Carrol College, WI Trinity University, TX Buena University, IA
Churches of Christ/ Disciples	52 7.0% of church-related colleges and universities 2.2% of all colleges and universities	Columbia College, MO Texas Christian University, TX Pepperdine University, CA Chapman University, CA Harding University, AR
Lutheran	43 5.8% of church-related colleges and universities 1.8% of all colleges and universities	Concordia University, WI Capital University, OH Valparaiso University, IN Pacific Lutheran University, WA Augsburg College, MN
Other Christian Affiliation	179 24.2% of church-related colleges and universities 7.6% of all colleges and universities	Brigham Young University, UT Brigham Young University, ID Indiana Wesleyan University, IN Azusa Pacific University, CA Biola University, NC The University of Findlay, OH Olivet Nazarene University, IL Bob Jones University, SC

SOURCE: Rhonda Hustedt Jacobsen and Douglas Jacobsen, *The American College in a Postsecular Age*. New York: Oxford University Press, 2008, 74. Used with permission.

Many persons in the academy have an unfortunate stereotype of faith-based institutions as institutions that isolate students from perspectives they do not share and indoctrinate them with narrow beliefs and doctrines. Certainly, some have that orientation, but the vast majority promote a value-based liberal education that is respectful and accepting of others. They help students define and develop a sense of vocation that includes engagement and involvement in social needs and problems. At their best, they help students make meaning and develop a commitment to the common good within an intellectually stimulating environment that asks hard questions and examines foundational presuppositions.

Braskamp, Trautvetter, and Ward (2006) in a study of ten faith-based colleges found "a rigorous intellectual challenge in which the head and heart are integrated in the search for truth, meaning and fulfillment" (xii). They also found that service-learning went beyond just doing good to become a way for students to express their faith. Students develop a service ethic that affects their life choices not only in college but throughout their lives.

Faith-based institutions have exemplary programs in civic engagement and service. In 2006, Elon College received the President's Higher Education Community Service Award for General Community Service, and faith-based colleges were represented in numbers higher than their national proportions on the President's Honor Roll with Distinction for Hurricane Relief Service and the President's Honor Roll with Distinction for General Community Service.

Faith-based programs of service and civic engagement share most perspectives with similar programs at other kinds of colleges. Good practices have universal application. However, as with other types of colleges and universities, faith-based ones develop a particular character and fill a particular niche in the broader movement. They provide an opportunity to work at some of the cutting-edge issues being discussed and debated in higher education.

Access through Particularity

Many faith-based institutions struggle to find their place in the academy because the academy has been dominated by an emphasis on objectivity, which has assumed that we know reality best when we are unencumbered by particularistic meanings and interpretations. The goal was to find objective truth independent of the observer's perspective, experience, and standpoint. That kind of scholarship was dominated by white, western heterosexual males, though the ways in which that particularity shaped understandings were often hidden. Education from that perspective too often focused on the intellect and neglected the spirit. It separated knowledge from application and action.

Within that frame, the faith perspectives of faith-based institutions were often seen as biases to be overcome, not only by the broad academy but sometimes by the faith-based institutions themselves. Too often, faith perspectives were devalued to be replaced by a generic spirituality. Some faith-based institutions marginalized things they did well, such as experiential education, service-learning, and the scholarship of teaching and learning, to imitate the "objective" approach of research universities.

The particularism of faith-based institutions and, for many of them, their rootedness in a community of faith give them a place to stand and a particular perspective to make

168

significant contributions to the academy. With the advent of perspectival scholarship such as feminist theory and postmodernism, a door has been opened to understanding that is hidden by traditional approaches. Conversation from a clearly articulated standpoint enhances and enriches conversation and dialogue with other perspectives.

Woltersdorf (2004) suggests that scholarship from a faith perspective, rather than bringing "bias," brings "access" to parts of reality hidden by other approaches. "Augustine believed that only if one departs from the condition of generic humanity and adopts that highly particular stance which consists of loving God above all else can one genuinely understand the fundamental structure of reality" (p. 240). The particular perspective of faith-based institutions provides a standpoint that opens access to perspectives on reality, and their rootedness in a particular community of faith provides stability and context (Wenger Shenk, 2003).

The particular impact of a faith perspective and of spirituality is recognized in a number of studies. The work of Colby, Ehrlich, Beaumont, and Stephens (2003) sponsored by the Carnegie Foundation for the Advancement of Teaching recognizes the unique contributions of faith in their reports of interviews at Messiah College, Alverno College, and the College of St. Catherine. They also point to the significant role spirituality plays in colleges in Native American communities. Turtle Mountain Community College has a circle of seven columns at their front entrance, each of which portrays one of the values that are central to the Ojibway heritage. Schulman, in public presentations, links faith to a "way of knowing" and frequently points to the contributions faith traditions, particularly his own, the Jewish faith, make to understanding and teaching, service, and learning.

Mission Statements

One way to see the diversity and rich resources faith-based institutions bring to the academy is to scan their mission statements and to hear the way they talk about themselves.

Messiah College's mission "is to educate men and women toward maturity of intellect, character, and Christian faith in preparation for lives of service, leadership, and reconciliation in the church and society" (Messiah College Catalog, 2007–2008, p. 6). The mention of "reconciliation" reflects Messiah's commitment to peace and social justice growing from the Anabaptist roots of the college. College-wide educational objectives include several statements that commit the educational process to help students develop a sense of civic responsibility and commitment to work with others for the common good, practice good stewardship of economic and natural resources, and make decisions that reflect an ethic of service, a concern for justice, and a desire for reconciliation (Messiah College Catalog, 2007–2008).

Calvin College describes its mission as a Christian collage as "education for shalom" (http://www.calvin.edu/about/shalom.htm). They seek through learning to be agents of renewal in the academy, church, and society. They maintain a very close relationship with the Christian Reformed denomination from which they receive the perspective that links faith to social change and justice.

Georgetown University's Center for Social Justice Research reflects the university's deep commitment to educating men and women to be reflective lifelong learners, to be responsible and active participants in civic life, and to live generously in service to others. As would be expected at a university with a strong Jesuit tradition, community service and volunteerism have long been defining characteristics of students' education and the university's mission. Georgetown, as would be the case at other Catholic institutions, places service within the broader context of social justice. They build on the rich heritage of scholarship in the social teachings of the Catholic tradition. Pope John Paul II says that one of the four "essential characteristics" of every Catholic university is "an institutional commitment to the service of the people of God and of the human family in their pilgrimage to the transcendental goal which gives meaning to life" (Weigert & Miller, 1996).

McNally's (2004) fascinating article about indigenous pedagogy identifies a number of characteristics of pedagogy rooted in Ojibway tradition and religion and explores ways service-learning "fits" with that pedagogy and is organized to exploit it. One of the foundational concepts suggests that "Ojibway pedagogy couples knowledge learned with responsibility to use that knowledge on behalf of community well-being." In that tradition, as in others, knowledge both serves the community and is shaped by it.

The Global Studies program at Azusa Pacific University, which the director describes as "pro poor and sustainable," includes a service-learning component oriented toward helping develop empathy for the poor and marginalized groups in society (Slimbach, 2008).

DePaul University, with more than twenty-three thousand students, is an urban university with a diverse student population. One of the many symbols across campus, at the Lincoln Park Student Center, is a life-sized statue of Monsignor John Egan with the question, "What are you doing for Justice?" (Dalton, 2006).

University of Notre Dame opens its website with a quotation from its founder, Rev. Edward Sorin: "This college will be one of the most powerful means for doing good in this country." It goes on to say,

> At Notre Dame, education has always been linked to values, among them living in community and volunteering in community service. . . . the University's Center for Social Concerns, serves as a catalyst for student volunteerism. About 80 percent of Notre Dame students engage in some form of voluntary community service during their years at the University and at least 10 percent devote a year or more after graduation to service in the United States and around the world. (www.nd.edu)

Statements like these are common in the mission and vision statements of faith-based institutions and their service centers. Although they share a general commitment to service and civic engagement, each is unique and particular in that they reflect the foundational faith perspectives of the institutions. This particularity enriches and deepens both the conceptualization and practice of service and civic engagement.

As suggested in the quotation heading this chapter, various forms of civic engagement, including service-learning, stand at the crossroads of several significant conversations in the academy. These include issues of service and social justice, the place of spirituality in higher education, discussions about the approach and outcomes of holistic education, and the importance of connections and relationships with community organizations and leaders. The rest of this chapter briefly addresses these issues and their relevance and the contributions made by faith-based institutions.

Service, Faith, and Spirituality

Because service is a sine qua non of Christian faith, it should come as no surprise that most faith-based institutions include a commitment to service and civic engagement at the center of their mission. Campus Compact takes an annual survey of service-related activity in its 1,145 member intuitions. About 19 percent identify themselves as faith-based or religious. In 2006, 580 responded to the survey. This is not a random sample, but the respondents were generally representative of the total membership.

Religious institutions report higher student participation rates than the national averages. About 49 percent of students at religious colleges participated in service activities, compared with 32 percent when all colleges, including religious ones, are included. The difference would be greater if the categories were separate.

Faith-based institutions tend to use "service" language rather than "civic engagement" language. They draw heavily on language from the Bible, particularly the Hebrew prophets and Jesus, to talk about service, community, vocation, mission, reconciliation, justice, prophetic ministries, or righteousness more frequently than the language of civic engagement, which would use concepts such as democracy, civic engagement, common good, or equality. This is more than just a difference in language. It reflects a connection to a religious purpose and mission that is understood as joining in God's work in the world through the Church, rather than primarily a social or political process. It also tends to be global rather than narrowly nationalistic. The spiritual dimension of service is not an "add on" but is foundational. The "Lord's Prayer" includes a phrase that reflects that centrality: "Thy kingdom come, thy will be done, on earth as it is in heaven" (Mt. 6:10 RSV). For Christians, service reflects the intersection between and the interconnectedness of "heaven" and "earth."

Because of their primary emphasis on student learning and experience, although they value research and civic engagement, faith-based institutions tend to focus their programs on community service and service-learning. This may reflect the way they understand human and social need. Emerson and Smith (2000), in their study of race, point out that Evangelical Christians tend to have an individualistic understanding of social issues growing from their individualistic understanding of salvation. They tend to see social problems as rooted in decisions made by individual persons rather than linked to social structures or social policy. This is one of the reasons they tend to focus on service that is individualistic rather than civic engagement, which is structural.

This emphasis on service is by no means exclusive. Goshen College in Indiana has a significant partnership with the community to work at understanding and serving the educational needs of the Latino community. Messiah College partners with local community organizations and the school system through the Harrisburg Institute. Xavier University in Louisiana works at urban development issues. Many faith-based institutions engage in voter registration and get-out-the-vote initiatives.

Faith has played a significant role in the development of academic service and civic engagement. Hesser (2003) points out that many of the early pioneers of experiential education and service-learning like himself had gone to faith-based colleges and had seminary connections: Bob Sigmon, John Duly, Tom Little, Steve Schultz, Dwight Giles, and

171

others (Stanton, Cruz, & Giles, 1999). That pattern continues with many faculty both at faith-based institutions and in the broader academy, indicating that it is their faith that both motivates and informs their involvement in service and civic engagement. Ernest Boyer, a strong advocate for engaged scholarship and service, traced his vision to his roots in the Brethren in Christ church. Any list of heroes of social change include many persons of faith such as Bishop Tutu, Mohandas Gandhi, William Wilberforce, Martin Luther King, Mother Teresa, Bishop Romero, Cesar Chavez, Paulo Freire, the native American Peace Chiefs, the prophets from the Bible, and of course Jesus. Faith and spirituality have had a major impact on the conceptualization and practice of service and civic engagement.

There are a number of other ways that faith impacts service and civic engagement. Faith is frequently listed by students at all institutions as a motivating factor for participation in service-learning. Spiritual growth is often listed as one of the anticipated outcomes of service by both institutions and individual students. Many service programs at faith-based institutions include activities specifically oriented toward faith development.

For many years, the academy seemed uncomfortable when ideas of spirituality entered the discussion. There were a number of reasons for this, including the strong emphasis on empiricism and a legitimate suspicion of subjective, unverifiable claims to knowledge (Woltersdorf, 2004). However, more recently spirituality has entered the mainstream. Chickering, Dalton, and Stamm (2006) argue eloquently that "our almost exclusive emphasis on rational empiricism must be balanced by similar concern for other ways of knowing, being and doing" (p. xiii). The spiritual domain, with its emphasis on qualitative and affective experiences and ways of knowing, is a legitimate part of academic inquiry and a foundation for service and civic engagement. Personal and subjective values and life commitments are important both as issues to be studied and as explanatory factors necessary to understand human behavior.

It is difficult to think of service and civic engagement apart from the impact of affective and qualitative domains of spirituality in general, and impossible to separate these factors at faith-based institutions.

In 2003, the Higher Education Research Institute (HERI, 2003) did an extensive study of 3,680 students at forty-six diverse colleges and universities. They found a strong interest in spirituality as measured both by student self-reports and by student interest in key indicators. They found strong empirical relationships between students' spirituality and things such as civic responsibility, empathy and understanding/caring for others, racial/ethnic awareness, and tolerance. Students with high scores on spirituality scored higher on measures of having a compassionate self-concept, charitable involvement, and an ethic of caring. The differences were significant both statistically and substantively.

Many students identify spirituality and religion as important motivations for doing service and service-learning. Eyler and Giles (1999) comment, "Although not all students link altruism with religious or spiritual values, finding reward in helping others was among the most often identified benefits in service-learning" (p. 37).

Persons can be religious without being spiritual and certainly can be spiritual without being religious. However, when spirituality is rooted in a particular faith tradition and religious community, it takes on added meaning and significance.

Service is at the center of Christian understandings of faith. This is expressed so clearly in what is perhaps the best-known story Jesus told, the story of the Good Samaritan (Luke 10:25–37 RSV). Although almost everyone knows the story, what is often overlooked is the question that stimulated it. The lawyer asked, "What shall I do to inherit eternal life?" Jesus affirmed his answer: "You shall love the Lord your God with all your heart, and with all your soul, and with all your strength, and with all your mind; and your neighbor as yourself." Love of neighbor illustrated by meeting the needs of an injured, robbed man is linked inextricably to the center of faith. For Christians, service is fundamentally a spiritual act.

At faith-based institutions, spiritual and religious values are frequently cited as the strongest forces motivating and sustaining service and civic engagement. This is reflected in their mission statements and statements of core values. Students who serve because of a religious call are more dependable than those who serve for other reasons, including merely getting course credit. Hesser (2003) predicts that in the future when service, civic engagement, and citizenship compete for increasingly scarce resources and the priorities of hard-pressed academic administrations, "faith based colleges and universities will be less likely to diminish their commitment to service-learning because it is now seen as intrinsic to their mission/ theology and linked to their commitment to effective teaching and learning" (p. 67). Service and civic engagement are deeply institutionalized in faith-based institutions because they are so integral to their faith-based identity.

Service from a faith perspective is oriented toward the alleviation of social needs in communities and toward fundamental social change. In addition, there is an intentional goal of faith development and spiritual growth for participants. A student at the Conservative Schul in Philadelphia, a Jewish high school, commented, "Doing service and educating others about social causes, that's how I've found my own Judaism." This statement reflects not only the goal of service-learning at faith-based institutions, but the reality of the experience. Service is a spiritual activity. By relating to the needs of others, students often develop a deeper and richer faith of their own. As with other spiritual disciplines, service is both a cause and a result of practicing the discipline.

A study of service involvement of Notre Dame students (Trozzolo & Brandenberger, 2001) found that students with higher service involvement also had higher involvement in Bible reading, church attendance, and prayer. The reciprocal nature of service and growth is found in the data showing that students who found daily guidance from their religion and took church teachings seriously also reported higher levels of service.

Faith Traditions

As suggested earlier, the spirituality of service and civic engagement at faith-based institutions is enriched and given specific content and meaning when part of an articulated faith tradition (Teasdale, 1999). This happens in several ways.

First, a faith tradition provides a codified set of beliefs and perspectives on social issues which have been developed and tested over a period of time and in various social contexts. For many, the tradition incorporates diverse national, racial, gender, and socioeconomic perspectives. Statements by groups such as the Catholic Bishops, denominational study groups, or even ad hoc groups reflect deep study and important dialogue. The U.S. Catholic Bishops' Pastoral Letter on Catholic Social Teaching and the U.S. Economy sets a solid theological and philosophical grounding for what has become known as "preferential option for the poor." (Economic Justice for All, 1986). Sider (1997) set a social agenda for several generations of Evangelical Christians. CS Statements by Evangelical leaders on environmental stewardship have been very influential in shaping a faith-based environmentalism.

A faith tradition also links colleges to an identifiable community and constituency that helps the college shape and maintain its vision and identity. Some institutions, such as Goshen College and Eastern Mennonite University, are controlled by denominations through the appointment of controlling boards. Some Catholic institutions are controlled by a particular order and reflect the particular perspective of the order. Notre Dame University stipulates that their president must be a member of the Fathers of the Holy Cross. For some institutions, an informal ad hoc but important constituency has developed over time. Messiah College now has a broad Evangelical constituency reflected in its board and student body. It also maintains a special relationship to its roots in the Brethren in Christ denomination through a mutually developed covenant relationship. Eight board members must be from the denomination, and the denomination takes particular responsibility to promote the college and raise funds in the Brethren in Christ constituency. Some institutions have denominational advisory committees or constituency councils to represent church interests. Others maintain informal but influential relationships.

A third way identification with a faith tradition is meaningful for institutions is through involvement with associations for interaction with similar institutions. These provide resources for member institutions and opportunities for staff and faculty to build a community of reference. The Council for Christian Colleges & Universities (CCCU) is an international higher education association of intentionally Christian colleges and universities. It has 105 members in North America and 77 affiliate institutions in 24 countries. Its goal is to advance the cause of Christ-centered higher education and to help its institutions transform lives by faithfully relating scholarship and service to biblical truth. It provides more than one hundred programs to promote this vision.

The Association of Catholic Colleges and Universities promotes and strengthens the mission and character of Catholic higher education in the United States and serves as its collective voice. Through research, publications, conferences, consultations, special programs, and standing relationships with other agencies, ACCU encourages and facilitates sharing of ideas and cooperative efforts among its member institutions. ACCU's journal, *Current Issues in Catholic Higher Education*, is published semiannually and articulates a vision for higher education from a Catholic perspective. Since 1935, the Association of Lutheran College Faculties has annually brought together members of faculties of Lutheran institutions of higher learning and Lutherans teaching at other institutions of higher learning in the United States and Canada. It provides a Christian forum for discussion of issues relating to teaching and learning. The Nazarene International Education Association provides an opportunity for fellowship and networking for those involved in Christian, public, private, and home schools by sponsoring an annual conference. Similar associations serve other denominations and colleges with similar commitments. The biennial conference on Service-Learning at

Faith-Based Colleges and Universities held at Messiah College since 2000 brings together service-learning practitioners. The papers from the 2004 conference provide a rich resource of theoretical and practical knowledge (Eby, 2005).

At the most basic level, faith brings moral and ethical values and perspectives derived from religion to the discussion. It is important for faith-based colleges and universities to be intentional about connecting to their faith traditions and for others to be aware of those traditions as they interact with faith-based institutions. Hughes (2001) suggests contributions particular traditions make to intellectual activity and scholarship. He examines Catholic, Reformed, Anabaptist, and Lutheran traditions. Each of these traditions supports institutions of higher learning with strong programs of service and civic engagement and worldwide programs of service, development, and social change.

Catholics bring a rich intellectual tradition, the sacramental principle that takes the world seriously on its own terms, a global church, and an understanding that the life of the mind translates into a community. They have well-articulated social teaching that provides a solid foundation for service and civic engagement.

Reformed traditions bring the notion of a Christian world view, often stated as "all truth is God's truth." They integrate faith and learning and the notion of secularization, both in the sense that they see God in the "secular" and also see the "secular" as a "threat to be overcome." The Reformed perspective that links them in a partnership with God transforming society motivates them for service and civic engagement.

Hughes says the Mennonite model, in contrast to the reformed model, which "transforms living by thinking," "transforms thinking by living," an action reflection model, if you will. This approach focuses on the hands and the heart, abandons narrow nationalism for a world citizenship, requires a point of view developed in a "story informed community" nurtured by critique, and humility. The Mennonite model historically emphasized the tension and incompatibilities between the "kingdoms of the world" and the "kingdom of God" and suggested that God works primarily through the church.

The Lutheran model, he says, offers an understanding of human finitude and the sovereignty of God in which doubt is a partner of faith, Luther's notion of paradox, particularly the paradoxes of the two kingdoms or nature and grace, the sacred and the secular. This understanding encourages dialogue between the world of ideas and Christian faith.

Each of these perspectives opens a particular window on the interaction of faith and learning, and together they structure a set of dialectics and paradoxes that, when interacting, lead to rich and nuanced understandings and actions. More specifically, each perspective suggests a particular approach to service, social action, and civic engagement. Each denomination has a rich and long history of doing service, justice, and social change that informs the service and civic engagement of its colleges.

Connections and Relationships

Faith-based colleges and universities have a particular opportunity to partner with faith-based local organizations in civic engagement and service because they share similar values and commitments.

Locally and internationally, faith-based service organizations are among the leaders in sponsoring programs addressing human need and working for development and justice. Organizations such as Voice of Calvary, Urban Promise, Catholic Charities, the Mennonite Central Committee, Lutheran World Service, and World Vision all have well-deserved reputations for efficiency and effectiveness. They have built up a high level of expertise and a rich body of action-informed literature that informs service and social change.

Some of the most innovative and effective programs of service and social change in local communities are sponsored by congregations. Church organizations and congregations are among the most viable, authentic, and deeply rooted organizations in many local communities. Much of the community leadership is found in churches. Pastors have respect and experience and often education that is needed for effective community work. Churches provide facilities for community meetings and in many other ways contribute strength to local communities. They are key actors in community development and service.

Because educational institutions are often isolated from the real needs and social networks of local communities, they need strong connections to the community provided by religious organizations. At the same time, the local community needs the expertise provided by colleges to help local organizations move beyond good intentions toward research-based practice. The professional expertise of the academy linked with the passion and deep community roots of local organizations makes for strong and effective programs. Shared faith commitments enhance these partnerships.

Challenges and Issues for the Future

It is important to look not only at the strengths and perspectives of faith-based colleges and universities, but at some of the challenges as well. Faith-based programs need to work with a range of motivations for service. They should move beyond direct service to incorporate programs that work at fundamental issues of social change and justice. They are also challenged to connect passion with objectivity. These issues are by no means unique to faith-based institutions, but they do take on particular dimensions when faith is part of the mix.

Mixed Motives

The particular contribution the academy makes to service, civic engagement, and social change is the symbiosis that emerges when the research and teaching strengths of the academy are linked creatively with the strengths and needs of local communities. Some persons approaching service from a faith perspective hesitate to link service to learning for fear that mixed objectives added by the learning component will dilute the spiritual motivation and benevolent character of service. A student leader at Messiah College, in the early stages of adding service-learning to a very strong community volunteer service program, commented that he did not want to "pollute Christian service with learning." What he was saying is, of course, legitimate. Christian service is given only because of love and should not have ulterior motives or mixed objectives. In addition, it should respond to community-defined needs and requests, which should not be subverted or replaced by learning goals for students.

When service and civic engagement is done by faith-based organizations, whether community organizations or colleges and universities, there is always a possible tension between service and proselytization. Fears of the inappropriate use of religion in faith-based service organizations, although certainly legitimate, are often exaggerated. Evangelism and church development are important goals for faith-based organizations. Service can be used inappropriately as an enticement for conversion or recruitment for church membership. Some programs limit service to members of a particular religious group or to persons who make a particular religious commitment. Civic engagement can include advocacy for narrowly defined religious positions in public policy. Such practices not only violate good principles of service practice, they violate the best understandings of Christian service and evangelism.

Service and Social Justice

The dominant form of civic engagement at faith-based institutions is service-learning and community volunteer service, most of which is direct service such as tutoring individual students, working with food distribution programs, helping in youth recreation programs, visiting older people, and similar kinds of programs that relate to individuals and individual needs (Vogelgesang & Rhodes 2006). These activities do meet real needs and are appropriate for the skill levels students bring. They provide needed staff for local programs and are to be affirmed. When done well, with quality reflection, they can promote greater awareness of social issues, and when combined with classroom instruction, they help students see how individual needs are related to larger social issues and structural problems (Colby et al., 2003).

Some Christians, because of their individualistic definition of salvation, extend that individualistic approach to their understanding of social issues. One of the real challenges of service programs is to move beyond ameliorative service to address structural and systemic issues. However, that emphasis ignores the deep and rich teaching of the Bible related to structural justice issues. There is no lack of critique of social class inequities and calls for building social structures to care for the marginalized. Over and over again, the prophets in the Hebrew Bible called for special concern for widows, the fatherless, and strangers. The call for a jubilee year in which slaves would be freed, debts forgiven, and land returned to its original owners would have had staggering effect on the accumulation of inequality over the generations (Leviticus 25:1–55).

Cuban and Anderson (2007) suggest that "social justice and service-learning are separate inter-related approaches to education and social change." They identify several barriers that prevent a social justice perspective from being more prevalent. Faculty lean toward outcomes of service-learning that help students develop academic skills rather than focusing on linking students to social change activities in communities. Many faculty and most students do not have the analytic skills needed for social justice work or the contacts in the community to facilitate them. There is also fear that social activism may generate controversy that colleges do not want because it impacts fund raising and marketing in negative ways. For many of the same reasons, local partner organizations find it easier and more appealing to work at direct service. The "feel good" rewards of direct service sustain both students and agency constituencies. They also make good publicity for the sponsoring college or university!

177

St. Mary's College of California is one example of a faith-based college that takes social justice seriously. Its Lasallian Heritage supports education that is truly transformative, both for the individual and for the society around them. They build on five core principles: Faith in the Presence of God, Concern for the Poor and Social Justice, Quality Education, Inclusive Community, and Respect for All Persons (http://www.stmarys-ca.edu/lasallian-approach/). Adler (2005) makes a strong case for giving greater attention to social justice in the curriculum and in institutional life and describes two projects that reflect that emphasis. One was a student-led effort toward adopting a "living wage" for employees on campus using student and staff organizing, advocacy, dialogue, and public action. The administration eventually adopted the policy. The other involved advocacy and awareness raising related to a movement to try to close the School of the Americas, now known as the Western Hemisphere Institute for Security Cooperation. Adler (2005) says the project provided an "opportunity to balance advocacy with inquiry, tutoring the skills of listening, research and presentation." It is important to help students understand what C. Wright Mills calls "public issues of social structure" in contrast to "personal troubles" (Mills, 1959).

One of the challenges for faith-based institutions is to move beyond direct service often reflecting a "charity" model to build on the social justice teachings of their faith traditions to include activities that help students understand underlying structural and political issues and engage in activities that are oriented to fundamental social change (Adler, 2005; Butin, 2006, 2007; Cuban & Anderson, 2007; Vogelgesang & Rhodes, 2006).

Linking Passion and Objectivity

One of the strengths of faith-based institutions is their deep and sustaining motivation and passion. The challenge is to build on that base with civic engagement and service that is informed by solid research and evaluation (Gelmon & Billig, 2007).

Illich (1990) wrote many years ago about the dangers of serving with "good intentions" but developing little solidarity with the people and having little real impact on alleviating the real needs of people. He warned of the paternalism embedded in that approach. McKnight (1989) comments that many church people have "substituted a vision for service for the only thing that can make people whole, community." His advocacy for asset-based development builds strong communities able to work at their own issues.

Service, however well intentioned, can actually do harm when it replaces local initiative or tempts local people to give ownership of the project to the persons who do it. A mission group from a church in the United States built a church for a community in South America. Several years later, when the roof developed a leak, the pastor of the congregation wrote to the group in the United States, "Your church has a leaky roof. Please come and fix it." There are numerous examples around the world where well-intentioned gifts of food or other goods such as used clothing destroyed the market for locally produced goods and led to long-term dependence. Service rooted in research-based theories of community change and development can build local strength and independence.

One kind of service-learning that has promise is community-based research. Making available the research expertise of the academy as a resource for local community action will enrich and strengthen community organizations. A knowledge base can be developed that will inform action and provide data for evaluation of program strategies and approaches. Asset identification and evaluation research can be particularly helpful.

When the passion of faith-based service is informed by the research and knowledge base of the academy, authentically rooted local organizations can be empowered to initiate genuine social and structural change.

Conclusion

Faith is a powerful source of motivation that leads to sustainable effort. Faith-based colleges and universities build on the richness of particular faith traditions and the history of social service and scholarship in those traditions. Faith-based colleges and universities play a significant role in service and civic engagement. They have relatively high rates of student participation in a broad range of programs. Because they share faith commitments and a world view based on faith, they develop rich and holistic partnerships with organizations with deep roots in local communities.

At their best, faith-based colleges and universities reflect the best practices of civic engagement and service developed in partnerships with local community organizations. These practices are enriched and strengthened with the perspectives and power of their faith tradition.

References

Adler, G. (2005). Taking justice seriously: Advocacy, the campus, and catholic social thought. In J. W. Eby (Ed.), *Spirituality, social justice, and service-learning* (pp. 83–91). Grantham, PA: Messiah College Press.

Braskamp, L. A., Trautvetter, L. C., & Ward, K. (2006). *Putting students first: How colleges develop students purposefully.* Bolton, MS: Anker Books.

Butin, D. W. (2006). The limits of service-learning in higher education. *Review of Higher Education, 29*(4), 473–493.

Butin, D. W. (2007). Justice-learning: Service-learning as justice-oriented education. *Equity and Excellence in Education, 40,* 177–183.

Chickering, A. W., Dalton, J., & Stamm, L. (2006). *Encouraging authenticity and spirituality in higher education.* San Francisco: Jossey-Bass.

Colby, A., Ehrlich T., Beaumont, E., & Stephens, J. (2003). *Educating citizens: Preparing America's undergraduates for lives of moral and civic responsibility.* San Francisco: Jossey-Bass.

Cuban, S., & Anderson, J. B. (2007). Where's the justice in service-learning? Institutionalizing service-learning from a social justice perspective at a Jesuit University. *Equity and Excellence in Education, 40,* 144–155.

Dalton, J. C. (2006). Community service and spirituality: Integrating faith, service, and social justice at DePaul University. *Journal of College & Character, 8*(1), 1–8.

Eby, J. W. (Ed.). (2005). *Spirituality, justice, and service-learning.* Grantham, PA: Messiah College Press.

Economic justice for all: Pastoral letter on Catholic social teaching and the U.S. economy. (1986). Washington, DC: National Conference of Catholic Bishops.

Emerson, M., & Smith, C. (2000). *Divided by faith divided by faith: Evangelical religion and the problem of race in America.* New York: Oxford University Press.

Eyler, J., & Giles, D. (1999). *Where's the learning in service-learning?* San Francisco: Jossey-Bass.

Gelmon, S. B., & Billig, S. H. (Eds.). (2007). *Service-learning: From passion to objectivity.* Charlotte, NC: Information Age Publishing.

Heffner, G. G., & Beversluis, C. D. (Eds.). (2002). *Commitment and connection: Service-learning and Christian higher education.* New York: University Press of America.

Hesser, G. (2003). Review essay: Faith-based service-learning: Back to the basics. *Michigan Journal of Community Service-learning, 10*(1), 59–69.

Higher Education Research Institute (HERI). (2003). *The spiritual life of college students: A national study of college students' search for meaning and purpose.* University of California, Los Angeles.

Hughes, R. T. (2001). *How Christian faith can sustain the life of the mind.* Grand Rapids, MI: Eerdmans.

Illich, I. (1990). To hell with good intentions. In J. Kendall and Associates (Eds.), *Combining Service and Learning.* Raleigh, NC: National Society for Internships and Experiential Education.

Jacobsen, R. H., & Jacobsen, D. (2008). *The American college in a post secular age.* New York: Oxford University Press.

McKnight, J. (1989, January/February). Why servanthood is bad. *The Other Side*, pp. 35–44.

McNally, M. D. (2004). Indigenous pedagogy in the classroom: A service learning model for discussion. *American Indian Quarterly, 28*(3&4), 604–617.

Messiah College catalog. (2007–2008). Grantham, PA: Messiah College Press.

Mills, C. W. (1959). *The sociological imagination.* New York: Oxford University Press.

Selingo, J. (2008, August 1). Trust ideas, not policy, to improve teaching, says departing leader. *Chronicle of Higher Education.*

Sider, R. J. (1997). *Rich Christians in an age of hunger.* Dallas, TX: Word Publishing.

Slimbach, R. (2008, May 30–June 1). *Stepping up: Making global service-learning pro-poor and sustainable.* Paper presented at the Fifth National Faith-Based Service-Learning Conference at Messiah College.

Stanton, T., Cruz, N., & Giles, D. (1999). *Service-learning: A movement's pioneers reflect on its origins, practice, and future.* San Francisco: Jossey-Bass.

Teasdale, W. (1999). *The mystic heart.* Novato, CA: New World Library.

Trozzolo, T. A., & Brandenberger, J. (2001). *Religious commitment and prosocial behavior: A study of undergraduates at University of Notre Dame.* Report Number 2, Center for Social Concerns. University of Notre Dame.

Vogelgesang, L., & Rhodes, R. (2006). Advancing a broad notion of public engagement: The limitations of contemporary service-learning *Journal of College Character.* Available at http://www.collegevalues.org/articles.cfmevalues.org/diaries.cfm?a=1&id=1017.

Weigert, K. M., and Miller, S. L. (1996). Identity and mission at a sample of Catholic colleges and universities: Students and service to society. *Current Issues in Catholic Higher Education, 16*(2), 33–62.

Wenger Shenk, S. (2003). *Anabaptist ways of knowing: A conversation about tradition-based critical education.* Telford, PA: Cascadia Publishing House.

Woltersdorf, N. (2004). Particularist perspectives: Bias or access in educating for shalom. In C. W. Joldersmith and G. G. Stronks (Eds.), *Essays on Christian higher education* (pp. 226–240). Grand Rapids, MI: Eerdmans.

Engaged Scholarship at Historically Black Colleges and Universities

Stephen L. Rozman

Michael Lomax, president and CEO of the United Negro College Fund (UNCF), observes:

> From their founding 150 years ago, historically black colleges and universities have been an exercise in engagement. For almost a century, they functioned not only as institutions dedicated to the education and betterment of their students, but very deliberately as engines for the improvement of a community and population toward whose well-being and social integrity society at large was at best indifferent, at worst hostile. (2006, p. 12)

Zlotkowski et al., in *One with the Community: Indicators of Engagement at Minority-Serving Institutions* (2005), compare historically black colleges and universities (HBCUs) with non-HBCUs by saying, "It is important to appreciate the degree to which interest in campus-based community engagement, a recent phenomenon for many institutions, has always been part of the core mission of HBCUs" (p. 39).

The traditionally strong identification of African Americans with their communities is apparent in African American students at both HBCUs and predominantly white institutions (PWIs). A sample of 276 African American students who attended either an HBCU or a PWI—two HBCUs and two PWIs—revealed that the strongest predictor for perceptions of community outreach was black racial identity, with racial identity playing a significant role in this bonding. The data help provide a framework for understanding the factors that build strong connections between African American students and African American community members, and support the hypothesis that racial identity "contributes a substantial variance to community outreach perceptions" (Lott, 2008, p. 11).

The importance of race as a variable is attested to by data from the 2005 National Survey of Student Engagement (NSSE), which showed that students at HBCUs "are far more likely to participate in a community project linked to a course (28 percent) than students at predominantly white institutions (16 percent)" (Indiana University, 2004, p. 1).

This result is bolstered by survey data from the Center for Information & Research on Civic Learning & Engagement (CIRCLE), which show that graduates of HBCUs "volunteer more and are more likely to attend political meetings than are graduates of other types of institutions" (Campus Compact, 2006, p. 2).

The commitment to community outreach at HBCUs is reflected in the priorities set by faculty development directors. Beach, Dawkins, Rozman, and Grant (2008) compare the perceptions of faculty development directors at HBCUs with those of faculty development directors affiliated with the Professional and Organizational Development Network in Higher Education (POD) with regard to issues of importance to faculty developers, and observe the following:

> Of particular interest is the very significant difference between the HBCU sample and the POD sample regarding the importance of "Community service learning." Given the unique historical circumstances of African Americans in their encounters with racism and racial injustice, they may have developed a greater sense of community than whites. Consequently, HBCUs have tended to have stronger identifications with their (African American) communities. (p. 166)

Faculty developers were also asked to respond to a number of new challenges and pressures on institutions that affect faculty work, both in terms of how important they think it is to address those issues through faculty development and the extent to which their institutions were already responding. HBCU faculty developers, by a significantly higher percentage than the POD developers, regarded "outreach/service activities" and "commitment to civic life/the public good" as important and claimed that their institutions were responding to these issues. The HBCU developers also placed a higher premium on "community-based research," and, according to the results of the survey, their institutions were collectively more involved in this type of research than those of the POD developers (p. 164).

The struggle for civil rights during the 1960s was a time of particular struggle for HBCUs, as the leaders of these institutions were confronted by this dilemma: encourage the engagement of their students and faculty in the civil rights movement and risk a white backlash; or suppress civil rights activity and risk alienation from their own campus and external communities. Public HBCUs were especially vulnerable because they were under the authority of governing boards controlled by whites who tended to be committed to the racial status quo.

Strong ties were in place between HBCUs and the faith-based community because of the strong religious identification of African Americans. These ties were reinforced during the civil rights period due to the fact the African American churches and their ministers often played key leadership roles in the civil rights struggle. The ministers tended to have more freedom for independent action because they were less vulnerable economically. HBCU administrators faced job loss and economic sanctions against their institutions if they challenged the existing order or allowed their campuses to become focal points for civil rights activities.

In the aftermath of the civil rights period, HBCUs gradually began to adopt community service requirements for student graduation, and these requirements led to the building of relationships with a wide variety of community organizations. These relationships provided an ideal foundation for service-learning programs that growing numbers of HBCUs have come to develop, either as options for students and faculty or as student graduation requirements.

Only recently have HBCUs, in significant number, become involved in engaged scholarship through community-based research. This research has been depicted as "action-oriented research" because it involves direct contact and interaction with community organizations and community representatives and active participation in the development and implementation of strategies to address community needs. The addition of this research dimension to community outreach serves to provide documentation of the long history of strong HBCU ties with the community. Indeed, it is often bemoaned that HBCUs have traditionally neglected to document their work with their community partners and have, thus, sacrificed the recognition they justly deserve.

Abbott and Beech (2007) provide a useful framework in comparing HBCUs with non-HBCUs:

> The university traditionally has had three roles: (a) student instruction, (b) pure research, and (c) community service. While these roles have become disconnected in the contemporary university, they have remained integrated in historically black colleges and universities. . . . In recent years, the concept of "service learning" has been used by HBCUs to further integrate traditional university roles. . . . Perhaps, though, it is the Historically black University (HBU) that provides the best model of what the fusion of these traditional roles might look like. Because of the nature of its students, the research pursuits of its faculty, and the obligations that are imposed upon it by its community, the HBU has been coerced to continue to treat the traditional roles of the university as one instead of three opposing tracts. . . . As an HBCU—especially one in a distressed urban area—it has been forced to accept its obligations as a major stakeholder in the African American community. (pp. 1–3)

Abbott and Beech then describe the initial success of their university, Harris-Stowe, in incorporating service-learning into business administration and other courses, and how the community, students, and faculty all benefited from the experience. With service-learning as a foundation, Harris-Stowe faculty went on to create a center devoted to strengthening the relationship between the campus and the community.

Many non-HBCUs, especially well-endowed liberal arts colleges, have developed infrastructures for community outreach prior to taking steps to expand their limited community ties, whereas HBCUs have had the community ties and have been working to develop their infrastructures. A growing number of HBCUs now have in place effective infrastructures, including specialized research centers, for engaging in community-based research and developing ongoing partnerships to address needs identified by both the community and engaged scholars—students and faculty. Howard University, Morgan State University, and Jackson State University have established major urban research centers and have developed a large number of projects to address the service needs of residents in their communities.

In their discussion of the extent to which minority serving institutions embrace the culture of engagement, Taylor, Dwyer, and Pacheco (2005b) argue:

> For many HBCUs, there is little difference between the power and resources of the institution and that of the community in which they are located. Often the business leaders, community agencies, and legislators neglect both the HBCU and its community. In fact, many HBCUs that are engaged in numerous community partnerships . . . are also struggling to remain financially and academically viable.

They add that "HBCUs are most likely to be integrated and engaged in their communities because the fortunes of one tend to be the fortunes of the other" (p. 34).

Taylor, Dwyer, and Pacheco go on to say that in the case of HBCUs, the community is not another culture that needs to be studied as a separate entity from the university, unlike the circumstances faced by a major research university that has a traditionally white faculty, staff, and student body, is located right in the middle of a blighted community, and is trying to form a partnership with that community. They believe that the HBCU has an advantage over the non-HBCU in that "the faculty, staff, and students at HBCUs more closely reflect the population of their communities in terms of race, socioeconomic status, and (sub) culture" (p. 35).

An impressive model for conducting community-based research was established at Johnson C. Smith University (JCSU) in Charlotte, North Carolina (Carter, Fox, Priest, & McBride, 2002). With the support of a grant from the Council of Independent Colleges Urban Missions project, a group of faculty from a variety of disciplines formed the Urban Research Group (URG), designed to conduct community research for community-based organizations (CBOs) with limited resources. Eighteen faculty members from twelve academic disciplines worked together to establish a method to assist CBOs in doing the necessary research to document their needs and concerns.

The URG was successful in completing sixteen student-assisted research projects, with six in process at the time this article was written. The projects involved the assistance of 250 faculty-trained student research assistants from nearly all JCSU disciplines. The research has included both projects linked to classes and unlinked projects, with students in the latter group receiving financial remuneration. The authors affirm, "Community leaders report that they have used the research results to create strategic plans and write successful grant proposals" (p. 56).

As Carter et al. note, the URG was formed in response to the need to strengthen the CBOs in the Charlotte area, based on the belief that people are not really empowered until they are given the tools to make informed decisions about community needs and become effective in their efforts to solve community problems. In addressing this need, the URG discovered that many faculty members showed an interest in conducting research to increase their skills and their connection with the community (p. 57).

Carter et al. describe their model of community research, which is a model based on responses to needs identified by the community. The process begins with CBO representatives sending research requests to the director of the URG, who then determines the type of expertise needed and seeks faculty members to conduct the necessary research. Interested faculty members give the URG research proposals that must include students. Once the proposal is approved by the URG and university administrators, faculty work closely with the CBO and students to plan and conduct the research. All URG faculty involved in student-assisted community research are members of the URG, which meets monthly to review and approve faculty proposals and research requests from the community (p. 59).

Carter et al. also describe the value of the community-based research related to a variety of purposes, most notably to secure funding for the organization and its programs. Timely data are highly important for writing strong proposals to funding agencies and meeting their deadlines. The authors refer to the example of an antipoverty agency that needed data related to community needs and to the effectiveness of this agency in meeting those needs. The agency was facing a deadline for submitting this information to avoid a loss of funding (p. 60).

Critical Issues Related to Engaged Scholarship

Perhaps the most critical issue related to engaged scholarship at HBCUs has been that of building trust. Given the historical treatment of African Americans, the suspicion African American communities have had about outsiders and their intentions has been endemic. However, the Tuskegee syphilis experiment probably did more to build distrust than any other outside intervention.

An article by Borgna Brunner (2003) on the Tuskegee University web page pays homage to the victims of this atrocity, with some essential background information. Brunner notes that between 1932 and 1972, the U.S. Public Health Service (PHS) conducted an experiment on 399 black men in the latter stages of syphilis. This group was mainly composed of illiterate sharecroppers from one of the poorest counties in Alabama, and the subjects were never informed as to what disease they were suffering from or how serious it was. They were simply told that they were being treated for "bad blood," and the doctors had no intention of treating them for syphilis. The data for the experiment were to be collected from autopsies of the men, and they were thus deliberately left to suffer the effects of tertiary syphilis—which can include tumors, heart disease, paralysis, blindness, insanity, and death. Brunner quotes one of the physicians as saying: "As I see it, we have no further interest in these patients until they die." The experimenters would then collect data from the autopsies of the men, with the goal of comparing the effects of syphilis on African Americans with the effects on whites (p. 1).

Brunner observes that the real nature of the experiment had to be concealed from the subjects to ensure their cooperation, and they cooperated because of what they saw as the benefit of receiving free medical care. Twenty-eight of the men in the experiment died directly from syphilis, whereas one hundred more died from related complications. Forty of their wives were infected, and nineteen of their children were born with congenital syphilis.

Brunner continues:

> One of the most chilling aspects of the experiment was how zealously the PHS kept these men from receiving treatment. When several nationwide campaigns came to Macon County, the men were prevented from participating. Even when penicillin—the first real cure for syphilis—was discovered in the 1940s, the Tuskegee men were deliberately denied the medication. (pp. 1–2)

185

In discussing "The Legacy of Tuskegee," Brunner cites a 1990 survey which found that 10 percent of African Americans believed that the U.S. government created AIDS as a plot to exterminate blacks, and another 20 percent accepted the possibility that this was true (p. 3).

Another important issue in engaged scholarship at HBCUs has been oral history, to capture and document the experiences of African Americans, ranging from the slave narratives to the Jim Crow years to the civil rights period and its aftermath, including the Tuskegee syphilis experiment. The University of the District of Columbia, as one example, has recently engaged its students in a community-based research and oral history project (Jowers-Barber, 2008) to document and chronicle the experiences of community residents.

Jowers-Barber observes that community members are becoming increasingly active and vocal about the preservation of their history, which may relate distinctively to their respective neighborhood or may be connected to a broader regional, national, or international history. The community members are also concerned about the loss of the neighborhood itself, together with its historic structures and their cultural significance.

Perhaps the most important current issue related to engaged scholarship has been health disparities in African Americans, the subject of a variety of studies, including the Jackson Heart Study, which is the largest single-site, epidemiological investigation of cardiovascular disease among African Americans ever undertaken. This population-based longitudinal study has been taking place in Jackson, Mississippi, with the collaboration of two HBCUs— Tougaloo College and Jackson State University—and the University of Mississippi Medical Center, the Jackson community, and the National Institutes of Health, to discover and test best practices for eliminating health disparities.

Taylor et al. (2005a) affirm that the Jackson Heart Study "seeks not only to study disparities in CVD health and health care but also to address these disparities." They add, "Public health scientists have increasingly recognized the value of community participation in defining key questions, carrying out protocols and interpreting and responding to research findings" (p. S6-6).

In discussing the process of developing of the Jackson Heart Study, Taylor et al. (2005a) note:

> an active community outreach program was developed well before the start of JHS recruitment. This program is intended to build an atmosphere of trust and support in the community but also to better understand sociocultural factors that might influence the success and findings of the study and to address the documented need for increased knowledge of CVD prevention among African Americans. (p. S6-6)

Although their primary goal was to generate broad awareness of the Jackson Heart Study across the nation, their long-range goal was to create a sense of trust within the African American community to enable the JHS project to continue regardless of the findings that might emerge from the study (p. S6-6).

To help build this trust, the organizers of the JHS recruited members of the African American community to participate in all components of the program. They first turned to the Council of Elders, generally respected members of community, to get their inputs into the planning process at its initial stages. They subsequently brought in other community members to serve on most of the operating committees. Public relations were not over-looked, as the JHS used television and print advertisements that featured local sports figures and other recognized leaders. They also promoted the JHS at sports events and other gather-ings (S 6-6).

In addition, The Partnership for Community Awareness and Health Education (PCAHE) set up a cardiovascular Community Health Advisers Network and trained members of the Jackson metropolitan area to provide counseling on a heart-healthy diet and lifestyle changes that contribute to good health. The counseling also included monitoring community mem-bers to make certain they were taking their prescribed medications, and providing informa-tion to assist people in locating health care resources.

The strategic importance of the African American faith-based community is emphasized in the following statement by Taylor et al. (2005a):

> Community outreach efforts have been based on an awareness of the central role of churches in African American communities. Many area churches have willingly embraced the JHS. Other contacts have been made through schools, beauty shops, and civic organizations. The involve-ment of local students in Undergraduate Training Center activities has created valuable inciden-tal interactions with their friends and relatives. (p. S6-6)

It should also be mentioned that the Jackson Heart Study Undergraduate Training Center (UTC) has been established at Tougaloo College to increase the number of African American students entering public health and health-related fields.

Another important example of a collaborative campus-community relationship involv-ing HBCUs and other institutions has been the relationship between Shaw University and the University of North Carolina at Chapel Hill (UNC-CH), described by Carey, Goldmon, Roberson, Godley, and Ammerman (2005). The two universities developed a number of research initiatives to address health disparities. Shaw faculty participated in a variety of faculty development activities, engaged in pilot studies with the UNC-CH faculty, and worked with their UNC-CH counterparts to get grants from the Agency for Health Care Research and Quality of the federal Department of Health and Human Services and the National Institutes of Health (p. 47).

The most substantive collaborative project between Shaw and UNC-CH has been the Project EXPORT center's five-year grant on health disparities, which "solidified the relation-ship" between the two institutions. The goal statements included "training young investiga-tors in research methods in health disparities, collaboration between the universities on major community-based research projects, and enhancing Shaw University's capacity to conduct independent research."

The Shaw–UNC-CH partnership also targeted health disparities through community engagement. Again, the importance of partnering with religious organizations was empha-sized, and Shaw worked to develop a network with African American churches throughout North Carolina. The stated long-term goal of the Shaw Divinity School was to establish a dialogue with the congregations of these churches related to health. Shaw and UNC-CH would team up with the North Carolina Office of Minority Health to provide health informa-tion to the churches, which the latter would then share with their congregations. Instead of anticipating the needs of the church members, they invited the congregations to discuss their health concerns with Shaw and its partners. They also invited the church members to indicate whether they were interested in joint research projects on health disparities (Carey et al., 2005, pp. 50–51).

North Carolina Central University (NCCU) offers another important example of a community-campus partnership to address health disparities, as described by Reid, Hatch, and Parrish (2003) in an article entitled "The Role of a Historically black University and the black Church in Community-Based Health Initiatives: The Project DIRECT Experience." Project DIRECT, an acronym that refers to Project Diabetes Interventions Reaching and Educating Community Together, is a federally funded participatory research project sponsored by the Centers for Disease Control and Prevention.

Reid, Hatch, and Parrish note that "faith-centered strategies were used in local churches to create social and environmental changes to support diabetes prevention and control" and add, "Involving historically black colleges and universities and black churches in health promotion at the community level represents an excellent example of how local institutional resources can help eliminate health disparities." Project DIRECT was implemented to increase the awareness of African American residents in Raleigh, North Carolina, neighborhoods of the importance of following recommended guidelines for exercise, diet, and diabetes self-management (p. S70).

NCCU believed that Project DIRECT could play a key role in meeting the health needs of the African American community. As an initial step, NCCU sought to determine the level of understanding that project staff and members of the community had about outreach and to discover steps they were taking or hoped to take to facilitate their outreach goals. To gain this knowledge, they engaged in one-to-one conversations with key stakeholders, who included leaders of various community organizations, tenants' associations, civic leaders, Project DIRECT board and staff members, health professionals, and clergy. Two of the authors played key roles among the NCCU faculty dedicated to Project DIRECT.

Reid, Hatch, and Parrish (2003) add that the team found it necessary to clarify the overall goals of the project in its early stages, and that "outreach to churches was considered an effective way to increase awareness and participation." NCCU and Project DIRECT staff were in agreement that it was essential to build trust and increase understanding of Project DIRECT's mission through formal and informal networks throughout the community.

One of the most effective strategies used by Project DIRECT staff was to engage in dialogues with patients living with diabetes who visited a local health center. These dialogues gave the staff information about local beliefs and actions that contributed to Project DIRECT's outreach and educational initiatives (Reid et al., 2003, p. S71).

They illustrate the stature of churches and church officials in the African American community with the comment that:

> Historically, African American people have turned to the church for information about services of value and importance to them. Our challenge was to gain support from clergy and key leadership for community-based diabetes control. . . . NCCU faculty, graduate and undergraduate health education majors at NCCU, made visits to churches regularly. . . . NCCU faculty designed the congregational needs assessment tool (CHAT) and the congregational health action plan

(CHAP), both tailored to the need of each congregation. . . . NCCU consultants and Project DIRECT staff presented church leaders with the results of the CHAT and CHAP. NCCU referred church leaderships to (or facilitated their contacts with) organizations and experts who could help their churches develop comprehensive responses to address health priorities, particularly diabetes. Several churches have reorganized their social or health ministries based on findings from the CHAP. (p. 71–72)

Another critical issue has been the housing in inner cities and the impact of substandard houses on minority populations. The Research and Evaluation Division of Howard University's Center for Urban Progress (CUP) has collaborated with the Lincoln Heights Community Partnership, the District of Columbia Government, and the D.C. Housing Authority to determine the needs of community residents (Howard University Center for Urban Progress, 2008). CUP "used multiple approaches to data collection in pursuance of this research, including one-on-one household surveys, focus groups, video taped interviews, and the community dollar game."

CUP has also been involved in the assessment of the HOPE (Housing Opportunities for People Everywhere) VI Program, a program designed to address problems related to severely distressed public housing. A Community and Supportive Services Program (CSSP) was designed to address the needs of residents who were relocated as a result of community revitalization efforts, and CUP assessed the impact of CSSP on the displaced residents.

CUP has also received federal government funding to conduct a Lead Technical Study in Washington, DC, using a community-based participatory approach to research and partnering with four local churches in the city, together with local agencies that dealt with problems related to lead poisoning, which has been a serious problem for children in the inner cities (http://www.coas.howard.edu/hucup/research_hvi.html).

Environmental issues, such as lead poisoning, have been researched by other HBCUs, including North Carolina Central University (NCCU), which has utilized federal funding to assess exposure in communities impacted by environmental hazards and to develop the research infrastructure of the NCCU Environmental Science Program for sustainable service to local communities. (R. S. Messick, Assistant Director, Academic Community Service Learning Program, NCCU, personal communication, September 9, 2008). The NCCU/ National Exposure Research Laboratory project developed a process for collecting data to gain greater awareness of environmental hazards and help apply needed remedies.

LeMoyne-Owen College in Memphis, Tennessee, and Benedict College in Columbia, South Carolina, are examples of private HBCUs that have worked closely with the community to revitalize the surrounding neighborhoods. Both have done so through the creation of Community Development Corporations. LeMoyne-Owen established a Community Development Corporation and has received funding from the HUD Office of University Partnerships (OUP) to address inner city economic development and housing needs, with emphasis on job creation, affordable housing, and access to health and wellness activities (OUP, 2007).

Benedict College promoted its mission of community development and neighborhood revitalization through the Benedict-Allen Community Development Center (CDC) (Greene, 2006). The Benedict-Allen CDC, in collaboration with the local community councils and the city of Columbia, has renovated and built homes for low- to moderate-income families. Their acquisition, rehabilitation, and resale of existing substandard housing and new home development has served to promote home ownership (p. 55).

The Institute for Urban Research (IUR) at Morgan State University is involved in many types of action research and community service activities, and provides technical assistance to Morgan State University and the Baltimore urban community (Morgan State, 2008). It also facilitates research opportunities for Morgan State faculty and students.

IUR research projects have included assessing the impact of a comprehensive school-based health, educational, and social services program at a Baltimore school, through the use of "an integrated framework of quantitative and qualitative data analysis;" "evaluation of a school-based partnership program for the prevention of crime and violence at a Baltimore school; and doing a variety of needs assessments for nonprofit organizations in Baltimore and in other geographical areas" (http://iur.morgan.edu/AboutUs/index1/htm).

The Mississippi Urban Research Center (MURC) at Jackson State University uses multi-disciplinary approaches and a variety of methods to provide "a structure and setting for conducting research, analyzing public policies and managing research data" (MURC, 2008). MURC also serves as a clearinghouse for dissemination of research data on critical issues found in urban settings related to health, crime, violence, substance abuse, urban education, and urban policy. MURC also reviews and analyzes these data to make projections concerning policies and initiatives that have an effect on urban life. It provides relevant data to urban planners, policymakers, service providers, educators, and community leaders (http://www.murc.org/).

Another example of collaboration between HBCUs and non-HBCUs directed toward the promotion of community-based participatory research has been the "Building Campus to Campus Partnerships to Serve Community Needs" program, which has brought together faculty from seven HBCUs—Tougaloo College, Benedict College, Jackson State University, Norfolk State University, Tuskegee University, Morehouse College, and Prairie View A&M University—and Michigan State University faculty and graduate students to develop a model for a partnership linking Michigan State University with the HBCU Faculty Development Network (HBCUFDN) and its member institutions; and, second, to development models for transforming service learning programs into community-based participatory research opportunities for faculty and students (Campus to Campus Partnerships, 2007).

The purpose of the "Campus to Campus" initiative was to "create a partnership between MSU faculty and students and those at the HBCUFDN institutions to co-create models of community engagement that emphasize CBPR research practices and scholarship opportunities related to service learning/civic engagement activities as well as independent CBPR projects."

Representatives from the participating institutions participated in a workshop in May 2007 at Michigan State University and, among other actions, developed logic models that "identified how faculty, community partners, and individual institutions can advance CBPR, with a goal of increasing the number of publications by HBCU faculty on CBPR projects." Participating faculty have been giving presentations at the annual *HBCU Faculty Development Symposium*—sponsored by the HBCUFDN—to promote CBPR at additional HBCUs.

One of the academic institutions in the "Campus to Campus" partnership, Tougaloo College, was responsible for founding the HBCUFDN in 1994 and continues to host this organization. Its Center for Civic Engagement & Social Responsibility (CCESR) has worked closely with the HBCUFDN to sponsor workshops and summer institutions on CBPR, including a June 2007 summer institute on "Community-Based Participatory Research: A Pathway to Sustainable Partnerships" that attracted representatives from a variety of HBCUs, non-HBCUs, and community organizations. For further information on the relationship between the CCESR and the HBCUFDN, please see the article by Rozman and Roberts (2006) on "Tougaloo College and the HBCU Faculty Development Network: Networking for Mutual Reinforcement."

Tougaloo College has also been participating in the National Community-Based Research Networking Initiative—directed by Princeton University and the Bonner Foundation—designed to "support the development of high-quality community-based research as a form of service-learning and create a national networking structure that assists and connects practitioners" (National CBR Networking Initiative, 2008). Tougaloo faculty, from a variety of academic disciplines, have partnered designated classes with community organizations, with students in these classes doing research on issues of relevance to these organizations.

Another issue has been justice, as a response to the long history of racial discrimination in the criminal justice system. Winston-Salem State University's Center for Community Safety's research, outreach, and training center (see Harvey & Mitchell, 2006) has undertaken a "data-driven, community-based partnership approach to solving local problems," with WSSU faculty serving on the local evaluation team.

The center has defined its mission as one of engaging communities to undertake research to develop policies for addressing community safety issues. The "action-oriented research" included community-mapping workshops using geographic information systems (GIS) software. This research contributed to solving community problems and to the development of partnerships among criminal justice, social service, civic, community development, faith-based, neighborhood organizations, and individual community residents (Harvey & Mitchell, 2006, p. 44).

Fayetteville State University, in Fayetteville, North Carolina, is another institution that has linked community engagement to community justice, based on the argument that "there is no place in U.S. society where racial minorities face greater danger and discrimination than with the police and the entire criminal justice system" (Barlow, Barlow, DeValve, & DeValve, 2007). They observe that HBCUs "are well positioned to bridge the divide between those who create and apply justice policy and the communities most affected by them." (p. 2)

Collaborative relationships between HBCUs and community partners have been facilitated by modern technology. Tennessee State University (TSU) (see Maddux, Bradley, Fuller, Darnell, & Wright, 2006) serves as an important example, as it created an Office of Technology Integration (OTI) that serves as the coordinator of service-learning and community engagement activities. TSU students, faculty, and staff collaborated with several community centers to establish education computer laboratories "to provide tools and training that will build capacity," with a "focus on how technology (through e-commerce and e-philanthropy) can help drive community partners' missions" (Maddux et al., 2006, pp. 70–71).

Future Trends

For the scholarship of engagement at HBCUs to move forward, there is a pressing need for both the documentation of community outreach activities and a commitment to publishing the results. The rich body of experience and achievement of HBCU faculty and students in service to their surrounding communities remains as a legacy in the minds and, perhaps, official records of individual institutions, but sadly has not become a major segment of the growing body of literature on community engagement.

This is a loss for both the HBCUs and the general community of scholars because HBCUs have much to teach us from their extensive and productive relationship with the community. Colleagues from HBCUs have related their experiences to me about attending academic meetings on community engagement where only a handful of representatives from HBCUs have been present. Presentations from the African American faculty at HBCUs have been very well attended, with white faculty from non-HBCUs wanting to learn strategies for building trust with minority communities and developing suitable research projects. These faculty often come from institutions with well-developed infrastructures for community engagement and generously funded programs.

Faculty and staff at HBCUs—often serving in service-learning and research centers—are often productive in proposal writing and grant management and do commendable work in fulfilling the grant objectives and reporting to the funding agency. However, the opportunity to publish their work in a scholarly journal to model their achievements with the community is often lost. The fact that faculty at most HBCUs have a full teaching load—generally four courses per semester—greatly limits their time for engaged scholarship, especially when they are often encouraged to generate funding through proposal writing more than they are encouraged to publish.

A second critical need is to create genuine community-based participatory research, with community representatives as actual partners rather than facilitators of research. This would best be accomplished by doing three things: (1) recognizing the wisdom of the community generated by its collective experience, as a step toward bringing together the academic skills of the campus and the practical skills of the community; (2) preparing a budget in collaboration with community representatives that places equal value on the time and effort of community representatives and academic representatives in the management of the project, and sharing the funding in an equitable manner; and (3) making it clear to the community that the research is much more than an intellectual exercise; that it is designed to address community needs—as they are identified by community representatives—by developing effective responses and possible solutions. (A Jackson-area community representative, at one of our community-campus meetings held in the inner city, put our academic team on notice that "We don't want an intellectual drive-by.")

A third critical need is to combine the resources of the campus and the community to develop strategies for addressing the health needs of the community. Mississippi, for example, has the highest obesity rate in the country, with growing numbers of children becoming obese and contracting diseases such as type 2 diabetes. Mississippi also has a high rate of sexually transmitted diseases, including HIV-AIDS. Both of these problems are particularly acute in the African American community. Many HBCUs have established service-learning and community-based research programs to address community health concerns, but, again, documentation of activities and publication of results in academic literature have often been absent.

A fourth critical need is to address concerns about the police and the criminal justice system in strategic relationships between HBCUs and community organizations, including the documentation of treatment of members of the minority population relative to treatment of the majority population by law enforcement officials. African Americans in many communities--particularly young males—insist that they are sometimes routinely stopped by police when they are "driving while black" in white communities.

Related to this need are possible strategies for addressing the high incidence of violent crimes committed by African American males. Several HBCUs have received funding to partner with area schools in violence prevention projects, and many HBCUs have tutoring programs to help students stay in school to at least receive their high school diploma. Such projects lend themselves to engaged scholarship.

A fifth critical need relates to the economic well-being of inner city residents, especially during a time of national economic challenges, including high unemployment, home foreclosures, low salaries relative to rising costs for food and energy, and unmanageable debt burdens. HBCUs have the expertise to provide assistance with such activities as budget preparation and, perhaps, renegotiation of loans. This type of assistance may already be provided by many HBCUs, and, if so, the publication of the accomplishments of effective community-campus partnerships as models to be emulated would be a great act of service.

HBCUs have been making progress in developing infrastructures and positioning themselves to expand their level of scholarly research and publication. The partnerships with PWI institutions previously discussed have contributed to this progress, as the HBCUs and PWIs have much to offer one another. PWI partners, in many cases, have well-funded research centers and faculty versed in cutting-edge methodology with the most advanced computer software. Many HBCUs have had extensive experience in community outreach and have built levels of trust in minority communities that greatly facilitate community-based participatory research.

PWIs have traditionally enjoyed access to funds far beyond the reach of most HBCUs. However, HBCUs have been gaining access to funding, due both to sources that are targeted to them and to a growing emphasis on grantsmanship at these institutions, bringing them into greater competition for available funds.

Increasingly, funding sources are encouraging—sometimes demanding—collaborations between institutions in their grant guidelines, including partnerships between PWIs and HBCUs. They are also targeting more of their funding to community organizations and demanding that community-campus partnerships be genuine partnerships that include joint management of the grant and a sharing of funds, with community involvement at all stages of the project.

Given these developments, collaboration is in the self-interest of all parties—HBCUs, PWIs, and community organizations. This is especially true during these challenging economic times, where competition will need to give way to growing levels of cooperation in the interest of survival. Minority communities will likely face some of the greatest challenges, and HBCUs will be called upon to step up their community outreach and involve growing numbers of faculty and students in service-learning and community-based research.

With all this in mind, the future of engaged scholarship at HBCUs looks promising. These institutions, collectively, have built up a track record with their long history of community engagement. They have never functioned as ivory tower institutions dedicated solely to intellectual pursuits, and they are increasingly moving forward in establishing community service and service-learning requirements and developing community-based research programs. The climate is favorable for engaged scholarship, as the number of HBCU faculty who are contributing to the body of literature on community engagement is growing.

References

Abbott, M., & Beech, R. (2006, October). *Service learning, non-traditional students, and the historic black university: the Harris-Stowe model.* Paper presented at the Midwest Research-to-Practice in Adult, Continuing, and Community Education meeting, St. Louis, MO.

Barlow, M. H., Barlow, D., DeValve, M., & DeValve, E. (2007, November). *Community engagement and community justice at an HBCU.* Paper presented at the annual meeting of the American Society of Criminology, Atlanta.

Beach, A., Dawkins, P. W., Rozman, S. L., & Grant, J. L. (2008). Faculty development at historically black colleges and universities. In M. Gasman, B. Baez, & C. S. Viernes Turner (Eds.), *Understanding minority-serving institutions* (pp. 156–168). Albany: State University of New York.

Brunner, B. (2003). The Tuskegee syphilis experiment. Available at http://www.tuskegee.edu/Global/Story.asp?s=1207586.

Campus Compact. (2006, October 17). *New data links college education with civic engagement.* National Campus Compact press release, available at http://www.compact.org/news/press/release/536.

Campus to Campus Partnerships. (2007, May). *Executive summary* (unpublished).

Carey, T. S., Howard, D. L., Goldmon, M., Roberson, J. T., Godley, P. A., & Ammerman, A. (2005). Developing effective interuniversity partnerships and community-based research to address health disparities. *Academic Medicine, 80,* 1039–1045.

Carter, D., Fox, L., Priest, T., & McBride, F. (2002). Student involvement in community-based research. *Metropolitan Universities Journal, 13*(1), 56–63.

Greene, G. R. (2006). Cultivating reciprocity: The guiding framework for Benedict College in partnership with the community to garner economic and community growth. *Journal of Higher Education Outreach and Engagement, 11,* 53–63.

Harvey, L. K., & Mitchell, A. D. (2006). Beyond the criminal arena: The justice studies program at Winston-Salem State University. *Journal of Higher Education Outreach and Engagement, 11,* 41–52.

Howard University Center for Urban Progress Research and Evaluation Division (2008). *Research and evaluation projects.* Available at http://www.coas.howard.edu/hucup/research_hvi.html.

Indiana University. (2004, November 15). Survey: College students benefit from civic engagement, study less than expected. Available at http://newsinfo.iu.edu/news/page/normal/1723.html.

Jowers-Barber, S. (2008, October). *Community based research and oral history: Engaging students to research, document and chronicle the experiences of community residents.* Abstract for presentation at Fifteenth National HBCU Faculty Development Symposium, Washington, DC.

Lomax, M. L. (2006). Historically black colleges and universities: Bringing a tradition of engagement into the twenty-first century. *Journal of Higher Education Outreach and Engagement, 11*, 5–13.

Lott, J. L. II. (2008, Winter). Racial identity and black students' perceptions of community outreach: Implications for bonding social capital. *Journal of Negro Education, 77*, 3–14.

Maddux, H. C., Bradley, B., Fuller, D. S., Darnell, C. Z., & Wright, B. D. (2006). Active learning, action research: A case study in community engagement, service-learning, and technology integration. *Journal of Higher Education Outreach and Engagement, 11*, 65–79.

Mississippi Urban Research Center. (2008). *Overview.* Available at http://www.murc.org/.

Morgan State Institute for Urban Research. (2008). *Empowering urban communities through intervention, understanding, research.* Available at http://iur.morgan.edu/AboutUs/index1/htm.

National CBR Networking Initiative (2008). *National community-based research networking initiative.* Available at http://www.bonner/.org/campus/cbr/home/htm.

Office of University Partnerships (OUP). (2007). *Grantee details: LeMoyne-Owen College.* Available at http:// www.oup.org/grantee/org.

Reid, L., Hatch, J., & Parrish, T. (2003, November). The role of a historically black university and the black church in community-based health initiatives: The Project DIRECT Experience. *Journal of Public Health Management Practice* (Suppl), S70–S73.

Rozman, S. L., & Roberts, G. (2006). Tougaloo College and the HBCU Faculty Development Network: Networking for mutual reinforcement. *Journal of Higher Education Outreach and Engagement, 11,* 81–93.

Taylor, H. A., Jr., Wilson, J. G., Jones, D. W., Sarpong, D. F. Srinivasan, A. Garrison, R. J., et al. (2005a). Toward resolution of cardiovascular health disparities in African Americans: Design and methods of the Jackson Heart Study. *Ethnicity & Disease, 15,* S6-4 to S6-16.

Taylor, M. C., Dwyer, B., & Pacheco, S. (2005b). Mission and community: The culture of engagement and minority serving institutions. In P. A. Pasque, R. E. Smerek, B. Dwyer, N. Bowman, & B. L. Mallory (Eds.), *Higher education collaboratives for community engagement and improvement* (pp. 32–37). Ann Arbor: University of Michigan National Forum on Higher Education for the Public Good.

Zlotkowski, E., Jones, R. J., Lenk, M. M., Meeropol, J., Gelmon, S. B., Norvell, K. H., et al. (2005). *One with the community: Indicators of engagement at minority-serving institutions* (p. 39). Providence, RI: Campus Compact.

Engaged Scholarship in Hispanic-Serving Institutions

Jaime Chahin and Noe Ortega

Principle of Education: the school, when it is truly a functional organ of the nation, depends far more on the atmosphere of national culture in which it is immersed than it does on the pedagogical atmosphere created artificially within it. A condition of equilibrium between this inward and outward pressure is essential to produce a good school.—Ortega y Gasset

The importance of the mutually beneficial interactive nature of universities and the national culture was first acknowledged when Congress passed the Morrill Act, also known as the Land Grant Act, in 1862. Pressure from farmers and laborers who recognized the importance of an education to improving their social and economic status led to the federal government providing thirty thousand acres of public land to each state for each senator and representative in Congress, based on the 1860 census. The act "specified that the income from the land was to be used to support at least one college that would 'teach such branches of learning as are related to agriculture and mechanical arts . . . in order to promote the liberal and practical education of the industrial classes in the several pursuits and professions of life'" (Webb, Metha, & Jordan, 2007, p. 145). This call for universities to engage with the community could be viewed as the first model of university-community partnerships for the public good.

As these land-grant institutions became more comprehensive, their outreach evolved into widening access to undergraduate and graduate education, student volunteers, internships, extension, and research. Today, numerous public and private universities and community colleges, many of them Hispanic-serving institutions (HSIs) that have emerged throughout the country, emulate land-grant institutions to various degrees in that they also provide access to undergraduates, graduate and professional education, internships, outreach, training programs, promotion of the arts and culture, and solving local problems.

Even though all of these are viable activities, they have usually been kept peripheral to the main mission of the university and not fully integrated to create reciprocity and mutual benefits that are sustainable and that connect communities to the institutions.

Given the shift in the mission of institutions and the continued need to improve the economic and social status of the population served by these institutions, particularly HSIs, there exists an even greater need for engaged partnerships to be sensitive to the communities, as well as respectful and understanding of the community. These partnerships must happen in order to establish a continuous engagement that moves from the periphery of the institution so they become an integral component of programs, departments, and colleges and reflect a level of applied scholarship that contributes to the development and involvement of the partners. However, the question remains: What are the models of engagement that have the greatest potential for wider application and that will promote the optimal development of institutions and communities?

In this chapter, we examine the historical precedents of engaged practice and explore some of the engagement-centered trends that are impacting the higher education landscape and helping to shift the focus of institutions back to a mission driven by civic engagement and a renewed commitment to the public good. We also discuss how a new generation of HSIs is challenging the traditional view of scholarship, so we therefore make recommendations that will ensure that Hispanic-serving institutions continue to play a central role in ensuring the success of our nation's rapidly growing minority population.

Pertinent Literature

Historically, leading educators have been at the forefront of espousing the many contributions of institutions of higher education (IHEs) to society. Daniel Coft Gilman, in his inaugural address in 1876 as the first president of Johns Hopkins University, America's first modern research university, first expressed the hope that universities should "make for less misery among the poor, less ignorance in the schools, less bigotry in the temple, less suffering in the hospital, less fraud in business, less folly in politeness" (Long, 1992, p. 184). In 1908, Harvard's president Charles Eliot stated that "at bottom most of American institutions of higher education are filled with the democratic spirit of serviceableness. Teachers and students alike are profoundly moved by the desire to serve a democratic Community." (Veysey, 1965, p. 119). The emphasis of the preeminent role of education in individual and societal success is also reflected in John Dewey's work, specifically in a 1902 essay in which he indicates that during the twentieth century, the schooling system would be the strategic institution that would serve the complex industrial system. In 1927, Dewey added that the existence of a "neighborly community" was critical to a well-functioning democratic society.

There is thus a need to examine contemporary institutions that are engaged in partnerships with communities in order to assess the results of their collaborative endeavors. It is imperative that institutions not only analyze a problem, but also provide sustained attention to the identification of solutions to determine who is changing and what needs to be changed in a collaborative environment. Furthermore, institutions should be interested in optimizing the ways that community-university partnerships function by developing a sustainable culture. Additionally, leaders within the partnerships need to be cognizant of what should be done by whom (e.g., schools, institutions of higher education, churches, business, government, community-based organizations, and individuals) to ensure that mutually beneficial engagements occur between institutions and communities.

Four institutions that can be cited that were actively engaged in the community in the late nineteenth and early twentieth centuries were Johns Hopkins in Maryland, Columbia University in New York City, the University of Chicago, and the Wharton School of Business (Harkavy & Benson, 1998). Daniel Coit Gilman, president at Johns Hopkins (1876), provided the leadership necessary for the establishment of the Charity Organization Society. The intent of this organization was to provide a scientific approach to helping Baltimore's poor. Professors collected and analyzed data to determine the root causes of poverty and the interventions needed to ameliorate that plight. Faculty and students at Johns Hopkins were engaged with the city, which was the most logical laboratory to apply their theory to practice during this period of social reform. At Columbia University, President Seth Low called on faculty and students to become directly engaged with the city and its communities and people. In "The University and the Working Man," Low states that "the working man of America should know that at Columbia College the disposition exists to teach the truth, but we also ask the working man to enable us to see the truth as it appears to them" (Bender, 1987, p. 279). During this same period at the University of Chicago, Jane Addams's social work emanating from the Hull House had very close ties to the locality. The Hull House was also a site for labor union activities that surfaced issues and led to interventions that served as a forum for social, political, educational, humanitarian, civic, and economic reform that impacted the community (Harkavy & Puckett, 1994). In later years, perhaps the most notable work at the University of Chicago was the Laboratory School, established by Dewey, which immersed itself in developing educational solutions for the problems of the city.

Likewise, in Philadelphia, the Wharton School of Business—under the leadership of Edmund James—was established to respond to the problems of industrialization. The institution linked academics and citizens to the study of social problems. Wharton's foundation believed that the active engagement of the institution in public affairs would also contribute to the academic success of the institution (Sass, 1982). These partnerships were predicated on the concept of a partnership between academics and reformers. Ironically, none of the Progressive Era initiatives (1895–1915) became dominant, despite the significant expansion of higher education after World Wars I and II.

What can Hispanic-serving institutions learn from Johns Hopkins, Wharton, Columbia, and the University of Chicago, in terms of how they responded to the needs of the community? Clearly, they analyzed the problem and engaged and embraced communities of immigrants to meet their basic needs in order to integrate them into society. Given the skills that are required in the twenty-first century, HSIs have a more daunting challenge today, as they attempt to meet the needs of first-generation students and immigrants with limited financial resources and with a lack of public school experiences. Underresourced families and school districts are at the core of the challenge for Latino students and HSIs.

The Changing Landscape

Never has the impact of scholarship been more central to the discussion of community engagement than with the case of minority-serving institutions (MSIs) and the role they play in the higher education landscape of the twenty-first century. This is especially true when examining HSIs and the impact the U.S. demographic shift has had on their institutional priorities. The minority population of the United States has surpassed 102 million people, and Hispanics represent the fastest-growing minority group in the country (U.S. Census Bureau, 2008a, 2008b). The estimated 45.5 million Hispanics living in the United States make up 15 percent of the total population, and their number is projected to reach 102.6 million people by 2050 (U.S. Census Bureau, 2008a, 2008b).

Parallel to this demographic shift is the continual widening of the economic and social disparities that exist between people of Hispanic origin and Whites in this country. The census reflects that an estimated 20 percent of the U.S. Hispanic population lives in poverty (U.S. Census Bureau, 2008) and that only 59 percent have a high school diploma or higher, compared with 91 percent of non-Hispanic Whites (U.S. Census Bureau, 2006). The challenges and uncertainties of an ailing economy and the increased demand for a highly educated workforce are causes of great concern. Institutions of higher education, long viewed as agents of change committed to the education and preparation of its citizenry, are being called upon to apply their scholarly knowledge and resources to address societal concerns (Rice, 1996). The future success of this country with its rapidly growing Hispanic population rests in the belief that "better education is the single resource that in the long run will improve the economic and social integration of the burgeoning Hispanic population" (Tienda & Mitchell, 2006).

The Mission of a University

In 1930, Jose Ortega y Gasset delivered a series of lectures at the University of Madrid where he described "the mission of the university" as one that is highly dependent on the "atmosphere of national culture in which it is immersed in" (Ortega y Gasset, Nostrand, Kerr, & Webster, 1930/1992, p. 19). Almost a century later, much of the literature on engagement and the role scholarship plays in addressing the needs of our communities continues to reflect similar ideas. The milieu of the United States in the twenty-first century, or "national culture," as it was referred to by Ortega y Gasset, is one characterized by tremendous change. The United States currently finds itself in the midst of what some scholars have referred to as a *perfect storm*—where powerful forces are driving change in America and are having a significant impact on the country (Kirsch, Bruaun, Yamamoto, & Sum, 2007). This change is not only attributable to the rapidly growing minority population, but to a divergent distribution of skills among U.S. minority groups and a changing global economy, that demands a highly skilled workforce (Kirsch et al., 2007).

The changing landscape of the United States and the increased value placed on higher education in our society make it difficult for institutions to ignore the urban deterioration at their gates. Hispanic-serving institutions, most of which are located in areas with high concentrations of Hispanics and which enroll almost half of all Hispanics in the U.S. (Marin-Kennen & Aguilar, 2005), are finding it imperative to engage in partnerships aimed at addressing the concerns of the communities they serve.

Hispanic-Serving Institutions

Before we examine the role of engaged scholarship at Hispanic-serving institutions, it is important to describe their brief history and highlight some of the unique characteristics that make these institutions different from other minority-serving institutions in the United States. The concept of HSIs, or what at the time were referred to as "significantly Hispanic institutions" (Barry, 1991), first surfaced in the early part of the 1980s when educational leaders from Texas and New Mexico convened to discuss the creation of a coalition that would advocate on behalf of institutions with large concentrations of Hispanic enrollment (Santiago, 2006). It was the collective efforts of these educational leaders advocating for increased funding and raising awareness for "significantly Hispanic institutions" that eventually led to the national recognition of HSIs by the federal government (*The Voice*, 2006, p. 4).

But the road to national recognition was not an easy one, as advocates failed repeatedly to get the HSI agenda on the Higher Education Act (HEA) of 1984 and then again in 1989. The coalition would have to wait until the HEA of 1992 before the federal government officially recognized HSIs. Today, according to the HEA, 20 USCA Section 1101a, a Hispanic-Serving Institution is defined as follows: "A degree granting institution of higher education that has an enrollment of undergraduate full-time equivalent students that is at least 25 percent or more Hispanic students; and no less than 50 percent of the institution's Hispanic students are low-income individuals." (Note that low income is defined as 150 percent of the poverty level as determined by the U.S. Census Bureau.)

Today, Hispanic-serving institutions make up 7 percent of the U.S colleges and universities and enroll half of the Hispanic students in the country (Marin-Kenner & Aguilar 2005). HSIs are classified in the same category as other minority-serving institutions (MSIs), a category that includes, but is not limited to, historically Black colleges and universities (HBCUs) and Tribal colleges and universities (TCUs). However, unlike HBCUs and TCUs, which were created with the mission of serving a very specific and clearly defined population, HSIs were not formally created to serve Hispanic students and are identified solely on enrollment percentages and not their institutional mission. The only exceptions are several institutions in Puerto Rico, Hostos Community College, Boricua College, and the National Hispanic University, which were established with a mission to serve the Hispanic community. Therefore, as the number of Hispanics enrolling in higher education increases, so does the number of HSIs (Marin-Kenner & Aguilar, 2005).

The Higher Education Act of 1992 was also responsible for creating a competitive grant that provides federal support to improve and expand the capacity of HSIs to serve Hispanics and other low-income students. Of the estimated 236 HSIs, approximately 185 have benefited from the more than $550 million that has been awarded by federal government agencies in multiple disciplines since 1992 (Santiago, 2006).

Engagement Initiatives

The federal funding set aside for HSIs impacted the program development of the institutions, especially Title V and Gear Up, which provide funding for institutional initiatives and outreach that HSIs cannot sustain with their limited resources. The U.S. Office of Education (USOE), U.S. Department of Agriculture (USDA), Health and Human Services (HHS), the Department of Energy (DOE), Housing and Urban Development (HUD), and the Department of the Interior have used the HSI designation to set aside resources for HSI projects at HSI institutions that have the faculty and academic programs to undertake specific projects. This federal outreach has also created internship opportunities for Hispanic students (*The Voice*, 2006, pp. 4–5).

Charitable foundations have, likewise, enabled HSIs to continue developing programs that partner with the community and enhance learning opportunities for students. For example, the Kellogg ENLACE project (Engaging Latino Communities for Education), initiated in 1997, consisted of thirteen partnerships in seven states that were designed to increase the number of Latino graduates from high school and college. In Spanish, "enlace" means to link or weave together in such a way that the new entity is stronger than its parts (ENLACE, 2007). ENLACE partnerships include universities, community colleges, K–12 schools, community-based organizations, students, and parents. Numerous lessons have been learned from these partnerships and institutional engagement. For example, in San Marcos, the San Marcos Consolidated Independent School District adopted the policy of offering all high school juniors the opportunity to take the PSAT at no cost to the student, based on a practice developed and implemented by the local ENLACE partnership. New Mexico (www4.unm.edu/enlace) and Florida institutionalized statewide initiatives as a result of Kellogg Foundation funding (http://usfweb2.usf.edu/enlace/).

The Lumina Foundation is another example of effective involvement with community college HSIs in developing partnerships to increase college access and success. The foundation funded 75 projects to develop sustainable projects to increase college awareness, retention, literacy, and the development of sustainable community partnerships that will expand community participation (Lumina Foundation, 2005). These initiatives are critical because the majority, 60 percent of Hispanic students in America, are enrolled in community colleges (*Chronicle*, 2008, p. 14).

The recent move by a number of institutional leaders to adopt a policy of engagement at the center of their institution's mission has been recognized by other national organizations and disciplinary associations committed to recognizing institutions for their impact on their communities. National organizations, such as the National Science Foundation and Campus Compact, which was established in 1996 with the purpose of reinvigorating the service role in higher education, have begun to target scholarship aimed at addressing the social and economic concerns of their community. Many of the initiatives embarked on by these institutions may have otherwise never materialized without the availability of financial resources made available through the organizations just mentioned.

Key to enabling the momentum of engagement among HSIs are the efforts of several government and state agencies to encourage institutions of higher education to explore ways of addressing the social and economic concerns of their communities. Many states have targeted funding for initiatives aimed at improving college going rates and have begun holding institutions accountable for the gaps that exist in the low educational attainment levels of their students. In October 2000, for instance, the Texas Higher Education Coordinating Board (THECB), a state agency responsible for overseeing higher education in Texas, approved the "Closing the Gaps Higher Education Plan." This plan seeks to improve the postsecondary participation and success rates of students in the state. This move by the THECB prompted institutions of higher education across the state to implement initiatives that target underrepresented students and help address some of the social and economic disparities in the state.

Community Engagement

The movement toward a policy of engagement at HSIs has benefited from the activities of the federal, state, and foundational initiatives that have contributed to an agenda to promote the increased educational attainment and success of the nation's rapidly growing Hispanic population. These resulting partnerships are a positive step toward regaining public trust in our institutions of higher education and in reestablishing them as "a community of scholars, serving both internal and external audiences in addition to the academic and the public good" (Boyer, 1990, p. 10; Kellogg Commission, 1999, 2000). Ultimately, the true measure of the success of these initiatives rests on the impact they have on society and their ability to provide long-term, sustainable, and viable solutions to problems impacting the communities they serve.

Engaged Scholarship

A number of HSIs around the country have undertaken successful partnerships worthy of praise in this book; however, for the purpose of this chapter, we have elected to highlight a few of the initiatives currently taking place in the states of Texas, New Mexico, Arizona, and California. All are Southwestern states, which have experienced a significant increase in their Hispanic population in recent years and have seen the numbers of Hispanics residing in their states rise to over 30 percent, respectively (Bernstein, 2008). The initiatives highlighted in the next couple of sections have paralleled and, in some cases, preceded many of the current national, state, and institutional trends of engagement. The following sections sheds light on these trends and highlights some of the engaged scholarship taking place at HSIs around the country; ultimately, it demonstrates how HSIs not only have benefited from a national movement toward engagement, but in some cases, have succeeded in changing the culture of their institutions.

The Culture of Engagement at HSIs

As institutions develop outreach and retention programs, they become engaged with the community, families, and the public schools. In the past several years, we have witnessed a push among institutional leaders to successfully make community engagement a core value of their mission statements. Whether driven by social and economic concerns or a reaction to the changing demographic landscape of the country, a number of HSIs are discovering the tremendous impact outreach and community engagements have on the success of their institutions. This recent move has resulted in a number of partnerships that are either administratively driven or faculty-led.

Perhaps the movement toward administrative support of engaged scholarship at HSIs can best be summed up by the following excerpt from an essay written by the president of the University of Texas-El Paso for the 20th Anniversary of Campus Compact, in which she writes:

> Universities can create access to higher education for non-traditional groups while simultaneously reinforcing their commitment to excellence in education and research. To be effective community partners we must be context-sensitive, that is to be aware of, understand and respect the community in which they live and work. Universities have a special responsibility to respond to the needs of their surrounding communities, particularly through K–16 initiatives and economically distressed areas. (Natalacio, 2006, p. 5)

The University of Texas-El Paso (UTEP), located on the border between Texas and Mexico, has a total Hispanic enrollment of 14,484 (73 percent) ("Diversity in Academe," 2008, p. B38), made up largely from the surrounding community,,, which has historically struggled with the low educational attainment levels of its Hispanic population. This concern prompted President Natalicio to urge faculty and staff to engage in partnerships that provide increased educational opportunities for the community's Hispanic citizens. Under the leadership of its current president, the university defined its primary mission as a university-wide commitment to meeting the needs of the community. The university made an effort to recruit staff and faculty reflective of the El Paso community and have aggressively targeted students from predominant Hispanic-serving secondary institutions with their recruitment efforts (De Los Santos, 1991). UTEP created a culture of collaboration across disciplines and urged its faculty and staff to find ways to address the gaps in educational attainment of first-generation Hispanic students. Much of the success at UTEP has been attributed to the faculty's commitment to reach out to minority students in the community and help increase the institutions efforts to help "socialize first-generation college students in to the university culture while building a community environment supportive of higher education" (De Los Santos, 1991, p. 80). The outreach for training and community health partnered with community health clinics in the community's different neighborhoods. Furthermore, partnerships with public schools and community colleges promoted college attendance at the university. This continues and has been sustained for more than two decades.

Another example of sustained engagement is the University of New Mexico (UNM), located in Albuquerque. UNM enrolls an estimated 24,000 students, 7,400 (30 percent) of whom are Hispanic. Since its inception in 2001, the ENLACE New Mexico collaborative has served more than 20,000 students and parents through a number of its outreach programs that resulted from these regional partnerships. In an impact report issued by ENLACE, they reported that 83 percent of the students participating in their regional programs went on to college. In addition, ENLACE has seen a number of its programs replicated throughout the state and adopted as a public policy model by the New Mexico state legislature. One of the most critical measures of the ENLACE model's success has been its ability to impact education policy and acquire legislatively appropriated funds to help expand its initiatives and allow some of the more successful programs to continue operating around the state.

Texas A&M University-Corpus Christi (TAMUCC), an HSI located in south Texas, with a student body that is 38 percent Hispanic ("Diversity in Academe," 2008, p. B36), is an example of a faculty-led initiative. TAMUCC has committed intellectual resources to help meet the Closing the Gaps campaign through its faculty-led initiatives. Recognizing the challenges school districts were facing in meeting the needs of students from low-income, predominantly Hispanic communities, the university embarked on the Colonias ("neighborhood") Learning Project. Colonias, which are scattered throughout the South Texas border, are home to approximately four hundred thousand predominately Spanish-speaking, low-income Mexican Americans, the majority of whom are U.S. citizens. Families from colonias often face issues of high mobility, poverty, and language differences. These challenges can often lead to poor performance in school for the children of these communities. School districts in south Texas have made attempts to reach out to the parents of the children in these poor communities and search continuously for strategies aimed at helping to involve parents in the education of their children. Their limited success has created a need in many school districts in South Texas for information and resources on successful intervention strategies to help encourage minority parents from disadvantaged communities to become involved in their children's education.

The research embarked on by the faculty of TAMUCC aimed at investigating how participation in a family-learning partnership program would empower parents of pre-K to grade-3 students living in colonias to become advocates for their children's mathematics and science education (McDonald & Canales, 2008). Through their initiative, TAMUCC faculty were able to provide the community with useful strategies in the areas of program delivery targeted at minority students, ways to reconceptualize the use of funding resources, and new parental involvement models that can help educators engage parents in their students' learning (McDonald & Canales, 2008). The Colonias Family Learning Project serves as a model for community engagement and exemplifies the institution's commitment to the community it serves. Lessons learned from this project led to an additional NSF-funded project to train math and science faculty in preparing future teachers at two HSIs to integrate the strategies into their curricula. This venue has created more than four hundred teachers equipped with the strategies and skills to engage Hispanic students and their parents in learning math and science (McCullough, McDonald, & Canales, 2008).

The Culture of Engagement at Emerging HSIs

In 2003, an Office of the Vice President for Educational Partnerships (VPEP) was established by the president of Arizona State University (ASU) with a mission aimed at "improving the academic performance of students in Arizona from early childhood through high school completion and promotes attainment of college degrees" (Arizona State University, 2008). Arizona

State University's main campus is located in Tempe. It enrolls more than 51,000 students, more than 7,000 (13.6 percent) of them Hispanic. Through its VPEP division, ASU has made a commitment to providing "responsible and responsive leadership with regard to Arizona's pre-K–12 sector by collaborating across departments to advance scholarship and engagement across the educational pipeline and the public sector" (ASU, 2008). Various departments at the institution work to deliver support for early childhood development and professional development for educators, and they actively engage faculty in scholarship that targets students, schools, and families. In addition to the work done in teacher preparation by the College of Education, ASU also encourages faculty across disciplines in the areas of sociology, family studies, social work, psychology, and neurosciences to consider the implications of interdisciplinary research and develop strategies and interventions in early childhood education.

Many of the faculty-led initiatives at ASU draw on scientifically based, empirical data regarding child development and school success. The data acquired from these initiatives lead to a deeper understanding of the long-term implications of sustained improvements in school readiness and achievement for minority students in the community. ASU is committed to investing both human and intellectual resources in the arena of education and is working on finding ways to address the gaps that exist between the pre-K–12 educational systems and university enrollment. The multiple and comprehensive approaches are continuously assessed by ASU to determine their successful impact and the long-term success of the institution.

Since the creation of the VPEP, ASU has impacted the lives of more than four thousand students from the surrounding areas with its early childhood support and family initiatives. The programs embarked on in the community provide multiple opportunities for students to develop the knowledge and skills needed to be successful learners. In addition, many of these initiatives have also provided support to more than 150 teachers, principals, and administrators to enhance their ability to make to provide equal access and educational success to students (ASU, 2008). Arizona State University has succeeded in obtaining public and private funds to sustain its activities and continues to pursue additional partnerships in the community and throughout the state (ASU, 2008).

The University of California—Irvine is another institution that has been engaging for the past several decades in educational partnerships with the community and Hispanic-serving institutions such as Cal State Fullerton and Rancho Santiago Community College. In 1983, UC Irvine developed the Student/Teacher Educational Partnership (Project STEP). Project STEP served as a partnership model aimed at improving the educational performance of students in its community. What originally began as a partnership between UC Irvine and the Santa Ana School District evolved to include Rancho Santiago Community College and California State University at Fullerton. The project brought K–12 educators and institutional leaders together to develop and implement programs targeting the following general areas: (1) curriculum revision projects, especially in the areas of mathematics, science, and language arts; (2) faculty development programs for improved preparation for teaching, particularly with regard to students in multicultural and multilingual classrooms; and (3) a comprehensive and continuous system of support and curricular guidance for students in secondary schools (Gomez, Bissel, Danzinger, & Casselman, 1990).

Project STEP was successfully able to raise the academic aspirations and achievements of students in surrounding communities. Annual surveys by the school district reported dramatic increases in the higher educational expectations of faculty and students (Gomez et al., 1990). The project is credited with serving as a catalyst for change, helping to bridge the disconnects between K–12 education and postsecondary institutions (Gomez et al., 1990). The success of Project STEP is attributed not only to the design of the STEP model, but to the educators in the community who were committed to ensuring the academic success of their students. Although the project was initially designed to address the particular needs of a regional K–12 institution composed primarily of minority students, UC Irvine realized the impact their findings had in addressing the needs of the state of California and that of the changing demographic landscape of an entire nation (Gomez et al., 1990).

In the following statement, Manuel N. Gomez, Vice Chancellor of Student Services at the University of California—Irvine, best describes the role collaborative partnerships play in bringing about educational reform: "Bringing together schools, colleges, universities, parents and community leaders, collaborative projects have attempted to renew the democratic value of education, equalize educational opportunity, support our nation's teachers, break down institutional barriers and share resources for maximum benefit" (Gomez, 1998, p. 30).

Likewise, at an emerging HSI such as Texas State University—San Marcos (24 percent Hispanic), the president established the strategic goal of becoming an HSI. Faculty have led initiatives such as "The Forgotten Americans," a colonia project funded by the W. K. Kellogg Foundation that engaged border communities, students, and nonprofits in creating a documentary that used film, photography, and testimonials to document the economic and social conditions in the United States-Mexico border (Chahin, 2005). As a result of informing policy makers, Texans voted in November 2001 to approve $175 million in bond money to improve the infrastructure of colonias (Taylor, 2001).

Furthermore, the commitment of the engaged professor contributed guidance and service to a local housing project (Proyecto Azteca), which became a sustainable community development bank (CDB) that for the past six years has continued building affordable homes, providing low-interest loans, and matching savings accounts for residents of colonias in south Texas (Chahin, 1998). This project led to the establishment of a partnership (Caminos) with the San Marcos Consolidated School District that provides academic training for at-risk middle school students in algebra, English, technology, and leadership. This program, funded by the Texas Pioneer Foundation and operated by faculty, college student mentors, and public school teachers, has served more than three hundred students and their families and continues to have a presence at the local high school.

In addition, in 2004, the University Provost at Texas State established and funded a graduate fellows program to invite diverse and upcoming doctoral candidates to spend eight weeks on campus conducting research with faculty. The fellows apply and are selected by the Graduate College faculty with the intent of identifying mutual research interests and then joining the Texas State faculty on completion of the program and their doctorate programs. In addition, the provost also awards target-of-opportunity faculty positions to departments that are experiencing growth and that need to enhance their faculty diversity. The senior faculty and chair identify and select that potential faculty. All of the aforementioned activities have created an institutional climate and sustainable university culture that promotes the engagement of scholars and students (Shelly Yates, 2008).

Critical Issues

If we believe in the ideals of democracy and are cognizant of the fact that "all advanced nations depend increasingly on three critical elements: new discoveries, highly trained personnel, and expert knowledge," then institutions that are a primary source of these elements should act responsibly to engage and embrace their communities (Bok, 1990, p. 3).

The changing role of higher education and the demographic distribution of Hispanics in the United States make it essential for institutions of higher education, not just HSIs, to engage in scholarship focused on the common good. The reasons for doing so are quite compelling when one looks closely at the social and economic disparities that continue to exist and that will challenge higher education in the twenty-first century. HSIs and universities, as well as outside organizations, need to make an explicit commitment to serving Hispanic students as an integral component of the institution's mission and view this mission as an investment in educating the next generation of ethnically different or immigrant-origin students.

If IHEs, and particularly HSIs, are to fulfill their primary mission of advancing and transmitting knowledge for a democratic society, the application of knowledge and the dedication of resources must be focused on transformative change. The examination of engaged institutions revealed the following critical elements worthy of serious consideration: community stewardship, cultural infrastructure, faculty diversity, institutional leadership, and acknowledgment and recognition.

Community Stewardship

There is a need in our society to examine the HSIs that are engaged in partnerships with their communities around the country and focus attention to identifying some of the viable solutions that are making an impact on society. It is imperative that we learn from those endeavors and seek to replicate some of these initiatives in our own communities. Given the complex, interconnected, systemic, and seemingly intractable problems affecting our schools and communities, institutions of higher education have a role in developing partnerships and collaborations that will result in long-term, sustainable, and viable solutions to problems impacting the community. Systemic change must encompass higher education because its institutions have intellectual capital and yield influence on policy at both the regional and state levels. Homegrown human investment by states and institutions will impact the workforce and economic development in communities and states with large Hispanic populations. The University needs to listen and be sensitive to the needs and cultural challenges of the community as it develops partnerships.

Cultural Infrastructure

If institutions are to function as the core subsystem of modern information societies and seek to educate a greater number of citizens, it is imperative that universities serve as a primary partner in community endeavors. In order to develop long-term sustainable partnerships, universities need to establish community advisory boards, in academically linked partnership, and must be fully able to engage their faculty with students, teachers, parents, and key stakeholders in the community. As demonstrated by the faculty-led initiatives highlighted in this chapter, before an institution can successfully begin to engage with the community, it has to be sensitive and cognizant of the culture of the community. Institutions need to recognize that reliance on collective intellectual capital versus the individual expertise of faculty is the only way to successfully make a difference in the lives of the people in their communities.

Institutions need to develop an internal discourse about the proper relationships between the university and the community. Essential to this development are the following: Universities must continue to integrate teaching, research, service, and students so faculty can continue to engage and be rewarded for their scholarship application, and institutions must also provide opportunities for faculty release time or matching resources to leverage funding to sustain community-based activities. Institutions should develop an infrastructure that will be conducive to the development of faculty research clusters that will promote interdisciplinary opportunities to collaborate. This will enhance the collaborative process between the university and the community and ensure the reciprocity that will impact the core curricula.

Faculty Diversity

Institutions of higher education need to recruit diverse faculty or staff that are sensitive to the needs of students and who understand the community. In addition, we need to invest in diverse graduate students to continue to support the infrastructure. HSIs will need to partner with research institutions to develop faculty and refer graduate students in some disciplines. Incorporating concepts of community service in meetings, orientations of new faculty, and seminars will create an atmosphere of outreach and service among faculty. By initiating this, the university tackles another obstacle: recruiting faculty members who value engagement. If it is already understood that outreach is important within the university, the colleges and departments will be able to recruit faculty who possess a willingness to engage in the community as well as meet the requirements of teaching in the department or college. This will also impact the diversity of the graduate enrollment.

Institutional Leadership

The engaged and emerging HSIs of the twenty-first century are involved in activities that are connected to the needs of the community, that are mutually beneficial, and that have moved from the periphery of the institution to being an integral part of programs, departments, and colleges. These engagements between the institutions and the communities also reflect a level of leadership and commitment from university presidents that is critical to creating a collective and strategic vision that creates a culture of support for students, faculty, and staff. HSIs, as well as all of the other institutions of higher education, must continue to collaborate with their communities to enhance the fulfillment of their primary mission of advancing and transmitting knowledge for a democratic society. Even more important is the application of their knowledge and resources to ensure transformative change in the community and the university.

To integrate engaged scholarship within an institution successfully will require a comprehensive assessment by faculty and administrators and the development of an incremental plan that will outline the steps, roles, resources, and expectations of the partnerships, to promote and sustain a culture of engagement. Institutions need to develop strategies that are well integrated into the culture of the institution and sensitive to the needs of the community. Besides commitment to their communities, institutions need to develop strategies that are well integrated and designed to promote and sustain engagement with the community. It can be at the departmental, college, or university level, but it requires institutional support, student involvement, and recognition. It should recognize the fact that community-based efforts are an integral part of the scholarship of the institution and the development of the community.

Acknowledgment and Recognition

The acknowledgment of these types of academic endeavors by the institution and its peers will set the precedent that community engagement is important. Faculty, students, staff, and community members have to work collectively to engage in work that makes a difference in people's lives. A culture of true collaborative practice has to be established between the partners in order for community-based partnerships to prosper.

Moreover, the application of this scholarship needs to be published. If scholarship involves the community, faculty, and students and has implications for the curriculum, it will diminish the perceived boundaries existing between teaching, research, and service. This level of commitment and engagement will result in mutual reciprocity that will impact the community and academia. The key is to uncover community needs rather than impose an agenda on the community. The changing landscape of the United States and its increasing interconnectedness with higher education requires that we view communities and local schools as essential to the survival of our institutions.

Conclusion

As demonstrated by initiatives in Texas and New Mexico, government and foundations should have macro fiscal responsibilities to support the engagement between institutions of higher education and communities. Universities need to create community-based schools and activities that are designed to engage, educate, and interact with all members of the community. This will increase the number of partnerships that enhance community inclusiveness in developing solutions to local problems. University students that are involved in areas of education should learn to apply what they learn in the classroom to real-world problems. Institutions that are engaged with their communities can tap numerous community resources that will impact their students and transform how we teach and develop curricula at the university level. The elements of a good model should also include a governance structure that is of a smaller scale to permit a participatory structure that allows for collective initiative and action. Institutions have to function as collaborating partners that facilitate cooperation among all key stakeholders in the community.

Ultimately, Hispanic-serving institutions and universities need to focus on the application of scholarship and reward faculty, departments, and colleges that use their collective intellectual capital to benefit communities, especially underrepresented groups. We need to measure and reward institutions that create partnerships of engagement that foster citizenship and democracy. Furthermore, foundations, national organizations, and government agencies should recognize and reward the performance and results of engaged institutions.

As Lewis V. Gerstner, Jr., president of IBM, once stated, universities have to adopt the "Noah Principle"—No more prizes for predicting rain, prizes only for building the arks. In essence, there needs to be recognition not only of the problems, but also of those institutions that provide solutions (Gerstner, 1998, p. 42). The changing demographics and the continual widening of the educational gaps in the United States are compelling reasons for universities to act. We need to do the right thing, or else students, especially minority students, will not constitute the critical mass of citizens needed to contribute and be engaged in our democracy. The investment in this new generation of human capital composed of immigrants and ethnic minorities represents the mutual self-interest of our economic well-being and democracy.

References

Almanac Issue. (2008, August 29). *Chronicle of Higher Education.* 15(1), 14.

Arizona State University (ASU). (2008). *Education partnerships: Collaboration and the collective good.* White Paper III. Available at http://vpep.asu.edu/.

Barry, P. (1991, Summer). A new voice for Hispanics higher education: A conversation with Antonio Rigual. *College Board Review, 160,* 2–7, 337.

Bender, T. (1987). *The New York intellect: A history of intellectual life in New York City from 1750 to the beginning of our time.* Baltimore: Johns Hopkins Press.

Bernstein, R. (2008). U.S. Hispanic population surpasses 40.5 million, now 15 percent of total. *U.S. Census Bureau News.* Retrieved September 3, 2008, from http://www.census.gov/Press-Release/www/releases/archives/population/011910.html.

Bok, D. C. (1990). *Universities and the future of America.* Durham, NC: Duke University Press.

Boyer, E. L. (1990). *Scholarship reconsidered.* Princeton, NJ: Carnegie Foundation for the Advancement of Teaching.

Chahin, J. (2005). The forgotten Americans: A voice for colonia residents. *Children, Youth and Environments, 15*(1), 318–330.

Chahin, T. J. (1998). *Las colonias: Children of the colonias.* Paper 1, Faculty Publications—College of Applied Arts. Available at http://ecommons.txstate.edu/appafacp/1.

De Los Santos, A.G., Jr. (1991). *Achieving quality and diversity.* New York: American Council on Education and Macmillan.

Dewey, J. (1902). The school as social center. *Elementary School Teacher, 3*(2), 73–86.

Dewey, J. (1927). The public and its problems. Cited in *Fortune,* November 7, 1988, p. 47.

Diversity in Academe. (2008, September 26). Whatever Happened to all those plans to hire more minority professor? By Ben Rose. *Chronicle of Higher Education.*

ENLACE. (2007). *ENLACE Connection: What makes a difference in the education of Latino U.S. Students: Learning from the experience of 13 ENLACE partnerships.* W. K. Kellogg Foundation.

Gerstner, L. V., Jr. (1998, November 7). *Fortune*, p. 42.

Gomez, M. N. (1998). On the path to democracy: The role of partnership in American education. *On Common Ground, 8,* 29–31.

Gomez, M. N., Bissell, J., Danziger, L., & Casselman, R. (1990). To advance learning: A handbook on developing K–12 postsecondary partnerships. Lanham, MD: University Press of America.

Harkavy, I., & Benson, L. (1998). De-platonizing and democratizing education as a basis of service learning, In R. Rhoads & J. Howard (Eds.), *Academic service learning: A pedagogy of action and reflection.* San Francisco: Jossey-Bass.

Harkavy, I., & Puckett, J. L. (1994), Lessons from Hull House, for the contemporary urban university. *Social Science Review, 68*(3), 299–321.

Kellogg Commission on the Future of State and Land-Grant Universities. (1999). *Returning to our roots: The engaged institution.* Third Report. Washington, DC: National Association of State Universities and Land-Grant Colleges.

Kellogg Commission on the Future of State and Land-Grant Universities. (2000). *Returning to our roots: A learning society.* Fourth Report. Washington, DC: National Association of State Universities and Land-Grant Colleges.

Kirsch, I., Braun, H., Yamamoto, K., & Sum, A. (2007). *America's perfect storm: Three forces changing our nation's future.* Princeton, NJ: Educational Testing Service (ETS).

Long, E. L., Jr. (1992). *Higher education as a moral enterprise.* Washington, DC: Georgetown University Press.

Lumina Foundation. (2005). Available at http://luminafoundation.org.

Marin-Kennen, E., & Aguilar, W. (2005). Defining Hispanic-serving institution and living up to the definition. *Hispanic Outlook in Higher Education, 15*(21), 27.

McCullough, C., McDonald, J., & Canales, J. (2008). The power of family science learning events: All stakeholders benefit. In *The Center for Educational Development, Evaluation, and Research (CEDER) yearbook.* Corpus Christi: Texas A&M University—Corpus Christi.

McDonald, J. M., & Canales, J. (2008). Bridging the gap: Developing a school/family/community partnership model to enhance early mathematics and science literacy of children living in the colonias, Corpus Christi, TX.

NASULGC. (1995). *The land-grant tradition.* Washington, DC: Office of Public Affairs.

Natalacio, D. (2006). *20-20: Building access, engaged learning and excellence.* Paper presented at UTEP, El Paso, Texas. www.utep.edu/aboututep/speeches/campus compact.doc

Ortega y Gasset, J., Nostrand, H. L., Kerr, C., & Webster, D. S. (1992). *Mission of the university.* New Jersey: Transaction Publishers. (Original work published 1930)

Rice, E. R. (1996). *Making a place for the new American scholar.* American Association for Higher Education Forum on Faculty Roles and Responsibilities, The New Pathways Working Paper Series, Inquiry #1.

Santiago, D. A. (2006). *Inventing Hispanic Serving Institutions (HSIs): The basics.* Washington, DC: Excelencia in Education.

Sass, S. A. (1982). *The pragmatic imagination: A history of the Wharton School 1881–1981.* University of Pennsylvania Press.

Shelly Yates, C. (2008, February/March). Study finds keys to Hispanic student success. *Public Purpose (American Association of State Colleges and Universities),* pp. 10–12. Retrieved February 18, 2009, from http://www.aascu.org/media/public_purpose/08_0203aossey.pdf.

Taylor, S. (2001, November 7). Valley lawmakers pleased with prop results. *Brownsville Herald,* p. A11.

The Voice of Hispanic Higher Education. (2006, Fall). 20th Annual Conference edition. *HACU Milestones, 15,* 4–5.

Tienda, M., & Mitchell, F. (2006). *Multiple origins, uncertain destinies.* Washington, DC: National Academies Press.

Texas Higher Education Board (THCEB). (2000). *Closing the Gaps in Higher Education Plan.* Available at http://www.thecb.state.tx.us/reports/pdf/0379.pdf.

U.S. Census Bureau. (2008a). *Hispanic Heritage Month 2008: Sept. 15–Oct. 15.* Census Bureau News. Washington, DC: Author. Retrieved September 3, 2008, from http://www.census.gov/Press-Release/www/releases/archives/cb08ff-15.pdf

U.S. Census Bureau. (2008b). *Earnings gap highlighted by Census Bureau data on educational attainment.* Census Bureau News. Washington, DC: Author. Retrieved September 3, 2008, from http://www.census.gov/Press-Release/www/releases/archives/education/009749.html.

Veysey, L. R. (1965). *The emergence of the American university* (p. 119). Chicago: University of Chicago Press.

Webb, L. D., Metha, A., & Jordan, K. F. (2007). *Foundations of American education* (5th ed.). Columbus, OH: Prentice-Hall.

Engaged Scholarship with Tribal Communities

Michelle Sarche, Douglas Novins, and Annie Belcourt-Dittloff

A merican Indian and Alaska Native (AIAN) tribal communities have long been the subject of intense interest by outside groups. Like indigenous people around the world, they have been observed, named, and evaluated by outsiders since the time of first contact (Smith, 1999). Academic scholars representing the gamut of Western scientific disciplines are included among those interested in tribal culture, life, health, and development. The research that this interest has generated has led to the perception among AIAN people that they are among the most researched groups in the United States (Burhansstipanov, Christopher, & Schumacher, 2005; Sahota, 2007); given the small percentage of the general population that they represent, this perception is likely well-grounded. Unfortunately, AIAN communities have not always been well-served by this research—whether because they have received little apparent benefit, or because they have been overtly harmed by the research that has been conducted in their communities (Beals, Manson, Mitchell, Spicer, & AISUPERPFP-Team, 2003; Norton & Manson, 1996). In response, tribes have become increasingly wary of research, casting a critical eye upon the enterprise as a whole. As Smith writes, "Indigenous peoples have been, in many ways, oppressed by theory. Any consideration of the ways our origins have been examined, our histories recounted, our arts analyzed, our cultures dissected, measured, torn apart and distorted back to us will suggest that theories have not looked sympathetically or ethically at us" (Smith, 1999, p. 38).

Despite these experiences, AIAN communities acknowledge that research, with the appropriate protections, is a (potentially) powerful tool to address the pervasive health disparities AIAN people experience (Bird, 2002; Harris, 2002; Roubideaux, 2002); as a result, there is arguably no community more receptive to the concept of engaged scholarship and participatory research than tribal communities (Burhansstipanov et al., 2005). Indeed, engaged scholarship is at the core of the research process that tribes, as uniquely sovereign entities, require (National Congress of American Indians, 2005). In this chapter, we focus on engaged scholarship as it relates to research in tribal communities. Our goals are to describe the tribal context in which research occurs; review existing models of research engagement with tribes; offer a set of guiding principles, extracted from the current literature, as well as our own experiences, for working with tribal communities to conduct meaningful research; and identify next steps for deepening the engaged relationship between universities and tribal communities.

The Tribal Context of Research

Numbering 4.5 million, American Indians and Alaska Natives (AIANs) represent 1.5 percent of the United States population (U.S. Census Bureau, 2000). Within the United States, there are 562 federally recognized tribes, 69 state-recognized tribes, and a large percentage of "urban Indians" who reside in major cities across the country (Bureau of Indian Affairs; Indian Health Service; National Congress of State Legislatures, 2007). The AIAN population represents a rich diversity of tribally specific cultures, histories, and languages; at the same time, there are important shared experiences among the indigenous peoples of this land, including a history of colonization, a commitment to cultural preservation and revitalization, and ongoing sources of strength and challenge in their communities (Roubideaux, 2002). As researchers approach tribes to partner in research, they must be aware of the broader context in which this research is situated, including tribal jurisdiction, history, and culture.

Tribal Jurisdiction and Regulation of Research

The AIAN population is unique among all other racial/ethnic groups in the United States in that tribes maintain sovereign status as nations within a nation (Biolsi, 2005). This sovereignty affords tribes a significant degree of control over the affairs of their communities, including whether or not research is welcome, and if so, on what terms (Sahota, 2007). The National Congress of American Indians (NCAI) asserts that tribes are the "exclusive owner(s) of indigenous knowledge, cultural and biogenetic resources, and intellectual property," and thus, researchers must submit to the authority of tribes to approve research protocols, control research data, and oversee the interpretation and presentation of findings (National Congress of American Indians, 2005). As Sahota (2007) and Rhoades, Rhoades, and Freeman (2000) argue, the Belmont Report principles of respect for individuals (informed consent), beneficence (assessment of risk and benefit), and justice (selection of subjects) must be considered for the tribal community as a whole. Whereas the principles of beneficence and justice might be readily applicable at the community level, it may be more difficult for researchers to understand how "respect for individuals" is applied—but "respect" is at the heart of statements such as the NCAI's about tribal ownership of data and control of research in their communities. Thus, in tribal contexts, "respect" for the community means that tribes should be fully informed about the purpose of the research, the research methods, and the potential risks and benefits to their communities. Once informed, they may elect or decline to participate as a community in the research.

Statements about tribal control over the research process are instantiated in the resources provided by a number of AIAN organizations. The Indigenous Peoples Council on Biocolonialism (www.ipcb.org), the American Indian Law Center (www.ailc-inc.org), the National Congress of American Indians Policy Research Council (www.ncaiprc.org), the Indian Health Service (www.ihs.gov), and the Canadian Institutes for Health Research (www.cihr-irsc.gc.ca) have all offered extensive guidance to both tribes and researchers, by providing model research agreements, model research codes for tribes, and in-depth guidelines for the ethical conduct of research in tribal communities.

The strong stance that tribes take with respect to the oversight and control of research in their communities may be difficult to understand for those unfamiliar with the history of research in tribal communities. As Salois, Holkup, Tripp-Reimer, and Weinert (2006) have summarized, research in tribal communities has too often failed communities because it identified problems without benefit or solution, resulted in the publication of protected cultural material, served the needs of the academic but not the tribal community, or presented inaccurate findings due to the cultural misinterpretation of data. One of the most well-known cases of harm to a tribal community due to research is the 1979 Barrow Alaska study of alcohol use among the Inupiat (Foulks, 1989). Following a press release about the study's findings, prominent headlines read, "Alcohol Plagues Eskimos," and "Sudden Wealth Sparks Epidemic of Alcoholism." As Manson and Norton (Norton & Manson, 1996) discuss, these provocative headlines, understandably, caused conflict among all parties involved—the community, the investigators, and the funding agency—and overshadowed any scientific merit the study may have had. Furthermore, the Standard and Poor's rating of the community dropped precipitously, and as a consequence, the tribe was precluded from obtaining funds for municipal projects needed to improve community members' lives.

In another more recent example, the Havasupai tribe filed suit against the Arizona Board of Regents alleging that the tribe's rights had been violated by research conducted by university investigators (Dalton, 2004; Jaschik, 2008). The case concerns blood samples collected in the early 1990s from two hundred tribal members, who had consented to the samples being used in a study of the genetics of diabetes. According to the suit, blood samples were subsequently used, without the tribe's or individual participants' knowledge or consent, in studies on schizophrenia, and in studies that examined the genetic origins of the tribe that challenged the tribe's own beliefs and creation histories (Jaschik, 2008). Had the tribe or the individual participants known about the ways that their blood would be used and for what purpose, they likely would have never consented to the samples being drawn. Furthermore, the tribe's experience with this project seriously undermined trust in the entire biomedical system, such that tribal members were reluctant to seek medical care and suffered physical health problems as a result. Researchers involved in the case have denied allegations and fear that because of the breakdown in this process, tribes will be left out of studies that promise to address some of the significant health problems their communities face (Dalton, 2004).

Although these two examples are extreme and do not represent the overwhelming majority of research that occurs in tribal communities, such cases nonetheless remain at the forefront of tribal consciousness with respect to research. Against a backdrop of more than five hundred years of overt attempts to colonize Native lands, subjugate Native peoples, and destroy or appropriate Native cultures, research can appear as yet another assault on Native existence (Duran & Duran, 1995; Smith, 1999). At the same time, tribal communities experience ongoing and pervasive disparities in health, including rates of morbidity and mortality due to diabetes, alcoholism, accidents, and suicide that far exceed those of the general U.S. or other minority populations (Jones, 2006; Shalala, Trujillo, Harry, Skupien, & D'Angelo, 1997; Shalala, Trujillo, Hartz, & D'Angelo, 1999). In light of these disparities, tribes recognize that research developed in partnership with university investigators is one approach to improving the health and well-being of their communities (Bird, 2002; Harris, 2002; Roubideaux, 2002). The mission statement of the Navajo Nation's research review board reflects a positive and proactive stance toward research, by stating,

> The mission of the Navajo Nation Research Program is to support research that promotes and enhances the interests and the visions of the Navajo people; to encourage a mutual and beneficial partnership between the Navajo people and researchers; and to create an interface where different cultures, lifestyles, disciplines, and ideologies can come together in a way that improves, promotes, and strengthens the health of the Navajo people. (http://www.nnhrrb.navajo.org/index.htm)

The Regulation of Research in Tribal Communities

Thus, as researchers approach partnerships with tribal communities, they must both be aware of the broader history and context of research in tribal communities, and understand the particulars of tribal research review and regulation in a given community. As a sovereign nation, each tribe determines its own regulations with regard to research. There are therefore arguably as many models for research regulation in tribal communities as there are tribes. Most often, however, research is reviewed by one or more tribal entities, such as the tribal health board, the tribal council, a tribal research review board, and/or the Indian Health Service (IHS) area office institutional review board (IRB). In many (but not all) cases, the tribe requires that a tribal council resolution be passed in support of a particular research project prior to its inception. The reach of tribal jurisdiction over research varies by community. Whereas many tribes limit their jurisdiction to participation in research occurring within the geographic boundaries of the reservation community, others require that participation by a tribal member in a research project anywhere in the United States requires tribal review of the research prior to his or her participation. Although the majority of tribal communities do not have formal IRBs as defined under the U.S. Department of Health and Human Services Title 45 Code of Federal Regulations Part 46 (45 CFR 46; http://www.hhs.gov/ohrp/humansubjects/guidance/45cfr46.htm#46.102), a small but growing number of tribes have constituted tribal IRBs that meet these regulatory criteria, including the California Rural Indian Health Board, and the Cherokee, Chickasaw, Choctaw, and Navajo Nations.

A review of all the models for tribal review of research is beyond the scope of this chapter. Indeed, such a review might well encompass an entire volume itself. It is also beyond the purpose of this chapter. Rather, we raise this important issue early in this chapter to alert researchers to the fact that tribal review of research is part and parcel of doing research in tribal communities and is integral to the process of engagement in tribal contexts. Knowing this, it is imperative that researchers understand the process for research review in the tribal community with whom they seek to partner. Furthermore, researchers must understand that this process is subject to change as each tribal community continues to adapt and refine its approach to research review, and the process may be affected by broader political issues occurring in the tribe at a given time (Burhansstipanov et al., 2005).

The Cultural Context for Research in Tribal Communities

In addition to the jurisdictional and regulatory processes within a given tribal community, researchers must also be prepared to understand and navigate the cultural processes (Beals et al., 2003). Although these cultural processes also vary widely and therefore cannot be generalized across tribal communities, the literature provides examples of ways in which the university "culture" may come into contrast (or even be at odds) with certain aspects of tribal culture. One aspect of many tribal cultures that comes into rapid contrast with university culture is differing notions of time. Pickering (2004) discusses this in terms of "task-orientation" versus "clock time," stating, "externally imposed time values are simply flouted when they contradict the internally defined, socially embedded requirements of material life" (p. 96). Because members of AIAN communities are often deeply connected to one another through blood and traditional relationship ties, the needs and demands of family and community are immediate and often take priority over what outsiders may perceive as the demands of one's occupation. Or, again, as Pickering states, "the clock is irrelevant when people are engaged in accomplishing tasks required for ceremonies, births, illnesses, funerals, or family crises. Because of the resources and safety nets they represent, social networks of support are as, or more, critical than the paycheck received for 14 weeks out of the year" (Pickering, 2004, p. 96). It is not uncommon for tribal offices to close or workers to be absent to attend important community-wide events—such as sporting events, graduations, ceremonies, pow-wows, or funerals. These and other realities of tribal community life can compound delays to researcher-defined timelines, including severe weather and the lack of reliable public transportation in many tribal communities.

It can be very frustrating to those outside of the community to understand this different orientation to time, or to appreciate other facts of life in tribal communities that interfere with timelines. To minimize frustration on both sides, and avert misunderstandings that can undermine important partnerships, researchers are well served to let go of rigid expectations for what needs to be done when, and to develop generous and flexible timelines to accommodate the inevitable competing demands that arise for their tribal partners. A generous timeline also allows researchers time to just "be" in the tribal community, and to witness, if not participate, in the natural ebb and flow of tribal life in order to more deeply appreciate where their community partners are coming from (both literally and figuratively).

Another aspect of tribal culture that is critically important to understand includes customs for how to relate to others. Such customs govern everything, from how to shake someone's hand to the appropriateness of certain topics for conversation. Perhaps most relevant for research are questions about what is appropriate to discuss and with whom. Among certain tribes, there are protocols limiting the ways in which one speaks of tragic events, such as death or harm that has befallen someone. This poses a challenge if, for example, one is conducting a mental health survey that is likely to include such topics as loss or trauma. Among other tribes, it may be inappropriate to broach certain topics with certain individuals —such as asking an elder about topics that could be construed as disrespectful, or asking opposite-sex participants about topics that are considered inappropriate. There are also protocols in different tribes for how individuals are approached. For example, when going to the home of a research participant, it is custom in some tribal communities to wait in the car for someone in the home to come out to greet you, as opposed to going to the door and knocking. In other communities, one might need an introduction by a trusted fellow community member before a research participant is willing to talk to a stranger, especially about research. Finally, researchers should understand community concerns about confidentiality. In some small tribal communities, sharing personal information (as in a research interview) with an outsider may be preferable to confiding in another community member for fear that the information will not stay confidential. In other communities, any concerns about confidentiality may be outweighed by the sense of trust and familiarity inherent in speaking with someone from the same community.

Such cultural customs are too numerous and too diverse to describe here, but should be well understood on a *tribally specific* basis, before any partnership is approached or research activities begin, through consultation with tribal partners. We have highlighted these examples not to provide the reader with a comprehensive review of all the ways that tribal and university cultures can differ, but rather, to illustrate the need for researchers to understand that such differences exist and to be prepared to effectively navigate these differences. In the following section, we review several models of university-tribal engagement with respect to research that have been effective.

Fulfilling the Promise of Research: Models of Engagement with Tribal Communities

With such potentially difficult processes to navigate, the enthusiasm for research on both the tribe's and the university researcher's sides can be challenged. Outweighing the challenges however, is the potential mutual benefit. On the tribal side, communities can use research data to better understand the health concerns and challenges of their communities and to advocate (with the researcher) for funding to improve or implement needed services these challenges, or they can work with researchers to develop intervention or prevention programs to address the health concerns of their communities. Furthermore, individual community members can benefit from the jobs and job training when they are employed as members of the research team, or can benefit from access to services (as in the case of intervention research) or technology they might not otherwise have. Researchers, on the other hand, have the opportunity to participate in real-world change by helping to address serious health disparities among a population that has not historically been well served by research or health care, and can also gain a culturally based understanding of their work.

Considerable thought has been given to the ways in which university researchers must approach partnerships with tribal communities to collaboratively produce meaningful research that stands a chance of affecting real-world change in tribal communities (Beauvais, 1999; Mohatt, 1989; Stubben, 2001). To this end, a number of authors have proposed models or guidelines for how university researchers and tribal communities can form meaningful research partnerships. Here, we review several perspectives on research engagement with tribes that may help researchers and communities alike navigate this sometimes difficult terrain.

Fisher and Ball have proposed the "Tribal Participatory Research Model" (TPRM) (Fisher & Ball, 2003) in which they advocate the following four mechanisms to guide research with AIAN communities: tribal oversight, use of a facilitator, training and employment of community members as project staff, and the use of culturally specific assessment and intervention methods. These mechanisms are grounded in the same principles of tribal sovereignty, tribal self-governance, and tribal self-determination that guide the relationship between tribes and other entities, such as the government or private corporations, and are intended to ensure meaningful tribal involvement throughout the scientific process. Tribal oversight involves three components, each related to different phases of the research. In the beginning of the research, investigators are directed to obtain a formal resolution from the tribal council, or other tribal entity, which, as Fisher and Ball point out, carries the legal authority of the tribe (in contrast to letters of support). Once the research is active, the TPRM advocates the use of an oversight committee composed of tribal members who are compensated for their time, to monitor project activities and ensure adherence to tribal regulations and cultural standards. Finally, the TPRM suggests the development and ongoing implementation of a tribal research code that articulates tribal expectations for the research process. Model tribal research codes have been provided by AIAN organizations such as the American Indian Law Center and the Indigenous Peoples Council on Biocolonialism, as mentioned previously.

The second mechanism suggested by the TPRM involves the use of a facilitator to serve the interests of both the researcher and the community, through presiding over meetings between the researcher and the community and through encouraging communication by clarifying terminology for both parties and keeping the process balanced so that one side does not dominate conversations. The TPRM argues that the presence of a facilitator is essential in the early phases of a project, while relationships and roles are being established. The third mechanism proposed by the TPRM concerns employing community members as research staff. Community members are valuable members of the research team, because they bring their familiarity with the community, trust from other community members, and cultural perspective. Furthermore, they receive job training and skills they might not otherwise have received. The final mechanism promoted by the TPRM involves the use of culturally specific assessment and intervention methods. In particular, the TPRM questions the use of certain methodologies (such as randomized controlled trials) that can conflict with tribal values of community—favoring instead, other scientifically grounded methodologies such as multiple-baseline designs that allow all to receive the benefits of an intervention at some point.

The set of guiding assumptions for partnering with tribal communities proposed by Whitbeck (2006) underscores and expands upon the TPRM call to use culturally specific assessment and intervention methods, stressing the primacy of Native culture in moving research forward to best serve the needs of AIAN people. Although Whitbeck's guiding assumptions were developed with prevention research in mind, they apply equally as well to research more generally. Whitbeck argues that prevention research (and, we argue, research in general) must (1) proceed nation by nation; (2) recognize that AIAN cultures contain all of the information needed to socialize mentally healthy children (and, we argue, to promote the health of AIAN communities); (3) view cultural ways and knowledge as equal to social science (prevention) knowledge; (4) acknowledge there are risk and protective factors unique to AIAN communities/cultures that operate both independently of and in interaction with risk and protective factors known to majority populations; (5) facilitate ownership of culturally specific prevention programs (or, we argue, research models) to be successful; and (6) recognize that there is a hunger for cultural knowledge among AIAN communities.

The guiding assumptions proposed by Whitbeck highlight the need for meaningful engagement with tribal communities in ways such as the TPRM suggests, and call to mind what Salois et al. (2006) described as the "spiritual covenant" that researchers have with tribal communities when engaged in research. From their experience working in three Northwest tribal communities, the authors proposed five principles that have grounded the work between them (outsiders, non-Natives) and their tribal partners. The first of the five principles is to view research as a "spiritual covenant" between researchers and communities such that prayer is used in project meetings, both researchers and the communities feel indebted to one another, and that individual's (and the community's) stories are treated as sacred. The second principle of reciprocity impels the research team to give something of immediate value back to the community (such as direct service). The third principle of harmony recognizes the need to respect different perspectives and is nurtured through a "memorandum of understanding" and the involvement of a "cultural insider" to assist with data analysis and interpretation in order to guard against cultural misinterpretations. The fourth principle of respect for all acknowledges the need to respect not only individuals but communities as well (as in respecting community-level confidentiality), and ways of being and communicating that are different between researchers and tribal communities. Finally, the fifth principle of cultural humility involves the researcher's commitment to self-evaluation and critique, such that s/he does not presume to be the expert and instead gives equal weight to the perspectives of the community.

Informed by the work of these and other authors, our own research team advocates the use of clearly articulated principles to guide research with AIAN communities. Table 1 provides an overview of the principles that have guided some of our own projects (Novins et al., 2006), as well as a comparison to how these principles relate to those of Israel et al. (2003), whose work on community-based participatory research (CBPR) provides a reference for anyone seeking to meaningfully engage communities in research (whether AIAN or otherwise), as well as to those proposed by Freeman, Iron Cloud-Two Dogs, Novins, and LeMaster (2005) based on their work with the Circles of Care Initiative for improving the systems of care for AIAN children's mental health.

Table 1 Guiding Principles for Conducting Research with AIAN Communities and Their Relationships to Principles Described by Israel et al. (2003) and Freeman et al. (2005)

Draft Guiding Principles	Corresponding Principles from Israel et al.	Corresponding Principles from Freeman et al.
The project will be community-based, building upon the strengths of all research partners, and recognizing the diversity of viewpoints and traditions within the community.	• Recognizes community as a unit of identity. Builds on strengths and resources within the community.	• In effective strategic planning, the unique characteristics and needs of different tribal entities are recognized, including recognizing tensions among traditions, culture, and rural-urban-reservation factors.
The project will rely on the development of a collaborative, inclusive investigative approach in which all participants share their skills, learn from each other, and appreciate the contributions of all team members. We will utilize an iterative process that assures effective participation of all key stakeholders.	• Promotes a co-learning and empowering process. . . . Facilitates collaborative, equitable involvement of all partners in all phases of the research. Involves a cyclical and iterative process.	• Effective strategic planning requires the direct participation of key stakeholders. Successful strategic planning necessitates establishing staff credibility.
The project will focus on the needs of (specify group)	• . . . attends to social inequalities.	
The project will delineate and achieve specific outcomes as developed through this inclusive research process.		• Effective strategic planning encompasses an outcome-oriented approach, with outcomes determined by participatory action research methods.
The project is based on the belief that change is possible—for individuals, families, and communities—and that research can be a positive agent in the change process.	• Addresses health from both positive and ecological perspectives.	• Effective strategic planning includes a central belief in change and change processes.
The project involves a long-standing and productive collaboration and represents an ongoing commitment to improving health for community members through high-quality research projects. Collaboration will continue beyond this project.	• Involves a long-term commitment by all partners.	
By disseminating study results to all key stakeholders and pursing scholarly publications, a knowledge base for similar efforts in this and other communities will be built.	• Disseminates findings and knowledge gained to all partners.	• Strategic planning processes need to be documented through process evaluation.

Guiding Principles for Engaged Scholarship with Tribal Communities

As reviewed, there are a number of models for and perspectives on engaged scholarship with respect to research in tribal communities. Here, we have extracted a set of guiding principles that are cross-cutting and should be considered essential in promoting successful researcher-AIAN community research partnerships.

1. *Invest in relationships:* The building and maintenance of relationships with tribal communities is at the core of university-tribal partnerships for research. As with all relationships, relationships between researchers and communities take time. Thus, the foundations of the relationship should be laid prior to the research, so that the community and the researcher together can develop research agendas. Furthermore, the relationship should continue beyond the life of a particular research project such that researchers and communities together can strategize and be proactive about next steps in the partnership.

2. *Know and respect community customs and practices:* Because of the diversity between tribes, researchers should familiarize themselves with the community customs and cultural practices of their particular tribal partner with respect to such things as the involvement of elders in the research project, the role of prayer or spirituality in project activities, the development of project timelines, and perceptions or concerns about confidentiality at the individual participant or community level. The involvement of a cultural consultant is essential in this regard.

3. *Honor tribal control of research:* It is not acceptable to conduct research in AIAN tribal communities without the knowledge and consent of the tribe as a whole. Though the process for research review and regulation varies by tribe, every tribe has some form of research review and regulation, and researchers must understand what that process is in their partner community. The scope of research review and regulation should also be understood on a community-by-community basis, with respect to the tribe's position on the review and approval of manuscripts and presentations that result from the research, control of research data following study completion, and the reach of tribal jurisdiction beyond the community's geographic boundaries.

4. *Seek meaningful involvement of tribal community members in the research process:* Members of the partner AIAN community should be involved in all phases of the research, including design, data collection and interpretation, and the publication of research findings as co-authors on papers and/or presentations. Involvement of community members can occur through tribal community advisory boards or oversight committees, and through the employment of community members as project personnel or as consultants. The identification of who should be involved depends on recommendations from the community as well as the needs of the project.

5. *Adapt methods, measures, and approach:* Because standard research methods and measures were generally not developed with AIAN communities or people in mind, they should be closely examined with the community and modified and/or interpreted with the appropriate context or precautions. This iterative process should be built into the research design and timeline, such that protocols can be reviewed by the community,

modified, and returned to the community for further review and/or acceptance. Community advisory or oversight boards can be helpful in this process, as can tribal members of the research team and community focus groups. Although some work has been done to develop and/or adapt such measures (Beals et al., 2003), there is much that remains to be done.

6. *Give back and think ahead:* At a minimum, research findings should be shared with the community. Target audiences within the community include the tribal council, tribal health boards, community advisory or oversight boards, and the community at large. In presenting findings, researchers should identify next steps that the community, the researcher, or the community and researcher together can take to bring about needed change in the community in light of the findings in a manner that is accessible, concise, practical, and clear. For example, researchers should identify implications for policies or practices within existing institutions, plans for follow-up studies, or plans to directly address any problems identified by the research. Because the community may seek to independently use research data to support their own efforts (e.g., grant writing to secure funding for services), researchers should be an ongoing technical resource to the tribe.

7. *Contribute to the expansion of local capacity for research:* Tribes are working continually to position themselves to do research of their own. Researchers can contribute to this capacity by hiring and training local research assistants, providing professional development opportunities to the community at large (e.g., offering to give a lecture at a local tribal college), involving tribal partners in the development of applications for funding and the analysis and presentation of data, keeping their tribal partners informed about funding opportunities even if not related to the researchers' own particular area of research, and supporting the development of new AIAN researchers through mentorship and training opportunities.

8. *Understand the broader context of life in this community:* By spending time in the tribal partner's community, researchers will have the opportunity to understand day-to-day life in the community, as well as the broader history of the community—both of which will situate research methods and questions in context and give added meaning to research findings. Spending time in the community forming personal and professional relationships and participating in some aspects of tribal life promotes a richer understanding of the complexities of tribal life and its sources of stress and strength.

9. *Educate the institution:* Institutions in the majority society are often woefully uninformed about tribal communities. Researchers partnering with tribal communities for research must be prepared to educate funders about the unique demands of conducting research in tribal communities (e.g., with respect to research methods and timelines) and the need to support projects that are by definition loosely defined in terms of method, but well defined in terms of process for engagement that will lead to a well-defined, culturally informed approach. Researchers must also be prepared to educate their own institutional IRBs about tribal review processes and how these may impact university institutional review processes.

225

Next Steps

Research has come a long way in tribal communities, as researchers have been more thoughtful about their responsibilities to tribal communities, and as tribal communities have become proactive in their relationship with researchers. As we look forward to what the future can bring for engaged research in tribal communities, the following next steps emerge.

1. There will be financial support for tribal IRBs and research review boards built into research grants.
2. The availability of research grants that support partnership building will increase.
3. Grant reviewers will be better educated about the developmental work involved in AIAN research.
4. Tribes will be better positioned to conduct their own independent research, as the numbers of AIAN research-trained faculty increase and as tribal colleges and universities become positioned to compete for funding of their own.
5. Research findings and funding priorities will be readily accessible to AIAN communities through the development of a clearinghouse of all tribally related research findings.

Conclusion

The discourse on engaged scholarship with respect to research in tribal communities is not new, but continues to evolve and inform the relationship between university researchers and tribal communities. As we have reviewed in this chapter, those relationships continue to be forged on a tribe-by-tribe and individual basis to a large degree. Nonetheless, the *process* by which tribes and university researchers engage has coalesced based on greater awareness on both sides of the promises and pitfalls of research with tribal communities. It is a fact that tribes must be involved in some meaningful way in the development of research agendas, the implementation of research projects, the interpretation of findings, and the ongoing control of research data. The particulars of how tribes and university researchers work out the details of this arrangement vary considerably from tribe to tribe—from informal agreements between researchers and representatives of the tribe on the one hand, to tribal IRBs on the other. Despite the progress that has been made, a number of broader shifts must occur to deepen engaged scholarship processes. As we have outlined here, these next steps are ambitious, but not outside the realm of the possible, given the important strides that have already been made.

Acknowledgments

Findings reported in this chapter were supported in part by grants ACF ACF/OPRE 90-YF-0053/05-AIH-002; NIAAA R21AA17596, NIH P01-MH4247; NIH P60-MD000507; NIMH R34-MH077802, NIDA R01-DA022239; R01 MH073965.

References

Beals, J., Manson, S. M., Mitchell, C. M., Spicer, P., & AISUPERPFP-Team. (2003). Cultural specificity and comparison in psychiatric epidemiology: Walking the tightrope in American Indian research. *Culture, Medicine, & Psychiatry, 27,* 259–289.

Beauvais, F. (1999). Obtaining consent and other ethical issues in the conduct of research in American Indian communities. *Drugs and Society, 14,* 167–184.

Biolsi, T. (2005). Imagined geographies: Sovereignty, indigenous space, and American Indian struggle. *American Ethnologist, 32*(2), 239–259.

Bird, M. E. (2002). Health and indigenous people: Recommendations for the next generation. *American Journal of Public Health, 92*(9), 1391–1392. Bureau of Indian Affairs. Retrieved February 20, 2009, from http://www.doi.gov/bia/.

Burhansstipanov, L., Christopher, S., & Schumacher, S. A. (2005, November). Lessons learned from community-based participatory research in Indian country. *Cancer Control,* 70–76.

Dalton, R. (2004). When two tribes go to war. *Nature, 430,* 500–502.

Duran, E., & Duran, B. (1995). *Native American postcolonial psychology.* Albany: State University of New York Press.

Fisher, P. A., & Ball, T. J. (2003). Tribal participatory research: Mechanisms of a collaborative model. *American Journal of Community Psychology, 32*(3), 207–216.

Foulks, E. F. (1989). Misalliances in the Barrow Alaska Study. *American Indian and Alaska Native Mental Health Research, 2,* 7–17.

Freeman, B., Iron Cloud-Two Dogs, E., Novins, D. K., & LeMaster, P. L. (2005). Contextual issues for strategic planning and evaluation of systems of care for American Indian and Alaska Native communities: An introduction to Circles of Care. *American Indian and Alaska Native Mental Health Research Journal, 11*(2), 1–29.

Harris, C. H. (2002). Indigenous health: Fulfilling our obligation to future generations. *American Journal of Public Health, 92*(9), 1390. Indian Health Service. *Urban Indian Health Program.* Retrieved January 20, 2009, from www.ihs.gov/nonmedicalprograms/urban/overview.asp.

Israel, B. A., Schulz, A. J., Parker, E. A., Becker, A. B., Allen, A. J., & Guzman, J. R. (2003). Critical issues in developing and following community-based participatory research principles. In M. Minkler & N. Wallertstein (Eds.), *Community-based participatory research for health.* San Francisco: Jossey-Bass.

Jaschik, S. (2008). *Whose blood is it?* Retrieved January 15, 2009, from www.insidehighered.com/news/2008/12/01/blood.

Jones, D. S. (2006). The persistence of American Indian health disparities. *American Journal of Public Health, 96*(12), 2122–2134.

Mohatt, G. V. (1989). The community as informant or collaborator? *American Indian and Alaska Native Mental Health Research, 2,* 64–70.

National Congress of American Indians. (2005). *Resolution #TUL-05-059: Tribal Ownership of Health-Related Data.* Retrieved November 10, 2008, from http://www.ncai.org/ncai/data/resolution/annual2005/TUL-05-059.pdf.

National Congress of State Legislatures. (2007). *Federal and state recognized tribes.* Retrieved January 20, 2009, from www.ncsl.org/programs/statetribe/tribes.htm#state.

Norton, I. M., & Manson, S. M. (1996). Research in American Indian and Alaska Native communities: Navigating the cultural universe of values and process. *Journal of Consulting and Clinical Psychology, 64*(5), 856–860.

Novins, D. K., Freeman, B., Thurman, P. J., Iron Cloud-Two Dogs, E., Allen, J., LeMaster, P. L., et al. (2006). Principles for participatory research with American Indian and Alaska Native communities: Lessons from the Circles of Care Initiative. Paper presented at conference Indigenous Suicide Prevention Research and Programs in Canada and the United States: Setting a Collaborative Agenda. Albuquerque, NM.

Pickering, K. (2004). Decolonizing time regimes: Lakota conceptions of work, economy, and society. *American Anthropologist, 106,* 85–97.

Rhoades, E. R., Rhoades, D. A., & Freeman, W. (2000). Research ethics and the American Indian. In E. R. Rhoades (Ed.), *American Indian health: Innovations in health care, promotion, and policy* (pp. 426–433). Baltimore: Johns Hopkins University Press.

Roubideaux, Y. (2002). Perspectives on American Indian health. *American Journal of Public Health, 92*(9), 1401–1403.

Sahota, P. C. (2007). *Research regulation in American Indian/Alaska Native communities: Policy and practice considerations.* Retrieved December 15, 2008, from http://www.ncaiprc.org/indexphp?todo=page&which=313.

Salois, E. M., Holkup, P. A., Tripp-Reimer, T., & Weinert, C. (2006). Research as spiritual covenant. *Western Journal of Nursing Research, 28*(5), 505.

Shalala, D. E., Trujillo, M. H., Harry, R. H., Skupien, M. B., & D'Angelo, A. J. (1997). *Regional differences in Indian health.* Rockville, MD: Indian Health Service.

Shalala, D. E., Trujillo, M. H., Hartz, G. J., & D'Angelo, A. J. (1999). *Regional differences in Indian health: 1998–1999.* Rockville, MD: Indian Health Service.

Smith, L. T. (1999). *Decolonizing methodologies: Research and Indigenous Peoples.* New York: Zed Books.

Stubben, J. D. (2001). Working with and conducting research among American Indian families. *American Behavioral Scientist, 44,* 1466–1481.

U.S. Census Bureau. (2000). *The American Indian and Alaska Native population: 2000.* Retrieved November 1, 2004, from http://www.census.gov/prod/2002pubs/c2kbr01 15.pdf.

Whitbeck, L. B. (2006). Some guiding assumptions and a theoretical model for developing culturally specific preventions with Native American people. *Journal of Community Psychology, 34*(2), 183.

PART 3

Engaged Faculty and Emerging Scholars

Edited by KerryAnn O'Meara

Engaged Faculty and Emerging Scholars

KerryAnn O'Meara

It can be argued that much of the research on faculty roles and rewards over the past two decades has been written from a constraint narrative. This is perhaps especially so in discussions of faculty engagement. By constraint, I refer to a story of why faculty are not socialized toward engagement, why they cannot prioritize it, the barriers to its practice, and its lack of reward or recognition. This narrative has served us well in that it has allowed us to see concrete areas where our campuses need to change in order to socialize and recruit more faculty toward this work, and help and sustain them throughout their experiences. It has perhaps not served us well, however, in considering the long-term investments faculty are making in engagement, the ways that they are growing and learning in it, and how it is integrated into the daily fabric of their lives.

The chapters in this part do not ignore constraints, but they lean toward what I will call critical investments or opportunities to extend faculty learning, agency, relationships, and commitments. Each chapter takes on key questions that challenge assumptions that shape how faculty are socialized and rewarded, and what knowledge and scholarship is valued. For example, Austin and Beck question the set of values and assumptions that have prioritized research over other forms of scholarship since World War II. In my chapter, I question, "if only" assumptions about how engaged scholars might be better prepared for promotion and tenure, as well as whether engaged scholars need to become more involved in remaking promotion and tenure systems as opposed to conforming or accommodating the norms of systems that were built to favor traditional research. Jordan questions previous practices of peer review, noting how exclusion of community members from peer review of engaged scholarship devalues the contribution the work is having in practice. Peters and Alter question the framing of the scholarship of engagement as neutral and objective, apolitical.

Through all of these questions, authors acknowledge constraint. And yet, every author then turns from such questions to suggest we build something new.

The chapter by Austin and Beck is perhaps the most far reaching, as they consider multiple "levers for change" or concrete strategies for building engagement into the fabric of faculty work-life. They carefully consider each aspect of "the problem," from the knowledge and skills faculty need to learn in graduate education to the reflection and strategy they need to embed and weave it into various roles. Austin and Beck do not let institutions off the hook. They chart a course for how institutional mission and rhetoric might be aligned with concrete investments in the careers of engaged scholars and what role institutional leaders can play in creating cultures conducive to engaged scholarship.

Next, Peters and Alter invest in this issue by shining a spotlight on the political roles and work of academic professionals that are already in play. Their research sheds light on the roles faculty play in civic and community engaged scholarship that are rarely described, such as civic actor, community organizer, facilitator, change agent, critic, and partner. While they acknowledge that the role of faculty member—as provider of scientific information, technical expertise, and assistance—receives the bigger headlines, they argue for a spotlight on the growth and learning faculty experience in these other extremely important aspects of that work. Finally, Peters and Alter invest in faculty and the scholarship of engagement by setting out a research agenda, one that is rich and storied and likely to capture the multitude of roles faculty play across the span of a long career.

In my own chapter, I take on a specific aspect of reward systems, one that has received much attention, despite its availability to a smaller number of academics: promotion and tenure. After considering the meaning and relevance of reward systems, I suggest that we invest in making faculty engagement work more public, publicly available, and visible. I also suggest we hold scholars going up for promotion and tenure who do not necessarily consider themselves engaged scholars accountable for relevance, impact, and contribution to public purpose. Finally, rather than the "publish or perish," "archery in the dark" and "don't do engagement until you are post-tenure" adages that seem to shape so many views of promotion and tenure, I suggest we make the process more growth focused, building in opportunities for faculty to extend relationships, feel civic agency, celebrate accomplishments, and reflect on learning.

Jordan's chapter has a heavy investment or growth focus as she suggests very concrete strategies she and other leaders in Community Campus Partnerships for Health have devised to value community-engaged scholarship through promotion and tenure. In this chapter, she takes on issues of assessing nontraditional products of community-engaged scholarship: She considers mechanisms for their peer review, standards for assessment, and publication outlets. In doing so, she unpacks rarely questioned assumptions regarding what peer review is supposed to accomplish, as well as scholarly process versus scholarly product, expertise, and impact. This chapter provides a real road map for academic leaders who want to invest in the careers of engaged scholars by honoring engaged scholarship. There are major implications for the reform of promotion and tenure materials, faculty development, and the peer review process.

In summary, these chapters do not just tear down what engaged scholars might not like about the academy; rather, they look critically at its faults in order to invest in its future. It is clear from reading the chapters that these are all scholars who love higher education and know that its faculty are at the heart of its future. Whether as academic leaders, as policy makers, as individual faculty, or as institutions, the authors offer new ways to rewrite the narrative, so that the work of faculty in engaged scholarship can be honored and grow.

Integrating Outreach and Engagement into Faculty Work

Ann E. Austin and John P. Beck

The history of higher education includes commitments to teaching the next generation, preparing thoughtful citizens, discovering new knowledge, and addressing and improving issues and problems confronting society. Higher education institutions stand solidly as pillars of society, without which the quality, meaning, and opportunities in the human experience would be much diminished. Part of the history of American higher education includes a trend in the past six decades toward heavy emphasis on the research productivity mission. As important as this contribution is, over the past decade and a half, many higher education leaders, faculty members, and observers have highlighted the full array of missions of higher education institutions, including the responsibility to engage deeply with the problems and issues of society (Boyer, 1990, 1996; Diamond & Adam, 1995; Glassick, Huber, & Maeroff, 1997). Building on Boyer's (1990) call for an expanded understanding of scholarship to include application, discovery, teaching, and integration, and his later call for a scholarship of engagement (Boyer, 1996), many higher education leaders and faculty members, across institutional types, are thinking more deeply about the roles and responsibilities of universities and colleges in the broader society.

This volume is simultaneously an outcome of and a tribute to the growing interest in the importance of outreach and engagement in academic work, while also being a call for an even greater effort to embed such commitment into the daily fabric of work in higher education. Because faculty are critically important to the fulfillment of the missions of universities and colleges, efforts to strengthen the scholarship of engagement and outreach must be linked to attention to how individual faculty members understand and carry out their work. This chapter takes up that question: How can outreach and engagement be integrated more fully into faculty work?

Faculty members are socialized from the start of their careers in graduate school to a set of values and assumptions that gained strength in post–World War II academe (Rice, 1986, 1996). These assumptions include the valuing of research productivity expressed through publication in scholarly journals, the dominance of disciplinary culture and identity in shaping an academic's life, the importance of the autonomy of the individual faculty member, and the recognition that career advancement and quality assurance are related to peer review. These assumptions have been instrumental in propelling forward and ensuring excellence in research activity and have had an impact on teaching-oriented as well as research-oriented higher education institutions. They have shaped the preparation process for graduate education and the reward structure for academic careers. Although for more than half a century these assumptions have formed the core of the American higher education system, recognized for its excellence and quality across the world, they also can be barriers to efforts to increase the attention of faculty members to scholarly work that involves explicit engagement with their communities and the broader world. Efforts to integrate engagement and outreach more fully into the work of faculty members must recognize and build on this assumptive world while also opening the way for expanded understandings of strategies to create responsible, effective, respected faculty careers.

Theoretical work and research findings concerning institutional change and faculty work satisfaction and motivation inform the analysis and ideas offered in this chapter. Research on organizational change highlights the importance of aligning multiple levers for change (Austin, 1998; Votruba, 2005). Specifically, changes in higher education are encouraged when there is attention to and alignment between such elements of the organization as leadership actions (including communication strategies and attention to cultural symbols), institutional infrastructure (including financing procedures and the organization of units), professional development, and incentive and reward structures. Focusing on only one of these elements—or levers—for change is often not sufficient to encourage substantive change within complex higher education systems; engaging a set of levers for change is likely to have a greater impact.

In addition to the work on organizational change, key findings concerning work satisfaction and motivation (Gappa, Austin, & Trice, 2007) are useful in regard to understanding strategies that may influence faculty members (although detailed discussion of this work is beyond the scope of this chapter). Specifically, employees' satisfaction is enhanced with the presence of these factors: challenging work, including opportunities for creativity and personal growth; meaningful relationships; a sense of responsibility; and opportunities to receive feedback, respect, and recognition. Intrinsic factors—interest in the work itself, achievement, and recognition—are especially important in motivating faculty members. Motivation is also enhanced when some degree of challenge is coupled with the sense that one has the ability to succeed at the challenge.

These theoretical and research findings suggest that efforts to encourage faculty to integrate outreach and engagement into their work should recognize the importance of multiple levers for change. Strategies that do not take into account the organizational and cultural factors that affect how faculty understand and make choices about their work are unlikely to be effective. At the same time, the literature on work satisfaction and motivation reminds us that faculty members, like other employees, are motivated when they understand what is being asked, know how to do the work, have opportunities for creativity, achievement, and autonomy, and receive recognition and reward for their efforts. Recognizing these literature-based implications, this chapter focuses on four areas—levers for change—that can encourage and help faculty members integrate outreach and engagement more fully into their work: (1) increasing faculty knowledge and abilities concerning outreach and engagement in relationship to faculty work; (2) providing opportunities for faculty to integrate outreach and engagement into their work; (3) aligning the incentive and reward structure with these goals; and (4) ensuring that the institutional culture encourages and supports faculty efforts to integrate outreach and engagement into their work. The chapter discusses each of these four strategic approaches and offers practical examples.

We note that, although these levers are effective, individual faculty members will always construct the details of their work in the context of their own interests, proclivities, and disciplines (Austin, 1992, 1994). That is, how faculty members integrate outreach and engagement into their work will always, and arguably should always, be characterized by much variation. Building on the four strategic levers for change, the chapter concludes with several specific suggestions for institutional leaders.

Increasing Faculty Knowledge and Abilities regarding Outreach and Engagement

If faculty members are to integrate outreach and engagement more fully into their work, they need to have a solid understanding of what this kind of scholarship is, why it is an important form of scholarly work, and what it might involve within the context of their disciplines. Because the preparation and socialization for an academic career begins during graduate study, one way to help faculty members integrate outreach and engagement into their work is to include attention to this form of scholarship within their graduate experiences. A second and equally important way to increase faculty knowledge and abilities to do this form of work is through faculty development once they have embarked on the career.

Using Doctoral Education as Preparation for Engagement

A growing body of research over the past fifteen years has been examining the nature of graduate education. Recognizing that the doctoral experience involves socialization to what it means to be a scholar, either within academe or in other positions (Austin & McDaniels, 2006), this body of work has highlighted some of the facets of doctoral education that could be improved to better prepare future faculty. Several key concerns stand out. First, doctoral students often receive mixed messages about what is valued within academe (Austin, 2002; Nyquist et al., 1999). For example, although they may be told that teaching and outreach are valued and important parts of academic careers, they often report observing that the reward structures of their universities appear to honor research over other forms of scholarship. Furthermore, some doctoral students find that their advisors do not encourage participation in workshops or seminars designed to help students prepare as teachers or learn about outreach opportunities.

237

Second, research shows that doctoral students often do not understand in detail what faculty works involves (including the multiple forms of scholarship in which faculty members might engage), nor do they typically learn about the history of higher education's role in society or the different institutional types and their missions (Austin, 2002; Golde & Dore, 2001; Wulff, Austin, Nyquist, & Sprague, 2004). In particular, doctoral education devotes little attention to preparing students for the scholarship of outreach and engagement. When asked about their understanding of public service, engagement, or outreach in a longitudinal, qualitative study involving ongoing interviews with students across their doctoral careers, the future faculty respondents had little understanding of these terms and concepts (Austin, 2002; Wulff et al., 2004).

Although doctoral education usually has not provided systematic ways for future faculty to learn about the various kinds of scholarship, doctoral students typically indicate that they want careers that include meaningful work, characterized by a sense of connection (Austin, 2002; Rice, Sorcinelli, & Austin, 2000). In their large-scale quantitative study of doctoral students' perceptions of their experiences, Golde and Dore (2001) found that more than half of their doctoral respondents wanted to provide community service as part of their careers. Furthermore, other research has shown that future faculty members want work and careers that feature balance and integration (Austin, 2002; Golde & Dore, 2001; Rice et al., 2000; Trower, Austin, & Sorcinelli, 2001). One respondent presented a preferred vision of a faculty career that includes elements of the scholarship of engagement: "What I want most in a faculty career is a profession that makes me feel connected to my students, to my colleagues, to the larger community, and to myself" (Rice et al., 2000, p. 11).

What issues and topics should doctoral education address if future faculty are to be prepared more fully to integrate outreach and engagement in their work? Austin and McDaniels (2006) have presented a set of competencies that they propose be included in doctoral education; several of these competencies, if addressed, would do much to prepare the next generation of faculty members for careers that include the scholarship of engagement. Prospective faculty members, they assert, need to learn the core purposes and values of higher education, including the role and history of higher education institutions in a democratic society in preparing leaders and citizens and in linking the discovery of knowledge to the solution of problems and the betterment of society. An aspect of learning about the purposes and history of higher education includes considering the responsibilities of faculty members to contribute to the public good.

Second, doctoral students should be introduced explicitly to the concepts of outreach, public service, and engagement. They should explore the relationships among theory, research, and application in their own disciplines and have opportunities to see how faculty members in their fields include outreach and engagement as part of their work.

Third, they should develop excellent skills as researchers, and, depending on their fields, learn about such forms of scholarly work as community-based research and action research. They should be prepared to teach, including learning how to help students engage in critical thinking (a skill important for an engaged citizenry) and how to incorporate service learning into their class plans. In addition to learning to research and teach, they should learn skills that are specifically relevant to incorporating outreach and engagement into their work. For example, a comprehensive doctoral experience would include opportunities for future faculty to learn teamwork, collaboration, and conflict resolution skills, so that they are able to work across disciplines and with people from many walks of life. Future faculty should also learn to communicate effectively with diverse groups, and to engage in forms of writing appropriate for various audiences, including government and community agencies.

Fourth, future faculty should be exposed in graduate school to the idea that universities and colleges, functioning at their best, model for students and for the community effective democratic processes at work. In this context, faculty members have the responsibility to participate as citizens of the institutions where they have the privilege of serving on the faculty.

If the universities where doctoral education occurs take seriously their responsibility for preparing future faculty who have an understanding of the full range of faculty work, including the scholarship of outreach and engagement, this form of work would be carried out more extensively in the work of the faculty (Austin & Barnes, 2005). What specific strategies might graduate deans, department chairs, and advisors incorporate into doctoral programs?

Graduate schools could organize and host workshops that help graduate students develop the competencies just discussed. Such workshops, for example, might highlight the work of faculty members who explicitly integrate outreach and engagement into their work or help students learn to translate research reports into forms appropriate for other audiences. At Michigan State University, the Graduate School has developed an extensive program entitled Setting Expectations and Resolving Conflicts. This program, which has received national attention, includes workshops in which doctoral students learn to set expectations in working relationships and productively address conflicts that arise in their work (www.grad.msu.edu/conflict.htm; Klomparens & Beck, 2004).

Faculty involvement in outreach and engagement projects may also present valuable opportunities for graduate students to "shadow" faculty as they take part in off-campus teaching and/or facilitation. Shadowing opportunities (for example, taking graduate students in labor relations to collective bargaining sessions or arbitrations) can be linked directly to lessons within the classroom or can be explored deeply in theory-to-practice reflection groups. Such graduate student shadowing also is extremely valuable in giving graduate students a realistic look at alternatives to traditional faculty jobs.

Graduate programs can also offer courses that help students explore ways in which their disciplines connect with community issues. For example, the Delta Program at the University of Wisconsin, affiliated with the Center for the Integration of Research, Teaching, and Learning (a National Science Foundation Center that focuses on preparing doctoral students in sciences, engineering, and mathematics for academic careers) offers a course on "informal education." This course enables participants to develop projects designed to connect their disciplinary expertise with the community beyond the university. For example, students might develop programs for museums, schools, or news organizations that highlight science or engineering topics. Graduate deans might encourage campus audits that investigate, categorize, and ultimately make public the courses and experiences that explicitly address the competencies discussed earlier.

Within departments, chairpersons or program coordinators could encourage faculty committees to review the program curricula to examine whether graduate students have opportunities to learn about the scholarship of engagement in their fields, ethical issues relevant to their particular areas, and ways to communicate with diverse audiences about their work. Individual faculty members who work with graduate students might consider whether they discuss they own efforts to include engagement in their work and provide opportunities for aspiring faculty members to discuss their career aspirations and explore questions about how outreach and engagement relate to other forms of scholarship.

Providing Faculty Development That Emphasizes Outreach and Engagement

Although graduate education ideally prepares future faculty for the work they will encounter in their careers, those who are already faculty members also benefit from institutional strategies to help them understand and develop the proclivities and abilities to integrate outreach and engagement into their work. Many faculty members have limited understanding of the meaning of the scholarship of engagement, and they do not see how their teaching, research, and service relate to this form of scholarship. Ward argues that outreach and engagement require "an integrated view of faculty work" (2005, p. 231). She continues by explaining: "To fulfill the goals of the scholarship of engagement, scholars must link their teaching, research, and service to community problems, challenges, and goals, whether the community served is the department, the university, the town, state, or nation, or the global community" (2005, p. 231). Ward then explains how engagement can be integrated into all aspects of faculty work.

How does engagement relate to teaching? Ward (2005) suggests that faculty members can use teaching strategies that strengthen students' preparation for participation in civic life. Colby, Ehrlich, Beaumont, and Stephens (2003) suggest the use of service learning, problem-based and other experiential learning, and collaborative learning to advance skills useful in responsible citizenship. In service learning, for example, students see how their academic work relates to community work. In problem-based learning, students encounter real problems to which they apply concepts they are learning. In collaborative learning experiences, students learn to interact with others as involved citizens must do. Each of these teaching strategies is a way to integrate engagement into the instructional aspect of a faculty member's work (Ward, 2005).

In terms of the relationship of engagement and outreach to research and the discovery of knowledge, faculty members can learn about the range of choices available to them. As Ward explains (2005), they can learn about content, process, and outcomes in regard to integrating engagement into their research. For example, they may choose topics directly relevant to community needs. In terms of process, faculty members can involve community members in framing topics, designing studies, conducting research, interpreting data, and disseminating findings in ways that community audiences find useful. Many faculty members need to learn how to use their projects both to meet expectations for traditional research (such as publishing in scholarly journals) and to address community needs (such as expectations for feedback to action groups or short articles in the daily paper).

How does engagement and commitment to the public good relate to service? Faculty members may choose to engage in service directly related to their expertise (such as when a professor of environmental studies serves on a local water use board). Furthermore, Ward (2005) points out that when faculty members consult for groups beyond the university, they are actually carrying out a form of engagement and outreach. Faculty members are sharing their knowledge with community-based groups, often in a form useful for action.

Integrating outreach and engagement into their teaching, research, and service, in the ways described, requires new learning for many faculty members. They must become aware of these forms of scholarship, understand how the scholarship of engagement relates to their institution's missions and their discipline's values, and develop the skills and abilities to do a form of work that is unusual for many. James Votruba, a university president with a long history of articulating the importance of and supporting the scholarship of engagement, explained the kind of qualifications and abilities that faculty members need to develop in order to be successful at integrating engagement into their work: "Faculty who are good at this work know how to listen, are sensitive as learners as well as teachers, speak in a language that the community can understand, and always seek first to understand, then to be understood" (2005, p. 270).

Faculty development opportunities can help faculty members become more aware of what the scholarship of engagement means and ways to incorporate it into their work. As faculty members join a university or college, an initial form of faculty development is to highlight the importance of the scholarship of engagement as part of the orientation process. Although a faculty member's interview should have included some discussion of expectations for engagement, the welcome orientation is a time to reinforce institutional values and to frame for new colleagues the institution's commitment to the integration of outreach and engagement into faculty work. Once faculty members are settled, institutions can ensure that they see examples of the scholarship of engagement and ways in which their colleagues have been involved with outreach and engagement. A typical strategy is to provide workshops or seminars at which scholars from various fields present and describe examples of their work. The benefits of seminars are that they raise awareness and give information to those who attend. The limitations are that they are typically one-time events and do not provide explicit help to faculty members in regard to trying new kinds of scholarly work. Thus, additional faculty development efforts need to be incorporated into a systematic strategy for supporting and encouraging this kind of work.

Some universities, including Michigan State University and the University of Georgia, take a creative and more time-intensive approach. In order to raise awareness and help faculty members consider the relationship between outreach and engagement and their own work, these universities invite newcomers to a traveling seminar focused on their geographic regions. One annual traveling seminar at Michigan State involves a bus trip that occurs over three days, during which faculty members see examples of how colleagues integrate outreach and engagement into their work, hear administrators provide short seminars on the bus about aspects of the institution's support for the scholarship of engagement, and visit sites within the state where faculty members are engaging with community members on societal issues. These traveling seminars often have a theme, such as health-related partnerships, science and environmental projects, or university-community collaborations to advance the arts. Evaluations indicate that this opportunity is a powerful experience for participants, during which they deepen their appreciation for the institutional mission of engagement with society, discuss the implications of the outreach mission in their own work, and, often, forge new cross-field collaborations with other colleagues involved in the trip.

Other forms of faculty development can also deepen faculty awareness and help them develop their approaches to integrating outreach and engagement into their work. Some institutions hold grant competitions that encourage faculty members to propose projects that integrate outreach and engagement into their research or teaching. Ward (2005) urges creativity in how funds from such competitions can be used. For example, grant awardees should be allowed to share some of their award money with community partners. Application instructions may remind faculty members to be creative in finding ways to fulfill institutional goals and faculty interests at the same time. Another strategy is to offer release time to faculty members who propose specific projects that involve integrating outreach and engagement more fully into their work. Mentoring is another strategy popular as part of the faculty development programs at many institutions. Although mentoring programs often focus on teaching or research development, they can be organized to encourage outreach and engagement. For example, faculty members experienced in integrating outreach and engagement might agree to mentor early-career colleagues striving to learn about and develop this focus in their work. Another strategy used by many faculty development programs is to provide materials and resources about various aspects of faculty work, including engagement, in a website, where busy faculty members can find information at their convenience.

Offering Opportunities for Faculty to Integrate Outreach and Engagement

In addition to learning about how outreach and engagement might be integrated into their work, and participating in faculty development opportunities that help them develop relevant abilities and skills, faculty members new to the idea of engaging in outreach and engagement can benefit from explicitly offered opportunities to do such work. Such opportunities may be made available at the institution level, through faculty development or service-learning offices, or at the college or department level (Benson, Harkavy, & Hartley, 2005; O'Meara, 2005).

At the institution level, some universities and colleges identify specific institution-wide outreach endeavors in which all faculty and students are invited to participate. One liberal arts college, for example, responded to some incidents of town-gown tension by deciding to make an institution-wide commitment to contributing to the improvement of life within the community. All members of the college are invited to participate in college-supported efforts to enhance the quality of life for the community. Freshmen are challenged to participate in some kind of service organization or project, including working in tutoring programs within the community for second-language English speakers, volunteering with social action groups, tutoring in elementary or secondary schools, or working in soup kitchens. Faculty members are encouraged to include in their courses service learning projects that link course content with issues in the community. In sum, the institution works collaboratively to identify creative ways in which community members and members of the college community can interact productively for the betterment of the town. One outcome of this institution-wide commitment is that each faculty member can see a variety of ways in which outreach and engagement can be integrated into his or her daily work as a professor at the college.

Many universities and colleges have offices, often led by senior-level administrators, that organize and focus institutional efforts toward outreach and engagement. Such offices can help faculty integrate outreach and engagement into their work by convening meetings of faculty members in related areas of work (e.g., those whose work relates to environmental issues or health issues or issues of children, youth, and families) with members of relevant community agencies. Through the interactions, faculty members can learn of specific ways to incorporate engagement in their work. Such offices may also offer competitions for grant funding for projects related to outreach and engagement as ways to provide encouragement and opportunities for faculty members to develop projects in which they link their expertise with community issues. Many institutions also have offices specifically devoted to coordinating service learning. Part of the purpose of such offices is to provide opportunities for faculty members to integrate outreach and engagement into their courses by ensuring that instructors have the knowledge, resources, and logistical help to do so.

In addition to institution-level strategies for making opportunities available to faculty members to integrate outreach and engagement into their work, deans and department chairs can also highlight such opportunities. One dean of education in a large university has invited faculty members to travel with her to China to explore ways to connect their educational expertise with international problems. In the department of one of this chapter's authors, the department chair provided funds for an early career faculty member to accompany a more senior professor who has long-established outreach and engagement work in South Africa. Working together, the two faculty members led a team of graduate students, and together the team collaborated for several weeks with colleagues at a South African university on ways to enhance the undergraduate learning experience at that institution. The early career faculty member has extensive experience conducting research on student learning and development and on the relationship between out-of-class and in-class learning. The collaborative work in which the team was involved in South Africa helped the early-career colleague—as well as the graduate students involved—see new ways to integrate outreach and engagement into academic work. One outcome is a research project collaboratively designed and now underway in South Africa; the results will be used to guide decision making and program development intended to deepen the learning experience for undergraduates at the South African university. The department chair made a strategic decision in regard to encouraging outreach and engagement when she provided funds to support the travel expenses of the junior colleague.

In academic departments that have affiliated outreach units, "outreach faculty" can help "academic faculty" connect with settings and constituencies outside the university. For example, academic faculty, working with outreach faculty offering noncredit education in such settings as agencies or factories, can use the opportunity to negotiate future entry for the purpose of research. Faculty members may gain access to organizational archives and opportunities for oral history interviews, surveys, or other avenues for data collection. Relationships with constituencies outside higher education can also provide faculty members with feedback about their current research, and its tone, perspective, and conclusions. For example, the annual law conference of MSU's School of Labor and Industrial Relations gives faculty members an appreciative, interested, and informed audience of field-based constituents (more than a hundred union leaders, activists, and staff) who are ready to give frank feedback and offer practical challenges and questions. Audiences may force presenters to adjust their language to accommodate the needs of those outside academe; such expectations can lead to simpler, more straightforward delivery of concepts and findings, which aids all future listeners or readers. Faculty members can also feel the satisfaction of seeing that an audience is planning to make immediate use of the information or tools being presented. Nothing is quite as satisfying as having a conference participant say some time later, "I tried what you suggested a few years back, and it worked."

Designing Reward Structures to Encourage Engagement

In addition to ensuring that faculty members understand why outreach and engagement are important forms of scholarly work, that they have the abilities and skills to carry out this work, and that they have opportunities to do so, higher education institutions need to be sure that their reward structures recognize and encourage this form of scholarship. Research has shown that faculty members feel encouraged to pursue the scholarships of teaching or engagement if these forms of scholarship are assessed and rewarded (Driscoll & Lynton, 1999; Hutchings & Shulman, 1999; Lynton, 1995). Often, however, faculty work in service to the public good is not held in high prestige or adequately rewarded (O'Meara, 2002). Rather, the traditional reward system, particularly in major universities, typically privileges research. The values and beliefs embedded in such traditional reward structures do not encourage the advancement of diverse institutional missions (Rice et al., 2000). Furthermore, the scholarship of application and engagement is valued differently depending on particular academic disciplinary cultures (Austin, 1992, 1994; see Braxton & Luckey chapter in this volume). Clear messages about how engagement and outreach are valued, assessed, and rewarded are important at the department, college, and institutional level. An explicit, understandable, and consistent evaluation and tenure and promotion system is a key factor in encouraging faculty members to integrate outreach and engagement into their work.

How can institutions develop tenure and promotion systems that carry clear signals about the value of outreach and engagement and encourage faculty members to carry out this form of scholarship? First, promotion and tenure guidelines, as well as annual review guidelines, should define faculty work for the public good. Statements might emphasize, for example, that the scholarship of outreach and engagement involves "the application of existing knowledge in a practical setting and/or the creation of new knowledge about practice" (O'Meara, 2002, p. 72). They might also explain that this kind of work involves a dynamic interplay between theory and practice. Whatever an institution's specific definition, an explicit statement explaining and defining the scholarship of engagement as a recognized and valued form of faculty work sends a clear message to faculty members that integrating outreach and engagement into their work fits with institutional missions. In addition to definitions, specific examples of how the scholarship of outreach and engagement is carried out in various disciplines help faculty members envision possibilities for their own work.

Handbooks explaining institutional tenure and promotion systems should also include clear criteria that will be used to evaluate the quality and impact of each form of scholarship. Such criteria might include the extent to which the work is a product of collaboration between the faculty member and the community, evidence of products or outcomes of importance in the community as well as outcomes important in the academic world, and the extent and evidence of impact within the community. Along with a statement of criteria for evaluation, useful handbooks include examples of specific documentation presented in successful tenure and promotion files (Ward, 2005). Such specificity helps faculty members determine how to present their own work and encourages them to feel that their efforts to integrate engagement into their work will be fairly reviewed.

Another strategy for using the reward system to encourage the scholarship of engagement is to highlight examples of this form of scholarship in any meetings to inform early career faculty members about the reward system. New faculty orientation, individual annual review meetings that deans and chairs hold with early career faculty, and cross-institutional workshops to explain the tenure and promotion system are each occasions for using the reward system as a strategy to encourage faculty members to integrate outreach and engagement into their work.

When institutions include in their tenure and promotion and annual review guidelines explicit statements about the value of the scholarship of engagement, they also need to be sure that the faculty committees that review, assess, and make recommendations concerning their colleagues' work and career progress firmly understand that the scholarship of engagement is a respected form of academic work. Deans and provosts must be prepared to stand firm in the face of faculty members who do not agree with or understand the role of the scholarship of engagement in faculty work.

Other incentives, in addition to a clear and consistent faculty evaluation and tenure system, include awards to individual faculty members or to departments that excel in the scholarship of engagement. Institutions may provide access to travel or bookstore funds for individual faculty members who develop projects involving the scholarship of engagement. Another incentive is to provide grants or awards to departments that develop outreach projects in which department members collaborate as a team with external partners, or that integrate service learning or other teaching-related outreach activities into their curricula.

Nurturing Institutional Cultures That Encourage Engagement

Faculty members need to understand the scholarship of engagement, have the relevant skills and abilities, see opportunities, and know that assessment and rewards accrue from involving themselves in this form of scholarship. In addition to the strategies in these areas that we have discussed, the overall institutional culture and environment play a large role in how faculty members choose to focus and organize their work. Various components of the culture can be used to send messages about the relevance and importance of the scholarship of engagement in faculty work.

As suggested by the discussion throughout the chapter, the infrastructure of a university or college is important. Is there a faculty development program, as already discussed, that encourages and nurtures faculty members as they pursue the scholarship of engagement? Is there a unit that has the responsibility to focus the institution and its faculty on the importance of outreach and engagement?

The budget priorities within an institution also help convey messages and institutional priorities. As mentioned, colleges and universities can provide resources to support grant programs through which faculty members can begin outreach activities. Resources may also be budgeted for release time when faculty members need time to work on long-term projects that take them away from campus or to fund special awards that recognize faculty members who excel in this form of scholarship. Such resource allocations help faculty members understand what is valued within the institutional culture and to make choices about how they will direct their own scholarly efforts.

The conversations that occur on campus also are part of the culture and context within which faculty members work. Do faculty members have opportunities to discuss with colleagues the nature of their work in outreach and engagement, perhaps through a seminar series that highlights projects in which faculty members are engaged? Are there gatherings that convene faculty members with community members to share their work, the challenges they are encountering, and their successes? Conversations and gatherings help create institutional cultures in which the scholarship of engagement is valued and in which faculty members feel encouraged on a regular basis to integrate outreach and engagement into their work.

Symbols also are part of institutional culture and can be used to convey messages to faculty about the importance of the scholarship of engagement. Where is the service-learning office or the office of engagement and outreach placed geographically on campus? If these offices are in accessible locations and appointed with pleasant furnishings, faculty members and community members alike perceive the message that the activities on which they focus are important. Does the institution include periodic celebrations that highlight the accomplishments of faculty members whose outreach and engagement work has received acclaim or has had a strong impact? These celebrations and symbols convey to faculty members that the scholarship of engagement is valued and encourages them to include this form of scholarship in their own work.

Institutional leaders have a particularly strong influence on the nature of institutional culture. They have the ability to frame and articulate institutional priorities, to connect current institutional activities to the history of the university or college, and to help faculty members understand how their individual work contributes to a larger mission. Sometimes senior leaders underestimate the importance of their comments and the benefits associated with consistent and frequent messages about the value the institution places on the scholarship of engagement.

Suggestions for Practice

This chapter acknowledges the premise that faculty members are at the heart of institutional efforts to connect the university and its work to the broader society. Yet, many faculty members need to learn about and be encouraged to integrate outreach and engagement into their work. Strategies to encourage faculty members can build on theoretical work about organizations and individuals, including these two research-based findings: (1) multiple levers are needed to encourage institutional change; and (2) individual faculty members must understand what they are being asked to do, know why it is important, have relevant skills and abilities, and know that the work will be valued, assessed, and rewarded. Key strategies for higher education institutions to use to encourage faculty members to integrate outreach and engagement into their work include the following:

1. Increase faculty knowledge and abilities regarding outreach and engagement by (a) ensuring that doctoral programs help prospective faculty develop knowledge and skills that enable them to include the scholarship of engagement as part of their careers, and (b) developing comprehensive faculty development plans that provide a variety of ways for faculty members to learn about and develop expertise in carrying out the scholarship of engagement.
2. Provide opportunities for faculty members to participate in the scholarship of engagement (i.e., invitations for campus-wide projects that connect with the community, information sessions and seminars, funding or release time to support participation in outreach projects).
3. Ensure that institutional reward structures acknowledge the scholarship of engagement and that the criteria for evaluating this form of scholarship are clear, and provide guidelines to faculty members concerning how to document and present this form of scholarship.
4. Nurture institutional cultures (attending to infrastructure, budget processes, conversations and gatherings, symbols, and especially, thoughtful leadership) that convey clear messages about the value of the scholarship of engagement and that encourage faculty members to integrate outreach and engagement into their work.

References

Austin, A. E. (1992). Faculty cultures. In B. R. Clark & G. Neave (Eds.) & A. I. Morey (Vol. Ed.), *The encyclopedia of higher education* (Vol. 4, pp. 1623–1634). New York: Pergamon.

Austin, A. E. (1994). Understanding and assessing faculty cultures and climates. In M. K. Kinnick (Ed.), *Providing useful information for deans and department chairs* (pp. 47–63). New Directions for Institutional Research. San Francisco: Jossey-Bass.

Austin, A. E. (1998, July). *A systems approach to institutional change and transformation: Strategies and lessons from American and South African universities.* Paper presented at the World Congress of Comparative Education Societies, Cape Town, South Africa.

Austin, A. E. (2002, January/February). Preparing the next generation of faculty: Graduate school as socialization to the academic career. *Journal of Higher Education, 73*(1), 94–122.

Austin, A., & Barnes, B. J. (2005). Preparing doctoral students for faculty careers that contribute to the public good. In A. Kezar, T. C. Chambers, & J. C. Burkhardt (Eds.), *Higher education for the public good* (pp. 272–292). San Francisco: Jossey-Bass.

Austin, A. E., & McDaniels, M. (2006, Spring). Using doctoral education to prepare faculty to work within Boyer's four domains of scholarship. In J. M. Braxton (Ed.), *Analyzing faculty work and rewards: Using Boyer's four domains of scholarship.* New Directions for Institutional Research No. 129 (pp. 51–65). San Francisco: Jossey-Bass.

Benson, L., Harkavy, I., & Hartley, M. (2005). Integrating a commitment to the public good into the institutional fabric. In A. Kezar, T. C. Chambers, & J. C. Burkhardt (Eds.), *Higher education for the public good* (pp. 185–216). San Francisco: Jossey-Bass.

Boyer, E. L. (1990). *Scholarship reconsidered: Priorities of the professoriate.* Princeton, NJ: Carnegie Foundation for the Advancement of Teaching.

Boyer, E. L. (1996). The scholarship of engagement. *Journal of Public Service and Outreach, 1*(1), 11–20.

Colby, A., Ehrlich, T., Beaumont, E., & Stephens, J. (2003). *Educating citizens: Preparing undergraduates for lives of moral and civic responsibility.* San Francisco: Jossey-Bass.

Diamond, R. M., & Adam, B. E. (Eds.). (1995). *The disciplines speak: Rewarding the scholarly, professional, and creative work of faculty.* Washington, DC: American Association for Higher Education.

Driscoll, A., & Lynton, E. A. (1999). *Making outreach visible: A guide to documenting professional service and outreach.* Washington, DC: American Association for Higher Education.

Gappa, J. M., Austin, A. E., & Trice, A. G. (2007). *Rethinking faculty work: Higher education's strategic imperative.* San Francisco: Jossey-Bass.

Glassick, C. E., Huber, M. T., & Maeroff, G. I. (1997). *Scholarship assessed: Evaluation of the professoriate.* San Francisco: Jossey-Bass.

Golde, C. M., & Dore, T. M. (2001). *At cross purposes: What the experiences of doctoral students reveal about doctoral education.* Philadelphia: The Pew Charitable Trusts. Available at www.phd-survey.org.

Hutchings, P., & Shulman, L. S. (1999). Scholarship of teaching. *Change, 31*(5), 11–15.

Klomparens, K. L., & Beck, J. P. (2004). Michigan State University's Conflict Resolution Program: Setting expectations and resolving conflicts. In D. H. Wulff & A. E. Austin (Eds.), *Paths to the professoriate: Strategies for enriching the preparation of future faculty* (pp. 250–263). San Francisco: Jossey-Bass.

Lynton, E. A. (1995). *Making the case for professional service.* Washington, DC: American Association for Higher Education.

Nyquist, J. D., Manning, L. Wulff, D. H., Austin, A. E., Sprague, J., Fraser, P. K., et al. (1999). On the road to becoming a professor: The graduate student experience. *Change, 31*(3), 18–27.

O'Meara, K. A. (2002). Uncovering the values in faculty evaluation of service as scholarship. *Review of Higher Education, 26,* 57–80.

O'Meara, K. A. (2005). Principles of good practice: Encouraging multiple forms of scholarship in policy and practice. In K. O'Meara & R. E. Rice (Eds.), *Faculty priorities reconsidered: Rewarding multiple forms of scholarship* (pp. 290–302). San Francisco; Jossey-Bass.

Rice, R. E. (1986). The academic profession in transition: Toward a new social fiction. *Teaching Sociology, 41,* 12–23.

Rice, R. E. (1996). *Making a place for the new American scholar.* New Pathways Inquiry No. 1. Washington, DC: American Association for Higher Education.

Rice, R., Sorcinelli, M., & Austin, A. E. (2000). *Heeding new voices: Academic career for a new generation.* New Pathways Working Paper Series No. 7. Washington, DC: American Association for Higher Education.

Trower, C. A., Austin, A. E., & Sorcinelli, M. D. (2001, May). Paradise lost: How the academy converts enthusiastic recruits into early-career doubters. *AAHE Bulletin, 53*(9), 3–6.

Votruba, J. C. (2005). Leading the engaged institution. In A. Kezar, T. C. Chambers, & J. C. Burkhardt (Eds.), *Higher education for the public good* (pp. 263–271). San Francisco: Jossey-Bass.

Ward, K. (2005). Rethinking faculty roles and rewards for the public good. In A. Kezar, T. C. Chambers, & J. C. Burkhardt (Eds.), *Higher education for the public good* (pp. 217–234). San Francisco: Jossey-Bass.

Wulff, D. H., Austin, A. E., Nyquist, J. D., & Sprague, J. (2004). The development of graduate students as teachings scholars: A four-year longitudinal study. In D. H. Wulff & A. E. Austin (Eds.), *Paths to the Professoriate: Strategies for enriching the preparation of future faculty* (pp. 250–263). San Francisco: Jossey-Bass.

Civic Engagement across the Career Stages of Faculty Life: A Proposal for a New Line of Inquiry

Scott J. Peters and Theodore R. Alter

In a piece she wrote on the "engaged academy" that was published in 2000, Carol Schneider noted the discussion that scholars and others were having about the roles mediating institutions play in addressing public issues and problems in American society, including the problem of civic disengagement. In this discussion, she observed, "there has been surprisingly little attention to the role that higher education institutions in particular might play in the renewal of civic engagement." She went on to say that there is a "crucial need for exploration of potential connections between the core missions of colleges and universities as educational institutions and the quality of our civic life" (Schneider, 2000, pp. 99, 100).

The topic Schneider pointed to in her piece is vast and enormously complex. There are all kinds of roles that higher education institutions might play in the renewal of civic engagement, and all kinds of potential connections that could be made between core missions of colleges and universities and the quality of our civic life. In the American higher education studies literature, the conversation about such roles and connections often focuses on preparing undergraduate students for citizenship (e.g., Colby, Beaumont, Ehrlich, & Corngold, 2007; Colby, Ehrlich, Beaumont, & Stephens, 2003). This is important work, and it deserves our attention. But if we wish to both understand and improve higher education's roles in renewing civic engagement and enhancing the quality of our civic life, we also need to attend to the broader topic of the work of faculty members (and other academic professionals) as active participants in and contributors to civic life. The issues to be explored in relation to this topic are not only the roles faculty *might* play in civic renewal, and the *potential* connections they *might* make between core academic missions and the task of improving the quality of our civic life. They are also the roles and connections they *already have and are* playing and making as they step off their campuses and become engaged in civic life. Of course, the work of preparing students for citizenship through community service-learning pedagogies and courses can and often does engage faculty members as active participants in civic life (Jacoby & Associates, 2003). But faculty members have been and are engaged in civic life in many other ways, and for many other reasons.

Here, we come to the problem we take up in this chapter. Beyond service-learning as a means of preparing undergraduates for citizenship, much if not most of the civic engagement work and roles of faculty members has been overlooked as a topic of inquiry, assessment, and discussion, both in the organizational and administrative workings of academic institutions and in the American higher education studies literature. (By "the American higher education studies literature," we are referring only to books and articles published by scholars working in the official academic field of higher education studies. We are well aware of the fact that there are many books and articles written by scholars in other academic fields [e.g., sociology, political theory, history, cultural studies, and philosophy] that address the issue of the political roles and work of academic professionals.) Jane Wellman made this point in 2000, in the same book in which Schneider's piece appeared. Despite all the attention to assessment and accountability in American higher education, Wellman (2000, p. 323) observed, "the civic educational and service roles of higher education remain invisible, unreported, and largely undefined." We want to sharpen her observation by noting that the *political* roles and work of academic professionals and institutions in civic life remain invisible, unreported, undefined, and largely unexplored.

Our purpose in this chapter is to propose a new line of inquiry in the field of higher education studies that attends to this largely unexplored topic. The line of inquiry we propose is not designed to pursue the goal of establishing causal, statistically significant relationships between factors or variables in order to inform attempts by administrators, policy makers, or others to predict, control, and/or intervene for some specific end. Rather, it is designed to stimulate and contribute to conversations within and beyond the academy about the nature, meaning, significance, and value of civic engagement across the career stages of faculty life. Utilizing knowledge, methodological approaches, and theoretical frameworks and tools from several fields and sources, it is designed to catalyze and inform processes of institutional change and faculty and organizational development that contribute to the project of strengthening and deepening higher education's roles in renewing civic engagement and enhancing the quality of our civic life.

The Political Roles and Work of Academic Professionals in Civic Life

In both the American higher education studies literature and the organizational and administrative workings of academic institutions, words such as "political," "politics," and "civic engagement" are rarely used in the ways and for the purposes that we are using them. We therefore want to be clear about what we do and don't mean by these words. We also want to be clear about why we think scholars in the academic field of higher education studies need to open a new line of inquiry that attends to the political roles and work of academic professionals in civic life.

With respect to the words political and politics, we aren't referring to elections, the legislative process, the workings of political parties and elected officials, or activities that are "partisan" in a political party sense. We aren't referring to personal and/or institutional behavior, as in "She's just being political," or "That's just politics." Rather, we are referring to public work, which Harry Boyte (2004, p. 5) defines as "sustained effort by a mix of people who solve public problems or create goods, material or cultural, of general benefit." Public work is pursued through what Boyte calls "everyday politics." Everyday politics is centered on people rather than government (Mathews, 1999). It is the means by which individuals and groups develop and exercise power in neighborhood and community settings as they seek to understand and address technical and social problems, stand for and further key normative ideals and values, and promote, consider, deliberate about, negotiate, and take action to pursue their self-interests, their common interests, and larger public interests.

The meanings we give to the terms politics and political shape our view of the meaning of civic engagement. For us, civic engagement means engaging in civic life by participating in the everyday politics of public work. When we refer in this chapter to faculty members' civic engagement work, we are not referring to their on-campus activities and work with students and others, even if such work has political dimensions and civic motivations, intentions, and indirect or future consequences. We are not referring to what faculty members do in their communities during their off-hours as "private" citizens. Rather, *we are referring to their on-the-clock, off-campus participation as professional scholars, educators, scientists, engineers, architects, designers, and/or artists in the everyday politics of public work.*

There is a robust conversation in several academic fields (e.g., sociology, political theory, philosophy, history, anthropology, cultural studies, science and technology studies) about the political roles and work of "intellectuals"—a category of people that includes academic professionals—in civic life (e.g., Bauman, 1987; Bender, 1993; Boggs, 1993; Coser, 1965; Etzioni & Bowditch, 2006; Eyerman, 1994; Fink, 1997; Fink, Leonard, & Reid, 1996; Foucault, 1970; Furner, 1975; Goldfarb, 1998; Gramsci, 1949; Habermas, 1972; Hale, 2008; Jacoby, 1987; Mannheim, 1936; Merod, 1987; Nichols, 2007; Perry, 1984; Recchiuti, 2007; Rouse, 1987; Said, 1994; Smith, 1994; Tyrrell, 2005; Znaniecki, 1940). Growing out of the epistemological and political transformations of the Enlightenment, intellectuals took up two main political roles in civic life. These are the distinctly different but related roles of expert and critic. Contributors to the conversation about how intellectuals have taken up these roles have explored two main themes. First, they have explored how intellectuals have served the interests of dominant social classes, groups, or powers by reproducing or legitimizing an oppressive status quo, and/or facilitating and legitimizing oppressive social change projects and agendas. Second, they have explored how intellectuals have served the interests of oppressed or marginalized social classes by resisting, subverting, undermining, and delegitimizing oppressive status quos and social change projects and agendas, and/or by facilitating and legitimizing emancipatory social change projects and agendas, including the project of creating and defending a public sphere that is devoted to open, free, and rational public debate.

In contrast with other academic fields, until quite recently there has been effectively no conversation in the field of higher education studies about the political roles and work of faculty members and other academic professionals in civic life. In every book reporting the findings of studies of the academic profession that we reviewed (e.g., Altbach & Finkelstein, 1997; Blackburn & Lawrence, 1995; Clark, 1987; Fairweather, 1996; Finkelstein, 1984; Finkelstein, Seal, & Schuster, 1998; Graubard, 2001; Gappa, Austin, & Trice, 2007; Schuster & Finkelstein, 2008; Wilson, 1942, 1979), the political roles and work of faculty members in civic life were either not mentioned at all, or mentioned only in passing. They are similarly absent from or only briefly mentioned in most contemporary studies of higher education institutions, including a recent book by Altbach, Berdahl, and Gumport (2005) that explores critical dynamics in the American higher education/society nexus in the twenty-first century.

In our review of the literature in the field of higher education studies, we also found that scholars in the field have given little attention to the related—but not synonymous—topic of higher education's "public service" mission. In his extensive review and synthesis of the literature on the academic profession in the post–World War II era, published in 1984, Finkelstein observed that "we know very little about faculty performance in their administrative or extra-institutional professional service (to the discipline and the community at large) capacities" (p. 127). A decade after Finkelstein's study was published, Blackburn and Lawrence (1995, pp. 125, 127) not only found that "there is almost no research on faculty in service roles," but also that "empirical evidence with respect to the role is nonexistent." Although scholars in the higher education studies field have begun over the past fifteen years to attend to the topics of outreach, engagement, and civic responsibility (e.g., Ehrlich, 2000; Kezar, Chambers, & Burkhardt, 2005; Tierney, 1998; Walshok, 1995; Ward, 2003;), they have mainly done so in theoretical or hortatory ways. Beyond service-learning, few—if any—of the scholars working in the field of higher education studies have systematically examined the *political* aspects of faculty members' civic engagement work, roles, views, and experiences.

The reason why a new line of inquiry about the political roles and work of academic professionals in civic life is needed is not just because the topic has been neglected in the field of higher education studies. Rather, it is because such a line of inquiry can offer a powerful means of both understanding and improving higher education's roles in renewing civic engagement and enhancing the quality of our civic life at a critical moment in the nation's history. It can do so in two main ways. First, it can illuminate unwarranted presumptions and blind spots in the dominant framing of and narrative about higher education's public purposes and work. Centered on the concepts of "service," "outreach," and "extension," the dominant framing and narrative both overlooks faculty members' civic engagement work and obscures its political nature and significance. It provides us not only with an incomplete but also an untrustworthy and misleading view of the nature and value of American higher education's public purposes and work. Second, if—and in our view, *only* if—it is approached as action research (Greenwood & Levin, 2007; Reason & Bradbury, 2008), a new line of inquiry can help to illuminate and stimulate a more complete fulfillment of the positive democratic promise and potential of the academic profession in every academic discipline and field, all institutional types, and each stage of a faculty member's career.

Background

Before we lay out our design for the new line of inquiry we are proposing, we want to explain how we came to see that it was needed. In 2000, we launched a study of the practice of "public scholarship" in the state and land-grant university system (Peters, Jordan, Adamek, & Alter, 2005). (Some scholars [e.g., Mitchell, 2008] view "public scholarship" as being essentially the same thing as the "public intellectual" tradition. We do not. The central work of public intellectuals is to engage in social criticism by speaking to or writing for the general public about public problems and issues. Public scholarship, as we define it, is not limited to social criticism. It is not mainly about speaking to or writing for general public audiences. Rather, it is creative intellectual work that is conducted in the context of public settings and relationships, facilitating social learning and producing knowledge, theory, technologies, and other kinds of products that advance both public and academic interests and ends.) As a part of that study, in June 2001 we interviewed Don Wyse (his real name, not a pseudonym), a full professor in the Department of Agronomy and Plant Genetics in the University of Minnesota's College of Food, Agricultural and Natural Resource Sciences. During the interview, we asked Don to tell us about the origins and evolution of his academic career. In response, he traced his life story from his youth on a farm in northwestern Ohio during the 1950s and '60s to his present work as a full professor. About three-quarters of the way through the interview, he said the following:

> I would find it very difficult to go out and just conduct research on corn, soybeans, and wheat that would increase the yield of those crops. That's what most researchers do. Most researchers are basically in research programs that are designed to enhance the productivity per unit area of major crops. I think that's what they consider their role to be. The role is defined that way by a number of different messengers, like financial messengers that support research programs. At the state level, commodity organizations fund research. What are they funding? They are funding things that increase yield, and the stability of yield, and now new uses for those crops. It is basically a commodity-enhancement focus. Most of our federal programs, whether they are supporting basic or applied research, are designed to focus on those commodities. There's a full array of political and economic signals to scientists that that's their role. And it isn't just to the scientists; the signals come to administrators as well. Policies are built around those crops. That sends signals to administrators within institutions that if you're going to fill faculty positions, you fill them in the context of that model. But what I've learned in my experience here is that there is, in fact, greater opportunity than that—that we as land-grant scientists have a greater obligation and a greater opportunity. It's to look at the system as a whole and provide the framework for the conversation as to how you deal with social issues facing rural America, environmental issues facing rural America, climate change that is facing rural America, invasive species facing not only the United States, but the world, and on and on. It is, in fact, that level of conversation that I think land-grant scientists need to provide the framework for, because that's really the framework of the public trust that is historically placed in land-grant institutions: to look out for the public good and to provide leadership for the issues that are not going to be highlighted by the business sector, or in many cases by the political sector. We with tenure within land-grant institutions have an obligation to raise these issues for public conversation, to help determine a direction and approaches to these problems.

As we read and reread the transcript of our interview with Don, we kept coming back to this passage. We found it to be both surprising and provocative, particularly when we considered the fact that according to his own self-description, Don is a "weed scientist." Most people (including us, before we interviewed Don) probably don't have the foggiest idea what a "weed scientist" is and does. Nor, for that matter, do they know much if anything about what *any* kind of scientist who holds a faculty position in a land-grant college of agriculture is and does. One might presume that the work and roles of such people are narrowly technical in nature: that is, that they are focused only on teaching technical knowledge and skills to students, and identifying and solving technical problems related to agriculture and horticulture in order to increase efficiency and/or productivity for the economic benefit of farmers, consumers, agribusinesses, states, the nation, and/or the world. Don effectively affirms this presumption in the foregoing passage. He tells us that most researchers think their role is "to enhance the productivity per unit area of major crops." He suggests that this role is not necessarily self-assigned. It is taken up, he claims, in response to "a full array of political and economic signals" from "messengers" external to the university, including agricultural commodity organizations and federal programs. According to Don, the "signals" from external messengers also influence administrators to set policies and hire faculty to fit and support a model of research that is focused on enhancing the productivity of commodities such as corn, wheat, and soybeans.

The most interesting thing to us about the quoted passage is the way in which Don situates himself as standing *against* this model of research. He tells us in the first sentence that he "would find it very difficult" to be limited to the model's narrow role of conducting research to increase the yield of commodity crops such as corn, soybeans, and wheat. Why does Don feel this way? Because he thinks that "land-grant scientists have a greater obligation and a greater opportunity." The greater opportunity he articulates is civic and political in nature. In Don's words, it is "to look at the system as a whole and provide the framework for the conversation as to how you deal with social issues facing rural America, environmental issues facing rural America, climate change that is facing rural America, invasive species facing not only the United States but the world, and on and on." Where does this greater obligation come from? According to Don, it comes from an institutional mission: from the "framework of the public trust that is historically placed in land-grant institutions: to look out for the public good and to provide leadership for the issues that are not going to be highlighted by the business sector, or in many cases by the political sector." It also comes from his view of the obligation that tenure provides. "We with tenure within land-grant institutions," Don says, "have an obligation to raise these issues for public conversation, to help determine a direction and approaches to these problems."

Although we find what Don tells us in this passage to be interesting, surprising, and provocative, by itself it doesn't hold much value. It's easy to dismiss as being preachy, politically correct, naïve, romantic, mere rhetoric (and thus inconsequential), or just simply wrong. And it's too thin to be of much use in serious inquiries about the nature, meaning, significance, and value of civic engagement in the academic profession. But there is a line in the passage that points to something that would be of great use in such inquiries. It's when Don says, "But what I've learned in my experience here is. . . ." When we read this line, we find ourselves wanting to hear not just the *lesson* he draws from his experience, but the *story* of his experience. The lesson by itself is not enough. We need to hear the story (or more accurately, stories) of Don's experience in order to understand how he came to draw his lesson about the greater opportunity and obligation of land-grant scientists, how—or if—he pursues it in his work, and most importantly, what its larger meaning, significance, and value may be.

Acting on our intuition rather than a deliberate design, we conducted our interview with Don as a life story interview (Atkinson 1998), with a focus on the origins and development of his work as a civically engaged academic professional. We invited Don to tell us the story of where he grew up and what it was like, how his experiences led him to decide to go to college and then on to graduate school, how he ended up on the faculty at the University of Minnesota, how he developed his research and teaching program, when, where, how, and why he has interacted and worked with people off-campus as he has performed his job, and how his academic work changed and evolved as he moved through the ranks from assistant to full professor. Inspired by Forester (1999), we edited the transcript into a "practitioner profile" that is composed only of Don's words, with our questions edited out. (On the development and use of practitioner profiles, see http://courses.cit.cornell.edu/practicestories.)

As we read and sought to make sense of Don's profile, we began to feel that we had accidentally stumbled onto something important. We started to see that the profile is heavily and densely *storied*. The profile as a whole is a story of the origins and evolution of Don's career. It also both includes or hints at many small stories from his life experience—stories about his youth on a farm, his father's teachings and influence, his graduate education, his early career as an assistant professor, and his current work as a full professor. But we found that the profile isn't just storied in a personal way. It's also richly storied in larger ways. It includes or hints at larger social, cultural, political, economic, and institutional narratives—narratives about struggles people have faced and are facing in rural Minnesota, battles and conflicts involved in the development of American agriculture, fights over the meaning of the land-grant mission and its implications for the work and roles of scientists, and more. Remarkably, Don links and relates these personal and larger stories and narratives in his discourse. He weaves stories about his father, his graduate education, his job interview, rural Minnesota, American agriculture, the land-grant mission, and his early career as an assistant professor together with the stories he tells of his contemporary civic engagement work as a full professor. We found that the stories about his life prior to his employment at the University of Minnesota and stories about larger issues relating to rural America, American agriculture, and the land-grant mission were vitally important in helping us understand the meaning, significance, and value of his civic engagement work as a faculty member. Although we had placed the focus of the research we were conducting at the time on the construction and interpretation of case studies and practice stories of a couple of dozen faculty members' work and experiences as publicly engaged scholars, Don's profile convinced us that we could greatly enhance our interpretation and analysis of our cases and practice stories by situating them in the context not only of faculty members' *life* stories, but also of larger social, cultural, political, economic, and institutional narratives. With this realization, we began to see

257

the value of opening a new line of inquiry that examines the nature, meaning, significance, and value of civic engagement across the career stages of faculty life.

A New Line of Inquiry

In this section, we provide a brief sketch of the new line of inquiry we are proposing, following Maxwell's (2005) "interactive" approach to qualitative research design. Maxwell's approach consists of a model with five interrelated parts: goals, conceptual framework, research questions, methods, and validity. We provide only a general sketch of these parts. Researchers who wish to pursue this line of inquiry must flesh out the details of each part of the design in ways that are informed by the judgments, knowledge, experience, and interests of their research participants, as well as situational and contextual realities related to participants' institutions, institutional types, academic fields and disciplines, and geographical locations.

Goals

We propose the establishment of a new line of inquiry in the field of higher education studies that pursues three related goals:

1. The goal of advancing our understanding of the nature, meaning, significance, and value of faculty members' civic engagement work, both within and across each stage of their careers;
2. The goal of catalyzing and informing processes of institutional change and faculty and organizational development; and
3. The goal of advancing the project of strengthening and deepening higher education's roles in renewing civic engagement and enhancing the quality of our civic life.

We propose that these goals be pursued not only simultaneously, but also with equal weight and attention. Goals two and three are not to be treated as secondary afterthoughts. Also, goals one and two are not ends in and of themselves, but rather means to an end. The end they are a means to is expressed in goal three. Given the change and action-oriented nature of goals two and three, researchers must take an action research approach in all stages of their inquiry, including research design.

Conceptual Framework

Maxwell's model of qualitative research design includes the articulation of a conceptual framework that consists of the main assumptions, presumptions, concepts, beliefs, and theories that inform and support the study of a particular issue or problem. A conceptual framework serves as an answer to the question of what scholars think is going on with the issue and/or problem they wish to examine and understand in their inquiry, based on their review of prior research and relevant academic literatures, their personal experience, and their preliminary research.

Despite the lack of attention (beyond service-learning) in the academic field of higher education studies to the political roles and civic engagement work of faculty members and other academic professionals, there are explicit and implicit presumptions about this issue in the field's literature, and in the organizational and administrative workings of academic institutions. The central presumption is normative: namely, that faculty members should limit their civic engagement work and roles to a responsive "service" function that consists of the provision of scientific information (usually in the form of the results of or findings from a faculty member's own research), technical expertise and assistance, and/or criticism, all of which are to be supplied from a stance of disinterested and unbiased neutrality. If they wish to be engaged in the everyday politics of public work in other ways, they are free to do so—but only in their "private" lives as citizens. It is simply inappropriate for them to do so as professionals. [This normative presumption was included in one of American higher education's most important documents: the "Report of the Committee on Academic Freedom and Tenure," published in 1915 by the American Association of University Professors. For the full statement, see Hofstadter & Smith (1961).] The main reasons why this is so have to do with issues of epistemology, professional and institutional identity, and public trust. More specifically, it has to do with judgments and theories about how trustworthy knowledge is discovered, constructed, and communicated (answer: from a stance of disinterested, unbiased objectivity), how academic professionals and institutions should behave themselves if they are to stay true to their appropriate functions and missions (answer: they should stay out of politics in all ways except the responsive service function noted earlier), and how academic professionals and institutions are to secure and hold the public trust (answer: by staying out of politics in all ways except the responsive service function noted earlier).

A second presumption we want to note is particularly prevalent in research universities: the presumption that faculty members should not spend much (if any) time being engaged in civic life until after they have been tenured and promoted. There are two main reasons why this is so. First, it's partly due to realities about what will and won't get faculty members tenured and promoted. In many if not most cases, a record of civic engagement not only won't help, it may well hurt. [There are efforts underway to encourage and support institutions that wish to include and value civic engagement in the tenure and promotion process (e.g., Ellison & Eatmon, 2008).] As a result, junior faculty members are encouraged to avoid civic engagement until they reach the associate professor stage of their careers. Second, it's a reflection of the view that civic engagement is mainly or even only about the provision of the results of a faculty member's research. In line with this view, civic engagement is seen as being inappropriate during the early, pretenure, assistant professor stage of a faculty member's career. Faculty members who wish to become engaged should wait until they have research results to provide, which (according to the logic of this presumption) isn't until after they've been tenured and promoted.

We readily acknowledge that these presumptions are not universally and consistently held and articulated across the whole of American higher education. We are not saying they are. What we are saying is that they have been and continue to be voiced and accepted in ways that influence and shape our individual and collective perceptions and beliefs—particularly in the research-university context. We think this is one of the things that is going on with respect to the topic of faculty members' engagement in civic life, and we think it is a serious problem. We are deeply skeptical about the truth and value of these presumptions, based on our experience, our preliminary research, and our review of various literatures about the political roles and work of intellectuals.

In our view, there are three other things we think are going on that both warrant and guide our proposal for a new line of inquiry:

1. We think the normative presumption that faculty members *should* limit their civic engagement work and roles to a responsive "service" function is problematic, on three counts: (1) We think it unnecessarily limits the scope of higher education's public purposes and work, (2) we think it is widely violated in actual practice, and (3) we think it obscures the ways in which the political roles and work of faculty members are deeply contested, both in theoretical and normative terms. In our experience and previous research (Peters et al., 2005; Peters, Alter, & Schwartzbach, 2008), we have learned that faculty members' political roles and civic engagement work are not in practice limited to the provision of scientific information, technical expertise and assistance, and/or criticism from a stance of disinterested and unbiased neutrality. Likewise, the public purposes faculty members pursue in their civic engagement work are not limited to technical and social problem solving. Faculty members are engaged in civic life in other ways and for other purposes. They may become engaged as experts, critics, leaders, servants, educators, change agents, facilitators, and/or organizers. In taking up these roles, they may seek to pursue public purposes that have to do with much more than technical and social problem solving. They may seek to stand for and pursue cultural, political, environmental, and economic ideals and interests related to such things as sustainability, democracy, equity, and justice. As we learned from our interview with Don Wyse, they may interweave a wide range of roles in pursuit of technical as well as cultural, political, environmental, and economic ideals and interests. And as we also learned from Don, they may seriously disagree with each other about not only what counts as "proper" roles and work, but also how to understand the meaning and significance of their roles and work.

2. We think that the political roles and work of faculty members in civic life involve developmental, relational, situational, and contextual dynamics of trust, interests, agendas, and power that take a good deal of time to establish, negotiate, build, and exercise. As a result, we would expect to see changes in the nature and quality of work and relationships over time, across the span of a faculty member's career. This is the main reason why we think that career stage is an important issue to attend to in the study of civic engagement in the academic profession. We think that both the nature and scope of civic engagement in the academic profession are likely to vary across not only the career stage of faculty life, but also the different kinds of intellectual projects faculty members choose to pursue in their scholarly work, the disciplines in which they work, the kinds of academic appointments they hold, and the types of institutions in which they are employed. Some faculty members' research and teaching agendas and projects—particularly but not only if they involve action research and/or service-learning—may *require* deep and sustained levels of civic engagement *from the very beginning* in order for them to be successful. In these cases, civic engagement can't be put off until after tenure and promotion. Given all this, we believe that the study of faculty members' engagement in civic life

must be approached and situated within the unique contexts of specific institutional types, in ways that are attentive to differences in faculty members' academic appointments, disciplines, and intellectual projects.

3. We think that civic engagement in the academic profession involves serious questions and problems that are not being attended to as much as or in the manner in which they should be. They include challenging epistemological, pedagogical, and methodological questions and problems related to the implications of civic engagement—both positive and negative—for the trustworthiness, quality, integrity, and effectiveness of academic professionals' research and teaching. Most importantly, in our view, they also include the problem of understanding and working through what Thomas Bender (1993, p. 128) has called "the dilemma of the relation of expertise and democracy." The dilemma for academic professionals is to decide, among various options, how and for what purposes they should contribute their specialized knowledge and skills to the everyday politics of public work. The ways faculty members perceive and work through this dilemma is not just a reflection of "what works." It is also a reflection of their normative views about not only democracy and politics, but also their roles and responsibilities as professionals in a democratic society. As Brint (1994) notes, there are two main aspects of professional practice: a technical aspect having to do with the competent performance of skilled work, and a social aspect that grounds and guides professionals in an appreciation of the larger public ends they serve. Those professionals whom Sullivan (2003, p. 10) refers to as "civic professionals" attend in equal ways to both by making a "public pledge to deploy technical expertise and judgment not only skillfully but also for public-regarding ends and in a public-regarding way." The question of what it means and looks like to work for public-regarding ends in public-regarding ways is perhaps the most important one that can be raised in the context of conversations about the political roles and work of faculty members in civic life. This question has no single answer that is equally true or applicable across the diversity of institutional types, academic disciplines and fields, and stage of career. Therefore, to borrow from Ernest Boyer (1990, p. xiii), there is a need for many conversations, each informed by the values that are reflected in a college or university's "distinctive mission," by situational and contextual realities, and by a quality and level of reflexivity that illuminates rather than obscures the wide range of political roles and non-neutral commitments faculty pursue in their civic engagement work.

Questions

In line with the goals and conceptual framework just outlined, the line of inquiry we are proposing should include the following set of questions:

1. With respect to the nature of faculty members' civic engagement work:

   • When, where, how, and for what purposes do faculty members become engaged in the everyday politics of public work? What different forms does their civic engagement work take, what political roles do they play, and what contributions do they make? Are there patterns in forms, roles, and contributions within and across each stage of faculty life? What challenges, dilemmas, tensions, and difficulties does civic engagement involve, and how do faculty members perceive and deal with them? How do faculty members understand and articulate what the public-regarding ends of their work are or should be? How do they understand and describe the public regarding ways they do or should pursue these ends?

2. With respect to the meaning, significance, and value of faculty members' civic engagement work:

   • How are we to understand the meaning, significance, and value of faculty members' civic engagement work? Specifically, what meaning, significance, and value does it hold for the pursuit of core academic missions, and the pursuit of the project of renewing civic engagement and enhancing the quality of our civic life?

3. With respect to the goals of catalyzing and informing processes of institutional change and faculty and organizational development, and advancing the project of strengthening and deepening higher education's roles in renewing civic engagement and enhancing the quality of our civic life:

   • How and why do institutions change? How, in particular, are problematic presumptions in institutional cultures changed? How and why do faculty and academic organizations develop? How can a line of inquiry about faculty members' civic engagement work be designed and conducted in ways that are more rather than less likely to catalyze and inform processes of institutional change and faculty and organizational development that enable academic professionals and institutions to make significant contributions to the project of strengthening and deepening higher education's roles in renewing civic engagement and enhancing the quality of our civic life?

Methods

In line with the goals and conceptual framework just articulated, we propose the following methods, broadly and briefly described under three headings.

1. Recruiting participants, refining the research design.

In line with principles from action-research, researchers must take an organizing approach to the tasks of recruiting participants and refining their research designs. [It is important to note, in line with Maxwell's (2005) approach, that the task of developing a research design is an interactive and iterative (rather than linear) process. Therefore, a design must be refined and revisited throughout the life span of a research project.] In our view, a robust organizing approach must be centered on one essential and irreplaceable method: the discipline, art, and skill of the one-on-one relational meeting (Chambers, 2003; Rogers, 1990). The central purpose of a relational meeting is to explore the potential of building an ongoing public relationship with someone. In the context of this line of inquiry, relational meetings should be designed to identify and recruit participants who have a deep self-interest in pursuing change and action goals related to faculty members' civic engagement work. Participants must include faculty members who are and/or have been significantly engaged in civic life in one or more stages of their academic careers. Instead of aiming for the recruitment of a random or representative sample of participants, the aim must be to recruit a purposeful sample that includes not only faculty members who have civic engagement experiences, but also faculty members (and others) who have a self-interest in acting to strengthen and deepen higher education's roles in renewing civic engagement and enhancing the quality of our civic life. In engaging participants in the task of refining the research design, the additional organizing methods of power and interest mapping (Boyte, 2004) should be used. These methods engage participants in a process of identifying not only who the main players in their contexts are, but also and more importantly what their self-interests are, and what kinds and levels of power they have. Power and interest mapping is not to be done only as an intellectual exercise (although it is an intellectual exercise), but also as a means of informing strategic actions.

2. Producing and gathering data.

The specific set of methods researchers and their participants use to produce and gather data is likely to vary across the different contexts in which this line of inquiry is pursued. However, we believe that life story (Atkinson, 1998) and narrative interviews (Chase, 1995; Forester, 2006; Jovchelovitch & Bauer, 2000; Seidman, 1998) of faculty members who are or have been engaged in civic life should be conducted and recorded in every context as a central method of generating data. Life story and narrative interviews are deliberately designed to avoid questions that elicit only or mainly participants' views and opinions and/ or second- and third-person reports of other people's actions. Instead, they are designed to invite participants to tell first-person stories from their life experience that feature themselves as primary actors. The interview protocol for this line of inquiry should consist of four sections of open-ended questions: the first section on participants' personal and professional life experiences and backgrounds, the second on the origins and evolution of their political roles and work in civic life, the third on their accounts of their work, roles, and experiences in specific civic engagement practice stories, and the fourth on their reflections on the meaning and significance of their experiences. To elicit stories, interviewers should ask "how" questions. For example, they might ask how participants ended up becoming a faculty member, how they came to be engaged in civic life, how they came to be involved in a particular civic project, how they came to take up specific roles in their projects, what kinds of challenges they encountered and how they dealt with them, and how they assess the meaning, significance, and value of their work, roles, and experiences. Although individual life story and narrative interviews should be one of the main means of generating data, it should not be the only means. Other means that should be used include autoethnography (Chang, 2007; Fear, Rosaen, Bawden, & Foster-Fishman, 2006), focus group interviews, ethnographic field notes that document aspects of interview and research experience that are not captured in recordings of interviews, and the collection of historical and contemporary documents related to the research context.

3. Conducting analysis, writing up and communicating findings, taking action.

In this line of inquiry, the work of managing, analyzing, and interpreting data from individual interviews includes not only transcribing them, but also editing them into what we (following Forester, 1999) refer to as "practitioner profiles." Practitioner profiles include only the words of interviewees, with the interviewers' questions edited out. [The process of editing interview transcripts into profiles is explained and discussed at the following website: http://courses.cit.cornell.edu/practicestories.] Utilizing tools and approaches from narrative analysis (Chase, 2005; Clandinin, 2007; Riessman, 1995) and critical discourse analysis (Rogers, 2004), researchers who pursue this line of inquiry must work to identify, interpret, and analyze not only the stories and narratives that are included in a profile, but also the ways in which interviewees narrate their life experiences and practice stories, and the discourses they use in doing so. Researchers and their participants should look for ways that both their context(s) and data are storied and/or restoried, utilizing conceptual tools such as meta- and counternarratives. In doing so, they must focus their attention "not only on individuals' experiences but also on the social, cultural, and institutional narratives within which individuals' experiences are constituted, shaped, expressed, and enacted" (Clandinin & Rosiek, 2007, pp. 42–43). Data analysis and interpretation should be centered on the task of discovering the meaning, significance, and value of faculty members' narratives of and discourse about their civic engagement experiences and their political roles and work with respect to the dilemma of the relation of democracy and expertise, the pursuit of core academic missions, and the pursuit of the project of renewing civic engagement and enhancing the quality of our civic life. In doing so, researchers must utilize a carefully selected set of conceptual tools, frameworks, and approaches from political theory, philosophy, sociology, cultural studies, adult learning, anthropology, and history. The analysis and interpretation of meaning, significance, and value must be conducted not only by researchers, but also by and with research participants. This can (and we think should) be done by organizing and facilitating collective reflection sessions during which participants are asked to read, critique, and make sense of the stories and narratives in their edited profiles. Such sessions should be captured as data by being recorded and transcribed. Implications for action from the analysis and interpretation process must not only be named, but also pursued, tested, documented, and evaluated through organized cycles of action and reflection. Actions should include making profiles public and using them as resources in faculty and organizational development workshops and sessions. Research findings should be written up and communicated not only for and in academic journals, but also for and in other venues that are strategically selected to reach audiences in and beyond the academy.

Validity

Under Maxwell's model of qualitative inquiry, "validity" refers to the trustworthiness of researchers' findings, analysis, interpretation, and conclusions. Maxwell suggests that researchers ask themselves to think of the reasons and ways they might get things wrong in their research, and what they will do about it. The key is to identify specific threats to validity and incorporate specific strategies for addressing the threats into the research design.

In the line of inquiry we are proposing, there are two main categories of validity threats.

- First, there are threats to the trustworthiness of narrative interview data. Specifically, interviewees may intentionally or unintentionally get things wrong or leave things out in relating stories from their work and experience. Researchers should address this threat in five main ways: (1) by probing during individual interviews for additional details of the stories interviewees tell; (2) by sharing transcripts and/or edited profiles of interviews with interviewees and asking them to correct mistakes, add missing details, and clarify and/or elaborate on particular passages, points, or aspects of their stories, a move that is sometimes referred to as conducting "member checks" (Guba & Lincoln, 1989); (3) by guaranteeing interviewees anonymity if they so choose (see the following section on ethics); (4) by triangulating interview data with other data related to interviewees' stories; and (5) by organizing and facilitating collective reflection sessions during which interviewees and their colleagues have an opportunity to provide their perspectives on the trustworthiness, meaning, significance, and value of the stories interviewees tell.

- Second, there are threats to the trustworthiness of the analyses and interpretations researchers and their research participants conduct and make of narrative interview and other data. In interpretive research, there is no such thing as a single "correct" interpretation and analysis of a narrative or set of narratives, or of a data set. But analyses and interpretations can be better or worse, or more or less trustworthy. Generally speaking, there are three main ways researchers can address threats to the validity of their analyses and interpretations of narrative data: (1) by situating narratives of individuals' experiences and work in the context of larger social, cultural, and institutional narratives; (2) by asking interviewees to contribute their own analyses and interpretations; and (3) by organizing and facilitating collective reflection sessions during which interviewees and their colleagues have an opportunity to both provide their own and respond to others' analyses and interpretations of the meaning, significance, and value of the stories our interviewees tell.

Ethics

Finally, it would be a major mistake to gloss over the ethics of the line of inquiry we are proposing here. Because this line of inquiry is centered on drawing out, documenting, analyzing and interpreting, and taking action on the implications of personal stories from faculty members' life experiences and civic engagement work, there are numerous risks involved. If the stories and experiences faculty members tell about their political commitments, roles, and work become known to others, it may get them and/or others in various kinds of trouble. Reputations may be damaged or even destroyed, and public relationships and/or support may be lost or destroyed. It may become harder rather than easier for faculty members to continue to pursue civic engagement work. They may even lose their jobs. In light of these and other potentially negative implications of making narrative data about faculty members' political commitments, roles, and work, every effort must be taken to protect their anonymity, unless or until such a time as they permit their stories and names to be made public. Because this line of inquiry is grounded in an action research orientation, the issue of anonymity is problematic. In most cases, unless real names are used in publishing and communicating findings, including profiles, the power of the research will be greatly diminished. People rarely care about or are moved by anonymous stories and information. Making the data real and personal is absolutely essential to making it matter. It is also absolutely essential to do so in ways that meet the highest standards of ethical responsibility.

Conclusion

As we noted at the beginning of this chapter, if we wish to both understand and improve higher education's roles in renewing civic engagement and enhancing the quality of our civic life, we need to illuminate and examine the nature, meaning, significance, and value of the political roles and work faculty members (and other academic professionals) have and are playing and pursuing as active participants in and contributors to civic life. With the exception of service-learning, scholars working in the academic field of higher education studies have mostly ignored or glossed over this topic. Our proposal for a new line of inquiry on this topic is designed to stimulate and contribute to conversations within and beyond the academy about the nature, meaning, significance, and value of civic engagement across the career stages of faculty life. Our motivation in proposing this new line of inquiry is not only or mainly because scholars in the field have ignored it. Rather, it is because we are convinced that it can help us rethink problematic presumptions and realize positive democratic possibilities—but only if it is deliberately and effectively designed to address action and institutional change-oriented goals.

We are well aware of the fact that what we have proposed in this chapter is extraordinarily ambitious and difficult. The task of illuminating, analyzing, and interpreting the nature, meaning, significance, and value of faculty members' political roles and work in civic life will require the creative use of complex conceptual and theoretical frameworks and approaches from many different fields. It will require deep, careful, and close attention to the particular and the contextual, rather than the general. It will take a good deal of time and effort by many people in many different contexts. And it will involve levels of personal exposure and political and ethical risk that are not typically experienced—or wanted—by faculty members, and by scholars working in the field of higher education studies. Despite the complexities and difficulties of this line of inquiry, we firmly believe in its potential and promise not only to advance the leading edge of inquiry in the field, but also to catalyze and inform positive institutional change processes in the American academy in ways that advance the larger project of renewing civic engagement and enhancing the quality of our civic life.

References

Altbach, P. G., Berdahl, R. O., & Gumport, P. J. (Eds.). (2005). *American higher education in the twenty-first century: Social, political, and economic challenges.* Baltimore: Johns Hopkins University Press.

Altbach, P. G., & Finkelstein, M. J. (Eds.). (1997). *The academic profession: The professoriate in crisis.* New York: Garland.

Atkinson, R. (1998). *The life story interview.* Thousand Oaks, CA: Sage.

Bauman, Z. (1987). *Legislators and interpreters: On modernity, post-modernity, and intellectuals.* Ithaca, NY: Cornell University Press.

Bender, T. (1993). *Intellect and public life.* Baltimore: Johns Hopkins University Press.

Blackburn, R. T., & Lawrence, J. H. (1995). *Faculty at work: Motivation, expectation, satisfaction.* Baltimore: Johns Hopkins University Press.

Boggs, C. (1993). *Intellectuals and the crisis of modernity.* Albany: State University of New York Press.

Boyer, E. L. (1990). *Scholarship reconsidered: Priorities of the professoriate.* San Francisco: Jossey-Bass.

Boyte, H. C. (2004). *Everyday politics: Reconnecting citizens and public life.* Philadelphia: University of Pennsylvania Press.

Brint, S. (1994). *In an age of experts: The changing role of professionals in politics and public life.* Princeton, NJ: Princeton University Press.

Chambers, E. T. (2003). *Roots for radicals: Organizing for power, action, and justice.* New York: Continuum.

Chang, H. (2007). *Autoethnography as method.* Walnut Creek, CA: Left Coast Press.

Chase, S. E. (1995). Taking narrative seriously: Consequences for method and theory in interview studies. In R. Josselson and A. Lieblich (Eds.), *Interpreting experience: The narrative study of lives* (pp. 1–26). Thousand Oaks, CA: Sage.

Chase, S. (2005). Narrative inquiry: Multiple lenses, approaches, voices. In N. K. Denzin & Y. S. Lincoln (Eds.), *Handbook of qualitative research* (3rd ed., pp. 651–680). Thousand Oaks, CA: Sage.

Clandinin, D. J. (Ed.). (2007). *Handbook of narrative inquiry: Mapping a methodology.* Thousand Oaks, CA: Sage.

Clandinin, D. J., & Rosiek, J. (2007). Mapping a landscape of narrative inquiry: Borderland spaces and tensions. In D. J. Clandinin (Ed.), *Handbook of narrative inquiry: Mapping a methodology.* Thousand Oaks, CA: Sage.

Clark, B. R. (1987). *The academic profession: National, disciplinary, and institutional settings.* Berkeley: University of California Press.

Colby, A., Ehrlich, T., Beaumont, E., & Stephens, J. (2003). *Educating citizens: Preparing America's undergraduates for lives of moral and civic responsibility.* San Francisco: Jossey-Bass.

Colby, A., Beaumont, E., Ehrlich, T., & Corngold, J. (2007). *Educating for democracy: Preparing under-graduates for responsible political engagement.* San Francisco: Jossey-Bass.

Coser, L. A. (1965). *Men of ideas: A sociologist's view.* New York: Free Press.

Ehrlich, T. (Ed.). (2000). *Civic responsibility and higher education.* Westport, CT: Oryx Press.

Ellison, J., & Eatman, T. K. (2008). *Scholarship in public: Knowledge creation and tenure policy in the engaged university.* Syracuse, NY: Imagining America.

Etzioni, A., & Bowditch, A. (Eds.). (2006). *Public intellectuals: An endangered species?* Lanham, MD: Rowman & Littlefield.

Eyerman, R. (1994). *Between culture and politics: Intellectuals in modern society.* Cambridge, MA: Polity Press.

Fairweather, J. S. (1996). *Faculty work and public trust: Restoring the value of teaching and public service in American academic life.* Boston: Allyn & Bacon.

Fear, F., Rosaen, C. L., Bawden, R. J., & Foster-Fishman, P. G. (2006). *Coming to critical engagement: An autoethnographic exploration.* Lanham, MD: University Press of America.

Fink, L. (1997). *Progressive intellectuals and the dilemmas of democratic commitment.* Cambridge, MA: Harvard University Press.

Fink, L., Leonard, S. T., & Reid, D. M. (1996). *Intellectuals and public life: Between radicalism and reform.* Ithaca, NY: Cornell University Press.

Finkelstein, M. J. (1984). *The American academic profession: A synthesis of social scientific inquiry since World War II.* Columbus: Ohio State University Press.

Finkelstein, M. J., Seal, R. K., & Schuster, J. H. (1998). *The new academic generation: A profession in transformation.* Baltimore: Johns Hopkins University Press.

267

Forester, J. (1999). *The deliberative practitioner: Encouraging participatory planning processes*. Cambridge, MA: MIT Press.

Forester, J. (2006). Exploring urban practice in a democratising society: Opportunities, techniques and challenges. *Development Southern Africa, 23*(5), 569–586.

Foucault, M. (1970). *The order of things: An archeology of the human sciences*. New York: Random House.

Furner, M. O. (1975). *Advocacy and objectivity: A crisis in the professionalization of American social science, 1865–1905*. Lexington: University Press of Kentucky.

Gappa, J. M., Austin, A. E., & Trice, A. G. (2007). *Rethinking academic work: Higher education's strategic imperative*. San Francisco: Jossey-Bass.

Goldfarb, J. C. (1998). *Civility and subversion: The intellectual in democratic society*. New York: Cambridge University Press.

Gramsci, A. (1949). *Selections from the prison notebooks of Antonio Gramsci*. New York: Lawrence and Wishart.

Graubard, S. R. (Ed.). (2001). *The American academic profession*. New Brunswick, NJ: Transaction.

Greenwood, D. J., & Levin, M. (2007). *Introduction to action research: Social research for social change* (2nd ed.). Thousand Oaks, CA: Sage.

Guba, E. G., and Lincoln, Y. S. (1989). *Fourth generation evaluation*. Newbury Park, CA: Sage.

Habermas, J. (1972). *Knowledge and human interests* (2nd ed.). London: Heinemann.

Hale, C. R. (Ed.). (2008). *Engaging contradictions: Theory, politics, and methods of activist scholarship*. Berkeley: University of California Press.

Hofstadter, R., & Smith, W. (Eds.). (1961). *American higher education: A documentary history* (Vol. 2). Chicago: University of Chicago Press.

Jacoby, B., & Associates. (2003). *Building partnerships for service-learning*. San Francisco: Jossey-Bass.

Jacoby, R. (1987). *The last intellectuals: American culture in the age of academe*. New York: The Noonday Press.

Jovchelovitch, S., & Bauer, M. W. (2000). Narrative interviewing. In M. W. Bauer & G. Gaskell (Eds.), *Qualitative researching with text, image and sound: A practical handbook*. Thousand Oaks, CA: Sage.

Kezar, A. J., Chambers, T. C., & Burkhardt, J. C. (Eds.). (2005). *Higher education for the public good: Emerging voices from a national movement*. San Francisco: Jossey-Bass.

Mannheim, K. (1936). *Ideology and utopia: An introduction to the sociology of knowledge*. San Diego, CA: Harcourt.

Mathews, D. (1999). *Politics for people: Finding a responsible public voice* (2nd ed.). Urbana: University of Illinois Press.

Maxwell, J. A. (2005). *Qualitative research design: An interactive approach* (2nd ed.). Thousand Oaks, CA: Sage.

Merod, J. (1987). *The political responsibility of the critic*. Ithaca, NY: Cornell University Press.

Mitchell, K. (Ed.). (2008). *Practising public scholarship: Experiences and possibilities beyond the academy*. West Sussex, UK: Wiley-Blackwell.

Nichols, L. T. (Ed.). (2007). *Public sociology: The contemporary debate*. New Brunswick, NJ: Transaction.

Perry, L. (1984). *Intellectual life in America: A history*. Chicago: University of Chicago Press.

Peters, S. J., Alter, T. R., & Schwartzbach, N. (2008). Unsettling a settled discourse: Faculty views of the meaning and significance of the land-grant mission. *Journal of Higher Education Outreach and Engagement, 12*(2), 33–66.

Peters, S. J., Jordan, N. R., Adamek, M., & Alter, T. R. (Eds.). (2005). *Engaging campus and community: The practice of public scholarship in the state and land-grant university system.* Dayton, OH: Kettering Foundation Press.

Reason, P., & Bradbury, H. (Eds.). (2008). *The handbook of action research: Participative inquiry and practice* (2nd ed.). Thousand Oaks, CA: Sage.

Recchiuti, J. L. (2007). *Civic engagement: Social science and progressive-era reform in New York City.* Philadelphia: University of Pennsylvania Press.

Riessman, C. K. (1993). *Narrative analysis.* Newbury Park, CA: Sage.

Rogers, M. B. (1990). *Cold anger: A story of faith and power politics.* Denton: University of North Texas Press.

Rogers, R. (Ed.). (2004). *An introduction to critical discourse analysis in education.* Mahwah, NJ: Erlbaum.

Rouse, J. (1987). *Knowledge and power: Toward a political philosophy of science.* Ithaca, NY: Cornell University Press.

Said, E. W. (1994). *Representations of the intellectual.* New York: Vintage Books.

Schneider, C. G. (2000). Educational missions and civic responsibility: Toward the engaged = academy. In T. Ehrlich (Ed.), *Civic responsibility and higher education.* Westport, CT: Oryx Press.

Schuster, J. H., & Finkelstein, M. J. (2008). *The American faculty: The restructuring of academic work and careers.* Baltimore: Johns Hopkins University Press.

Seidman, I. (2006). *Interviewing as qualitative research: A guide for researchers in education and the social sciences* (3rd ed.). New York: Teachers College Press.

Smith, M. C. (1994). *Social science in the crucible: The American debate over objectivity and purpose, 1918–1941.* Durham, NC: Duke University Press.

Sullivan, W. M. (2003, Summer). Engaging the civic option: A new academic professionalism? *Campus Compact Reader,* 10–17.

Tierney, W. G. (Ed.). (1998). *The responsive university: Restructuring for high performance.* Baltimore: Johns Hopkins University Press.

Tyrrell, I. (2005). *Historians in public: The practice of American history, 1890–1970.* Chicago: University of Chicago Press.

Walshok, M. L. (1995). *Knowledge without boundaries: What America's research universities can do for the economy, the workplace, and the community.* San Francisco: Jossey-Bass.

Ward, K. (2003). *Faculty service roles and the scholarship of engagement.* ASHE-ERIC Higher Education Report: Vol. 29, No. 5. San Francisco: Jossey-Bass.

Wellman, J. V. (2000). Accounting for the civic role: Assessment and accountability strategies for civic education and institutional service. In T. Ehrlich (Ed.), *Civic responsibility and higher education.* Westport, CT: Oryx Press.

Wilson, L. (1942). *The academic man: A study in the sociology of a profession.* London: Oxford University Press.

Wilson, L. (1979). *American academics: Then and now.* New York: Oxford University Press.

Znaniecki, F. (1940). *The social role of the man of knowledge.* New York: Columbia University Press.

Rewarding Multiple Forms of Scholarship: Promotion and Tenure

KerryAnn O'Meara

The purpose of this chapter is to review recent research and literature on reward systems and how they regard faculty engagement. Promotion and tenure remains a dominant part of the reward system landscape, despite the smaller number of tenure-track appointments. Thus, I consider the current state of promotion and tenure within reward systems as well as enduring dilemmas in the scaffolding that surrounds the assessment of engagement in reward systems. Finally, I outline major areas for reform, advocacy, and organizational and cultural change in higher education to more effectively encourage faculty engagement and move it to the center of our institutions.

Efforts are made to broadly consider the landscape of reward systems and promotion and tenure. Other chapters in this volume should be considered in "close conversation with" this broader topic of promotion and tenure and reward systems and in fact are key aspects of it. For example, Catherine M. Jordan's chapter considers the use of nontraditional products in promotion and tenure, good review standards, and peer reviewers. The chapter by Ann Austin and John Beck reviews research and integrating engagement into faculty roles and across institutional missions. The issues of integrating faculty engagement into faculty work in different career stages are covered in the chapter by Scott Peters and Theodore Alter, and in other places in this book, and are critical aspects of the big picture of how faculty engagement is woven into the fabric of faculty professional lives.

The Meaning of Reward Systems

For the purposes of this chapter, I build on work done previously with colleagues to define faculty reward systems as *"the many ways in which an institution regards faculty—including*

271

but not limited to how it recruits, sustains, assesses, and advances faculty throughout their careers" (O'Meara, Terosky, & Neumann, 2008). This broad definition recognizes the etymology of the word "reward," which is closely related to the word "regard" or care for, and the meaning of the word "system" as a group of interacting elements that make a whole (O'Meara et al., 2008). Although we often tend to talk about reward systems and promotion and tenure processes interchangeably, it is important to recognize that the promotion and tenure process is only one of several ways faculty are "regarded" or rewarded. Increasingly, faculty are hired onto non-tenure-track positions and part-time positions (Schuster & Finkelstein, 2006), which also have embedded reward systems, but do not offer tenure. Thus, we need to consider promotion and tenure as one key aspect of a reward system, but also consider how else tenure-track faculty and non-tenure-track faculty might be rewarded throughout their careers.

What do we know about faculty reward systems from recent research? A quick review of the literature tells us that faculty are indeed influenced by their reward systems to prioritize some work activities over others. Several comprehensive analyses of faculty behavior have shown us that faculty respond to positive reinforcement such as awards, travel funds, professional development monies, merit pay, tenure, and promotion (Austin & Gamson, 1983; Blackburn & Lawrence, 1995). Whether referred to as "extrinsic" sources of motivation (Austin & Gamson, 1983) or as the social knowledge faculty have of what their institution values (Blackburn & Lawrence, 1995), these factors or sources of support have been found to influence faculty behaviors, work priorities, productivity, and satisfaction (Bland, Center, Finstad, Risbey, & Staples, 2006; Deming, 2000; Senge, 1990). Likewise, we know from many decades of research on academic environments that extrinsic motivators sometimes come in the form of less tangible resources such as the approval of a department chair and senior colleagues who favor one type of scholarship over another. Appointments to important committees on campus or in disciplinary associations may be offered in return for certain kinds of faculty priorities and work. Also, extrinsic motivation systems do not work alone but in concert with faculty socialization and preferences. Thus, a reward system should be considered not only in terms of the formal and structural policies in place but as a more complex set of interacting social, cultural, political, and economic factors that encourage some behaviors over others. One thing is certain, however: Reward systems matter in the professional lives of faculty. Even when faculty seemingly operate against the current of reward systems or completely outside of them, reward systems are shaping how faculty present and understand their work. Also, reward systems are an important cultural and symbolic way departments, colleges, and institutions say what matters. It is for these reasons that reward systems deserve our attention.

Promotion and Tenure: Current Conditions

Perhaps the most researched and discussed aspects of reward systems in higher education today are promotion and tenure systems. With notable deviation across institutions, most promotion and tenure systems work in the following way. Faculty are recruited onto a tenure track, usually into an assistant professor position. They have six or more years "on the tenure track" and then submit their materials for promotion to associate professor, which comes with tenure. This is usually an "up or out" decision, with successful faculty being tenured and promoted and unsuccessful faculty being given one extra year before their appointments are terminated. If faculty are successful, they then wait another five to eight years and submit materials to be promoted to full professor, although the timing between associate and full professor is highly variable. Also, this second decision is not up or out, because the person is already tenured. Faculty can apply more than once for full professor. Most faculty submit an overall personal statement discussing their professional work, a curriculum vitae, annual faculty reports, teaching evaluations and philosophies, research publications, and documentation of grants, awards, fellowships, and committee assignments as part of their portfolios.

In reviewing research and commentary on promotion and tenure systems over the past two decades, three observations seem important, especially in light of the topic of this volume of faculty community engagement. First, although there was a maelstrom of critique against the idea of tenure in the late 1980s and throughout the 1990s, tenure seems to have remained stable with a few modifications. It is available, however, as a career track for a smaller number of new academics (Chait, 2002; Schuster & Finkelstein, 2006). The modifications that seem to be most prevalent across higher education systems are post-tenure review, stopping the clock for family reasons, and broadening of the definitions of scholarship (O'Meara et al., 2008). Although each of these modifications has its own record of research in terms of successes and failures, they have all struggled to become embedded in academic cultures and reward systems as opposed to "virtually adopted" (Birnbaum, 2000). For example, research shows that many academic parents have noted that they wanted to take advantage of new stop-the-clock policies, wherein the tenure decision year is extended for the addition of the child to the family, but have not because of bias in their departments and fear that taking advantage of the policy would hurt their careers (Colbeck & Drago, 2005; Erskine & Spalter-Roth, 2005; Williams, Alon, & Bornstein, 2006). Likewise, post-tenure review has helped some institutions provide meaningful professional development for mid- and late-career faculty (Licata & Morreale, 1997; O'Meara, 2003, 2004). However, in other institutions or even departments in the same institution, post-tenure has been scorned and virtually ignored because of faculty feelings that it goes counter to valued norms of autonomy, academic freedom, and collegiality (O'Meara, 2003, 2004). As such, context is key in implementing any modifications to promotion and tenure policies (Wood & Johnsrud, 2005). This point will be underscored in discussing modifications to acknowledge a broader definition of scholarship and to recognize and reward engagement.

A second observation is that for those who actually go up for tenure, the odds are actually in their favor. In 2002, Chait estimated the chances of achieving promotion and tenure for those who submit applications to be about 3 in 4. This is an average; it is slightly less in research universities and slightly higher in small four-year liberal arts colleges.

Yet, these statistics are not the full story. For although three of four faculty who apply may be awarded tenure, not all of the faculty who started on the tenure track make it from the first appointment year to the tenure decision year. In fact, women and faculty of color have been found to have more trouble within existing reward systems than their white male counterparts (Aquirre, 2000; Morrison, Rudd, Nerad, & Picciano, 2007). For example, when compared to their male White counterparts, women faculty have been found more likely to: not enter the tenure track, leave institutions prior to receiving tenure, or take longer to achieve tenure or promotion for family-related reasons (varying of course by discipline and institutional type) (Morrison et al., 2007; Perna, 2001a, 2005).

When compared to their White male counterparts, faculty of color have been found more likely to be dissatisfied with their institution's tenure process (its fairness, sense of their own prospects of achieving tenure) and feel less of control over their research trajectory (Aguirre, 2000; Trower & Bleak, 2004b; Trower & Chait, 2002). It must be noted, however, that recent studies show that when appointment type, career stage, and institutional type are controlled, fewer differences emerge between faculty of color and white faculty (Trower & Bleak, 2004b).

Often the issue in looking at equity is not evident at face value. For example, in a recent review of the status of women at the University of Maryland, completed by a summer 2008 class of mine, it was found that among tenure-track faculty, women and men had the same chance of receiving tenure once they went up, but women were more likely than men to leave the tenure track before the decision (Campbell, Huang, & Stamps, 2008). Likewise, students found that although men and women who go up for full professor have the same chances of success, eligible women are less likely than eligible men to submit their bid for full professor. This of course becomes one negative influence on the percentage of women full professors on campus.

There have been more good explanations and analyses of why women and faculty of color seem to be disadvantaged within current promotion and tenure systems than can be described here. However, I observe that some of the explanations have to do with the social and human capital women and faculty of color bring to their positions vis-à-vis their colleagues (Perna, 2001a, 2001b, 2005), whereas others have focused on the cultural schemas, gender stereotyping, and implicit bias that are inherent in all who work in higher education organizations and limit the progress of women and faculty of color (Callister, Hult, & Sullivan, 2006; Valian, 2000; Williams, Alon, & Bornstein, 2006).

The reason faculty demographics are important to the discussion of reward systems and community engagement is that many studies have shown that women and faculty of color self-report greater involvements in service-learning and community engagement (Antonio, 2002; Antonio, Astin, & Cress, 2000; Baez, 2000; Rosser, 2004, Umbach, 2006). Given that a majority of faculty involved in community engagement do so as part of their teaching, vis-à-vis service-learning, it is important to consider how the teaching goals and intentions of women and faculty of color may differ and how this may influence their standing within reward systems.

Recent survey research found that in comparison to their White male counterparts, faculty of color were more likely to report commitments to the holistic development of students and to out-of-class experiences, goals for social change, community engagement, and the scholarship of application in their work lives (Umbach, 2006). In comparison to male faculty, women faculty were significantly more likely to use student-centered pedagogies such as collaborative learning and diversity-related classroom activities, spend significant time preparing for teaching and advising, and embrace liberal arts goals (Umbach, 2006). Yet Fairweather's (1993, 1996, 2005) research on reward systems consistently shows that faculty who emphasize research over teaching receive higher salaries and accrue greater prestige. Although context is key when discussing reward systems—that is, good teaching will matter more in a small liberal arts college than a research university—it is nonetheless instructive to note that those who preference engagement, either by teaching or by research, do so at the very least not in the service of their professional careers but in some cases to their own jeopardy. Women and faculty of color who engage in such work may be in a double bind, because implicit bias and stereotyping may be their first barrier and then work priorities their second.

A third, closely related observation is that the promotion and tenure system has been critiqued for other reasons unrelated to gender and race and unrelated to a failure to acknowledge the scholarship of engagement. For more than two decades research on tenure-track faculty has shown that junior faculty feel the process is ambiguous and difficult to navigate in terms of standards and expectations, and that it seems to almost always emphasize research in ways disproportionate to the weight given to it in institutional rhetoric, mission statements, formal workload assignments, and even promotion and tenure guidelines (Rice, Sorcinelli & Austin, 2000; Rice & Sorcinelli, 2002). In addition, promotion and tenure processes have been critiqued for disadvantaging interdisciplinary work, encouraging siloed/individual work over collaboration, and not recognizing multiple forms of scholarship (O'Meara & Rice, 2005; Trower, 2008).

It is critical to look at the issue of reward systems and promotion and tenure for community-engaged scholars within this broader context. Oftentimes, I have attended well-intentioned presentations on supporting faculty in community engagement where the central premise of the conversation and advice seemed to be a series of "if only assumptions." Such assumptions regarding faculty documentation of engaged work for promotion and tenure were that engaged scholars will be successful and their work valued in reward systems:

- If only we could show the rigor of the engaged work
- If only we could prove it is the best way to promote student learning
- If only we could document its impact on the field, students, the institution, community and policy through multiple products for multiple audiences
- If only the peer reviewers could be expanded to include community partners and policy makers
- If only the promotion and tenure policy language itself would laud the value of engaged work and its importance to tenure decisions.

The problem with these "if only's" is not that they are wrong in and of themselves—they are just out of context. As other chapters in this volume point out—making a clear case for the rigor of engaged work for peers through careful documentation *will* make a difference to both the quality of the work and to reviewers who are willing to hear the case made. Expanding who is considered peer and changing institutional missions and reward system policies to laud engagement *are* important cultural armor for engaged faculty going up for tenure. My research with Gene Rice suggests the importance of redefining scholarship in promotion and tenure criteria, workload, and mission documents for engaged scholars as well as teacher-scholars (O'Meara & Rice, 2005).

However, the crux of the issue is that much of the work we do in support of engaged faculty—while cognizant of discipline, and while encouraging linking of mission to engaged work—seems to miss the point that that each engaged scholar is not a blank slate around the edges of his or her engagement. Nor is every environment the same—even within an institutional type—in terms of relevant "currencies" sought and exchanged in reward systems.

Instead, each person who stands before a tenure or promotion committee, or in the case of a non-tenure-track faculty member, for renewal of a contract, brings with them certain currencies or assets to offer in their particular institutional political economy. One faculty member may be in a second career and bring significant professional contacts and networks. Another faculty member who joined the faculty straight from graduate school is an expert in how to use a new instrument in the laboratory. One faculty member is a favorite among students, and another recently received a large grant to implement a new curricular strategy in the local school district. As such, their engagement is part of a total picture. The prestige one faculty member offers through peer-reviewed journals may be considered equal to the currency of a new engagement-oriented NSF grant or outstanding teaching award, depending on the institutional economy at that time.

To make things more complicated, one of these faculty members is a Latina woman, one is a White man, and one is African American. One of these faculty members, while going up for tenure, is on her second maternity leave. One faculty member's research is interdisciplinary, and another faculty member is publishing much of his work online and in new media. Furthermore, whereas one faculty member has been taken in by the senior faculty in his department, another is somewhat isolated.

Each of these faculty members is going up for tenure in places that are not static but constantly evolving as well in terms of campus leadership, reward system priorities, and membership of promotion and tenure committees. Each institution also has local traditions or expectations not stated in formal policies but understood in everyday practice, such as whether it is appropriate to go up early for tenure, how much service a faculty member should have done, and what kinds of relationships with the external community are most valued. For example, I have worked several times with campuses where service to undergraduates is considered preeminent. I have heard discouragement from senior faculty of what was called "selfish research" that took junior faculty away from students as opposed to supervision of undergraduate research projects fulfilling the research role. In these environments, engagement that promotes civic responsibility among students while improving town-gown relationships has high currency.

In addition, each discipline has its own tensions, completely separate from issues of public work, regarding what is considered important to study, how to study it, and where to publish it (Sterett, 2008). These issues will have been raised in disciplinary journals, from granting agencies, and within conversations among the top scholars of a field. These conversations will inevitably also influence the scholars involved in promotion and tenure decisions, whether on a campus committee or as external reviewers.

If the original point was that we oversimplify the problems inherent in regard for faculty community engagement, I may have overcompensated by painting a picture of promotion and tenure processes that is too complex. However, both my experiences studying faculty reward systems and my own experiences as a faculty member suggest that the same two faculty members can be going up for tenure in the same department and have a completely different set of experiences based on individual demographics, their work contributions, and the priorities of the institution at that time.

What this means is that faculty members have to figure out for themselves how their public work will fit into the unique career that they are building at a particular institution and in their field. Not all faculty doing engaged work will have to struggle to make a case for their work. In more environments than we recognize, it will be regarded well or at minimum not be held against the faculty member. Even in some research-oriented institutions, the other assets engaged scholars bring with their engagement to the tenure table, whether they be peer-reviewed articles or a teaching award or a grant, offset any perceived disadvantages of time not spent on something that brings more prestige. For other faculty, it may not be their engaged scholarship holding them back at all as much as cultures not supportive of women or faculty of color, an institution that is resource-thirsty and needs faculty to bring in more grants, or preference by faculty for a different type of research, such as quantitative or qualitative.

Given that faculty live their daily lives in departments, programs, with students and colleagues, and in particular locations, we need to look at what assets and currencies faculty engagement can bring to the more intimate spaces where faculty live their professional lives. Much of the conversation about integrating the scholarship of engagement into reward systems seems highly aware of how the work differs from a perceived norm of traditional scholarship. This deficits approach attempts to prove how community engagement is as good as if not superior to traditional scholarship using criteria related to rigor, peer review, and dissemination. This is done for some good reasons—reflection on goals, dissemination, reflection, and critique can in fact improve the quality of the work. Also, it is done as a recognition that the norms of academic culture prefer traditional scholarship—at least in research and doctoral institutions, and so for the career success of the engaged scholar—and so it is better to make your argument in these terms. Likewise, the majority of faculty are socialized toward these sets of expectations in graduate school, and therefore they govern across many institutional types. However, one has to wonder whether by taking this approach, engaged scholars are in some ways cloaking the true values and value of the work. For example, commentators have noted on several occasions that there are different epistemologies, modes of work, and values around dissemination that govern engagement. One of these is the value of genuine collaboration, and another is the value of inviting in and facilitating partner knowledge and expertise in projects (O'Meara, 2008; Strand, Marullo, Cutforth, Stoecker, & Donohue, 2003). Currently, our advice to faculty is to work hard to point out in their portfolios what parts of a collaboration were their individual contribution and to have products with their name as solo author on them. We likewise advise faculty to go to great pains to demonstrate exactly what knowledge they themselves brought to bear on the issue and the impact of their individual knowledge.

However, what if all of the engaged scholars who have been successfully promoted and tenured at each university were actually in charge? What criteria and values would we then apply not only to engagement but to all scholarship? Clearly, the practice of engagement and the discussion around multiple forms of scholarship have pushed many campuses to add the criteria of impact (e.g., on communities and students) to their promotion and tenure processes. But I posit that at times this can still seem like adding to the edges of a system fundamentally at odds with the epistemology of engagement. Thinking any other way, though, requires our imaginations to consider not what is, but what we think should be, and to work toward those goals. Also, it requires engagement scholars to consider the possibility that they may not all be in agreement as to what ideal requirements might be for demonstrating excellence in engagement.

The next section reviews reforms that seem to have made the biggest impact so far on the recognition of faculty engagement in current reward systems. After describing the accomplishments of these reforms, I consider where we still need to go to strengthen the overall reward "systems" that support engaged faculty and all faculty in higher education, in ways that take into account individual and institutional contexts, and currencies. I also raise the question I posed above—what would we do to reward engagement if "we" were in charge?

Reform in Reward Systems

As is well known to readers of this volume, in 1990, Ernest Boyer advocated in the landmark Carnegie report *Scholarship Reconsidered* that campuses transform their reward systems to align mission and reward system and to acknowledge multiple forms of scholarship including discovery, teaching, integration, and application of knowledge. In subsequent work the term "application" was amended to "engagement" in consideration of the reciprocal nature of relationships and knowledge flow. This framework, which built directly off of earlier work by Gene Rice, resonated with provosts, deans, and department chairs struggling with striving academic cultures that did not seem to be rewarding teaching and service, much less community engagement. Glassick, Huber, and Maeroff (1997) followed the initial report with *Scholarship Assessed*, which provided actual criteria for assessing excellence in these four forms of scholarship. These criteria include clear goals, adequate preparation, appropriate methods, significant results, effective presentation, and reflective critique. We know that hundreds of campuses adopted the Boyer framework and put it into their promotion and tenure and related reward system and evaluation policies (O'Meara, 1997; O'Meara & Rice, 2005).

Only a few studies have tried to look comprehensively at the impact of reforms to acknowledge a broader definition of scholarship on institutions and faculty (Braxton, Luckey, & Helland, 2006; Huber, 2002, 2004; O'Meara, 2002, 2005a, 2005b; O'Meara & Rice, 2005). For example, Braxton et al. (2006) have tried to understand whether reforms made at the institutional level have trickled down to influence actual faculty understandings of scholarship or involvements in different forms of scholarship. The authors found that while teaching and discovery remain institutionalized in workload, only discovery or research was considered fully adopted into faculty values and assumptions. My own research (O'Meara, 2002) involved case studies at four colleges and universities to assess the extent to which community engagement was considered a form of scholarship for promotion and tenure. I found that each of the four campuses had reformed their promotion and tenure policies and were experiencing slight improvements in balance across reward systems, faculty involvement in alternative forms of scholarship, and faculty satisfaction with institutional work life. A key finding of the study, though, was that institutional type played a huge role in assessment of service as scholarship. Also, there were specific values and beliefs that worked for and against the assessment of engagement as scholarship, even among its advocates.

Gene Rice and I (O'Meara & Rice, 2005) conducted a three-year study that included a national survey of chief academic officers (CAOs) at four-year institutions, regional focus groups with CAOs, and demonstration projects with nine campuses all amending their reward systems as suggested by Boyer (1990). CAOs from reform institutions where changes had been made (in the previous five to ten years) to acknowledge, support, and reward multiple forms of scholarship were significantly more likely than CAOs at institutions that had not made similar reforms to observe that at their institutions innovation was encouraged and rewarded, the primary interests of new faculty hires matched the institution's primary goals and direction, and that over the previous ten years their institutions had found a greater balance in the faculty evaluation process, that is, research was not rewarded over teaching and service for promotion and tenure (O'Meara, 2005b, 2006). In contrast, CAOs at nonreform institutions were significantly more likely to report that the institutions found it hard to initiate innovations that did not conform to norms at peer institutions and that faculty at their institutions wanted strategic decisions to make the institution more like peer institutions. Likewise, survey research found that CAOs at reform institutions were more likely than those at nonreform institutions to say that they had seen faculty involvement in the scholarships of teaching, integration, and engagement increase and to report that the impact of scholarship on the local community or state, the institution, students, the mission of the institution, and the priorities of the academic unit influenced promotion and tenure decisions. And CAOs at reform institutions reported a higher percentage of tenure and promotion cases that emphasized their work in teaching and engagement scholarship. They were more likely as well to report that chances of achieving tenure and promotion based on teaching or engagement had increased over the previous decade (O'Meara, 2005b, 2006).

Both the Braxton et al. (2006) and O'Meara (2005b, 2006) studies drew on representative samples of four-year institutions, and they complement each other in that the former explored institutionalization of Boyer's conceptions of scholarship from the perspective of faculty and the latter from the perspective of CAOs. Braxton et al.'s study (2006) also contributed significantly to the literature by creating measurable constructs to measure faculty work activity in each of the areas of scholarship. Huber's in-depth anthropological exploration (2004) of faculty crafting careers around the scholarship of teaching complements qualitatively these other two studies by examining the nature of faculty teaching scholarship and how it has played out in reward systems.

As the overall movement to acknowledge broader definitions of scholarship has permeated national discussion and individual campus faculty senates and promotion and tenure committees, two movements within the larger one have quietly made inroads under this bigger tent. First, under the leadership of the Carnegie Foundation for the Advancement of Teaching, significant efforts have been made to differentiate effective teaching from the scholarship of teaching and assess it for promotion and tenure (Huber, 2002; Hutchings & Shulman, 1999).

Second, and most pertinent to this volume, there have been more than two decades of work by national associations, college presidents, provosts, deans, and department chairs, as well as individual faculty leaders, to change promotion and tenure to reward community engagement in and of itself and, in relevant cases, as a form of scholarship.

Although some early advocates of this process (Diamond & Adam, 1995; Elman & Smock, 1985) must be recognized, no one really ignited the conversation as effectively as Ernest Lynton in *Making the Case for Faculty Professional Service*. Subsequently, with Amy Driscoll, Ernest Lynton worked to "make the case" for why partnerships for the public good enriched scholarship and the academy as well as the community (Driscoll & Lynton, 1999). Lynton's (1995) early work provided rich cases of what this work was, and the aspects of it that made it scholarship, including consideration of the process and products of the work and the criteria by which they might be evaluated (Lynton, 1995). Examples were provided from multiple disciplines to demonstrate this was work for faculty not just in the social sciences or professional schools, but also in the sciences and humanities (Driscoll & Lynton, 1999).

Since then, many leaders and advocates in the engagement movement have added layers practically and conceptually to how we might transform reward systems to acknowledge the complexity of faculty engagement (Bringle & Hatcher, 2000; Driscoll & Sandmann, 2001; Holland, 1999; Ward, 2003). A major contribution to assessing engaged scholarship was made by the National Review Board for the Scholarship of Engagement and National Clear-inghouse on Engagement (headed by Lorilee Sandmann and Amy Driscoll) (http://schoe. coe.uga.edu/index.html).

Perhaps most encouraging to those who have been advocates of higher education reward systems that encourage public work are fairly recent efforts by national disciplinary associations to weigh in on this matter. Although there are many more, I note several here that seem likely to have significant impact in terms of specific colleges and departments making judgments about engaged work.

In 2007, the Modern Language Association of America put out a report of the MLA task force on evaluating scholarship for tenure and promotion. The context of the report was that the association was concerned about the ever-increasing demands for publication for promotion and tenure among their members at a time when it has become even more difficult to publish single-author books with university and other presses. From this initial concern, the task force considered the status of graduate education and career options for MLA members and what might need to be done to ensure both reasonable and flexible standards for faculty. They concluded that institutions and departments affiliated with MLA need to do a better job of connecting institutional mission and reward systems and amending reward systems to acknowledge broader forms of scholarship, as well as the newer venues that these come in, such as new media. They also acknowledged the importance of the "applied work of citizenship" wherein faculty partner with public organizations, and suggest that this work be better included in reward systems (Modern Language Association Task Force on Tenure and Promotion [www.mla.org/tenure_promotion].

Likewise, in 2007, the American Sociological Association (ASA) recognized the long-standing contributions of sociologists to the public's understanding of, and ability to act on, the social issues of our time by asking a task force to develop guidelines for the evaluation of public sociology for promotion and tenure. The report, entitled "Standards of Public Sociology: Guidelines for Use by Academic Departments in Personnel Reviews," was submitted by the Task Force on the Institutionalization of Public Sociology. These guidelines suggest ways to define and assess what public sociology is and contains, noting that it builds on previous literature and is research-based, upholds rigorous methodological standards, is subject to peer review, and includes or should include an expanded definition of the "peer" in peer review, and identification of how portfolios can be used to display and evaluate public sociology.

The Community-Campus Partnerships for Health Collaborative, under the auspices of Cathy Jordan (2007), developed the *Community Engaged Scholarship Review, Promotion and Tenure Package and Toolkit,* which, although applicable to faculty in many disciplines, provides very concrete tools for faculty in the health fields to define their community engagement for promotion and tenure and develop a portfolio that demonstrates rigor in both teaching and research aspects of community engagement. A mock dossier and tips for highlighting different aspects of engagement that have contributed to institutional teaching, research, and service missions are included, as well as advice for suggesting peer reviewers and creating multiple products for multiple audiences (http://depts.washington.edu/ccph/toolkit.html).

Last but certainly not least is Imagining America's newest report (Ellison & Eatman, 2008) entitled *Scholarship in Public: Knowledge Creation and Tenure Policy in the Engaged University: A Resource on Promotion and Tenure in the Arts, Humanities, and Design,* created by Julie Ellison and Timothy Eatman and the Tenure Team Initiative. This project advocates in the report for recognition and assessment of a "continuum of scholarship" (p. iv) that includes work created with specific publics and communities outside academe and thereby embracing of multiple products and expanded notions of peer review. Concrete examples are given of public engagement in the arts, humanities, and design. Some strengths of this work in terms of building from what came before are that it considers how interdisciplinary and intercultural engagement interact with assessment of engagement. This report also considers different paths to civic agency throughout the career of the faculty member in arts, humanities, and design.

There is no doubt that the recent efforts of these disciplinary associations in showing how public work might be conducted, assessed, and rewarded in their disciplines are a major step forward for the engagement movement. Vivid examples in such publications, as well as the national awards such as the Ernest Lynton and Thomas Ehrlich awards, respond directly to naysayers who said earlier in the movement, "Well, that is very nice for education and social work, but I am in medicine"—or English, or even engineering. We know because of such projects that there are roles for public scholars in every field and discipline, and we know there are concrete ways to assess the work.

Likewise, reforms in mission, planning documents, promotion and tenure, and other reward system documents that emphasize multiple forms of scholarship have helped support and—perhaps as importantly—regard the work of engaged faculty.

The recent work of disciplinary associations and interdisciplinary partnerships has also moved the issue forward by better defining engagement, identifying its benefits in specific disciplines and areas of public life, and providing concrete ways to assess its excellence.

Yet, returning to the earlier discussions, it does seem as if the entire movement operates on the defensive when it comes to faculty evaluation and promotion and tenure. We seem to develop better and better ways to "make cases" for what we assume to be hostile receptions to engaged teaching and scholarship. Clearly, there are good reasons for this, as the very research and personal experiences of engaged scholars suggest those hostile rooms that prize more traditional work over engaged scholarship.

However, this situation seems very similar to that of the dominant narrative on faculty in higher education, which tends to emphasize constraints on faculty work lives and careers (O'Meara et al., 2008). Although it is true that there are serious constraints in terms of equity, workload, reward systems, mission creep, balance of work and family, and other major factors that limit faculty capacity to thrive in their careers, it is also true that these differ greatly by institutional type and discipline, and that these are also careers that are highly sought after with comparably high satisfaction rates. By revealing the constraints, we help provide paths to ameliorate them; but our focus is also not on other key aspects of faculty work life—such as growth (O'Meara et al., 2008).

Likewise, by taking the defensive and devising strategies to make cases for engagement in environments that prize research above all else, we sometimes obscure the environments (of which there are likely more) that are already interested in engagement and in tenuring engaged scholars. We also shift attention from what we might do to better develop the entire pipeline of faculty learning and growth in community engagement. In the next section I outline major issues I see remaining in terms of the overall system of rewards and regard for community engagement, and then discuss four critical areas for reform.

Enduring Dilemmas and Issues

This volume provides a comprehensive examination of the many issues propelling and holding the scholarship of engagement back. The topic of this chapter is reward systems and promotion and tenure. However, it is impossible to observe what needs to be done specifically with reward systems and promotion and tenure without also acknowledging broader work that must be done to embed community engagement in supportive cultures and systems of support. I offer each of these three areas on top of the areas already mentioned in terms of improving equity for women and faculty of color, lessening ambiguity in the tenure process, and recognition of multiple faculty talents and scholarships. Because each of the following is covered in more detail elsewhere, I touch on each issue briefly and then turn to three critical issues for improving the regard for community engagement in higher education reward systems.

Issue One: There is no widespread system of graduate education providing opportunities to learn the skills and values of engaged work. There are some excellent enclaves, but no systems.

Although important work is being done by new enclaves within disciplines and interdisciplinary research centers, there is no widespread system wherein doctoral students are learning the knowledge sets, skills, or professional orientation of engaged work. This is really the long-term problem of the movement, as we know from decades of higher education research that it is during graduate programs that doctoral students develop their identity as scholars, develop networks with others doing similar work, and develop a sense of competency and then priority for some types of work over others (Austin & McDaniels, 2006; Colbeck, O'Meara, & Austin, 2008; Golde, 2008; Weidman, Twale, & Stein, 2001). This means the current generation of future faculty are missing opportunities for critical experiences that help them to see how their topics connect to public work (O'Meara, 2007, 2008; O'Meara & Jaeger, 2007). It also means that they are not receiving an apprenticeship with senior engaged scholars that shapes their professional identity toward public work (Colbeck, 2008; Golde, 2008; O'Meara, 2008).

Perhaps as important, it means that community engagement is not being mainstreamed into department cultures and expectations in such a way that even graduate students who do not wish to become involved nonetheless see it as a legitimate pathway for their classmates and something common in their field. As a result, these graduate students become future faculty who have no experience with engagement when a colleague presents it as scholarship in their new department.

Also, the requirements of the dissertation still focus predominantly on individual rather than collaborative work, with choice of topics focused on contributions to academic knowledge as opposed to public knowledge. Many of the values inherent in the process of creating the dissertation are thus in conflict with the values of engaged scholarship, which encourages problems identified with community partners, in collaboration (Strand et al., 2003; O'Meara, 2008).

It is true, however, that these problems are not central concerns in all institutional types, because many faculty eschew their research training to intentionally choose colleges that prioritize teaching and engagement and are thus more open to regard of such work in their departments. Yet the residue of such socialization seems to impact even these scholars, even if in ways they do not realize as they evaluate community engagement as a form of scholarship (O'Meara, 2002). Thus, a central concern for future generations is the reform of graduate education to be more focused on public work.

Issue Two: Most reward systems privatize faculty work toward the interests of individual faculty, departments, colleges, and institutions, as well as disciplines.

Although there are some notable exceptions, most junior faculty enter departments without a focus on public work but rather with very private interests, reinforced through private rewards. The reward of tenure is given to an individual and its private benefits to the individual reinforced through a pay increase, greater autonomy, and prestige.

In reflecting on his own academic experiences, John Saltmarsh (2004) observed that while at Northeastern, "The deeper I got involved in service-learning the less my work was private.

I was dealing with public issues." (p. 14). He goes on to note that after leaving Northeastern, he began to work with Campus Compact and stepping out into this role made him

> see academic culture in ways that I hadn't seen so clearly before. I never quite appreciated how we are socialized to be accountable only to ourselves. I was socialized to believe that my first loyalty was to my profession (a loyalty that was fairly undefined but meant something about my scholarship adhering to the standards of the craft) and after that there were no loyalties, not to institution, department, colleagues or students. This deep socialization fostering the privatization of the faculty role led to inherent disengagement in social and political affairs (p. 15).

I would add to Saltmarsh's observations that as mentioned earlier, I have been involved in research with graduate students on the status of women on my campus for our Women's Commission. This collaboration invites a kind of accountability into the work that I am not subject to in the same way when submitting work to a peer-reviewed journal. In the latter process three or four well-known scholars in the field weigh in on the quality of the ideas, methods, and findings. Their deliberation and feedback no doubt makes the next draft better. But in the former case, because the questions about the status of women are asked publicly, members from across the campus in very different types of positions and with very different viewpoints get to ask questions of the work and have a say in what we might do with the findings. This kind of public work actually invites greater scrutiny, but also at times seems more relevant to the daily life of my academic home.

Indeed, a great challenge at the root of the community engagement movement is the degree to which the structure of faculty careers as well as the cultures of departments, colleges, institutions, and disciplines privatizes faculty work. This is a complex issue worthy of many pages, but the brief point I make here is that as long as faculty appointments are made in such a way as to stake the faculty member's work in the immediate needs of departments and institutions as well as to prioritize cosmopolitan interests over local interests (Rhoades, Kiyama, McCormick, & Quiroz, 2008), public access to faculty work and capacity to hold them accountable for relevance of their work is severely limited.

Issue Three: Faculty work is rarely held to standards related to public relevance, impact, and long-term contributions and relationships.

Although I argued earlier that cases made for engaged scholarship seem to take the defensive and assume that if only engaged scholars could show the rigor of their work to the more traditional scholars, they would be successful in achieving promotion and tenure, I now make a complementary point.

Too often, those engaged scholars who make it through the promotion and tenure process, do not push traditional scholars on criteria most exemplary in their own scholarship. Alan Bloomgarden (2008) recently completed a study of fifteen engaged scholars on prestigious liberal arts campuses and found that although these engaged scholars tended to support their more junior colleagues in the promotion and tenure process, helping these individuals to make their cases, they did not seem interested in or willing to take on the very epistemological assumptions of the process that disadvantaged their and their colleagues work to begin with. In fact, many engaged faculty seemed relieved that they were through with the promotion and tenure process, and having had the process work for them, they were satisfied to continue their work and ignore rather than transform the institution's reward system.

The engagement movement needs strong advocates who have tenure and full professor status to question the criteria and standards by which engaged work is disadvantaged. Perhaps even more importantly, such faculty need to speak up and inject their own sense of values and beliefs about scholarship and criteria into judgment of traditional scholarship. For example, why hasn't the movement pushed back and suggested that all scholarship—including theoretical work in journals and basic science—be considered for issues of impact, relevance, and contribution to public issues? Why are there not more faculty asking of their colleagues, "Who will use this research?" or "How will it make a difference?" Why does no one ask if researchers provided any findings to the subjects of their studies or if there was any reciprocal collaboration? This would not be done in such a way as to suggest every piece of scholarship must look the same or make the same contributions. Rather, I pose here that part of the enduring dilemma the engagement field faces is the silence of its own advocates within reward systems and the failure to push for more of the values of engaged scholarship to be considered in assessment of all scholarship, not just engaged work.

The next section considers these three embedded, somewhat enduring dilemmas in efforts to move community engagement to the center of reward systems.

Three Critical Issues for the Next Decade

Each of the following three issues is offered in the spirit of recognizing both the accomplishments and the limitations of where the engagement movement is today. Rather than addressing how all of higher education needs to change in order to be more connected to communities and public life, I consider how promotion and tenure and reward systems need to change to cause the kinds of change that engagement scholars seek, and to reflect that change in a deep way.

Making Faculty Appointments, Work, and Rewards More Public

A critical piece of how faculty are regarded is how they are held accountable and in conversation with their different constituencies. Although there are benefits to the ivory tower model of colleges and universities in terms of space for reflection and cultivation of intellect and free inquiry, these things can still be preserved in academic cultures that strive to create more intimate relationships with their alumni, grant-making agencies, community partners or organizations, the media, and colleagues from other disciplines.

Although a large-scale change in the governance of institutions and how faculty are appointed to give community members greater voice, create more joint appointments, exchange programs, and invite such partners into reward systems as external reviewers is important, there are smaller ways in which faculty professional lives might be connected with the public that would ultimately help change reward systems. First, many interdisciplinary centers have for some time had advisory boards that help the center develop priorities for research, grant funding, and to comment on curriculum. Such advisory boards are a way of inviting constituencies into conversation about where the field is going, what research matters, and where it can make the biggest difference. Likewise, in the area of pedagogy, such advisory boards can connect courses to public problems and issues that prepare students for careers while connecting the institution and community.

Second, each year faculty complete many research projects and publications with ideas and findings very relevant to public debate, but they are not circulated in any meaningful way on campus or off. If more campuses developed strategies for writing policy briefs or short summaries of findings and how they may be relevant to current national, state, or regional issues, and if these were more intentionally posted in libraries, discussed with local reporters, and shared electronically, even posted in places where public comment was possible, we would do much to open up our campuses and research to the public. Granted, this is a one-way strategy and does not solve the problem aptly described by Boyte (2008) and others of technocracy wherein the experts talk and the community is supposed to listen. However, by at least opening the research up for the public, we take another step toward a conversation from which partnerships and important action may form. Likewise, descriptions of what faculty are doing on sabbaticals could be posted on websites and in community newspapers each semester so that the public knows that these faculty members are working on and can connect with them on issues of common interest.

Third, the scholarship of teaching movement has pushed many faculty to consider how to make their teaching more public—moving beyond teaching evaluations from students to ways in which peers might be invited into consideration of teaching and learning in classrooms. Many faculty who are at institutions that prioritize service to undergraduates do not consider themselves part of a civic engagement movement, but nonetheless are everyday passionately engaged in teaching that prepares citizens with valuable skills for a democracy. For example, higher education institutions value thinking systematically about issues, using evidence to make points, and considering issues from multiple perspectives (Sterett, 2008). As good teachers, they have students debate issues, consider alternatives, role play, and engage in collaborative deliberation. Many of these classroom conversations would be enriched by participation from local voices and indigenous knowledge on the topics. Institutions could open many windows by having regularly scheduled days in which community members could join classes on campus, in local schools, or in conjunction with public events so that what is happening in those classrooms is more transparent and so that students and community members can enrich each other's learning.

There are many more small ways that the actual work of faculty and what they do might be made more public. Some are more realistic and appropriate for some disciplines, local contexts, and missions than others. Regardless, making the daily work of faculty more public will help in making the basis for faculty appointments more public. This will in turn raise public expectations regarding faculty work and its potential relevance to their communities. It could act to change public perception of faculty work as unrelated to the real world and thereby put external pressure on campuses to "open up" their reward systems and be accountable for rewarding engaged scholarship that benefits the public.

Making Reward Systems More Growth Focused

In a recent monograph with my colleagues Aimee Terosky and Anna Neumann, we have argued for a national narrative on faculty that is less focused on constraints and more focused on growth. By faculty growth we referred specifically to the following:

> Change that occurs in a person through the course of her or his academic career or personal life and that allows her or him to bring new and diverse knowledge, skills, values, and professional orientations to her or his work (O'Meara et al., 2008).

We further define growth with four aspects:

- Learning (ability to engage, personally and professionally)
- Agency (ability to assume)
- Professional relationships (ability to create, nurture, and sustain)
- Commitments (ability to act on and form).

This framework for faculty growth has significant implications for the entire system of faculty recruitment, support, and reward with regard to engagement. There are deep problems with approaching the tenure track as both a sprint and a marathon where faculty members must move as quickly as possible to publish as much as possible over a six-year period to prove themselves as teachers and scholars. I believe that a key issue for the improvement of reward systems overall, and for engaged scholars specifically, is to focus more on how faculty might learn through their work and what they are learning. This includes what faculty are learning through professional relationships with community partners and through long-term commitments to address particular social issues. It also means "regarding" faculty relationship building, leadership, social entrepreneurship, and impacts alongside the grants, articles, new media, books, and other products that come with it. This also has serious implications for faculty development for engagement.

Those vested with supporting faculty development and preparing faculty for success in reward systems might consider what supports they can provide faculty along a "learning continuum" as opposed to simply a career stage or tenure-track continuum, as different faculty members will come to their engagement with various levels of knowledge and community-building skills. Also, regardless of appointment type, we know that faculty are attracted to their positions out of a desire for learning. As such, faculty new to an area might benefit right off from "orientations to place" so that opportunities to make long-term commitments to specific neighbors might be understood earlier in careers and considered part of faculty learning and career building.

Faculty growth in engagement also requires a sense of civic agency. A reward system truly trying to help everyone succeed in engagement will help faculty develop a sense of self-efficacy in developing partnerships and facilitating public dialogue on key issues. It will facilitate skills in integrating service-learning or community-based research into their classes and studying the impact on student sense of civic responsibility and civic agency. Small faculty learning communities, peer networks, and encouragement of exchanges where faculty reside in community and public organizations and community partners reside in departments will facilitate such faculty growth. In sum, a reward system that truly contributes to and reflects an engaged university is one where faculty learning in engagement is nurtured in very concrete ways and regarded as central to evaluation.

Making Cases That Resist Accommodation

Finally, the bottom line in supporting engaged scholars through reward systems is that we need a new "script." This new script needs to take into account the unique assets and accomplishments of the engaged scholar and place them in context. This means avoiding the tendency to assume, "If all engaged scholars do X, then . . ." and instead make cases based on the quality of the work as we define it. By this last point I mean resisting the temptation to accommodate the criteria and epistemology of traditional research if it is not relevant, and instead to call the work what it is and make the case for why that is important for institutions, students, and public life.

The first point relates to the issue of context. A valid critique of exemplar studies are that they try to make practice seem generalizable that in fact is very bound in context. Thus, it seems as if the critical issue advocates of engagement need to help faculty with is less how to make "the" case or an exemplar case, and more how to make his/her individual case, which changes the focus from the important contributions of engagement overall and turns it toward the ways in which engagement is fostering learning, growth, and contribution in different parts of the faculty member's work, enhancing student learning and sense of civic responsibility and positive outcomes in communities.

Here I think some of the most recent conventional wisdom on integration of engagement within the triad of teaching, research, and service and of attendance to different audiences and to different purposes is most wise. Rather than arguments that may sound overly altruistic and moralistic, or praise engagement for its importance in and of itself, cases for promotion and tenure and within broader reward systems should put questions and methods—including public issues, collaborations, pedagogies, and outcomes—at their center.

This type of case also involves taking into account the unique context of the institution at that point in time. It would also consider the currencies an individual is bringing to the institution through her or his work—which may come in things other than scholarly outcomes.

Perhaps one of the biggest challenges that civic engagement faces is resisting attempts to compromise the major priorities, process, and values of civic engagement either to institutionalize it within higher education institutions or for civically engaged faculty to secure more prestigious and secure positions. For example, many faculty engaged in the scholarship of engagement espouse values of collaboration, reciprocal relationships with community partners, and dissemination of outcomes to as broad an audience as possible, privileging those that reach interested citizens over academic audiences (O'Meara, 2008; Strand et al., 2003). Many engaged scholars have written of their primary interest in capacity building in citizens, eschewing the traditional technocratic role of expert for the facilitator and catalyst, the partner in activism to address common social environmental or educational problems (Boyte, 2004, 2008). Likewise, there is a political and activist agenda with regard to much engagement work. As Peter Levine (2008) notes, the best examples of service-learning are "true collaborations among students, professors, and community members; they have a political dimension (that is, they organize people to tackle fundamental problems collectively)" (p. 21). Likewise, Butin (2006) argues that service-learning "embodies a liberal agenda under the guise of universalistic garb" (p. 485). Whether an individual engaged scholar agrees with this perspective or not, the point is that many engaged scholars may describe their work and operate with their colleagues in what Vogelgesang and Rhoads (2003) refer to as a "zone of indifference," in order to minimize controversy related to their work in their institutions. Yet, there is something lost, in terms of both the visibility of the work and understanding of its goals, by not making its more progressive, activist dimensions public and holding the work accountable to those values.

What is lost? Perhaps the way to remake the system. Rhoades et al. (2008) point out that much of the literature on faculty of color and women points out obstacles confronting new entrants to the profession and chronicles challenges in a system that is structured in the interest of the dominant group. Likewise, O'Meara et al. (2008) observe a "narrative of constraint" in research on faculty in higher education and note that the focus on constraint at times obscures the contributions of faculty and opportunities for faculty growth. Furthermore, Rhoades et al. (2008) observe that advice for faculty of color and women often suggests how faculty members should "fit within existing incentive structures" (p. 215). They go on to note that "the advice is more about how to 'make it' than how to remake it" (p. 215).

This seems an apt description of where we are with promotion and tenure and reward systems for engaged scholars. We need to extend beyond helping engaged faculty make it within a system that was not developed with them or their work in mind, and instead help them over the next generation to remake it in their own image. This image will involve more public work, more open doors, more regard for collaboration, and more accountability to the public. And this is how we will remake promotion and tenure systems.

References

Antonio, A. L. (2002). Faculty of color reconsidered: Reassessing contributions to scholarship. *Journal of Higher Education, 73*(5), 582–602.

Antonio, A., Astin, H., & Cress, C. (2000). Community service in higher education: A look at the nation's faculty. *Review of Higher Education, 23*(4), 373–397.

Aquirre, A., Jr. (2000). *Women and minority faculty in the workplace: Recruitment, retention, and academic culture.* ASHE-ERIC Higher Education Report, No. 27. Washington, DC: Association for the Study of Higher Education.

Austin, A. E., & Gamson, Z. F. (1983). *Academic workplace: New demands, heightened tensions.* ASHE-ERIC higher education research report, no. 10. Washington, DC: Association for the Study of Higher Education.

Austin, A. E., & McDaniels, M. (2006). Using doctoral education to prepare faculty to work within Boyer's four domains of scholarship. In J. M. Braxton (Ed.), *Analyzing faculty work and rewards using Boyer's four domains of scholarship* (pp. 51–65). New directions for institutional research, No. 129. San Francisco: Jossey-Bass.

Baez, B. (2000). Race-related service and faculty of color: Conceptualizing critical agency in academe. *Higher Education, 39*(3), 363–391.

Birnbaum, R. (2000). The life cycle of academic management fads. *Journal of Higher Education, 71*(1), 1–16.

Blackburn, R. T., & Lawrence, J. H. (1995). *Faculty at work: Motivation, expectation, satisfaction.* Baltimore: Johns Hopkins University Press.

Bland, C., Center, B., Finstad, D., Risbey, K., & Staples, J. (2006). The impact of appointment type on the productivity and commitment of full-time faculty in research and doctoral institutions. *Journal of Higher Education, 77*(1), 89–123.

Bloomgarden, A. (2008). *Prestige culture and community-based faculty support.* Unpublished doctoral dissertation, University of Massachusetts, Amherst.

Boyer, E. (1990). *Scholarship reconsidered.* Princeton, NJ: Carnegie Foundation for the Advancement of Teaching.

Boyte, H. C. (Ed.). (2004). *Going public: Academics and public life.* Dayton, OH: Kettering Foundation.

Boyte, H. C. (2008). Against the current: Developing the civic agency of students. *Change, 40*(3), 8–15.

Braxton, J. M., Luckey, W. T., & Helland, P. A. (2006). Ideal and actual value patterns toward domains of scholarship in three types of colleges and universities. In *Analyzing faculty work and rewards using Boyer's four domains of scholarship* (pp. 67–76). New Directions for Institutional Research, No. 129. San Francisco: Jossey-Bass.

Bringle, R. G., & Hatcher, J. A. (2000). Institutionalization of service learning in higher education. *Journal of Higher Education, 71*(3), 273–290.

Butin, D. W. (2006). The limits of service-learning in higher education. *Review of Higher Education, 29*(4), 473–498.

Callister, R., Hult, C., & Sullivan, K. (2006). Is there a global warming toward women in academia? *Liberal Education, 91*(3), 50–57.

Campbell, C., Huang, B., & Stamps, L. (2008). *Report on the status of women faculty at the University of Maryland.* College Park: University of Maryland.

Chait, R. (2002). *Why tenure? Why now? Questions of tenure.* Cambridge, MA: Harvard University Press.

Colbeck, C. L. (2008). Professional identity development theory and doctoral education. *New Directions for Teaching and Learning, 113,* 9–16.

Colbeck, C. L., & Drago, R. (2005). Accept, avoid, resist. *Change, 37*(6), 10–17.

Colbeck, C. L., O'Meara, K., & Austin, A. (Eds). (2008). *Educating integrated professionals: Theory and practice on preparation for the professoriate.* New Directions for Teaching and Learning, Vol. 113. San Francisco: Jossey-Bass.

Deming, W. E. (2000). *Out of the crisis.* Cambridge, MA: MIT Press.

Diamond, R. M., & Adam, B. E. (Eds). (1995). *The disciplines speak: Rewarding the scholarly, professional, and creative work of faculty.* Washington, DC: American Association for Higher Education.

Driscoll, A., & Lynton, E. (Eds.). (1999). *Making outreach visible: A workbook on documenting professional service and outreach.* Washington, DC: American Association for Higher Education.

Driscoll, A., & Sandmann, L. R. (2001). From maverick to mainstream: The scholarship of engagement. *Journal of Higher Education Outreach and Engagement, 6*(2), 9–19.

Ellison, J., & Eatman, T. (2008). *Scholarship in Public: Knowledge Creation and Tenure policy in the Engaged University: A Resource on Promotion and Tenure in the Arts, Humanities, and Design.* Imagining America.

Elman, S. E., & Smock, S. M. (1985). *Professional service and faculty rewards: Toward an integrated structure.* Washington, DC: National Association of State Universities and Land-Grant Colleges.

Erskine, W., & Spalter-Roth, R. (2005). Beyond the fear factor. *Change, 37*(6), 18–25.

Fairweather, J. S. (1993). *Teaching, research and faculty rewards.* University Park, PA: National Center on Postsecondary Teaching, Learning, and Assessment.

Fairweather, J. S. (1996). *Faculty work and public trust: Restoring the value of teaching and public service in American academic life.* Boston: Allyn & Bacon.

Fairweather, J. S. (2005). Beyond the rhetoric: Trends in the relative value of teaching and research in faculty salaries. *Journal of Higher Education, 76*(4), 401–422.

Glassick, C. E., Huber, M. T., & Maeroff, G. I. (1997). *Scholarship assessed: Evaluation of the professoriate.* San Francisco: Jossey-Bass.

Golde, C. (2008). Applying lessons from professional education to the preparation of the professoriate. In C. L. Colbeck, K. O'Meara, and A. Austin (Eds.), *Educating integrated professionals: Theory and practice on preparation for the professoriate* (pp. 17–26). New Directions for Teaching and Learning, No. 113. San Francisco: Jossey-Bass.

Holland, B. A. (1999). Factors and strategies that influence faculty involvement in public service. *Journal of Public Service and Outreach, 4*(1), 37–43.

Huber, M. T. (2002). Faculty evaluation and the development of academic careers. In C. L. Colbeck (Ed.), *Evaluating faculty performance* (pp. 17–26). New Directions for Institutional Research, No. 114. San Francisco: Jossey-Bass.

Huber, M. T. (2004). *Balancing acts: The scholarship of teaching and learning in academic careers.* Washington, DC: American Association for Higher Education and the Carnegie Foundation for the Advancement of Teaching.

Hutchings, P., & Shulman, L. S. (1999). The scholarship of teaching: New elaborations. New developments. *Change, 31*(5), 11–15.

Jordan, C. (2007). *Practical tools for overcoming the challenges of advancing your career as a community-engaged scholar.* Available at http://www.compact.org/wpcontent/uploads/2009/04/jordan-final1.pdf.

Levine, P. (2008). The landscape of higher education. In Brown, D. & Witte, D. (Eds.), *Agent of democracy: Higher education and the HEX journey.* Dayton, OH: Kettering.

Licata, C. M., & Morreale, J. C. (1997). Post-tenure review: Policies, practices, precautions, new pathways. In *Faculty careers and employment for the 21st century.* Washington, DC: American Association for Higher Education.

Lynton, E. A. (1995). *Making the case for professional service.* Washington, DC: American Association for Higher Education.

Morrison, E., Rudd, E., Nerad, M., & Picciano, J. (2007, November 8). *The more things change? Gender inequality in careers of recent social science Ph.D.s.* Paper presented at the annual conference of the Association for the Study of Higher Education, Louisville, KY.

O'Meara, K. (1997). *Rewarding faculty professional service.* Working Paper No. 19. Boston: New England Resource Center for Higher Education (NERCHE).

O'Meara, K. A. (2002). Uncovering the values in faculty evaluation of service as scholarship. *Review of Higher Education, 26,* 57–80.

O'Meara, K. A. (2003). Believing is seeing: The influence of beliefs and expectations on post tenure review in one state system. *Review of Higher Education, 27*(1), 17–44.

O'Meara, K. A. (2004). Beliefs about post-tenure review: The influence of autonomy, collegiality, career stage, and institutional context. *Journal of Higher Education, 75*(2), 178–202.

O'Meara, K. A. (2005a). Effects of encouraging multiple forms of scholarship nationwide and across institutional types. In K. A. O'Meara and R. E. Rice (Eds.), *Faculty priorities reconsidered: Encouraging multiple forms of scholarship* (pp. 77–95). San Francisco: Jossey-Bass.

O'Meara, K. (2005b). Encouraging multiple forms of scholarship in faculty reward systems: Does it make a difference? *Research in Higher Education, 46*(5), 479–510.

O'Meara, K. (2006). Encouraging multiple forms of scholarship in faculty reward systems: Have academic cultures really changed? In J. Braxton (Ed.), *Analyzing faculty work and rewards: Using Boyer's four domains of scholarship* (pp. 77–96). New Directions for Institutional Research, No. 129. San Francisco: Jossey-Bass.

O'Meara, K. (2007, February). *Graduate education and civic engagement.* NERCHE Working Brief, No. 20, pp. 1–8.

O'Meara, K. (2008). Graduate education and community engagement. In Colbeck, C. L., O'Meara, K., & Austin, A. (Eds.), *Educating integrated professionals: Theory and practice on preparation for the professoriate.* New Directions for Teaching and Learning, No. 113. San Francisco: Jossey-Bass.

O'Meara, K. A., & Jaeger, A. (2007). Preparing future faculty for community engagement: History, barriers, facilitators, models and recommendations. *Journal of Higher Education Outreach and Engagement, 11*(4), 3–26.

O'Meara, K. A., & Rice, R. E. (Eds.). (2005). *Faculty priorities reconsidered: Encouraging multiple forms of scholarship.* San Francisco: Jossey-Bass.

O'Meara, K., Terosky, A., & Neumann, A. (2008). *Faculty careers and work-lives: A professional growth perspective.* ASHE Higher Education Report, 34 (3) San Francisco: Jossey-Bass.

Perna, L. W. (2001a). Sex and race differences in faculty tenure and promotion. *Research in Higher Education, 42*(5), 541–567.

Perna, L. W. (2001b). Sex differences in faculty salaries: A cohort analysis. *Review of Higher Education, 24*(3), 283–307.

Perna, L. W. (2005). Sex differences in faculty tenure and promotion: The contribution of family ties. *Research in Higher Education, 46*(3), 277–307.

Rhoades, G., Kiyama, J. M., McCormick, R., & Quiroz, M. (2008). Local cosmopolitans and cosmopolitan locals: New models of professionals in the academy. *Review of Higher Education, 31*(2), 209–235.

Rice, R. E., & Sorcinelli, M. D. (2002). Can the tenure process be improved? In R. Chait (Ed.), *The questions of tenure* (pp. 101–124). Cambridge, MA: Harvard University Press.

Rice, R. E., Sorcinelli, M. D., & Austin, A. E. (2000). *Heeding new voices: Academic careers for a new generation.* New pathways, inquiry no. 7. Washington, DC: American Association for Higher Education.

Rhoades, G., Kiyama, J. M., McCormick, R., & Quiroz, M. (2008). Local cosmopolitans and cosmopolitan locals: New models of professionals in the academy. *Review of Higher Education, 31*(2), 209–235.

Rosser, V. J. (2004). Faculty members' intentions to leave: A national study on their worklife and satisfaction. *Research in Higher Education, 45*(3), 285–309.

Saltmarsh, J. (2004). Building bridges. In Boyte, H. (Ed.). *Going public: Academics and public life* (pp. 14–15). Dayton, OH: Kettering Foundation.

Schuster, J. H., & Finkelstein, M. J. (2006). *The American faculty: The restructuring of academic work and careers.* Baltimore: Johns Hopkins University Press.

Senge, P. S. (1990). *The fifth discipline.* New York: Currency Doubleday.

Sterett, S. (2008). *Speaking prose all Along? Public good research and teaching.* Denver, CO: University of Denver.

Strand, K., Marullo, S., Cutforth, N., Stoecker, R., & Donohue, P. (2003). *Community based research and higher education: Principles and practices.* San Francisco: Jossey-Bass.

Trower, C. A. (2008, January 28). *Promoting interdisciplinarity: Aligning faculty rewards with curricular and institutional realities.* Presentation at the American Association of Colleges and Universities Annual Conference.

Trower, C. A., & Bleak, J. L. (2004b). *Study of new scholars: Race: Statistical report [Universities]. Cambridge, MA: Harvard Graduate School of Education.* Retrieved February 15, 2007, from http://www.gse.harvard.edu/~newscholars/newscholars/downloads/racereport.pdf.

Trower, C. A., & Chait, R. (2002). Faculty diversity: Too little for too long. *Harvard Magazine, 104*(4), 33–38.

Umbach, P. D. (2006). The contribution of faculty of color to undergraduate education. *Research in Higher Education, 47*(3), 317–345.

Valian, V. (2000). Schemas that explain behavior. In J. Glazer-Raymo, B. K. Townsend, and B. Ropers-Huilman (Eds.), *Women in higher education: A feminist perspective* (2nd ed., pp. 22–33). ASHE Reader Series. Boston: Pearson Custom Publishing.

Vogelgesang, L., & Rhoads, R. (2003). *Advancing a broad notion of public engagement: The limitations of contemporary service learning.* Retrieved February 13, 2007, from http://www.collegevalues.org/seereview.cfm?id=1017.

Ward, K. (2003). *Faculty service roles and the scholarship of engagement.* ASHE-ERIC Higher Education Report, Vol. 29, No. 5. San Francisco: Jossey-Bass.

Weidman, J. C., Twale, D. J., & Stein, E. L. (2001). *Socialization of graduate and professional students in higher education—A perilous passage?* ASHE-ERIC higher education report No. 28(3). Washington, DC: The George Washington University, School of Education and Human Development.

Williams, J. C., Alon, T., & Bornstein, S. (2006). Beyond the "Chilly Climate": Eliminating bias against women. *Thought & Action, 22,* 79–96.

Wood, M., & Johnsrud, L. K. (2005). Post-tenure review. What matters to faculty. *Review of Higher Education, 28*(3), 393–420.

Redefining Peer Review and Products of Engaged Scholarship

Catherine M. Jordan

Community-engaged scholarship (CES) is increasingly discussed as a vehicle for enhancing science, improving the relevance of the academy, increasing the impact universities can make on their stakeholder communities, and making real change in societal conditions. Engaged faculty have recognized that in order to be relevant and to have impact, knowledge needs to be communicated in new ways and to more diverse audiences. This calls for generation of additional types of scholarly products targeted for the audiences to be impacted. Much as the peer-reviewed journal article, the traditional "gold standard" of evidence of scholarship, is tailored for the academic reader, products of engaged scholarship must be tailored to nonacademic audiences such as practitioners, policy makers, and citizens. As stated in *Linking Scholarship and Communities: Report of the Commission on Community-Engaged Scholarship in the Health Professions* (Commission, 2005),

> Peer-reviewed publications are essential for communicating the results of community-engaged scholarship to academic audiences, but they are not sufficient and are often not the most important mechanism for disseminating results. They do little, if anything, to reach community members, practitioners, policymakers, and other key audiences. Community-engaged scholarship *requires* diverse pathways and products for dissemination, including those that communities value most.

These pathways and products (referred to from here on as nontraditional products of CES) may take a myriad of forms based on content as well as the learning styles and preferred forms of communication of intended audiences. Examples include training materials, resource guides, policy briefing reports, intervention program manuals, curricula, online case studies, videos, CD-ROMs, websites, and TV or radio pieces. These products may result from diverse faculty activities such as research, teaching, program development, and policy education. Such nontraditional products concentrate on the immediate transfer of knowledge into application, "strengthen collaborative ties between academics and practice," and enable faculty to "apply disciplinary knowledge to practice" with communities (Aday & Quill, 2000).

Although faculty work and, to some degree, expectations on faculty have expanded to respond to the need for such diverse pathways and products for dissemination, peer-review mechanisms and the ability of promotion and tenure (P and T) committees to acknowledge nontraditional products in the P and T review have not kept pace. This chapter discusses the challenges faced by faculty members creating nontraditional products of CES, the debates that have shaped these challenges over recent decades, and a set of critical issues that must be tackled in the coming decade if CES is to have the expected benefit to communities, make contributions to our knowledge base, and facilitate the career advancement of community-engaged scholars.

The Debates of Recent Decades
What Is Scholarship?

Sometimes faculty themselves fail to appreciate the scholarly opportunities, both traditional and nontraditional, that exist within their community-engaged work and end up devoting considerable time and effort to an activity that will satisfy "service" requirements but not contribute to the scholarship of the faculty member. Most definitions suggest that for work to be scholarly it "requires a high level of discipline-related expertise, breaks new ground or is innovative, can be replicated, documented, and peer-reviewed and has significant impact" (Diamond & Adam, 1993). Traditionally, scholarship has been thought of as research, and the typical and most acceptable form of documenting scholarship has been the peer-reviewed journal article. This has resulted in an undervaluing of other forms of faculty work and of products that are not peer-reviewed journal articles.

The need for an expanded view of scholarship was recognized nearly two decades ago and articulated by Ernest Boyer in *Scholarship Reconsidered* (Boyer, 1990). Boyer offered a four-part view of scholarship that recognized the potential for faculty to create scholarship from most of their activities and for P and T committees to recognize those activities as scholarly. Boyer states, "Surely, scholarship means engaging in original research. But the work of the scholar also means stepping back from one's investigation, looking for connections, building bridges between theory and practice and communicating one's knowledge effectively to students" (Boyer, 1996). He proposed four interrelated dimensions of scholarship: *teaching, discovery, integration,* and *application.* These forms of scholarship often interact, and a particular piece of faculty work may represent multiple forms of scholarship.

Maurana, Wolff, Beck, and Simpson (2000) emphasize that "Boyer's model of scholarship of discovery, integration, application, and teaching all apply to community scholarship, but the principles, processes, outcomes and products may differ in a community setting." Boyer himself recognized the need to think about the community, later expanding his definition to include the *scholarship of engagement:* activities within teaching, discovery, integration, and application that connect universities and communities and focus the work of the academy on understanding and solving community problems (Boyer, 1996).

Glassick, Huber, and Maeroff (1997) extended Boyer's work and expanded the limited view of the peer-reviewed article as the most important criteria for academic recognition and reward. Their proposed standards (scholars must have clear goals, be adequately prepared, use appropriate methods, achieve outstanding results, communicate effectively, and reflectively critique their work) allow review of a range of products intended for both academic and nonacademic audiences. Numerous academic departments, professional schools, and colleges/universities have adopted some version of the definitions of Boyer or Glassick et al., though peer review, specifically, continues to be seen as a critical feature of scholarship at many institutions.

How Should Nontraditional Products Be Reviewed?

If, for a work product to be scholarly, it should be able to be submitted to the critical review of peers, how should nontraditional products be judged, and who should judge them? These questions require attention to three issues: mechanisms for peer review of nontraditional products, criteria for review of these products, and the role of community members in the peer-review process.

A need for peer review of nontraditional products of CES has begun to be recognized, but we sorely lack mechanisms to facilitate such review as well as vehicles for the dissemination of reviewed products to a wide audience. Models do exist, however. MedEdPORTAL (http://www.mededportal.org), developed and launched by the Association of American Medical Colleges, provides rigorous peer review and online dissemination of medical and dental educational resources. Its reviewers are primarily medical and dental educators. The Multimedia Education Resource for Learning and Online Teaching (MERLOT; http://www.merlot.org) provides peer review of online learning and teaching resources within a myriad of disciplines. Its reviewers are peer users of online resources who are faculty with experience using technology in teaching and learning. There are other examples of online repositories of peer-reviewed teaching resources. However, there has not been a mechanism available specifically for the peer review of products of CES.

If there were mechanisms to review nontraditional products of CES, questions might arise regarding criteria to be used to judge these products. Do review criteria that are used to assess manuscripts for journal publication apply to review of nontraditional products? What are the unique features of CES and of nontraditional products that would require thinking differently about the criteria for their peer reviewing?

Academics have traditionally served as reviewers in the peer-review process based on an understanding of "peer" as the professional colleagues within our disciplines. However, in CES it is reasonable to ask whether our community partners, those with whom we share intellectual contribution, project tasks, and decision-making power, should be considered as legitimate and qualified reviewers. For some, the answer is yes; community peers are in the best position to judge qualities such as the authenticity of the community engagement process and the real or potential impact of the work on the community. For example, the print journal *Progress in Community Health Partnerships: Research, Education and Action* asks submitting authors to recommend several community members unaffiliated with the work as potential reviewers. The editor chooses at least one to review the article to determine the utility of the information in the article to their own and other communities and to assess the quality and quantity of the input community members had into the work being described. Although the appropriateness of using community members as reviewers may seem self-evident to community-engaged scholars and those who create publication venues for their work, it is not necessarily a position that would be shared by others, including many sitting on P and T committees.

Should Nontraditional Products "Count" in Promotion and Tenure?

"With no currently accepted method for rigorously peer reviewing these alternative means of dissemination or documenting any peer review that has taken place, they are often perceived by P and T committees as being of less importance, quality, credibility, and value than peer-reviewed journal articles" (Commission on Community-Engaged Scholarship in the Health Professions, 2005). Peer review is a stamp of approval by a set of reviewers not unlike P and T committee members, and positive review of a scholarly product communicates to the P and T committee that, were they to have been the ones reviewing the scholarly product, they would likely agree that the scholarship was worthy.

Would concerns about import, quality, credibility, and value be allayed if mechanisms for rigorous peer review and dissemination of nontraditional products existed? Very possibly, with education of P and T committee members regarding the scholarly qualities of these products and the rigor of the review process. However, the products that result from CES present additional challenges for P and T committee members. CES tends to be a social undertaking, and the contributions of various members of the collaboration can be difficult to tease apart. Products of CES frequently have multiple authors, across disciplines, the university, and the community, and community-engaged scholars tend to emphasize the work of the collective, rather than stressing credit for themselves. This can be problematic in a P and T process that focuses on the contributions of the individual.

The definition of "impact," and impact on what audiences, can also be points of divergence between community-engaged scholars and P and T committees. Traditionally, P and T committees have stressed impact on the field and contribution to the disciplinary knowledge base. The measure most often taken as evidence of such impact is publication in journals with high "impact factor" scores. Community-engaged scholars often see benefit to stakeholder communities, better informed policies, and systems change as the desired goals. A need for an expanded definition of impact, recognizing the relevance of community impact in the P and T process, has been a topic of discussion on numerous campuses, and several have been explicit in adding community impact to their traditional definition of impact in their P and T guidelines (http://depts.washington.edu/ccph/pdf_files/Developing%20Criteria%20for%20Review%20of%20CES.pdf).

Critical Issues for the Coming Decade

In many ways, the same debates that have taken place over the past twenty years shape the issues to be addressed in the next decade. Fortunately, the attention invested in these issues in recent years has resulted in progress in some cases and sometimes in limited ways.

Mechanisms for Peer Review

Many products that could be peer reviewed are not because there are few mechanisms of peer review for products that are not journal article submissions. Some disciplines are recognizing this gap and calling for change. The Commission on Community-Engaged Scholarship in the Health Professions (2005) recommended that a national board be established to provide a mechanism for the peer review of nontraditional products of health-related CES as well as P and T dossiers of engaged faculty.

Though not a national board, and more limited in scope than the board recommended by the Commission, "CES4Health.info" is being developed by a working group of the Faculty for the Engaged Campus, a Community-Campus Partnerships for Health project funded by the Department of Education Fund for the Improvement of Postsecondary Education. CES4Health.info will serve as a rigorous peer-review mechanism and online repository of nontraditional products of CES relevant to clinical health professions, public health, social work, related disciplines, and the social determinants of health. Additional peer-review and dissemination mechanisms will need to be developed within other disciplines or, more broadly, across disciplines in order to meet the peer-review needs of scholars working in areas other than health.

Even without established mechanisms for peer review, faculty can accomplish some of the goals of peer review through less formal strategies. Peer review serves to provide an impartial critique of the work to the author that may be used to make improvements in the work or its presentation. Peer review also ensures that disseminated work meets certain standards and prevents work that is irrelevant, incredible, biased or misrepresents the research from being published. It increases the likelihood that the body of research and knowledge available for other scholars, practitioners, policy makers and citizens to apply and build upon is reliable and valid. In the absence of established peer-review mechanisms, faculty can submit their nontraditional products of CES to a set of professional and community colleagues, removed from the work itself but familiar with the practices of CES, willing to provide a critique and suggestions for revision. The constructive criticism that results can lead to considerable improvements in the product and greater likelihood that the product will be a useful tool or reliable source of information for end users.

This form of peer review is not likely to be judged by P and T committees as equivalent to established peer-review mechanisms because the review criteria used would be idiosyncratic and not transparent, and the critique would be less impartial than blinded peer-review processes because the faculty member hand-selected reviewers. This type of peer review should be thought of as a mechanism to provide feedback for improvement and an opportunity to, in the terms of Glassick et al. (1997), reflectively critique one's work. These are important outcomes, though, and P and T committees at institutions incorporating the work of Glassick et al. into their P and T guidelines would likely respect a faculty member that made the effort to seek such peer review, made improvements based on reflection on the feedback, and discussed within their dossier essays the role of peer review in the development of their scholarship.

The Right Standards

As noted earlier, nontraditional products of CES take many forms, for example, print, web-based, and video. Their content is similarly varied. Nontraditional products arise from undertakings as diverse as research, teaching, policy education, and practice activities. For example, a researcher and leaders of an American Indian service organization may conduct a study of health and well-being in rural and urban American Indian communities. One product of this investigation might be a documentary video presenting the stories of individuals recounting times of health and illness in their lives, their beliefs about health, and their experiences in the health care system and with traditional approaches. This video may be accompanied by a discussion guide and documentation about the interview process conducted. In another example, a law professor and students in her service-learning course on culture, ethnicity, and the law collaborated with staff at a free legal clinic in an inner city community to design a service related to restitution. Staff at the clinic recognized the need to enhance their capacity to work with the diverse clients seeking their services. The professor and students reviewed the literature on cultural competency training and interviewed clinic staff and clients. The professor, students, and several staff members produced a cultural competency training manual tailored for attorneys.

These products have in common only that they resulted from work completed in collaboration between faculty and community partners. Should a set of guidelines for review be developed that is relevant and appropriate for all types and formats of products? Particularly for review of nontraditional products of CES, with which P and T committees and peer reviewers have relatively less experience, a standard and transparent set of criteria would be quite valuable. Such criteria would help P and T committee members understand and trust the review process and enhance the credibility of reviewers' determinations regarding quality, rigor and impact of reviewed products. Peer reviewers would also appreciate a standard set of criteria. Since peer review of nontraditional products is a relatively new charge, even reviewers with experience in reviewing manuscripts for traditional journals or reviewing grant applications may feel less prepared to review the breadth of nontraditional products of CES. Developing some consensus around review criteria also communicates a level of sophistication or maturity within the field that would reassure P and T committee members.

The Glassick et al. (1997) criteria have been adopted or modified by MedEdPortal for evaluating medical and dental education resources, CES4Health.info for reviewing nontraditional products related to health CES, the Clearinghouse and National Review Board for the Scholarship of Engagement (http://schoe.coe.uga.edu/) for the evaluation of P and T candidate dossiers, and the Community-engaged Scholarship Review, Promotion and Tenure Package (Jordan, 2007; http://depts.washington.edu/ccph/toolkit.html) to educate candidates and P and T committee members about characteristics of quality CES. Developers of these peer-review mechanisms have found the Glassick et al. criteria to be flexible and generalizable to a range of situations. These criteria might serve as a standard, yet adaptable, set of criteria for the peer review of nontraditional products of CES across all topics and disciplines.

The Role of Community Members

Community-engaged scholars view community members as possessing important and relevant expertise and knowledge that qualifies them as partners in the intellectual effort of scholarship creation. Increasingly, faculty and community members are co-authoring manuscripts, copresenting, and cocreating nontraditional products of CES. Publication outlets are also increasingly recognizing community members as qualified and appropriate co-authors. As mentioned previously, some publication and dissemination outlets also recognize community members as legitimate peers with an important role to play in the peer-review process. However, promotion guidelines and P and T committees have been slower to embrace community members in the peer-review process. Beliefs that community members are not really peers may lead committee members to place less weight on the peer review and publication of manuscripts or products in outlets that utilize community members as reviewers. Letters of support from community members are not weighted particularly heavily in a review of a dossier compared to internal and external letters from academic peers. And, it is a rare occurrence for community members to sit on promotion and tenure committees.

If characteristics such as authenticity of the collaboration, relevance, and appropriateness of the product for intended audiences and potential for the product to make real community impact are to be taken seriously in peer review and in the P and T process, community members with experience in partnering with university faculty will need to be appreciated for the unique knowledge and expertise they bring. Community members will need to be part of the peer-review process for traditional and nontraditional products of CES and will need to be involved in the evaluation of engaged scholars in the P and T process. It will be important for community members serving in the role of peer reviewers to receive appropriate training and support, because peer review is part of the academic rather than community culture, and they are likely to be less familiar with the norms and mores of this process than novice academic peer reviewers would be. Likewise, academic reviewers need training about CES and the role of nontraditional products in broad dissemination and creating community impact in order to perform their review duties appropriately. Community members should be considered the preferred trainers for these reviewers.

Publication Outlets

It is critical that community-engaged scholars have a range of high-quality, credible, high-impact outlets for disseminating the information and tools resulting from their community-engaged work. Likewise, readers, both academic and community-based, need access to an array of trustworthy sources of information and materials relevant to their activities. For greatest impact, outlets need to be directed at both academic and community audiences, including practitioners, policy makers, organization leaders, community activists, and citizens. Reaching such a diverse audience requires expanding the options of acceptable journals in which CES can be credibly published as well as developing rigorously reviewed repositories for nontraditional scholarly products, easily accessible to the public as well as members of the academy, such as CES4Health.info mentioned earlier.

The premier academic journals (such as those with high "impact factor" scores) may be less likely to publish articles based on CES than other journals (Nyden, 2003). Therefore, it will be important not only to create new outlets for peer review and publication of CES, but to convince those existing outlets that are particularly well respected within disciplines and by P and T committees to solicit and publish more examples of CES, either as part of their regular publication schedule or as special issues. This has begun to happen. New print and online journals dedicated to CES have emerged, such as the *Journal of Higher Education,*

Outreach and Engagement or the *Journal of Community Engagement and Higher Education*. Journals such as the *Journal of General Internal Medicine* (July 2003 issue) have published special issues on topics relevant to CES, such as community-based participatory research.

Making It "Count"

P and T guidelines and the committee members charged with evaluating dossiers according to those guidelines place value on some achievements more than others. Rigor of scholarship, professional distinction in the form of a national or international reputation (depending on rank), and evidence of impact are three areas that tend to receive special attention. It will be important to examine each of these in relation to the development, peer review, and dissemination of nontraditional products of CES.

CES is sometimes misunderstood to be necessarily "soft" or of less rigor. This misperception is partly the result of assumptions about the methods used in CES and partly the result of beliefs about the influence community member participation has on rigor and objectivity. CES is scholarship that results from an equitable collaboration between a faculty member and the community. Design, methods, procedures, and content are not prescribed; any form of research or educational activity may result in CES. CES is not limited to a particular branch of the academy or discipline. Therefore, the scholarship that emerges from a community-engaged activity is not necessarily of less rigor and may be of considerable rigor depending on the methods employed. It is the job of peer reviewers and P and T committee members to make that determination of rigor without capitulating to preconceived notions about methods used in community-engaged approaches.

The sharing of decision-making power and the participation of community members in various stages of an engaged activity provokes a concern for some that community members will influence the outcome of the work, resulting in bias. However, humans view the world through their own frames of reference, whether those frames be formed by academic training, disciplinary loyalties, or lived experience. All scholarly efforts are vulnerable to a restricted field of vision and personal biases and academics are as likely to allow these phenomena to unconsciously enter the process as are community members. Rather than bias the work, including the perspectives and expertise of community members can guard against the bias inherent in the faculty member's frame of reference and in scientific epistemology. In the case of community-based research (CBR):

> The participation of all collaborators in this process provides a system of checking the accuracy and rationality of interpretations against each other. Rather than create subjectivity, this part of the CBR process tends to create a balance between various "takes" on the data, and therefore, greater objectivity. Consideration of multiple and sometimes diverse interpretations of the data can lead to appreciation of the complexities inherent in the object of investigation and prevents oversimplification of the model constructed to explain the phenomenon (Jordan, Gust, & Scheman, 2005).

The reputation of nontraditional products resulting from community-engaged activities suffers both from biases about the rigor and objectivity of the community-engaged work on which the product is based and from adherence to beliefs about peer-reviewed manuscripts as the defining example of what is scholarly. Although rigorous peer-review mechanisms can dispel some myths and enhance appreciation of these products as scholarship, improving the reputation of nontraditional products of CES will require a cultural shift within the disciplines and across our campuses.

Professional distinction is evidenced primarily by prestigious invitations of various sorts, presumably related to the high visibility and substantial impact of one's scholarship, such as requests to provide keynote addresses at national and international academic meetings, be an editor for a journal, serve on commissions and task forces, or provide expert testimony. Earning this reputation can be a challenge for community-engaged scholars focused on developing nontraditional products of CES. Such products are often developed, disseminated, and have impact in a local context. The community-engaged scholar tends to, at least initially, earn a local reputation. The scholar may earn invitations based on this local reputation to, for example, present at community meetings, give interviews to local media, or serve on the boards of community-based organizations. Such invitations must be appreciated as evidence of an earned reputation. However, the community-engaged scholar will also need to leverage this local reputation to build evidence of national or international distinction. It is therefore important for the scholar to increase the visibility of his or her CES by publishing manuscripts in prominent journals and subjecting his or her nontraditional products to peer review and broad dissemination through online mechanisms. These actions, of course, are dependent on the willingness of journals and the existence of online mechanisms, as mentioned earlier in the discussion of publication outlets.

Issues related to the need for an expanded definition of impact, to include the impact that CES and specifically nontraditional products of CES can have on communities, systems change, policy decision making, and the like, were discussed earlier. Development of an understanding of evidence for community impact, and effective ways of documenting it, will be critical for acceptance of this expanded definition by P and T committee members. The Community-Engaged Scholarship Review, Promotion and Tenure Package (Jordan, 2007; http://depts.washington.edu/ccph/toolkit.html), developed by a working group of Community-Campus Partnerships for Health's Community-Engaged Scholarship for Health Collaborative, is one resource that could be of assistance. This package presents characteristics of quality CES, numerous examples of evidence of each characteristic, and ideas for documenting the evidence in the P and T dossier. It is intended to help P and T candidates make their best case for promotion or tenure as community-engaged scholars, but also to assist P and T committee members in recognizing within dossiers evidence of rigor, community impact, authentic partnership, socially responsible conduct, and other characteristics of best practices in CES.

Conclusion

In closing, the following is a proposed action plan for achieving rigorous peer review of nontraditional products and their recognition in the P and T process, based on the foregoing discussions of past debates and critical issues for the future:

1. Develop, or agree to an existing, set of standard but adaptable criteria for peer review of nontraditional products. Ensure that evaluation of the quality and authenticity of community partnership is included.

2. Create mechanisms for peer review of these products. Such mechanisms can function just as review processes for journals do, but attending to the need for community members to contribute to the review process.

3. Create additional dissemination outlets, taking advantage of web-based technology. Track hits and downloads to provide a rudimentary indicator of impact of the product.

4. Solicit the support of professional and disciplinary societies for increasing the visibility of and appreciation for nontraditional products of CES.

5. Solicit support from the highest levels of higher education administration for widespread culture change on campuses to enhance the acceptance of CES and nontraditional products within the academy.

6. Advocate for changes in P and T guidelines, as one of the most important reflections of an institution's culture and values, to recognize nontraditional products of CES.

7. Provide training to P and T committee members about expanded definitions of scholarship and impact and the role of nontraditional products in broad dissemination and enhancing community benefit.

8. Provide training to faculty about the importance of, and effective routes to, creating nontraditional scholarly products from their community-engaged work.

9. Provide training for faculty in documenting evidence of the rigor of their CES, the authenticity and quality of their community collaborations, and the impact of their community-engaged work. Provide tools for faculty to use to make their best case for promotion or tenure as a community-engaged scholar.

10. Showcase exemplary nontraditional products of CES and candidates who are successful in achieving promotion or tenure as community-engaged scholars who use, in part, nontraditional products to communicate information and achieve benefit.

CES is an important mechanism for increasing the validity and relevance of science, adding consequentially to our knowledge base, and making positive impact on communities. Although traditional manuscripts do often result from community-engaged work, nontraditional products are critical for disseminating information to a broader audience and making impact. The broader audience includes practitioners, policy makers, community organizations, community activists, citizens, and others, in addition to academics. For faculty to be able to invest time, energy, and resources into the development of these products, they must contribute to the faculty member's ability to pass performance reviews and achieve promotion or tenure. Peer review, given its central place in our conceptualization of what is scholarly and therefore what "counts" in P and T, needs to be extended in a systematic and rigorous manner to the assessment of nontraditional products.

References

Aday, L. A., & Quill, B. E. (2001). A framework for assessing practice-oriented scholarship in schools of public health. *Journal of Public Health Management Practice, 6*(1), 38–46.

Association of American Medical Colleges. (n.d.). *MedEdPortal.* Available at http://www.mededportal. org.

Boyer, E. L. (1990). *Scholarship reconsidered: Priorities of the professoriate.* The Carnegie Foundation for the Advancement of Teaching.

Boyer, E. (1996). The scholarship of engagement. *Journal of Public Service and Outreach, 1,* 11–20.

Clearinghouse and National Review Board for the Scholarship of Engagement. (n.d.). Available at http://schoe.coe.uga.edu/.

Commission on Community-Engaged Scholarship in the Health Professions. (2005). *Linking Scholarship and Communities: Report of the Commission on Community-Engaged Scholarship in the Health Professions.* Seattle, WA: Community-Campus Partnerships for Health.

Diamond, R. M., & Adam, B. E. (1993). *Recognizing faculty work: Reward systems for the year 2000.* San Francisco: Jossey-Bass.

Glassick, C. E., Huber, M. T., and Maeroff, G. (1997). *Scholarship assessed: Evaluation of the professoriate.* San Francisco: Jossey-Bass.

Jordan, C. (Ed.). (2007). *Community-engaged scholarship review, promotion &tenure package.* Peer Review Workgroup, Community-Engaged Scholarship for Health Collaborative, Community-Campus Partnerships for Health. Available at http://depts.washington.edu/ccph/toolkit.html.

Jordan, C., Gust, S., & Scheman, N. (2005). The trustworthiness of research: The paradigm of community-based research. *Metropolitan Universities Journal, 16*(1), 39–57.

Maurana, C., Wolff, M., Beck, N., & Simpson, D. E. (2000). *Working with our communities: Moving from service to scholarship in the health professions.* San Francisco: Community-Campus Partnerships for Health.

MERLOT. (n.d.) *The Multimedia Educational Resource for Learning and Online Teaching.* Available at http://www.merlot.org.

Nyden, P. (2003). Academic incentives for faculty participation in community-based participatory research. *Journal of General Internal Medicine, 18*(7), 576–585.

PART 4

Student Learning in the Engaged Academy

Edited by Eric J. Fretz

Student Learning in the Engaged Academy

Eric J. Fretz

This handbook is part of the developing literature on engaged scholarship that reflects the intellectual maturation and the "thickening" of the movement. As the theories and practices of engagement evolve, the movement itself is, happily, acquiring a critical edge that it lacked in its nascent stages.

The essays in this part serve up a series of critiques about the way higher education has organized itself, especially as it relates to the role that students can and should play within the engaged university. They question the way knowledge is produced and who can and should produce knowledge. They argue for a reinvigoration of teaching and learning models and improving the quality of graduate and undergraduate education. They question how we are shaping students' professional lives and public imaginations. They critique the expert model of higher education. They worry that education practices have drifted from democratic principles and an attention to the civic roles of students and faculty. And they show how global and corporate trends are outpacing higher education practice.

The authors in this part see a number of problems within higher education:

They question the way knowledge is produced and who can and should produce knowledge. They argue for a reinvigoration of teaching and learning models and for improving the quality of graduate and undergraduate education. They question how we are shaping students' professional lives and public imaginations. They critique the expert model of higher education. They worry that education practices have drifted from democratic principles and an attention to the civic roles of students and faculty. And they show how global and corporate trends are outpacing higher education practice.

Hope and idealism, the hallmarks of the civic engagement movement, balance these critiques. All of the essays in this part articulate a belief that engaged scholarship has the

309

potential to change higher education. They believe that engaged scholarship and learning can make higher education more relevant to a larger audience and that this movement can counter the powerful trends of consumerism that have so deeply affected higher education. They see hope in incorporating deliberative democracy and collaborative learning techniques into the classroom. For the authors in this part, engaged scholarship and learning is not an add-on to an already overloaded curriculum or research agenda—it is a robust way of thinking and generating knowledge that can change the way institutions accomplish their work and mission. Most importantly, they see students as agents of change within institutions, and they see students playing powerful roles in knowledge generation.

The critical edge of the civic engagement movement is reflected in two major themes within this part. The first theme is about the need for the engagement movement to think beyond individual, faculty-led projects, and the second theme is about the changing nature of scholarship. Both of these themes are critical for engaged scholars, administrators, and students to consider.

The everyday practices of higher education work against the collaborative practices that are the heart of the engaged-scholarship and service-learning movements. Faculty members are educated—and rewarded—to work in isolation or to work primarily with colleagues within their own academic disciplines. This set of received professional practices works against the fundamental sensibility of the engaged scholarship movement which, as John Saltmarsh writes in his essay, is "localized, relational, practice-based, active collaborative, experiential, and reflective." There is a serious tension between engaged scholarship projects that are inspired by individual faculty members (the default mode) and department or institutional-wide commitments to civic education (a more challenging prospect). It's an important question to consider as the engagement movement moves forward. Too often, civic engagement initiatives rest on the shoulders of individual faculty members. As a result, engagement activities are often isolated within academic units and not fully integrated into larger curricular initiatives. One of the arguments being made in these essays, then, is that students have the capacities and interests to shoulder some of the civic engagement weight of higher education institutions. As Judith Ramaley notes, "engagement has grown beyond primarily to individual experiences—how students learn and how faculty choose the questions they wish to pursue in their research—to encompass the collective work and institutional relationships that connect an institution to the broader community." She argues, further, that as engagement initiatives move from individuals to institutions, "scholarship itself begins to change."

Universities that are serious about engagement will need to critically reflect upon and promote campus-wide discussions about the nature of scholarship and knowledge generation. In short, as Saltmarsh notes, knowledge production in the engaged university will need to be defined as collaborative and constructivist as well as developed by a variety of constituents that include faculty, community partners, and students.

In this way, the essays in this part extend and even critique the foundational ideas of public scholarship and teaching that Ernest Boyer articulated in the 1990s.

As Nick Longo and I argue in our piece, including students in the movement is actually a return to the roots of the civic engagement movement in higher education. We argue that efforts to institutionalize service learning and civic engagement within curricula have marginalized student voices and taken decision-making capacities away from students. We see students as critical in the continuing evolution of the engaged scholarship and learning movements, and we call for a course correction that "reclaims the voices, experiences, and talents of our students" and brings them into the movement as active agents and "co-producers" of knowledge. For Nick and I, engaging students as co-producers in the movement will involve faculty members rethinking and reconstituting their roles (from experts on top to experts on tap), providing long-term opportunities for student engagement and helping students see the larger public purposes of their education.

Change serves as the operating trope of John Saltmarsh's essay. For Saltmarsh, "changing pedagogy" has a double meaning: on one hand it reflects the ways that service learning teaching methods transform traditional classroom practices, and on the other hand, it alludes to the way that service learning teaching methods are agents of institutional change. There is a centrifugal force at work in Saltmarsh's engaged academy—engaged pedagogies practiced in the classroom radiate outward in order to transform institutions. "Engaged pedagogy" he argues, "compels institutional change." Saltmarsh asserts that service learning is a "change" pedagogy that has the ability to transform student's understanding of the world as well as help them develop a public imagination. Some of Saltmarsh's most provocative critiques emerge when he argues that this new pedagogy of service learning actually needs a new epistemology. For Saltmarsh, this new epistemology should emerge from the theoretical frameworks of Donald Schoen and John Dewey and will, ultimately, be a rebuke of the technical rationality that has governed academic discourse and knowledge production.

Timothy Stanton and Jon Wagner argue for a vigorous infusion of civic-mindedness into graduate education. They show how civic education at the graduate level lags significantly behind undergraduate civic engagement opportunities, and they note that graduate students, many of whom were engaged in civic activities as undergraduates, "experience the transition to graduate study as a withdrawal from public and community service." Graduate students are required to check their public imaginations at the door as they enter their graduate studies. This phenomenon has a stultifying effect on the civic skills that (some) graduate students developed during their undergraduate studies, the potential for graduate students to engage their academic interests in salient community issues and problems, and, perhaps more importantly, the ability of graduate students to develop a set of civic practices and habits that will inform their professional lives. Happily, there is a movement afoot to correct this lack of civic engagement in graduate programs, and Stanton and Wagner spend a significant portion of their essay describing the (California-based) efforts to connect graduate students to engagement opportunities.

In a companion piece to Stanton and Wagner's, Doberneck, Brown, and Allen look at what happens when graduate students are actively developing an ethic of public work in their professional lives. The authors are interested in the question of how to foster future faculty members who are interested in developing research agendas around public scholarship. If, as Stanton and Wagner argue, the logic of graduate education is to instill graduate students with a set of professional skills and practices that set them up for successful careers within their disciplines, it makes sense for the engaged scholarship movement to take seriously the challenge of creating effective professional development projects for future faculty members.

Judith Ramaley examines the changing nature of the community engagement movement alongside trends related to student learning and professional development. For Ramaley, engagement offers students a set of opportunities and skills that allow them to compete in the marketplace as well as augment democratic practices within their communities. Ramaley, like other authors in this part, asks us to rethink our conceptions of students—what they are capable of and how they can contribute to their education process. She understands the role that traditional disciplines play in the university, but she also argues that engaged learning and scholarship has a pivotal role to play in students' professional development and their future roles as "scholar practitioners." Ramaley looks at the veritable chaos of the undergraduate curriculum, arguing that students move in "swirling pathways across the educational landscape, taking courses from many institutions, often enrolling in two or more in any given semester." She argues that the engagement movement has a role to play in bringing coherence to the student experience, and she calls for institutions to develop integrated learning models that "link learning to life in our curriculum, in our relationships with the community, in our approach to scholarship and in our partnerships with students."

In "Students as Change Agents in the Engagement Movement," Amanda L. Vogel, Caroline Fichtenberg, and Mindi B. Levin relate the powerful story of a group of enterprising students in the Johns Hopkins Bloomberg School of Public Health who affected real institutional change by developing a student-run organization that marshaled university resources to improve life for residents in East Baltimore. Vogel et al.'s essay is an important contribution to this volume because it demonstrates in a real and practical way how students have played key leadership roles in the engaged academy.

In case it is not clear by now, the arguments in these essays offer up radical critiques, as well as real solutions, to the problematic everyday practices of higher education.

Students Co-creating an Engaged Academy

Eric J. Fretz and Nicholas V. Longo

Much progress has been made over the past decade in higher education to activate civic and political engagement, as the other chapters in this book clearly illustrate. The concepts and practices associated with service-learning and the scholarship of engagement have moved from the margins to the mainstream in even some of our most prestigious institutions of higher education. Yet, there is also a growing sense that the civic engagement movement in higher education is at a crossroads and in need of new vision and energy for democratic progress to be further realized. This is especially the case given the rising pressures of the consumer model in higher education, along with the critiques of civic engagement from the more traditional wings of academia.

These issues and questions were on the minds of John Saltmarsh, Matthew Hartley, and leaders at the Kettering Foundation when in February 2008 they called together a group of forty-five community-engaged scholars and practitioners to address the idea that, "While the [civic engagement] movement [to date] has created some change, it has also plateaued and requires a more comprehensive effort to ensure lasting institutional commitment and capacity." [See the virtual forum for the "Democracy and Higher Education: The Future of Engagement" colloquium at http://futureofengagement. wordpress.com/

If the civic engagement movement has indeed leveled off, we believe it is partly a matter of the narrow focus on faculty development as a method of building service-learning and public scholarship on campuses. We have been part of the important efforts to develop courses and/or research agendas that include service-learning and community-engaged scholarship. These efforts have been largely led by faculty, and this shift to a broadening of the public dimensions of faculty work has been essential for civic engagement to not simply be another institutional fad or a separate "civic moment" detached from core priorities and institutional cultures of colleges and universities.

It is time, though, for a course correction that reclaims the voices, experiences, and talents of our students and that understands students to be central agents and architects of the democratic change. In this essay, we argue that theorists and practitioners of civic engagement initiatives often view students as an afterthought or as receptors of courses and research projects, rather than colleagues or co-investigators. To take this agenda to a point where civic engagement in higher education meets the lofty goals of helping to revitalize democracy, it is essential to include students more fully in the development and implementation of civic engagement initiatives.

Our argument goes a bit against the grain of how many faculty members think about student engagement. Ted Marchese levels a fairly typical complaint against university students:

> By far the most disturbing stories I've picked up on campus these past two years have been ones of student disengagement. These aren't the complaints we've heard for years about student under preparation (though that's still real). They're stories about a 1990s generation described to me as consumerist, uncivil, demanding, preoccupied with work, and as caring more for GPAs and degrees than the life of the mind. (Quoted in Gould, 2003, p. 46)

Without disavowing or glibly explaining away these concerning trends in student behavior, we wonder if perceived patterns of student disengagement are partly a manifestation of students being cut off from the production of knowledge and, consequently, treated as consumers of higher education. In other words, could student disengagement be a subtle, even insidious, manifestation of a creeping market culture within higher education? "The market," as noted by William Galston (2004), "has become more pervasive during the past generation as organizing metaphor and as daily experience, [and] the range of opportunities to develop non-market skills and dispositions has narrowed" (p. 263). We must ask, however, could concerted efforts to include students as real partners in the production of knowledge serve as an effective antidote for student disengagement and possibly even the broader consumer culture?

The idea of seeing students as co-producers is rooted in Harry Boyte's (2004) definition of public work, which is "sustained effort by a mix of people who solve public problems or create goods, material or cultural, of general benefit" (p. 5). As students become co-creators, as opposed to customers or clients, they develop "the broader set of capacities and skills required to take confident, skillful, imaginative, collective action in fluid and open environments where there is no script," what Boyte (2008a) has referred to as developing "civic agency." Involving students as co-producers in civic engagement initiatives, then, means that we will need to go beyond offering them opportunities to participate in focus groups and surveys, or even sit on boards and task forces. When we talk about building student civic agency, it means including students in the planning, developing, and implementing of civic engagement opportunities. Education, like politics, is not a spectator sport, and seeing students as co-producers is about including them in the central effort of higher education: the pursuit and dissemination of knowledge (see Saltmarsh, this volume).

In this chapter, after reviewing the landscape of student civic engagement in higher education, we offer two programmatic cases where students are invited to be civic actors and producers of knowledge. We conclude by outlining some of the critical issues facing higher education over the next decade, along with recommendations for ways that colleges and universities can best utilize the assets that students contribute to an engaged university.

Lost in the Shuffle? Students and the Engaged Campus

When it comes to thinking about and bringing service-learning and community-engaged scholarship into the academy, students have largely been left out of the equation, even though it was students who helped catalyze the most current iteration of engagement in higher education in the 1980s. This history was well documented by Liu (1996). Drawing on his experience as a student leader at Stanford before going to work as a program officer for the Corporation for National and Community Service, Liu writes:

> Our story begins with the generational stereotype of college students in the 1980s. The "me generation" label is especially familiar to those of us who came to social consciousness during this period. . . . It was against this backdrop that students of a different sort made their mark. (p. 5–6)

In talking about the dramatic founding of Campus Outreach Opportunity League (COOL) in 1984 and other student-led efforts on campuses during that time, he notes that "*students catalyzed the contemporary service movement in higher education*" (p. 6). Liu then reflects on the movement in the 1990s to begin to focus on institutionalization, a focus that has only deepened in the more than ten years since his writing.

The institutionalization of community engagement began in the early 1990s, and its success is seen in the growth of Campus Compact, an organization dedicated to promoting the civic purposes of higher education that just celebrated its twentieth year and has grown impressively to more than 1,100 member campuses served by thirty-one state offices. Moreover, there are centers of service-learning and civic engagement on more than three-quarters of colleges and universities that are members of Campus Compact, along with majors, minors, and a new career track for directors of community engagement in higher education. There is also significant support for community engagement, including federal funding through the Corporation for National and Community Service, a growing number of refereed journals dedicated to service-learning and community engagement, the impressive twenty volumes in the American Association for Higher Education's series on service-learning in the academic disciplines edited by Edward Zlotkowski (1997–2004), and countless conferences, books, and new initiatives by national and international associations in higher education.

As Liu points out, increasing interest in community engagement from an institutional perspective may have had a detrimental effect on the role that students can and have played within the effort. For example, institutions that take seriously their civic mission most often push to institutionalize service and community-based learning on a curricular level. Indeed, a great deal has been written about and support has been provided to institutionalize service-learning on a curricular level beginning with the project on Integrating Service with Academic Study (ISAS) in 1989 (Stanton, Giles, & Cruz, 1999). Likewise, many of the essays published by the *Michigan Journal of Community Service Learning,* the first and, arguably, the most influential refereed journal dedicated to advancing service-learning in higher education, demonstrate the movement's high priority of institutionalizing service-learning within the university (Buchanan, 1998; Fenzel & Peyrot, 2005; Holland, 1997, 2000; Howard, Gelmon, & Giles, 2000; Hudson & Trudeau, 1995; Kahne, Westheimer, & Rogers, 2000; Koliba, 2004; Lowery et al., 2006; Stanton, 1994; Strand, Marullo, Cutforth, Stoecker, & Donohue, 2003; Wallace, 2000; Ward, 1996).

Institutionalization is certainly essential, as service-learning initiatives and courses could never be sustained outside of curricular commitments. However, increased attempts to institutionalize community engagement also seem to have had an impact on student leadership by taking decision-making capacities away from students. Liu tellingly writes in a footnote that evaluating the progress of "student empowerment" is also an especially important criterion "as institutionalization gradually shifts control and resources away from students to people who have formal power and bureaucratic authority on campus." He concludes, "Whether or not institutionalization has dampened student leadership on individual campuses is a question that requires serious study" (p. 18).

The literature on the engaged academy reveals a powerful tip toward faculty development and a lack of thinking about how to strategically include students into the implementation and development of civic engagement initiatives. Consider, for instance, the Institutional Assessment Model of Gelmon and colleagues (Gelmon, Seifer, Kauper-Brown, & Mikkelsen, 2005), which provides a useful and detailed twelve-page rubric of characteristics of what the engaged academy looks like. The model's rubrics are largely focused on the role of faculty and chief academic officers (with brief mention of community partners). Students are mostly included as recipients of community-engaged initiatives, with the potential role of students as agents in the engaged campus largely omitted. For instance, the model includes several dimensions of engagement, including defining and visioning community engagement; determining faculty, student, and community support for engagement; and assessing institutional leadership as well as the levels of community-engaged scholarship. Each dimension includes factoring elements that are designed to help institutions measure their capacity for community engagement. Only one of the model's dimensions is concerned with students, and that dimension itself includes the fewest factoring elements (three), whereas other dimensions, mostly dealing with faculty, have as many as twelve assessment elements.

Furthermore, the language of the rubric casts students as passive agents of community engagement. Measuring students' awareness of community engagement is a matter of "informing" students of community engagement opportunities. It is assumed that this process is mostly transmitted by faculty members, and, perhaps, staff that work on community-engaged initiatives. The model lacks an assessment element that allows institutions to grade themselves on the level of student participation in the development and implementation of community-engaged projects and courses. And even the highest level of assessment for the element of measuring student involvement stops short of asking institutions to imagine their students as co-producers; instead, it measures students according to their ability to "recruit" other students to participate in existing community-based projects.

Likewise, even some of the finest monographs on the engaged university leave out students as actors and developers of community-based activities. Consider, for instance, *Creating a New Kind of University* (Percy, Zimpher, & Brukardt, 2006), and *Higher Education for the Public Good* (Kezar, Chambers, Burkhardt, & Associates, 2005), volumes that make important contributions toward questions of what an engaged institution looks like, but which, except for an essay on the role of graduate students in the civic engagement movement (Quaye, 2005), are largely silent on the role of students as assets for developing rich and sustained engagement activities.

Finally, a survey of some of the most influential literature in this area reveals a lack of thinking around the role(s) that students can play in development and implementation of community engaged efforts. For instance, consider the nature of essays published in the *Michigan Journal of Community Service Learning* as they relate to this issue of student involvement in the construction and implementation of the engaged academy. Articles that place students as front-liners in community engagement efforts only skim the surface in immersing students in the leadership roles we envision (Barber, 1994; Bullard & Maloney, 1997; Cummings, 2000; Desplaces, Steinberg, Coleman & Kenworthy-U'Renn, 2006; Koliba, 1998; Varlotta, 1996; Werner & McVaugh, 2000).

This is less of a critique of the good work of scholars who are writing about institutionalizing civic engagement in higher education than it is of the underlying structures of higher education that preclude many faculty members from even seeing their students as possible co-creators of knowledge and knowledge frameworks.

We are not advocating that higher education professionals give up on efforts to institutionalize service-learning and community-engaged scholarship. Rather, we are recommending a course correction that directly involves students in the necessary institutionalization work and has an understanding of the power and agency of student voice to accomplish community-engaged work. Strong institutional culture and practices demand that faculty members be the keepers of disciplinary knowledge and administrators establish the guidelines of the institution's everyday practice and long-term goals. Faculty members also rightly drive curriculum and university research agendas. We are not proposing to fundamentally alter this dynamic. However, when institutions make commitments to fully engaging with communities, faculty and student roles change and should naturally become more dynamic, cooperative, reciprocal, and shared than they are in more traditional faculty/student roles. Institutions fully committed to community engagement must adapt to these changing roles.

Recent Developments

Despite the lack of scholarship about including student voice and experience in the engaged academy, there is a strain in the literature that positions students as co-creators of knowledge and imagines them as actors on a public stage.

In 2001, thirty-three college students met at the Wingspread Conference Center in Racine, Wisconsin, to discuss their "civic experiences" in higher education. This conversation led to

317

the student-written *New Student Politics* (Long, 2002), which forcefully argues that student work in communities is not an alternative to politics, but rather an "alternative politics." This new politics enables students to blend the personal and the political and address public issues through community-based work. Although many of the students at Wingspread expressed frustration with politics-as-usual, they were not apathetic or disengaged. To the contrary, they point out that what many perceive as disengagement may actually be a conscious choice; they argued that, in fact, many students are deeply involved in nontraditional forms of engagement. These students saw their "service politics" as the bridge between community service and conventional politics, combining public power with community and relationships. This new politics connects individual acts of service to a broader framework of systemic social change. The students at Wingspread further noted that they see democracy as richly participatory; that negotiating differences is a key element of politics; that their service in communities was done in the context of systemic change; and that higher education needs to do more to promote civic education.

A look at the current generation of college students and their understanding and experiences with civic engagement is also helpful for making the case that students should be partners in the engaged academy (Longo & Meyer, 2006). As Richard Battistoni (2003) has observed:

> What stands out to me is that our students see the whole question of civic engagement, and its connection to service, quite differently from those of us who philosophize about the connections. On many of our campuses students who are engaged in significant community-based work are deepening their learning about the issues that matter to them. They are getting to know their neighbors, to work with people across differences of race, gender, class, religion, and interest. And they are challenging faculty to do more than pay lip service to civic engagement, by bringing their practices in the classroom and/or community into sync with democratic values. I would call this significant "civic engagement" learning, and yet, most studies fail to unearth this aspect of student learning and community service.

A number of studies have illustrated a rather dramatic shift in the way college students understand civic and political engagement. A study done by CIRCLE, which was commissioned by the Kettering Foundation, found a difference in civic attitudes and practices among the current generation of college students—an age cohort known as the Millennials (those born after 1982). Based on focus groups with more than four hundred college students on a dozen college campuses, *Millennials Talk Politics* (Kiesa et al., 2007) discovered that today's college students (1) are more engaged than GenXers; (2) are involved locally but are ambivalent about formal politics; (3) dislike spin and are looking for authentic opportunities to discuss public issues; and (4) are getting uneven opportunities for civic engagement depending on the college or university they attend. The report concludes that although students are not fully engaged with the political system or fully informed on issues, they are "aware of the importance of policy and politics, conscious that it is desirable to be informed and engaged, and fairly optimistic about the power of collective action" (p. 10). At least partially, the report contends, these changes can be attributed to the increase in the institutional infrastructure for engagement, beginning in the 1990s. The authors conclude,

"It is clear that today's college students, compared to students from Generation X, have more structured opportunities to engage in community service and are presented with more messages about the importance of civic participation" (p. 11).

Likewise, *Educating for Democracy* (Colby, Beaumont, Ehrlich, & Corngold, 2007) details findings from the Carnegie Foundation Political Engagement Project (PEP) examination of twenty-one college and university courses and co-curricular programs that address preparation for democratic participation. The study found that (1) participation in PEP courses results in "greater political understanding, skills, motivation and expectations for future political action" (p. 6); (2) contrary to claims that education for political development will indoctrinate students, increased political learning does not change student party identification or political ideology; and (3) students with little initial interest in political issues made especially substantial learning gains. The authors contend that "high-quality education for political development increases students' political understanding, skill, motivation and involvement while contributing to many aspects of general academic learning" (p. 5).

Some of the best programmatic, research, and course-related models for including students as "colleagues" in the engaged academy are presented in *Students as Colleagues* (Zlotkowski, Longo, & Williams, 2006), an edited collection that includes nineteen chapters (most of which are co-authored by students) and numerous vignettes that document examples of student collaboration with faculty, staff, and community partners. The book offers promising models for developing students with an interest in service and civic engagement to campus through scholarship programs at campuses such as DePaul, Bentley, and IUPUI. Like students with sports scholarships, these civic-minded students are asked to play a variety of leadership roles on campus in support of community engagement. Another growing practice that is highlighted is the way students are given responsibilities as staff members in service-learning centers, and community liaisons to community partners in service-learning courses. Chapters from students and staff from the University of Pennsylvania and Duke University reveal the possibilities of student-generated community-based research, whereas an essay on North Carolina State focuses on student-faculty co-creation in the development of a reflective leadership program. Finally, a chapter from University of Massachusetts–Amherst describes "the professorless classroom," part of an innovative program where students teach an alternative spring break course with training and mentoring from a distinguished faculty member.

In one powerful example of a university being aware of these pressures, Colgate University organized a multiyear campaign led by the dean of students, Adam Weinberg, to rebuild campus life around the principles of civic learning, including using residence halls as "sites for democracy" (Weinberg, 2005, 2008). Colgate redefined the role of residence advisers from rule enforcers to coaches who catalyze teams of students. Student leaders in the residence halls are trained as community organizers, as they move from a programming model to a mentorship model. In trying to move from a culture of student entitlement to a culture of student responsibility, they also created community councils in each residential unit that function as neighborhood associations. "This required a lot of faith in our students, a keen and specific sense for what we are trying to accomplish, and an eternal vigilance to educate for democracy across the campus," Weinberg concludes (2005, p. 44).

Like Weinberg's work at Colgate, our work with students at Miami University in Ohio and the University of Denver also provides insights into the challenges and possibilities for infusing student voice into the engaged academy.

Acting Locally at Miami University

At Miami University, the Wilks Institute sponsors a series of innovative civic engagement programs, including courses focused on public engagement and community learning, a high school leadership program, international leadership courses, engaged scholarship, and a series of speakers and symposiums promoting leadership for the public good. Founded through a $5 million gift from philanthropist and alumnus Harry T. Wilks, the institute was launched in 2003 with a sense of urgency about the lack of leadership in our democracy.

In an effort to infuse civic engagement into the curriculum, the Wilks Institute offers three years of funding called a "think tank" through a proposal process to one academic department/program to develop a series of public engagement courses. Some of the lessons from the first think tank in American Studies have been instructive.

Acting Locally: Civic Learning and Civic Leadership in Southwestern Ohio was the first intensive experiment with community engagement and student/faculty partnerships. Conceived in the fall of 2003 by Peggy Shaffer, director of the American Studies program, along with faculty associated with American Studies, the curriculum explores the ways in which local communities of different sorts are created, challenged, transformed, and sustained in a world where global and local forces intersect in complex ways. The first cohort of students was enrolled in the two-year think tank curriculum in the fall of 2006 (see Longo & Shaffer, 2009).

Acting Locally involves students (Wilks Scholars) taking one course per semester for two years with an interdisciplinary group of faculty focusing on three locales in southwest Ohio—the Over-the-Rhine Neighborhood, the city of Hamilton, and rural Butler County—to explore how globalization has affected a decaying urban center, an expanding postindustrial metropolitan city, and a rural agricultural community.

The first group of Wilks Scholars, who completed the sequence in the spring of 2008, developed projects that emerged from the students and faculty collaborations in the community. Students partnered with Latino immigrants in Hamilton to create a series of ongoing Spanish-English language and cultural exchanges in local restaurants, churches, and community organizations using a nonprofessional, democratic approach that centers on one-on-one learning partnerships. Students also worked with Latino business owners to host a series of community events, including a neighborhood clean-up and festival, to celebrate and make visible the contribution that immigrants make to this changing industrial city. Students worked with local farmers to create and sustain a local food network in rural Butler County, including hosting a local-foods dinner to build support for local farmers and the creation of a local food guide to publicize local food options, farmer stories, and recipes.

The role of student voice in the courses developed over time. As one Wilks Scholar explains, "This process has made me see that as students we have so much more power and credibility than I ever thought possible." To institutionalize the role of student leadership, the next group of Wilks Scholars, which began in the fall of 2008, are being mentored by four Community Assistants, seniors at Miami who are former Wilks Scholars. These students are helping to introduce the new Wilks Scholars to community partners and issues by setting up one-on-one interviews, meetings, and service projects with key community partners in southwest Ohio.

This kind of engaged learning can lead to the development of civic agency described earlier. As one Wilks Scholar explains, "I realize I am an asset. Though I am younger and have little/no money, my presence still matters and I can still influence what is happening in my communities. My voice is not softer than others and I am at an institute where I can have the backing of my peers and as a member of such a large group I have the ability to be noticed and make changes."

Public Achievement at the University of Denver

The Center for Community Engagement and Service-Learning and its academic partners at the University of Denver have a long-standing tradition of including students in the development and implementation of its programs and scholarly production, including student involvement in an international youth civic engagement program called Public Achievement (PA).

The PA program at the Center for Community Engagement and Service-Learning provides curricular and co-curricular opportunities for DU students to act as co-creators in civic engagement initiatives with local youth. Public Achievement, an initiative founded by the Center for Democracy and Citizenship at the University of Minnesota, focuses on building civic agency among young people by enabling high school and college students to collaborate on public work projects that produce tangible community results.

In PA, diverse teams of youth and college students discuss their individual interests and passions, the community's needs and assets, and strategies for community change initiatives. Youth participate in an "issues convention," a public forum where all can express their concern for a particular issue and persuade others to join them in their efforts. Teams of six to eight participants are created around issues that resonate most, and each is assigned a "coach"—in this case, a student from the University of Denver. The teams, with support from their coaches, research issues and develop action projects. Coaches also work with their teams to reflect throughout, and at the same time, are reflecting on their own civic identities as they develop a set of civic skills through the coaching process.

Public Achievement teams have organized school and community dialogues about pressing public issues and have organized students and community members to pay attention and then do something about critical community matters. Past projects have addressed a range of issues from graffiti and gangs, to racism and immigration, to environmental issues such as global warming and pollution in local rivers and streams.

Throughout the process, students develop civic skills and learn to think and act in a way that places them at the center of community change efforts. For instance, they learn how to analyze an issue, write persuasive letters, speak in public settings, understand who makes policy decisions, and develop public relationships with those people. They use their collective imaginations to practice active listening, build consensus, define community problems, and implement actions to solve the problems. One former PA coach noted the way that PA acknowledged her as a co-producer by comparing her experience with PA to previous experiences tutoring in the community:

> The only engagement in schools I knew of before this program was things like tutoring and after school programs. Now I see the students as contributing members to the way the education system works and I see school engagement as more of a collaborative program rather than a bunch of outside "professionals" coming in and "fixing" the school.

PA's model of viewing students as co-producers also forces students to question more traditional ways of teaching and learning. "I feel like in the traditional classroom children are taught at, whereas in programs like PA, children help create the curriculum, and it is so much more useful to their lives," explains one University of Denver student. "I love the feeling of empowering children, and someday I would love to find a way to incorporate programs like this into everyday schooling."

Critical Issues over the Next Decade

It seems clear that students are interested in playing more active roles in community community-engagement initiatives, and we believe that they have the capacities to do so as well, but they need more support and opportunities from faculty members. In effect, our work with students in community-engaged projects leads us to believe that students are encouraging faculty members to reconstitute their roles; want opportunities for longer-term engagement; and are hoping that their learning has a larger purpose. No small task for faculty members who have, by and large, not been trained to think and act this way, but one that we take seriously in this final section where we outline critical issues as we involve students in the engaged academy over the next decade.

Reconstituting Faculty Roles

Our first critical issue—about reconstituting faculty roles—may seem unlikely for an essay about students in the engaged academy. But student collaboration is integrally linked to the practice of faculty. We are framing our first critical issue around faculty roles because we believe that faculty members and administrators who are interested in engaging students as co-producers in civic engagement initiatives will need to find new models for engaging students in their community-based teaching and research practices and to essentially rethink their roles as scholars. Faculty members will need to model the engagement they'd like to see from their students and become more engaged themselves in community-based work, and in the process act more as "coaches" or facilitators of civic learning for students as they get more involved in co-teaching and joint research efforts. This argument is rooted in the new professional practices associated with the scholarship of engagement as developed by Ernest Boyer (1990, 1997), William Sullivan's emphasis on "civic professionalism" (1995), Harry Boyte's (2004, 2008a, 2008b) notion of "public work," and Dzur's (2007) idea of "democratic professionalism."

As part of his promotion of the scholarship of engagement, Boyer (1997) called for campuses to be viewed by *both* students and professors "not as isolated islands, but as staging grounds for action" (p. 92). Boyer's work has led to a national conversation on the scholarship of engagement, including a new National Review Board on the Scholarship of Engagement to promote and review scholarly work in this area, along with a series of conversations and research led by Eugene Rice, Kerry Ann O'Meara, and John Saltmarsh.

The concept of "civic professionalism," as defined by Sullivan (1995), will also continue to be important for the scholarship of engagement as it captures the understanding that there should not be a separation between technical expertise and civic action.

Likewise, Harry Boyte (2008b) argues that for our institutions of higher education to become "agents and architects" of democracy requires a radical shift in the way scholars see themselves and their work. Scholars cannot simply be dispassionate researchers, critics, service providers, or educators of future leaders; rather, scholars must also be "engaged public figures" who "stimulate conversations to expand the sense of the possible, and to activate broader civic and political energies" (p. 79). This must also include the energies and talents of their students as we include them as partners in this effort. Thus, when faculty are able to catalyze students, they often can help develop what Evans and Boyte termed "free spaces" (Evans & Boyte, 1986), "places in which powerless people have a measure of autonomy for self-organization and engagement with alternative ideas" (Boyte, 2004, p. 61).

More recently, in *Democratic Professionalism*, Dzur (2007) locates a "democratic significance" within the professions, which he views as places where public life and public culture can be nurtured and facilitated. Specifically, he examines recent innovations in the fields of public journalism, restorative justice, and bioethics as a way to encourage other "helping" professions to develop a culture of professional practice that shares tasks and responsibilities with laypeople in order to bring laypeople into problem-solving relationships.

Dzur describes democratic professionals as facilitators of public knowledge and public work. They seek out common interests that link professional inquiry and local knowledge, and they work to develop systems of communication and knowledge production that involve laypeople in the solution of public problems. Democratic professionals "refuse to dominate discussion" and are capable of "stepping back and allowing laypeople the chance to take up responsibilities" (Dzur, 2007, p. 41). Most importantly, though, democratic professionals accomplish public work with ordinary citizens and engage in the co-creative process of imaginative public problem solving into everyday institutional life.

Despite the significant efforts to institutionalize service-learning and community engaged scholarship, very little ground has been gained in the area of updating promotion and tenure guidelines to reward faculty members who engage in this work. Consequently, even though a good deal has already been written about this issue, there remains a need to update tenure and promotion guidelines to reflect faculty member's growing interest in community-based work (Bringle, Hatcher & Clayton, 2006; Shomberg, 2006; Ward, 2005). One of the many promising inroads in this area is the promotion and tenure task force organized by Imaging America. In *Scholarship in Public* (Ellison & Eatman, 2008), Imagining America's Tenure Team Initiative developed a series of recommendations for updating tenure and promotion guidelines that range from further defining public scholarly and creative work to advocating for policy changes on the departmental level.

Creating Opportunities and Incentives for Longer-Term Engagement

As a second critical issue, we think it is essential to create incentives for student voice and broader student civic engagement on campus. This is especially relevant given the rising cost of higher education and the mounting debt that comes with unprecedented tuition increases.

According to the National Center for Education Statistics, about two-thirds of college students graduate with educational loans, with the average student graduating from a four-year public institution $18,000 in debt. One in four graduates $25,000 in debt or higher. By contrast, in 1993, less than one-half of four-year graduates had student loans with an average of less than half of the debt level of current graduates.

This has an impact on the way students view higher education and their ability to participate in civic engagement. Undoubtedly, the cost of higher education contributes to the consumer mindset and the increasing focus on workforce preparation. Students today, for example, are almost twice as likely to view the goal of higher education as "becoming well off financially" (almost 80 percent) as opposed to "developing a meaningful philosophy of life" (just over 40 percent)—numbers that have reversed since the 1960s, according to the Higher Education Research Institute (HERI).

At the same time, however, there have been increases in youth participation in public life, most especially through volunteering in communities (Longo & Meyer, 2006). And colleges and universities offer implicit and explicit incentives to be involved in community service—not least of which is the criteria for admissions. A recent study from CIRCLE illustrated the power of these incentives in finding that "resume padding" is a major reason that young people volunteer. One of the authors of the study, Lew Friedland, writes, "Much of the reported volunteerism was shaped by the perception that voluntary and civic activity is necessary to get into any college; and the better the college (or, more precisely, the higher the perception of the college in the status system) the more volunteerism students believed was necessary" (Friedland & Morimoto, 2005).

Those of us in the civic engagement movement need to do a better job of addressing the financial pressures many of our students face by building in incentives for authentic student leadership in every aspect of engagement work (Gibson, 2004). This can begin with admissions and scholarship funds. Campuses serious about civic engagement need to develop the kinds of service scholarship programs found at Bentley, DePaul, IUPUI (Zlotkowski et al., 2006), and other schools, including the University of Denver and Providence College, which identify and reward students involved in their communities during high school and then ask them to make a commitment to be part of formal civic leadership programs on campus. Not unlike sports scholarships, programs like these offer incentives for (in this case, civic) participation in high school, and also create recognized opportunities for peer leadership on campus.

Likewise, we need more opportunities for students to get credit, funding, and pay for providing leadership in service-learning courses on campus, such as acting as teaching assistants leading reflection in the classroom or community assistants serving as liaisons for their peers in the community.

We should also rethink undergraduate research funding and expectations. Specifically, this entails asking that the substantial research funding colleges and universities provide to undergraduate students *always* include a public dimension.

Finally, as we noted earlier, with the level of student debt that seems likely to continue to rise over the next decade, we need to provide more postgraduate opportunities that enable students to continue to act as social entrepreneurs, while getting debt relief and/or money for graduate school in the process.

Making Learning Transformational as Part of a Larger Public Purpose

As a final critical issue, we offer the tension between *tactical* and *transformational* learning in the context of student leadership in the engaged academy. Much of the growth in engaged scholarship, and more specifically, service-learning, has been focused on convincing faculty that community engagement is good pedagogy. There are a series of toolkits and a vast array of sample syllabi that help faculty use community-based experiences as another course "text" (see, for example, Heffernan, 2001), which helps them view service as another way for students to achieve predetermined learning outcomes.

Although service as part of a course may add to the faculty workload, having students engage in real-world experience is a good way to learn about almost any topic. And if it has some impact on the community or students' future lives, that's an added benefit. Given the preponderance of this approach, service-learning courses have tended to be measured according to student acquisition of a set of skills, dispositions, values, and knowledge. We view this approach as essentially tactical—it makes community-based learning a tool to transmit knowledge as part of the existing framework for higher education.

The tactical success in this area is a chief reason why service-learning has grown so rapidly over the past decade. Service-learning has become an effective pedagogical tool for a host of educational outcomes—from disciplinary knowledge to, more recently, civic development. However, we must also constantly challenge the notion that community engagement is simply a good way to acquire knowledge. When students are given serious roles in the construction of an engaged campus, we believe that the learning will have to have a larger purpose: it will also need to bring about transformation.

This issue goes to the very core of the future of higher education: we can choose to reinforce the dominant way of knowing in higher education that tends to ignore the capacities and experiences of the very people we most want to engage—in this case, our students (but this also applies to community partners); or we can take student empowerment seriously as part of the larger civic mission of higher education. When this happens, our goal becomes transforming students, communities, institutions, and ideas.

Student transformation, of course, is the most direct potential consequence of making students central actors in the engaged academy. When we truly engage our students in meaningful learning partnerships and knowledge is "mutually constructed via the sharing of experience and authority" (Baxter Magolda & King, 2004, p. xix), there is the possibility for learning to become transformational. We found this in focus groups and interviews with students at the University of Denver and Miami University in which students spoke eloquently about how community learning projects gave them opportunities to work with people who are different from themselves, people with whom they would not ordinarily develop a relationship. Moreover, students who came from privileged backgrounds also talked a great deal about the transformative quality of their community learning experiences, especially when it challenges their identities and asks them to expand the way they think about their education. One Miami student involved in the two-year Wilks program explained: "Before, I thought my time as a Miami student was merely an opportunity to gather information in classes and then disengage when I stepped out of the classroom. I now view my time as a student as an opportunity to learn from both my classes and from the community, as a time to build new relationships, and as a chance to understand my place as a member of a community."

It's worth noting, too, that these transformations generally take place in relationship with skillful faculty "coaches" who understand how to mentor students in these areas, an important connection with our first critical issue on reconstituting faculty roles.

At the same time, when students are part of reciprocal and ongoing partnerships with the community, this also allows for community and even institutional transformation. A transformational model is at the center of the best campus-community partnerships, and seen, for example, in projects like the Jane Addams School for Democracy. Jane Addams School partners college students from campuses across the Twin Cities in Minnesota with new immigrants from the West Side of St. Paul in reciprocal learning exchanges. The mantra of these partnerships is "everyone's a teacher, everyone's a learner" (Kari & Skelton, 2007). "People who work in open-ended spaces like Jane Addams School, find wider latitude for experimentation and co-creation," explains Nan Kari, one of the founders of the School. "When prescribed roles and boundaries are suspended, the spaces framed by public work philosophy can be transformative" (p. 35).

Over the next decade, student learning should be focused on larger public purposes, rather than instrumental advances. If we are able to create more open-ended spaces between campuses and communities where students and community members are involved in the co-creation of knowledge, there are sure to be dramatic shifts in the very way we understand the concepts of practices of ideas such as "democracy," "politics," "service," "public," and "leadership." John Dewey (1916/1993) famously stated that "democracy must be reborn in every generation" (p. 122), and this can occur rather naturally if we give the next generation opportunities to struggle with and then rewrite its very meaning.

This can happen if we create multiple opportunities for various forms of dialogue and deliberation, especially in connection with service and community engagement. In this process, space must also be created for ongoing reflection and evaluation, along with real, public products.

The evidence seems to illustrate that developing programs that invite long-term relationships are more likely to lead to the kind of transformation we are hoping to accomplish. Our priority should be to create long-term developmental programs, with both curricular and co-curricular components, that allow students to develop deep relationships and establish more integrated public work projects. These types of approaches to the engaged academy help civic engagement and service-learning become about transforming, rather than simply accommodating higher education.

If we involve students as colleagues in the work of higher education, the critical issues of reconstituting faculty roles, creating incentives for long-term engagement, and making learning transformative as part of a larger public purpose, along with a multitude of others, are sure to emerge in ways we cannot imagine over the next decade. But that is exactly the point. When we unleash the powers, voices, and energies of students, they will be sure to critically challenge our assumptions and our work. An engaged academy—with engaged students—will become a more dynamic and messy place. But at the same time, this opens up the possibility for co-creating lively, democratic spaces on campuses, in communities, and at the same time, a more vibrant democracy.

References

Barber, B. (1994). A proposal for mandatory citizen education and community service. *Michigan Journal of Community Service-Learning, 1*(1), 86–93.

Battistoni, R. (2003). Interviewed by Barbara Roswell. From service-learning to service politics. *Reflections, 3,* 1–6.

Baxter Magolda, M., & King, P. (Eds.). (2004). *Learning partnerships: Theory and models of practice to educate for self-authorship.* Sterling, VA: Stylus.

Boyer, E. (1990). *Scholarship reconsidered: Priorities of the professoriate.* New York: The Carnegie Foundation for the Advancement of Teaching.

Boyer, E. (1997). *Selected speeches 1979–1995.* Princeton, NJ: The Carnegie Foundation for the Advancement of Teaching.

Boyte, H. (2004). *Everyday politics: Reconnecting citizens and public life.* Philadelphia: University of Pennsylvania Press.

Boyte, H. (2008a). Against the current: Developing the civic agency of students. *Change, 40,* No. 3.

Boyte, H. (2008b). Public work: Civic populism versus technocracy in higher education. In D. W. Brown and D. Witte (Eds.), *Agent of democracy.* Dayton, OH: Kettering Foundation Press.

Bringle, R. G., Hatcher, J. A., & Clayton, P. H. (2006). The scholarship of civic engagement: Defining, documenting, and evaluating faculty work. *To Improve the Academy, 25,* 257–279.

Buchanan, R. (1998). Integrating service-learning into the mainstream: A case study. *Michigan Journal of Community Service Learning, 5,* 114–119.

Bullard, J., & Maloney, J. (1997). Curious minds after-school program: A creative solution to a community need. *Michigan Journal of Community Service Learning, 4,* 116–121.

Colby, A., Beaumont, E., Ehrlich, T., & Corngold, J. (2007). *Educating for democracy: Preparing undergraduates for responsible political engagement.* Stanford, CA: Carnegie Foundation for the Advancement of Teaching.

Cummings, K. (2000). John Dewey and the rebuilding of urban community: Engaging undergraduates as neighborhood organizers. *Michigan Journal of Community Service Learning, 7,* 97–109.

Desplaces, D., Steinberg, M., Coleman, S., & Kenworth-U'Renn, A. (2006). A human capital model: Service-learning in the micro business incubator program. *Michigan Journal of Community Service Learning, 13*(1), 66–80.

Dewey, J. (1916/1993). The need of an industrial education in an industrial democracy. In *The political writings*. Cambridge, MA: Hackett.

Dzur, A. (2007). *Democratic professionalism: Citizen participation and the reconstruction of professional ethics, identity, and practice*. University Park: Pennsylvania University Press.

Ellison, J., & Eatman, T. (2008). *Scholarship in public: Knowledge creation and tenure policy in the engaged university*. Imagining America: Artists and Scholars in Public Life Tenure Team Initiative on Public Scholarship. Available at www.imaginingamerica.org/TTI/TTI_FINAL.pdf.

Evans, S., & Boyte, H. (1986). *Free spaces. The sources of democratic change in America*. Chicago: University of Chicago Press.

Fenzel, L. M., & Peyrot, M. (2005). Relationship of college service-learning and community service participation with subsequent service-related attitudes and behavior of alumni. *Michigan Journal of Community Service Learning, 12*, 23–31.

Friedland, L., & Morimoto, S. (2005). *The changing lifeworld of young people: Risk, resume padding, and civic engagement*. Circle Working Paper 40. College Park, MD: CIRCLE.

Galston, W. (2004). Civic education and political participation. *PS: Political Science & Politics, 37*, 263–266.

Gelmon, S., Seifer, S., Kauper-Brown, J., & Mikkelsen, M. (2005). *Building capacity for community engagement: Institutional self-assessment*. Seattle, WA: Community-Campus Partnerships for Health

Gibson, C. (2004). Thinking outside the (ballot) box: A broader engagement for America's civic organizations. *National Civic Review, 93*, 20–30.

Gould, E. (2003). *The university in a corporate culture*. New Haven, CT: Yale University Press.

Heffernan, K. (2001). *Fundamentals of service-learning course construction*. Providence, RI: Campus Compact.

Holland, B. (1997). Analyzing institutional commitment to service: A model of key organizational factors. *Michigan Journal of Community Service Learning, 4*, 30–41.

Holland, B. (2000). Institutional impacts and organizational issues related to service-learning. *Michigan Journal of Community Service Learning, 7*(1), 52–60.

Howard, J., Gelmon, S., & Giles, D. (2000). From yesterday to tomorrow: Strategic directions for service-learning research. *Michigan Journal of Community Service Learning, 7*(1), 5–10.

Hudson, W., & Trudeau, R. (1995). An essay on the institutionalization of service-learning: The genesis of the Feinstein Institute for Public Service. *Michigan Journal of Community Service Learning, 2*, 150–158.

Kahne, J., Westheimer, J., & Rogers, B. (2000). Service-learning and citizenship: directions for research. *Michigan Journal of Community Service Learning, 7*(1), 42–51.

Kari, N., & Skelton, N. (2007). *Voices of hope: The Story of the Jane Addams School for Democracy*. Dayton, OH: Kettering Foundation Press.

Kezar, A., Chambers, T., Burkhardt, J., & Associates. (2005). *Higher education for the public good: Emerging voices from a national movement*. Jossey-Bass, 2005.

Kiesa, A., Orlowski, A. P., Levine, P., Both, D., Kirby, E. H., Lopez, M. H., et al. (2007). *Millennials talk politics*. College Park, MD: CIRCLE.

Koliba, C. (1998). Lessons in citizen forums and democratic decision-making: A service-learning case study. *Michigan Journal of Community Service Learning, 5*, 75–85.

Liu, G. (1996). Origins, evolution, and progress: Reflections on the community service movement in higher education 1985–1995. In *Community service in higher education: A decade of development.* Providence, RI: Providence College.

Long, S. (2002.). *The new student politics: The wingspread statement on student civic engagement.* Providence, RI: Campus Compact.

Longo, N., & Meyer, R. (2006). College students and politics: A literature review. Circle Working Paper 46. College Park, MD: CIRCLE.

Longo, N., & Shaffer, M. (2009). Leadership education and the revitalization of public life. In B. Jacoby (Ed.), *Civic engagement in higher education* (pp. 154–173). San Francisco: Jossey-Bass.

Lowery, D., May, D. L., Duchan, K. A., Coulter-Kern, R., De'Bryant, Morris, P. V., et al. (2006). A logic model of service-learning: Tensions and issues for further consideration. *Michigan Journal of Community Service Learning, 12*(2), 47–60.

Percy, S., Zimpher, N., & Brukardt, M. (2006). *Creating a new kind of university: Institutionalizing community-university engagement.* Bolton, MA: Anker.

Quaye, S. (2005). Let us speak: Including students' voices in the public good of higher education. In A. Kezar, T. Chambers, J. Burkhardt, & Associates (Eds.), *Higher education for public good: Emerging voices from a national movement* (pp. 293–307). San Francisco: Jossey-Bass.

Shomberg, S. (2006). Hope tempered by reality: Integrating public engagement into promotion and tenure decisions. *Metropolitan Universities: An International Forum, 17*(3).

Stanton, T. (1994). The experience of faculty participants in an instructional development seminar on service-learning. *Michigan Journal of Community Service Learning, 1*(1), 7–20.

Stanton, T., Giles, D., & Cruz, H. (1999). *Service-learning: A movement's pioneers reflect on its origins, practice, and future.* San Francisco: Jossey-Bass.

Strand, K., Marullo, S., Cutforth, N., Stoecker, R., & Donohue, P. (2003). Principles of best practice for community-based research. *Michigan Journal of Community Service Learning, 9*(3), 5–15.

Sullivan, W. (1995). *Work and integrity: The crisis and promise of professionalism in America.* New York: Harper Collins.

Varlotta, L. (1996). Service-learning: A catalyst for constructing democratic progressive communities. *Michigan Journal of Community Service Learning, 3*, 22–30.

Wallace, J. (2000). The problem of time: Enabling students to make long-term commitments to community-based learning. *Michigan Journal of Community Service Learning, 7*, 133–141.

Ward, K. (1996). Service-learning and student volunteerism: Reflections on institutional commitment. *Michigan Journal of Community Service Learning, 3*, 55–65.

Ward, K. (2005). Rethinking faculty roles and rewards for the public good. In A. Kezar, T. Chambers, J. Burkhardt, & Associates (Eds.), *Higher education for public good: Emerging voices from a national movement* (pp. 217–234). San Francisco: Jossey-Bass.

Weinberg, A. (2005). Residential education for democracy. In *Learning for democracy,* Vol. 1, No. 2.

Weinberg, A. (2008). Public work at Colgate: An interview. In D. W. Brown & D. Witte (Eds.), *Agent of Democracy: Higher Education and HEX Journey* (pp. 102–120). Dayton, OH: Kettering Foundation.

Werner, C., & McVaugh, N. (2000). Service-learning "rules" that encourage or discourage long term service: Implications for practice and research. *Michigan Journal of Community Service Learning, 7*, 117–125.

Zlotkowski, E., Longo, N., & Williams, J. (Eds.). (2006). *Students as colleagues: Expanding the circle of service-learning leadership.* Providence, RI: Campus Compact.

Changing Pedagogies

John Saltmarsh

When efforts emerge in higher education to change pedagogical practice, it is likely a sign that something is fundamentally wrong. In the current period of reform, which began in the late 1970s, efforts to change pedagogy have been fueled by two critical failures in higher education. One is a failure of teaching and learning in undergraduate education; the other a failure of higher education to fulfill its civic mission. Changes in pedagogy are reflected in experimentation with active and collaborative forms of teaching and learning tied to community-based public problem solving. New community-based, engaged pedagogies—most prominently, service-learning—connect structured student activities in communities with academic study, de-center the teacher as the singular authority of knowledge, incorporate a reflective teaching methodology, and shift the model of education from "banking" to "dialogue," to use Freire's distinction (1970/1994). To assert their civic relevance, higher education institutions strive to revive their founding missions, which in some dimension express the aim of serving American democracy by educating students for productive citizenship. Campuses encourage pedagogies of engagement to prepare students with the knowledge, skills, and values needed for democratic citizenship.

"Changing pedagogies," however, has a double meaning, because community-engaged pedagogies are also associated with efforts to transform higher education institutions. Changes in teaching and learning are not confined to alterations in classroom dynamics; they have wider institutional implications. They involve reconsideration of fundamental epistemological assumptions; they are aligned with disciplinary border-crossing in the curriculum; they are integrated seamlessly into faculty roles along with engaged research and engaged service; and they thrive in an institutional culture that changes in ways that support all these dimensions of engagement. Engaged pedagogy compels institutional

331

change, and it is necessary to account for the institutional implications of changes in teaching and learning. Deep, pervasive institutional changes align across the institution in the emergence of an engaged campus. Indeed, the engaged campus is a relatively recent phenomenon in higher education that emerged, ironically, during the same period when higher education lost its image as a social institution fostering the public good and instead became widely perceived as a market-driven institution existing for the private economic benefit of upwardly mobile individuals—what William Sullivan calls "the default program of instrumental individualism" (2000, p. 21).

For those of us in higher education who are interested in the multiple meanings of changed pedagogies, we are often involved in subversive activity. In changing teaching and learning we seek to teach the content knowledge of our disciplines more effectively, but we also seek to cross disciplinary boundaries. We seek to change our classrooms, but we also seek to change institutional structures and cultures that delegitimize new forms of knowledge creation and different ways of knowing. We view educational practice not as a commercialized, credentialized, commodified end in itself but as a means to the larger end of active participation in a diverse democratic society. Changing pedagogy changes everything.

This chapter explores many of the dimensions of changing pedagogy by first describing the inner workings of changed teaching and learning through engaged pedagogy. It then conceptualizes the place of changed pedagogical practice within a larger framework of change and explores the deeper implications of changed pedagogies for students and community partners. Finally, it examines the kind of institutional change necessary for this pedagogy to thrive in higher education.

Engaged Pedagogy

Adopting and implementing changed pedagogy begins with the critical teaching and learning challenges facing higher education. One of these challenges is how to improve the quality of undergraduate education. The focus here is on developing and assessing effective educational practices that engage students in the learning process to develop higher-order thinking skills and improve learning outcomes. The second challenge relates to changing student demographics as increasing numbers of traditionally underrepresented students pursue higher education. The focus here is on developing educational practices that recognize different cognitive preferences and learning styles while educating *all* students effectively.

Addressing these challenges begins with bringing the past twenty years' worth of research in the cognitive sciences to bear on improving teaching and learning, and then incorporating that research into our thinking about pedagogy. Peter Ewell summarizes what the research reveals about "what we know about learning" (1997, pp. 3–4):

1. The Learner is not a "receptacle" of knowledge, but rather creates his or her learning actively and uniquely

2. Learning is about making meaning for each individual learner by establishing and reworking patterns, relationships, and connections

3. Every student learns all the time, both with us and despite us
4. Direct experience decisively shapes individual understanding [cf. "situated learning"]
5. Learning occurs best in the context of a compelling "presenting problem" [cf. Freire]
6. Beyond stimulation, learning requires reflection
7. Learning occurs best in a cultural context that provides both enjoyable interaction and substantial personal support

Based on research findings, Ewell suggests that the cognitive sciences provide six foci for designing teaching and learning environments that promote learning:

1. Approaches that emphasize application and experience
2. Approaches in which faculty constructively model the learning process
3. Approaches that emphasize linking established concepts to new situations
4. Approaches that emphasize interpersonal collaboration
5. Approaches that emphasize rich and frequent feedback on performance
6. Curricula that consistently develop a limited set of clearly identified, cross-disciplinary skills that are publicly held to be important

These foci form the basis for designing engaged pedagogies that address the teaching and learning challenges facing higher education. As Barr and Tagg explain in their seminal essay "From Teaching to Learning," the "purpose is not to transfer knowledge but to create environments and experiences that bring students to discover and construct knowledge for themselves, to make students members of communities of learners that make discoveries and solve problems" (1995, p. 15). Further, they point out that in a shift to more engaged teaching and learning, "the goal for underrepresented students (and *all* students) becomes not simply access but success. By 'success' we mean the achievement of overall educational objectives . . . [aiming] for ever-higher graduation rates while maintaining or even increasing learning standards" (p. 15). The research on learning indicates that although the student in the twenty-first century must learn what John Abbott has called "a whole series of new competencies," there is doubt that "such abilities can be taught solely in the classroom, or be developed solely by teachers." Abbott notes that "higher order thinking and problem solving skills grow out of direct experience, not simply teaching; they require more than a classroom activity. They develop through active involvement and real life experiences in workplaces and the community" (Marchese, 1996).

In her profoundly reflective essay on "reclaiming a pedagogy of integrity," Patricia Owen-Smith, a professor of psychology and women's studies, recalls the transformation she experienced when she confronted the challenges of improving teaching and learning in her courses. She explains that

> when I began teaching in 1986, I reinvented the model I was educated with. It was, after all, the only one I knew. But at some level I recognized that this model worked for me neither as a learner nor a teacher. My students were performing well on exams, but it was increasingly clear to me that they did not have the conceptual clarity or the ability to "uncover" material that would serve them well as learners.

She made the decision that something would have to change. Thus, she reexamined both what she knew about teaching and what she knew about her students:

> One aspect of the change in my attitude was that I looked at my students and myself differently, and realized that I had to leave the lectern, figuratively and literally. I abandoned essentialist assumptions about pedagogy—that some universal template of the teaching transaction existed —and began to introduce multiple pedagogical methods into my work to accommodate the multiple styles of learning expressed by my students.

The first thing she did was de-center herself in the classroom, an explicit symbolic recognition that she was no longer the sole authority of knowledge. Students possess significant authority of knowledge and contribute that authority as a valuable asset to the learning environment. Owen-Smith also employed new pedagogical techniques in the classroom and lectured less often:

> I stopped lecturing on a routine basis. When I did lecture, I made two assumptions about the place and quality of lectures in my classes. I believed that my students could read and comprehend the basic facts presented in the text, and I believed that maximum content coverage by me in lecture did not necessarily maximize student conceptual understanding. Therefore, my lectures were directed, more times than not, toward the philosophical issues and dilemmas surrounding the factual material (i.e., the why and how and the unexamined assumptions and implications).

Finally, as an extension of introducing active and collaborative teaching methods into her course, she added a community-based component, creating an engaged pedagogy that combined community-based service with academic study to improve teaching and learning:

> I also began sending students out into the community to experience the connection between theory and praxis. Many educational psychologists remind us that the absence of experience might explain why students misunderstand. Through theory/practice or service learning opportunities students were challenged to negotiate the tension between their strongly held beliefs and the discrepant images and information gained from their actual experiences in social service agency work. They were compelled to reflect on the limitations of theories and assumptions in making sense out of and reconciling real world problems. (Owen-Smith, 2001)

Owen-Smith's strategies exemplify "service learning," a prominent pedagogical approach that has emerged in the past quarter century and which incorporates design characteristics meant to improve learning and connect teaching and learning to experiences in community. Service learning has been defined as "a credit-bearing, educational experience in which students participate in organized service activity that meets identified community needs and reflects on the service activity in such a way as to gain further understanding of course content, a broader appreciation of the discipline, and an enhanced sense of civic responsibility" (Bringle & Hatcher, 1996, p. 222). This definition incorporates the key elements of service-learning educational design: it is an academically legitimate, course-based activity; students participate in carefully identified community-based activities that are aimed at fulfilling the learning goals of the course; the community-based service activity is determined by those in the community who have greater community-based knowledge and will have to live with the results of the activity the students are involved with; reflection is an essential component of course design and is the process for creating meaning and understanding out of the community-based experience in the context of the academic course content; the outcome of the integration of community-based activity and the course content in the discipline is greater understanding of the disciplinary knowledge base of the course; and the development of the student's civic engagement—which includes an appreciation of what civic engagement means in the context of a particular disciplinary or professional perspective—is a specific outcome.

Service learning has proved particularly effective as a pedagogy that engages students in the process of teaching and learning in deeper ways. As the National Survey of Student Engagement reports,

> complementary learning opportunities inside and outside the classroom augment the academic program . . . [and] provide students with opportunities to synthesize, integrate, and apply their knowledge. Such experiences make learning more meaningful, and ultimately more useful because what students know becomes a part of who they are. (2002, p. 11)

This last finding has a remarkably Deweyian ring to it: Dewey described what he called "embodied intelligence" or "embodied knowledge" as knowledge that students acquired in such a way that it not only became what they knew but shaped who they were as individuals.

A key element of service-learning pedagogy is that it provides an educational design that acknowledges students' different learning styles. All students come into our classes with certain cognitive preferences and styles of learning. The greater diversity of students in higher education means that there is a greater diversity of cultural backgrounds and a greater diversity of preferred ways of knowing and learning. Service learning offers an opportunity to teach to a variety of learning styles, engaging all students in learning and contributing to the academic success of all students. David Kolb explained experiential learning as a cyclical process that involves concrete experience, reflection on the experience, abstract conceptualization contextualizing the experience, and application of abstract concepts in real-world situations to test their validity. Kolb's work is grounded in Dewey, who conceived of learning taking place through a reflective process involving a concrete activity. This for Dewey formed the basis of "experience." To make his point, Dewey claimed that "mere activity does not constitute experience" (1916/1966, p. 139). Experiential education, as Kolb explains, entails more than "concrete experience"—it includes reflection, abstract conceptualization, and active experimentation (see figure 1; adapted from Kolb, 1981).

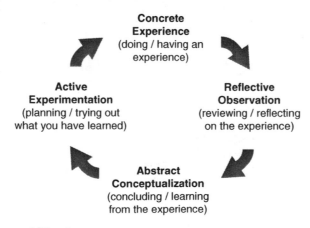

FIGURE 23.1. Experience and Education
SOURCE: David A. Kolb, "Learning Styles and Disciplinary Differences," in A.W. Chickering and Associates, *The Modern American College: Responding to the Realities of Diverse Students in a Changing Society*, San Francisco: Jossey-Bass

With service-learning pedagogy, students engage in the learning process through their preferred mode of learning and improve their ability to learn through the other modes of learning. For example, a student who learns best through hands-on experience can learn through a concrete experience in the community as his or her preferred mode of learning; having engaged in the learning process through his or her preferred mode of learning, the student can then reflect on the experience, can read academic material related to the experience, and can devise ways to participate in the experience more effectively. Another student whose preferred mode of learning is through abstract conceptualization can read academic material as a way of making sense of the community-based experience before participating in it; reflection helps the student connect the experience in the community to the course material, allowing him or her to read and understand the academic concepts in more complex and deeper ways as the student thinks through how he or she can participate in the community experience more effectively. The key is that service-learning provides the opportunity to learn through multiple modes of learning without privileging any single cognitive preference.

Through this understanding of experiential learning, Kolb identified learning styles associated with preferred modes of learning. Kolb's model has been adapted for service learning as a way to understand the educational design and its implications for learning (see figure 2.

This model explicates the educational design in a number of ways. It highlights different preferred modes of learning and different learning styles, and it explicitly connects affective and cognitive development. It also identifies a number of stages in the learning process, including exploration, clarification, realization, activation, and internalization; however, these stages comprise not a cyclical process but a spiral, leading to higher and deeper learning.

Let me offer an example from a course that I taught using service-learning pedagogy. One of the students, a sociology major in her junior year of study (we'll call her Michelle—not her real name), chose to provide service to a homeless shelter for women in a neighborhood near the campus, in fulfillment of her community-based experience for the course. In a reflection session during the first week of class, I asked all the students, including Michelle, why they wanted to be at the community-based agency they had chosen. Michelle avoided the question, and when pressed, she answered: "I don't care how the women at the shelter got there; I just want to help them." I had expected an academic answer, one more in line with a sociological analysis of the situation of homelessness and women's experience with homelessness. Yet, Michelle's response was an affective one. The service-learning model explains that individuals do not move to higher levels of cognitive development without connecting it to their affective development. How would that happen? Again, the model explains that the process entails (1) concrete experience and (2) reflection on that experience, (3) in the context of contextualization of the experience, and (4) ways to reconceptualize participation in the experience. This will lead to movement to the next stage in the learning process.

For Michelle, the transformational process was revealed six weeks later, when during a reflection exercise in class, I reminded her of her response to the question on the first day of class. She was visibly stunned at her previous response, and then proceeded to talk with the other students about her experience at the shelter. She explained that her work at the

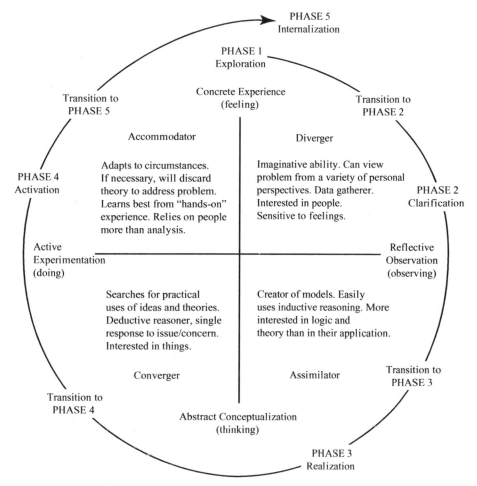

FIGURE 23.2 Comparison of Kolb's Experiential Learning Cycle with the Service Learning Model
SOURCE: Delve, C. I., Mintz, S. D., and Stewart, G. I. (Eds.). *Community Service as Values Education.* New Directions for Student Services, no. 50. San Francisco: Jossey-Bass, 1990, p. 37.

shelter consisted of intake—taking information from the women who came into the shelter. She told the class that she spent more time doing intake than anyone else at the shelter. Then she proceeded to provide a detailed, sophisticated, and complex sociological explanation for why women ended up at the shelter. According to the model, she was somewhere in the phase of realization and had reached higher levels of cognitive development. To complete the story and the cycle, Michelle finished the course and graduated the following year. Her first job after graduation was as the volunteer coordinator at the shelter. According to the model, her learning had become internalized. What she knew became part of who she is.

Service-learning, through relevant and meaningful community-service activity, is designed to achieve learning outcomes in two primary areas—academic learning and civic learning (see figure 3).

In the example of Michelle's experience, purposeful civic learning was structured into the course primarily through reflection that framed questions within a civic dimension. In *Civic Engagement across the Curriculum,* Richard Battistoni provides examples of reflection

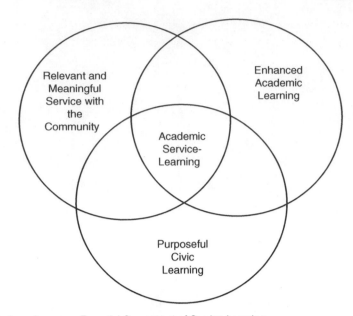

FIGURE 23.3. Civic Learning as an Essential Component of Service-Learning

SOURCE: Jeffrey Howard, 2001. Service-Learning Course Design Workbook, Michigan Journal of Community Service Learning, summer, p. 12.

questions with a civic dimension: "What is the civic role of your chosen profession/discipline? What are the public/civic dimensions of your anticipated work? What expectations does a democratic community place upon you as an individual? Upon you in your professional capacity?" (2002, p. 72).

Civic learning is an essential thread in the fabric of service-learning pedagogy. While at the Carnegie Foundation for the Advancement of Teaching in the early 1980s, Frank Newman, a leading service-learning proponent, asserted that "the most critical demand is to restore to higher education its original purpose of preparing graduates for a life of involved and committed citizenship . . . The advancement of civic learning, therefore, must become higher education's most central goal" (1985, xiv). More recently, the U.S. Department of Education's Fund for the Improvement of Postsecondary Education claimed:

> A good understanding of the democratic principles and institutions embodied in our history, government, and law provide the foundation for civic engagement and commitment, but the classroom alone is not enough. Research shows that students are more likely to have a sense of social responsibility, more likely to commit to addressing community or social problems in their adult lives as workers and citizens, and more likely to demonstrate political efficacy when they engage in structured, conscious reflection on experience in the larger community. To achieve these outcomes, students need structured, real-world experiences that are informed by classroom learning. (Fund for the Improvement of Postsecondary Education, 2003)

Jeffrey Howard, editor of the *Michigan Journal of Community Service Learning*, defines civic learning as "any learning that contributes to student preparation for community or public involvement in a diverse democratic society."

A loose interpretation of civic learning would lead one to believe that education in general prepares one for citizenship in our democracy. And it certainly does. However, we have in mind here a strict interpretation of civic learning—knowledge, skills and values that make an explicitly direct and purposeful contribution to the preparation of students for active civic participation. (2001, p. 38)

Civic learning draws attention to the civic dimensions of education, emphasizing the need not only for the development of disciplinary mastery and competence, but also for civic awareness and purpose. Civic learning illuminates the socially responsive aspects of disciplinary knowledge, those dimensions that expand the view of education to include learning and developing the knowledge, skills, and values of democratic citizenship.

Engaged pedagogies such as service-learning are defined in part by learning outcomes that have a civic dimension. An essential point made by Edgerton and Schulman in reflecting on the 2002 National Survey of Student Engagement results is relevant here: "Students can be engaged in a range of effective practices and still not be learning with understanding; we know that students can be learning with understanding and still not be acquiring the knowledge, skills, and dispositions that are related to effective citizenship" (National Survey of Student Engagement, 2002, p. 3). A focus on civic learning builds upon effective teaching and learning practices by *linking them more deliberately to civic outcomes.*

A New Pedagogy Requires a New Epistemology

Donald Schon's writings help to situate changes in pedagogy within a broader framework of changes that begin with shifts in epistemology and extend to shifts in institutional culture. Schon's most influential writings focus on reflective practice and are grounded in Dewey's educational thought. He describes a way of knowing and a form of knowledge that are associated with practice and action:

> In the domain of practice, we see what John Dewey called inquiry: thought intertwined with action—reflection in and on action—which proceeds from doubt to the resolution of doubt, to the generation of new doubt. For Dewey, doubt lies not in the mind but in the situation. Inquiry begins with situations that are problematic—that are confusing, uncertain, or conflicted, and block the free flow of action. The inquirer is in, and in transaction with, the problematic situation. He or she must construct the meaning and frame the problem of the situation, thereby setting the stage for problem-solving, which, in combination with changes in the external context, brings a new problematic situation into being. (Schon, 1995, p. 31)

Here, Schon identifies practitioner knowledge, or "knowing in action" (p. 27), which represents a particular way of constructing and using knowledge.

What concerns Schon is that colleges and universities in the United States are dominated by technical rationality—what he called their "institutional epistemology (p. 27)"—which shuns other forms of rationality. "Educational institutions," he writes, "have epistemologies. They hold conceptions of what counts as legitimate knowledge and how you know what you claim to know" (p. 27). Further, he explains that

> all of us who live in research universities are bound up in technical rationality, regardless of our personal attitudes toward it, because it is built into the institutional arrangements—the formal and informal rules and norms—that govern such processes as the screening of candidates for

tenure and promotion. Even liberal arts colleges, community colleges, and other institutions of higher education appear to be subject to the influence of technical rationality by a kind of echo effect or by imitation. (p. 32)

For Schon, all the work being done to change higher education by broadening what is viewed as legitimate scholarly work in the academy—particularly the influential work of Ernest Boyer in his *Scholarship Reconsidered* (1990)—raises issues not only of scholarship but fundamentally of epistemology. If faculty were to engage in new forms of scholarship, Schon writes in a essay called "The New Scholarship Requires a New Epistemology," then "we cannot avoid questions of epistemology, since the new forms of scholarship . . . challenge the epistemology built into the modern research university . . . if the new scholarship is to mean anything, it must imply a kind of action research with norms of its own, which will conflict with the norms of technical rationality—the prevailing epistemology built into the research universities" (p. 27).

Schon uses the example of community-based scholarship to make his point. "If community outreach is to be seen as a form of scholarship," he writes, "then it is the practice of reaching out and providing service to a community that must be seen as raising important issues whose investigation may lead to generalizations of prospective relevance and actionability" (p. 31). This requires institutional change. "The problem of changing the universities so as to incorporate the new scholarship," he explains, "must include, then, how to introduce action research as a legitimate and appropriately rigorous way of knowing and generating knowledge . . . If we are prepared to take [on this task], then we have to deal with what it means to introduce an epistemology of reflective practice into institutions of higher education dominated by technical rationality" (pp. 31–32). Schon links issues of scholarship to what he calls "the epistemological, institutional, and political issues it raises within the university." He further connects questions of scholarship and epistemology to "institutional arrangements—the formal and informal rules and norms of the campus, or the institutional culture." He argues that "in order to legitimize the new scholarship, higher education institutions will have to learn organizationally to open up the prevailing epistemology so as to foster new forms of reflective action research" (p. 34).

Schon's insights into new forms of scholarship are useful in thinking about new forms of pedagogy. In the same way that a new scholarship requires a new epistemology, a new pedagogy—localized, relational, practice-based, active, collaborative, experiential, and reflective—requires a new epistemology consistent with changed pedagogical practice. Schon offers a framework that suggests that a shift in how knowledge is constructed (how we know what we know and what is legitimate knowledge in the academy) will lead to a change in how knowledge is organized in the curriculum, to a change in how the curriculum is delivered through instruction (pedagogy), to a change in how knowledge is created and shared, and to a change in the institutional cultures that support change in all these educational dimensions. Each relates to the other, none can be considered in isolation, and all lead to issues of institutional transformation (see figure 4).

Community-based pedagogy raises issues of institutional change that are centered, as the framework suggests, in questions of epistemology. An example of this framework in practice comes from a group of multidisciplinary faculty at a small liberal arts college who

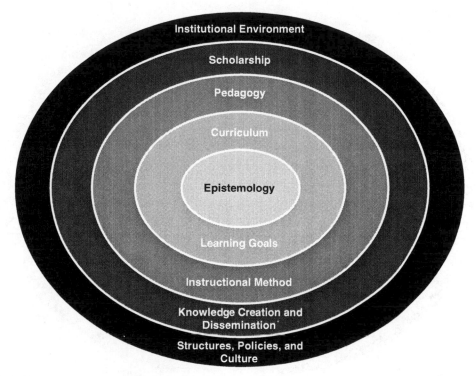

FIGURE 23.4. Components of Service-Learning

were teaching community-based experiential courses. The campus was involved in a strategic planning process, and the faculty determined that the central question that they wanted to discuss was the following: "For the sake of creating new knowledge, what is the intellectual space for complementary epistemologies at X College." These faculty wanted to legitimize a different kind of epistemology that aligned with their conception of both how knowledge is constructed and how learning occurred in their classes. The "intellectual space" alluded to broader systemic issues at the institution, linking "complementary epistemologies" with interdisciplinarity, community-based teaching and learning, and engaged scholarship, as well as the structures, policies, and cultures of the institution. The situation on this campus is not unlike what is happening on many campuses, where introducing new pedagogies into institutions of higher education, Schon suggests, "means becoming involved in an epistemological battle. It is a battle of snails, proceeding so slowly that you have to look very carefully in order to see it going on. But it is happening nonetheless" (p. 32).

Implications of Changed Pedagogy

Drawing on Schon's insights, changed pedagogy results from changed epistemology. Understanding the role of students and community partners as co-creators of knowledge and collaborators in the design and delivery of the curriculum coincides with a fundamental shift in understanding how we know what we know, how knowledge is constructed, and what is considered legitimate knowledge within the academy.

341

Implications for Students

Community-based teaching and learning is grounded in the position that knowledge is socially constructed, and that the lived experience and cultural frameworks that the teacher and learner bring to the educational setting form the basis for the discovery of new knowledge. This position is antithetical to the dominant epistemological position that holds knowledge as being objectified and separate from the knower, in which case the knowledge and experience that the learner brings to the learning environment is of little consequence. In this way, valuing the lived experience and the cultural frameworks that the teacher and learners bring to the educational environment directly challenges the position that all valid knowledge is rational, analytic, and positivist. Rather, this new framework legitimizes knowledge that emerges from experience. Knowledge, according to Mary Walshok, "is something more than highly intellectualized, analytical, and symbolic material. It includes working knowledge, a component of experience, of hands-on practice knowledge" (1995, p. 14).

Closely related to this epistemological position is the perspective that looks at students as assets to the educational process, challenging the deficit thinking that accompanies a traditional epistemological perspective. The student's assets are embraced because the experience and knowledge they contribute to the learning process, and the authority of knowledge that they possess, contribute necessarily to the construction of new knowledge. This is the essence of learner-centered education. The educational value of diversity is enhanced proportionate to the greater ethnic, racial, cultural, religious, gender, and socio-economic diversity present in the educational setting. This means that a conventional university education

> cannot offer nearly enough on its own to a huge range of students with starting-points, aspirations, and destinations immensely varied but mostly well outside the confines of the theoretical discipline . . . [It is necessary] to situate our university courses as far as possible in the context of the students' experience at work and in the world they come from, go back to, and where they expect to exercise understanding and practical intelligence. To do that means rooting much of our teaching in our own engaged understanding of that world. (Bjarnason & Coldstream, 2003, p. 335)

From an asset-based perspective, the student is fundamentally a knowledge producer instead of a knowledge consumer, an active participant in the creation of new knowledge. In order to facilitate socially constructed knowledge, an educational design is needed that fosters active participation in teaching and learning—in a Freireian sense, everyone involved is both a teacher and a learner. Instruction, therefore, is designed to be active, collaborative, and engaged rather than passive, rote, and disengaged (in a deficit model, there is no need to involve the student except as the recipient of knowledge that is "out there" and that needs to be brought, by the instructor at the center of the classroom and in sole possession of authority of knowledge, to the student—typically in a lecture format). The civic corollary to this epistemological position is that education instills active participation in learning and in civic life; students, as knowledge producers, are educated to become active participants in democratic life instead of being spectators to a shallow form of democracy.

Positioning the student as a knowledge producer is associated with the design of educational experiences that reinforce democratic values and experiences. The works of Myles

Horton (1998, 2003), Paulo Freire (1970/1994), and Bell Hooks (1994) take the position that democracy in the process of teaching and learning is shaped by a framework of equality— equality defined as the equal respect for the knowledge and experience of all the participants in the learning process. When Myles Horton designed the learning experience at Highlander Folk School in the 1930s, he understood that "one of the best ways of educating people is to give them an experience that embodies what you are trying to teach" (p. 68). This meant creating a "circle of learners" (de-centering the teacher) with the commitment of all the participants "to respect other people's ideas" (p. 71). This kind of educational design for democracy, influenced by Dewey and Jane Addams, played itself out in the Citizenship Schools that became a catalyst for action during the civil rights era. Equal respect for the knowledge and experience of everyone involved in learning presupposes a shift in epistemology. Horton explained it this way:

> The biggest stumbling block was that all of us at Highlander had academic backgrounds. We thought that the way we had learned and what we had learned could somehow be tailored to the needs of poor people, the working people of Appalachia . . . We still thought our job was to give students information about what we thought would be good for them . . . we saw problems that we thought we had the answers to, rather than seeing the problems and the answers that the people had themselves. (p. 68)

Ordinary citizens from communities in the South came to Highlander with the goal of collectively working toward the solution of a public problem. They each came with a body of knowledge and experience that had relevance to the problem at hand. And they participated in a process of learning from each other and creating new understandings and knowledge to take back to their communities to address social issues. While at Highlander they participated with a certain authority of knowledge that was respected by others. They participated in community-based public problem-solving through a process that afforded equal respect for the knowledge and experience that everyone brought to the educational enterprise. It is this process of democratic knowledge creation that is at the heart of education that integrates pedagogies of engagement with civic engagement.

Horton's educational approach was consistent with John Dewey's educational philosophy in that it explicitly linked education and democracy. Dewey wrote that "unless education has some frame of reference it is bound to be aimless, lacking a unified objective. The necessity for a frame of reference must be admitted. There exists in this country such a unified frame. It is called democracy" (1937b, p. 415). Dewey's conception of democratic education first broadens the meaning of democracy to encompass widespread, cooperative, participatory experience: "A democracy is more than a form of government; it is primarily a mode of associated living, of co-joint communicated experience. The extension in space of the number of individuals who participate in an interest so that each has to refer to his own action and to that of others, and to consider the action of others to give point and direction to his own, is equivalent to the breaking down of those barriers of class, race, and national territory which keep men form perceiving the full import of their activity" (1916/1966, p. 87). Second, by "associated living, co-joint communicated experience," Dewey maintains that "the foundation of democracy is faith in the power of pooled and cooperative experience" and "it is the democratic faith that . . . each individual has something to contribute whose value can be assessed only as it enters into the final pooled intelligence constituted by the contributions of all" (1937a, p. 219). Both democracy and education require wide and diverse participation, and this participation cannot be limited because everyone has something to contribute to education and to the public culture of democracy. Dewey argued forcefully that "the democratic idea itself demands that the thinking and activity proceed cooperatively" (1937a, p. 220). In democratic education, learning takes place through a process "constituted by the contributions of all."

For Dewey, "whether this educative process is carried on in a predominantly democratic or non-democratic way becomes therefore a question of transcendent importance not only for education itself but for its final effect upon all the interests and activities of a society that is committed to the democratic way of life" (1937a, p. 225). The result of nondemocratic education—*both for engagement in learning and engagement in democracy*—is that "absence of participation tends to produce lack of interest and concern on the part of those shut out. The result is a corresponding lack of effective responsibility" (1937a, p. 223). "What the argument for democracy implies," Dewey noted, "is that the best way to produce initiative and constructive power is to exercise it" (1937a, p. 224).

In his book *Democratic Professionalism* (2008), Albert Dzur points out that "Dewey's democratic educators foster cooperation and creative problem solving by structuring learning environments for students to work and deliberate together . . . Dewey's students learn about democracy by acting democratically; the very structure of their schools gives students a taste for collective self-determination" (p. 21). According to Dzur, Dewey "directs educators to facilitate cooperative situations in the classroom in which 'associated thought' and the democratic habits that go along with it can thrive" and in which students are "initiated into the participatory and deliberative mode of associated living characteristic of a task-sharing democracy" (p. 21). Dewey was consistent and explicit in his meaning of democracy: it requires wide and diverse participation, drawing on the rich assets of knowledge and experience of individuals that contributes to the public culture of democracy.

A shift from a deficit-based to an asset-based approach compels a shift from knowledge as the sole possession of the academic expert to something that is shared among all those involved in the learning process. Students, then, share in the authority of knowledge in the classroom and contribute to the learning process. They are not viewed through the dominant deficit framework, as having little or nothing to contribute to their education; rather, through diverse knowledge and experiences, they help shape the learning that collectively takes place. Similarly, an asset-based approach affects how community partners relate to the educational process (see figure 5)

Implications for Community Partners

Engaged academics in higher education relate to external community partners largely as a function of reconceptualized faculty work—that is from that of expert application to collaborative engagement. O'Meara and Rice make this distinction when they assess the developments in engagement in higher education since the publication of Boyer's *Scholarship Reconsidered*. Specifically, they maintain that what Boyer called the "Scholarship of

	Deficit-Based Approach	Asset-Based Approach
Implications for Students	Student as knowledge consumer	Student as knowledge producer
	Knowledge is rational, analytic, positivist	Knowledge is relational, contextual, socially constructed
	Instruction is passive, rote, disengaged	Learning is active, collaborative, experiential
Implications for Community Partners	Expert generation and application of knowledge	Collaborative and reciprocal knowledge production and use
	Traditional knowledge generation—the dominant position in the academy that all valid knowledge is rational, analytic, and positivist (pure, disciplinary, homogeneous, expert-led, supply-driven, hierarchical, peer reviewed, and almost exclusively university-based)	Engaged knowledge generation—problem-centered, transdisciplinary, heterogeneous, hybrid, demand-driven, entrepreneurial, network-embedded, etc. (Gibbons et al., 1994)

FIGURE 23.5. Pedagogy, Epistemology, and Institutional Change

Application" "builds on established academic epistemology, assumes that knowledge is generated in the university or college and then applied to external contexts with knowledge flowing in one direction, out of the academy." In contrast, they explain that the

> Scholarship of Engagement . . . requires going beyond the expert model that often gets in the way of constructive university-community collaboration . . . calls on faculty to move beyond "outreach," . . . asks scholars to go beyond "service," with its overtones of noblesse oblige. What it emphasizes is genuine *collaboration:* that the learning and teaching be multidirectional and the expertise shared. It represents a basic reconceptualization of faculty involvement in community-based work. (2005, pp. 27–28)

An "expert-centered" framework of engagement (Saltmarsh, Hartley, & Clayton, 2009; Saltmarsh & Hartley, in press), often identified as technocratic, scientific, or positivist, defines the dominant paradigm of engagement in higher education and is grounded in an institutional epistemology of expert knowledge housed in the university and applied externally. "This epistemology," William Sullivan has noted, "is firmly entrenched as the operating system of much of the American university" (2000, p. 29). There exists, Sullivan writes, an "affinity of positivist understandings of research for 'applying' knowledge to the social world on the model of the way engineers 'apply' expert understanding to the problems of structures." Knowledge produced by credentialed, detached experts is embedded in hierarchies of knowledge generation and knowledge use, creating a division between knowledge producers (in the university) and knowledge consumers (in the community). In the positivist scheme, "researchers 'produce' knowledge, which is then 'applied' to problems and problematic populations" (p. 29). Academic expertise, writes Greenwood (2008), focuses on "building theory, being 'objective,' writing mainly for each other in a language of their own creation, building professional associations, and staying away from political controversies" (p. 321). Valued more than community-based knowledge, academic knowledge flows

345

unilaterally, from inside the boundaries of the university outward to its place of need and application in the community.

This expert-centered framework of engagement locates the university at the center of solutions to public problems and educates students through service as proto-experts who will be able to perform civic tasks in communities they work with because they will have the knowledge and credentials to help communities improve. In the expert-centered paradigm, students, in their developing citizen roles, will not be taught the political dimensions of their activities, because questions of power are left out of the context of objectified knowledge production and the way that "service" is provided to communities. Higher education that includes civic engagement activities characterized by the expert-centered paradigm perpetuates a kind of politics that rejects popularly informed decision-making in favor of expert-informed knowledge application. Politics is something to be kept separate from the dispassionate pursuit of knowledge because it is understood in terms of competing partisan positions and opposing ideologies, and thus not only is avoided by academics who perceive such work as "activist scholarship" but is prohibited by federal mandate when community-service programs are funded through federal agencies. On many campuses what has emerged are remarkably apolitical "civic" engagement efforts.

Expert-driven, hierarchical knowledge generation and dissemination is not only an epistemological position but, as Harry Boyte points out, a political one. Traditional academic epistemology, with its embedded values, methods, and practices, signifies a "pattern of power" relationships and creates a "technocracy" and a particular politics that is "the core obstacle to higher education's engagement." As Boyte asserts, the power and politics of expert academic knowledge is "the largest obstacle in higher education to authentic engagement with communities," and is "a significant contributor to the general crisis of democracy." Its core negative functions," he explains, "are to undermine the standing and to delegitimate the knowledge of those without credentials, degrees, and university training . . . It conceives of people without credentials as needy clients to be rescued or as customers to be manipulated" (2008, p. 108). In this way of thinking and acting, he notes, genuine reciprocal learning is just not possible.

Community partnerships in the expert-centered framework of engagement do not have an explicit and intentional democratic dimension in which academics share knowledge-generating tasks with the public and involve community partners as participants in public problem solving. A shift in discourse from "partnerships" and "mutuality" to that of "reciprocity" is grounded in democratic values of sharing previously academic tasks with nonacademics and encouraging the participation of nonacademics in ways that enhance and enable broader engagement and deliberation about major social issues inside and outside the university. A democratic framework seeks the public good *with* the public—not merely *for* it—as a means for facilitating a more active and engaged democracy. Reciprocity signals an epistemological shift that values not only expert knowledge that is rational, analytic, and positivist, but also a different kind of rationality that is more relational, localized, and contextual and favors mutual deference between laypersons and academics. Knowledge generation is a process of co-creation, breaking down the distinctions between knowledge producers and knowledge consumers. It further implies scholarly work that is conducted by

	Expert-Centered	Democratic-Centered
Community Relationships	Partnerships and mutuality	Reciprocity
	Deficit-based understanding of community	Asset-based understanding of community
	Academic work done *for* the public	Academic work done *with* the public
Knowledge Production/ Research	Applied	Inclusive, collaborative, problem-oriented
	Unidirectional flow of knowledge	Multidirectional flow of knowledge
Epistemology	Positivist/scientific/technocratic	Relational, localized, contextual
	Distinction between knowledge producers and knowledge consumers	Co-creation of knowledge
	Primacy of academic knowledge	Shared authority for knowledge creation
	University as the center of public problem solving	University as a part of an ecosystem of knowledge production addressing public problem solving
Political Dimension	Apolitical engagement	Facilitating an inclusive, collaborative, and deliberative democracy

FIGURE 23.6. Comparing Civic Engagement Frameworks

sharing authority and power with those in the community in all aspects of the relationship: defining problems, choosing approaches, addressing issues, developing the final products, and participating in assessment. Reciprocity operates to facilitate the involvement of individuals in the community not just as consumers of knowledge and services but as participants in the larger public culture of democracy (see figure 6).

Implications for Teaching and Learning

A "democratic-centered" framework of engagement locates the university within what Ernest Lynton called an "interconnected and interdependent ecosystem of knowledge" (1994, p. 90), requiring interaction with other knowledge producers outside the university through a multidirectional flow of knowledge and expertise. In an ecosystem of knowledge, Lynton explained, "knowledge does not move from the locus of research to the place of application, from scholar to practitioner, teacher to student, expert to client. It is everywhere fed back, constantly enhanced" (1994, p. 10). "The design of problem-solving actions through collaborative knowledge construction with the legitimate stakeholders in the problem," writes Davydd Greenwood, takes place in

> collaborative arenas for knowledge development in which the professional researcher's knowledge is combined with the local knowledge of the stakeholders in defining the problem to be

347

addressed. Together, they design and implement the actions to be taken on the basis of their shared understanding of the problem. Together, the parties develop plans of action to improve the situation together, and they evaluate the adequacy of what was done. (2008, p. 327)

This interactive and interdependent process of knowledge creation is what Greenwood describes as "a democratizing form of content-specific knowledge creation, theorization, analysis, and action design in which the goals are democratically set, learning capacity is shared, and success is collaboratively evaluated" (p. 329).

In this collaborative framework, students learn cooperative and creative problem-solving within learning environments in which faculty, students, and individuals from the community work and deliberate together. Politics is understood through explicit awareness and experience of patterns of power that are present in the relationship between the university and the community; that is, politics is not reduced to partisanship. In the democratic-centered paradigm, academics are not on the front lines of partisan politics, but, as described by Dzur, they "have sown the seeds of a more deliberative democracy . . . by cultivating norms of equality, collaboration, reflection, and communication" (2008, p. 121). Civic engagement in the democratic-centered framework is intentionally political in that all those involved in the learning process learn about democracy by acting democratically.

A developing critique of a unidirectional, applied, expert-centered approach to knowledge generation, teaching, and learning, especially in the social sciences, recognizes that complex social problems can be addressed only if the intended recipients' motivations and contexts are taken into account. In the expert-centered framework of engagement, "the terms of engagement, the ways of studying the issues, and the ownership of the actions and the intellectual products are not negotiated with the legitimate local stakeholders" (Weerts & Sandmann, 2008, p. 333). A democratic-centered framework, conversely, "must involve a true partnership, based on both sides bringing their own experience and expertise to the project," noted Lynton, and "this kind of collaboration requires a substantial change in the prevalent culture of academic institutions" (1995, p. xii). A democratic-centered framework is premised on the understanding that "the pursuit of knowledge itself demands engagement" and that "a greater number of academics need to define their territory more widely and accept that they share much of it with other knowledge-professionals; engagement with those beyond the ivory tower may greatly enrich their own thinking" (Bjarnason & Coldstream, 2003, p. 323). A "more inclusive, two-way approach to knowledge flow" accompanied by "an epistemological shift . . . from a rational or objectivist worldview to a constructivist worldview" (Weerts & Sandmann, 2008, p. 78) is marked by movement away from traditional academic knowledge generation (i.e., pure, disciplinary, homogeneous, expert-led, supply-driven, hierarchical, peer-reviewed, and almost exclusively university-based) to engaged knowledge generation (i.e., applied, problem-centered, transdisciplinary, heterogeneous, hybrid, demand-driven, entrepreneurial, and network-embedded) (Gibbons et al., 1994).

The implication of this shift for teaching and learning is that it relocates students and community partners as co-producers of knowledge, valuing the knowledge and experience they contribute to the educational process, sharing authority for the process of knowledge generation and pedagogy, and allowing them to practice and experiment with a public culture of democracy as part of the work of higher education.

Changing Higher Education from the Inside Out

Drawing on Schon's observations, if changed pedagogies are going to be adopted and sustained as part of the academic mainstream in higher education, then changes in teaching and learning practice alone will not be enough. Also necessary are changes in the institutional cultures in which the practices are embedded. This, in turn, will require new ways of thinking about teaching, learning, and institutional change.

Changes in practice are associated with what Larry Cuban describes as "first order change," which aims to improve "the efficiency and effectiveness of what is done . . . to make what already exists more efficient and more effective, without disturbing the basic organizational features, without substantially altering the ways in which [faculty and students] perform their roles" (1988, p. 342). Change in pedagogical practice as a matter of new technique need not fundamentally alter the established organizational structures and culture of higher education. It does not require what Eckel, Hill, and Green refer to as changes that "alter the culture of the institution," those that require "major shifts in an institution's culture—the common set of beliefs and values that creates a shared interpretation and understanding of events and actions" (1998, p. 3). Changes in pedagogy that perpetuate the dominant expert-centered educational paradigm do not compel change that transforms institutional culture. Civic engagement within the "democratic-centered" framework, with its explicit value of reciprocity and implications for students and community partners, points to change in the institutional culture of colleges and universities, or what Cuban identifies as "second-order changes" that

> seek to alter the fundamental ways in which organizations are put together. These changes reflect major dissatisfaction with present arrangements. Second-order changes introduce new goals, structures, and roles that transform familiar ways of doing things into new ways of solving persistent problems. (1988, p. 342)

"Those who propose first-order changes," he writes, "believe that the existing goals and structures . . . are both adequate and desirable" (p. 342); therefore, there is no need to fundamentally alter the established organizational structures and culture of higher education.

Whereas first-order changes largely involve improving existing practice, those of the second order require significant restructuring of academic work aligned with a democratic conception of civic engagement. Second-order changes are associated with transformational change, what Eckel, Hill, and Green define as change that "(1) alters the culture of the institution by changing select underlying assumptions and institutional behaviors, processes, and products; (2) is deep and pervasive, affecting the whole institution; (3) is intentional; and (4) occurs over time" (p. 3). Cultural change focuses on "institution-wide patterns of perceiving, thinking, and feeling; shared understandings; collective assumptions; and common interpretive frameworks [that] are the ingredients of this 'invisible glue' called institutional culture" (p. 3). From this perspective, innovative practices that shift epistemology, reshape the curriculum, alter pedagogy, and redefine scholarship must be supported through academic norms and institutional reward policies that shape the academic cultures of the academy.

For changed pedagogies that foster civic engagement to be sustained as institutionalized practices, they will need to be embedded in the shared norms, beliefs, and values of the

349

institution—embedded in the institutional culture. They will need to be seamlessly woven into what Schon calls "the formal and informal rules and norms that govern such processes as the screening of candidates for promotion and tenure" (1995, p. 32). If civic engagement is practiced in such a way that it compels changes in institutional culture, then engaged faculty work not only may be sustained but can thrive amid a supportive environment that encourages such work. Sullivan observes that efforts of civic engagement in higher education "seem to succeed best in actually becoming institutionalized as standard academic procedure when they develop as actual partnerships in which knowledge and practices evolve cooperatively rather than proceeding in a one-directional way from experts to outsiders" (2000, p. 34).

Although higher education's reliance on an expert-centered paradigm has emphasized individual and institutional expert self-interest at the expense of the public purposes of higher education, an alternative paradigm is possible—and can contribute to the reshaping of higher education to better meet its academic and civic missions in the twenty-first century. As Sullivan reminds us, "campuses educate their students for citizenship most effectively to the degree that they become sites for constructive exchange and cooperation among diverse groups of citizens from the larger community" (2000, p. 20). It is this democratic-centered paradigm that holds the promise of not only changing pedagogies but changing the institutional identity of colleges and universities, thus cultivating the values of long-term democracy-building and contributing to the public culture of democracy itself.

References

Barr, R. B., & Tagg, J. (1995). From teaching to learning: A new paradigm for undergraduate education. *Change, 27*(6), 12–25.

Battistoni, R. (2002). *Civic engagement across the curriculum.* Providence, RI: Campus Compact.

Bjarnason, S., & Coldstream, P. (Eds.). (2003). *The idea of engagement: Universities in society.* London: Association of Commonwealth Universities.

Boyer, E., (1990). *Scholarship reconsidered: Priorities of the professorate.* Princeton, NJ: The Carnegie Foundation for the Advancement of Teaching.

Boyte, H. (2008, May/June). Against the current: Developing the civic agency of students. *Change, 40*(3), 8–15.

Bringle, R., & Hatcher, J. (1996). Implementing service learning in higher education. *The Journal of Higher Education, 67*(2), 221–239.

Cuban, L. (1988). A fundamental puzzle of school reform. *Phi Delta Kappan, 69*(5), 341–342.

Delve, C. I., Mintz, S. D., & Stewart, G. I. (Eds.). (1990). *Community service as values education.* New Directions for Student Services, No. 50. San Francisco: Jossey-Bass.

Dewey, J. (1937a). Democracy and educational administration. Reprinted in J. A. Boydston (Ed.): *John Dewey: The later works* (Vol. 11). Carbondale: Southern Illinois University Press, 1981–1990.

Dewey, J. (1937b). Education and social change. Reprinted in J. A. Boydston (Ed.): *John Dewey: The later works* (Vol. 11, p. 415). Carbondale: Southern Illinois University Press, 1981–1990.

Dewey, J. (1966). *Democracy and education* (p. 87). New York: Free Press. (Original work published 1916)

Dzur, A. W. (2008). *Democratic professionalism: Citizen participation and the reconstruction of professional ethics, identity, and practice.* University Park: Pennsylvania State University Press.

Eckel, P. Hill, B., & Green, M. (1998). *On change: En route to transformation.* Washington, DC: American Council on Education.

Ewell, P. (1997, December). Organizing for learning. *AAHE Bulletin,* pp. 3–6.

Freire, P. (1994). *Pedagogy of the oppressed.* New York: Continuum. (Original work published 1970)

Fund for the Improvement of Postsecondary Education. (2003). *The comprehensive program. FY 2003.* Washington, DC: U.S. Department of Education.

Gibbons, M., Limoges, C., Nowotny, H., Schwartzman, S., Scott, P., & Trow, M. (1994). *The new production of knowledge: The dynamics of science and research in contemporary societies.* London: Sage.

Greenwood, D. J. (2008). Theoretical research, applied research, and action research: The deinstitutionalization of activist research. In C. R. Hale (Ed.), *Engaging contradictions: Theory, politics, and methods of activist scholarship* (pp. 319–340). Berkeley: University of California Press.

hooks, b. (1994). *Teaching to transgress: Education as the practice of freedom.* New York: Routledge.

Horton, M. (1998). *The long haul: An autobiography.* New York: Teachers College.

Howard, J. (2001, Summer). Service-learning course design workbook. *Michigan Journal of Community Service Learning.*

Kolb, D. A. (1981). Learning styles and disciplinary differences. In A. W. Chickering & Associates (Eds.), *The modern American college: Responding to the realities of diverse students in a changing society.* San Francisco: Jossey-Bass.

Lynton, E. A. (1994, Summer). Knowledge and scholarship. *Metropolitan Universities: An International Forum, 5*(1), 9–17.

Lynton, E. A. (1995). Foreword: What is a metropolitan university?. In D. M. Johnson & D. A. Bell (Eds.), *Metropolitan universities: An emerging model in American higher education.* Denton, TX : University of North Texas Press.

Marchese, T. (1996, March). The search for the next century learning, an interview with John Abbott, director of the Education 2000 Trust. *AAHE Bulletin, 48*(7), 3–6.

National Survey of Student Engagement. (2002). *From promise to progress: How colleges and universities are using student engagement results to improve collegiate quality.* Bloomington: Indiana University Center for Postsecondary Research and Planning.

Newman, F. (1985). *Higher education and the American resurgence.* Stanford, CA: Carnegie Foundation for the Advancement of Teaching.

O'Meara, K. A., & Rice, R. E. (Eds.). (2005). *Faculty priorities reconsidered: Encouraging multiple forms of scholarship* (pp. 27–28). San Francisco: Jossey-Bass.

Owen-Smith, P. (2001). Reclaiming a pedagogy of integrity. *National Teaching and Learning Forum Newsletter, 11*(1), 3, 5–6.

Saltmarsh, J., Hartley, M., & Clayton, P. H. (2009). *Democratic engagement white paper.* Boston: New England Resource Center for Higher Education

Saltmarsh, J., & Hartley, M. (Eds.). (In press). *"To serve a larger purpose:" Engagement for democracy and the transformation of higher education.*

Schon, D. (1995). The new scholarship requires a new epistemology. *Change, 27*(6), 26–35.

Sullivan, W. M. (2000). Institutional identity and social responsibility in higher education. In T. Ehrlich (Ed.), *Civic responsibility and higher education* (pp. 19–36). Phoenix, AZ: Oryx Press.

Walshok, M. (1995). *Knowledge without boundaries: What America's research universities can do for the economy, the workplace, and the community.* San Francisco: Jossey-Bass.

Weerts, D. J., & Sandmann, L. R. (2008). Building a two-way street: Challenges and opportunities for community engagement at research universities. *Review of Higher Education, 32*(1), 73–106.

Students as Scholars: Integrating Research, Education, and Professional Practice

Judith A. Ramaley

During the past twenty years, two patterns have converged to alter in substantive ways our ideas about how to prepare our students for life and work. One trend is the changing nature of the concept of engagement itself and the relationships that have developed between colleges and universities and the communities they serve (Peters, Jordan, Adamek, & Alter, 2005; Ramaley, 2007). The other trend is our growing understanding of the habits of mind and inclinations that will allow our graduates to put their education to the best possible use in a world of ever-changing complexity (AAC&U, 2008). As both themes have come into focus, each has strengthened and supported the other. The result is that students now are not simply the object of our instructional attention. They are now also critical participants in developing and delivering on the promise of university-community engagement. In the process of contributing to our university-community partnerships, our students are also learning how to address emerging and volatile challenges that require new forms of thinking and new ways of working together.

In this essay, I address the challenges of advanced education in the twenty-first century. I argue that a twenty-first-century curriculum must incorporate engagement and public scholarship. The experience of engagement will become the pathway to a fresh interpretation of the role of higher education in American life. This conception rests on a rethinking of the core of the academy: the nature of scholarship itself and our expectations for the undergraduate experience. The goal of engaged scholarship is not to define and serve the public good directly on behalf of society, but to create conditions for the public good to be interpreted and pursued in a collaborative mode with members of the community. In contemporary life, the exercise of citizenship requires constant learning and the thoughtful and ethical application of knowledge. By including our students in engaged scholarship, we

353

introduce them to basic concepts and, at the same time, offer them a chance to explore the application and consequences of ideas in the company of mature scholars and practitioners. Clearly, the dissection of the process of observation, action, and reflection into three separate facets of a scholarly life, either for faculty members or for students, is much too restrictive. The pattern does not foster the creative approaches that are needed in the world today.

The Nature of Engagement and Public Scholarship

Before the term "engagement" was used by Russ Edgerton in 1995 to describe the theme of the American Association of Higher Education Annual meeting that year, we usually talked about volunteer service or community service. By 1999, the term had been adopted widely in the higher education community, as evidenced by the Presidents' Declaration on the Civic Responsibility of Higher Education (Campus Compact, 1999) in which the signatories affirmed their commitment to "to re-examine [our] public purposes and [our] commitments to the democratic ideal. We also challenge higher education to become engaged, through actions and teaching, with its communities." These activities, pursued because of individual interests or a sense of commitment to the public good, were rarely connected in a meaningful way to faculty or student scholarship, teaching, or learning. In fact, for a long time, service was understood as a separate activity that faculty or students undertook apart from their scholarship and coursework. In many promotion and tenure policies, service is still listed as a separate category of activities, given little weight, and often not held up to any rigorous scrutiny. Increasingly, however, activities that can lead to public benefit are integrated into a scholarly agenda or connected to clear educational goals and incorporated into the design of a course or an entire sequence of experiences in a program of study (Colby, Beaumont, Ehrlich, & Corngold, 2008; Kuh, 2008; Kuh, Kinzie, Schuh, & Whitt, 2005).

As service has been folded into scholarship, teaching, and learning, the educational focus has been increasingly to apply the knowledge learned in a classroom setting to contemporary and practical challenges in order to accomplish clear educational goals. An integrated approach changes the working relationships among the disciplines within an institution. Engaged work also requires a significant change in how campuses interact with the communities around them and with other knowledge-based organizations such as K–12, social service agencies, business alliances, and other collections of knowledgeable people who depend on accurate and timely information to do their work. This form of integration can be called truly *engaged*. In such a setting, the gaps that limit new working relationships between the professions and the liberal arts, general education and the in-depth study of the major, formal study and daily life, academic affairs and student affairs, research and teaching can be closed. Engagement is a natural and powerful vehicle for spanning institutional boundaries (Holland, 2005), but it is also a powerful vehicle for creating a coherent and progressively more demanding and meaningful experience for students as they progress through their education. Engaged scholarship and learning offer an especially attractive vehicle for achieving the aspirations and goals of Liberal Education and America's Promise (LEAP) (AAC&U, 2008).

If our students are to be ready for the demands of the twenty-first century, they must make sense of the insights and perspectives of all of the disciplines in order to foster their growing understanding of the world. To achieve this, attention must be paid to the integration and application of knowledge and perspectives across the disciplines, not only through the general studies component of an undergraduate experience but also throughout the rest of the curriculum and related student experiences such as internships or undergraduate research. Students must also apply their growing understanding to a series of challenges of increasing complexity and importance, some of which, at least, are posed by the realities of daily life in the communities around them. This does not mean that we should abandon our efforts to engage our students in the exploration of questions that arise at the frontiers of the traditional disciplines or that have been conundrums and challenges across time. Traditional forms of undergraduate research still matter, and those students who are interested in exploring a scholarly career should seek experiences as undergraduate researchers. For others, however, who are pursuing a professional career in a field of practice or who are using a liberal education to prepare for postgraduate study in a professional field, the work of a scholar practitioner may be more meaningful. A good place to work out these connections and to design the continuum of experiences that can draw our students toward greater sophistication, purpose, and capability is the kinds of community-based learning or service-learning that we have been exploring across this nation since the idea was first articulated by Campus Compact and explored in a series of Wingspread Conference Conferences in the 1980s and 1990s (Ramaley, 2007). Engaged learning can make the creation and application of knowledge both visible and compelling, and at the same time, these experiences can be put to good use as students make the challenging transition from the more intentional and predictable environment of a college campus to the complex and ever-changing world of citizenship and professional practice beyond.

Along with changes taking place in the experience of students and in the design of the curriculum, integrative activities have begun to emerge as legitimate forms of faculty work as well. For as long as most of us can remember, the intellectual work of the academy has been artificially separated for purposes of evaluating the work of faculty into research, teaching, and service. Seen through the research lens, a form of scholarship is beginning to emerge that is closely guided by the experience of society at large and the challenges faced by people in their daily lives. Its participants can be called public intellectuals or public scholars (Ramaley, 2006) and their work can offer insights that can guide and support policymakers and community leaders as well as engaged citizens who seek to contribute to the public good. Their work can be distinguished from the valuable contributions of scholars who use methodologies such as participatory action research or service-learning to draw community members into the articulation of problems that address the public interest and to generate and interpret information that can be applied to economic and community development and the solution of community problems.

Through the teaching lens, we are seeing a new, more intentional approach to the curriculum, accompanied by new "greater expectations" for our students as well as for ourselves as their mentors. Seen through the service lens, we are changing the dimensions of application of research to community problems from an outreach model of service

355

delivery in which experts apply well-researched answers to clearly characterized problems to a collaborative model in which solutions to often highly contested and poorly defined problems (the "swampy lowlands" of Donald A. Schoen, 1997, p. 3) are developed in a collaborative mode.

Expanding the Concept of Scholarship

It has become increasingly clear that the dissection of the process of observation, action, and reflection into three separate facets of a scholarly life, either for faculty members or for students, is much too restrictive. A milestone conception along the pathway toward an integration of these aspects of scholarship was the work of Ernest Boyer. In 1990, Boyer proposed a grand synthesis in his monograph *Scholarship Reconsidered: Priorities of the Professoriate*. He began by "looking at the way the work of the academy has changed throughout the years-moving from teaching, to service, and then research, reflecting the shifting priorities both within the academy and beyond" (Boyer, 1990, p. xi). Examining the changing context within which higher education operates, Boyer concluded, "At no time in our history has the need been greater for connecting the work of the academy to the social and environmental challenges beyond the campus" (p. xii). He then wrote an entire monograph addressing his core theme: "The most important obligation now confronting the nation's colleges and universities is to break out of the old tired teaching versus research debate and define, in creative ways, what it means to be a scholar" (p. xii).

The result of Boyer's wonderfully integrative reflection on this challenge was a model of scholarship that could no longer be broken into separate parts. He developed a concept of four views of scholarship: discovery, integration, application, and teaching. In recent years, many have chosen to develop more fully the idea of the scholarship of teaching in order to make clear that instructors can and must approach their work as teachers in the same scholarly fashion that they would address a research question of interest to them. As in other realms of scholarly work, the questions of concern to all of us about how people learn now require a much more cross-disciplinary approach and the active revisiting of the habits of mind and the standards of excellence of individual disciplines.

Others, myself included (Ramaley, 2006), have elected to add an additional component of scholarship, namely, *interpretation*, and argue that anyone—student, faculty member, staff member, or community participant—can engage in all four aspects of scholarly work (*discovery, integration, interpretation, and application*). What varies is who defines the questions, who does the work, who interprets the results, and who puts the results to good use. What does *not* change is the importance of rigorous and well-founded work upon which we can reliably base responsible actions on behalf of the public good (Glassick, Huber, & Maeroff, 1997). If the focus is a matter of shared concern and the arena of study is community-based, it is public scholarship. Boyer set in motion the first line of engagement, that of the interaction across realms of scholarly activity. As we shall see, this way of thinking has grown since his initial contributions and has expanded into more and more aspects of academic life.

The next major milestone along the path to a richer conception of public scholarship emerged from the work of the Kellogg Commission on the Future of State and Land-Grant

Universities (Kellogg Commission, 1999), which shifted the terms *research, teaching,* and *service* to the words *discovery, learning,* and *engagement.* In so doing, the commission opened up a consideration of who participates in scholarly work, where that work is done, who defines the questions of significance, who cares about the answers obtained, and who is responsible for putting the resulting insights and knowledge to effective use in addressing complex, societal problems either in a particular community or on a global scale. This shift in emphasis opened the door for thinking about the ways in which concepts of scholarship apply to the student experience and the role that students can play in advancing knowledge, while, at the same time, deepening their own exploration of ideas that have powerfully shaped our experience and our understanding of the human condition.

Since the work of the Kellogg Commission, some observers have begun to think both about the large domain encompassed by a scholarly agenda and about the way in which both research (defined broadly as discovery, integration, interpretation, and application) and teaching (also defined broadly as an approach to the collective enterprise called "the curriculum") can be approached in an engaged manner and thus can become public scholarship (Ramaley, 2005.) The portfolio of work that makes up Liberal Education and America's Promise (LEAP), the successor to Greater Expectations, has taken these ideas and used them to shape an entire toolkit of ideas, approaches to learning, and curricular design that any institution can adapt to its own purposes and mission in order to draw on its distinctive history, institutional resources, and community relationships to create an environment in which the integration of scholarship and learning can be offered in distinctive ways.

Putting It All Together: What It Means to Be Educated in the Twenty-first Century

The Greater Expectations Panel (2002) assembled by the Association of American Colleges and Universities issued a report calling for a fresh approach to liberal education that would produce graduates who are prepared for life and work in the twenty-first century and who are "*intentional* about the process of acquiring learning, *empowered* by the mastery of intellectual and practical skills, *informed* by knowledge from various disciplines and *responsible* for their actions and those of society" (foreword by Andrea Leskes in Huber and Hutchings, 2004, p. iv). To accomplish the formidable charge set forth by the Greater Expectations panel and since embraced in large measure by many institutions across this country, an education must create an environment in which students can bring together their formal studies and their life experiences, explore and understand the worldviews of different fields, learn how to examine a complex issue from multiple perspectives, and bridge the often daunting gaps between theory and practice, contemplation and action.

There are many impediments to achieving this goal of a grand reweaving of the often fragmented ways in which our colleges and universities choose to organize their scholarly life. The goal is easy to articulate but difficult to realize in practice. According to the joint statement by the Association of American Colleges and Universities (AAC&U) and the Carnegie Foundation for the Advancement of Teaching on Integrative Learning, "Integrative learning comes in many varieties: connecting skills and knowledge from multiple sources and experiences; applying theory to practice in various settings utilizing diverse and even contradictory points of view; and, understanding issues and positions contextually" (Huber & Hutchings, 2004, p. 13). Such learning goes against the grain of our own scholarly lives as well as the structure and organization of our colleges and universities. We have not recovered from the invention of the Carnegie Unit that broke our curriculum into courses and credits. To this historic pattern we can add the strong influence of the massive national investment in university-based research that reshaped our institutions into vital contributors to the nation-building and economic development goals of the federal government and reinforced the research university model of organizational structure and purpose. The infusion of such capital left the undergraduate teaching function as a secondary role of our major universities. Compounding this reshaping of the university enterprise, we have seen in recent years a growing complexity of enrollments in postsecondary education as students have moved in swirling pathways across the educational landscape, taking courses from many institutions, often enrolling in two or more in any given semester. The task of creating educational coherence has become harder than ever.

Such trends and patterns of societal influence and changing participation have led to a series of gaps between the professions and the liberal arts, general education and the in-depth study of the major, formal study and daily life, academic affairs and student affairs, research and teaching. As Gerald Graff puts it (quoted in Huber & Hutchings, 2004),

> One of the oddest things about the university is that it calls itself a "community of scholars," yet it organizes itself in a way that conceals the intellectual links of that community from those who don't already see them. I trace this oddity to . . . the assumption that the natural unit of instruction is the autonomous course, one not in direct dialogue with other courses. The classes being taught at any moment on a campus represent rich potential conversations between scholars and across disciplines. But since these conversations are experienced as a series of monologues, the possible links are apparent only to the minority of students who can connect ideas on their own. (p. 4)

At its best, an integrated program of scholarship, learning, and application to practice can become a working prototype of what all students should experience as intentional, empowered, informed, and responsible people ready to lead productive, responsible, and creative lives (Greater Expectations, 2002, and further developed in AAC&U, 2008). In reality, however, many degree programs are built on a set of courses in which some integration is attempted within each individual course or seminar, but as in the larger curriculum, there is often very little intentional alignment or connection from one course to another. Each course may be a dialogue, but the whole still consists of a series of monologues. One way to resolve this problem is to map out the curriculum and look for where in the sequence students encounter each major concept and when and how they build essential skills and habits of mind. One way to construct such a model is to link learning to life in our curriculum, in our relationships with the community, in our approach to scholarship, and in our partnerships with students. By introducing our students to engaged research and learning, we offer them a way to make sense of the courses they take and the connections across disciplines that their instructors can see but they often cannot. The kind of thinking required to work with others and to explore what AAC&U would call an "unscripted problem" can offer powerful integration no matter what path a student takes through his or her educational experiences.

The experience obtained through engaged scholarship and learning is still based firmly upon a liberal education, a philosophy of learning that draws inspiration from challenging encounters with important issues and with difficult differences that make us question our ideas and assumptions about life. We must ask our students to join us in exploring the complexities of the human condition in ways that provide benefits to our community partners as well (Sandy & Holland, 2006). Together, we can advance knowledge and put what we learn to good use in service to others.

In colleges and universities, we must do our best to model the essential traits of an educated person: open-mindedness, informed judgment, and empathy. We must seek to exercise moral imagination (Nussbaum, 2004, p. 42) and to view with sympathy and understanding the experience of people who live at a distance from us, or who look different from ourselves, or who have different values and cultural experiences (Nussbaum, 1997, p. 8). Such openness allows us to take seriously the lives of other people and to be concerned about their well-being. In a world that is now connected in new and intimate ways, the qualities of empathy and moral imagination are more important than ever, and our efforts to expand the international dimensions of the campus community and the scope of our international programs reflect our commitment to preparing our students and ourselves for what some futurists are calling "the Conceptual Age" (Pink, 2005).

Building on the Promise Offered by Greater Expectations

Since the publication of the Greater Expectations Report (2002), the Association of American Colleges and Universities (AAC&U) has partnered with a number of other organizations to probe more deeply into the core concepts that the panel articulated and to test the assumptions upon which those recommendations were based. This collection of studies and a toolkit of strategies for curricular reform to accompany them can be found as a package under the section on Liberal Education and America's Promise (LEAP) on the AAC&U website. From these studies and reflections, several themes emerge:

1. A contemporary curriculum must incorporate both formal study and a reflection upon life experiences.
2. The curriculum must provide conditions for the fostering of creativity.
3. The educational experience must build across time in both intellectual complexity and significance of the outcomes.
4. Learning must be built on an integrated concept of scholarship.

Supporting Public Scholarship by Faculty Members and Students

There are many motivations for considering public scholarship as legitimate work for both faculty and students (Holland, 2005). At its most basic level, it offers a way for scholars as well as students to integrate their scholarly interests and their personal experiences and motivations. As David Cooper (2002) expresses it, "Could I bring my 'whole self' to a vocation in higher education? Could I practice a scholarship that nourished an active inner life, while forging strong and meaningful links to the public sphere? What would scholarship, teaching and service look like if they supported both personal wholeness and the fulfillments of an engaged public life?" (p. 26). For this kind of authenticity to be possible, the entire scholarly and learning environment must expand and open up. This idea leads us to explore further the concept of engaged institutions.

In the past several years, engagement has begun to grow beyond primarily individual experiences—how students learn and how faculty choose the questions they wish to pursue in their research—to encompass the collective work and institutional relationships that connect an institution to the broader community. As engagement spreads from individual experiences to shared experiences within departments and across disciplines, scholarship itself begins to change. The traditional distinctions of teaching, research, and service begin to blur, and research ceases to be the exclusive purview of faculty and their most advanced students. As engagement progresses, the distinctions articulated by Boyer (1990)—discovery, integration, application, and the scholarship of teaching—cease to matter as much. Discovery and application can occur together in what Donald Stokes (1997) calls Pasteur's Quadrant, where theoretical advances and practical utility combine. The scholarship of teaching blends with discovery, and all forms of scholarship can occur in a complex "cycle of innovation" that draws upon observation and experience to challenge theory and that applies theory to the understanding of experience (Ramaley, Olds, & Earle, 2005). Universities and colleges are in an especially good position to be the locus of work of this kind and can, by doing so, accomplish their public responsibilities as stewards of public resources and contributors to community development. Although a full realization of this integrative pattern is only beginning to emerge, the promise of this development is compelling. Aspects of this approach are being incorporated into a portfolio of high-impact practices (Kuh, 2008) that can promote student success and a deepening of intellectual and personal engagement. In all of these approaches, knowledge has consequences well beyond the experience of individual students. For numerous examples from the state university and land-grant community, see Peters et al. (2005).

As the different forms of scholarly activity come together in an engagement model, we must find a new vocabulary to describe what we are doing. We may find it useful to retire the term *service* from our lexicon, except for faculty contributions to institutional committee work and institutional governance or to the advancement of their disciplines that are customarily documented in promotion and tenure files. Now, research is often *engaged research* and teaching and learning are becoming *engaged learning*. More commonly, engaged research takes place as an integration of theory and practice, with utility being one intended outcome and advancement of our fundamental knowledge being the other outcome. Active or hands-on learning can take place in a campus setting or off campus. In either environment, learning has meaningful consequences that can influence the thinking and the lives of others. Recent research shows clearly that this kind of learning fosters deeper, more lasting insights and promotes greater confidence and competence (summarized in Bransford, Brown, & Cocking, 1999; Pascarella & Terenzini, 2005).

The engaged institution, which today takes many forms ranging from state and land-grant universities to regional comprehensive institutions, urban universities, community colleges, and liberal arts colleges, is committed to direct interaction with external constituencies and communities through mutually beneficial exchange, exploration, and application of knowledge, expertise, resources, and information. These interactions enrich and expand the learning and discovery functions of the academic institution while also enhancing community capacity. The work of the engaged institution is responsive to (and respectful of) community-identified needs, opportunities, and goals in ways that are appropriate to the campus' mission and academic strengthens.

Living in the Conceptual Age: Global, Multidisciplinary, Collaborative and Open

A recent report on undergraduate education, entitled "The Curriculum at Forty: A Plan for Strengthening the Undergraduate Experience at Brown" (Brown University, 2008), was based on several key assumptions that also underlie the approach to the undergraduate experience in this chapter. These assumptions provide the bridge that can take us from a discussion of how the integration of scholarship, learning, and engagement can enrich the student experience to a consideration of the context and climate in which many of these experiences will take shape: (1) A curriculum should be more about context than content and the basic conditions that foster learning rather than the subjects learned; (2) the most important social, political, scientific, and moral challenges of any era have always demanded the ability to navigate multiple points of view and the application of the tools of many disciplines; and (3) the curriculum has always reflected the changing landscape of American culture and the challenges of nation-building, but often lags behind.

These basic assumptions can lead us to a consideration of the nature of that changing landscape of American culture and the increasingly global context in which our lives and work will surely unfold. The nature of innovation and creativity is changing as business, technology, and society increasingly intersect and influence each other. These new forms of interactions and new opportunities for collaboration are changing some of the fundamental concepts that have driven our approach to education, knowledge transfer, and the management of human capital, intellectual capital, and social capital.

In 2006, IBM Corporation brought together 248 thought leaders from nearly three dozen countries and regions representing 178 organizations on four continents and asked them to explore the evolving nature of innovation. The first conversation about the Global Innovation Outlook (referred to as GIO 1.0), conducted in 2004, concluded that innovation is increasingly *global, multidisciplinary, collaborative*, and *open* (summarized in IBM Corporation, 2006).

Global

New ideas are driven by interactions made possible by networked technology and open standards that are removing geographic barriers to interaction and moving the economy from a reliance on natural resources to a reliance on people resources. In this environment, people can work together across both time and space, but location still matters because the quality of life in a particular region affects who will choose to live there. No longer, however, are the options open to a particular geographic area bounded by or limited by the people and ideas and natural resources found there.

361

Multidisciplinary

A number of years ago, Michael Gibbons et al. (1994) developed the concept of *transdisciplinary* to describe the remarkable changes that are taking place in how and where knowledge is generated and how and where it is put to use. The GIO conception is very closely related to the concept of *transdisciplinary*. GIO 2.0 is based on the observation that the challenges and opportunities we now experience are complex. If we are to respond to them in an innovative way, we need a "diverse mix of talent and expertise" (IBM Corporation, 2006, p. 2).

Collaborative and Open

GIO 2.0 argues that increasingly, "innovation results from people working together in new and integrated ways" (p. 2). This is occurring within our more traditionally organized enterprises, both public and for-profit, and in modes that bring shifting networks of people and organizations together, shaped by common interests rather than by unique institutional affiliations or identities. In these environments, we need new definitions of such classic concepts as enterprise, intellectual property, risk and benefit, trust and responsibility, and brand identity. As we shall see, we also need fresh interpretations of the classic university functions of research, teaching, and service that embrace new ways of working together, new standards of proof and warrants for action, and new participants. We will explore this further when we discuss new ways in which knowledge is being generated and utilized.

It is becoming clear that changes in the very nature of business and how it develops will have significant implications for how we organize and operate our societal institutions, both public and private, how the field of competition changes, what individual and collective behaviors will be rewarded, and how the workings of industry will be judged in the broader context of the social and environmental impacts of their operations. GIO 2.0 offers some tantalizing glimpses of a new reality that will be earth-shaking. The impact of these changes will also shake the foundations of our social systems—how we organize and deliver health care, how we act as stewards of the natural environment and work together to ensure that we leave sufficient resources for coming generations, how we educate, how we work together, and how we learn. It is important to explore what all of this means for how we prepare our students who will begin their professional careers in the rapidly changing context of practice. These changes also have implications for how we view our own work as scholars and how the culture of the academy must change in order to reflect the emerging realities of how knowledge is generated and applied in the world today. We are, alas, far behind.

The Changing Nature of Knowledge Production and Use

The changing nature of knowledge production and international competition and collaboration will affect the organization, working relationships, educational strategies, and societal roles and expectations that we attribute to our nation's colleges and universities, as well as the functions of K–12 and how our educational system prepares its students for the workplace, for citizenship, and for postsecondary education. As we change what we do at the college level, our definition of what it means to be "college ready" will also have to change. It will expand from an emphasis on content knowledge to a more comprehensive conception of what students will need to know and be able to do and how they can respond to changing conditions and needs innovatively and creatively.

We have a long way to go to match our environments, habits, and expectations to the realities of the growing number of enterprises that are working in global, multidisciplinary, collaborative, and open modes. We will only see an alignment between the realities of the creative economy and the goals and aspirations of higher education when these realities are reflected in the policy environments that govern and assess the quality and productivity of postsecondary institutions and in the policies and expectations of most governing boards that oversee public and private higher education. In these environments today, enterprises are still considered as self-contained and solely responsible for whether their students learn and progress successfully to graduation and for how intellectual capital is distributed and used. Within public educational systems in the United States, resources are generally distributed according to the student credit hours generated (i.e.,), according to enrollments) and attributed to individual institutions. Assessments of productivity such as retention and graduation rates of students are still measured within the context of individual institutions even though increasingly students move through a complex pattern of participation in K–12 and postsecondary education and enroll in multiple institutions, often concurrently. Intellectual capital is still regarded as intellectual property to be owned and protected and treated as a means for institutions and their employees (usually academic staff) to generate much-needed revenues. It is rarely considered to be "open source" to be used by a social network of interactive and creative people. With some exceptions, knowledge production by such social networks takes place beyond the bounds of higher education.

Measures of learning are still being approached as a means to assess quality and mete out rewards or punishments rather than as a mechanism to gauge the overall intellectual assets of a state or a region and to guide further investment in the human, social, and intellectual capital that will allow a community to thrive in a networked and global environment. According to Paul Lingenfelter (2007), "meaningful, collective, self-disciplined accountability requires evidence—monitoring results and working for improvement." Note especially the mention of the concept of *collective*. It is the introduction of the concept of shared responsibility that will most characterize the educational environment of the future, both within the context of individual institutions and across the educational sector.

The production and use of knowledge is changing in dramatic ways that will challenge the traditional organization of the disciplines and their reflection in the typical undergraduate and graduate/professional curriculum. A decade ago, Michael Gibbons et al. (1994) foreshadowed these developments in *The New Production of Knowledge*. They argued that a second form of knowledge production that they called Mode 2 was emerging from within the classic research model (Mode 1) and that both how knowledge was being developed and where the work was being done were starting to change. Donald Stokes captured the essence of this new model in *Pasteur's Quadrant* (Stokes, 1997). In his conception of knowledge transfer, Stokes argues that the original linear model—in which basic research leads to applied research, which leads to development and then application on a large scale—offers only a limited understanding of how knowledge is generated and put to use today. He developed the concept of Pasteur's Quadrant to describe a model in which theoretical research and practical research and application come together, as they did in the career of Louis Pasteur, to create a continuously turning *cycle of innovation* driven by changing environmental conditions and the competitive landscape.

Research and learning as well as innovation and invention are becoming concurrent, iterative, and ever-shifting in their focus and their participants. As Gibbons et al. (1994) explain, a new mode of knowledge production is emerging alongside the traditional one "affecting the context in which knowledge is being produced, the very way it is organized, the reward system it uses and the mechanism of quality control" (p. 1) used to validate the work. This new mode is not approached in the frame of a particular discipline. It is not vetted through the usual hierarchical, discipline-based set of warrants for validity. It is not conducted primarily within research universities or their associated laboratories, and it depends on a community of investigators and experimenters drawn from a variety of fields and representing multiple interests. These interactions are supported by the networking capabilities of cyberspace as well as by new and more innovative mindsets and institutional models that foster collaboration. If we are to prepare our students for a world in which knowledge is generated, validated, and applied by communities that form and then shift constantly across traditional boundaries, we must find ways to emulate these new forms and engage our students in the kind of integrative work that they will be asked to undertake once they graduate. We are starting to see a gradual blending of models and methods to create a different, more integrated approach that Gibbons et al. call "transdisciplinary" to distinguish the phenomenon from "interdisciplinary," where a common problem is studied from several angles but the different perspectives do not commingle.

What might this new mode of inquiry and application mean for the intellectual and structural organization of a university and how its intellectual resources are applied to regional innovation? The question is critical because the emerging Mode 2 models appear to hold great promise for supporting the kind of outreach and engagement that will best utilize the resources that society has underwritten in public universities to support the formation of creative centers and competitive regions in a creative economy.

Consider how very different Mode 2 work is from the structure of universities with their departments and carefully codified disciplines. In this environment, even interdisciplinary work is often difficult. In universities, the unit of measure is the individual, not a group or team. It is necessary to distinguish the contributions of a particular person or department to either the generation of intellectual capital or the attraction of prestige and recognition. Meanwhile, in society at large, knowledge workers and their inclination to experimentation and intentional learning continue to spread throughout the professions and organizations, both for-profit and nonprofit, and the locus of research within the research university continues to shift. Much intellectual work and innovation occurs in situations often quite remote from universities. In fact, knowledge and capacity for innovation are increasingly being seen by economists as a valuable, if hard to measure, commodity whose movement and trading resembles a marketplace (Foray, 2004). Gibbons et al. (1994, p. 14) calls this "socially distributed knowledge production." Increasingly, new ideas and knowledge are being generated in many places, involving many types of people and organizations interacting with each other in a variety of ways. With the opening of cyberspace, these relationships appear to be expanding endlessly through a series of social networks supported by a rapidly expanding set of cyber-communities. Our students know about this, and most are active in them. What will be the role of the disciplines in providing quality assurance for ideas and "facts" or observations generated by such a distributed system of people working in increasingly different settings on complicated, multidimensional problems? How must we prepare our students to function as professionals and knowledge workers in a genuine learning society? What should our educational objectives be? How will we deal with the fact that we are no longer the primary or dominant arbiters of what is true and valid and what is not? What will be the role of higher education in the knowledge-based economy and society of the future? What will we do as technological solutions cease to derive from previous experience or existing science but instead represent adaptive solutions to previously unforeseen problems and opportunities? How, in fact, can we cope with adaptive problems in the first place? Designing our curriculum and our expectations of students to model this new and more fluid and improvisational approach to defining and solving problems will require a major overhaul of our approach to teaching and our understanding of what it means to know something and to have confidence in that knowledge.

Making Engagement Legitimate

Unless the institution as a whole embraces the value and validity of engagement as legitimate scholarly work and provides both moral support and concrete resources to sustain it, engagement will remain individually defined and sporadic. Such limited interventions cannot influence larger systems on a scale necessary to address community issues. Significant change to incorporate a strong community base for research and education requires (1) the possibility of reward or benefit for faculty and staff; (2) individual influence and inspired leadership throughout the institution, not just at the top; (3) an institution that is responsive to the needs of the community it serves; (4) educational planning and purposefulness that recognizes the value of active and responsible community service that has a real community impact; (5) a willingness to adopt a shared agenda and a shared resource base over which the institution has only partial control; and finally, (6) the capacity to change (Ramaley, 2006.)

Regardless of local circumstances and institutional traditions and history, there are a few conditions that must be in place for a community-based strategy to work. First, community-based work must be valued as a meaningful educational experience and a legitimate mode of scholarly work. Second, the evaluation of faculty and student work must include rigorous measures of the quality and impact of community-based scholarship, and professional service must be recognized as a component of staff work as well.

Third, mediating structures must be provided to help faculty and students identify community-based learning and research opportunities, and technical support must be available to help faculty and students use these opportunities and assess the results of such programs, both from their own points of view and from the perspectives of the community and its priorities and experiences. Finally, opportunities must be provided for faculty, staff, and students to develop the skills to participate in research and curricular programs in a collaborative mode with partners from different academic disciplines and with significant community involvement.

The Challenges Ahead

As we continue to rethink our approach to educating our students, we have a number of issues to keep in mind: (1) the rapidly changing state of knowledge and how knowledge is used; (2) the increasing fluidity of disciplines through the convergence and integration of fields and methodologies—a phenomenon rarely reflected in the design or content of the undergraduate curriculum; (3) new technologies that create new opportunities and allow us to model, simulate, and experiment in cyberspace-supported collaborative environments; (4) new undergraduate populations; (5) a rapidly changing professoriate; and (6) new expectations for college graduates and new demands in the workplace.

In the past decade, we have experienced a fresh wave of thinking about the relationship between education and democracy and a careful examination of the concept of a public good and the role of higher education in contributing to democratic life and the practice of good citizenship. At the same time, we have begun to appreciate that the intellectual, social, and cultural demands of a truly global environment will place new expectations on higher education. We must educate for a new age where the traditional categories of academic life—research, teaching, and service—must be integrated, both in the life of our faculty and in the experiences of our students. We must move beyond the boundaries that we have held so dear and explore new concepts of what it means to be educated in the twenty-first century and what it means to be a scholar and teacher.

We now return to the issue of a twenty-first-century curriculum. I have argued that the curriculum must incorporate engagement and public scholarship and that to accomplish this we must rethink the core of the academy: the nature of scholarship itself and our expectations for the undergraduate experience. We must work together across the disciplines to create conditions for the public good to be interpreted and pursued in a collaborative mode with the community in order to foster the creative approaches that are needed in the world today.

The integration of research and education has become a powerful tool for preparing students for the responsibilities of the twenty-first-century workplace, where approaches to the generation and use of knowledge will increasingly transcend disciplinary boundaries, as well as for the demands of effective citizenship and the exercise of social responsibility. We must integrate research experiences with a broader conception of what it means to be educated, and link together research opportunities as well as curricular designs that promote a mindset of informed and responsible decision making. Our challenge is to examine research opportunities for undergraduates not only as a means to interest a select group of students in going on to advanced study, but also as a vital component of the educational environment for *all* students and a means to attain our expectations for our graduates.

Whenever we invest in research capacity, we are creating an educational asset. This asset can be deployed in a number of ways: to provide research experiences for undergraduate students, high school students, and K–12 teachers and to promote public understanding of the value of learning. In some instances, the research activities themselves can be designed in such a way that the general public can also contribute to the work, through gathering of observations and data.

In some instances, research can be incorporated into the design of educational experiences for all students, not just those who can be accommodated on a research team or in a field or laboratory research project. This can be done through such pedagogies as service-learning, inquiry-based learning, and project-based learning. In all cases, a scientific mindset and an approach that promotes quantitative literacy can be introduced into the classroom so that students learn in a mode comparable to that employed by an investigator, even if the work they are doing is not an original contribution.

Taken as a whole, the growing relationships of the disciplines to each other, the opportunities to link life experiences with scholarly inquiry, and the growing connections between learning and life will ensure that we are preparing our students for life in a Conceptual Age. In such a world, learning will have visible and compelling consequences and a meaning far beyond the impact of an education on our students individually. In sum, the path of integration and coherence offers a way to return to the true public purposes of higher education. *We shall all benefit.*

References

Association of American Colleges and Universities (AAC&U). (2008). *College learning for the new global century.* Executive summary. Washington DC: Author. Full text of the LEAP Report is available at www.aacu.org.

Boyer, E. L. (1990) *Scholarship reconsidered: Priorities of the professoriate.* Princeton, NJ: Carnegie Foundation for the Advancement of Teaching.

Bransford, J. D., Brown, A. N., & Cocking, R. R. (Eds.). (1999). *How people learn, brain, mind, experience and school.* Washington, DC: National Academies Press.

Brown University. (2008). *The curriculum at forty: A plan for strengthening the undergraduate experience at Brown.* Retrieved February 1, 2009, from http://www.brown.edu/Administration/Dean_of_the_College/tue/downloads/Task_Force_Final_Report.pdf.

Campus Compact. (1999). *The presidents' declaration on the civic responsibility of higher education.* Retrieved February 1, 2009, from http://www.compact.org/resources/declaration/.

Colby, A., Beaumont, E., Ehrlich, T., & Corngold, J. (2008) *Educating for democracy. Preparing undergraduates for responsible political engagement.* San Francisco: Jossey-Bass.

Cooper, D. D. (2002). Bus rides and forks in the road: The making of a public scholar. In D. W. Brown & D. Witte (Eds.), *Higher education exchange* (pp. 24–48). Dayton, OH: Kettering Foundation.

Foray, D. (2004). *The economics of knowledge.* Boston: MIT Press.

Gibbons, M., Limoges, C., Nowotny, H., Schwartz, S., Scott, P., & Trow, M. (1994). *The new production of knowledge: The dynamics of science and research in contemporary societies.* London: Sage.

Glassick, C. E., Huber, M. T., & Maeroff, G. I. (1997). *Scholarship assessed: Evaluation of the professoriate.* Carnegie Foundation for the Advancement of Teaching. San Francisco: Jossey-Bass.

Greater Expectations Panel. (2002) *A new vision for learning as a nation goes to college.* National Panel Report 2002. Washington, DC: Association of American Colleges and Universities.

Holland, B. A. (2005). Real Change in Higher Education: Understanding Differences in Institutional Commitment to Engagement. In A. Kezar, T. Chambers, J. Burkhardt, & Associates (Eds.), *Higher education for the public good: Emerging voices from a national movement*. San Francisco: Jossey-Bass.

Huber, M. T., & Hutchings, P. (2004). *Integrative learning, mapping the terrain*. Washington DC: Association of American Colleges and Universities.

IBM Corporation. (2006, March). *Global Innovation Outlook 2.0*. IBM Monograph. Armonk, NY: Author.

Kellogg Commission on the Future of State and Land-Grant Universities. (1999). *Returning to our roots: The engaged institution*. Washington, DC: National Association of State Universities and Land-Grant Colleges.

Kuh, G. (2008). *High impact educational practices: What they are, who has access to them, and why they matter*. Washington, DC: AAC&U.

Kuh, G., Kinzie, J., Schuh, J. H., & Whitt, E. J. (2005). *Student success in college, creating conditions that matter*. San Francisco: Jossey-Bass.

Lingenfelter, P. E. (2007, January 29). *What should the states require—and not require of accreditation, and why?* Paper presented at the Council for Higher Education Accreditation (CHEA) Annual Conference.

Nussbaum, M. C. (1997). *Cultivating humanity: A classical defense of reform in liberal education*. Cambridge, MA: Harvard University Press.

Nussbaum, M. C. (2004, Winter). Liberal education and global community. *Change*, 42–47.

Pascarella, E. T., & Terenzini, P. T. (2005). *How college affects students: Vol. 2. A third decade of research*. San Francisco: Jossey-Bass.

Peters, S. J., Jordan, N. R., Adamek, M., & Alter, T. R. (Eds.). (2005). *Engaging campus and community. The practice of public scholarship in the state and land-grant university system*. Dayton, OH: Kettering Foundation Press.

Pink, D. H. (2005). *A whole new mind: Moving from the Information Age to the Conceptual Age*. New York: Riverhead Books.

Ramaley, J. A. (2005). Scholarship for the public good: Living in Pasteur's quadrant. In A. J. Kezar, T. C. Chambers, J. C. Burkhardt, & Associates (Eds.), *Higher education for the public good. Emerging voices from a national movement* (pp. 166–182). San Francisco: Jossey-Bass.

Ramaley, J. A. (2006). Public scholarship: Making sense of an emerging synthesis. In R. Eberly & J. Cohen (Eds.), *A laboratory for public scholarship and democracy: New directions for teaching and learning* (Vol. 105, pp. 85–97).

Ramaley, J. A. (2007, Summer). Reflections on the public purposes of higher education. *Wingspread Journal Education*, 5–10.

Ramaley, J. A., Olds, B., & Earle, J. (2005). Becoming a learning organization: New directions in science education research at the National Science Foundation. *Journal of Science Education and Technology*, available at http://dx.doi.org/10.1007/s10956–0054420–8.

Sandy, M., & Holland, B. A. (2006, Fall). Different worlds and common ground: Community partner perspectives on campus-community partnerships. *Michigan Journal of Community Service Learning*, 30–43.

Schoen, D. A. (1997). *Educating the reflective practitioner*. San Francisco: Jossey-Bass.

Stokes, D. E. (1997). *Pasteur's Quadrant: Basic science and technological innovation*. Washington, DC: Brookings Institution.

Students as Change Agents in the Engagement Movement

Amanda L. Vogel, Caroline Fichtenberg, and Mindi B. Levin

Since the start of the contemporary engagement movement in higher education, students have made important contributions as leaders and change agents. A number of authors credit students with catalyzing today's engagement movement, through the creation of the Campus Outreach Opportunity League (COOL) in 1984 (Liu, 1996; Zlotkowski, Longo, & Williams, 2006). Multiple publications document the development, in the 1990s, of a national student-driven service movement, which existed within the broader engagement movement, and in which students were participating in "unprecedented numbers" (Levine & Cureton, 1998, p. 39; Liu, 1996; Loeb, 1994). Student founders of that service movement laid the groundwork for the thriving student engagement movement that exists today, by creating a model for student engagement that was sustainable in large part because it was rooted in their generation's politics. Issue-oriented, pragmatic, localized, nonpartisan, and rooted in a desire for social change—the overarching traits of their movement continue to define student engagement today (Levine & Cureton, 1998; Loeb, 1994).

Throughout the past twenty-five years, students have also been vocal proponents of the civic responsibilities of higher education. In the 1980s, students led the highly successful national campaign for institutions of higher education to divest from South Africa, which in turn triggered the national divestment movement (Boren, 2001; Loeb, 1994). They also provided outspoken leadership at their colleges and universities to promote gender and race/ethnic diversity in faculty hiring and retention (Wilson, 1989). In the 1990s and 2000s, students advocated for their higher education institutions to adopt a stance of greater social responsibility through the Living Wage Campaign, United Students Against Sweatshops, and Universities Allied for Essential Medicines (Featherstone, 2002; Harvard Living Wage Campaign, 2002; UAEM, 2008).

369

Despite this history of consistent contributions to the engagement movement, until recently, students' leadership role was not widely recognized (Bastress & Beilenson, 1996; Liu, 1996; Zlotkowski et al., 2006). A number of authors trace this oversight to strategic decisions that were made in the 1990s in order to sustain the movement. National leaders in the movement adopted two main strategies for sustainability. They created resources to support the institutionalization of engagement on campuses nationwide, and they fostered the integration of engagement into the core activities of academia, through service-learning, and more recently, engaged research. These approaches were highly effective, leading to the founding of Campus Compact, the creation of the Learn and Serve America program within the federal Corporation for National and Community Service, the increasing adoption of service-learning and engaged research, and the flowering of a new body of engaged scholarship. But a number of authors have argued that by focusing only on the activities of administrators and faculty, these strategies marginalized students' past contributions to the movement (Bastress & Beilenson, 1996; Liu, 1996; Zlotkowski et al., 2006). In doing so, they also missed an opportunity to capitalize on students' natural role as co-leaders, which was also important to the movement's future.

But over the past decade the broader engagement movement has been paying growing attention to students' past, current, and future leadership roles, because of a new awareness that students contribute to the movement in ways that are distinct from faculty and administrators. Leading organizations in the movement, with Campus Compact in the forefront, increasingly are seeing student co-leadership as essential to the next phase of the movement (Cone, Keisa, & Longo, 2006; Long, Saltmarsh, & Heffernan, 2002; Zlotkowski et al., 2006). The Campus Compact-published book, *Students as Colleagues: Expanding the Circle of Service-Learning Leadership* asserts, "just as the service movement once needed resources that students alone could *not* supply, so the movement has now reached a point where it needs resources that students alone *can* supply" (Zlotkowski, et al., 2006; page 3). It argues that student co-leadership can enrich the quality of community engaged learning experiences and ensure continued student interest in service-learning. Similar assertions can be made about the added value of student co-leadership for engaged research and practice. *Students as Colleagues* includes twenty case studies describing how students nationwide are providing extraordinary co-leadership in service-learning and other forms of engagement on their campuses. The cases also demonstrate widespread support for student co-leadership among faculty and administrators nationally.

Recent interest in student co-leadership in the engagement movement is also informed by the dramatic contributions that today's youth are making to civil society. It is widely perceived that the hallmark of the "millenial" generation is civic engagement. Reflecting on the current boom of youth-led social entrepreneurship, a recent *New York Times* op-ed describes social entrepreneurship as this generation's answer to the youth activism of the 1960s (Kristof, 2008). National news outlets including the *Times,* CNN, and *Newsweek* are following the youth civic engagement movement and have featured stories on innovative student-led service projects, engaged research, activism, and social entrepreneurship (CNN, 2008; Ellin, 2001; Foote, 2008; Kuchment, 2008). There has also been noteworthy growth in youth voter participation over the last decade, and this has been credited with contributing to change in the political environment (CIRCLE, 2008; Lopez, Kirby, & Sagoff 2005; Market Watch, 2008). Persons aged 18 to 29 made up a disproportionate 20 percent of the electorate in the Presidential election of 2008, and voted for President Obama over Senator McCain by more than two-to-one, contributing a major part of the winning coalition (CIRCLE, 2008; Market Watch, 2008). They also voted nearly two-to-one for House Democrats (Market Watch, 2008).

With regard to the role of students in the engagement movement, two main questions stand out today. First, given the remarkable contribution that the current generation of students is making to civil society, what innovative roles can current and future students play in the engagement movement, particularly if included as co-leaders? Second, in order to fully realize their role as co-leaders, what additional support will students need from the national engagement movement and their local institutions?

In this chapter, we offer some answers to these questions. First, we describe three ways in which today's students are contributing unique leadership to push the engagement movement forward in new directions. Then we present a case study of one student organization, with which we were involved as founding members, that is an example of students' leadership in the engagement movement today. This case study highlights the distinct contributions that student leaders can make as compared to faculty, administrators, and staff. It also identifies ways that students can capitalize on their strengths and work around their limitations as contributors to the engagement movement at their institutions; and it provides examples of how faculty and administrative allies can provide critical support for student co-leaders. Based on lessons from the case study, we end this chapter with five key considerations for how to foster effective student co-leadership in the engagement movement in the next decade.

Today's Students Are Providing Unique Leadership in the Engagement Movement

Higher education students today are building on a long tradition of student service and activism. But the contributions of the current generation of students are unique because of the social forces that have shaped these students and the resources they have available. Today's students have been influenced by the culture of volunteerism, the growth of service-learning in K–12 education, and the trend of social entrepreneurship that have characterized the past two decades. When they enter higher education, they have a firsthand understanding of how engagement can be structured and what social goals it can pursue. Today's students also have the support of the resources created by the broader engagement movement, including campus engagement centers, a growing number of faculty and staff allies, and the support of national organizations. These resources provide critical instrumental support, enabling students to maximize their leadership potential in the movement.

As a result of these unique circumstances, today's students are serving as change agents in the engagement movement, providing innovative leadership that is helping to push the engagement movement forward in new directions. Three methods, in particular, characterize their contributions: social entrepreneurship, academic entrepreneurship, and activism for institutional culture change in higher education. The following examples describe the activities of a number of leading national student engagement organizations, highlighting aspects of their work that exemplify each of these methods. It should be noted, though, that these methods are interdependent, and often they are used in tandem by student organizations, including some of the ones we describe here.

As *social entrepreneurs,* students are designing and implementing ambitious models of community outreach and service delivery, in order to address important social problems. These programs' sophisticated design, and their remarkable scope, and impact, are challenging our understanding of the limits of engaged scholarship. Unite for Sight (UFS) is a powerful example. Founded in 2000 by an undergraduate student, UFS initially provided eye health education and screenings to the poor and underserved in New Haven. But its founder radically transformed the organization to address wider population eye health needs and focus on building local capacity. Now a nonprofit organization, but still run by its founder, who is a medical resident, UFS has expanded to include chapters at over seventy colleges and universities, each serving its local community. It also has a growing program in developing countries, where its volunteers work with local eye clinics to deliver eye care in communities that had no prior access to care, with financing from UFS. Through these innovations, the organization has provided services to over six hundred thousand persons (Unite for Sight, 2008).

Teach for America (TFA) was designed by an undergraduate student as her senior thesis project. She then went on to found the organization upon graduating in 1990. Through TFA, outstanding college graduates commit to teach for two years in high-need public schools. The organization currently provides teachers to more than a thousand schools in twenty-nine high-need areas nationally. It has served three million students and employed twenty thousand individuals. Some see the organization as a training ground for future leaders in the education field (Foote, 2008; Graves, 2008; Teach for America, 2008).

As *academic entrepreneurs,* today's students are creating new curricula and infrastructure to support engaged learning at their institutions. In this role, students are capitalizing on their position as the experts on their own educational needs. Independently and in collaboration with faculty and administrative allies, students are developing and teaching service-learning courses and co-curricular learning experiences, creating student-run engaged research projects, reaching out to communities to lay the foundations for long-term community-academic partnerships, and establishing coordinated service-learning programs and student engagement centers at their schools (Addes & Keene, 2006; Alden & Norman, 2006; Chatwin, Gillespie, Looser, & Welch, 2006; Meyer, 2006; Mohan & Mohan, 2006; Vogel, Ghanbarpour, Mistry, & Levin, 2007). These activities are being led by both undergraduate and graduate students across a spectrum of disciplines.

One of the most important contributions students are making as academic entrepreneurs is by establishing innovative co-curricular engaged learning programs. These programs are introducing sustainable engaged learning opportunities and providing ongoing benefits for communities. For example, in the health professions, students are founding and operating community-based clinics in community centers, churches, and homeless shelters, both to enhance their training and to provide care to the poor and underserved

(Beck, 2005; Eckenfels, 1997). Participation in the clinics is becoming a widely accepted training method; a recent survey identified student-run clinics at forty-nine U.S. medical schools (40 percent) (Beck, 2005; Buchanan & Witlen, 2006; Eckenfels, 1997; Simpson & Long, 2007). Law students are creating similar sustainable co-curricular engaged learning programs. Founded at the New York University Law School, the Unemployment Action Center is a student-run nonprofit organization that provides real-world litigation experiences for law students who supply free legal representation at unemployment hearings. Since it was founded in 1981, the organization has expanded to seven New York City law schools and served more than eleven thousand claimants (Unemployment Action Center, 2008).

Finally, students today are providing unique leadership in the engagement movement as *activists for institutional-culture change*, who are working to promote a culture of civic engagement in higher education. These students are continuing a tradition of student activism calling for greater social responsibility by academic institutions. But as part of the engagement movement, they are advocating for universities to ensure that their central activities—namely, research and teaching—are being used for the public good. Students are playing a unique leadership role in these efforts because they are able to use advocacy methods that may not be available to faculty and administrators. For example, Universities Allied for Essential Medicines (UAEM) advocates for universities to ensure that lifesaving biomedical products developed in academic laboratories are financially accessible in developing countries. Founded in 2001 by a Yale Law student, UAEM now has chapters at forty-four universities in North America and Europe that work with faculty and administrators to examine and improve the research, licensing, and patenting practices at their respective institutions (UAEM, 2008).

Students for a Positive Academic Partnership with the East Baltimore Community (SPARC) was created in 2005 by students at the Johns Hopkins Bloomberg School of Public Health (JHSPH) to promote a greater institutional commitment to investing in the health of the school's local community, which faces many public health challenges. As described in the following case study, SPARC collaborated with faculty and administrators to make policy and curriculum changes to increase institutional support for engaged scholarship and create more opportunities for student engagement in the community. It also engaged in awareness-raising activities to foster an organizational culture of civic responsibility to the local community. SPARC's activities were among a variety of student, faculty, and staff efforts that contributed to a visible increase in community engagement at the school over the past five years.

Case Study of SPARC

Background

The East Baltimore community where JHSPH is located faces many challenges, including poverty, disproportionate levels of preventable disease, and environmental hazards. In the neighborhood immediately around the School, median household income was $14,900, and 70 percent of residents earned less than $25,000 annually in the year 2000 (Baltimore City Health Department, 2008). The area currently ranks among the least healthy third of Baltimore's fifty-five neighborhoods for HIV/AIDS deaths, drug-induced deaths, low-birth-weight births, and childhood lead poisoning (Baltimore City Health Department, 2008). Residents

373

are also disproportionately affected by heart disease, stroke, diabetes, and homicide (Baltimore City Health Department, 2008). Finally, there are a striking number of abandoned and boarded-up homes in the neighborhood, and this is a source of multiple health threats, including lead paint exposure, rat infestations, dumping, drug trade, and violence (Cohen, 2005; Farfel et al., 2003; Gomez, 2005; Gomez & Muntaner, 2005). Despite these challenges, the neighborhood is also home to dozens of community-based organizations devoted to improving community health and well-being.

JHSPH has plentiful resources for addressing complex public health problems. The school has a global reputation as a premier research and teaching institution for public health. It has adopted the motto "Protecting Health, Saving Lives—Millions at a Time," reflecting the transformative impact of a number of its scientific discoveries. As the largest school of public health in the world, JHSPH has an annual budget of $360 million and receives one-fifth of all federal research funds awarded to the thirty-nine accredited public health schools in the United States (Johns Hopkins Bloomberg School of Public Health, 2008). It employs 530 full-time faculty members, many of whom have expertise in addressing the health of the global poor, and a number of whom have dedicated their careers to community-engaged research abroad and in Baltimore. But despite these resources, the health of residents in the surrounding community has continued to suffer for the past several decades (Gomez & Muntaner, 2005).

In the five years before SPARC was founded, some steps were taken to invest more university resources in the health of East Baltimore. In 2000, the university established the Johns Hopkins Urban Health Institute to foster engaged research by faculty. In early 2005 the Johns Hopkins Medical Institutions established SOURCE (Student Outreach Resource Center), the community service and service-learning center for students at the Johns Hopkins University Schools of Medicine, Nursing, and Public Health. But these initiatives were constrained by small budgets and staff, and neither was implemented at the level of the school.

Uniting around Shared Values and Goals

The founding members of SPARC came together around a shared sense that, as members of the JHSPH community, they could contribute to catalyzing greater community engagement at the school to address the social, economic, and public health problems facing the East Baltimore neighborhood. These students were frustrated by what seemed to them to be the insufficient attention the school was paying to the health problems in the local community, particularly given the school's unique resources to address public health challenges. These students believed that although existing efforts were focused in the right direction, they were too limited and too uncoordinated considering the magnitude of the health challenges in the community. The students wanted the school to make it an institutional priority to address the public health problems right outside its door. They believed that the school could make a significant positive contribution to the health of the local community if it adopted a coordinated schoolwide approach.

These students formed SPARC as a student organization to promote this goal. The founding group included eight students (including authors ALV and CF) as well as two community-engaged staff members who became key allies and advisors. They were a representative from a community-academic environmental justice partnership, and the director of SOURCE (author MBL).

From the outset, the goal of the group was to foster a change in the organizational culture of the School. In an early visioning document, they wrote:

> We believe JHSPH has an ethical responsibility as an educational institution, as a public health institution, as an employer and as a neighbor to use its financial, intellectual and technical resources to help improve the quality of life of East Baltimore "residents. ... We" would like the School to publicly recognize its responsibility toward the community in which it resides. We envision an institutional culture change whereby a community perspective would be acknowledged at the highest levels of the institution and incorporated into all aspects of the institution: teaching, learning, research and social activities.

The students identified several school-level responses that could help achieve this vision: (1) curriculum changes that would facilitate service-learning in the local community; (2) direct financial aid to East Baltimore community-based organizations addressing health issues; and (3) a center for community-academic partnerships that would coordinate all ongoing community engaged projects at the school, support community-engaged faculty, and serve as a portal for community members who wished to tap into the school's expertise.

Mobilizing Students' Voices to Foster Community Engagement
The SPARC Student Body Survey

SPARC's founders decided that in order to effectively advocate for these changes, they first needed to demonstrate widespread student support for their goals. Earlier that year, a student-led initiative to improve student health benefits had been a success after demonstrating widespread student support through a student-body survey. SPARC believed that survey was effective because it appealed to the data-driven culture of this research-focused institution, and they decided to follow the same strategy.

The SPARC survey was fielded in spring 2005 over the school's student electronic mailing list. It assessed student attitudes about institutional and personal engagement in the community, and student support for specific institutional changes that would promote greater engagement. The survey included both multiple-choice questions and opportunities for student comments.

Despite fielding the survey at one of the most challenging times for students—during the last two weeks of the academic year—nearly three hundred students (16 percent) participated. An overwhelming majority of respondents (90 percent) felt that JHSPH had a responsibility to be more involved with the East Baltimore community, and nearly three-quarters (73 percent) thought that the school's lack of emphasis on community involvement was contrary to the philosophy of public health.

More than two-thirds (69 percent) of respondents wanted to increase their personal engagement in the community, and there was widespread support for institutional changes that would support greater engagement by students and the entire school community.

Almost all of the respondents supported a greater emphasis on community involvement in the school's mission statement (95 percent) and were in favor of having more courses that included community involvement (97 percent). One respondent wrote, "Everyone wants to pass off community involvement to the students—but it is at the level of the school that it needs to happen." In fall 2005, SPARC's founders wrote up the survey findings and related recommendations in a report to the school's administration. They offered ten recommendations for actions, listed below.

Recommendations for Action from SPARC'S Report to the Administration

Curriculum:
1. Greater Encouragement and Support of Service-Learning
2. Academic Credit for Self-Directed Community-Based Learning
3. Community-Based Masters Degree Capstone Projects
4. Public Health in Baltimore Course
5. Community-Based Participatory Research (CBPR) Methods Course

Institutional Infrastructure:
6. Recruitment and Retention of Community-Engaged Faculty Members
7. Community-Based Participatory Research and Outreach Center
8. Visible Direct Aid to East Baltimore Community Agencies
9. Financial Support for Student Community Involvement
10. Encourage Use of Community Based Participatory Research Principles

SPARC Communications Campaign

Over the next six months, SPARC members engaged in a communications campaign to publicize their report to the school's administration, faculty, and students. SPARC began by meeting directly with high-level administrators to discuss the report. Their reactions to SPARC's report were mixed. One high-ranking dean was enthusiastic about SPARC's ability to support ongoing efforts to develop more engaged training opportunities. He invited SPARC to become involved in this work. He also gave a copy of SPARC's report to the new Dean of the School. But other deans believed SPARC's advocacy was unnecessary. He also gave a copy of the report to the new Dean of the School. In response to SPARC's curriculum recommendations, they suggested there were extracurricular opportunities for student engagement in the community that students were not utilizing enough. In response to SPARC's institutional recommendations, they informed the group of past and ongoing efforts at the school to engage with the local community. The fact that SPARC members were hearing about many of these efforts for the first time indicated to them that the school needed to enhance its communication about its existing community engagement activities.

At the same time SPARC was reaching out to administrators, the group disseminated its report broadly to the school community. With the support of SOURCE, SPARC developed a website where it posted the survey findings and report. It then sent announcements to the school's student, faculty, and staff electronic mailing lists, summarizing the survey findings and recommendations and providing a link to the website. SPARC members also spoke at School Town Hall meetings, which are organized by the Student Assembly for students to discuss their concerns with the deans of the school and attended by hundreds of students, faculty, and administrators. SPARC members highlighted particular survey results and recommendations and asked the deans how the school planned to increase its engagement in the community. Finally, SPARC members presented their report to the Student Assembly, where they discussed how SPARC's activities could complement Student Assembly's work on behalf of student interests.

The SPARC Student Assembly Resolution

In response to SPARC's survey and report, a number of faculty and administrative allies approached SPARC to offer their support, as did allies outside the school who were involved in the engagement movement. But the school did not respond in any direct way to SPARC regarding its recommendations. SPARC needed to keep its agenda in the spotlight.

Acting on the advice of its new allies, SPARC drafted a Student Assembly resolution calling on the school to adopt an institution-wide commitment to investing in the local community. Student Assembly is the main voice for students at the school and an elected representative body. The resolution put the weight of Student Assembly behind SPARC's recommendations. It also had additional power because the last Student Assembly resolution had been for institutional divestment from South Africa in the mid-1980s. The resolution recommended that the school (1) adopt a coordinated schoolwide planning process for engagement that would involve both community and student representatives, and (2) develop infrastructure to enhance communication about its engagement in the local community.

Resolution to Support a Greater Institutional Commitment to Improving Public Health in East Baltimore

JHSPH is widely recognized as a leader in public health both domestically and internationally. Yet the East Baltimore neighborhood where the School is located is one of the least healthy in Baltimore City and the nation. The JHSPH student body recognizes that longstanding socioeconomic and political factors have contributed to the poor health of East Baltimore residents, and that JHSPH supports many activities that work to promote health in the community. However, our current efforts are not commensurate with the scope of the public health concerns. We believe that *JHSPH has the resources and the social responsibility to undertake more visible and effective efforts to improve the health of its neighbors.*

We therefore call upon the administration to adopt an institution-wide commitment to help improve the health of East Baltimore residents, beginning with the following three steps:

1. **Coordination**—Create a strategic planning group to develop goals for how JHSPH can help to improve the health of East Baltimore residents, both by coordinating existing resources and by creating new resources.

2. **Representation**—Designate seats for JHSPH student and meaningful East Baltimore representation on the proposed strategic planning group and on all existing JHSPH decision-making bodies that impact the health of East Baltimore residents.

3. **Communication**—Create a permanent infrastructure to continually communicate with the student body and East Baltimore residents about the School's activities to improve the health of the East Baltimore community.

The Student Assembly will support the administration in implementing the above resolution through facilitating ongoing dialogue between students and administrators.

Student Assembly passed the resolution unanimously, and SPARC publicized the outcome to the school community over the student, faculty, and staff electronic mailing lists. However, mirroring SPARC's experience with its report, there was no direct response from the administration to the recommendations in the resolution.

Nevertheless, the SPARC survey, communications campaign, and resolution were effective in many ways. Most important, these activities injected student voices into the growing group of stakeholders at the school who wanted a greater institutional investment in the health of the local community, and were working toward this goal. These activities also established SPARC as a new public presence at the school that spoke for students committed to engagement. It become a group where like-minded students could gather to become involved in these issues, and that faculty and administrators could tap to involve interested students in their own efforts to increase engagement at the School.

Finally, the feedback SPARC received from faculty and administrators helped the group to refine its aims and strategies, which ultimately improved SPARC's effectiveness. The lack of a direct response to SPARC's recommendations from the administration suggested to SPARC that, as a student group, it was limited in its power to catalyze policy changes at the school. But the active support SPARC received from many individual faculty members and administrators showed that student efforts, to promote greater institutional engagement nonetheless were considered valuable. In fact, these allies asserted that students had a unique and valuable contribution to make to fostering engagement. SPARC recognized that it could be most effective by capitalizing on its role as a student group. SPARC also learned that faculty and administrators who were also working to increase engagement at the school were natural allies for SPARC. SPARC might be able to collaborate with them in the future to achieve goals they could not accomplish independently.

Strategic Planning: Capitalizing on Students' Unique Roles in the Academy

At about this time, SPARC became an official student group through Student Assembly. To fulfill requirements for student groups, it engaged in a process of writing mission and vision statements, planning a long-term strategy, and developing an organizational structure. This provided an opportunity for SPARC to reevaluate its strategies, based on the lessons it had learned from the responses to its activities up to that time.

SPARC decided to pursue two main strategies moving forward that would capitalize on its strengths as a student group. First, SPARC would promote curriculum changes to create greater opportunities for community-engaged learning for students. If successful, these curriculum changes could institutionalize greater support for engaged scholarship. SPARC members recognized that whatever limitations they faced to changing the school's other policies, students had unique leverage to advocate for curriculum change, because they were experts on their own educational goals and they had firsthand knowledge of the scope of the existing curriculum.

Second, SPARC would continue to encourage broader investments of school resources in the community. But it would do so by working to consolidate general opinion at the school in favor of greater institutional investments in the local community, which it hoped would then lead the school to act. This strategy was based on SPARC's recognition that students play an important role in the school community, and student activities have a significant impact on the school. It also reflected SPARC's experience with the survey and resolution, demonstrating that students could say and do things to foster institutional change that faculty and administrators could not.

SPARC created a two-part mission statement reflecting these two strategies and established two action committees—one to pursue each strategy. SPARC also recognized it would need to work around its limitations. It could do this by collaborating with faculty and administrative allies.

SPARC's Mission and Vision Statements

SPARC is a JHSPH student advocacy group promoting greater institutional commitment to the East Baltimore community. We advocate for:

1. Improved training opportunities in community-based research and public health practice for JHSPH students through sustained, reciprocal community-academic partnerships; and

2. A greater investment of JHSPH institutional resources in supporting East Baltimore community organizations and improving the health of East Baltimore residents.

SPARC envisions an institutional commitment at JHSPH to improving the health of the East Baltimore Community through sustained, reciprocal community-academic partnerships based upon a foundation of mutual respect and trust.

Academic Entrepreneurship to Create Engaged Training Opportunities

SPARC used two methods to create more opportunities for community engaged training for students. First, it provided support for work being led by faculty, staff, and administrators that would create new engaged coursework or foster support for engaged learning. Second, it led a major curriculum reform project, in which it engaged faculty and staff allies, that led to the creation of an integrated curriculum in engaged public health at the school.

SPARC's initial curriculum related project provided support for the school to meet a new accreditation requirement for engaged training that would be implemented in fall 2006. This developed from SPARC's conversation with the Associate Dean for Academic Affairs in fall 2005. At the same time that SPARC was developing its survey, it compiled a list of courses at the school that provided training that SPARC believed would prepare students for careers in engaged public health. The list was intended to help incoming students to identify this coursework, because it was not designated in any other way. The Senior Associate Dean believed the course list would help satisfy the new accreditation requirements. On his recommendation, SPARC enhanced the list to support the accreditation process, identifying courses that included engaged learning opportunities. SPARC believed that successful adherence to this requirement would increase interest in engaged training and scholarship at the school.

The same accreditation requirement prompted SOURCE to develop a new course for Master of Public Health students that included a community-based practicum in the local community. SPARC provided support for the course in its ten recommendations to the administration. SPARC also advocated for SOURCE to receive funding to hire an additional staff member to facilitate engaged learning with local community organizations. SPARC's support was among a number of factors that helped to obtain this funding.

At the same time, SPARC began focusing on how it could lead more comprehensive efforts to create new opportunities for engaged training. Having identified a need for students to be able to identify course work in engaged public health, SPARC wanted to create a coordinated course of study in this area. However, the group did not know how to work within the school's systems to achieve this goal, or even whether a proposal submitted by students would be considered.

SPARC asked faculty and administrative allies for guidance. In late 2006, the group invited faculty who were interested in promoting greater institutional engagement, and who understood how decisions were made at the school, to meet with them to discuss their curriculum goals. This began a process of sustained collaboration with many of these faculty members over the next two years. They recommended that SPARC develop a proposal for a certificate program because it would be the easiest type of curriculum change to make. They believed that SPARC could lead this effort, as a student group, and that its survey findings would provide a strong argument for the certificate. But they recommended that SPARC replicate the survey, adding a question specifically to assess student support for a certificate. SPARC did this in May 2007. This time, 447 (34%) students responded of these 97%, or one-third of the student body, supported the idea of a "new certificate or track in community-based and practice-based public health." These data provided the support SPARC needed to propose the certificate.

Over the next year, SPARC developed a proposal for a Certificate in Community-Based Public Health, combining existing coursework at the Schools of Public Health and Nursing into a single integrated course sequence. The proposed certificate would provide training in the content areas and methods needed for careers in engaged public health and offer a series of engaged learning opportunities in the local community. Faculty allies provided important insights that shaped the scope and content of the proposed certificate. In addition based on faculty members' advice, SPARC developed a supporting document providing the rationale for the certificate. It summarized the public health competencies the certificate would teach, the value of the experiential teaching methods it would use, and SPARC's survey findings demonstrating strong student demand.

With these documents complete, in spring 2008, SPARC approached the Chair of the Department of Health, Behavior and Society and a departmental faculty member who is an engaged scholar, to solicit their advice on next steps. Both immediately agreed to sponsor the proposal. The faculty member became a critical partner, working with SPARC and SOURCE to see the proposal through multiple reviews by the Department and the school, which led to a series of revisions. The Certificate in Community-Based Public Health was approved in January 2009 and was opened for enrollment in September 2009.

Activism to Promote a Culture of Civic Engagement

Meanwhile, SPARC was engaging in activities aimed at consolidating public opinion at the school in favor of greater institutional investments in the local community SPARC hoped this would lead the school to pursue greater engagement across the spectrum of its activities. From fall 2006 to spring 2008, SPARC engaged in two approaches to foster these beliefs among the school community. First, it organized high-visibility awareness raising activities that aimed to convince students, faculty, staff, and administrators of the need for the school to invest in the East Baltimore community. Second, SPARC members became involved in multiple schoolwide committees and student groups whose work had, or could have, an impact on engagement in the community.

SPARC's awareness-raising activities highlighted the public health needs in East Baltimore, the school's relationship with the community, community members' desire to partner with the school to support the health of the community, and specific actions the school could take. The centerpiece of this work was a series of public events at the school that addressed pressing public health needs in the community. SPARC's first event examined the public health consequences of an urban redevelopment project immediately adjacent to the school that will impact eight-eight largely residential acres to make room for a biotechnology park in which the university is a major stakeholder, and new mixed-income housing (Cohen, 2008; EBDI, 2008; Gomez, 2005). The event featured a panel discussion involving academics, community activists, and local developers. SPARC's second event featured a talk by a prominent community activist working to address poverty in East Baltimore. He facilitated a discussion among the audience members about how the school and community could collaborate to address the problem of structural poverty. More than three hundred faculty, staff, students, and community members participated. SPARC included SOURCE, student groups, the school's Center for Environmental Health, and a new administrative initiative to foster applied public health research as co-sponsors of these events. SPARC also co-sponsored other student groups' events highlighting public health issues relevant to the local community.

SPARC also collaborated with SOURCE and Student Assembly to institutionalize awareness-raising activities about health in the local community. Together, they launched Baltimore Week, an annual weeklong series of lectures, discussions, and films about health in Baltimore on campus, and opportunities for student, faculty, and staff to provide service in the local community. Baltimore Week is now sponsored by SOURCE, with co-sponsorship from Student Assembly. It was held for the fourth time in October 2009. These events have created a new focus on the health of the East Baltimore community at the school. Notably, this event brings community members into the school and creates dialogue between members of the community and the school about how the school can support the health of the community.

SPARC also engaged in awareness raising through articles, letters to the editor, and petitions that highlighted health needs in the community, recommended ways the school could respond, and pointed out the value of involving students. SPARC's articles and letters were published in the school's official magazine and student publications, and a Baltimore magazine dedicated to urban issues. SPARC's petitions called on the school to implement the SPARC resolution and to invest substantial resources in a student-run tutoring program serving a local elementary school. Although the petitions did not lead to action by the administration, they contributed to raising awareness of specific ways the school could respond to the health challenges in the local community.

SPARC's second strategy to foster culture change was to join schoolwide committees and student groups whose activities had, or could have, some influence on the school's engagement in the community. SPARC learned about these committees, and their inclusion of student representatives, during its first year of activities. SPARC members nominated themselves for these positions. They served on a total of eight schoolwide committees that addressed topics ranging from curriculum development to diversity in faculty hiring. They used these positions to encourage engagement and policies that would support engagement.

SPARC members also joined other student groups interested in issues relevant to the local community, in order to foster greater student engagement in the community. These included student groups addressing such issues as human rights and minority health. This led these student groups to co-sponsor activities with SPARC, and produced a collaboration on a grant proposal to support a local community-based organization. SPARC's membership in Student Assembly was particularly fruitful, leading to permanent infrastructure to support student engagement. With SPARC's encouragement, Student Assembly created a new position for Student Assembly Vice President of Community Affairs and established the Community Service Fund, a competitive small grants program to support community-engaged projects by student groups.

SPARC's Impact on the School

SPARC created or helped to create important new sources of support for engagement at the school, including the Certificate in Community-Based Public Health, Baltimore Week, and the Student Assembly Vice President position and Community Service Fund. These innovations are now institutionalized in the fabric of the school. The impact of SPARC's awareness-raising activities—including its survey and report, resolution, public events, publications, petitions, and participation in schoolwide committees—is harder to measure. But we believe that these activities contributed to a meaningful trend at the school toward greater commitment to community engagement.

Since SPARC made its ten recommendations to the administration, six have been realized: there is now greater support for service-learning through the Certificate program (recommendation 1); there is a new practical course with placements in the local community (3); a community-based participatory research course was established (5); the Urban Health Institute (UHI) was reorganized and expanded to better fulfill the role of a community-based research and outreach center (7); the UHI is now providing direct aid to East Baltimore community-based organizations through a small grant program (8); and the Student Assembly established the Community Service Fund (9). The school has also created a new position for Dean for Public Health Practice, whose work will foster engaged public health research and teaching. SPARC contributed directly to three of these developments, and may have contributed indirectly to the others, by adding student voices to the growing group of faculty and administrators promoting greater community engagement at the school.

The Challenge of Sustainability

Student groups always face the challenge to sustainability posed by student turnover. Early in its activities, SPARC invested attention in institutionalizing the group and creating avenues for member recruitment and leadership development. SPARC became an official student group under Student Assembly, which gave the group a level of permanence and visibility. It recruited new members through quarterly meetings and awareness-raising events, enhanced its website to better communicate with supporters, and developed a SPARC electronic mailing list, which had more than two hundred subscribers. Most important, SPARC's founders hand-selected and nurtured what it hoped would be the next generation of SPARC leaders. Despite these efforts, as the original student founders of SPARC graduated, new leaders did not step in to take their places.

In response, SPARC turned to SOURCE to sustain the group. As SPARC's ally since the group was founded, SOURCE will provide institutional memory for SPARC. SOURCE is also able to identify incoming students whose interests match SPARC's goals, providing a source of new members and leaders. In additions, SPARC added extensive resources to its website to support the group's continuity. The website now documents all of SPARC's activities and includes resources to help future SPARC leaders build on the lessons learned in SPARC's first four years, including articles about advocacy methods, the health of East Baltimore, and the relationship between the school and the community. These resources are also available for use by others in the engagement movement, and we hope that in this way, SPARC's activities will be sustained in their work, as well.

Five Key Considerations for Student Co-leadership in the Engagement Movement

The SPARC case study highlights key lessons about the unique contributions of student co-leaders to the engagement movement, and how students and their faculty and administrative allies can maximize the impact of students' contributions to fostering engagement. In this section we present five related considerations.

1. *Student leaders make valuable contributions to the engagement movement that are distinct from the contributions of faculty and administrators because of the unique methods students can use for organizational change, and the perspectives students bring to their engagement work. In these ways, student contributions complement those of faculty and administrators.*

Students have a unique role in the academy that allows them to use organizational change techniques that are distinct from those of faculty and administrators and prove to have a particular advantage for making organizational change. Although students are understood to be a central reason why these institutions exist, as transient members of the school community they are not bound by the same loyalties as faculty, staff, and administrators. For these reasons, students are able to use the methods of both insiders and outsiders to create organizational change. For example, SPARC used traditional pathways for organizational change, including submitting a formal certificate proposal and sitting on schoolwide committees. But the group also used nontraditional change methods involving vocal critiques, including the student body survey report to the administrating student assembly resolution, published articles and letters, and petitions. These methods are particularly useful to create a sense of urgency for organizational change, but they are outside of the activities that are typically appropriate for faculty, staff, and administrators. Using a combination of insider and outsider methods (also called moderate and vanguard methods) is considered a particularly effective way to create organizational change (Chapman, 2001).

Students also bring new perspectives and priorities to the engagement movement. Students enter an academic setting with fresh eyes, which allows them to see issues of community engagement in new ways. It was this fresh perspective that motivated SPARC students to advocate for the school to invest more resources in the community. Students also act based on the hallmark attitudes of their generation. For today's students, these attitudes include a strong sense of social purpose and a belief in their generation's ability to contribute to society (Market Watch, 2008). These perspectives have inspired today's students to engage in the social entrepreneurship, academic entrepreneurship, and activism for organizational change described in this chapter. In these ways, students may help to catalyze new investments to address community problems.

2. *Student leaders can make the strongest contribution to promoting engagement at their institutions by capitalizing on their strengths, and recognizing their limitations, as institutional change agents. Students have unique leverage to make institutional change where it concerns traditional student issues, and where they can have an influence through their unique role in the public life of the school community.*

Students may be best able to foster new opportunities for community engagement when they are related to traditional student issues, including student learning opportunities and community service. The curriculum is perhaps the one area of academic policy in which students are seen as having unique expertise. Students also have leverage as the consumers of higher education, who can enroll in greater numbers in institutions that are best meeting their educational goals. For these reasons, students can be particularly successful in promoting engaged teaching and learning opportunities. Community service projects are another traditional student issue that students may be able to leverage to foster greater institutional engagement. Students can advocate successfully for more resources for student service, such as grants for student service activities and institutional support for campus student engagement centers. In addition, student activities have a significant impact on the school community, and students can use this influence to foster a culture of interest in, and support for, engagement at their institutions.

3. *All student-led initiatives to promote engagement face challenges to their effectiveness and sustainability due to student turnover. Student groups can address this challenge by working through existing avenues for organizational change, creating durable impacts, and collaborating with faculty and administrative allies.*

Students promoting greater engagement can enhance their efficiency by tapping into existing pathways for students to contribute to the school culture—for example, through student groups, student seats on schoolwide committees, and existing communications outlets.

Students can also turn to faculty and administrative allies for guidance as to the most effective ways to promote engagement at their institutions, the pathways for making an impact, and how student-led activities can complement other ongoing initiatives. SPARC's long-term collaboration with SOURCE, and the close partnership of faculty to develop the certificate proposal, were critical to the group's successes. Finally, allies who are involved in the engagement movement, nationally, can provide important perspectives, based on their knowledge of how engagement has been fostered at other institutions, and the contributions students may have made.

Students promoting engagement can make a lasting impact by creating permanent infrastructure and durable products. SPARC's activities provide examples of a number of ways to do this. If there are limited opportunities for students to influence the culture of their school—for example, if student seats are not included on schoolwide committees—students can advocate for these opportunities to be created. Finally, student groups promoting engagement can plan for sustainability by partnering with their campus student engagement center, as SPARC did with SOURCE.

4. *Academic institutions can ensure that they benefit from the unique contributions that student leaders have to make to the engagement movement by involving students in decision-making processes around institutional engagement, and by engaging in open dialogue and collaboration with student leaders. In both these ways, institutions can ensure that student leaders' activities are directed in ways where they are most effective, and most needed.*

Students can be included in decision-making processes that have an impact on engagement at the levels of the university, college, school, or department. Committees that address issues of policy around faculty hiring, retention, and diversity; engaged scholarship; the curriculum; and even student scholarships and awards all can have an impact on engagement and can include positions for student representatives. Through student membership in these groups, institutions will be able to directly benefit from students' unique perspectives and priorities related to engagement.

By providing support to student engagement leaders, schools can help to ensure that students' activities are focused on goals that students can achieve and that can complement other ongoing engagement efforts. Individual faculty and administrators can provide this support through informal advising and collaboration on projects, as demonstrated by the SPARC case. Institutions, too, can initiate open, public dialogue with the student body about the institution's work toward greater engagement and students' goals for engagement. Town hall meetings, letters to the student body, and school websites are existing methods of communicating with students about engagement efforts and exploring how students can contribute.

5. *Some disciplines may be especially fertile ground for student leadership in the engagement movement. Fostering student leadership for engagement in these fields may have benefits for the future of engagement in these fields, and for the engagement movement more broadly.*

Earlier in this chapter, when describing the three methods that today's students are using to act as change agents in the engagement movement, we offered a number of examples of exceptional student leadership that were taken from a review of scholarly and media articles and websites about relevant student organizations. All of these examples came from the fields of health, law, and education.

Although medicine and law are traditionally conservative fields, all three of these fields may provide more support for student leadership for engagement because they have traditions of engaged learning. These fields may also attract students who are more inclined toward engagement. A challenge, however, is to sustain the idealism of students in these fields who are interested in engagement. Law and medicine students, in particular, often enter their training with a desire to pursue work that will improve community well-being, but exit with this idealism undermined. Supporting student leadership for engagement in these fields may help to maintain students' initial interest in community issues and lead them to pursue engaged careers, either inside or outside the academy. It may also provide models of student leadership for engagement that may be of benefit to other fields.

Conclusions

In the past, leaders of the engagement movement did not see a role for students as co-leaders in the future of the movement, and as a result, they missed the opportunity to fully benefit from student leaders' contributions. The new emphasis in the engagement movement on engaging students as co-leaders promises to help schools benefit from student leaders' ingenuity and energy, their unique methods for contributing to organizational change, and their distinctive perspectives and priorities. The effectiveness of students' contributions, however, is interconnected with the level of support they receive from faculty and administrative allies. Engaging students as true co-leaders in the engagement movement will harness student leaders' contributions to advance the movement in the coming decade. It will also foster the next generation of academic leaders for engagement, to ensure the vitality of the engagement movement into the future.

Resources

For more information about SPARC, and for online resources for student leaders in the engagement movement, please visit our website at www.jhsph.edu/SOURCE/SPARC.

References

Addes, D., & Keene, A. (2006). Grassroots community development at UMass Amherst: The professorless classroom. In E. Zlotkowski, N. V. Longo, & J. R. William (Eds.), *Students as colleagues* (pp. 227–240). Providence, RI: Campus Compact.

Alden, B., & Norman, J. (2006). Students as engaged partners at Duke: A continuum of engagement. In E. Zlotkowski, N. V. Longo, & J. R. William (Eds.), *Students as colleagues* (pp. 213–225). Providence, RI: Campus Compact.

Baltimore City Health Department Office of Epidemiology and Planning. (2008, October). Perkins/ Middle East Health Profile 2008. Baltimore City, MD: Baltimore City Health Department.

Bastress, J., & Beilenson, J. (1996, Fall). Response to: Origins, Evolution, and Progress: Reflections or a Movement. In *Community service in higher education: A decade of development* (pp. 19–20). Providence, RI: Providence College.

Beck, E. (2005). The UCSD student-run free clinic project: Transdisciplinary health professional education. *Journal of Health Care for the Poor and Underserved, 16*, 207–219.

Boren, M. E. (2001). *Student resistance: A history of the unruly subject.* New York: Routledge.

Buchanan, D., & Witlen, R. (2006). Balancing service and education: Ethical management of student-run clinics. *Journal of Health Care for the Poor and Underserved, 17*, 477–485.

Center for Information and Research on Civic Learning and Engagement (CIRCLE). (2008, November). *Youth turnout rate rises to at least 52%.* Available at http://www.civicyouth.org.

Chapman, S. (2001). Advocacy in public health: roles and challenges. *International Journal of Epidemiology, 30*, 1226–1232.

Chatwin, W., Gillespie, S., Looser, A., & Welch, M. (2006). The University of Utah's SPACE Program: Service-politics and civic engagement. In E. Zlotkowski, N. V. Longo, & J. R. William (Eds.), *Students as colleagues* (pp. 241–253). Providence, RI: Campus Compact.

CNN. (2008). *Be the change.* Available at http://www.cnn.com/CNNI/Programs/bethechange/.

Cohen, C. (2005, March 16). Danger zone. *Baltimore City Paper.* Available at http://www.citypaper.com/ news/story.asp?id=9754.

Cohen, C. (2008, October 22). Unbuilding community: East Baltimore residents fret as residential construction sputters in biotech park. *Baltimore City Paper.* Retrieved February 12, 2010, from http://www.citypaper.com/news/story.asp?id=16909.

Cone, R. E., Kiesa, A. Y., & Longo, N. V. (2006). Introduction. In R. E. Cone, A. Kiesa, & N. V. Longo (Eds.), *Raise your voice: A student guide to making positive social change* (pp. 1–5). Providence, RI: Campus Compact.

East Baltimore Development, Inc. (EBDI). (2008, July). *The story.* Available at http://www.ebdi.org/ thestory.html.

Eckenfels, E. K. (1997). Contemporary medical students' quest for self-fulfillment through community service. *Academic Medicine, 72*(2), 1043–1050.

Ellin, A. (2001). The making of a student activist. *New York Times.* Retrieved February 12, 2010, from http://www.nytimes.com/2001/11/11/education/the-making-of-a-student-activist.html? pagewanted=1.

Farfel, M. R., Orlova, A. O., Lees, P. J. S., Rohde, C., Ashley, P. J., & Chisolm, J. J., Jr. (2003). A study of urban housing demolitions as sources of lead in ambient dust: Demolition practices and exterior dustfall. *Environmental Health Perspectives, 111*, 1228–1234.

Featherstone, L., & United Students Against Sweatshops. (2002). *Students against sweatshops: The making of a movement.* New York: Verso.

Foote, D. (2008, August 2). Lessons from Locke. *Newsweek.* Retrieved February 12, 2010, from http:// www.newsweek.com/id/150463.

Gomez, M. (2005, November/December). *Demanding a better deal.* Shelterforce Online, issue 144. National Housing Institute. Available at http://www.nhi.org/online/issues/144/organize.html.

Gomez, M. B., & Muntaner, C. (2005). Urban redevelopment and neighborhood health in East Baltimore, Maryland: The role of communitarian and institutional social capital. *Critical Public Health, 15*(2), 83–102.

Graves, L. (2008, March 5). What is Teach for America really like? A new book looks at the lives of four recruits. *U.S. News and World Report.* Retrieved February 15, 2010, from http://www.usnews.com/articles/education/k-12/2008/03/05/what-is-teach-for-america-really-like.html.

Harvard Living Wage Campaign. (2008, October 2). http://www.hcs.harvard.edu/~pslm/livingwage/portal.html. Updated 2002.

Johns Hopkins Bloomberg School of Public Health. (2008, July 28). *The school at a glance.* Available at http://www.jhsph.edu/school_at_a_glance/index.html.

Kristof, N. D. (2008, January). The age of ambition. *New York Times.* Available at http://www.nytimes.com/2008/01/27/opinion/27kristof.html.

Kuchment, A. (2008, August 11). Into the wilds of Oakland, Calif. *Newsweek,* pp. 49–50.

Levine, A., & Cureton, J. S. (1998). *When hope and fear collide.* San Francisco: Jossey-Bass.

Liu, G. (1996). Origins, evolution and progress: Reflections on a movement. *Metropolitan Universities, 7*(1), 25–38.

Loeb, P. R. (1994). *Generation at the crossroads: Apathy and action on the American campus.* New Brunswick, NJ: Rutgers University Press.

Long, S.E., Saltmarsh, J., & Heffernan, K. (2002). *The new student politics: The Wingspread statement on student civic engagement* (2nd ed.). Providence, RI: Campus Compact.

Lopez, M. H., Kirby E., & Sagoff, J. (2005, July). The Center for Information & Research on Civic Learning & Engagement (CIRCLE) fact sheet: The youth vote 2004. Available at http://www.civicyouth.org/PopUps/FactSheets/FS_Youth_Voting_72–04.pdf.

Market Watch. (2008, November 11). *18–29 voter landslide is a new generation flexing their activism.* Available at http://www.marketwatch.com/news/story/18–29-Voter Landslide-Is/story.aspx?guid=%7B37ADC2AF-70A7–4684–8179–9C77F0846C65%7D.

Meyer R. (2006). Social action at Miami University: Lessons from building service-learning. In E. Zlotkowski, N. V. Longo, & J. R. William (Eds.), *Students as colleagues* (pp. 255–263). Providence, RI: Campus Compact.

Mohan, C.P., & Mohan, A. (2007). HealthSTAT: A student approach to building skills needed to serve poor communities. *Journal of Health Care for the Poor and Underserved, 18,* 523–531.

Simpson, S. A., & Long, J. A. (2007). Medical student-run health clinics: Important contributors to patient care and medical education. *Journal of General Internal Medicine, 22*(3), 352–356.

Teach for America. (2008). *Teach for America—Help ensure educational opportunity for all.* Retrieved November 2, 2008, from http://www.teachforamerica.org.

Unite for Sight. (2008). *Unite for Sight.* Retrieved September 6, 2008, from http://www.uniteforsight.org.

UAEM. (2008). *Universities allied for essential medicines.* Retrieved September 6, 2008, from http://www.essentialmedicine.org.

Unemployment Action Center. (2008). *About the Unemployment Action Center.* Retrieved November 13, 2008, from http://www.uac-ny.org.

Vogel, A. L., Ghanbarpour, S. A., Mistry, K., & Levin, M. B. (2007, April). *SPARCing change: Adventures of a student advocacy group at the Johns Hopkins School of Public Health.* Oral presentation at the 10th Anniversary Conference of Community-Campus Partnerships for Health, Toronto, Canada.

Wilson, R. (1989, September 20). Student leaders from Big 10 Campuses organize to revitalize activism. *Chronicle of Higher Education, 36*(3), A40–A41.

Zlotkowski, E., Longo, N. V., & Williams, J. R. (2006). Introduction. In E. Zlotkowski, N. V. Longo, & J. R. Williams (Eds.), *Students as colleagues: Expanding the circle of service-learning leadership* (pp. 1–11). Providence, RI: Campus Compact.

Professional Development for Emerging Engaged Scholars

Diane M. Doberneck, Robert E. Brown, and Angela D. Allen

U.S. institutions of higher education face unprecedented challenges about their fundamental commitment to communities and society at large. Critics question whether research has trumped teaching, basic science has supplanted research addressing "real world" problems, and faculty members have succumbed to careerism over answering the call to serve the greater good (Bridger & Alter, 2006). Others argue that institutions of higher learning have lost a sense of civic duty and have become commercial enterprises differing in name only from their counterparts in the business world (Bok, 2003; Gould, 2003; Kirp, 2004; Washburn, 2005). Such calls for improved responsiveness to and collaboration with communities and society increase the pressure on institutions to abandon (real or perceived) "out of touch, out of date" relationships with their public. Some institutions of higher education are beginning to respond to these calls for public accountability with professional development programs aimed at preparing the next generation of engaged scholars.

Research about graduate student expectations clearly highlights their interest in "meaningful" and engaged work (Austin & McDaniels, 2006; Rice, Sorcinelli, & Austin, 2000). Aspiring future faculty speak of commitment to their disciplines, their eagerness to have an impact on younger scholars and the next generation, their interest in working with diverse people, their love of creative work, and their desire to make a positive contribution to society (Anderson & Swazey, 1998; Austin, 1992, 2002; Austin & McDaniels, 2006; Rice et al., 2000). Despite an interest in making scholarly contributions to society, graduate students feel that their doctoral programs have not adequately prepared them to do so. A 2001 survey of graduate students sponsored by The Pew Charitable Trusts revealed the significant gap between graduate student interest in "service to the external community" (51 percent) and

391

their self-reported preparation to apply their expertise to community beyond campus (13.8 percent) (Golde & Dore, 2001, p. 26).

As demands and expectations have increased, scholars of higher education and engagement have begun to focus their research on the preparation of graduate students and junior faculty as emerging engaged scholars. This recent literature provides insight into the challenges of socialization, identity, apprenticeship, mentoring, and networking as graduate students prepare for future roles as engaged scholars in the academy and in communities (Austin, Connolly, & Colbeck, 2008; Colbeck, 2008; Golde, 2008; Janke & Colbeck, 2008; O'Meara, 2008; Sweitzer, 2008). Together, they advocate that aspiring faculty "must see with new eyes the more complex array of possibilities of their research and embrace a commitment to the common good and to their status as public intellectuals. They must develop an engaged vision of scholarship, pursue it with passion, [and] commit to action" (Applegate, 2002, p. 10).

In this chapter, we explore professional development for emerging engaged scholars and suggest practical ways to support them as they envision career paths that combine scholarship, passion, and action. First, we review the literature related to professional development for emerging engaged scholars and identify key challenge themes. Next, we describe five examples of professional development programs for emerging engaged scholars and summarize the extent to which they address key challenge themes from the literature. Based on the literature and current practice, we make recommendations for future professional development programs for emerging engaged scholars. Finally, we look to the future of professional development for emerging engaged scholars and suggest another perspective for strengthening the preparation of the next generation of engaged scholars. To be clear, we are not advocating that all graduate students become engaged scholars. Instead, we believe that graduate students who wish to become engaged scholars should have multiple opportunities to pursue intentional, effective professional development in ways that support their vision and continued success over the course of their careers. The purpose of our chapter is to explore what that means from scholarly and practical perspectives.

Review of Selected Literature

The following literature review focuses on the major ideas and challenges facing emerging engaged scholars and those who wish to develop professional development programs for them. We acknowledge that other scholars have addressed this issue in greater depth, but recognize that a complete review of this literature is beyond the scope of the handbook chapter. Drawing heavily on Stanton and Wagner (2006), we focus our literature review on challenges of becoming an engaged scholar, competencies of engaged scholarship, and organizing professional development programs for emerging engaged scholars. In this chapter, we define "emerging engaged scholars" as both advanced graduate students and junior faculty members with scholarly interests in engaged research, teaching, and service.

Becoming an Engaged Scholar

Unlike undergraduate education, most graduate education programs have not been influenced by the service learning and civic engagement movement (O'Meara, 2007). Many students, as they enter graduate school, experience a withdrawal from the public and community life of service that was a vital part of their undergraduate experience. Graduate students are often encouraged to leave their civic-minded values and behaviors behind in order to concentrate on more serious and scholarly matters as graduate and professional students. The gap between undergraduate and graduate school creates a divide between meaningful work and advanced study toward a faculty career (Stanton & Wagner, 2006). The pathway from an engaged undergraduate experience to becoming an engaged scholar is an uncertain one for many.

Becoming an engaged scholar is a challenge because historically, the "pursuit of specialized, scientific research has shaped the requirements and culture of graduate education" (O'Meara & Jaeger, 2006; Stanton & Wagner, 2006). This science model, based on historical traditions of German research universities as "elite institutions for the preparation of the elite," influences contemporary institutions of higher education. Research universities, as a result, place greater emphasis on basic over applied research, science-based over professional study, and research over liberal arts and creative activities (O'Meara & Jaeger, 2006, p. 6). Because most of today's faculty members receive their Ph.D. at research universities, the bias against engaged scholarship continues to be (even inadvertently) passed on to subsequent generations of scholars (Applegate, 2002; Golde, 2008; O'Meara & Jaeger, 2006). Graduate students often complete their doctoral programs and enter the academy as new faculty without understanding how they might go about engaging communities as part of their scholarship. As faculty mentors of new graduate students, they pass on their perspectives of research as a highly specialized, narrowly focused endeavor, separate from public discourse. This "cycle of disengagement" permits history to repeat itself and diminishes the potential of engaged scholarship (Applegate, 2002; Bloomfield & Dubrow, 2006; O'Meara, 2007; O'Meara & Jaeger, 2006; Stanton & Wagner, 2006). To become engaged scholars, aspiring future faculty "must see with new eyes the more complex array of possibilities for their research" and connect to a commitment to the common good and to their status as public intellectuals (Applegate, 2002, p. 8).

Broadening the definition of scholarship has been one major response to this challenge. In 1990, Ernest Boyer's *Scholarship Reconsidered* called for an expansion of the definition of scholarship to include synthesis, application, teaching, as well as the more traditional forms of discovery through research (Boyer, 1990). Since Boyer, other scholars have furthered his work and examined the implications of broader definitions of scholarship for promotion and tenure, faculty development, faculty career stages, and graduate education (Driscoll & Lynton, 1999; Glassick, Huber, & Maeroff, 1997; Lynton, 1995).

More recently, Ellison and Eatman's Imagining America tenure study has promoted a "continuum" approach to expanded definitions of scholarship. Their continuum includes four domains: continuum of scholarship within which academic public engagement has full and equal standing; continuum of scholarly and creative artifacts; a continuum of professional pathways for faculty; and a continuum of actions for institutional change. The continuum concept allows for multiple scholarships, is inclusive of many sorts and conditions of knowledge, assigns equal value to places along the continuum (without penalty), and encourages movement along the continuum over careers (Ellison & Eatman, 2008).

Integration across faculty responsibilities of teaching, research, and service has been a second response to the challenge of engaged scholarship. "Faculty work has long been departmentalized by discipline, and it is becoming increasingly subdivided by distinct and separate teaching, research, and service tasks" (Colbeck, 2002; Colbeck & Wharton-Michael, 2006, p. 18). Reframing engagement as a form of scholarship that cuts across the traditional missions of higher education—teaching, research and creative activities, and service—allows scholars to benefit from synergies across their responsibilities, instead of juggling them separately (Provost's Committee on University Outreach, 1993; Toews & Yazedjian, 2007). Many current professional development programs perpetuate these subdivisions (i.e., workshops on teaching, research methods, or working with communities) instead of promoting integrated scholarship. For emerging engaged scholars to develop an integrated approach to engaged scholarship, they must have the opportunity to learn about intentional strategies for integrating all forms of intellectual activity (i.e., teaching, research, service) into public scholarship that emphasizes the "public nature of academic work, democratic obligation of schools and citizens, and idea of knowledge as a public good" (Cohen, 2005, pp. 506–507; Boyer, 1996; Boyte, 2005; Matthews, 2006).

Competencies for Engaged Scholarship

In addition to disciplinary knowledge and methodological practices, graduate students need to master an additional set of competencies associated with engaged scholarship (Austin & McDaniels, 2006; O'Meara, 2008). Mentors should introduce them to the complexities of collaborative inquiry and coach them on negotiating the significant questions that inevitably arise at the engagement interface (Fear, Rosaen, Bawden, & Foster-Fishman, 2006). Key questions include: Whose knowledge counts? Who has the right to disseminate it? How will the scholarly products have the most impact? Who has the right to benefit from them? (Bloomfield & Dubrow, 2006; Hutchings & Shulman, 1999). Achieving competency in community collaboration skills such as listening, dialogue, understanding power and privilege, and group decision-making will assist emerging engaged scholars in their effort to balance quality scholarship with respectful community engagement.

Organizing Professional Development Programs for Emerging Engaged Scholars

Higher education scholars have focused their scholarship on how professional development programs should be organized to support the success of emerging engaged scholars (Austin & McDaniels, 2006; Ellison & Eatman, 2008; O'Meara, 2008). Based on Weideman, Twale, and Stein's overlapping stages of graduate student development (2001), O'Meara suggests embedding community engagement in the socialization and preparation of future scholars (O'Meara, 2008). She recommends helping graduate students to acquire specific understandings, skills, and competencies in four stages: anticipatory stage; formal and knowledge acquisition stage; developing mastery stage; and making commitments stage with an intentional emphasis on values and beliefs related to the process, products, and location of engaged scholarship.

Similarly, Ellison and Eatman's tenure study includes career stages of engaged faculty. Their research reveals a need to understand how engaged scholarship takes shape over the course of an individual's career. As part of Imagining America's Tenure Team Initiative, Ellison and Eatman propose a "continuum of professional choices" and delineate pathways for public engagement at five career stages—graduate student, assistant professor (years 1–3), assistant professor (years 4–6), associate professor, and full professor (Ellison & Eatman, 2008, p. 21). Across these five career stages, they make recommendations about becoming a public scholar; building knowledge for public scholarship; developing public scholarship skills; mentoring public scholarship; doing public scholarship; and exercising leadership for public scholarship.

Instead of stages of professional development, Austin and McDaniels propose a three-dimensional framework based on (1) multiple definitions of scholarship (i.e., application, discovery, integration, and teaching), (2) various stakeholders responsible for graduate education (i.e., faculty, graduate programs universities, agencies and foundations, and professional associations), and (3) preparation strategies (i.e., modeling, professional seminars, certificate, internships, and informal and formal conversations). They point out that "some [preparation] strategies are best handled by specific stakeholders" (Austin & McDaniels, 2006, p. 59). What does this mean for the professional development of emerging engaged scholars? A wide range of professional development opportunities organized by different groups is optimal.

To summarize this literature, emerging engaged scholars face a number of key challenges as they pursue engaged research, teaching, and service for their academic careers. Initially, they may find it difficult to see scholarly engagement as a professional possibility and, as a result, find it difficult to establish an identity as an engaged scholar. Narrow definitions of "what counts" as scholarship in their programs, departments, institutions, and disciplines represents another key challenge to overcome—particularly if funding, opportunities, and awards focus on basic research and reward excellence in more traditionally defined ways. Emerging engaged scholars, in addition to mastering content and methods associated with their area of study, must also acquire mindsets and skills that support respectful, collaborative relationships with their community partners. In order to do so, they must search out and establish connections to other engaged colleagues for support, mentoring, and collegiality—sometimes in places and spaces beyond their own departments and institutions. Finally, emerging engaged scholars must craft integrated, meaningful, and holistic ways to frame their scholarly engagement, so that their work does not suffer from fragmentation and compartmentalization often reinforced by different levels of the higher education system, such as programs, departments, institutions, and disciplines.

Professional Development Programs for Emerging Engaged Scholars

Institutions of higher education, disciplinary associations, national conferences, and graduate students themselves are organizing a variety of programs to meet the professional development needs of emerging engaged scholars. Some professional development programs (i.e., the Professional Development and Community Engagement program at the University of Texas–Austin) help graduate students to learn about engaged scholarship as an occasional component of a broader set of professional development activities, such as writing for publication or preparation for academic job searches. Other programs focus specifically on supporting emerging engaged scholars. Intentional professional development programs for emerging engaged scholars differ in other significant ways as well. They may be:

- Offered for academic credit or pursued as co-curricular learning
- Open to graduate students nationally or limited to those enrolled at specific institutions
- Focused on engaged scholarship principles in general or include mentored community engaged scholarship or some combination
- Limited to specific disciplines or foster cross-disciplinary exchanges

To be clear, like Nelson (2004) and Gunzenhauser and Gerstl-Pepin (2006), we are not promoting a specific career path, methodology, or form of engagement for all graduate students. Instead, we advocate that graduate students who wish to become engaged scholars have multiple opportunities to pursue professional development in ways that support their vision and continued success over the course of their careers. In the next section, we describe five programs for emerging engaged scholars, specifically selected to illustrate a variety of institutional, cross-institutional, and interdisciplinary approaches to professional development for emerging engaged scholars.

The PAGE Fellows Program through Imagining America

In 2004, the PAGE (Publicly Active Graduate Education) Fellows Program was developed by Sylvia Gage, a University of Texas–Austin graduate student, and Julie Ellison, director emerita of Imagining America and professor of American Culture and Arts and Design at the University of Michigan (Publicly Active Graduate Education, 2008). Imagining America is a national consortium of colleges and universities committed to public scholarship in the arts, humanities, and design. The PAGE Fellows Program was originated by participating graduate students in direct response to their need for professional development, dialogue, and resources to support their own development as public scholars and artists.

Annually, ten new PAGE fellows and five returning PAGE Fellows are awarded competitive fellowships to travel to attend the PAGE Summit and Imagining America conference. Starting in 2008, PAGE applicants who were not selected as fellows become PAGE Associates and receive Imagining America resources and materials.

Fellows attend a preconference, day-long summit, where they build theoretical and practical foundations for their own public scholars. The summit includes "seminar-style discussions of readings in public scholarship, in-depth consideration of the theoretical language, practical skills, and models associated with public scholarship" (Publicly Active Graduate Education, 2007). The summit also offers participants an opportunity to work on their own projects and community-based programs in a supportive environment.

Following the Summit, PAGE Fellows attend Imagining America's annual conference, where they meet with leaders in the field of public scholarship and network with faculty members and administrators who support public engagement. On an ongoing basis, Imagining America provides PAGE Fellows with opportunities for mutual mentorship with faculty, interdisciplinary collaboration, and dialogue on experiences and achievements—"deliberately shaping a culture of peer mentoring and workshopping" (Ellison & Eatman, 2008, p. 20).

Kevin Bott, current director of the PAGE Fellows Program and doctoral student at Syracuse University, envisions a future website forum for online dialogue and debate, critical discourse, and social networking. Other future plans include a "toolbox" to assist graduate students in establishing a PAGE "chapter" at their home institution, a PAGE postdoctoral fellowship, and an edited volume documenting the pathways to engaged graduate education.

Emerging Engagement Scholars Workshop at National Outreach Scholarship Conference

In 2006, the Emerging Engagement Scholars Workshop (EESW) was launched by two doctoral students, Angela Allen from Michigan State University and Tami Moore from Washington State University, as a preconference professional development opportunity for both advanced graduate students and early career faculty (Emerging Engagement Scholars Workshop, 2008).

EESW scholars are selected through a nationally competitive application process. Selection criteria include interest in conducting research that contributes to a discipline and impacts external stakeholders, a demonstrated desire to learn about outreach scholarship, interest in working with faculty across disciplines to explore how outreach scholarship is conducted, and capacity to effectively communicate the results of the research to public, academic, and other audiences. EESW participants attend the preconference workshop for a minimal fee and receive waived conference fees for the associated National Outreach Scholarship Conference. Michigan State University's National Center for the Study of University Engagement, the Higher Education Network for Community Engagement (HENCE), and the member institutions of the National Outreach Scholarship Conference all provide funding and in-kind support for EESW.

EESW preconference activities include a master class on the foundations of engaged scholarship, panel discussions on community-engaged methods and with community partners, and sessions on publishing outreach scholarship. In addition, EESW participants are matched with faculty mentors with similar research interests and expertise. The mentors are attendees of the National Outreach Scholarship Conference who volunteer to welcome the emerging engagement scholars to the community of scholars and practitioners. The mentoring relationship is expected to continue beyond the conference.

Each year, four doctoral students (two of whom serve as co-chairs for the program) join National Outreach Scholarship Conference organizers, veteran scholars in outreach and engagement, and a representative from HENCE in constituting the EESW planning committee. They organize the workshop sessions, select EESW participants, and conduct evaluations on the experience.

Future plans for the EESW include an increased emphasis on discussions about each participant's research project during the workshop, and the inclusion of past EESW participants on the planning committee.

The Houle Engaged Scholars Program

In 2008, the Houle Engaged Scholars Program was initiated by North Carolina State University, Pennsylvania State University, University of Georgia, and University of North Carolina–Chapel Hill as a cross-institutional effort to build capacity of emerging and current scholars to do community-engaged scholarship (Houle Engaged Scholars program, 2008).

Each cohort of Houle Engaged Scholars includes a faculty mentor–graduate student pair from each institution (total of four pairs in 2008–2009). Selection criteria include interest in community-engaged research by both graduate students and faculty mentors; stage in doc-toral program where exploration of dissertation related research is appropriate; willingness by both graduate students and faculty mentors to participate in program activities; an iden-tified community partner community to community-engaged research; and diverse repre-sentation of disciplines in the cohort. Each institution nominates its pair to the Houle Engaged Scholars program leaders, who confirm participation. Dissertation mini-grants will be awarded by each institution to their pair to support the community-engaged research associated with the program.

Houle Engaged Scholars participate in the program for an academic year. Program activities include attendance at the Outreach Scholarship conference the first fall semester; written resources, materials, and discussions about community-engaged research; individ-ual meetings and mentoring sessions; a retreat for graduate students and mentors; a cross-institutional, virtual meeting of all Houle Engaged Scholars; and presentations of their community-engaged research at the Outreach Scholarship conference the following fall. In addition, Houle Engaged Scholars are expected to produce at least two of the following: conference presentation, journal article, grant proposal, or other type of scholarly publica-tion at the conclusion of the project. Along with their community partners, Houle Engaged Scholars are required to disseminate their work to communities in appropriate formats, such as white papers, policy briefings, or focus groups. Graduate students may earn aca-demic credit from either their home department or the University of Georgia, whose Program in Adult Education, along with collaborative administration from faculty members at the North Carolina State University's Department of Higher Education, is the home of the Houle Engaged Scholars program.

Future directions include evaluation of outcomes by institutional pair and by cohort; funding to support the expansion of this pilot program; and scholarship on the advisor-advisee relationship regarding community-engaged research.

Service-Learning Certificate at Portland State University

Portland State University has offered a 15-credit Service-Learning Certificate available to undergraduates, graduate students, elementary through higher education teachers, admin-istrators, community-based organization staff, and others interested in building strong com-munity development programs (Service Learning Certificate at Portland State University, 2010). This certificate emphasizes essential skills necessary to be a more effective leader of change, an expanded resource network of other service-learning professionals, and a certificate of completion for those who take all 15 credits.

Required courses include Service-Learning Design and Practice; Planning for Service-Learning; Sustaining Service Learning through Effective Resource Development and Marketing; Service Learning Best Practice: Collaboration; and Service Learning Best Practice: Youth Voice. These courses are structured to be accessible both locally and at a distance and are taught primar-ily online with typically two Saturday, on-campus classes. Video-streaming and email exchanges support learning from a distance. Two courses are offered during most academic terms.

All courses can be taken for graduate credit, and those credits can potentially be applied toward a degree from the Graduate School of Education or transferred to other university programs (with the approval of the student's adviser). For those who do not desire graduate credit, these courses are also offered on an undergraduate basis.

The Graduate Certificate in Community Engagement at Michigan State University

During 2007–2008, Michigan State University's (MSU) Office of University Outreach and Engagement and the Graduate School designed a Graduate Certificate in Community Engagement (Michigan State University Graduate Certification in Community Engagement, 2010). The certificate, when completed, appears on students' transcripts signifying mastery of defined core competencies in outreach scholarship and community engagement. Its purpose is to prepare the next generation of engaged scholars by exposing them to mindsets, knowledge, and practices about community engagement in systemic, thoughtful, and scholarly ways.

To complete the certificate, graduate students must be accepted into the program based on an application and departmental recommendation; demonstrate mastery of core competencies; participate in a mentored community engagement experience; and write a reflection on the experience for their engagement portfolio. The Associate Provost of University Outreach and Engagement officially certifies completion of the graduate certificates.

There are five core competencies, which include knowledge about the following: attending to my career, community-based participatory research and evaluation, co-building effective partnerships, capacity-building for mutual benefit, and logic modeling. These core competencies may be met through departmentally approved courses or experiences, through seminars offered by University Outreach and Engagement, or in a combination of both.

The mentored community-engagement experience is intentionally flexible to accommodate different disciplinary, professional, and engagement traditions within and across MSU's departments and colleges and is expected to augment the graduate student's progress toward completion of the degree. These experiences may be arranged and overseen by either department faculty or University Outreach and Engagement faculty and may address aspects of outreach-research, outreach-teaching, outreach-service, or outreach and engagement activities integrated across university missions.

The reflection component requires graduate students to critically examine their engagement experience in the broader context of their discipline, their scholarship, their career, and their contribution to communities. The reflection is also a significant component of the student's engagement portfolio, an ongoing scholarly process of documenting impact, quality, and meaning of engaged scholarship.

In addition, through the Graduate Certificate in Community Engagement, University Outreach and Engagement supports the professional identity development of emerging engaged scholars, maintains supportive structures and connective networks (inside and outside the academy), and sustains a culture of engaged scholarship across the colleges and departments.

Future directions for the Graduate Certificate in Community Engagement include additional collaboration with campus departments and colleges, expansion of resource materials available to graduate students in the program, and exploration of ways to offer the certificate to students at other institutions of higher education.

In summary, Table 1 shows how the five professional development programs for emerging engaged scholars address the key challenge themes identified in the literature.

Table 1. Key Challenges and Professional Development Programs

Program	Key Challenges					
	Engaged Scholar Identity	Expanded Definition of Scholarship	Mindsets and Skills	Negotiating Engaged Career	Cross-Disciplinary Spaces	Integration, Meaning, Wholeness
PAGE Fellows	Yes	Yes	Yes	Yes	Yes, also cross-institutional	Yes
Emerging Engagement Scholars Workshop	Yes	Yes	Yes, engaged research	Yes	Yes, also cross-institutional	Yes
Houle Engaged Scholars program at NCSU, PSU, Georgia, & UNC-CH	Yes	Yes	Yes, engaged research	Yes	Yes, also cross-institutional	No
Service Learning Certificate at Portland State	Yes	Yes	Yes, engaged teaching	Yes	No	No
Graduate Certificate in Community Engagement at MSU	Yes	Yes	Yes, all forms of engagement	Yes	Yes, not cross-institutional	Yes, in portfolio

Recommendations

Our recommendations are based on ideas found in the literature, from current professional development programs, and from our experience as organizers of educational programs for emerging engaged scholars. Because professional development for emerging engaged scholars is in its initial phases, we have identified nine key recommendations as a starting point, in the hope that they are further refined by engaged scholars themselves, faculty, community partners, disciplinary associations, outreach administrators, and others interested in preparing the next generation of engaged scholars. The nine recommendations are for individuals and institutions and address the salient issues of identity, skills, culture, structure, and practices supportive of emerging engaged scholars.

1. Becoming intentional and collaborative

Just as the scholarship of teaching movement has focused on intentionally preparing the next generation of college and university teachers, the scholarship of engagement movement needs to deliberately and collaboratively focus on preparing the next generation of engaged scholars. Instead of top-down or bottom-up approaches, we suggest a deliberate, systemic approach that strengthens the preparation of engaged scholars at multiple levels, on multiple dimensions, at the same time. We also recommend that doctoral students, community members, and other responsible stakeholders, such as disciplinary associations and foundations, have a voice in creating these new programs, so that the professional development programs not only focus on engagement as a content area but also model principles of engagement as part of their practice. The PAGE Fellows Program and the Emerging Engaged Scholars Workshop clearly embody intentional, collaborative, and engaged leadership by graduate students with support from interdisciplinary groups at national conferences.

2. Learning about multiple forms of engaged scholarship

In order to develop an identity as an engaged scholar, graduate students need to "see engagement as a way of being a scholar" (Austin & McDaniels, 2006; Fear et al., 2006). Engagement as it is expressed in different contexts and for different purposes needs to be made more visible to potential emerging engaged scholars, particularly those in science, technology, engineering, and mathematics (STEM) disciplines (Stanton & Wagner, 2006). Emerging engaged scholars need to be introduced to the different ways scholarly engagement takes place as a form of research, teaching, and service. Although community-based participatory research and service learning are common examples of engaged research and engaged teaching, they may not be appropriate or feasible choices for all scholars or at all stages of a scholar's career. Research conducted in collaboration with industry, performance and public art, noncredit instruction, expert testimony, clinical services, evaluation research, and forms of public communications are additional types of scholarly engagement that should be introduced to emerging engaged scholars. In addition to different types of engagement, professional development for emerging engaged scholars must be sensitive to disciplinary differences. Using the language appropriate to the disciplines, discipline-specific examples of scholarly engagement activities across the university's traditional missions of teaching, research, and service will help emerging engaged scholars see possibilities for their own scholarship in their future department and disciplines.

3. Pursuing integration, meaning, and wholeness

Emerging engaged scholars, particularly graduate students, must be encouraged to view their engagement in integrated, meaningful, and holistic ways—not as a responsibility added on to their other teaching, research, and service obligations. To counteract the strong forces of fragmentation and departmentalization of research, teaching, and service (The Provost's Committee on University Outreach, 1993; Colbeck & Wharton-Michaels, 2006), professional development programs need to lift up examples of undivided faculty life and to introduce emerging engaged scholars to seamlessly integrated ways of thinking, being, and doing. By having the opportunity to intentionally explore possible ways to integrate their scholarship, they may find their journey to engagement more meaningful and significant (Palmer, 1997, 2004).

4. Learning mindsets and practices for engaged scholarship

As illustrated in the previous section, emerging engaged scholars should have a variety of opportunities to learn new ways of thinking about their relationship with community partners and new practices for working with them collaboratively, including engaged scholarship skills, community engagement skills, appropriate methodological choices, ethics and community engagement, interpersonal and cross-cultural skills, evidence-based practices, and funding and publishing opportunities. Each of these mindsets or practices is explained in greater detail in the following section.

Engaged Scholarship Skills

Skills in engaged scholarship include framing appropriate research questions, designing and implementing a scholarly project, and presenting results to communities and the academy (Austin & McDaniels, 2006; Stanton, 2007). "Academic researchers have an ethical as well as a practical responsibility to involve community partners deeply in the conceptualization, execution, and analysis of research. Tools for resolving conflicts that arise in the process of widespread consultation need to become an explicit part of the graduate curriculum" (Bloomfield & Dubrow, 2006).

Community Engagement Skills

Opportunities to learn and practice engagement skills including listening, dialogue, collaboration, responsiveness, capacity-building, and communication with community partners need to be made available to potential engaged scholars (Michigan State University, 2008a, 2008b).

Appropriate Methodological Choices

Emerging engaged scholars need to be introduced to a wide range of methods, so that their work is both scholarly and responsive to community needs. Applied research and participatory action research methods are a start (Austin & McDaniels, 2006). However, truly responsive approaches to community-engaged research rely on mixed methods approaches to honor epistemological perspectives and sources of knowledge associated with both academic and community settings (Greene, 2007; Gunzenhauser & Gerstl-Pepin, 2006; Stanton & Wagner, 2006).

Ethics and Community Engagement

Emerging engaged scholars also need to be introduced to the "ethical aspects of publicly engaged research, including IRB issues, formulating, reviewing, and publishing research in ways meaningful to community partners, addressing the imbalances of power that usually attend university-community partnerships . . . and attending to the potential uses and consequences of new knowledge" (Bloomfield & Dubrow, 2006). Research ethics education programs often emphasize ethical issues associated with traditional forms of research and, as a result, do not address the ethical issues specific to community-engaged scholarship. Case studies, exemplars, and modules could be developed to assist emerging engaged scholars, their mentors, and community partners to identify potential ethical issues and to seek solutions to them proactively.

Interpersonal Skills and Working Cross-Culturally

Engaged scholars must possess interpersonal skills, including skills in relationship building, establishing trust, building rapport, and maintaining open communications. Very often, engaged scholars find themselves working with community partners with backgrounds and experiences that differ from their own. Understanding power and privilege associated with race, class, gender, ethnicity, age, experience, or marital status is an important step in respectful, cross-cultural collaborations. Professional development for emerging engaged scholars should provide ample opportunities for reflexive self-evaluation for scholars to understand who they are and how their identity and privilege affect their relationships with community partners. Finally, giving and receiving critical, constructive feedback is another interpersonal skill essential for engaged scholars (Austin & McDaniels, 2006).

Evidence-Based Practices

Emerging engaged scholars need to be introduced to evidence-based practices—for both their work in/with communities and for documenting the quality and impact of their engaged scholarship. As a start, clear goals, adequate preparation, appropriate methods, significant results, effective presentation, and reflective critique should be incorporated into professional development programs (Ellison, 2006). Ideas for documenting quality outreach and engagement also include significance, context, scholarship, and impact (Michigan State University, 1996) and goals/questions; context of theory, literature, and "best practice"; methods; results; communication/dissemination; and reflective critique ("Evaluation Criteria," 2002). At the minimum, professional development programs for emerging engaged scholars should encourage reflective critique of the engaged scholarship and documentation of its quality and impact (Driscoll & Lynton, 1999; Fear et al., 2006).

Funding and Publishing Engaged Scholarship

Emerging engaged scholars also need assistance in "finding funding, securing grants, publishing" their engaged work (O'Meara & Jaeger, 2006). Professional development programs might help emerging engaged scholars identify peer-reviewed journals in their disciplines that are likely to published engaged scholarship as well as familiarize them with journals dedicated to engagement, such as the *Journal of Higher Education Outreach and Engagement, Michigan Journal of Community Service Learning, Metropolitan Universities, Journal of Community Engagement and Scholarship, Manifestations: Journal of Community Engaged Research and Learning Partnerships,* and *Journal of Community Engagement and Higher Education.* Expert panels from foundations and government funding agencies might also be convened to share strategies for successful grant writing to support engaged scholarship.

5. Negotiating a place for engaged scholarship

Emerging engaged scholars may benefit from assistance in negotiating a "home" for their engaged scholarship—in appropriate programs, centers, departments, institutions, disciplines, and communities (Sandmann, Saltmarsh, & O'Meara, 2008). Recognizing opportunities and managing critical tensions between university and communities are important skills for emerging engaged scholars to master (Sandmann, Foster-Fishman, Lloyd, Rauhe, & Rosaen, 2000). Finding creative and scholarly ways to manage the tensions among program, department, institution, and community/society is essential as well. How successful engaged scholars have negotiated a place for their work throughout their careers should be an explicit focus of both informal mentoring and more formal professional development programs.

6. Envisioning engaged scholarship across career stages

Emerging engaged scholars need to see engaged scholarship as a viable career path over the longer term. They need to understand how an engaged research, teaching, and service unfolds, develops, and deepens over time, throughout different stages of a scholar's career (O'Meara, 2008; Ellison & Eatman, 2008). Mentors should make this an explicit part of their coaching conversations because career trajectories for engaged scholars are not evident to most graduate students. Examples given to students should illustrate different options at different career stages, similar to the continuum idea offered by Imagining America.

7. Strengthening faculty culture to accept engaged scholarship

Although much progress has been made since Boyer's *Scholarship Reconsidered*, there is still a way to go to shift faculty culture to be more accepting of multiple forms of scholarship as legitimate. Emerging engaged scholars need to be sensitized to differences in how programs, departments, institutions, and disciplines *value* different forms of scholarship, so that they may make more informed decisions about their own scholarship in light of these differing priorities. Despite these differences, professional development programs need to encourage emerging scholars to pursue engagement and prepare to continue to lead the shift in faculty culture (Jaeger & Thornton, 2005; O'Meara & Jaeger, 2006; O'Meara & Rice, 2005).

8. Participating in cross-disciplinary, cross-institutional spaces

Emerging engaged scholars need to have access to cross-disciplinary, cross-institutional spaces to discuss and understand engagement; they must find a community of practice. "Reflective practices are not carried out in isolation of others, but rather in collaboration with others within and outside of the academy, and within and outside the scholar's discipline" (Nelson, 2004, p. 5). Graduate students need to seek out spaces that nurture their emerging identities as engaged scholars, strengthen their engagement skills, and support their reflective critique of their scholarship. They must have alternative spaces, especially if their departments or institutions are not supportive, for professional development and access to a network of mentors (Sorcinelli & Yun, 2007). Disciplinary associations and conferences focused on engagement are two places where emerging engaged scholars may find a community of support.

9. **Increasing scholarship about professional development for emerging engaged scholars**

As professional development programs for emerging engaged scholars continue to evolve, we need to "develop a research agenda . . . that looks critically at educational outcomes of embedding community engagement in graduate education" (O'Meara & Jaeger, 2006, p. 20). *We believe it is time to move beyond advocating for the establishment of professional development programs for engaged scholars to delivering them in scholarly ways and studying their outcomes.* We wholeheartedly agree that:

> Faculty advisors, graduate deans, and professional development specialists would benefit from knowing more about when in a doctoral program is the best time for providing professional development focused on integrating professional roles and which strategies have the most impact. Different types of professional development may be effective at different stages of doctoral education . . . Patterns may vary by discipline (Austin et al., 2008, p. 78).

Future Directions: A Systems Perspective on Preparing Engaged Scholars

Together, the literature and programs we reviewed about professional development for emerging engaged scholars emphasize different aspects the process of becoming an engaged scholar, but none are comprehensive in their treatment of the entire emerging engaged scholar experience. We believe these ideas can be brought together into a comprehensive, holistic framework that reveals potential synergies within and across different levels (i.e., individual, program/department, college, institutional, discipline/profession/tradition, and community/society at large) in which engaged scholars and their scholarship are located—physically, structurally, and culturally. Emerging engaged scholars both influence and are influenced by the values and priorities of different levels of the system in which they find themselves. As we look to the future of professional development for emerging engaged scholars, we believe that a systems perspective, capturing the complexity, interdependence, and interaction between levels, will be beneficial.

To be successful, emerging engaged scholars must be aware of different stages of development and different system levels; understand each level's focus and priorities; learn to negotiate between the levels in scholarly and creative ways; and craft professional lives that integrate their work into cohesive expressions of engaged scholarship over their lifetime as scholars. As we advance professional development for emerging engaged scholars, we must proceed in a manner that is complementary to and not contested by the current range and variation of graduate education ethos. The intention must be to not dismiss or denigrate the values of any systems level, but to use each level's currency to craft responses within and across levels that speak to the sensibilities of those levels. One-size-fits-all approaches will be difficult to establish and sustain as well as disingenuous to the complex realities of both the development of professional identity as an engaged scholar and the practice of respectful, collaborative community engagement.

References

Anderson, M. S., & Swazey, J. P. (1998). Reflections on the graduate student experience: An overview. In M. S. Anderson & J. P. Sawzey (Eds.), *The experience of being in graduate school: An exploration* (pp. 3–13). New Directions for Higher Education, No. 101. San Francisco: Jossey-Bass.

Applegate, J. L. (2002). *Engaged graduate education: Seeing with new eyes.* Preparing Future Faculty Occasional Paper. Washington, DC: Association of American Colleges and Universities.

Austin, A. E. (1992). Supporting junior faculty through a teaching fellows program. In M. D. Sorcinelli & A. E. Austin (Eds.), *Developing new and junior faculty* (pp. 73–86). New Directions for Teaching and Learning, No. 50. San Francisco: Jossey-Bass.

Austin, A. E. (2002). Preparing the next generation of faculty: Graduate school as socialization to the academic career. *Journal of Higher Education, 73*(1), 94–122.

Austin, A. E., Connolly, M., & Colbeck, C. L. (2008). Strategies for preparing integrated faculty: The center for the integration of research, teaching, and learning. In C. L. Colbeck & A. E. Austin (Eds.), *Educating integrated professionals: Theory and practice on preparation for the professoriate* (pp. 69–81). New Directions for Teaching and Learning, No. 113. San Francisco: Jossey-Bass.

Austin, A. E., & McDaniels, M. (2006). Using doctoral education to prepare faculty to work within Boyer's four domains of scholarship. In J. M. Braxton (Ed.), *Analyzing faculty work and rewards using Boyer's four domains of scholarship* (pp. 51–65). New Directions for Institutional Research, No. 129. San Francisco: Jossey-Bass.

Bloomfield, V., & Dubrow, G. (2006). Integrating engagement with research ethics in graduate education. In B. Holland & J. Meeropol (Eds.), *A more perfect vision: The future of campus engagement.* Providence, RI: Campus Compact. Retrieved October 15, 2008, from http://www.compact.org/20th/papers.

Bok, D. (2003). *Universities and the marketplace.* Princeton, NJ: Princeton University Press.

Boyer, E. L. (1990). *Scholarship reconsidered: Priorities of the professoriate.* Princeton, NJ: Carnegie Foundation for the Advancement of Teaching.

Boyer, E. L. (1996). The Scholarship of engagement. *Journal of Higher Education Outreach and Engagement 1*(1), 11–20.

Boyte, H. C. (2005). *Everyday politics: Reconnecting citizens and public life.* Philadelphia: University of Pennsylvania Press.

Bridger, J. C., & Alter, T. R. (2006). The engaged university, community development, and public scholarship. *Journal of Higher Education Outreach and Engagement, 11*(1), 163–178.

Cohen, J. (2005). Public scholarship. In L. Sherrod, C. Flanagan, R. Kassimir, & A. Bertelsen (Eds.), *Youth activism: An international encyclopedia* (pp. 506–507). Westport, CT: Greenwood.

Colbeck, C. L. (2002). Integration: Evaluating faculty work as a whole. In C. L. Colbeck (Ed.), *Evaluating faculty performance* (pp. 43–52). New Directions for Institutional Research, No. 114. San Francisco: Jossey-Bass.

Colbeck, C. L. (2008). Professional identity development theory and doctoral education. In C. L. Colbeck & A. E. Austin (Eds.), *Educating integrated professionals: Theory and practice on preparation for the professoriate* (pp. 9–16). New Directions for Teaching and Learning, No. 113. San Francisco: Jossey-Bass.

Colbeck, C. L., & Wharton-Michael, P. (2006). Individual and organizational influences on faculty members' engagement in public scholarship. In R. A. Eberly & J. Cohen (Eds.), *A laboratory for public scholarship and democracy* (pp. 17–26). New Directions for Teaching and Learning, No. 105. San Francisco: Jossey-Bass.

Driscoll, A., & Lynton, E. A. (1999). *Making outreach visible: A guide to documenting professional service and outreach.* Washington, DC: American Association for Higher Education.

Ellison, J. (2006). *Imagining America: Artists and scholars in public life. Background study.* Syracuse, NY: Imagining America.

Ellison, J., & Eatman, T. K. (2008). *Scholarship in public: Knowledge creation and tenure policy in the engaged university.* Syracuse, NY: Imagining America.

Emerging Engagement Scholars Workshop. (2008). Retrieved October 17, 2008, from http://ncsue.msu. edu/eesw.aspx.

Evaluation criteria for the scholarship of engagement. (2002). Retrieved October 16, 2008, from http://schoe.coe.uga.edu/evaluation/evaluation_criteria.html.

Fear, F. A., Rosaen, C. L., Bawden, R. J., & Foster-Fishman, P. G. (2006). *Coming to critical engagement: An autoethnographic exploration.* Lanham, MD: University Press of America.

Glassick, C. E., Huber, M. H., & Maeroff, G. I. (1997). *Scholarship assessed: Evaluation of the professoriate.* San Francisco: Jossey-Bass.

Golde, C. M. (2008). Applying lessons from professional education to the preparation of the professoriate. In C. L. Colbeck & A. E. Austin (Eds.), *Educating integrated professionals: Theory and practice on preparation for the professoriate* (pp. 17–25). New Directions for Teaching and Learning, No. 113. San Francisco: Jossey-Bass.

Golde, C. M. & Dore, T. M. (2001). *At cross-purposes: What the experience of today's graduate students reveal about doctoral education.* Philadelphia: The Pew Charitable Trusts.

Gould, E. (2003). *University in a corporate culture.* New Haven, CT: Yale University Press.

Greene, J. C. (2007). *Mixed methods in social inquiry.* San Francisco: Jossey-Bass.

Gunzenhauser, M. G., & Gerstl-Pepin, C. I. (2006). Engaging graduate education: A pedagogy for epistemological and theoretical diversity. *Review of Higher Education 29*(3), 319–346.

Houle engaged scholars program: Developing engaged scholars at research universities. (2008). Unpublished program documents.

Hutchings, P., & Shulman, L. S. (1999). The scholarship of teaching: New elaborations, new developments. *Change 31*(5), 10–15.

Jaeger, A. J., & Thornton, C. H. (2005). Moving toward the market and away from public service? Effects of resource dependency and academic capitalism. *Journal of Higher Education Outreach and Engagement, 10*(3), 53–67.

Janke, E. M., & Colbeck, C. L. (2008). Lost in translation: Learning professional roles through the situated curriculum. In C. L. Colbeck & A. E. Austin (Eds.), *Educating integrated professionals: Theory and practice on preparation for the professoriate* (pp. 57–68). New Directions for Teaching and Learning, No. 113. San Francisco: Jossey-Bass.

407

Kirp, D. L. (2004). *Shakespeare, Einstein, and the bottom line: The marketing of higher education.* Cambridge, MA: Harvard University Press.

Lynton, E. A. (1995). *Making the case for professional service.* Washington, DC: American Association for Higher Education.

Mathews, D. (2006). *Reclaiming public education by reclaiming democracy.* Dayton, OH: Kettering Foundation Press.

Michigan State University. (1996). *Points of distinction: A guidebook for planning and evaluating quality outreach.* East Lansing: Michigan State University.

Michigan State University. (2008a). *Tools of engagement: Collaborating with community partners.* East Lansing: University Outreach and Engagement, Michigan State University.

Michigan State University. (2008b). *Graduate certificate in community engagement.* East Lansing: University Outreach and Engagement, Michigan State University.

Michigan State University Graduate Certification in Community Engagement. (2010). Retrieved on February 12, 2010, from http://outreach.msu.edu/gradcert/.

Nelson, P. D. (2004). *Civic engagement and scholarship: Implications for graduate education in psychology.* American Psychology Association. Retrieved October 15, 2008, from http://www.apa.org/ed/slce/engage_nelson.pdf.

O'Meara, K. A. (2007). *Graduate education and civic engagement.* NERCHE Brief, No. 20. Retrieved October 16, 2008, from http://www.nerche.org/briefs/NERCHE_Brief_20__Graduate_Education_and_Civic_Engagement.doc.

O'Meara, K. A. (2008). Graduate education and community engagement. In C. L. Colbeck & A. E. Austin (Eds.), *Educating integrated professionals: Theory and practice on preparation for the professoriate* (pp. 27–42). New Directions for Teaching and Learning, No. 113. San Francisco: Jossey-Bass.

O'Meara, K. A., & Jaeger, A. J. (2006). Preparing future faculty for community engagement: Barriers, facilitators, models, and recommendations. *Journal of Higher Education Outreach and Engagement, 11*(3), 3–26.

O'Meara, K. A., & Rice, R. E. (2005). *Faculty priorities reconsidered: Encouraging multiple forms of scholarship.* San Francisco: Jossey-Bass.

Palmer, P. J. (1997). *The courage to teach: Exploring the inner landscape of a teacher's life.* San Francisco: Jossey-Bass.

Palmer, P. J. (2004). *A hidden wholeness: The journey toward an undivided life.* San Francisco: Jossey-Bass.

Provost's Committee on University Outreach. (1993). *University outreach at Michigan State University: Extending knowledge to serve society.* East Lansing: Michigan State University.

Publicly Active Graduate Education (PAGE). (2007). Pressing concerns. *IA News, 9,* 10–12.

Publicly Active Graduate Education (PAGE). (2008). *Publicly active graduate education.* Retrieved October 17, 2008, from http://pageia.com/.

Rice, R. E., Sorcinelli, M. D., & Austin, A. E. (2000). *Heeding new voices: Academic careers for a new generation.* Washington, DC: American Association for Higher Education.

Sandmann, L., Foster-Fishman, P. G., Lloyd, J., Rauhe, W., & Rosaen, C. (2000). Managing critical tensions: How to strengthen the scholarship component of outreach. *Change, 32*(1), 44–52.

Sandmann, L., Saltmarsh, J., & O'Meara, K. (2008). An integrated model for advancing the scholarship of engagement: Creating academic homes for the engaged scholar. *Journal of Higher Education Outreach and Engagement, 12*(1), 47–64.

Service Learning Certificate at Portland State University. (2010). Retrieved on February 12, 2010, from http://www.ceed.pdx.edu/service-learning/.

Sorcinelli, M. D., & Yun, J. (2007). From mentoring to mentoring network: Mentoring in the new academy. *Change 39*(6), 58–60.

Stanton, T. K. (2007). *New times demand new scholarship II: Research universities and civic engagement: Opportunities and challenges.* Retrieved on October 16, 2008, from http://www.compact.org/initiatives/research_universities/Civic_Engagement.pdf.

Stanton, T. K., & Wagner, J. (2006). *Educating for democratic citizenship: Renewing the civic mission of graduate and professional education at research universities.* Retrieved October 16, 2008, from http://www.cacampuscompact.org/download/programs/Final%20Paper%20(JR%20edit%206–30–06).pdf.

Sweitzer, V. L. (2008). Networking to develop a professional identity: A look at the first-semester experience of doctoral students in business. In C. L. Colbeck & A. E. Austin (Eds.), *Educating integrated professionals: Theory and practice on preparation for the professoriate* (pp. 43–56). New Directions for Teaching and Learning, No. 113. San Francisco: Jossey-Bass.

Toews, M. L., & Yazedjian, A. (2007). The three-ring circus of academia: How to become a ringmaster. *Innovative Higher Education, 32,* 113–122.

Washburn, J. (2005). *University, Inc.: The corporate corruption of higher education.* New York: Basic Books.

Weideman, J. C., Twale, D. J., & Stein, E. L. (2001). *Socialization of graduate and professional students in higher education: A perilous passage?* ASHE-ERIC Higher Education Report, No. 28. Washington, DC: George Washington University, School of Education and Human Development.

Educating for Democratic Citizenship: Antecedents, Prospects, and Models for Renewing the Civic Mission of Graduate Education at Research Universities

Timothy K. Stanton and Jon Wagner

Education for democratic citizenship involves human capacities relating to judgment, to choice, and, above all, to action. To be literate as a citizen requires more than knowledge and information; it includes the exercise of personal responsibility, active participation, and personal commitment to a set of values. Democratic literacy is a literacy of doing, not simply of knowing. Knowledge is a necessary, but not sufficient condition of democratic responsibility.

With these words Richard Morrill (1982, p. 365) challenged academicians to take seriously their historical mandate to "educate for democratic values." He suggested that education for civic engagement must combine doing with knowing, that it must be both "the empowerment of persons and the cultivation of minds" (p. 365).

The ideals underlying Morrill's challenge are embedded deeply in the foundation of the modern research university, but so too are related concerns and ambiguities about the purposes and practices of "active participation." These ambiguities can complicate the lives of students, faculty members, and administrators who value civic engagement. They do so by giving life to fundamental questions about individual action, the nature of knowledge and the methods through which it is developed, institutional accountability, and collective responsibility. These questions frequently find their way into public hearings about university plans to expand or contract visible public service programs, but they also emerge from the community engagement of individual students and faculty members.

This paper was originally prepared as background for the Stanford Symposium on Civic Engagement and Graduate Education at Research Universities, sponsored by California Campus Compact at Stanford University on April 24, 2006.

Some civic challenges facing research universities reflect the multiple and unshared goals of the university community. For example, is the primary purpose of a volunteer tutoring program to impart knowledge of chemistry, mathematics, or music to children; to acquaint graduate students with the needs and challenges of underprivileged children; or to build confidence and raise civic aspirations? Is the purpose of a community design agency to help individuals solve technical facilities problems or to build infrastructure in disenfranchised communities? Is a public lecture series about science and the citizen a showcase for representing new knowledge or a venue for stimulating community life? Is a public interest campaign designed to educate or persuade the public?

Other challenges involve articulation—or the lack of it—between civic engagement practices that differ substantially in scope and scale. What arrangements does a university provide, for example, to guide the student who wants to participate as a volunteer tutor? Is this a matter for the individual student, an extracurricular club, an integral part of a department or college curriculum, or a campus-wide graduation requirement? Pointing in the other direction, are campus- or system-wide commitments to public service recognized by student transcript notations or in defining criteria for faculty appointments and advancement? Are they reflected in budgeting for individual programs? And how do programs that emphasize or support civic involvement determine whether or not engagement strategies are consistent with campus ideals and the academic and professional needs of students?

Answers to these questions can only come through close attention to local circumstances that are well beyond the scope of this essay. What we have tried to provide here, however, is an account of the historical and organizational contexts that shape their contemporary relevance for graduate education. The two questions that we will try to answer can be stated as follows: What history has shaped current interest in enriching civic engagement within graduate programs at research universities? What dimensions of culture and social life can we draw upon in guiding or assessing programs designed with this in mind?

Defining the Problem

During the quarter century since Morrill's challenge to the academy, civic engagement has become increasingly important to colleges and universities in strengthening undergraduate education and forging stronger links with neighboring communities. Service-learning courses that include community service as a "text" to be read alongside assigned readings are well represented in undergraduate curricula. Numerous departments sponsor community-based undergraduate research opportunities. Campus centers for public service and service-learning have been established at many institutions to encourage and coordinate these activities with community partners.

At the graduate level, however, the picture is quite different. Although many law schools engage students in representing people who lack legal services, and medical students provide health care to the poor through "free clinics," more varied forms of graduate-student community engagement are few and far between, especially in the curriculum. As a result, many students experience the transition to graduate study as a withdrawal from public and community service that was a vital part of their undergraduate years. Far too often they shelve their civic interests, relegating them to the indulgences of a "youthful past," to focus on the more "serious" and mature challenges of professional training and advancement. As noted by Melissa Salazar (2006) during her doctoral studies in education at UC Davis, "Part of the problem is not the lack of desire on the part of graduate students to engage in civic life, but rather the need to abandon everything not directly connected to progress toward the degree. There is too much to do in a doctoral program and too little time to do it."

A consequence of this service asymmetry between undergraduate and graduate education is that the values of civic engagement have become increasingly separate from the values of advanced study and career development. As graduate students become enmeshed in hectic study schedules, student loans, and the challenges of forging new professional identities, they find it increasingly difficult to set aside time for volunteer work and attention to public issues. These difficulties are compounded for graduate students who are also working or starting families. Without institutional nurturing and support, the civic passions that students held as talented and engaged undergraduates can wither and die quickly in graduate school.

Disparities between how civic engagement is framed within undergraduate and graduate education exist at most colleges and universities, but they are particularly acute at research universities, for several reasons. First, research universities are more likely than other institutions to expect graduate students to make a full-time commitment to academic study. These expectations appear in the demands of coursework and in the timing and structure of program requirements. They also are embedded in the ideal of "fully socializing" graduate students to the academy or a profession and in admonitions by faculty advisors for students to "finish your dissertation first, then get on with your life."

Second, research universities and their faculties distinguish themselves from other institutions of higher education by a sometimes fervid commitment to basic instead of applied research. Though Clark Kerr (1963/2002) and other notable scholars of higher education have questioned the analytical soundness of this distinction, it is still invoked routinely in affirming the primacy of basic research over applied, and, by implication, the special significance of universities in which the former is paramount.

These distinctive elements of the research university ethos are tied closely to institutional features and practices. In contrast to other institutions, for example, research universities make few if any efforts to shape academic programs so that they can serve part-time students or working professionals. They champion instead provisions that help students stay focused 100 percent on their studies and/or select students for whom this is more likely to be possible than not. As another example, the kind of single-minded, entrepreneurial vigor with which many university faculty members pursue their research is presented within the research university as a valued attribute of professional calling and commitment. To encourage a similar single-mindedness among graduate students, faculty mentors frequently advise them to aim their extracurricular activities toward the profession, not a nearby community. This pattern of encouragement applies routinely to junior faculty members as well. Both graduate students and junior faculty are frequently counseled away from service activities that could interfere with their research productivity. Consistent with this ideal, both groups are much more likely to receive support (and even funding) for research travel and conference

413

presentations than for community service and civic engagement. Junior faculty may also be compensated with reduced teaching loads, summer salary, and research assistants, which are rarely if ever made available to graduate students.

This ethos of graduate education at a research university, its institutional supports, and its consequences deserves much more attention than it has received to date within discussions about both civic engagement and graduate study itself. As one step toward bringing attention to this condition, this chapter provides an overview of issues, challenges, and resources that could bring these related but largely separate discussions closer together. We begin by reviewing some of the policy and program antecedents that inform current discussions about integrating civic engagement and graduate education. We then turn to challenges and opportunities that characterize the current and prospective civic engagement of graduate students within the distinctive culture and organization of research universities. We summarize some program innovations that encourage civic engagement by graduate students in research universities, and conclude by posing questions that can help faculty and administrators think about how to best advance this work.

Antecedents and Foundations

In 2003, the Committee on Institutional Cooperation (CIC), an academic consortium of Big Ten universities and the University of Chicago, established a Committee on Engagement to help define, benchmark, and measure university-supported civic engagement activities. The Committee proposed the following definition:

> Engagement is the partnership of university knowledge and resources with those of the public and private sectors to enrich scholarship, research, and creative activity; enhance curriculum, teaching, and learning; prepare educated, engaged citizens; strengthen democratic values and civic responsibility; address critical societal issues; and contribute to the public good. (Bloomfield, 2005)

The CIC Engagement Committee identified three distinguishing elements of university-supported civic engagement:

- Engagement is scholarly. A scholarship-based model of engagement involves both the act of engaging (bringing universities and communities together) and the product of engagement (the spread of discipline-generated, evidence-based practices in communities).
- Engagement cuts across the mission of teaching, research, and service. It is not a separate activity, but a particular approach to campus-community collaboration.
- Engagement is reciprocal and mutually beneficial. There is mutual planning, implementation, and assessment among engagement partners. (Bloomfield, 2006)

The CIC Graduate Deans gathered in March 2006 with faculty, graduate student, and community leaders, as well as representatives of the National Science Foundation (NSF), North Central Association's Commission on Accreditation and School Improvement, and the Carnegie Foundation for the Advancement of Teaching, at a Wingspread conference on "Civic Engagement in Graduate Education: Preparing the Next Generation of Engaged Scholars." Co-sponsored by the Upper Midwest Campus Compact Consortium and The

> **Engaged higher education institutions:**
>
> - Seek out and cultivate reciprocal relationships with the communities in which they are located and actively enter into "shared tasks"—including service and research—to enhance the quality of life of those communities and the public good, overall (Kellogg Commission, 1999, p. 9, cited in USC, 2001, p. 1).
> - Support and promote the notion of "engaged scholarship"—that which addresses public problems and is of benefit to the wider community, can be applied to social practice, documents the effectiveness of community activities, and generates theories with respect to social practice (USC, 2001, p. 1).
> - Support and reward faculty members' professional service, public work, and/or community-based action research or "public scholarship" (Boyte & Hollander, 1999, p. 10).
> - Provide programs, curricula, and other opportunities for students to develop civic competencies and civic habits, including research opportunities that help them create knowledge and do scholarship relevant to and grounded in public problems but still within rigorous methodological frameworks (Boyte & Hollander, 1999, p. 10).
> - Have administrators that inculcate a civic ethos throughout the institution by giving voice to it in public forums, creating infrastructure to support it, and establishing policies that sustain it.
> - Promote student co-curricular civic engagement opportunities that include opportunities for reflection and leadership development.
> - Collaborate with community members to design partnerships that build on and enhance community assets, as well as increase community access to the intellectual, material, and human resources of the institution (J. Plaut, personal communication, March 29, 2006).

FIGURE 27.1. What Is An "Engaged" Higher Education Institution?
SOURCE: Adapted from Gibson, 2006.

Johnson Foundation, the meeting addressed the benefits and challenges of incorporating civic engagement in doctoral education, principles and indicators of success that might guide future engagement efforts, and promising strategies for preparing future scholars to use engaged pedagogies, to pursue public scholarship, and to support a culture of democratic dialogue and action in collaboration with community stakeholders (Upper Midwest Campus Compact Consortium, 2006).

Despite the thoughtfulness of the CIC efforts, most faculty members continue to consider the civic mission of universities as a matter of consequence only for those university administrators concerned with undergraduate education and community relations. In a 1993 assessment of research universities, Donald Kennedy, former president of Stanford, found that these institutions send few signals about their expectations regarding faculty citizenship.

> A striking example of this . . . [is] the way universities prepare their own doctoral candidates for academic careers. In the schools of law, medicine, and even business, one now sees well-taught, required courses with names like "Ethics for . . ." or "Professional Responsibility." Yet, one finds almost no systematic instruction of this kind for dissertation-level Ph.D. candidates. In this way, we broadcast the view that some form of civic education is in order for every profession except our own. (1993, p. 146).

Kennedy's observation more than a decade ago still holds true and does so despite the civic origins of universities themselves. Indeed, as Gibson notes (Gibson, 2006), the preparation of civic leadership was a primary role of the first universities in this country. In 1749,

Benjamin Franklin wrote that the "ability to serve" should be the rationale for all public schools—a mission that colonial colleges, including Harvard, William and Mary, Yale, Princeton, Columbia, Brown, Rutgers, and Dartmouth, adopted, to educate men "capable of creating good communities built on religious denominational principles" (Harkavy, 2004, p. 6; cited in Gibson, 2006). In 1876, Daniel Gilman, in his inaugural address as the first president of Johns Hopkins University, expressed the hope that universities would "make for less misery among the poor, less ignorance in the schools, less bigotry in the temple, less suffering in the hospitals, less fraud in business, less folly in politics" (Long, 1992, cited in Harkavy, 2004, p. 7).

These elements of civic engagement and public responsibility were also deeply embedded in the Morrill Act of 1862 that created the nation's land-grant institutions. The intent of this legislation was to establish a new generation of universities that could play a key role in rural economic and community development. The attention of land-grant institutions to "agriculture and the mechanic arts," and to enrolling populations that otherwise lack access to higher education, has persisted. However, the range of programs offered by these universities has evolved and diversified dramatically. As boundaries between "public" and "private" have blurred, the implications of the "land-grant ideal" have become increasingly apparent for private institutions as well.

As noted by Harry Boyte and Elizabeth Hollander in their 1999 report of a Wingspread Conference on "Renewing the Civic Mission of the American Research University,"

> research institutions of higher education in America have been, in Charles Eliot's words, "filled with the democratic spirit." Such spirit took many different forms. Columbia University, according to Seth Low, breathed the air of the city of New York, its working class population, its problems, and its opportunities. At the University of Chicago, America's pragmatic philosophy and world-renown sociology department emerged, in part, from vital partnerships between the Hull House settlement and scholars. At land grant institutions, the cooperative extension system of county agents saw itself as "building rural democracy" and helping to develop communities' capacities for cooperative action. (p. 7)

These historical antecedents are notable in shaping idealized notions of the social contract between research universities and the public. However, as higher education expanded dramatically in the twentieth century, increased demands to support technical scholarship and to prepare professional practitioners displaced attention to the university's civic mission. Although university ideals continued to affirm civic values, the civic contributions of university programs suffered increasing neglect.

Withdrawal from civic engagement over the last century was not just an institutional matter. At the individual level, as noted by Robert Putnam (2000) and other observers, there was a parallel withdrawal by American citizens from participation in public affairs. But having neglected their historic civic missions, higher education institutions did not perceive themselves "as part of this problem or of its solution" (Boyte & Hollander, 1999).

Some of the first challenges within the university to the eclipse of civic ideals took shape within efforts to strengthen and revitalize undergraduate student life. Efforts to engage university students in community service date back to the "YMCA movement" at the end of the nineteenth century (with the founding of Philips Brooks House at Harvard, Dwight Hall at Yale, etc.). However, in the first half of the twentieth century few national or institutional initiatives emerged to support and sustain these efforts. That began to change in the 1960s when a loosely connected band of "service-learning" pioneers began working to combine service activities with academic study (Stanton, Giles, & Cruz, 1999).

For this network of reformers, service-learning was a pedagogy that joined two complicated processes—community action by students, the "service," and efforts to learn from that action and connect what is learned to existing knowledge. Service-learning advocates wanted opportunities of this sort to be curriculum-based, designed and facilitated by faculty in collaboration with nonprofit-sector staff and/or community leaders. Within this pedagogy, community service and academic excellence would not be "competitive demands to be balanced [by students] through discipline and personal sacrifice, but rather . . . interdependent dimensions of good intellectual work" (Wagner, 1986, p. 17). The pedagogical challenge was to devise "ways to connect study and service so that the disciplines illuminate and inform experience and experience lends meaning and energy to the disciplines" (Eskow, 1980, p. 21). The roots of these early expressions of service-learning can be found in a number of "antecedent movements"—e.g., land-grant colleges and universities, settlement house education, "progressive educators," work programs in the 1930s, Peace Corps and VISTA, and the civil rights movement (Pollack, 1996).

Educators affiliated with this first wave of civic education reform developed several exemplary programs, and a diverse literature appeared in which theoretical propositions and best practices were examined and explicated through the federally funded National Student Volunteer Program's (NSVP) *Synergist* journal. However, the program-oriented, "bottom-up" thrust of these efforts had only marginal impact on curricula and modes of instruction.

A second wave of serious effort to restore civic engagement to a prominent place within colleges and universities emerged in the mid-1980s in connection with a national initiative to promote public service among undergraduate students. Early advocates of this initiative such as Stanford's President Kennedy cited the social obligation of students privileged to obtain a higher education degree: that they should "give back" to society through volunteer and/or government service while in school and throughout life after graduation. Others called for a return to the historical mission of higher education in the United States to educate and inform society's emerging leaders and prepare them for their civic roles and duties. And others advocated volunteer service as a means of connecting the privileged to the lives and problems of those less fortunate, in the hope of building knowledge and public will to solve societal problems.

Campus Compact stimulated a third wave of interest a few years later. Kennedy and two other research university presidents had founded the Compact in 1986 as a coalition for public and community service. In 1989 Kennedy and David Warren, then President of Ohio Wesleyan University, led an effort to link students' public and community service to the academic curriculum through service-learning pedagogy and community-based research. Naming their initiative the Project on Integrating Service with Academic Study (ISAS), they argued that by integrating community service with academic study, universities could more

417

effectively encourage student interest in and engagement with civic life. Service connected with study would ensure that students' service experiences were continually challenging and educational as well as useful for the communities they served. Most importantly, academically based community service would enable students to reflect critically on their experience in communities and connect these reflections both to broader social issues and to subject matter in the disciplines. Integrating service experience with academic study was key to ensuring the development of graduates who would participate in society actively, ethically, and with an informed, critical habit of mind.

This project marked a shift in the work of Campus Compact from promoting community and public service—service outside the curriculum—to an emphasis on service that is integrally connected to course content in a wide variety of disciplines. With its curricular focus, ISAS was aimed at the needs of faculty who adopt service-learning as a teaching methodology and sought to deepen its practice in their courses, in their department, and at their institutions.

A Fourth Wave of Reform

A fourth wave of reform to restore the civic foundation of higher education is reflected in a concerted effort over the past ten years to move beyond individual initiatives and special programs to increase the civic engagement of institutions themselves. Advocates argue that "engaged" institutions serve and strengthen the society of which they are a part. Through the learning, values, and commitment of faculty, staff, and students, our institutions create social capital, preparing students to contribute positively to local, national, and global communities. Universities have the responsibility to foster in faculty, staff, and students a sense of social responsibility and a commitment to the social good, which is central to the success of a democratic and just society (The Talloires Network, 2005).

The commitment to civic engagement outlined in statements such as this is no longer the special province of undergraduate education, but implicates the entire institution. Both undergraduate and graduate students and all other segments of the university community are called upon to engage in civic enterprises through teaching and learning, research, and administrative and service functions. (For example, university administrative policy could require purchasing officers to seek vendors in local communities with which the institution is partnered.) An "engaged" institution in which this ideal is realized would "foster partnerships between universities and communities to enhance economic opportunity, empower individuals and groups, increase mutual understanding and strengthen the relevance, reach and responsiveness of university education and research" (The Talloires Network, 2005). The University of Pennsylvania's embrace of West Philadelphia is a shining example of this kind of institutional commitment with students, faculty, and staff engaged in service, research, and economic development activities with community members.

Within this affirmation of institutional civic engagement, the asymmetries noted earlier between undergraduate and graduate orientations become increasingly apparent. Although civic engagement has been revitalized at the undergraduate level, it is still largely neglected at the graduate level, particularly at universities with a dominant research mission. This contrast can perplex and demoralize graduate students who enjoyed institutional support for community involvement in their undergraduate years, in part as a result of the reforms noted earlier. It has also become increasingly apparent and perplexing to faculty and administrators, some of whom were engaged in the undergraduate service-learning movement or who are civically engaged themselves. From the perspective of these students and faculty, inattention to civic engagement at the highest levels of academic study has unfortunate consequences for students, the research university, and the public. Among those most frequently noted are the following.

For students:

- The moral and civic development that many students enjoyed as undergraduates is suspended when they move on to graduate studies.
- The knowledge that graduate students acquire about professions and disciplines is frequently divorced from the contexts of social responsibility in which mature professionals work—to the detriment of intellectual, civic, and professional development.
- Graduate students lack opportunities to integrate their interests in liberal arts, graduate, and professional education with community service.
- Graduate students lack opportunities to learn community-based and collaborative research methodologies that are increasingly important to understanding and solving community problems.

For communities:

- Graduate students are not making the kinds of contributions that undergraduates make to community life and development.
- Communities have unmet information needs to which graduate students are capable of responding through community-based/responsive research and professional service.
- As they become academics and professionals, graduate students develop little if any familiarity with forms of teaching, service, and research that can enrich community and civic participation.

For research universities:

- The neglect of civic engagement in the fabric of graduate education strikes a false chord in the research university's social contract with the public.
- The social contributions of the research university are truncated by the relative isolation of graduate students and their faculty mentors from projects of public service and civic engagement.
- Universities lack opportunities to be of scholarly service to communities in ways that will strengthen public support.
- Taken together, these concerns suggest that the segregation between civic engagement and graduate education diminishes the vitality of graduate education itself and marks a problematic and glaring gap in the research university's social contract.

Prospects and Possibilities

In the past several years, the long-standing neglect of advanced academic study as a venue for inculcating ideals of civic engagement has been challenged by several reports and

419

proposals. As one example, a summary of Recommendations from National Studies on Doctoral Education (Nyquist & Wulff, 2000 cited in Bloomfield, 2005) calls for the production of "scholar-citizens who see their special training connected more closely to the needs of society and the global economy." As another, the Woodrow Wilson National Fellowship Foundation Responsive Ph.D. Initiative (2005) urges that "the goal of the doctorate [be] redefined as scholarly citizenship."

Similar concerns and ideals are beginning to percolate among professional school networks at both undergraduate and graduate levels. Health profession associations have recently called for an increased emphasis on community-based and community-focused education (Seifer, Hermanns, & Lewis, 2000, p. 1). The American Medical Association recently passed a resolution recommending that the Liaison Committee on Medical Education (LCME) consider a requirement for service-learning in its next review of LCME standards. Community-Campus Partnerships for Health (CCPH) has been a major force in promoting civic engagement by health profession schools, faculty, and students.

The health sciences and professions are not the only areas in which these developments are occurring. In its follow-up to a "Visions for Change Report," (2004, p. 10), ABET, the organization responsible for setting the standards of engineering education, called for reexamination of Engineering Criterion 3, Program Outcomes and Assessment, with the goal of "re-defining engineering for the public in a global context." In its "Criteria for Accrediting Computing Programs" (2007, p. 14), ABET lists "an understanding of professional, ethical, legal, security and social issues and responsibilities" and "an ability to analyze the local and global impact of computing on individuals, organizations, and society" as attributes for students to achieve by graduation. In a similar vein, the American Bar Association requires law schools to offer public service opportunities to law students and provide instruction in "professional responsibility." Some law schools (e.g., Tulane and the University of Pennsylvania) go farther and actually require law school students to do pro bono work (Rhode, 2005).

Limited but important developments have also occurred in individual academic disciplines. The National Communication Association focused a recent annual convention on "The Engaged Discipline." Issues of "public scholarship" were also featured themes for recent national conferences of the American Anthropological Association and the American Sociological Association.

Eloquent calls for increased attention to civic engagement in graduate education have also come from research sponsors. The National Science Foundation now reviews proposals based on two criteria: the intellectual merit of the proposed activity and its broader social impacts, defined to include engagement of underrepresented groups, strengthened partnerships, and integration of research and education. NSF is also supporting new models for graduate education through its Integrative Graduate Education and Research Traineeship Program, which seeks to "contribute to the development of a diverse, globally-engaged, science and engineering workforce," and it has expanded involvement of graduate students in community-university partnerships through grant programs such as the Math Science Partnerships.

These recent calls for action have a special significance for research universities, in two respects. First, they refer explicitly to issues of graduate education and to the development of graduate students as engaged researchers and professionals. Second, they affirm civic engagement as an ideal that needs to be embedded in the enterprise of research itself.

Public Scholarship

The concept of public scholarship is a key element of renewed conversations about the research university and civic engagement. Imagining America at Syracuse University, which has established a Publicly Active Graduate Education (PAGE) Fellows program, describes public scholarship as:

> Scholarly or creative work integral to a faculty member's academic area. It is jointly planned, carried out, and reflected on by co-equal university and community partners. And it yields one or more public good products.
>
> Subject to these three conditions, public scholarship may encompass artistic, design, historical, and critical work that contributes to public discourse and the formation of robust publics. It may also include disciplinary or interdisciplinary efforts to advance public engagement in higher education itself and reflection or research on the import of such efforts.
>
> Public good products may take diverse and plural forms, including but not limited to: peer-reviewed individual or co-authored publications; other forms of writing and publication; presentations at academic and non-academic conferences and meetings; oral histories or ethnographies; interviews with or reflections by participants; program development; performances, exhibitions, installations, murals, or festivals; new K–16 curricula; site designs or plans for "cultural corridors," and other place-making work; and policy recommendations. (Ellison, 2006)

Advocates argue that public scholarship of this sort brings about a greater "return on [research] investments" by joining university and community assets to yield better quality and availability of data; better questions, reflecting theory and practice; better methods, applied more effectively to specific populations; and integration of theory and practice, making science more useful and practice more effective (J. R. Cook, personal communication, June 7, 2006).

As another step toward reconsidering graduate education and civic engagement, the concept of public scholarship is beginning to make headway within the social science and humanities disciplines. In its "Interim Report and Recommendations" to the American Sociology Association, the ASA Task Force on Institutionalizing Public Sociologies addressed "the need for more explicit guidance of graduate students and junior faculty for integrating public sociology into their career development" (2005, p. 3) and recommended that the ASA Council "review and endorse" public sociology tenure and promotion guidelines "that could be used by sociology departments to . . . to recognize scholarship of public sociology." The American Historical Association established a "Task Force on Public History" in 2001 to facilitate better relations between the AHA and public historians (see http://www.historians.org/governance/tfph). Anthropologists have created a web page and journals to promote "public anthropology."

Public Anthropology

Public anthropology is "the ability of anthropology and anthropologists to effectively address problems beyond the discipline—illuminating the larger social issues of our times as well as encouraging broad, public conversations about them with the explicit goal of fostering social change. It affirms our responsibility, as scholars and citizens, to meaningfully contribute to communities beyond the academy—both local and global—that make the study of anthropology possible" (http://www.publicanthropology.org/).

Both regional and national initiatives have emerged as complements to these discipline specific recommendations. The Higher Learning Commission of the North Central Association of Colleges and Schools introduced in 2003 (and began applying in 2005) a new accreditation criterion—"Engagement and Service"—that requires institutions to demonstrate responsiveness to the constituencies and communities they serve, including connecting students with external communities through their educational programs. As part of recent revisions to its widely used institution classification system, the Carnegie Foundation for the Advancement of Teaching developed a new elective classification that focuses on community engagement and includes graduate education as one arena in which institutions can demonstrate engagement through the curriculum.

In 2005 Campus Compact and Tufts University convened scholars from research universities who had undertaken significant civic engagement efforts to discuss how their institutions are promoting engagement on their campuses and in their communities. The group shared program models and strategies and decided to take on more visible leadership nationally. As a first expression of this role, they developed a case statement (Gibson, 2006) that outlines why it is important for research universities to embrace and advance engaged scholarship as a central component of their activities and programs at every level—institutional, faculty, and student.

The newly formed group met a second time at UCLA in 2007 and published a second report (Stanton, 2007) that focuses on opportunities and challenges in four areas critical to expanding and institutionalizing civic engagement within research universities: engaged scholarship (research in any field that links university scholarship with public and private sector resources to enrich knowledge, address, and help solve critical societal issues and contribute to the public good); scholarship focused on civic and community engagement (research focused on civic participation in public life, including participation by engaged scholars, and on the impact of this work on all constituencies); educating students for civic and community engagement (what students need to know and be able to do as active, effective citizens of a diverse democracy); and advancing civic engagement within and across research universities. The group emphasized that recommendations addressing these issues should apply to graduate and professional education.

In February 2008 the group convened a third time at UNC–Chapel Hill to focus on civic and community-engaged scholarship. Discussions were aimed at clarifying definitions and developing a "resource toolkit" for advancing this work at research universities (Stanton & Howard, 2009). The group concluded this meeting by formally establishing itself as The Research University Civic Engagement Network (TRUCEN) and invited membership from other Carnegie Foundation–defined "very high research institutions." This new network enjoins research university colleagues to embrace its vision for civic and community engagement and work together to realize this vision in practice.

Graduate students themselves have played a role in some of these efforts. In 2004, Imagining America established a Publicly Active Graduate Education (PAGE) project, which recruits graduate student fellows to participate in a day-long institute held at its annual conference (http://pageia.com/). Graduate students also participated as planners and speakers for California Campus Compact's Symposium on Civic Engagement and Graduate Education at Stanford University in 2006 and at a follow-up symposium held at the University of California, Davis, in 2008.

The Logic of Graduate Education

An important recognition emerging from the discussions just noted is that graduate education is something more than an advanced form of undergraduate study. As a result, improvements proposed as logical extensions of undergraduate ideals may meet with skepticism or resistance by graduate program students, faculty, and administrators. At the very least, somewhat different arguments are called for in recommending civic engagement for graduate students than for undergraduates.

The most compelling of these arguments corresponds closely to the distinctive logic of graduate education and an emphasis on the professional and academic skill sets required of practicing academics and professionals. Beyond coursework and assignments, this underlying logic is tied closely to the induction and socialization of students as new members of professional and disciplinary communities. These communities make graduate education more specialized and intensive than undergraduate education. They also create distinctive opportunities and challenges for civic engagement.

Thoughtful efforts to embrace civic engagement need to respect these distinctions not only in general, but as they apply to a specific profession or discipline. What we ask of medical students, for example, is not the same as what we ask of Ph.D.s in comparative literature or physics. For all these reasons, developing a universal template for how civic engagement can serve the interests of all institutions, graduate students, and programs is unrealistic. For the same reasons, however, there is much to be gained from looking at best practices across institutions and programs, and increasingly, there are practices and programs worth looking at.

Our preliminary review of several recent efforts suggests that incorporating civic engagement as a vitalizing ideal in graduate education may also require and benefit from:

- A renewed understanding of the social contract between the research university, the professions and the public.
- Systematic, cross-institutional attention to assessing the individual and social outcomes of graduate and professional education programs.
- Broad-based efforts to improve the pedagogy of graduate and professional education within a context of social and technological change.
- Broad-based efforts to improve the social and economic welfare of graduate and professional students, including increased levels of financial support and family-friendly policies.

Against the backdrop of these related reforms, civic engagement discussions revolve around two different sets of questions. The first set focuses on the institutional contexts in which service or engagement is broached, exercised, assessed, or supported. Is it an individual student initiative, something sponsored through the curriculum or by a department,

423

or a broad institution-wide effort? The second set focuses on the purpose of direct service or engagement activities. What kind of service is intended? Does the service provide direct assistance to clients, or is it aimed more toward developing policy, research, or public discourse? As a framework for considering the potential contributions of different pilot efforts and exemplars, let us describe the two kinds of questions in more detail.

Institutional Contexts

Discussions of public service and civic engagement frequently confound the activities of individual students, curriculum-based programs or projects, and institutions (see Figure 27.2). In assessing opportunities for graduate student civic engagement, service by individual students may receive the most anecdotal attention, but all three of these contexts are important. Exemplary efforts within any one of the contexts can also serve as a catalyst for stimulating efforts in the other two. However, important differences appear across disciplines and professions in how they define and regard civic engagement within these different contexts. It is also possible for opportunities that emerge in one context to be neglected, trivialized, or resisted by policies associated with another.

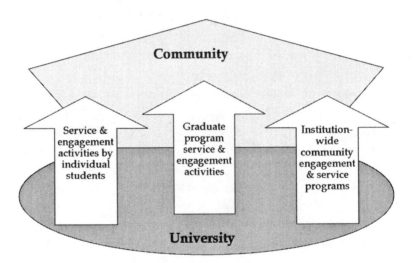

FIGURE 27.2. Three University Contexts of Service Design and Administration
SOURCE: Adapted from M. Salazar (2006).

Perhaps the most widely noted examples of public service and civic engagement involve individual students who become involved in community efforts entirely on their own initiative. Among graduate students, the range of this kind of engagement is suggested by the following activities:

- Volunteering to tutor students at a local school
- Working to establish a tutoring program at a local school
- Performing music or theater pieces for community audiences
- Teaching a class for adults in prison
- Helping residents assess environmental hazards

- Working to establish a community or school garden
- Providing nutritional counseling to children or adults
- Participating in political or social action campaigns
- Offering expert testimony in court cases and public hearings
- Offering legal assistance to indigent populations
- Helping a community organization prepare a funding or policy proposal

Individual graduate students undertake activities of this sort for many reasons—in some cases as an extension or component of their graduate studies, in others as respite from those same studies. In many cases this kind of engagement is relatively invisible. There's no expectation that it be reported as part of a student's graduate program of study, nor do the arrangements by which the student participates fall within the province of an official university office or program. The content of the engagement may also overlap or be divorced entirely from the focus of the student's graduate program.

Activities quite similar to those listed may also take place within programs and projects that enjoy institutional support. These include both academic programs leading directly to advanced degrees and centers and projects affiliated with campus academic units. In terms of academic degree programs, for example, public service internships of one sort or another are an integral part of graduate education in fields such as medicine, dentistry, social welfare, education (for teaching or administrative credential candidates), and public policy. Similar experiences are also included in some programs in other professions, including law, architecture, engineering, and clinical psychology. However, they rarely appear as an integral part of degree programs in core academic disciplines (e.g., biology, anthropology, economics, history, English literature).

Somewhat similar asymmetries by discipline and profession apply to public service projects that bear no direct relationship to degree requirements but are still supported by academic units and departments. Examples include:

- A community design center supported by a college of architecture
- An elementary laboratory school affiliated with a graduate school of education
- A university program for placing mathematics graduate students as co-teachers in high school mathematics classrooms
- A community lecture/discussion series on engineering and public interest
- An "arts in the schools" program associated with campus fine arts departments
- A public interest or legal aid clinic supported by a law school

In some cases, students have created projects or programs on their own that are passed down from one student generation to the next, without much institutional or faculty support. For example, the Board Fellows Program, founded by students at Stanford's Graduate School of Business in 1997, matches MBA students with the boards of directors of San Francisco Bay Area nonprofit organizations for eight-month apprenticeships. Fellows serve as nonvoting board members, gaining an understanding of the challenges and roles for nonprofit organizations as well as the complexities of nonprofit management (http://csi.gsb.stanford.edu/service). In other instances, campus or department staff members administer community service projects and centers and students participate as they can, without necessarily leading the overall effort.

425

Public service and civic engagement can also be supported through institutional policies and strategies. A notable example for faculty members is the inclusion of "public service" among criteria for faculty appointment and merit advancement. Another involves including "beneficence" and "justice" among the criteria for reviewing research involving human subjects. Yet another involves institutional efforts to form collaborative partnerships with community organizations that can support economic and community development of targeted neighborhoods or regions (e.g., the University of Pennsylvania's work in West Philadelphia; an initiative by the University of California, Davis Medical School to help revitalize surrounding low-income neighborhoods in Sacramento.)

Few if any institutional policies explicitly encourage civic engagement among graduate students, but some strategies can have that effect indirectly. For example, the University of Minnesota offers the Mary A. McEvoy Award for Public Engagement and Leadership annually to one graduate student and one professional student; graduate assistantships that support individuals working with the service-learning office and doing research with community organizations; and training on service-learning pedagogy. An institutional mission that emphasizes public service—as articulated in the land-grant ideal—can help create opportunities for graduate students to observe and learn from the extension involvement of faculty members. By supporting professional schools per se, research universities also establish close links with professional associations, some of which have their own ethics of service and civic engagement. To the extent that research universities actively assist graduate students in becoming members of these professions—through professional student associations and the like—these links can become vital enough to acquaint students with professional ethics and service principles.

Taken together, these observations support the following generalizations about institutional contexts:

- Civic engagement opportunities for graduate students can be created and supported through the initiatives of individual students, through curriculum and academic (research) programs and through institutional policies.
- The distribution of these opportunities across the research university is uneven; differences appear among different disciplines and professions at the program and institutional level, with a notable vacuum in doctoral education.
- Institutional attention to coordinating these opportunities as an explicit dimension of graduate education is weak, as are efforts to assess their contributions to pedagogic and professional ideals.

Few institutions have set about the task of assessing graduate student civic engagement opportunities across all three contexts. Fewer still have made deliberate efforts to link engagement in different contexts to pedagogical or professional ideals. A more thoughtful and coherent orientation toward these issues will require both attention and continuing inquiry.

Service and Engagement Purposes

As suggested by the questions we posed in the introduction to this essay, public service and civic engagement activities can be aimed toward multiple and at times conflicting goals. Intentions do not always reflect outcomes, and both intentions and outcomes can vary for different participants. These abiding uncertainties characterize a rich seam of transactions between research universities and the public. Involving graduate students in these transactions brings them face to face with these ambiguities and the challenge of balancing public and professional concerns.

In their tripartite commitment to teaching, research, and public service, research university faculty members have developed a valuable rubric for organizing these and at least some faculty members would draw the arrows in Figure 27.3 so that they point in both directions. Graduate students can benefit from having this same rubric incorporated within their programs of study, not just as a footnote about the academy, but also as the organizing foundation for thoughtful and engaged professional lives. Indeed, to prepare professionals who have an informed regard for the intersection of teaching, research, and public service, it makes good sense to place this intersection at the center, rather than the periphery, of graduate education.

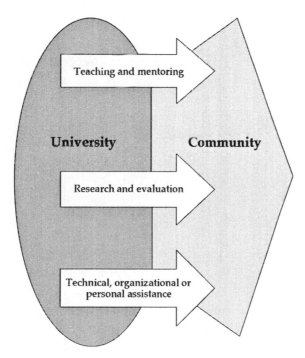

FIGURE 27.3. Three Service and Engagement Purposes

SOURCE: Adapted from M. Salazar (2006).

Authors' note: While many civic and community engagement practitioners advocate reciprocal, collaborative partnerships between campus and community as the foundation of their work, most projects continue to be sponsored by and managed by university staff and faculty. The one-directional arrows in figures 2 and 3 reflect this reality.

Some civic engagement programs rest on teaching or mentoring as a primary rationale, others on research, and still others on forms of service that are more akin to direct technical, administrative, or personal assistance (Figure 27.3). Overlap between these three purposes of service is common, but it is also useful to distinguish them, at least temporarily, for purposes of focused design and evaluation.

Programs that emphasize teaching and mentoring, for example, are best examined and refined by attending to concepts of pedagogy, curriculum, instruction, and so on. Programs that emphasize research unfold according to a somewhat different logic. They might raise questions about teaching as well, but they invite primary attention to data collection and analysis strategies, community concerns, and research reporting. Projects through which graduate students provide organizational leadership, counseling, or technical assistance are best examined and refined by attending to the logic and particulars of that kind of work. Running through each level and type of engagement are questions about equitable partnerships and the effectiveness of relationships between campus and community members.

But isn't the research university a service institution in its own right? Do not university teaching and research both provide valuable service to the public? Yes, on both counts. However, although research and teaching have a special place within the ideals of a research university, university members can also make valuable civic contributions that bear little relationship to their research or teaching interests. Indeed, citizenship and civic engagement can be built on a foundation of teaching or research, but they need not be.

Related closely to this proposition, the skills needed to design and evaluate programs may differ greatly from the skills required to deliver valued services over the long haul. In other cases, this asymmetry is less a matter of skills than of resources; people who run programs seldom have the time and attention required to examine them systematically. Research universities that seek to make their graduate students' public service and civic engagement as thoughtful and effective as possible need to find ways to bridge these asymmetries at the level of both programs and the institution as a whole.

Contexts and Purposes

The distinctions noted earlier about contexts and purposes help to define a rich array of civic and service activities in which graduate students can productively engage. As represented in Figure 27.4, a matrix framed by these two dimensions can serve as a tool for locating and inventorying public service and civic engagement opportunities for graduate students. It can also reveal points of correspondence or conflict between contexts of civic engagement within the same institutions. In particular, paying attention to both purposes and contexts of civic engagement can stimulate efforts to build opportunities of this sort more thoughtfully into graduate programs of study, broadly defined. Ideally, graduate students would have something more than lots of opportunities to "do good." They would also have opportunities to develop the moral and civic sensibilities of informed professionals, citizens who have special skills and responsibilities for supporting public and civil society.

Although innovative approaches to encouraging civic engagement among graduate students lag far behind those of undergraduate education, they do exist. Some have developed in the margins and persisted through the efforts of a single individual. Many others have

Service and Engagement Purposes	Individual	Program/Project	Institution
Teaching and Mentoring	A graduate student in chemistry tutors students taking chemistry at nearby high school * * * A food sciences graduate student conducts nutrition and meal planning workshops for school cafeteria workers	A graduate program in mathematics arranges for MA and Ph.D. students to co-teach mathematics classes with credentialed teachers at nearby high schools * * * Graduate students in the visual and performing arts organize and staff a Saturday arts academy in a nearby community	Through a campus-wide "science in the schools" program, graduate students from a wide range of science departments work with teachers in nearby elementary and high schools to strengthen curricula and develop enriched assessments of students' scientific literacy * * * Graduate students staff a summer "bridge" program that helps incoming freshman strengthen their writing and reading skills
Research and Evaluation	An engineering graduate student works with local high-tech employers to redesign production equipment so that it can accommodate the needs of disabled workers * * * A history graduate student helps a local newspaper organize its photo archives as part of her own dissertation research	A cohort of education doctoral students work with local school districts in a collaborative project to evaluate alternative approaches to second-language instruction * * * Medical students work with community agencies to study and discourage adolescent tobacco use	A campus-wide fellowship program supports collaboration between graduate students and local farmers in conducting research related to regionally sustainable agriculture * * * The office of graduate studies offers an annual award for a student dissertation that integrates disciplinary research with community service
Technical, Organizational, or Personal Assistance	A student helps a community advocacy group prepare proposals for extramural funding * * * A graduate student establishes a program through which undergraduate student volunteers provide counseling and social support to prisoners	Students enrolled in a graduate ecology program help community volunteers create and maintain a community garden * * * Students in a graduate school of architecture and city planning staff a community design center in a low-income community	A campus-wide faculty and graduate student group works with civic leaders from nearby communities to support and assess a wide range of community development projects * * * A group of faculty and graduate students from different departments transform a campus arboretum into an ecological study center for nearby schools and community members

FIGURE 27.4. Contexts of Service Design and Administration

been initiated in response to the recent sense of urgency outlined earlier. The civic engagement efforts described next reflect a range of institutional contexts and service activity genres identified across California. (We know there are many more across the United States.) Taken together, these examples can, we hope, enrich discussions about related challenges and opportunities that characterize research universities. Beyond that, we hope they can stimulate faculty, administrators, and students to develop more thoughtful and effective strategies for supporting the civic engagement of graduate students.

Engagement through Curriculum and Teaching

Scholarly Concentration in Community Health and Public Service. School of Medicine, Stanford University. Contact: Lisa Chamberlain, MD, MPH, Director: http://med.stanford. edu/chps.

All MD students at Stanford must complete requirements in a Scholarly Concentration. This concentration, distinguished by service-learning and community-based research, enables students to gain knowledge and skills necessary for addressing health challenges of diverse and often underserved communities domestically and overseas. Curriculum topics include the social role of physicians; community health assessment and health interventions; program planning and evaluation; community-based research methods; practice and politics of health-focused public service; and cultural competencies and organizing strategies necessary for working in diverse communities. The Concentration encourages the development of physicians with the commitment and capacity to become effective, lifelong leaders in community health and community-focused domestic and international health policy.

Humanities Out There (HOT). University of California, Irvine. Contact: Julia Reinhard Lupton, Professor of English and Comparative Literature, Director: http://www.humanities.uci.edu/ hot/program/menu.html.

Humanities Out There joins public school teachers, graduate students, and undergraduate tutors to develop and instruct age-appropriate curricula designed to help students of the Santa Ana Unified School District develop critical thinking and writing skills. Sponsored by UCI's School of Humanities, HOT takes its intellectual leadership from faculty members and advanced graduate students. These interests in turn drive the workshops that take place in the schools that are designed to develop basic literacy—reading, writing, and critical thinking—through exposure to intellectually challenging artifacts and exercises. The graduate students provide required intensive training to undergraduate tutors involved in these projects as well as ongoing mentorship.

Capital Area North Doctorate in Educational Leadership (CANDEL). University of California, Davis. Contact: Paul Heckman, Associate Dean, School of Education. UC Co-Director: http://candeljtdoc.org/.

CANDEL is a collaborative Ed.D. program that that combines doctoral training for students with service to regional schools and educators. The program was established in 2005 through a partnership between UC Davis, CSU Sonoma, and CSU Sacramento to integrate academic instruction for individual students with efforts to strengthen the educational leadership resources of California's Great Central Valley. [Note: CSU Sacramento has since withdrawn to establish a related doctoral program of its own.]

Engagement through Research

The Ralph and Goldy Lewis Center for Regional Policy Studies. UCLA School of Public Affairs, Los Angeles. Contact: Paul Ong, Director, Department of Urban Planning: http://lewis.spa. ucla.edu/index5.cfm.

The Ralph and Goldy Lewis Center for Regional Policy Studies promotes the study, understanding, and solution of regional policy issues, with special reference to Southern California, including problems of the environment, urban design, housing, community and neighborhood dynamics, transportation, and economic development. It is a locus for interdisciplinary activities, involving numerous faculty members and graduate students from many schools and departments. It also fosters links with researchers at other California universities and research institutes on issues of relevance to regional policy.

John Gardner Center for Youth and Their Communities, Stanford University, Stanford, California. Contact: Craig Baker, Director: http://gardnercenter.stanford.edu/index.html.

Founded at Stanford University in 2000 and situated in the School of Education, the Gardner Center works closely with three communities in the San Francisco Bay Area to integrate a community youth development perspective into the practices of schools, local governments, regional institutions, and policy-making systems, with the ultimate goal of maximizing the responsiveness of these systems to youths' developmental needs. Key strategies employed by the Center include bridging research and practice, supporting community action, and sharing what works, in response to pressing concerns of Bay Area youth and their communities. Graduate students are involved as staff and researchers.

Engagement through Institutional Collaboration

UCLA in LA. University of California, Los Angeles. Contact: William Vega, director, Luskin Center for Innovation: http://la.ucla.edu/.

UCLA in LA was established in 2002 as a chancellor's initiative that utilizes the scholarship of engagement to more intentionally and meaningfully connects university and community interests in the greater Los Angeles area. Operationalized through the Center for Community Partnerships, the initiative provides partnership support to UCLA faculty, staff, and graduate students and nonprofit organizations in the surrounding Los Angeles area to work together to address issues of concern in three areas: children, youth, and families; arts and culture; and economic development. Partnership projects have produced art installations in Chinatown to examine the impact of culture on economic development; created nanotechnology kits to improve mathematics and science pedagogy in secondary education; and built medicinal gardens in East LA to study the relationship between health outcomes and cultural practices.

431

Community Partnership Resource Center. University of California, San Francisco. Contact: Roberto Ariel Vargas, Coordinator: http://www.familymedicine.medschool.ucsf.edu/ community%5Fservice/cprc/.

The UCSF Community Partnership Resource Center seeks to promote the overall health and well-being of San Franciscans by facilitating partnerships between UCSF and local communities, focusing particularly on communities with significant health disparities compared to the rest of the city. Such collaborations link the skills and wisdom present within these communities with the specialized knowledge and academic discipline of the health professionals and staff of UCSF. By bringing partners together, the resource center fosters sharing of community and university resources, enriches the academic experience, and advances the overall health of local communities in a culturally and linguistically competent manner.

Community Based Learning Collaborative. University of Southern California, Los Angeles. Contact: Sharon Stewart http://www.usc.edu/neighborhoods/community/programs/c. html.

The CBLC was launched in 2003 as a university-wide "equitable partnership" among community-based organizations and faculty, students, and staff at the University of Southern California. The mission of the CBLC is to promote public service as an integral part of education and to foster reciprocal relationships between the university and the neighboring community. Specifically, the CBLC seeks to increase awareness among students—graduate and undergraduate—faculty, and community members about opportunities for civic engagement and to facilitate the development of innovative and interdisciplinary community-based/service-learning projects.

Questions, Strategies, and Ideals

Recent calls for renewing the civic mission of graduate education at research universities, and the development of innovative exemplars, such as those mentioned earlier, have set the stage for enhancing graduate-level civic engagement in both professional and doctoral education. These examples illustrate a range of strategies for moving in that direction—through community service, service-learning, community-based research, and institutionally supported community-university collaboratives. The following questions may be useful in guiding action by institutions and statewide associations concerned with these issues.

For institutions:

- What current opportunities exist for graduate student civic engagement in your institution?
- What patterns appear in how graduate students use or neglect these opportunities?
- What kinds of adjustments would make existing opportunities more attractive or feasible to graduate students?
- What new kinds of opportunities could be created to extend and deepen participation of this sort?

In trying to answer questions such as these, campus administrators could consider the following strategies:

- Conduct an institution-wide audit of civic engagement to identify and assess the extent of activity at the graduate level. The matrix included earlier may be a helpful way to organize findings.
- Give campus-wide visibility and recognition to exemplary efforts, including engaged community partners.
- Convene faculty and students who are involved in civic engagement activities so they may learn from and encourage each other.
- Offer incentives (e.g., teaching/research assistants, curriculum development funds, research incentive funds) to faculty members who propose innovative civic engagement courses, research, or other initiatives.

For statewide associations:

- What current opportunities exist for graduate student civic engagement among research universities in a state or region?
- Which of these opportunities could expand through increased collaboration among institutions?
- What kinds of cross-institutional collaboration would be useful in assessing the value and quality of these different opportunities?
- What new kinds of opportunities could be created through cross-institutional collaboration to extend and deepen participation of this sort?

In trying to answer questions such as these, association directors could consider the following strategies:

- Collaborate on conducting an audit of civic engagement activities across research universities statewide.
- Sponsor and organize colloquia, workshops, etc., in which interested faculty and graduate students from different institutions can come together to share and learn about civic engagement teaching, research, and development work.
- Encourage and disseminate research and publications that document, evaluate, and analyze civic engagement activities within and across disciplines at research universities.

A Special Role for the Research University

In attending to these related questions, research universities have a special set of challenges, but also a special role to play. In terms of challenges, the distinctive ethos and practices of research universities can make the civic engagement of graduate students difficult to promote and sustain, for all the reasons we have noted earlier. However, the same ethos and practices also leave research universities well positioned to investigate the scope and effectiveness of different civic engagement activities. This kind of investigation is essential to design and support effective programs on a campus-by-campus or program-by-program basis. It is also necessary to better understand the lives that graduate students lead while pursuing advanced degrees and the kinds of lives graduate study is preparing them to live as citizens, professionals, and scholars.

Stated in these terms, the current lack of policy and research attention to the civic engagement of graduate students is doubly problematic. On the one hand, it leaves graduate students adrift in trying to negotiate competing demands of research, teaching, and service. On the other, it forfeits for research universities an extraordinary opportunity to improve the quality and civic contributions of graduate education, by being better at what they already are: civic institutions with special resources for supporting reflection and investigation.

In writing about the special role of schools in encouraging reflection and civic attention, Lauren Resnick (1987) affirmed the value of learning in and out of school in terms that seem equally important to how we think about research universities. As she put it (p. 19), "School is not only a place to prepare people for the world of work and everyday practical problems. It is also a place in which a particular kind of work is done—intellectual work that engages reflection and reasoning. At its best such work steps back from the everyday world in order to consider and evaluate it, but it is engaged with that world as the object of reflection and reasoning."

When they begin their graduate studies, many students at research universities have some sense of what Resnick understands schooling to be "at its best." All too quickly, however, they encounter the unhappy prospect of sealing off the skills of reflection and reasoning being developed through graduate study from civic engagement in the larger world. In many cases, this prospect even comes to define what it means to succeed as a graduate student, but it bears little relationship to the lives and imagination of graduate students or to what it will take to succeed as future professionals and academics. To reflect better the complexities and virtues of the latter requires that ideas about civic engagement be woven through the very fabric of graduate studies. That has yet to happen for most research universities, but we remain hopeful that it can and will be done.

Acknowledgment

The authors wish to acknowledge Stacey Caillier, Barbara Holland, Elaine Ikeda, Nina Moore, Kerry Ann O'Meara, Julie Plaut, and Melissa Salazar, who generously read drafts and offered valuable suggestions as we prepared that paper. Its original printing and distribution was made possible by California Campus Compact with support from Learn and Serve America.

References

American Sociological Association Task Force on Institutionalizing Public Sociologies. (2005). *Public sociology and the roots of American sociology: Re-establishing our connections to the public.* Available at http://pubsoc.wisc.edu/news.php.

ABET, Inc. (2004). *Sustaining the change: A follow-up report to Vision for Change.* Available at http://www.abet.org/Linked%20Documents-UPDATE/White%20Papers/Sustaining%20the%20Change-Web.pdf.

ABET, Inc. (2007). *Criteria for accrediting computing programs.* Available at http://www.abet.org/Linked%20Documents-UPDATE/Criteria%20and%20PP/C001%2008-09%20CAC%20Criteria%2011-8-07.pdf.

Bloomfield, V. (2005). Civic engagement and graduate education. *Communicator, 38*(3), 1–2, 6. Washington, DC: Council of Graduate Schools.

Bloomfield, V. (2006). *Civic engagement and graduate education: Ten principles and five conclusions.* Minneapolis, MN: University of Minnesota. Available at www.grad.umn.edu.

Boyte, H., & Hollander, E. (1999, December). *Wingspread declaration on renewing the civic mission of the American research university.* Proceedings of the Wingspread Conference held on December 11–13, 1998. Racine, WI: Johnson Foundation. Available at http://www.compact.org/initiatives/ civic-engagement-at-research-universities/wingspread-declaration-on-the-civic-responsibilities-of-research-universities/.

Ellison, J. (2006). *On responsive tenure policies for public scholars in the humanities, arts, and design: Discussion draft for participants in Imagining America's Tenure Team Initiative.* Available at http:// www.imaginingamerica.org/IApdfs/tti-background-study%20DRAFT.pdf.

Eskow, S. (1980, Spring). A pedagogy of experience. *Synergist, 9,* 20–21.

Gibson, C. (2006). *New times demand new scholarship: Research universities and engagement.* Medford, MA: Tufts University. Available at http://www.compact.org/initiatives/civic-engagement-at-research-universities/trucen-intr/.

Harkavy, I. (2004). Service-learning and the development of democratic universities, democratic schools, and democratic good societies in the 21st century. In M. Welch & S. Billig (Eds.), *New perspectives on service-learning: Research to advance the field* (pp. 3–22). Greenwich, CT: Information Age Publishing.

Kellogg Commission on the Future of State and Land-Grant Universities. (1999). *Returning to our roots: The engaged institution.* Battle Creek, MI: W. K. Kellogg Foundation.

Kennedy, D. (1993). Making choices in the research university. *Daedalus: Journal of the American Academy of Arts and Sciences, 122*(4), 127–155.

Kerr, C. (2002). *The uses of the university: The Godkin lectures on the essentials of free government and the duties of the citizen* (5th ed.). Cambridge, MA: Harvard University Press. (Original work published 1963)

Morrill, R. L. (1982). Educating for democratic values. *Liberal education, 68*(4), 365–376.

Nyquist, J., & Wulff, D. H. (2000). *Recommendations from national studies on doctoral education.* Available at http://www.grad.washington.edu/envision/project_resources/national_recommend.html.

O'Meara, K. (2006). Graduate education and community engagement. In Colbeck, C.L., O'Meara, K.A., & Austin, A.E. (eds.), New directions for teaching and learning (pp. 27–42). San Francisco: Jossey-Bass Publishers.

Pollack, S. (1996). *Higher education's contested service role: A framework for analysis and historical survey.* Stanford, CA: Haas Center for Public Service.

Putnam, R. (2000). *Bowling alone: The collapse and revival of American community.* New York: Simon & Schuster.

Resnick, L. B. (1987). The 1987 Presidential Address: Learning in school and out. *Educational Researcher, 6*(9), 13–20, 54.

Rhode, D. L. (2005). *Pro bono in principle and in practice: Public service and the professions.* Stanford, CA: Stanford University.

Salazar, M. (2006, March 10). Personal communication.

Seifer, D., Hermanns, K., & Lewis, J. (2000). *Creating community-responsive physicians: Concepts and models for service-learning in medical education.* Washington, DC: American Association for Higher Education.

435

Stanton, T. (2007). *New times demand new scholarship II: Research universities and civic engagement— opportunities and challenges.* Los Angeles: University of California. Available at http://www. compact.org/initiatives/civic-engagement-at-research-universities/trucen-intr/.

Stanton, T., Giles, D., & Cruz, N (1999). *Service-learning: A movement's pioneers reflect on its origins, practice, and future.* San Francisco: Jossey-Bass.

Stanton, T., & Howard, J. (2009). *Research university engaged scholarship toolkit.* Boston: Campus Compact. Available at http://www.compact.org/initiatives/civic-engagement-at-research-universities/trucen-intr//.

The Talloires Network. (2005). *On the civic roles and social responsibilities of higher education: The Talloires declaration.* Available at http://www.tufts.edu/talloiresnetwork/?pid=17&c=7.

University of Southern California (USC). (2001). *The community and academic life at USC.* Unpublished white paper by Academic Senate. Available at http://www.usc.edu/academe/acsen/documents_whitepapers.shtml.

Upper Midwest Campus Compact Consortium (2006). *Civic engagement in graduate education: Preparing the ext generation of engaged scholars.* Wingspread conference report. Available at: http://www.mncampuscompact.org/index.asp?Type=B_LIST&SEC={93F35BCF-AE90-4093-952D-EBDABFD-F3BA6}.

Wagner, J. (1986). Academic excellence and community service through experiential learning: Encouraging students to teach. In *Proceedings of the Ninth Annual University of California Conference on Experiential Learning, Santa Barbara, CA.*

Woodrow Wilson National Fellowship Foundation (2005). *The responsive PhD.: Innovations in U.S. doctoral education.* Available at http://www.woodrow.org/responsivephd/agenda.html.

Contributors

Angela D. Allen provides community technical assistance for Public Agenda's department of Public Engagement programs, including the Center for Advances in Public Engagement (CAPE). Her focus includes capacity-building and cross-sector collaboration strategic planning, pre-community engagement research, and stakeholder engagement work. Angela was an ABD Research Associate at the Charles F. Kettering Foundation in Dayton, Ohio. Angela has a PhD in higher education administration with a specialization in applied developmental science from Michigan State University, a MSW in community organization administration from the University of Michigan-Ann Arbor, and a Bachelor's degree in urban and regional planning from Michigan State University. Dr. Allen's dissertation, "Faculty and Community Collaboration in Sustained Community-Campus Engagement Partnerships," was a case study analysis of nine community-campus partnerships and the collaboration factors that impacted partnership sustainability and the alignment of the academic and civic contexts through partnership knowledge dissemination. In her doctoral program, Dr. Allen spent three years as a graduate assistant with MSU University Outreach and Engagement, co-creating the Emerging Engagement Scholars Workshop of the National Outreach Scholarship, the National Center for the Scholarship of Engagement at MSU, and the Higher Education Network for Community Engagement in 2007. After more than fourteen years of professional experience in community-based program administration in her hometown of Detroit as well as a year as Research Associate at the Charles F. Kettering Foundation, Dr. Allen is establishing an independent consulting practice.

Theodore R. Alter is professor of agricultural, environmental and regional economics and Co-Director of the Center for Economic and Community Development in the Department of Agricultural Economics and Rural Sociology at Penn State University. He served as associate vice-president for outreach, director of Penn State Cooperative Extension, and associate dean in the College of Agricultural Sciences at Penn State from July 1997 through July 2004. His research focuses on the scholarship on engagement in higher education, agricultural economics and agribusiness management, community and rural development, development and public sector economics, and comparative rural development policy.

Ann E. Austin is a Professor of Higher, Adult, and Lifelong Education at Michigan State University, where she is also the director of the Global Institute for Higher Education (GIHE). Her scholarly interests focus on faculty roles and professional development, work and workplaces in academe, organizational change and transformation in universities and colleges, reform in doctoral education, the improvement of teaching and learning in higher education, and higher education issues in developing countries. She was the 2001–2002 president of the Association for the Study of Higher Education (ASHE) and a Fulbright Fellow in South Africa (1998). She is currently co-principal investigator of the Center for the Integration of Research, Teaching, and Learning (CIRTL), a National Science Foundation Center. She has authored or co-authored numerous articles, chapters, and books. Her most recent books are *Rethinking Faculty Work: Higher Education's Strategic Imperative* (2007, with J. M. Gappa and A. G. Trice) and *Educating Integrated Professionals: Theory and Practice on Preparation for the Professoriate* (2008, with C. Colbeck and K. O'Meara).

John P. Beck is an associate professor in the School of Labor and Industrial Relations at Michigan State University. He serves as associate director of the school in charge of two of the school's outreach units, the Labor Education Program and the Program on Innovative Employee Relations Systems (PIERS). He has worked primarily in change management, joint labor/management cooperation, and workplace transformation.

Annie Belcourt-Dittloff, Ph.D., is an American Indian research and clinical faculty member at the University of Colorado at Denver's Centers for American Indian and Alaska Native Health (enrolled tribal member: *Blackfeet, Chippewa, Mandan, & Hidatsa*). She is a clinical psychologist, and her research priorities include trauma, post-traumatic stress reactions, risk, resiliency, and psychiatric disorder within the cultural context of American Indian populations. She has provided clinical services to a diverse clientele in a variety of settings, recently completing an internship with the Department of Veterans Affairs Medical Center in Denver, Colorado, working with veterans and addressing post-trauma reactions. Dr. Belcourt-Dittloff has conducted multiple, grant-funded, collaborative research projects with American Indian communities. These projects have provided experience in both quantitative and qualitative analysis and were aimed at the investigation of factors, including post-traumatic stress disorder, trauma, cultural resiliency, spirituality, adversarial or post-traumatic growth, and psychosocial factors involved in depression and suicidal ideation. She has presented her research findings to numerous national conferences and tribal communities and has published in peer-reviewed journals including *Psychological Bulletin, American Psychologist,* and *Educational and Psychological Measurement.*

Charles Blaich currently serves as the director of inquiries at the Center of Inquiry in the Liberal Arts at Wabash College. He received his Ph.D. in psychology from the University of Connecticut in 1986. Blaich joined Wabash College in fall 1991 and assumed his current position at the Center of Inquiry in 2002. Blaich is also currently directing the Wabash National Study of Liberal Arts Education. Blaich's recent publications include "Do Liberal Arts Colleges Really Foster Good Practices in Undergraduate Education?" and "Liberal Arts Colleges and Liberal Arts Education: New Evidence on Impacts."

John M. Braxton is Professor of Education in the Higher Education Leadership and Policy Program in the Department of Leadership and Organizations at Peabody College, Vanderbilt University. His research interests include the sociology of the academic profession with particular interest in faculty teaching and scholarship role performance. His publications on this topic include *Institutionalizing a Broader View of Scholarship through Boyer's Four Domains* (2002), co-authored with William Luckey and Patricia Helland, and the edited volume *Analyzing Faculty Work and Rewards Using Boyer's Four Domains of Scholarship* (2006). Professor Braxton is a past president of the Association for the Study of Higher Education.

Robert E. Brown is the associate director at University-Community Partnerships. He works to support, nurture, and expand outreach and engagement at MSU through structural, collaborative, and curricular initiatives. He also promotes communities' use of actionable knowledge and evidence-based interventions/models. With his colleague Celeste Sturdevant Reed, Brown developed the Outcome-Asset Impact Model (Outcome/impact assessment model: Linking outcomes and assets, *Evaluation and Program Planning, 24,* 287–295). A description of their work can be found on the Capable Communities website.

Cathy Burack is a Senior Fellow for Higher Education at the Center for Youth and Communities (CYC) in the Heller School for Social Policy and Management at Brandeis University. Prior to coming to Brandeis, Cathy was the Associate Director of the New England Resource Center for Higher Education (NERCHE). For the past eighteen years Cathy has focused on ways faculty, students, and administrators can work together to fulfill the civic missions of their colleges and universities. This focus has been on two interrelated areas: access to higher education, especially by students who are among the first in their families to attend; and the ways in which college and universities engage with their communities. Cathy holds a bachelor's degree in psychology from the University of Rochester, and a doctorate in Administration, Planning and Social Policy from Harvard University. Cathy's work is undergirded by her core beliefs in the power of reflective practice, collaboration, importance of creating learning organizations, capacity building, and development of communities and the individuals who inhabit them.

Jaime Chahin is Professor and Dean of the College of Applied Arts at Texas State University San Marcos. He also served as Senior Policy Analyst for the Texas Select Committee for Higher Education and dean of students at a community college. He received two graduate degrees from the University of Michigan, in education (1977) and social work (1975), and his undergraduate degree in sociology (1974) from Texas A&I University in Kingsville. He teaches graduate and undergraduate courses in administration supervision and social policy. His research interests involve migrants, college access, bridge programs, and public policy issues that impact funding and retention in higher education.

Tony Chambers is Associate Professor, Director of the Centre for the Study of Students in Postsecondary Education, and program coordinator of the Higher Education program at

439

the Ontario Institute for Studies in Education/University of Toronto. He previously served as Associate Vice-Provost, Students at the University of Toronto. Tony was formerly Associate Director of the National Forum on Higher Education for the Public Good and an adjunct associate professor at the University of Michigan. He researches and teaches in the areas of student learning and development, as well as the social purposes of postsecondary education. His publications include the co-edited book *Higher Education for the Public Good: Emerging Voices from a National Movement* (Jossey-Bass, 2005).

David Cox serves as executive assistant to the president at the University of Memphis and holds the rank of professor in the Division of Public and Nonprofit Administration. His research has centered on the effect of urban governance on the responsiveness, equity, and effectiveness of public policies and on strategies for interorganizational collaboration. Awards he has received include the Dr. Martin Luther King, Jr. Human Rights Award from the National Conference on Community and Justice and the Superior Accomplishment in Community-University Partnerships Award from the U.S. Department of Housing and Urban Development.

Diane M. Doberneck, Ph.D., is a research specialist at the National Collaborative for the Study of University Engagement and an adjunct assistant professor in the Liberty Hyde Bailey Scholars Program. Doberneck's research interests include outreach and engagement in promotion and tenure processes; faculty integration of outreach and engagement across their teaching, research, and service responsibilities; faculty pathways to careers as engaged scholars; international community engagement; and effective strategies for teaching and learning community engagement. Informed by this research, Doberneck creates and supports the co-creation of professional development programs on community engagement—including Tools of Engagement (undergraduate students), the Graduate Certificate on Community Engagement (graduate students), the Emerging Engaged Scholars Workshop (graduate students and new/junior faculty), and the Engaged Scholar Speakers Series (faculty, community members). In addition, she coordinates an international collaborative with the Tochar Valley Rural Community Network (Co. Mayo, Ireland) that enhances rural community vitality through community engagement. Together, Tochar Valley community members and MSU students assist communities in developing their own deeper sense of place; individual, organizational, and community capacities; and cultural and natural heritage assets. In 2008, she won MSU's first annual Curricular Service-Learning and Civic Engagement Award in the College of Agriculture and Natural Resources for her international engagement work. Doberneck holds a Ph.D. in organizational and community resource development from Michigan State University.

John W. Eby is professor of Sociology at Messiah College, Grantham, PA, and was active in service-learning before it was given the name when he led summer seminars in New York City in 1971 and in Whitesburg, KY, in 1972. In 1998 he founded and served as the first director of the Agape Center for Service and Learning at Messiah College, and he incorporates service-learning in a number of courses he teaches. He received an M.S. and Ph.D. in development sociology from Cornell University in 1970 and 1972, respectively, and earlier a B.A. in chemistry from Eastern Mennonite University. He administered social service and development programs in the United States and internationally and served on numerous boards for local community service agencies. He has served as academic dean and chaired departments of sociology and also of business in several colleges and has served as a consultant in service-learning.

Caroline Fichtenberg is an Assistant Scientist in the Department of Epidemiology at the Johns Hopkins School of Public Health in Baltimore, MD. She previously served as the Director of the Office of Epidemiology and Planning at the Baltimore City Health Department, where she oversaw the collection, analysis, and dissemination of data to assess community health and support development and evaluation of city programs and policies. Dr. Fichtenberg earned her Ph.D. in epidemiology with an emphasis on social epidemiology from Johns Hopkins. As a graduate student she helped found and lead SPARC during its first year of existence.

Hiram E. Fitzgerald, Ph.D., is associate provost for university outreach and engagement and university distinguished professor of psychology at Michigan State University. He is actively involved with the APLU Council on Engagement and Outreach, the National Outreach Scholarship Conference, and the Higher Education Network for University Engagement. Fitzgerald is a member of the steering committees of the Early Head Start National Research Consortium, and of the American Indian/Alaska Native Head Start Research Center. He is a member of a variety of interdisciplinary research teams focusing on evaluation of community-based prevention programs. His major areas of funded research include the study of infant and family development in community contexts, the impact of fathers on early child development, implementation of systemic models of organizational process and change, the etiology of alcoholism, the digital divide and youth access to technologies, and broad issues related to the scholarship of engagement. From 1992–2008 Fitzgerald served as the executive director of the World Association for Infant Mental Health. Fitzgerald holds a Ph.D. in experimental child psychology (1967) from the University of Denver.

Robert W. Franco, Ph.D., is a recognized expert on contemporary Samoan, Polynesian, and Pacific Islander demographic, ecological, health, and cultural issues. He has published scholarly research on contemporary Samoan political and cultural change, traditional Hawaiian water management systems, and sociocultural factors affecting pelagic fisheries in Polynesia and Micronesia. At Kapiolani Community College, University of Hawaii, he is Director of Institutional Effectiveness, oversees a "Best Practice" Service-Learning and Civic Engagement Program, and supports six NSF grant-funded programs. He serves as the college's accreditation liaison to ACCJC/WASC, and liaison to the Association of American Colleges and Universities, American Council on Education, Community College Survey of Student Engagement, and the Carnegie Foundation for the Advancement of Teaching. As a Campus Compact Senior Faculty Fellow for Community Colleges, he conducts training, technical assistance and research dissemination in five states per year (thirty-five states total) and provides community college, university, and conference audiences with research-based training designed to improve retention, degree completion, and transfer rates through service-learning, community-based research, and authentic partnerships. His current national research and training focuses on service-learning and reducing the minority academic achievement gap, and strengthening the liberal arts, workforce development and civic missions of community colleges. In 2008, he was selected a NSF-SENCER (sencer.net) Leadership Fellow, and advisor to SENCER Center for Innovation (SCI)–Western Region.

Eric J. Fretz directs the Center for Community Engagement and Service Learning at the University of Denver. His writings include articles on civic engagement in higher education, community organizing, and the use of democratic practices in the classroom. He received a Ph.D. in English and American Studies from Michigan State University.

Chris R. Glass is a doctoral candidate in Higher, Adult, and Lifelong Education at Michigan State University. He works as a doctoral research associate at the Global Institute for Higher Education at Michigan State. His research interests include integrative learning, internationalization and civic engagement in higher education and how they overlap in undergraduate education.

Bryan Gopaul is a Ph.D. candidate in the Higher Education program at the Ontario Institute for Studies in Education at the University of Toronto (OISE/UT). His research focuses on the socialization of doctoral students in engineering and history and emphasizes aspects of power and inequality. Finally, Bryan works as a teaching assistant trainer providing workshops on critical pedagogy and is also a student co-representative of the American Educational Research Association.

Ira Harkavy is Associate Vice President and Director of the Barbara and Edward Netter Center for Community Partnerships, University of Pennsylvania. As director of the Netter Center since 1992, Harkavy has helped to develop service-learning courses as well as participatory action research projects that involve creating university-assisted community schools in Penn's local community of West Philadelphia. Harkavy is a member of the Advisory Committee of the Directorate for Education and Human Resources (EHR) of the National Science Foundation; the International Consortium on Higher Education, Civic Responsibility, and Democracy (U.S. chair); and the Coalition for Community Schools (chair). His recent publications include *Dewey's Dream: Universities and Democracies in an Age of Education Reform* (Temple Press, 2007), which he co-authored with Lee Benson and John Puckett, and *The Obesity Culture: Strategies for Change. Public Health and University-Community Partnerships* (Smith-Gordon, 2009), co-authored with Francis E. Johnston.

Matthew Hartley is associate professor of education and chair of the higher education division at the University of Pennsylvania's graduate school of education. A significant thread of his research focuses on the civic purposes of colleges and universities. He has served on the editorial boards of the Harvard Educational Review, the Review of Higher Education and the Journal of Higher Education Outreach and Engagement. Dr. Hartley received a National Academy of Education/Spencer Postdoctoral Fellowship in 2006–07 to conduct a study tracing the trajectory of the civic engagement movement. He recently completed a project with the Council of Europe in Strasburg, France that explored democratic partnerships between universities, schools, and civil society organizations. A monograph which he co-authored entitled "School-Community-University Partnerships," will be published this spring.

Catherine M. Jordan, Ph.D., is Associate Professor of Pediatrics and Neurology and Director of the Children, Youth, and Family Consortium at the University of Minnesota. She is a graduate of Wayne State University and a pediatric neuropsychologist by training. She has been engaged in community-based participatory research projects since 1993 and focuses her writing on community-university partnership formation and navigating promotion and tenure as a community-engaged scholar. She is editor of CES4Health.info, a new mechanism for the rigorous peer review and online publication of innovative products of health-related community-engaged scholarship.

Mindi B. Levin, M.S., CHES is the Founder and Director of SOURCE (Student Outreach Resource Center), the community service and service-learning center, serving the Johns Hopkins University (JHU) Schools of Medicine, Nursing, and Public Health. In this capacity, she is responsible for creating strategies to integrate community outreach activities into students' academic training in the health professions. Additionally, Ms. Levin holds faculty appointments in JHU Bloomberg School of Public Health's Department of Health Policy and Management and JHU School of Nursing's Department of Community Public Health Nursing. She teaches and supports a variety of service-learning and experiential learning courses on campus, as well as advising service-based student groups. She is a co-director for the HOP-SIP (Hopkins Social Innovations Partnerships) Program, and a faculty co-sponsor for a new certificate program in Community-Based Public Health.

Nicholas V. Longo, is the director of Global Studies and Associate professor in the Department of Public and Community Service Studies at Providence College. From 2006 to 2008 he was the director of the Harry T. Wilks Leadership Institute at Miami University, and he also directed a national student civic engagement project for Campus Compact from 2002 to 2004. Longo is the author of *Why Community Matters: Connecting Education with Civic Life* (SUNY Press, 2007) and numerous articles and chapters on service-learning and civic engagement.

William Luckey has been the eighth president of Lindsey Wilson College since July 1, 1998. He has served Lindsey Wilson since 1983, holding the positions of Vice President for Enrollment Management, Vice President for Development, and Vice President for Administration and Finance. As president of one of Kentucky's fastest-growing and most diverse independent liberal arts colleges, President Luckey leads a faculty and staff of more than 280 and a student body of more than 2,003. The college's annual budget is more than $37 million. The focus of President Luckey's administration is to continue Lindsey Wilson's development as a liberal arts, church-related college that is distinguished for being one of the best undergraduate teaching colleges in the nation. A native of Louisville, Kentucky, President Luckey holds a bachelor's degree in biology from Wabash College; a master's degree in business administration from Vanderbilt University's Owen Graduate School of Management; and a doctorate in higher education administration from Vanderbilt's prestigious Peabody College. He has been published and has lectured widely on the subject of the scholarship of teaching.

Tami L. Moore is assistant professor of higher education in the Educational Leadership Program at Oklahoma State University–Tulsa. Her research agenda focuses broadly on the role of higher education institutions in the communities they serve, employing social and critical theory in the reading of community engagement. Her current projects explore issues related to faculty work and community-engaged scholarship, and the relationship between geographic place and community engagement in the United States, the United Kingdom, and Australia. She is founding co-chair of the Emerging Engagement Scholars Workshop at the National Outreach Scholarship Conference, and recipient of the AERA-J Dissertation of the Year Award in 2009.

Douglas Novins, M.D., is associate professor of psychiatry in the Native American and Telehealth Programs and the Division of Child and Adolescent Psychiatry at the University of Colorado School of Medicine. He holds a secondary appointment as associate professor in the Centers for American Indian and Alaska Native Health at the University Colorado School of Public Health. Dr. Novins conducts research that is critical for improving the mental health of American Indian children, adolescents, and adults. These include ongoing and completed studies in the areas of psychiatric epidemiology, developmental psychopathology, and mental health services research. Dr. Novins's research is supported by grants from the National Institutes of Mental Health, Drug Abuse, and Alcohol Abuse and Alcoholism, as well as the Administration for Children and Families. Dr. Novins is also the director of the Circles of Care Evaluation Technical Assistance Center, which provides evaluation technical assistance to thirty-one diverse American Indian communities who are funded by the Federal Center for Mental Health Services to develop new models of mental health service delivery for their children and adolescents. In. the area of telemental health, Dr. Novins has guided the development and implementation of telemental health services linking the Center for Native American TeleHealth and TeleEducation (in Colorado) to clinical facilities serving tribal communities in Alaska, Arizona, Montana, South Dakota, and Wyoming.

KerryAnn O'Meara serves as an associate professor of higher education in the College of Education, at the University of Maryland, College Park. Her research and practice focus on the academic profession and the civic mission of higher education. She is currently principal investigator on a collaborative project with the Kettering Foundation to study the origins of faculty civic agency, and she serves as the Associate Editor for Research Articles for the *Journal of Higher Education Outreach and Engagement*, as well as Associate Editor for the *Journal of the Professoriate*. KerryAnn's work has appeared in the following academic journals: *Review of Higher Education, Journal of Higher Education, Research in Higher Education, Michigan Journal of Service-Learning, NASPA Journal, Planning in Higher Education, Journal of Higher Education Outreach and Engagement, Journal of Teaching Excellence, Journal of Faculty Development*, and the *Handbook on Higher Education Research*, among others.

Noe Ortega is currently pursuing a Ph.D. at the Center for the Study of Higher and Post-secondary Education at the University of Michigan. Prior to enrolling at the University of Michigan, Noe worked as a P-16 Field Specialist for the Texas Higher Education Coordinating Board, spent eight years working in the areas of enrollment management and financial assistance, and served as chair of the Early Awareness Committee for the board of the Texas Association of Student Financial Assistance (TASFAA). Noe also spent seven years working as an English instructor and director of an English as a Foreign Language (EFL) institute in Osaka, Japan.

Scott J. Peters is an associate professor of education at Cornell University. His research and teaching are focused on the theme of democracy and education. He pursues this theme in two lines of inquiry: a line that examines the origins and evolution of the land-grant system's cooperative extension work, and a line that takes a narrative approach to the study of

444

the civic engagement work and experiences of contemporary academic professionals and community educators. His latest book, *Democracy and Higher Education: Traditions and Stories of Civic Engagement,* will be published in 2010 by Michigan State University Press.

Judith A. Ramaley is President of Winona State University (WSU) in Minnesota. In 2004–2005, she served as a Visiting Senior Scientist at the National Academy of Sciences. From 2001 to 2004, she was Assistant Director, Education and Human Resources Directorate (EHR) at the National Science Foundation (NSF). Dr. Ramaley was president of the University of Vermont (UVM) and professor of biology from 1997 to 2001. She was president and professor of biology at Portland State University in Portland, Oregon, for seven years from 1990 to 1997. Dr. Ramaley has a special interest in higher-education reform and institutional change and has written extensively on civic responsibility and partnerships between higher education and community organizations as well as articles on science, technology, engineering, and mathematics education.

Stephen L. Rozman is a professor of political science and Director of the Center for Civic Engagement & Social Responsibility at Tougaloo College. He is the founder and president of the HBCU Faculty Development Network, which is housed at Tougaloo College and which sponsors the annual HBCU Faculty Development Symposium. Dr. Rozman has also directed several faculty development grants at Tougaloo College, most recently on service-learning/community-based research and global studies.

John Saltmarsh is the Director of the New England Resource Center for Higher Education (NERCHE) at the University of Massachusetts, Boston, as well as a professor in the Higher Education Administration Doctoral Program in the Department of Leadership in Education in the Graduate College of Education. He is the author of numerous book chapters and articles on civic engagement, service-learning, and experiential education, and the co-author of the Democratic Engagement White Paper (NERCHE, 2009) as well as co-editor of the forthcoming book *"To Serve a Larger Purpose:" Engagement for Democracy and the Transformation of Higher Education* (2010). He serves as the chair of the board of the International Association for Research on Service Learning and Community Engagement (IARSLCE), as well as on the editorial board of the *Michigan Journal of Community Service Learning* and the editorial board of the *Journal of Higher Education Outreach and Engagement.* He is a member of the National Review Board for the Scholarship of Engagement, a National Scholar with Imagining America's Tenure Team Initiative, and a member of the Advisory Committee for the Carnegie Foundation's Community Engagement Classification.

Michelle Sarche, Ph.D., is a clinical psychologist and assistant professor at the Centers for American Indian and Alaska Native Health at the University of Colorado, Denver Colorado, School of Public Health. Dr. Sarche has worked with both urban and reservation tribal communities for nearly twenty years, to better understand the challenges to and supports for health across the life span. Her work has largely focused on children's early development and parenting. Currently, she directs the American Indian and Alaska Native Head Start Research Center and is beginning a project in collaboration with a tribal community to develop a culturally informed fetal alcohol spectrum disorders preventive intervention. Her work has been supported by the National Institute of Mental Health, the Administration for

Children and Families, and the National Institute on Alcohol Abuse and Alcoholism. Dr. Sarche is a member of the Lac Courte Oreilles Band of Ojibwe.

Sarena D. Seifer is Founding Executive Director of Community-Campus Partnerships for Health (CCPH) Established in 1996, CCPH promotes health in its broadest sense through partnerships between communities and higher educational institutions. She has led a series of CCPH-sponsored multi-site initiatives that incorporated service-learning into health professions education, developed community-based participatory research partnerships, convened community partners for peer support and advocacy, prepared faculty for community-engaged careers in the academy, aligned faculty promotion and tenure policies with community engagement, and created mechanisms for peer-reviewed publication of diverse products of community-engaged scholarship. Throughout her career, Sarena has sought to combine the knowledge, wisdom and experience in communities and in academic institutions to solve health, social and economic challenges. She deeply believes that we will only solve these challenges through partnerships that bring communities and institutions together and build upon the assets, strengths, and capacities of each.

Lou Anna Kimsey Simon is the twentieth president of Michigan State University, leading the university's transformation from land-grant university to embracing the World Grant Ideal, a vision grounded in land-grant values adapted to address the challenges of the twenty-first century. After earning her doctorate in administration and higher education, Simon became a member of the Michigan State University faculty and worked in a variety of administrative roles, including assistant provost for general academic administration and associate provost. Simon served MSU as provost and vice president for academic affairs from 1993 to 2004, acting as interim president in 2003. She was appointed president by the MSU Board of Trustees in January 2005. Among other national leadership positions, Simon serves as a board member of the Association of Public and Land-grant Universities and the Council on Foreign Relations' Higher Education Working Group on Global Issues. She serves on the executive committee for the Council on Competitiveness and as chair of the Big Ten Council of Presidents/Chancellors. In addition, she serves on the National Higher Education Security Advisory Board, a group of presidents and chancellors of several prominent U.S. universities that consults regularly with national agencies responsible for security, intelligence, and law enforcement. Most recently, Simon was made a board member of the Detroit Branch of the Federal Reserve Bank of Chicago. Simon has served on the State of Michigan Governor's Emergency Financial Advisory Panel and as a member of the Lt. Governor's Commission on Higher Education and Economic Growth. She is a member of the Michigan Strategic Economic Investment and Commercialization Board (SEIC), the board of directors of Business Leaders for Michigan and a board member of mid-Michigan's economic development foundation, Prima Civitas. Internationally, Simon is a member of the American Council on Education Commission on International Initiatives and serves on the executive committee of the Partnership to Cut Hunger and Poverty in Africa.

Timothy K. Stanton is Director of Stanford University's Bing Overseas Studies Program in Cape Town, South Africa. Prior to joining Overseas Studies, he founded and directed the Scholarly Concentration in Community Health and Public Service at Stanford's School of Medicine. He helped found and served as Associate Director and Director of Stanford's Haas

Center for Public Service from 1985 to 1999. He has published numerous articles on service-learning and engaged scholarship, and he co-authored a book, *Service-Learning: A Movement's Pioneers Reflect on its Origins, Practice, and Future* (1999).

Scott VanderStoep is Assessment Director, Professor of Psychology and Department Chair at Hope College. He has a Ph.D. in education and psychology from the University of Michigan. His research interests include critical thinking and problem solving, epistemological beliefs of college students, and the role that religious beliefs play in college student cognitive development. He also serves as a Teagle Scholar through the Wabash National Study of Liberal Arts Education.

Amanda L. Vogel, Ph.D., MHS, is a fellow at the National Cancer Institute, where she evaluates large center grant programs that fund cross-disciplinary science to address complex public health problems. Dr. Vogel earned a Ph.D. in Health Policy and Management at the Johns Hopkins Bloomberg School of Public Health (JHSPH). Her dissertation research examined the ten-year sustainability and outcomes of a national demonstration program to integrate service-learning into health professions training. Building on this work, as a doctoral student she led a successful student-staff-faculty partnership to create a certificate program in engaged public health at JHSPH. While at JHSPH,she was a student leader for civic engagement and describes her experiences in this volume. Her dissertation research consisted of a ten-year follow-up study of the Health Professions Schools in Service to the Nation (HPSISN) program. From 1995 to 1998, HPSISN provided support for service-learning at seventeen U.S. health professional schools. The program was funded by the Pew Charitable Trusts, the federal Corporation for National and Community Service, and the Health Resources and Services Administration. Dr. Vogel's research explored what factors influence the sustainability of service-learning in the health professions, and it produced strategies for success and lessons learned from institutions that successfully sustained service-learning. In her past work, Dr. Vogel implemented and evaluated community-based health promotion programs in underserved urban areas. In that capacity, she served as a service-learning preceptor for health professional students. She is currently a postdoctoral fellow at the National Cancer Institute, National Institutes of Health.

James C. Votruba is president of Northern Kentucky University, a sixteen-thousand-student metropolitan campus located in the Greater Cincinnati area. The university is nationally recognized for its community engagement. Prior to NKU, he was Vice Provost for University Outreach and Professor of Higher Education at Michigan State University and Dean of the College of Education and Human Development at Binghamton University. Dr. Votruba has been a long-standing advocate for the public engagement role of colleges and universities.

Jon Wagner is Professor Emeritus in the School of Education at the University of California Davis. From 2006–2009 he served as Director of the campus' Teaching Resources Center. His teaching and research have focused on children's material culture, qualitative and visual research methods, school change, and the social and philosophical foundations of education. He is a past president of the International Visual Sociology Association and was the founding image editor of *Contexts*, the American Sociological Association's general-interest publication. The author of *Misfits and Missionaries* (1977), he also edited two volumes that

447

examine visual studies and social research: *Images of Information: Still Photography in the Social Sciences* (1979) and *Visual Sociology* 14(1 & 2): *Seeing Kids' Worlds* (1999).

Kelly Ward is a professor of higher education and student affairs at Washington State University–Pullman. Her research interests are in the areas of faculty development, campus and community engagement, and work and family in the academic career. She has also held faculty and administrative positions at Oklahoma State University and the University of Montana, where she worked as the Service Learning Director for the Montana Campus Compact. She earned her Ph.D. in higher education from Penn State University.

Kathleen S. Wise, associate director of the Center of Inquiry in the Liberal Arts at Wabash College, received an MBA from the University of Chicago. She previously worked in finance at Eli Lilly and Company in Indianapolis. She has been at the Center of Inquiry since 2004. Wise helps direct the Wabash National Study of Liberal Arts Education and has also taught an intensive summer program on entrepreneurship at Wabash College. She has been in her current position since 2007.

Index